Fodor's

D0872841

EUROPEAN CRUISE PORTS OF CALL

Where to Stay and Eat for All Budgets

Must-See Sights and Local Secrets

Ratings You Can Trust

Fodor's Travel Publications   New York, Toronto, London, Sydney, Auckland
www.fodors.com

Excerpted from *Fodor's Complete Guide to European Cruises.*

FODOR'S EUROPEAN CRUISE PORTS OF CALL

Editorial Contributors: Lola Akinmade-Åkerström, Alexia Amvrazi, Lindsay Bennett, Linda Coffman, David Dunne, Jane Foster, Mike Gonzalez, Liz Humphreys, Jennifer Ladonne, Bruce Leimsidor, Giulia Pines, Anne-Sophie Redisch, Ellin Stein, Jessica Steinberg, Paul Sullivan, Joanna Styles, Gelu Sulugiuc, Victoria Tang, Adrian Vrettos, Dorota Wąsik

Editors: Douglas Stallings (lead editor), Alexis Kelly, John Rambow

Production Editor: Carrie Parker

Maps & Illustrations: David Lindroth, *cartographer;* Rebecca Baer, *map editor;* William Wu, *information graphics*

Design: Fabrizio La Rocca, creative director; Tina Malaney, Chie Ushio, Jessica Ramirez, designers; Melanie Marin, associate director of photography; Jennifer Romains, photo research

Cover Photo: Front cover: Damir Fabijanic/Corbis *[Description: Dubrovnik, Croatia]*; Back cover (from left to right): Lucian Cretu/Shutterstock; Gator/Dreamstime.com; Hemera/Thinkstock. Spine: Hemera/Thinkstock.

Production Manager: Angela L. McLean

3rd Edition

ISBN 978-0-89141-947-1

ISSN 2327-0292

SPECIAL SALES

This book is available at special discounts for bulk purchases for sales promotions or premiums. Special editions, including personalized covers, excerpts of existing books, and corporate imprints, can be created in large quantities for special needs. For more information, write to Special Markets/Premium Sales, 1745 Broadway, MD 3-1, New York, NY 10019, or e-mail specialmarkets@randomhouse.com.

AN IMPORTANT TIP & AN INVITATION

Although all prices, opening times, and other details in this book are based on information supplied to us at press time, changes occur all the time in the travel world, and Fodor's cannot accept responsibility for facts that become outdated or for inadvertent errors or omissions. So **always confirm information when it matters**, especially if you're making a detour to visit a specific place. Your experiences—positive and negative—matter to us. If we have missed or misstated something, **please write to us.** Share your opinion instantly through our online feedback center at fodors.com/contact-us.

CONTENTS

1 CRUISING IN EUROPE 7
   Choosing Your Cruise 8
   Before You Go 14
   Cruise Lines 18

2 WESTERN MEDITERRANEAN . . 39
   A Coruña, Spain (for Santiago
   de Compostela) 40
   Ajaccio, Corsica 43
   Barcelona, Spain 52
   Bari, Italy 61
   Bordeaux, France 65
   Cádiz, Spain (for Seville
   and Jerez) 69
   Cannes, France (with the Iles
   de Lérins and Antibes) 76
   Civitavecchia, Italy (for Rome) . . . 80
   Genoa, Italy 90
   Gibraltar 97
   Ibiza, Spain 102
   Le Havre, France (for Normandy
   and Paris) 107
   Leixões, Portugal (for Porto) 116
   Lisbon, Portugal 123
   Livorno, Italy (for Florence
   and Pisa) 129
   Málaga, Spain (with Marbella,
   Nerja, and Granada) 138
   Mallorca, Spain 145
   Marseille, France 152
   Menorca, Spain (Mahón) 157
   Messina, Italy (for Taormina
   and Mt. Etna) 162
   Monte Carlo, Monaco 168
   Naples, Italy (with Herculaneum,
   Pompeii, and Capri) 173
   Nice, France 182
   Palermo, Italy 188

   Porto Cervo, Sardinia, Italy 194
   Portoferraio, Italy (Elba) 200
   Portofino, Italy 204
   St-Tropez, France 209
   Valencia, Spain 213
   Valletta, Malta 219
   Venice, Italy 227
   Vigo, Spain (for Santiago de
   Compostela) 236
   Villefranche-sur-Mer, France 241

3 EASTERN MEDITERRANEAN
   AND AEGEAN 247
   Alexandria, Egypt 248
   Ashdod, Israel 254
   Corfu, Greece 263
   Dubrovnik, Croatia 270
   Haifa, Israel 276
   Hvar, Croatia 282
   Istanbul, Turkey 286
   Katakolon, Greece
   (for Olympia) 294
   Koper, Slovenia 300
   Korčula, Croatia 305
   Kotor, Montenegro 309
   Kuşadası, Turkey
   (for Ephesus) 314
   Limassol, Cyprus 319
   Mykonos, Greece 328
   Piraeus, Greece (for Athens) . . . 335
   Port Said, Egypt (for Cairo) 345
   Rhodes, Greece 352
   Santorini, Greece 358
   Split, Croatia 364

4 THE NORTH SEA 371
   Amsterdam, Netherlands 372
   Antwerp, Belgium 382

Cobh, Ireland (for Cork) 390

Dover, United Kingdom 397

Dublin, Ireland 403

Greenock, Scotland
(for Glasgow) 413

Harwich, United Kingdom
(for London) 421

Invergordon, Scotland 431

Leith, Scotland (for Edinburgh). . 437

Rotterdam, Netherlands. 445

Southampton, United
Kingdom 452

Zeebrugge, Belgium
(for Bruges). 460

5 THE BALTIC 467

Copenhagen, Denmark. 468

Gdańsk, Poland. 477

Hamburg, Germany 484

Helsinki, Finland 491

Rīga, Latvia 500

St. Petersburg, Russian
Federation. 504

Stockholm, Sweden 511

Tallinn, Estonia 520

Visby, Sweden. 523

Warnemünde, Germany
(for Berlin). 528

6 NORWAY 539

Ålesund, Norway 540

Bergen, Norway 543

Flåm 549

Geiranger, Norway 549

Gudvangen, Norway. 550

Hammerfest, Norway 552

Honningsvåg, Norway 554

Kristiansand, Norway 556

Oslo, Norway 558

Tromsø, Norway 568

Trondheim, Norway 570

7 ATLANTIC ISLANDS. 575

Funchal, Madeira 576

Gran Canaria, Canary Islands
(Las Palmas) 583

Lanzarote, Canary Islands 591

Reykjavík, Iceland. 598

Tenerife, Canary Islands
(Santa Cruz de Tenerife). 605

INDEX 614

ABOUT OUR WRITERS. 624

MAPS

Major European Cruise
Ports 10–11

Corsica 44

Barcelona 54–55

Bari 62

Bordeaux. 67

Cádiz and Seville 71

Cannes 77

Rome. 82–83

Genoa. 92–93

Gibraltar 99

Ibiza. 104

Paris 110–111

Porto. 118

Lisbon 125

Florence 132–133

Málaga 139

Mallorca 147

Marseille 155

Mahón/Menorca 159

Northeastern Sicily. 164

Monaco. 170

Naples 176–177
Nice 184
Palermo 190
Northern Sardinia 196
Portoferrio/Elba 203
Italian Riviera 206
St-Tropez 210
Valencia 215
Valletta 221
Venice 228–229
Santiago de Compostela 239
Villefranche-sur-Mer 242
Alexandria 250
Old City Jerusalem 256
Corfu 265
Dubrovnik 272
Haifa 277
Hvar 283
Istanbul 288–289
Northern Peloponnese
(Olympia) 296
Ljubljana 302
Korčula Island 306
Kotor Old Town 310
Epheseus & Kuşadasi 315
Cyprus 321
Mykonos Town 329
Athens 336–337
Cairo 346–347
Rhodes 353
Santorini 359
Split 366
Amsterdam 374–375
Antwerp 383
Cork City 391
Dover and Vicinity 398

Dublin 404–405
Glasgow 414–415
London 422–423
The Great Glen 432
Edinburgh 438–439
Rotterdam 446
Hampshire 453
Brugge (Bruges) 461
Copenhagen 470–471
Gdańsk 479
Hamburg 486–487
Helsinki 494–495
Rīga 501
St. Petersburg 506
Stockholm 512–513
Tallinn 521
Visby 525
Berlin 530–531
Norway 541
Bergen 544
Hammerfest 552
Nordkapp 555
Oslo 560–561
Tromsø 569
Trondheim 571
Madeira 577
Las Palmas 586
Lanzarote 592
Reykjavik 599
Tenerife 607

ABOUT
THIS BOOK

Fodor's Ratings
Everything in this guide is worth doing—
we don't cover what isn't—but exceptional sights, hotels, and restaurants are
recognized with additional accolades.
Fodor's Choice★ indicates our top recommendations; ★ highlights places we deem
highly recommended. Care to nominate a
new place? Visit Fodors.com/contact-us.

Trip Costs
We list prices wherever possible to help
you budget well. Hotel and restaurant
price categories from **$** to **$$$$** are noted
alongside each recommendation. For
hotels, we include the lowest cost of a
standard double room in high season.
For restaurants, we cite the average price
of a main course at dinner or, if dinner
isn't served, at lunch. For attractions,
we always list adult admission fees; dis-
counts are usually available for children,
students, and senior citizens.

Hotels
Our local writers vet every hotel to recom-
mend the best overnights in each price cat-
egory, from budget to expensive. Unless
otherwise specified, you can expect pri-
vate bath, phone, and TV in your room.

For expanded hotel reviews, facilities, and
deals visit Fodors.com.

Restaurants
Unless we state otherwise, restaurants are
open for lunch and dinner daily. We men-
tion dress code only when there's a specific
requirement and reservations only when
they're essential or not accepted. To make
restaurant reservations, visit Fodors.com.

Credit Cards
The hotels and restaurants in this guide
typically accept credit cards. If not, we'll
say so.

Listings
★ Fodor's Choice
★ Highly recommended
⊠ Physical address
✛ Directions or Map coordinates
🕮 Mailing address
☎ Telephone
🖷 Fax
⊕ On the Web

✎ E-mail
🎟 Admission fee
🕓 Open/closed times
Ⓜ Metro stations
▭ No credit cards

Hotels & Restaurants
🏨 Hotel
↪ Number of rooms
🛁 Facilities
🍴 Meal plans
✕ Restaurant
🍽 Reservations
🎩 Dress code
☊ Smoking

Outdoors
⛳ Golf
⛺ Camping

Other
☕ Family-friendly
⇨ See also
⊠ Branch address
☞ Take note

Cruising in Europe

Canal in Amsterdam

WORD OF MOUTH

"We based our decision [about which European cruise to take] on where the cruise went. We wanted to see Athens, so we chose [a] cruise that included Athens. . . .You can explore most ports on your own. That way you can do what you want and spend as much time on shore as you want. Research is the key."

—BarbAnn

By Linda
Coffman

Second only to the Caribbean in popularity with cruise passengers, Europe has it all—beautifully preserved castles, romantic gardens, fabulous art treasures, antiquities, and some of the world's most breathtaking scenery. Great cities flourished along all the coasts of the Continent, which makes it possible to explore many of Europe's richest treasures by ship.

Every year major North American cruise lines satisfy the seasonal demand for what amounts to an old-fashioned Grand Tour afloat by repositioning a large portion of their Caribbean fleets to Europe. They join European-based ships that are ported in the Baltic for the summer and the Mediterranean year-round. The largest vessels generally stick to predictable routes that include major cities along the coasts such as Amsterdam, Venice, Barcelona, and Athens, or those, like Rome, close enough to visit during a port call. Small to midsize ships offer the advantage of visiting ports off the beaten path of the large ships and can call at intriguing destinations like the less-visited Greek Isles and jet-set favorite Ibiza without the necessity of tendering passengers ashore.

CHOOSING YOUR CRUISE

Are you intrigued by the glory that is Rome or the antiquities of Greece? Do you want to venture behind the former Iron Curtain and unlock the mysteries of Russia? Unlike the "if it's Tuesday, this must be St. Thomas" nature of predictable Caribbean sailings, European itineraries come in shapes and sizes to suit a variety of interests. One voyage might emphasize the highlights of Baltic capital cities, while another focuses on classic Mediterranean cultures and cuisine. Equally rewarding, they nonetheless offer different experiences. Where to go to satisfy your inner explorer is a highly personal decision and one of the first you must make.

After giving some thought to your itinerary and where in Europe you might wish to go, the ship you select is the most vital factor in your cruise vacation. Big ships offer stability and a huge variety of activities and facilities. Small ships feel more intimate—more like a private club. For every big-ship fan there is someone who would never set foot aboard a "floating resort." Examine your lifestyle to see which kind of ship best meets your needs. But realize also that the size of your ship will also impact which ports you visit as well as how you see them. Big ships visit major ports of call such as Barcelona, Civitavecchia (for Rome), Amsterdam, and Venice; when they call at smaller, shallower ports, passengers must disembark aboard shore tenders (small boats that ferry dozens of passengers to shore at a time). Or they may skip these smaller ports entirely. Small and midsize ships can visit smaller ports, such as Monte Carlo, Monaco, more easily; passengers are often

able to disembark directly onto the pier without having to wait for tenders to bring them ashore.

ITINERARIES

Ship size and cruise length have the greatest impact on the number of ports you can visit, but the itinerary type and embarkation port will also impact the number and variety of ports. **One-way cruises** are much more prevalent in European sailings than in the Caribbean and will allow you to visit a wider variety of ports and travel farther from your port of embarkation. **Loop cruises** begin and end at the same point and often visit ports in relatively close proximity to one another. After deciding where to go, take a hard look at the number of hours your preferred itinerary spends in individual ports. You don't want to be frustrated by a lack of time ashore to do what you've come so far to accomplish. A late departure or overnight stay may be attractive if you wish to enjoy the local nightlife in a particular port.

NORTHERN EUROPE AND BALTIC ITINERARIES
Typical one-week to 12-night cruises include a day or two at sea, but ships on these itineraries spend as much time as possible docked in Baltic capitals and major cities. Departing from such ports as Dover (United Kingdom), Amsterdam, Copenhagen, or Stockholm, highlights of Baltic itineraries may include Amsterdam, Oslo, Helsinki, Tallin (Estonia), and St. Petersburg (Russia); ships calling on St. Petersburg often dock for two or three nights there. Some itineraries may focus on a theme or specific region, such as cruises around the British Isles or Norwegian fjords and North Cape.

WESTERN MEDITERRANEAN ITINERARIES
Some of the most popular Mediterranean itineraries, especially for first-time cruisers to Europe, are one-week sailings that embark in Barcelona and stop in southern European ports that range from Nice to Civitavecchia (Rome), and may include more exotic off-the-beaten-path destinations like Malta and Corsica. A sea day might include a cruise through the narrow Strait of Messina or sailing past the volcanic island of Stromboli. Longer, one-way itineraries can even start in Lisbon and end as far away as Venice, while possibly calling at not only Gibraltar, the French Riviera, and Sicily, but Dubrovnik (Croatia) as well.

EASTERN MEDITERRANEAN, ADRIATIC, AND GREEK ISLES ITINERARIES
The most exotic and port-intensive cruises are those embarking in Venice, Athens, and Istanbul. Often one-way voyages, these cruises visit coastal centers of antiquity such as Kuşadasi (Ephesus) in Turkey and Katakolon (Olympia) in Greece, but also the Roman outposts of Dubrovnik and Korčula, Croatia. For a transit through Greece's historic Corinth Canal, you'll have to select an itinerary on one of the high-end, small cruise ships, such as Seabourn or SeaDream cruise lines' yacht-size vessels. A sea day might be spent cruising past the grandeur of Mount Athos after leaving Istanbul or along the coastline in the Adriatic Sea. Best explored by small ship—preferably one with sails that add to the allure—Greek Island itineraries that include Santorini, Corfu, Rhodes,

Reykjavik **ICELAND**

Tromsø

Norwegian Sea

Færoe Islands

0   3000 mi
0   3000 km

Trondheim

Ålesund

SWEDEN

Shetland Islands

Bergen **NORWAY**

Åland Islands

Orkney Islands

Oslo

Stockholm

ATLANTIC OCEAN

Invergordon

North Sea

Greenock Glasgow
Edinburgh

Skagerrak

Gothenburg Visb

IRELAND **UNITED KINGDOM**

Århus Copenhagen

Kattegat

Baltic Sea

Dublin

DENMARK

Cork Cobh

Warnemünde

Gdańsk

Greenwich Harwich **NETH.**
London Amsterdam Hamburg

Southampton Dover Rotterdam Berlin **POLAND**

English Channel Zeebrugge Antwerp
Bruges **BEL.** **GERMANY**

La Havre

LUX.

Honfleur

CZECH REP.

Paris

SLOV

FRANCE

SWITZ. LIECH. **AUSTRIA** HUNGAR

Bay of Biscay

Bordeaux

Monte Carlo (MONACO)

Venice SLOV

A Coruña

Villefranche-sur-Mer

Genoa Portofino **CROATIA**

Vigo Santiago de Compostela

Cannes

Marseille Nice Pisa Florence

BOSNIA HERZEGOVIN

Leixos (Porto)

St-Tropez Livorno

Hvar

PORTUGAL

Corsica Ajaccio Civitavecchia

Korčula Dubrov

Lisbon

(France)

Rome

SPAIN

Barcelona

Mallorca Menorca Poltu Naples Bari

Seville

Valencia Palma Quatu

Cádiz

Granada Ibiza Mahón **I T A L Y**

Gibraltar Málaga Town *Sardinia (Italy)*

Tyrrhenian Sea

Corfu

Strait of Gibraltar

← TO MADEIRA

Palermo *Sicily (Italy)* Messina

TO THE CANARY ISLANDS ↙

MOROCCO ALGERIA

Valleta **MALTA**

Ionian Sea

TUNISIA *Mediterranean Sea*

Major European
Cruise Ports

and Mykonos are popular with honeymooners and couples for the romantic ambience of sun-splashed beaches and leisurely alfresco meals accompanied by local wines and breathtaking sea views, but these ports are also visited by the larger ships, which must usually tender their passengers ashore.

WHEN TO GO

Baltic cruises are scheduled from May through September, with mid-summer being high season, when the weather is predictably more pleasant. Temperatures throughout the Baltic are somewhat unpredictable, but can range from balmy mid- to high-70sF on sunny days to chilly 50sF in the evening, even if the sun doesn't set until well into the night. Mediterranean cruises are available year-round, with high season from late April through October when temperatures range from the upper 70s to mid-90sF, depending on your ports of call. Early spring and late fall aren't the best times to cruise in the Mediterranean if your plans include spending time on the beaches, yet the cooler temperatures are ideal for touring. Weather can be unpredictable and damp in fall and winter, but days often warm up when the sun is shining.

CRUISE COSTS

Average cruise fares vary considerably by itinerary and season, as well as by the category of accommodations you select. Published rates are highest for the most unusual and desirable itineraries, as well as for cruises during peak summer months, when most North Americans plan for vacations in Europe. Europeans are known to prefer late-summer holidays, with August being the busiest month. Typical daily per diems on a luxury line such as Silversea or Seabourn can be as much as three times or more the cost of a cruise on a mainstream line such as Royal Caribbean or even a premium Celebrity Cruises ship. It goes without saying that longer cruises are naturally more expensive.

Solo travelers should be aware that single cabins have virtually disappeared from cruise ships, although they are available on P&O's *Azura*, Norwegian Cruise Line's *Norwegian Epic* (in a particularly successful format), and a few older vessels. Taking a double cabin can cost up to twice the advertised per-person rates (which are based on double occupancy). Some cruise lines will find same-sex roommates for singles; each then pays the per-person, double-occupancy rate.

Although the overall price you pay for your cruise is always a consideration, don't think of the bottom line in terms of the fare alone. You also have to figure in the cost of other shipboard charges beyond the basic fare. However, the ultimate cost isn't computed only in dollars spent; it is in what you get for your money. The real bottom line is value. Many cruise passengers don't mind spending a bit more to get the vacation they really want.

TIPS

1

One of the most delicate—yet frequently debated—topics of conversation among cruise passengers involves the matter of tipping. Who do you tip? How much? What's "customary" and "recommended?" Should parents tip the full amount for children or is just half adequate? Why do you have to tip at all?

When transfers to and from your ship are a part of your air-and-sea program, gratuities are generally included for luggage handling. In that case, do not worry about the interim tipping. However, if you take a taxi to the pier and hand over your bags to a stevedore, be sure to tip him. Treat him with respect and pass along the equivalent of at least $5.

During your cruise, room-service waiters generally receive a cash tip of $1 to $3 per delivery. A 15% to 18% gratuity will automatically be added to each bar bill during the cruise. If you use salon and spa services, a similar percentage might be added to the bills there as well. If you dine in a specialty restaurant, you may be asked to provide a one-time gratuity for the service staff.

There will be a "disembarkation talk" on the last day of the cruise that explains tipping procedures. If you are expected to tip in cash, small white "tip" envelopes will appear in your stateroom that day. If you tip in cash, you usually give the tip envelope directly to each person on the last night of the cruise. Tips generally add up to about $11.50 to $14 per person per day. You tip the same amount for each person who shares the cabin, including children, unless otherwise indicated.

Most cruise lines now either automatically add gratuities to passengers' onboard charge accounts or offer the option. If that suits you, then do nothing further. However, you are certainly free to adjust the amounts up or down to more appropriate levels or ask that the charge be removed altogether if you prefer distributing cash gratuities.

EXTRAS

In addition to the cost of your cruise, there are further expenses to consider, such as airfare to the port city. These days virtually all cruise lines offer air add-ons, which are sometimes—but not always—less expensive than the lowest available airline fare. Airfares to Europe can be considerably more expensive from May through September than during the rest of year.

Shore excursions can also be a substantial expense; the best shore excursions are not cheap. But if you skimp too much on your excursion budget you'll deprive yourself of an important part of the European cruising experience. European shore excursions can be as simple as a stroll through Copenhagen's fanciful Tivoli Gardens or as splendid as tours through the imperial residences of the czars in St. Petersburg. You can inspect the architecture of Gaudí in Barcelona, take an all-day guided tour of Rome with a stop at Vatican City, and climb to the top of the Acropolis in Athens. One of the most popular excursions is from the port of Kusadasi (Turkey) to the ancient excavated city of Ephesus. You will walk along the marble road that Mark Antony's and Cleopatra's chariots once passed over to reach the Great Theater, where

gladiatorial contests entertained up to 24,000 spectators and where St. Paul addressed the Ephesians. If you want to take a ship-sponsored shore excursion, prebooking is highly recommended, as they can sell out weeks before you reach the ship.

But you don't necessarily have to take the tour offered by your ship. Although there's a distinct advantage these days to having your shore excursions priced in dollars rather than euros, you can still have a high-quality (though perhaps not cheaper) experience by banding together with a group of like-minded travelers to arrange a private tour rather than relying on the ship's big-bus experience. Or if you are more intrepid, you can simply hop in a taxi or onto public transportation and do some independent exploring. Whether you choose to take ship-sponsored tours or go it alone, you do need to budget for off-ship touring because that's the reason you came to Europe in the first place.

Finally, there will be many extras added to your shipboard account during the cruise, including drinks (both alcoholic and nonalcoholic), activity fees (you pay to use that golf simulator), dining in specialty restaurants, spa services, gratuities, and even cappuccino and espresso on most ships.

BEFORE YOU GO

To expedite your preboarding paperwork, some cruise lines have convenient forms on their websites. As long as you have your reservation number, you can provide the required immigration information (usually your citizenship information and passport number), prereserve shore excursions, and even indicate any special requests from the comfort of your home. Less-wired cruise lines might mail preboarding paperwork to you or your travel agent for completion after you make your final payment and request that you return the forms by mail or fax. No matter how you submit them, be sure to make hard copies of any forms you fill out and bring them with you to the pier to smooth the embarkation process.

DOCUMENTS

It is every passenger's responsibility to have proper identification. If you arrive at the airport without it, you will not be allowed to board your plane. Should that happen, the cruise line will not issue a fare refund. Most travel agents know the requirements and can guide you to the proper agency to obtain what you need if you don't have it.

Everyone must have a valid passport to travel to Europe. Additionally, some countries to which cruise ships call require visas, though it's also true that tourist visas are sometimes not required for cruise passengers, even if they are generally required to visit a particular country. For instance, a visa is not necessary in Russia if you book all your shore excursions through your cruise line or through a private tour company that is licensed to participate in the visa-waiver program (in both cases you must sleep on board your ship), but a visa is required if you tour independently without any kind of tour company. If your itinerary

requires a visa of *all* passengers prior to boarding, you should receive an information letter from your cruise line with instructions and, possibly, application forms. It is your responsibility to obtain all necessary visas. Visa information and applications may also be obtained through the local embassy or consulate of the country you will be visiting. Although you can obtain visas yourself, a more hassle-free route is to use a visa service, such as Visa Central or Travisa, that specializes in the process. ■ TIP→ **If you arrive at the pier without a required visa, you will not be allowed to board your ship, and the cruise line will not issue a fare refund.**

Children under the age of 18—when they are not traveling with *both* parents—almost always require a letter of permission from the absent parent(s). Airlines, cruise lines, and immigration agents can deny children initial boarding or entry to foreign countries without proper proof of identification and citizenship *and* a notarized permission letter from absent or noncustodial parents. Your travel agent or cruise line can help with the wording of such a letter.

Contacts **Travisa** (⊕ www.travisa.com). **Visa Central** (⊕ www.visacentral.com).

GETTING OR RENEWING A PASSPORT

In light of changing government regulations, you should apply for a passport as far in advance of your cruise as possible. In normal times, the process usually takes at least six weeks, but it can take as long as 12 weeks during busy periods. You can expedite your passport application if you are traveling within two weeks by paying an additional fee of $60 (in addition to the regular passport fee) and appearing in person at a regional passport office. Also, several passport expediting services will handle your application for you (for a hefty fee, of course) and can get you a passport in as few as 48 hours. If you are a U.S. citizen, you can read all about the passport application process at the website of the U.S. Department of State; a passport costs $140 if you are 16 or older and is valid for 10 years, $110 if you are under 16, when it is only valid for five years.

If you have left your passport renewal to the last minute, you can call on a company like A. Briggs Passport & Visa Expeditors to help you get a renewal, sometimes in as little as 48 hours. Most visa expeditors can also help you expedite a passport renewal.

Contacts **A. Briggs Passport & Visa Expeditors** (☎ 800/806–0581 or 202/464–3000 ⊕ www.abriggs.com). **U.S. Department of State** (⊕ travel.state. gov/passport).

MONEY

On board your ship you won't have any worries about money, but you will need cash while ashore. If you have not arranged for transfers from the airport to the ship, you will need taxi fare in the local currency, which is the euro for most embarkation cities and the British pound in Great Britain. The Scandinavian countries Denmark, Norway, and Sweden also have their own currencies.

Currency exchange is almost always more costly in your home country than at your foreign destination, but many banks, as well as the

American Automobile Association (AAA), American Express, and Travelex bureaus offer the service. In addition, you may find a currency exchange booth in the international terminal at your departure airport. However, the simplest, and usually least expensive, method of obtaining local currency is from an ATM. Visa and MasterCard debit and credit cards are widely accepted at ATMs throughout the world; however, some banks impose a fee for international withdrawals. Before leaving home, make sure you have a PIN (personal identification number) for your card and understand any fees associated with its use. Also, notify the credit card company that you will be using your card overseas so they don't refuse your charges when they notice its repeated use in foreign locales.

For days in port you will also want some cash on hand for beverages, snacks, and small souvenir purchases. Your cruise ship may offer a foreign currency exchange service on board, but, like hotels, the exchange rate is not always the most favorable. We suggest that instead of carrying large amounts of cash when ashore, use a credit card for major purchases.

INSURANCE

It's a good idea to purchase travel insurance, which covers a variety of possible hazards and mishaps, when you book a cruise. One important concern for cruise passengers is being delayed en route to the port of embarkation and missing the ship. Another major consideration is lost luggage (⇨ *for more information on lost luggage, see Luggage*)—or even the delay of luggage. Both of these possibilities should be covered by your policy. You may miss the first day or two of your cruise, but all will not be lost financially. A travel policy will ensure that you can replace delayed necessities secure in the knowledge that you will be reimbursed for those unexpected expenditures. Save your receipts for all out-of-pocket expenses to file your claim and be sure to get an incident report from the airline at fault.

No one wants his or her cruise vacation spoiled by a broken arm, heart attack, or worse, but if one of life's tragedies occurs, you want to be covered. The medical insurance program you depend on at home might not extend coverage beyond the borders of the United States. Medicare assuredly will not cover you if you are hurt or sick while abroad. It is worth noting that all ships of foreign registry are considered to be "outside the United States" by Medicare. If there is any question in your mind, check your cruise-ship's registry—with very few exceptions, it will *not* be the United States. Without basic coverage, travelers should be prepared to pay for any care they require, either by credit card or wire transfer of funds to the provider.

U.S. Travel Insurers Allianz Travel Insurance (☎ *800/284–8300* ⊕ *www. allianztravelinsurance.com*). **CSA Travel Protection** (☎ *800/711–1197* ⊕ *www. csatravelprotection.com*). **HTH Worldwide** (☎ *610/254–8700 or 888/243–2358* ⊕ *www.hthworldwide.com*). **Travelex Insurance** (☎ *800/228–9792* ⊕ *www. travelex-insurance.com*). **Travel Guard International** (☎ *715/345–0505*

or 800/826–4919 ⊕ *www.travelguard.com*). **Travel Insured International** (✆ *800/243–3174* ⊕ *www.travelinsured.com*).

CUSTOMS AND DUTIES

TAXES

If you make any purchases while in Europe, you should ask for a V.A.T. refund form and find out whether the merchant gives refunds—not all stores do, nor are they required to. Have the form stamped like any customs form by customs officials when you leave the country or, if you're visiting several European Union countries, when you leave the EU. This has to be done at the airport on the day you are flying home. After you're through passport control, take the form to a refund-service counter for an on-the-spot refund (which is usually the quickest and easiest option), or mail it to the address on the form (or the envelope with it) after you arrive home. You receive the total refund stated on the form, but the processing time can be long, especially if you request a credit-card adjustment.

Global Blue (formerly known as Global Refund) is a Europe-wide service with 225,000 affiliated stores and more than 700 refund counters at major airports and border crossings. Its refund form, called a Tax Free Check, is the most common across the European continent. The service issues refunds in the form of cash, check, or credit-card adjustment.

V.A.T. Refunds Global Blue (✆ *800/566–9828* ⊕ *www.global-blue.com*).

U.S. CUSTOMS

Each individual or family returning to the United States must fill out a customs declaration form, which will be provided before your plane lands. If you owe any duties, you will have to pay them directly to the customs inspector, with cash or check. Be sure to keep receipts for all purchases; and you may be asked to show officials what you've bought. If your cruise is a transatlantic crossing, U.S. Customs clears ships sailing into arrival ports. After showing your passport to immigration officials, you must collect your luggage from the dock, then stand in line to pass through the inspection point. This can take up to an hour.

ALLOWANCES

You're always allowed to bring goods of a certain value back home without having to pay any duty or import tax. But there's a limit on the amount of tobacco and liquor you can bring back duty-free. The values of so-called duty-free goods are included in these amounts. When you shop abroad, save all your receipts, as customs inspectors may ask to see them as well as the items you purchased. If the total value of your goods is more than the duty-free limit, you'll have to pay a tax (most often a flat percentage) on the value of everything beyond that limit. For U.S. citizens who have been in Europe for at least 48 hours, the duty-free exemption is $800. But the duty-free exemption includes only 200 cigarettes, 100 cigars, and 1 liter of alcohol (this includes wine); above these limits, you have to pay duties, even if you didn't spend more than the $800 limit.

Contacts U.S. Customs and Border Protection (⊕ *www.cbp.gov*).

SENDING PACKAGES HOME

Although you probably won't want to spend your time looking for a post office, you can send packages home duty-free, with a limit of one parcel per addressee per day (except alcohol or tobacco products or perfume worth more than $5). You can mail up to $200 worth of goods to yourself, or $100 worth of goods to a friend or relative; label the package "personal use" or "unsolicited gift" (depending on which is the case) and attach a list of the contents and their retail value. If the package contains your used personal belongings, mark it "personal goods returned" to avoid paying duty on your laundry. You do not need to declare items that were sent home on your declaration forms for U.S. Customs.

CRUISE LINES

Just as trends and fashion evolve over time, cruise lines embrace the ebb and flow of change. To keep pace with today's lifestyles, some cruise lines strive to include something that will appeal to everyone on their ships. Others focus on narrower elements and are more traditional. Today's passengers have higher expectations and they sail on ships that are far superior to their predecessors. And they often do so at a much lower comparable fare than in the past.

So which cruise line is best? Only you can determine which is best for you. You won't find ratings by Fodor's—either quality stars or value scores. Why? Ratings are personal and heavily weighted to the reviewer's opinion. Your responsibility is to select the right cruise for you—no one knows your expectations better than you do yourself. It's your time, money, and vacation that are at stake. No matter how knowledgeable your travel agent is, how sincere your friends are, or what any expert can tell you, you are the only one who really knows what you like. The short wait for a table might not bother you because you would prefer a casual atmosphere with open seating; however, some people want the security of a set time at an assigned table served by a waiter who gets to know their preferences. You know what you are willing to trade off in order to get what you want.

TYPES OF CRUISE LINES

MAINSTREAM CRUISE LINES

The mainstream lines are the ones most often associated with modern cruising. They offer the advantage of something for everyone and nearly every available sports facility imaginable. Some ships even have ice-skating rinks, 18-hole miniature golf courses, bowling alleys, and rock-climbing walls.

Generally speaking, the mainstream lines have two basic ship sizes— large cruise ships and megaships—in their fleets. These vessels have plentiful outdoor deck space, and many have a wraparound outdoor promenade deck that allows you to stroll or jog the ship's perimeter. In the newest vessels, traditional meets trendy. You'll find atrium lobbies and expansive sun and sports decks, picture windows instead of

portholes, and cabins that open onto private verandas. For all their resort-style innovations, they still feature cruise-ship classics—afternoon tea, complimentary room service, and lavish pampering. The smallest ships carry 1,000 passengers or fewer, while the largest accommodate more than 5,000 passengers and are filled with diversions.

These ships tend to be big and boxy. Picture windows are standard equipment, and cabins in the top categories have private verandas. From their casinos and discos to their fitness centers, everything is bigger and more extravagant than on other ships. You'll pay for many extras on the mainstream ships, from drinks at the bar, to that cup of cappuccino, to spa treatments, to a game of bowling, to dinner in a specialty restaurant. You may want to rethink a cruise aboard one of these ships if you want a little downtime, since you'll be joined by 1,500 to 5,000 fellow passengers.

PREMIUM CRUISE LINES

Premium cruise lines have a lot in common with the mainstream cruise lines, but with a little more of everything. The atmosphere is more refined, surroundings more gracious, and service more polished and attentive. There are still activities like pool games, although they aren't quite the high jinks typical of mainstream ships. In addition to traditional cruise activities, onboard lectures are common. Production shows are somewhat more sophisticated than on mainstream lines.

Ships tend to be newer midsize to large vessels that carry fewer passengers than mainstream ships and have a more spacious feel. Decor is usually more glamorous and subtle, with toned-down colors and extensive original art. Staterooms range from inside cabins for three or four to outside cabins with or without balconies to suites with numerous amenities, including butlers on some lines.

Most premium ships offer traditional assigned seatings for dinner. High marks are afforded the quality cuisine and presentation. Many ships have upscale bistros or specialty restaurants, which usually require reservations and command an additional charge. Although premium lines usually have as many extra charges as mainstream lines, the overall quality of what you receive is higher.

LUXURY CRUISE LINES

Comprising only 5% of the market, the exclusive luxury cruise lines, such as Crystal, Cunard, Oceania, Regent Seven Seas, Seabourn, SeaDream, and Silversea offer high staff-to-guest ratios for personal service, superior cuisine in a single seating (except Crystal, with two assigned seatings, and Cunard, with dual-class dining assignments), and a highly inclusive product with few onboard charges. These small and midsize ships offer much more space per passenger than you will find on the mainstream lines' vessels. Lines differ in what they emphasize, with some touting luxurious accommodations and entertainment and others focusing on exotic destinations and onboard enrichment.

If you consider travel a necessity rather than a luxury and frequent posh resorts, then you will appreciate the extra attention and the higher level of comfort that luxury cruise lines offer. Itineraries on these ships often include the marquee ports, but luxury ships also visit some of the more

uncommon destinations. With an intimate size, the smaller luxury ships can visit such ports as Marbella, Spain, and Korčula, Croatia.

EUROPEAN CRUISE LINES

With more similarities to American-owned cruise lines than differences, these European-owned-and-operated cruise lines compare favorably to the mainstream cruise lines of a decade ago. Many lines have embarked upon shipbuilding programs that rival the most ambitious in the cruise industry, but some European fleets still consist of older, smaller, yet well-maintained vessels. These cruises cater to Europeans—announcements may be broadcast in as many as five languages—and Americans are generally in the minority. English is widely spoken by the crew, however.

RIVER CRUISES

Riverboats and barges present an entirely different perspective on European cruising. Smaller than even the smallest ocean cruise ships, they offer a convenient alternative to bus tours—you only unpack once—while navigating the rivers and canals to reach legendary inland cities. Just as on cruise ships, accommodations and meals are included. Some shore excursions might be part of the package as well.

OTHER CRUISE LINES

A few small cruise lines sail through Europe and offer boutique to nearly bed-and-breakfast experiences. Notably, Star Clippers, Lindblad Expeditions, and Hurtigruten appeal to passengers who eschew mainstream cruises. Most of these niche vessels accommodate 200 or fewer passengers, and their focus is on soft adventure; Hurtigruten's ships and itineraries are perfectly suited for scenic coastal cruising and have few other onboard amenities. Other lines cruise between nearby ports and drop anchor so passengers can swim and snorkel directly from the ship (as on Star Clippers), and they have itineraries that usually leave plenty of time for exploring and other activities on- or offshore. Many of these cruises schedule casual enrichment talks that often continue on decks, at meals, and during trips ashore.

MAJOR CRUISE LINES

Azamara Club Cruises. Designed to offer exotic destination-driven itineraries, Azamara Club Cruises presents an intimate onboard experience while allowing access to the less traveled ports of call experienced travelers want to visit. It's two ships, *Azamara Journey* and *Azamara Quest,* offer not quite luxury but more than premium cruising, a deluxe cruise with concierge-style amenities for which you'd have to upgrade to a suite on other cruise lines. In addition, since its launch Azamara Club Cruises has added a number of more inclusive amenities to passengers' fares, with no charge for a specific brand of bottled water, specialty coffees and teas; shuttle bus service to/from port communities, where available; standard spirits, wines, and international beers throughout the ships during bar hours; and complimentary self-service laundry.

Your Shipmates: Azamara is designed to appeal to discerning travelers, primarily American couples of any age who appreciate a high level of service in a nonstructured atmosphere.

Dress Code: While passengers who choose to wear formal attire are certainly welcome to do so, there are no scheduled formal nights. The nightly dress code is simply "sophisticated" casual—a jacket and tie are never required, but you may see many men who are accustomed to wearing them will do so anyway.

Tipping: Housekeeping and dining gratuities are included in the fare. A standard 18% is added to beverage charges. It is recommended that a $5-per-person gratuity be extended when dining in the specialty restaurants. ☎ *877/999–9553* ⊕ *www.azamaraclubcruises.com* ☞ *Cruise Style: Premium.*

Carnival Cruise Lines. The world's largest cruise line originated the Fun Ship concept in 1972. Sporting red-white-and-blue flared funnels, which are easily recognized from afar, new ships are continuously added to the fleet and rarely deviate from a successful pattern. If you find something you like on one vessel, you're likely to find something similar on another. Each vessel features themed public rooms, ranging from ancient Egypt to futuristic motifs, although many of those elements are being replaced with a more tropical decor as older ships are upgraded. Carnival is also introducing features either branded by the line itself, such as the poolside Blue Iguana Tequila Bar with an adjacent burrito cantina and the Red Frog Rum Bar that also serves Carnival's own brand of Thirsty Frog Red beer, or in partnership with well-known brands, such as EA SPORTS. Food Network star Guy Fieri, and Hasbro. Implementation of the new features is scheduled for completion in 2015.

Your Shipmates: Carnival's passengers are predominantly active Americans, mostly couples in their mid-thirties to mid-fifties. Many families enjoy Carnival cruises in the Caribbean year-round.

Dress Code: Two "cruise elegant" nights are standard on seven-night cruises; one is the norm on shorter sailings. Although men should feel free to wear tuxedos, dark suits (or sport coats) and ties are more prevalent. All other evenings are "cruise casual," with jeans and dress shorts permitted in the dining rooms. All ships request that no short-shorts or cutoffs be worn after 6 pm, but that policy is often ignored.

Tipping: A gratuity of $11.50 per passenger per day is automatically added to passenger accounts, and gratuities are distributed to stewards and waitstaff. Passengers may adjust the amount based on the level of service experienced. All beverage tabs at bars get an automatic 15% addition. ☎ *305/599–2600 or 800/227–6482* ⊕ *www.carnival.com* ☞ *Cruise Style: Mainstream.*

Celebrity Cruises. The Chandris Group, owners of budget Fantasy Cruises, founded Celebrity in 1989. Celebrity gained a reputation for professional service and fine food despite the shabby-chic vessel on which it was elegantly served. The cruise line eventually built premium sophisticated cruise ships. Signature amenities followed, including large standard staterooms with generous storage, fully equipped spas, and butler service. Valuable art collections grace the fleet. Although spacious accommodations in every category are a Celebrity standard, Concierge-class, an upscale element on all ships, makes certain premium

ocean-view and balcony staterooms almost the equivalent of suites in terms of service.

Your Shipmates: Celebrity caters to American cruise passengers, primarily couples from their mid-thirties to mid-fifties. Many families enjoy cruising on Celebrity's fleet during summer months and holiday periods, particularly in the Caribbean. Lengthier cruises and exotic itineraries attract passengers in the over-sixty age group.

Dress Code: Two formal nights are standard on seven-night cruises, and men are encouraged to wear tuxedos. Other evenings are designated "smart casual and above." Although jeans are discouraged in formal restaurants, they are appropriate for casual dining venues after 6 pm. Most people observe the dress code of the evening, unlike on some other cruise lines.

Tipping: Gratuities are automatically added daily to onboard accounts in the following amounts (which may be adjusted at your discretion): $11.50 per person per day for passengers in stateroom categories; $12 per person per day for Concierge-class and Aqua-class staterooms; and $15 per person per day for Suites. An automatic gratuity of 15% is added to all beverage tabs. ☎ *800/647–2251* ⊕ *www.celebritycruises. com* ☞ *Cruise Style: Premium.*

Costa Cruises. Europe's number-one cruise line combines a Continental experience, enticing itineraries, and Italy's classical design and style with relaxing days and romantic nights at sea. Genoa-based Costa Crociere, parent company of Costa Cruise Lines, was bought by Airtours and Carnival Corporation in 1997. In 2000 Carnival completed a buyout of the Costa line and began expanding the fleet with larger and more dynamic ships. An ongoing shipbuilding program has brought Costa ships into the 21st century with innovative large-ship designs that reflect their Italian heritage and style without overlooking the amenities expected by modern cruisers. Acknowledging changing habits (even among Europeans), Costa Cruises has eliminated smoking entirely in dining rooms and show lounges. However, smokers are permitted to light up in designated areas in other public rooms, as well as on the pool deck.

Your Shipmates: Couples in the 35- to 55-year-old range are attracted to Costa Cruises; on most itineraries, up to 80% of passengers are European, and many of them are of Italian descent. An international air prevails on board, and announcements are often made in a variety of languages. The vibe on Costa's newest megaships is most likely to appeal to American tastes and expectations.

Dress Code: Two formal nights are standard on seven-night cruises. Men are encouraged to wear tuxedos, but dark suits or sport coats and ties are appropriate and more common than black tie. All other evenings are resort casual, although jeans are discouraged in restaurants. It's requested that no shorts be worn in public areas after 6 pm.

Tipping: A standard gratuity of €7 per adult per day for cruises up to eight nights or €6 per adult per day on longer cruises is automatically added to shipboard accounts and distributed to cabin stewards and dining-room staff. The applicable charge for teens between the ages

of 14 and 17 is 50% of those amounts; there is no charge for children under the age of 14. Passengers may adjust the amount based on the level of service experienced. An automatic 15% gratuity is added to all beverage tabs, as well as to checks for spa treatments and salon services. ☎ *954/266–5600 or 800/462–6782* ⊕ *www.costacruise.com* ☞ *Cruise Style: Mainstream.*

Crystal Cruises. Winner of accolades and too many hospitality industry awards to count, Crystal Cruises offers a taste of the grandeur of the past along with all the modern touches discerning passengers demand today. Crystal ships, unlike other luxury vessels, are large, carrying upward of 900 passengers. What makes them distinctive are superior service, a variety of dining options, spacious accommodations, and some of the highest ratios of space per passenger of any cruise ship and Asian-inspired design.

Your Shipmates: Affluent, well-traveled couples, from their late thirties and up, are attracted to Crystal's destination-rich itineraries, shipboard enrichment programs, and elegant ambience. The average age of passengers is noticeably higher on longer itineraries.

Dress Code: Formal attire is required on at least two designated evenings, depending on the length of the cruise. Men are encouraged to wear tuxedos, and many do, although dark suits are also acceptable. Other evenings are informal or resort casual; the number of each is based on the number of sea days. The line requests that dress codes be observed in public areas after 6 pm, and few, if any, passengers disregard the suggestion. Most, in fact, dress up just a notch from guidelines.

Tipping: Housekeeping and dining gratuities are included in the fare. A 15% gratuity is suggested for spa and salon services. ☎ *888/799–4625 or 310/785–9300* ⊕ *www.crystalcruises.com* ☞ *Cruise Style: Luxury.*

Cruise and Maritime Voyages. Founded in 2009, U.K.-based Cruise and Maritime Voyages specializes in adults-only cruises for travelers over 60 who seek a low-key, traditional British experience. Two refurbished 800-passenger ships, *Marco Polo* and *Discovery,* offer classic cruising itineraries from 2-night mini-excursions to 44-night cruises and are designed to maximize time in ports of call. With departure from six U.K. cities, afternoon tea service, an English-speaking staff, and pounds sterling as onboard currency, the cruise line attracts a predominantly unpretentious, British crowd.

Your Shipmates: Expect an older crowd on all CMV cruises, with the minimum age in the mid-50s. While the staff and entertainers are a multicultural blend of British and international citizens, the cruise line attracts primarily British travelers since all points of departure are located in the United Kingdom.

Dress Code: Ships have traditional formal, informal, and casual nights. On most evenings, informal attire applies, making ties optional (but not jackets) for men. On casual evenings, passengers can choose what they want to wear. On formal nights, black tie or dinner jackets are suggested for men, cocktail dresses for women. Casual nights occur on evenings in port or during special events such as deck parties.

Tipping: An automatic tipping charge of £5 per person per night is added to onboard customer accounts (£4 per person per night for cruises lasting more than 16 days). At the end of the cruise, passengers can adjust the charged amount to reflect personal satisfaction levels. ☎ *0845/430–0274 in the U.K.* ⊕ *www.cruiseandmaritime.com* ☞ *Cruise Style: Mainstream*

Cunard Line. One of the world's most distinguished names in ocean travel since 1840, the Cunard Line has a long history of deluxe transatlantic crossings and worldwide cruising. The line's ships are legendary for their comfortable accommodations, excellent cuisine, and personal service. After a series of owners tried with little success to revive the company's flagging passenger-shipping business, Carnival Corporation offered an infusion of ready cash and the know-how to turn the line around in 1998. Exciting new ships have followed. Delightful daily events include afternoon tea and the maritime tradition of sounding the ship's bell at noon. The line offers North Atlantic crossings and seasonal shorter cruises, including Northern European and Mediterranean itineraries.

Your Shipmates: Discerning, well-traveled American and British couples from their late-thirties to retirees are drawn to Cunard's traditional style and the notion of a cruise aboard an ocean liner. The availability of spacious accommodations and complimentary self-service laundry facilities makes Cunard liners a good option for families, although there may be fewer children on board than on similar size ships.

Dress Code: Glamorous evenings are typical of Cunard cruises, and specified attire includes formal, informal, and casual. Although resort casual clothing prevails throughout the day, Cunard vessels are ocean liners at heart and, as expected, are dressier than most cruise ships at night. To maintain their high standards, the cruise line requests passengers to dress as they would for dining in fine restaurants.

Tipping: Suggested gratuities of $13 per person per day (for Grill Restaurant accommodations) or $11 per person per day (all other accommodations) are automatically charged to shipboard accounts for distribution to stewards and waitstaff. An automatic 15% gratuity is added to beverage tabs for bar service. Passengers can still tip individual crew members directly in cash for any special services. ☎ *661/753–1000 or 800/728–6273* ⊕ *www.cunard.com* ☞ *Cruise Style: Luxury.*

Disney Cruise Line. With the launch of Disney Cruise Line in 1998, families were offered yet another reason to take a cruise. The magic of a Walt Disney resort vacation plus the romance of a sea voyage are a tempting combination, especially for adults who discovered Disney movies and the Mickey Mouse Club as children. Mixed with traditional shipboard activities, who can resist scheduled opportunities for the young and young-at-heart to interact with their favorite Disney characters? Although Disney Cruise Line voyages stuck to tried-and-true Bahamas and Caribbean itineraries in their formative years, and sailed exclusively from Port Canaveral, Florida, where a terminal was designed especially for Disney ships, the line has branched out to other regions, including Europe.

Your Shipmates: Disney Cruises appeal to kids of all ages—the young and not so young, singles, couples, and families. Multigenerational family groups are the core audience for these ships, and the facilities are ideal for family gatherings. What you might not have expected are the numerous newlywed couples celebrating their honeymoons on board.

Dress Code: One-week cruises schedule a semiformal evening and a formal night, during which men are encouraged to wear tuxedos, but dark suits or sport coats and ties are acceptable for both. Resort casual is the evening dress code for dinner in the more laid-back dining rooms. A sport coat is appropriate for the restaurants designated as fancier, as well as the adults-only specialty restaurants; however, you won't be turned away and could probably get by without the sport coat.

Tipping: Suggested gratuity amounts are calculated on a per-person, per-cruise rather than per-night basis and can be added to onboard accounts or offered in cash on the last night of the cruise. Guidelines include gratuities for your dining-room server, assistant server, head server, and stateroom host–hostess for the following amounts: $36 for three-night cruises, $48 for four-night cruises, and $84 for seven-night cruises. Tips for room-service delivery, spa services, and the dining manager are at the passenger's discretion. An automatic 15% gratuity is added to all bar tabs. ☎ *407/566–3500 or 888/325–2500* ⊕ *www. disneycruise.com* ☞ *Cruise Style: Mainstream.*

Fred. Olsen Cruise Lines. With its Norwegian heritage of seamanship spanning over 150 years, family-owned Fred. Olsen Cruise Lines has built a solid reputation of reliability and comfort for its U.K.-based fleet of smaller ships. Major refitting and refurbishment of old and recently acquired ships since 2008 have earned the company high industry accolades. Shipboard ambience is friendly, relaxed, and unabashedly British. As Fred. Olsen Cruise Lines expands, the line takes pride in maintaining the consistency their passengers prefer and expect, both on board—in the self-described "British country house" atmosphere—and ashore. Activities and entertainment are traditional cruise-ship fare with a laid-back tempo, albeit on a much smaller scale compared to a typical American megaship. British pounds are used for all transactions on board. Although the line is destination-focused—itineraries are seldom repeated within any cruise season—itinerary planning is versatile.

Your Shipmates: Well-traveled, mature British passengers who enjoy the time-honored shipboard environment with a formal style make up the majority on board Fred. Olsen sailings. Children's programs are offered only during summer months and school holiday breaks.

Dress Code: Requested attire is appropriately casual during the day and consists of three types of traditional shipboard evening dress—formal, informal, and casual. Most passengers still "dress" for dinner, which includes black tie on formal nights and a regular jacket and tie for men on informal evenings.

Tipping: Recommended gratuities, which are added to your onboard account, are £4 per passenger per day for your cabin steward and dining room waiter. ☎ *01473/742–424 in the U.K.* ⊕ *www.fredolsencruises. com* ☞ *Cruise Style: Mainstream.*

Holland America. Holland America Line has enjoyed a distinguished record of traditional cruises, world exploration, and transatlantic crossings since 1873—all facets of its history that are reflected in the fleet's multimillion-dollar shipboard art and antiques collections. Noted for focusing on passenger comfort, Holland America Line cruises are classic in design and style, and with an infusion of younger adults and families on board, they remain refined without being stuffy or stodgy. Following a basic design theme, returning passengers feel as at home on the newest Holland America vessels as they do on older ones.

Your Shipmates: No longer just your grandparents' cruise line, today's Holland America sailings attract families and discerning couples, mostly from their late-thirties on up. Holidays and summer months are peak periods when you'll find more children in the mix. Comfortable retirees are often still in the majority, particularly on longer cruises.

Dress Code: Evenings on Holland America Line cruises fall into two categories: smart casual and formal. For the two formal nights standard on seven-night cruises, men are encouraged to wear tuxedos, but dark suits or sport coats and ties are acceptable, and you'll certainly see them. On smart-casual nights, expect the type of attire you'd see at a country club or upscale resort. It's requested that no T-shirts, jeans, swimsuits, tank tops, or shorts be worn in public areas after 6 pm.

Tipping: Gratuities of $11.50 per passenger per day are automatically added to shipboard accounts, and distributed to stewards and waitstaff. Passengers may adjust the amount based on the level of service experienced. Room-service tips are usually given in cash (it's at the passenger's discretion here). Gratuities for spa and salon services can be added to the bill or offered in cash. An automatic 15% gratuity is added to bar-service tabs. ☎ *206/281–3535 or 800/577–1728* ⊕ *www. hollandamerica.com* ☞ *Cruise Style: Premium.*

Hurtigruten. Originally a communications and travel link between the villages on Norway's western coast, Hurtigruten provides an up-close look at the fascinatingly intricate fjords, mountains, and villages that were once isolated and difficult to navigate. The Hurtigruten itineraries are often described as "the world's most beautiful voyages," as they provide access to some of the most stunning scenery and the unique cultures of Norway, many of them above the Arctic Circle. Nine Hurtigruten ships sail year-round on Norwegian coastal express routes. Options include 6-night northbound, 5-night southbound, or 12-night round-trip sailings, calling at 34 ports in each one-way segment. Others spend part of the year on Antarctic and Chilean Fjord itineraries or take trips to Spitsbergen, an island midway between Norway and the North Pole. The MS *Fram* also makes summer expeditions to Greenland as well as a world cruise. These are also working ships, transferring both cargo and passengers, but the ships have the look and feel of traditional cruise ships.

Your Shipmates: Europeans make up the larger number of passengers, but there is often a minority of Americans. Travelers who find this kind of cruising attractive tend to be independent—comfortable controlling their vacation experience and perfectly content enjoying spectacular

scenery and visiting picturesque communities mostly on their own. Families with small kids are few and far between.

Dress Code: Hurtigruten ships are truly casual, with no dress-up nights. Pack clothing suitable for the area and season in which you are traveling. During the day and throughout the voyage, weather fluctuations can occur rather quickly. It is recommended you dress in layers to accommodate the changes in temperature. Should you choose to pack light, all ships reviewed here are equipped with self-service laundry facilities, including irons and ironing boards. Detergent is included in the price.

Tipping: Tipping is neither required nor expected, though it is allowed if you feel you have received particularly good personal service from a crew member. ☎ *800/323–7436* ⊕ *www.hurtigruten.us* ⌕ *Cruise Style: Small-ship.*

Lindblad Expeditions. Every Lindblad cruise is educational, focusing on soft adventure and environmentally conscientious travel. Since 2004 the line has partnered with *National Geographic* to enhance the cruise experience by including experts and photographers on board to lead discussions and hold workshops and help balance "must-see" destinations and less-traveled spots. The ships of Lindblad Expeditions spend time looking for wildlife, exploring out-of-the-way inlets, and making Zodiac landings at isolated beaches. Each ship has a fleet of kayaks as well as a video-microphone: a hydrophone (underwater microphone) is combined with an underwater camera so passengers can listen to whale songs and watch live video of what's going on beneath the waves. All activities and shore excursions, from guided walks and hikes to museum entrance fees to water activities like kayaking and snorkeling, are included in the cost of every Lindblad Expedition. Guests always have the freedom to pick and choose activities as the day unfolds.

Your Shipmates: Lindblad attracts active, adventurous, well-traveled over-forties, and quite a few singles, as the line charges one of the industry's lowest single supplements. But the line is making a push to be more family-friendly by adding cruises aimed specifically at families and children.

Dress Code: Casual and comfortable attire is always appropriate. Recommendations are based on practicality and the likely weather conditions in the region you're exploring. Good walking shoes are essential.

Tipping: Although gratuities are at your discretion, tips of $12–$15 per person per day are suggested; these are pooled among the crew at journey's end. Tip the massage therapist individually following a treatment. ☎ *212/765–7740 or 800/397–3348* ⊕ *www.expeditions.com* ⌕ *Cruise Style: Small-ship.*

Louis Cruises. Louis Cruises was established in 1986, with a fleet of refurbished, well-maintained ships. Today, the value-oriented line has six ships, two of which are chartered by and sail under the Thomson brand (⇨ *see Thomson Cruises*). Ships vary in size, age, and available amenities, but all the ships' cabins and facilities are well maintained and clean. Lacking luxury appointments and the accompanying prices and pretension, a cruise on any of the four Louis Cruises vessels concentrates

more on destination than the actual shipboard experience. Some Louis ships may not meet the high expectations of well-heeled globe-trotters, but the itineraries can be outstanding.

Your Shipmates: A wide range of ages and nationalities embark on Louis Cruise voyages. While crew and staff are all local Greeks, Cypriots, and other Eastern Europeans, clientele are usually British, French, German, and a variety of northern Europeans, with a growing number of Americans and Canadians as passengers.

Dress Code: Casual attire is common by day, and the evening dress code is country club casual, with more formalwear visible during special dinners. Women tend to wear long trousers or cocktail dresses. Men wear a jacket and tie. "Greek Night" suggests attire in blue and white, the colors of Greece.

Tipping: Tipping is expected. The line will debit shipboard accounts €8 per person per day for adults over 16 and €4 per person per day for children ages 6–16. Amounts can be adjusted by speaking with the staff at reception. ☎ *(44) 0800/0183883 in the U.K.; (30) 210/4583400 in Greece ⊕ www.louiscruises.com ☞ Cruise Style: Mainstream.*

MSC Cruises. More widely known as one of the world's largest cargo shipping companies, MSC has operated cruises with an eclectic fleet since the late 1980s. This line is growing into a major player in both Europe and the Caribbean. MSC blankets the Mediterranean nearly year-round with a dizzying selection of cruise itineraries that allow a lot of time in ports of call and include few if any sea days. In summer months, several ships sail off to northern Europe to ply the Baltic. Itineraries planned for repositioning sailings visit some intriguing, off-the-beaten-track ports of call that other cruise lines bypass. No glitz, no clutter—just elegant simplicity—is the standard of MSC's seaworthy interior decor. Extensive use of marble, brass, and wood reflects the best of Italian styling and design; clean lines and bold colors set their modern sophisticated tone. MSC adopts some activities that appeal to American passengers without abandoning those preferred by Europeans; however, regardless of the itinerary, be prepared for an Italian-influenced experience.

Your Shipmates: Most passengers are couples in the 35- to 55-year-old range, as well as some family groups who prefer the international atmosphere prevalent on board. Although more than half the passengers on Caribbean itineraries are North Americans, expect a more international mix on European cruises, with North Americans in the minority.

Dress Code: Two formal nights are standard on seven-night cruises, and three may be scheduled on longer sailings. Men are encouraged to wear dark suits, but sport coats and ties are appropriate. All other evenings are casual, although jeans are discouraged in restaurants. It's requested that no shorts be worn in public areas after 6 pm.

Tipping: For cruises of eight nights or less, customary gratuities are added to your shipboard account in the amount of €7 per person per day for adults and half that amount for children; for longer cruises, the customary daily amount is €6. You can always adjust these amounts at the reception desk or even pay in cash, if you prefer. Automatic 15%

gratuities are incorporated into all bar purchases. You may also reward staff in the spa and casino for exceptional service. ☎ *800/666–9333* ⊕ *www.msccruisesusa.com* ☞ *Cruise Style: Premium.*

Norwegian Cruise Line. Norwegian Cruise Line (originally known as Norwegian Caribbean Line) set sail in 1966 with an entirely new concept: regularly scheduled Caribbean cruises from the then-obscure port of Miami. Good food and friendly service combined with value fares established Norwegian as a winner for active adults and families. Innovative and forward-looking, Norwegian has been a cruise-industry leader for four decades, and is as much at home in Europe as it is in the Caribbean.

Noted for top-quality, high-energy entertainment and emphasis on fitness facilities and programs, Norwegian combines action, activities, and a variety of dining options in a casual, free-flowing atmosphere. Freestyle cruising signaled an end to rigid dining schedules and dress codes. Norwegian ships now offer a host of flexible dining options that allow passengers to eat in the main dining rooms or any of a number of à la carte and specialty restaurants at any time and with whom they please. Now co-owned by Genting Hong Kong Limited and Apollo Management, a private equity company, Norwegian continues to be an industry innovator.

Your Shipmates: Norwegian's mostly American cruise passengers are active couples ranging from their mid-thirties to mid-fifties. Many families enjoy cruising on Norwegian ships during holidays and summer months. Longer cruises and more exotic itineraries attract passengers in the over-55 age group.

Dress Code: Resort casual attire is appropriate at all times; the option of one formal evening is available on all cruises of seven nights and longer. Most passengers actually raise the casual dress code a notch to what could be called casual-chic attire.

Tipping: A fixed service charge of $12 per person per day is added to shipboard accounts. An automatic 15% gratuity is added to bar tabs. Staff members may also accept cash gratuities. Passengers in suites who have access to concierge and butler services are asked to offer a cash gratuity at their own discretion. ☎ *305/436–4000 or 800/327–7030* ⊕ *www.ncl.com* ☞ *Cruise Style: Mainstream.*

Oceania Cruises. This distinctive cruise line was founded by Frank Del Rio and Joe Watters, cruise-industry veterans with the know-how to satisfy the wants of inquisitive passengers. By offering itineraries to interesting ports of call and upscale touches—all for fares much lower than you would expect—they are succeeding quite nicely. Intimate and cozy public spaces reflect the importance of socializing on Oceania ships. Waiters are on standby to offer chilled towels or serve passengers with beverages or snacks, whether they are on deck or in a lounge. In addition, you can request a spa service in your cabana. Varied, destination-rich itineraries are an important characteristic of Oceania Cruises, and most sailings are in the 10- to 12-night range.

Your Shipmates: Oceania Cruises appeal to singles and couples from their late-thirties to well-traveled retirees who have the time for and pre-

fer longer cruises. Most are American couples attracted to the casually sophisticated atmosphere, creative cuisine, and high level of service.

Dress Code: Leave the formal wear at home—attire on Oceania ships is country-club casual every evening, although some guests can't help dressing up to dine in the beautifully appointed restaurants. A jacket and tie are never required for dinner, but many men wear sport jackets, as they would to dine in an upscale restaurant ashore. Jeans, shorts, T-shirts, and tennis shoes are discouraged after 6 pm in public rooms.

Tipping: Gratuities of $14.50 per person per day are added to shipboard accounts for distribution to stewards and waitstaff; an additional $6 per person per day is added for occupants of suites with butler service. Passengers may adjust the amount based on the level of service experienced. An automatic 18% gratuity is added to all bar tabs for bartenders and drink servers and to all bills for salon and spa services. ☎ *305/514–2300 or 800/531–5658* ⊕ *www.oceaniacruises.com* ☞ *Cruise Style: Premium.*

P&O Cruises. P&O Cruises is the oldest cruise in the world and remains Britain's leading cruise line, sailing the U.K.'s largest and most modern fleet. The ships are equipped with every traditional big-ship amenity, including swimming pools, stylish restaurants, spas, bars, casinos, theaters, and showrooms. Seven ships in the P&O fleet offer a diverse range of venues for relaxation and entertainment, including cocktail bars, nightclubs, cinemas, games rooms, and cabaret lounges. To offer passengers a variety of choices, P&O has adapted their fleet to match the preferences of their primary markets. Although most of the ships cater to families as well as couples and singles of all ages, *Arcadia, Adonia,* and *Oriana* are adults-only ships. The *Aurora, Azura, Oceana,* and *Ventura* complete the P&O armada and welcome both adults and children. Following customer feedback, P&O announced major refurbishments for the *Ventura, Oceana,* and *Arcadia* in 2013.

Your Shipmates: Count on fellow passengers to be predominantly British singles, couples, and families. Depending on which ship you are sailing on, the age demographic and passenger profile will vary; you may find Scandinavians, Americans, Australians, and other Europeans on board for some sailings in addition to the primarily British clientele. Passengers must be 18 or older to sail aboard the all-adult ships.

Dress Code: Daytime attire is appropriately casual; evening wear falls into three traditional categories: formal, informal, and smart casual. Formal is either a tuxedo or dark suit for men and informal generally requires men to wear a jacket to dinner. For women, cocktail dresses or elegant ensembles are the norm. Check P&O's website for specific theme-night dress codes for each ship and itinerary.

Tipping: A daily amount of £3.10 per person over the age of 12 is added automatically to passengers' onboard accounts and is shared among the waitstaff and cabin stewards. Prepayment is not possible. Should you wish to amend this amount, you can do so by visiting Reception during your cruise. ☎ *0845/374–0111* ⊕ *www.pocruises.com* ☞ *Cruise Style: Mainstream.*

1

Paul Gauguin Cruises. With one ship built specifically to sail the waters of Tahiti, French Polynesia, and the South Pacific and synonymous with luxury and exotic destinations, Paul Gauguin Cruises remains a top choice for discerning travelers and honeymooners. Paul Gauguin Cruises was acquired in 2010 by Pacific Beachcomber SC, the largest luxury hotel and cruise operator in French Polynesia. In order to offer similarly luxurious cruises in other regions—Europe in summer months and the Caribbean during the winter season—the line introduced a second vessel, MV *Tere Moana* in 2012. Intimate and luxurious, Paul Gauguin ships offer a cruise experience tailored to the regions in which they sail. A relaxed atmosphere prevails throughout both vessels, but the cruise line definitely has a split personality, with voyages on MS *Paul Gauguin* limited to the South Pacific and those of MV *Tere Moana* as varied as the Caribbean and Europe.

Your Shipmates: Paul Gauguin Cruises attracts passengers of all ages, and on *Paul Gauguin* especially you'll see young honeymooners mingling with mature well-traveled couples. Most enjoy the relaxed atmosphere on board in addition to the exotic ports and unique experiences ashore.

Dress Code: Elegant resort-casual attire is appropriate at all times. Slacks and a golf or sport shirt for men and sporty dresses or skirts or pants with a sweater or blouse for women are suggested for evening. Jackets are not required, but many men bring along a sport coat for the Captain's Welcome Reception.

Tipping: Tipping is neither required nor expected. ☎ *800/848–6172* ⊕ *www.pgcruises.com* ☞ *Cruise Style: Luxury.*

Princess Cruises. Princess Cruises may be best known for introducing cruise travel to millions of viewers, when its flagship became the setting for *The Love Boat* television series in 1977. Since that heady time of small-screen stardom, the Princess fleet has grown both in the number and size of ships. Although most are large in scale, Princess vessels manage to create the illusion of intimacy through the use of color and decor in understated yet lovely public rooms graced by multimillion-dollar art collections. Princess has also become more flexible; Personal Choice Cruising offers alternatives for open seating dining (when you wish and with whom you please) and entertainment options as diverse as those found in resorts ashore.

Your Shipmates: Princess Cruises attract mostly American passengers, ranging from their midthirties to midfifties. Families enjoy cruising together on the Princess fleet, particularly during holiday seasons and in summer months, when many children are on board. Longer cruises appeal to well-traveled retirees and couples who have the time.

Dress Code: Two formal nights are standard on seven-night cruises; an additional formal night may be scheduled on longer sailings. Men are encouraged to wear tuxedos, but dark suits are appropriate. All other evenings are casual, although jeans are discouraged, and it's requested that no shorts be worn in public areas after 6 pm.

Tipping: A gratuity of $11.50 per person per day ($12 for passengers in suites and minisuites) is added to shipboard accounts for distribution

to stewards and waitstaff. Passengers may adjust the amount based on the level of service experienced. An automatic 15% is added to all bar tabs for bartenders and drink servers; gratuities to other staff members may be extended at passengers' discretion. ☎ *661/753–0000 or 800/774–6237* ⊕ *www.princess.com* ☞ *Cruise Style: Premium.*

Regent Seven Seas Cruises. The 1994 merger of Radisson Diamond Cruises and Seven Seas Cruise Line launched Radisson Seven Seas Cruises with an eclectic fleet of vessels that offers a nearly all-inclusive cruise experience in sumptuous, contemporary surroundings. The line was rebranded as Regent Seven Seas Cruises in 2006, and ownership passed to Prestige Cruise Holdings (which also owns Oceania Cruises) in 2008. Even more inclusive than in the past, the line has maintained its traditional tried-and-true formula—delightful ships offering exquisite service, generous staterooms with abundant amenities, a variety of dining options, and superior lecture and enrichment programs. Guests are greeted with champagne on boarding and find an all-inclusive beverage policy that offers not only soft drinks and bottled water, but also cocktails and select wines at all bars and restaurants throughout the ships. Some shore excursions are included in the cruise fare.

Your Shipmates: Regent Seven Seas Cruises are inviting to active, affluent, well-traveled couples ranging from their late thirties to retirees who enjoy the ship's chic ambience and destination-rich itineraries. Longer cruises attract veteran passengers in the over-sixty age group.

Dress Code: Elegant casual is the dress code for most nights; formal and semiformal attire is optional on sailings of 16 nights or longer, but it's no longer required. It's requested that dress codes be observed in public areas after 6 pm.

Tipping: Gratuities are included in the fare, and none are expected. To show their appreciation, passengers may elect to make a contribution to a crew welfare fund that benefits the ship's staff. ☎ *877/505–5370* ⊕ *www.rssc.com* ☞ *Cruise Style: Luxury.*

Royal Caribbean International. Big, bigger, biggest! In the early 1990s, Royal Caribbean launched Sovereign-class ships, the first of the modern megacruise liners, which continue to be the all-around favorite of passengers who enjoy traditional cruising ambience with a touch of daring and whimsy. Plunging into the 21st century, each ship in the current fleet carries more passengers than the entire Royal Caribbean fleet of the 1970s, and has amenities—such as new surfing pools—that were unheard of in the past. All Royal Caribbean ships are topped by the company's distinctive signature Viking Crown Lounge, a place to watch the seascape by day and dance at night. Expansive multideck atriums and promenades, as well as the generous use of brass and floor-to-ceiling glass windows, give each vessel a sense of spaciousness and style. The action is nonstop in casinos and dance clubs after dark, while daytime hours are filled with poolside games and traditional cruise activities.

Your Shipmates: Royal Caribbean cruises have a broad appeal for active couples and singles, mostly in their thirties to fifties. Families are partial to the newer vessels that have larger staterooms, huge facilities

for children and teens, and seemingly endless choices of activities and dining options.

Dress Code: Two formal nights are standard on seven-night cruises; one formal night is the norm on shorter sailings. Men are encouraged to wear tuxedos, but dark suits or sport coats and ties are more prevalent. All other evenings are casual, although jeans are discouraged in restaurants. It's requested that no shorts be worn in public areas after 6 pm, although there are passengers who can't wait to change into them after dinner.

Tipping: Tips can be prepaid when the cruise is booked, added on to shipboard accounts, or given in cash on the last night of the cruise. Suggested gratuities per passenger per day are $5 for the cabin steward ($7.25 for suites), $3.75 for the waiter, $2.15 for the assistant waiter, and $0.75 for the headwaiter. A 15% gratuity is automatically added to all bar tabs and spa and salon services. ☎ *305/539–6000 or 800/327–6700* ⊕ *www.royalcaribbean.com* ⊂ *Cruise Style: Mainstream.*

Saga Cruises. Saga Cruises purchased its first ship in 1996. Itineraries brim with longer sailings to far-flung corners of the globe, making Saga voyages destination-oriented. Classic cruisers in every sense of the word, Saga's passengers are travelers who expect inspiring itineraries coupled with traditional onboard amenities and comfortable surroundings. In the style of Saga Holidays' land-based tours, Saga Cruises takes care of the details that discerning passengers don't wish to leave to chance—from providing insurance and arranging visas to placing fruit and water in every cabin. Ships have card rooms, but you won't find casinos. With numerous accommodations designed for solo cruisers, Saga Cruises are particularly friendly for senior singles. Especially convenient on lengthy sailings, each ship features complimentary self-service launderettes and ironing facilities. In port, the line offers complimentary shuttle transfers to the town center from the cruise pier.

Your Shipmates: Saga Cruises are exclusively for passengers age 50 and older; the minimum age for traveling companions is 40. On a typical cruise—particularly one of the longer itineraries—the average age of passengers may be quite a bit higher than 50. The overwhelming majority of passengers are from Great Britain, with a sprinkling of North Americans in the mix.

Dress Code: Dress on Saga ships is very traditional. While the requested attire on board is generally casual during the day, including sea days, by night there are three dress codes—formal, informal, and smart casual.

Tipping: Gratuities are included in the fare, and additional tipping is not expected. ☎ *0800/096–0079 or (44) 1303/771–111* ⊕ *www.saga. co.U.K.* ⊂ *Cruise Style: Premium.*

Seabourn Cruise Line. Seabourn was founded on the principle that dedication to personal service in elegant surroundings would appeal to sophisticated, independent-minded passengers whose lifestyles demand the best. Lovingly maintained since their introduction in 1987—and routinely updated with new features—the original megayachts of Seabourn and their new fleetmates have proved to be a smashing success over the years. They remain favorites with people who can take care

of themselves but would rather do so aboard a ship that caters to their individual preferences. Recognized as a leader in small-ship, luxury cruising, Seabourn delivers all the expected extras—complimentary wines and spirits, a stocked minibar in all suites, and elegant amenities. Expect the unexpected as well—from exclusive travel-document portfolios and luggage tags to the pleasure of a complimentary minimassage while lounging at the pool. If you don't want to lift a finger, Seabourn will even arrange to have your luggage picked up at home and delivered directly to your suite—for a price. Peace and tranquility reign on these ships, so the daily roster of events is somewhat thin. The line launched a newer set of larger, even more luxurious triplets that were introduced in 2009 (*Seabourn Odyssey*), 2010 (*Seabourn Sojourn*), and 2011 (*Seabourn Quest*). The original trio of ships was sold to Windstar in 2013.

Your Shipmates: Seabourn's yacht-like vessels appeal to well-traveled, affluent couples of all ages who enjoy destination-intense itineraries, a subdued atmosphere, and exclusive service. Passengers tend to be fifty-plus and retired couples who are accustomed to evening formality.

Dress Code: At least one formal night is standard on seven-night cruises and three to four nights, depending on the itinerary, on two- to three-week cruises. Men are required to wear tuxedos or dark suits after 6 pm, and the majority prefers black tie. All other evenings are elegant casual, and slacks with a jacket over a sweater or shirt for men and a sundress or skirt or pants with a sweater or blouse for women are suggested.

Tipping: Tipping is neither required nor expected. ☎ *800/929–9391* ⊕ *www.seabourn.com* ☞ *Cruise Style: Luxury.*

SeaDream Yacht Club. SeaDream yachts began sailing in 1984 beneath the Sea Goddess banner, and after a couple of changes of ownership and total renovations, they have evolved into the ultimate boutique ships. A voyage on one of these sleek megayachts is all about personal choice. Passengers enjoy an unstructured holiday at sea doing what they please, making it easy to imagine the diminutive vessel really is a private yacht. The ambience is refined and elegantly casual. Fine dining and socializing with fellow passengers and the ships' captains and officers are preferred yachting pastimes.

The weekly picnic on a private beach is considered by many passengers as their most memorable experience ashore during a SeaDream cruise. SeaDream yachts are often chartered by families, corporations, and other affinity groups, but the company does not charter both ships at the same time.

Your Shipmates: SeaDream yachts attract energetic, affluent travelers of all ages, as well as groups. Passengers tend to be couples in their mid-forties up to retirees who enjoy the unstructured informality, subdued ambience, and utterly exclusive service.

These ships are not recommended for passengers who use wheelchairs. Although there's one accessible stateroom, public facilities have thresholds and the elevator doesn't reach the uppermost deck. Tide conditions can cause the gangway to be steep when docked, and negotiating shore tenders would be impossible.

Dress Code: Leave the formal duds at home—every night is yacht casual on SeaDream. Men wear open-collar shirts and slacks; sport coats are preferred but not required. A tie is never necessary. For women, sundresses, dressy casual skirts and sweaters, or pants and tops are the norm.

Tipping: Tipping is neither required nor expected. ☎ *305/631–6100 or 800/707–4911* ⊕ *www.seadream.com* ⌖ *Cruise Style: Luxury.*

Silversea Cruises. Silversea Cruises was launched in 1994 by the former owners of Sitmar Cruises, the Lefebvre family of Rome, whose concept for the new cruise line was to build and sail the highest-quality luxury ships at sea. Intimate ships, paired with exclusive amenities and unparalleled hospitality, are the hallmarks of Silversea cruises. All-inclusive air-and-sea fares can be customized to include not just round-trip airfare but all transfers, porterage, and deluxe precruise accommodations as well. Personalization is a Silversea maxim. Their ships offer more activities than other comparably sized luxury vessels. Take part in those that interest you, or opt instead for a good book and any number of quiet spots to read or snooze in the shade. Silversea's third generation of ships introduced even more luxurious features when the 36,000-ton *Silver Spirit* launched late in 2009. Silversea's *Silver Explorer* is the top choice for luxurious, soft-adventure, expedition cruising, and in 2013 Silversea will add a second exploration ship that will sail exclusively in the Galapagos Islands.

Your Shipmates: Silversea Cruises appeal to sophisticated, affluent couples who enjoy the country-club-like atmosphere, exquisite cuisine, and polished service on board, not to mention the exotic ports and unique experiences ashore.

Dress Code: Two formal nights are standard on seven-night cruises and three to four nights, depending on the itinerary, on longer sailings. Men are required to wear tuxedos or dark suits after 6 pm. All other evenings are either informal, when a jacket is called for (a tie is optional, but most men wear them), or casual, when slacks with a jacket over an open-collar shirt for men and sporty dresses or skirts or pants with a sweater or blouse for women are suggested.

Tipping: Tipping is neither required nor expected. ☎ *954/522–2299 or 877/276–6816* ⊕ *www.silversea.com* ⌖ *Cruise Style: Luxury.*

Star Clippers. Star Clippers vessels are four- and five-masted sailing beauties—the world's largest barkentine and full-rigged sailing ships. Filled with modern, high-tech equipment as well as the amenities of private yachts, the ships rely on sail power while at sea unless conditions require the assistance of the engines. Minimal heeling, usually less than 6%, is achieved through judicious control of the sails. A lack of rigid scheduling is one of Star Clippers' most appealing attractions. As attractive as the ships' interiors are, the focal point of Star Clippers cruises is the outdoors. Plan to spend a lot of time on deck soaking in the sun, sea, and sky. Although the Star Clippers ships are motorized, their engines are shut down whenever crews unfurl the sails (36,000 square feet on *Star Clipper* and *Star Flyer*, and 56,000 square feet on *Royal Clipper*)

to capture the wind. On a typical cruise, the ships rely exclusively on sail power any time favorable conditions prevail.

Your Shipmates: Star Clippers cruises draw active, upscale American and European couples in their thirties and up, who enjoy sailing but in a casually sophisticated atmosphere with modern conveniences. Many sailings are equally divided between North Americans and Europeans. This is not a cruise line for the physically challenged: there are no elevators or ramps, nor are staterooms or bathrooms wheelchair accessible. Gangways and shore launches can also be difficult to negotiate.

Dress Code: All evenings are elegant casual, so slacks and open-collar shirts are fine for men, and sundresses, skirts, or pants with a sweater or blouse are suggested for women. Coats and ties are never required. Shorts and T-shirts are not allowed in the dining room at dinner.

Tipping: Gratuities are not included in the cruise fare and are extended at the sole discretion of passengers. The recommended amount is €8 per person per day. Tips are pooled and shared; individual tipping is discouraged. You can either put cash in the tip envelope provided and drop it at the Purser's Office or charge gratuities to your shipboard account. An automatic 15% gratuity is added to each passenger's bar bill. ☎ *305/442–0550 or 800/442–0551* ⊕ *www.starclippers.com* ☞ *Cruise Style: Small Ship.*

Thomson Cruises. In 1973, the UK-based travel operator Thomson Holidays officially entered the cruising market under the umbrella company Thomson Travel Group, a subsidiary of the larger German enterprise TUI. Since its inception, Thomson has operated, scrapped, and rehauled almost a dozen ships. Thomson sails four vessels, including the *Thomson Dream, Thomson Majesty, Thomson Celebration,* and *Thomson Spirit.* Itineraries include the Caribbean; the Canary Islands and Morocco; the Western and Eastern Mediterranean, and Black Sea; Egypt and the Red Sea; and Scandinavia, Baltic, and the UK. The range of accommodations on Thomson's other ships offer well-appointed suites and staterooms worthy of a four-star luxury hotel. At this writing, a multimillion dollar makeover of two vessels in 2013 will bring cruising to a more upscale level. An attentive and friendly staff coupled with seasoned entertainment professionals attract a loyal following of happy cruisegoers traveling alone or together, with or without children.

Your Shipmates: The majority of passengers are British couples between the ages of 50 and 75. Families and groups are also well-represented. Attracting a mostly budget-conscious UK clientele, ships may include a diverse range of ages and other nationalities, many of whom are first-time cruisers.

Dress Code: Expect an informal atmosphere, although there is a dress code in the evening. Evenings are designated as "smart casual." Women tend to wear dresses, pantsuits, or an ensemble of trousers and blouse. For men, pack trousers, shirts, and a sports jacket. One formal night on each seven-night cruise requires evening wear, translated to cocktail dresses for women and jacket plus tie for men. No dress code applies on the *Island Escape,* which is always casual.

Tipping: Passengers are not required to tip crew and officers. All tips are included in the cruise price. Supplementary gratuity is accepted and completely at the discretion of passengers but is not expected. ☎ *(44) 870/165–0079 or 0871/230–2800, both in the UK* ⊕ *www.thomson. co.uk/cruise* ☞ *Cruise Style: Mainstream.*

Windstar Cruises. Since 1986, these masted sailing yachts have filled an upscale niche. They often visit ports of call inaccessible to huge, traditional cruise ships and offer a unique perspective of any cruising region. Though Windstar ships seldom depend on wind alone to sail, if you're fortunate and conditions are perfect, as they sometimes are, the complete silence of pure sailing is heavenly. Stabilizers and computer-controlled ballast systems ensure no more than a mere few degrees of lean. Onboard diversions are for the most part social, laid-back, and impromptu. Multimillion-dollar upgrades in 2012 enhanced each ship from stern to stern with chic new decor that mimics the colors of the sky and sandy beaches. In addition, all accommodations and bathrooms have been remodeled with updated materials; new weights and televisions were added to the gym; a couples massage room enhances the *Wind Surf* spa; the casual Veranda was expanded; the decks now have Balinese sun beds; and cooling mist sprayers are near the pools. Windstar's original sailing ships will be joined by three Seabourn vessels, which were purchased in 2013 and which will join the fleet beginning as early as 2014.

Your Shipmates: Windstar Cruises appeal to upscale professional couples in their late thirties to sixties who enjoy the unpretentious, yet casually sophisticated atmosphere, creative cuisine, and refined service. However, Windstar's ships were not designed for accessibility, and are not a good choice for the physically challenged.

Dress Code: All evenings are country-club casual, and slacks with a jacket over a sweater or shirt for men, and sundresses, skirts, or pants with a sweater or blouse for women are suggested. Coats and ties for men are not necessary, but some male passengers prefer to wear a jacket with open-collar shirt to dinner.

Tipping: A service charge of $12 per guest per day (including children) is added to each shipboard account. A 15% service charge is added to all bar bills. All these proceeds are paid directly to the crew. ☎ *206/292–9606 or 800/258–7245* ⊕ *www.windstarcruises.com* ☞ *Cruise Style: Luxury.*

Western Mediterranean

PORTS IN FRANCE, ITALY, MALTA, PORTUGAL, AND SPAIN

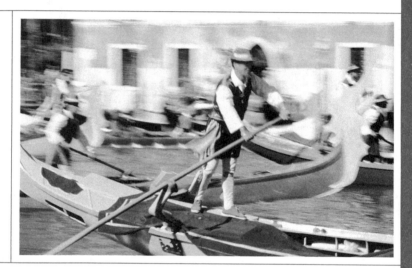

Gondolas, Venice

WORD OF MOUTH

"My wife and I are going on a trip of a lifetime next June—12-day Mediterranean/Greece cruise starting [in] Rome and ending in Venice. . . . Probably our biggest dilemma is in Naples. With only one day, do you go to Isle of Capri, try to see Pompeii and Mount Vesuvius, or see the Amalfi Coast?"

—MurrayMartin

If you're a first-time cruiser in Europe and want to stop at some of the most popular European destinations, a Western Mediterranean itinerary might be ideal for you.

Western Mediterranean itineraries often begin in either Barcelona or Civitavecchia (for Rome) and may be one-way or round-trip cruises. More one-week cruises in Europe tend to be one-way cruises than in other cruise regions, while those of 10 days or more are sometimes loop cruises. A few of these itineraries may take you as far as Venice, though that city is a more popular jumping-off point for cruises through the Adriatic and Aegean. Although some of the ports included in this chapter (such as Venice or Bari in Italy) are more likely to be on Eastern Mediterranean itineraries, others (such as Le Havre or Bordeaux in France) may be a part of some Northern European cruise routes. We've kept all the ports in Italy and France together in this chapter to make them easier to find. Larger ships will be limited in the ports at which they can call, but smaller ships may hit some of the lesser-visited spots on the French or Italian Riviera.

ABOUT THE RESTAURANTS
All the restaurants we recommend serve lunch, and many also serve dinner. If your cruise ship stays late in port, you may choose to dine off the ship. Although the cuisine in Europe is varied, one thing is constant across the continent: Europeans tend to eat a leisurely meal at lunch. In most ports there are quicker and simpler alternatives for those who just want to grab a quick bite before returning to the ship.

A CORUÑA, SPAIN (FOR SANTIAGO DE COMPOSTELA)

Updated by
Joanna Styles

One of Spain's busiest ports, A Coruña (La Coruña in Castilian) prides itself on being the most progressive city in the region. The weather can be fierce, wet, and windy—hence the glass-enclosed, white-pane galleries on the houses lining the harbor. This is one of two main ports at which cruise ships call so they can offer an overland trek to the pilgrimage city of Santiago de Compostela; the other is Vigo (⇨ *Vigo, below, for information on Santiago de Compostela, including a map*). Though at 57 km (35 miles) to the north, A Coruña is marginally closer. Occasionally, a cruise ship will offer an overland excursion beginning in one port and ending in the other.

ESSENTIALS
CURRENCY
The euro.

HOURS
Museums are generally open from 9 until 7 or 8, many are closed on Monday, and some close in the afternoon. Most stores are open Monday through Saturday 9 to 1:30 and 5 to 8, but tourist shops may open in the afternoon and also on Sunday between May and September.

2

PRIVATE TOURS

SECCHI organizes half- and full-day tours exploring Galician towns, cities, coastline, and countryside.

Contacts SECCHI. ☎ *981/554176* ⊕ *www.turismosecchi.com.*

TELEPHONES

Most tri- and quad-band GSM phones work in Spain, which has a 3G-compatible network. Public kiosks accept phone cards that support international calls (cards sold in press shops, bars, and telecom shops). Major companies include Vodafone.

COMING ASHORE

Ships dock at Liners Quay in the interior of the port. There are few services at the port itself, but from the port entrance you can explore the town on foot.

Bus 1 runs from the port to the main bus station every 15 minutes for €1.20. There is at least one train per hour to Santiago de Compostela. Journey time is 40 minutes, and tickets cost approximately €12 return.

Taxis wait at the port entrance and can be hired by the day for tourist itineraries. Renting a car will allow you to explore Santiago de Compostela plus the rugged countryside of this wild corner of Spain, but prices are expensive. Prices begin at €50 per day for a manual economy vehicle.

EXPLORING A CORUÑA

Castillo de San Antón. At the northeastern tip of the Old Town is the Castillo de San Antón (St. Anthony's Castle), a 16th-century fort. Inside is A Coruña's **Museum of Archaeology,** with remnants of the prehistoric Celtic culture that once thrived in these parts. The collection includes silver artifacts as well as pieces of the Celtic stone forts called *castros.* ⊠ *Paseo do Parrote s/n* ☎ *981/189850* ▨ *Free* ☉ *Sept.–June, Tues.–Sat 10–7:30, Sun. 10–2:30; July and Aug., Tues.–Sat., 10–9, Sun. 10–3.*

Colexiata de Santa María do Campo. Called "St. Mary of the Field" because the building was once beyond the city's walls, this Romanesque beauty dates to the mid-13th century. The facade depicts the Adoration of the Magi; the celestial figures include St. Peter, holding the keys to heaven. Because of an architectural miscalculation the roof is too heavy for its supports, so the columns inside lean outward and the buttresses outside have been thickened. ⊠ *Pl. de Santa María 1.*

Iglesia de Santiago. This 12th-century church, the oldest church in A Coruña, was the first stop on the *camino inglés* (English route) toward Santiago de Compostela. Originally Romanesque, it's now a hodge-podge that includes Gothic arches, a baroque altarpiece, and two 18th-century rose windows. ⊠ *Pl. de la Constitución s/n.*

Paseo Marítimo. To see why sailors once nicknamed A Coruña *la ciudad de cristal* (the glass city), stroll the Paseo Marítimo, said to be the longest seaside promenade in Europe. Although the congregation of boats is charming, the real sight is across the street: a long, gracefully curved row of houses. Built by fishermen in the 18th century, they face *away* from the sea—at the end of a long day, these men were tired of

looking at the water. Nets were hung from the porches to dry, and fish was sold on the street below. When Galicia's first glass factory opened nearby, someone thought to enclose these porches in glass, like the latticed stern galleries of oceangoing galleons, to keep wind and rain at bay. The resulting **glass galleries** ultimately spread across the harbor and eventually throughout Galicia.

Plaza de María Pita. The focal point of the *ciudad vieja* (Old Town), this stirring plaza has a north side that's given over to the neoclassical **Palacio Municipal**, or city hall, built 1908–12 with three Italianate domes. The **monument** in the center, built in 1998, depicts the heroine Maior (María) Pita. When England's Sir Francis Drake arrived to sack A Coruña in 1589, the locals were only half finished building the defensive Castillo de San Antón, and a 13-day battle ensued. When María Pita's husband died, she took up his lance, slew the Briton who tried to plant the Union Jack here, and revived the exhausted Coruñesos, inspiring other women to join the battle.

Torre de Hércules. Much of A Coruña sits on a peninsula, on the tip of which is the Torre de Hércules—the oldest still-functioning lighthouse in the world. Originally built during the reign of Trajan, the Roman emperor born in Spain in AD 98, the lighthouse was rebuilt in the 18th century and looks strikingly modern; all that remains from Roman times are inscribed foundation stones. Lining the approach to the lighthouse are sculptures depicting figures from Galician and Celtic legends. At this writing, the interior is closed for renovation, but the park is still worth a visit, whether or not you can get inside the lighthouse. ⊠ *Av. de Navarra s/n* 🕾 *981/223730* ⊕ *www.torredeherculesacoruna.com* 🖃 *€3* ⊙ *Apr.–June and Sept., daily 10–6:45; July and Aug., Mon.–Thurs. and Sun. 10–8:45, Fri. and Sat. 10–11:45; Oct.–Mar. daily 10–5:45.*

SHOPPING

Calle Real has boutiques with contemporary fashions. A stroll down **Calle San Andrés,** two blocks inland from Calle Real, or **Avenida Juan Flórez,** leading into the newer town, can yield some sartorial treasures.

José López Rama. Authentic Galician *zuecos* (hand-painted wooden clogs) are still worn in some villages to navigate mud; the cobbler José López Rama has a workshop 15 minutes south of A Coruña in the village of Carballo. ⊠ *Rúa do Muiño 7, Carballo* 🕾 *981/701068.*

Sastrería Iglesias. For hats and Galician folk clothing, stop into Sastrería Iglesias —founded in 1864—where artisan José Luis Iglesias Rodrígues sells his textiles. ⊠ *Rúa Rego do Auga 14* 🕾 *981/221634.*

WHERE TO EAT

$
SPANISH
★
✕ **Adega O Bebedeiro.** Steps from the ultramodern Domus, this tiny restaurant is beloved by locals for its authentic food. It feels like an old farmhouse, with stone walls and floors, a fireplace, pine tables and stools, and dusty wine bottles (*adega* is Gallego for bodega, or wine cellar). Appetizers such as *pulpo con almejas al ajillo* (octopus with clams in garlic sauce) are followed by fresh fish at market prices and

an ever-changing array of delicious desserts. $ *Average main: €15* ⊠ *C. Ángel Rebollo 34* ☎ *981/210609* ✆ *Closed Mon. and first week in Jan. No dinner Sun.*

$ ✕ **La Penela.** The smart, contemporary, bottle-green dining room is the
SEAFOOD   perfect place to feast on fresh fish while sipping Albariño—try at least a
★   few crabs or mussels with béchamel, for which this restaurant is locally famous. If shellfish isn't your speed, the roast veal is also popular. The restaurant occupies a modernist building on a corner of the lively Praza María Pita. Some tables have views of the harbor, or you can eat in a glassed-in terrace on the square. $ *Average main: €15* ⊠ *Praza María Pita 12* ☎ *981/209200* ✆ *Closed Sun. and Jan. 10–25.*

AJACCIO, CORSICA

Updated by
Victoria Tang

"The best way to know Corsica," according to Napoléon, "is to be born there." Not everyone has had his luck. This vertical chalky granite world of its own, rising in the Mediterranean between Provence and Tuscany, remains France's very own Wild West: a powerful natural setting and, literally, a breath of fresh air. Its strategic location 168 km (105 miles) south of Monaco and 81 km (50 miles) west of Italy made Corsica a prize hotly contested by a succession of Mediterranean powers, notably Genoa, Pisa, and France. Corsica gives an impression of immensity, seeming far larger than its 215 km (133 miles) length and 81 km (50 miles) width, partly because its rugged, mountainous terrain makes for very slow traveling and partly because the landscape and the culture vary greatly from one microregion to another. Much of the terrain of Corsica that is not wooded or cultivated is covered with a dense thicket of undergrowth, which along with chestnut trees makes up the maquis, a variety of wild and aromatic plants including lavender, myrtle, and heather that gave Corsica one of its sobriquets, "the perfumed isle."

ESSENTIALS
CURRENCY
The euro.

HOURS
Stores are generally open Monday through Saturday 9–7, but many close at lunchtime (usually noon–2 or 3) and some will open later and on Sunday during July and August. Museums open 10–5, but most are closed on either Monday or Tuesday.

TELEPHONES
Tri-band GSM phones work in France. You can buy prepaid phone cards at telecom shops, news vendors, and tobacconists in all towns and cities. Phone cards can be used for local or international calls. Orange, SFR, Bouygues Telecom, and Virgin are leading telecom companies. If you have an unlocked GSM phone, LeFrenchMobile (⊕ *www. lefrenchmobile.com*) offers SIM cards (and micro SIM cards) with support in English, unlimited validity of credits, and prepurchase online.

COMING ASHORE
Ships dock in Ajaccio port, a short walk from the town of Ajaccio. Cafés and shops can be found immediately outside the port gates.

Corsica

Ajaccio

- Musée Fesch ◆
- Chapelle Impériale ◆
- Jetée des Capucins
- av. Imperatore Eugénie
- sq. César Campinchi
- Marché Central (food market) ◆
- Port
- 1/16 mi
- 1/16 km
- Hôtel de Ville ◆
- Place Maréchal-Foch ◆
- Maison Bonaparte ◆
- Eglise St-Jean Baptiste ◆
- pl. Charles de Gaulle
- Cathédrale Notre Dame de L'Assomption ◆
- Notre Dame
- Citadelle

cours Napoléon · *quai l'Herminier* · r. S. Casalonga · r. Gl. Levie · d'Ornano · c. Grandval · av. de Paris · r. Bonaparte · r. Roi de Rome · r. F. Conti · bd. Lantivy · Charles

Map labels

- Cap Corse Peninsula
- Centuri
- Macinaggio
- Rogliano
- Pino
- Canari
- Monte Stello
- Canelle
- Sisco
- Nonza
- Erbalunga
- San Martino di Lota
- Patrimonio
- St-Florent
- Bastia
- L'Ile Rousse
- Oletta
- Lama
- Murato
- Casamozza
- Mariana
- Golo
- Algajola
- Pigna
- Sant'Antonino
- Calvi
- Catteri
- Cassano
- Calenzana
- Asco
- Ponte Leccia
- La Porta
- Folelli
- Haut-Asco
- Asco Valley
- Morosaglia
- Réserve Naturel de Scandola
- Monte Cinto
- Calacuccia
- Piedicroce
- Prunete
- Partinello
- Col de Verghio
- Scala di Santa Regina
- Corte
- Les Calanches
- Porto
- Evisa
- Ota
- Gorges de la Restonica
- Piana
- Vico
- Vivario
- Ghisoni
- Aléria
- Cargèse
- Sagone
- Tiuccia
- Ghisonaccia
- Golfe de Sagone
- Ajaccio see detail map
- Cauro
- Solenzara
- Iles Sanguinaires
- Golfe d'Ajaccio
- Porticcio
- Petreto-Bicchisano
- Parc Naturel Régional
- Col de Bavella
- Capo di Muro
- Filitosa
- Quenza
- Zonza
- Olmeto
- Propriano
- Ste-Lucie-de-Tallano
- Golfe de Porto-Vecchio
- Sartène
- Cauria
- Porto-Vecchio
- Figari
- Tyrrhenian Sea
- Mediterranean Sea
- Bonifacio
- Iles Lavezzi
- Ostricone Valley
- Golfe de Porto
- Tavignano
- Gravona · Prunelli · Taravo

Road numbers: D80, D180, D81, D82, N193, N197, N47, D151, D84, D515, D506, N193, D71, N200, N198, D344, N198, N196, D69, D268, D859, D368

The local bus network, catering to locals (not tourists), operates at least two buses a day to connect all the southern towns with Ajaccio, but timetables may not coincide with your ship's departure time, so check carefully.

Renting a vehicle would allow you to explore several towns and surrounding attractions during your stay on the island; however, be aware that travel times may be longer than map distances suggest, because the mountain roads can be narrow and winding. Vehicle rental costs approximately €60 per day for an economy manual car. Delivery to the port will be an additional charge. Hertz serves the entire island; its 18 offices are at all airports and harbors and in the major towns. Be sure to reserve at least two weeks in advance in July and August.

> **CORSICA BEST BETS**
>
> **Bonifacio.** Rising seemingly out of the living rock, this medieval stronghold is now a maze of tourist-friendly cafés and shops.
>
> **The Calanques de Piana.** Russet red inlets of jagged rocks lapped by azure waters, this vista, which you can see if you drive between Ajaccio and Calvi, is truly breathtaking.
>
> **Calvi.** A picture-perfect little town topped by a walled citadel, Calvi also offers some of the finest beaches on the island.

EXPLORING CORSICA

AJACCIO

Ajaccio, Napoléon's birthplace and Corsica's modern capital, is a busy, French-flavored town with a bustling port and ancient streets. The city has a long history dating back to its founding in 1492, and some of the original buildings can still be seen on rue Roie-de-Rome, near the Musée du Capitellu.

Cathédrale Notre Dame de L'Assomption. The 16th-century baroque cathedral where Napoléon was baptized is at the end of rue St-Charles. The interior is covered with trompe-l'oeil frescoes, and the high altar, from a church in Lucca, Italy, was donated by Napoléon's sister Eliza after he made her princess of Tuscany. Eugène Delacroix's *The Triumph of Religion* hangs above the Virgin of the Sacred Heart marble altar from the 17th-century. ⊠ *Rue F.-Conti.* ☎ *04–95–21–41–14* ⊕ *www.ajaccio-tourisme.com/* ▦ *Free* ☽ *Daily 9–11 am.*

Chapelle Impériale. Located on the south wing of the Palais Fesch, the neo-Renaissance-style Imperial Chapel was built in 1857 by Napoléon's nephew, Napoléon III, to accommodate the tombs of the Bonaparte family. The Coptic crucifix over the altar was taken from Egypt during the general's 1798 campaign. Renovated in 2012, the somber chapel officially classified as a historic monument is constructed worth a visit to view its neoclassical cupola and ecclesiastical iconography. ⊠ *50-52 rue Cardinal Fesch* ☎ *04–95–21–48–17* ⊕ *www.ajaccio.fr/La-Chapelle-Imperiale_a353.html* ▦ *€1.50; children under 15 free* ☽ *Tues.–Sat. 10–12:30 and 3–7.*

Eglise St-Jean Baptiste. Wander narrow streets lined with Ajaccio's oldest houses built around 1492, when the city was founded. At the intersection of rue du Roi-de-Rome and rue Saint Charles, you can visit the *confrérie*, or religious brotherhood, of St. Jean Baptiste. On June 24, the patron saint is honored with a solemn mass conducted by the city's bishop and Corsican music concert. Follow the ancestral religious procession from the chapel to the Old Town and Place Charles de Gaulle, where the celebration ends with traditional fire lighting in the evening. ⊠ *rue du Roi-de-Rome* ☎ *04–95–22–27– 38* ⊕ *www.ajaccio.fr/ Confreries-et-pelerinages_a21.html.*

Hôtel de Ville (*town hall*). Ajaccio's town hall has an Empire-style grand salon hung with portraits of a long line of Bonapartes. You'll find a fine bust of Letizia, Napóleon's formidable mother; a bronze death mask of the emperor himself; and a frescoed ceiling depicting Napóleon's meteoric rise. ⊠ *Pl. Maréchal-Foch, Avenue Antoine Serafini* ☎ *04–95– 51–52–53* ⊕ *www.ajaccio.fr* 🎫 *€2.30* ⊗ *Weekdays 9–noon and 2–6.*

Fodor'sChoice
★ **Maison Bonaparte** (*Bonaparte House*). One of four national historic museums dedicated to Napóleon, the multilevel house where the emperor was born on August 15, 1769, contains memorabilia and paintings of the extended Bonaparte family. History aficionados can tour bedrooms, dining rooms, and salons where Charles and Letitzia Bonaparte raised their eight children. Period furnishings and antiques in Corsican and Empire styles are scattered about and pay tribute to the family's bourgeoisie upbringing. Head downstairs below the Gallery to see the cellars and granite oil-pressing mill acquired by Napóleon III in 1860. Visit the trapdoor room and find the ground opening located next to the door through which Napóleon allegedly escaped in 1799. The building itself changed hands multiple times through Bonaparte heirs until 1923, when it was donated to the state of France by Prince Victor, elder son of Prince Jérôme Napoleon. ⊠ *Rue St-Charles* ☎ *04–95–21– 43–89* 🖨 *04–95–21–61–32* ⊕ *www.musee-maisonbonaparte.fr* 🎫 *€7 (Apr.–Oct.); €6 (low season); under 26 free* ⊗ *Oct.–Mar., Tue.–Sun. 10–noon and 2–4:45; Apr.–Sep., Tue.–Sun. 10:30–12:30 and 1:15–6* ⊗ *Last admission 30 min prior to closing.*

★ **Marché Central (food market).** For an authentic view of daily Corsican
☾ life, tour this wonderful open-air food market brimming with gastronomic delights. There is an array of local cheeses, charcuterie, breads, pastries, olives, condiments, and aromatic meats for sale. Taste samples of chorizo, nougat, liqueur, honeys, and oils from friendly foodstalls managed by original producers and farmers. Everything from artisanal candy to fresh-from-the-field vegetables and fruits, spices, and traditional indulgences like chestnut-infused beignets can be savored in an atmosphere guaranteed to be lively and local. Bring your euros—cash is the preferred method of payment. ⊠ *Square César Campinchi, boulevard du Roi Jérôme* ⊕ *www.ajaccio-tourisme.com* ⊗ *Tues.–Sun. 8–1; hours may vary due to weather.*

Fodor'sChoice
★ **Musée des Beaux Arts-Palais Fesch.** Adjacent to the Chapelle Impérial, this
☾ internationally recognized museum houses one of the most important collections from the Napoleonic era; it's undoubtedly one of the most

significant displays in France of ancient Italian masterpieces spanning the 14th–20th centuries. The massive treasure trove of objets d'art, sculptures, and paintings is impressive on scale alone—there are nearly 18,000 items, including nearly 16,000 awe-inspiring works from Italian painters. Seek out the dramatic realism of Neapolitan baroque artists Giordano and Giaquinto; view Renaissance masters Botticelli, Titian, Veronese and Fra Bartolomeo—all part of an astounding inventory that belonged to Napoléon's uncle, Cardinal Fesch, archbishop of Lyon and art lover, following the French Revolution. Thanks to his nephew's military conquests, the cardinal was able to amass (steal, some would say) many celebrated old master paintings, the most famous of which are now in Paris's Louvre. The museum's beautiful vaulted corridors, recently renovated for nearly €7 million, also showcase 700 paintings, portraits, still lifes, and sculptures from the First and Second Empire from the French school. ⊠ *50–52 rue Cardinal Fesch* ☎ *04–95–21–48–17* ⊕ *www. musee-fesch.com* ⊠ *€8* ⊘ *Oct.–Apr., Mon., Wed., and Sat. 10–5; Thurs., Fri., and 3rd Sun. of each month noon–5. May–Sept., Mon., Wed. and Sat. 10:30–6; Thur., Fri., and Sun. noon–6* ⊘ *Closed Tues.*

Place Maréchal-Foch. Surrounded by a row of stately palm trees, the Place Foch, also called the Place des Palmiers, is the city's magnificent central triangle, easily recognizable with its fountain of four Corsican granite lions encircling the commanding statue of Napoléon, a work by sculptor Jérôme Maglioli. Popular as a spot to people-watch on a sunny day, the place is surrounded by cafés, pharmacies, banks, and opens up to the Ajaccio port. ⊠ *Place Marechal Foch.*

FILITOSA

★ **Filitosa.** Filitosa is the site of Corsica's largest grouping of megalithic
Ⓒ menhir statues. The sensorial tour begins with a beautiful stroll down a bucolic tree-lined path with mesmerizing instrumental music emanating from hidden speakers. Discover enigmatic life-size stone figures of ancient warriors that rise up mysteriously from the undulating terrain, many with human faces whose features have been flattened over time by erosion. A small museum on the site houses archaeological finds, including the menhir known as *Scalsa Murta,* whose delicately carved spine and rib cage are surprisingly contemporary for a work dating from some 5,000 years ago. The guidebook in English (€5) by experts Cesari and Acquaviva is supplemented by information in English at each site. After your tour, enjoy a beverage at the small brasserie, where members of the Cesari family proudly discuss the site's historic discoveries on the personal property of Charles-Antoine Cesari in 1946. ⊠ *Centre Préhistorique Filitosa, Petreto-Bicchisano* ⊹ *Route 196 to col de Celaccia; right at Dept 57* ☎ *04–95–74–00–91 for information* ⊕ *www.filitosa. fr* ⊠ *Guided tours in English €5* ⊘ *June–October, daily 8–7.*

SARTÈNE

27 km (16 miles) southeast of Filitosa on N196.

Described as the "most Corsican of all Corsican towns" by French novelist Prosper Mérimée, Sartène, founded in the 16th century, has survived pirate raids and bloody feuding among the town's families. The word *vendetta* is believed to have originated here as the result of

a 19th-century family feud so serious that French troops were brought in to serve as a peacekeeping buffer force. Centuries of fighting have left the town with a somewhat eerie and menacing atmosphere. Perhaps adding to this is the annual Good Friday *catenacciu* (enchaining) procession, in which an anonymous penitent, dragging ankle chains, lugs a heavy cross through the village streets.

Surrounded by ancient ramparts, **Vieux Sartène** (Old Sartène) begins at place de la Libération, the main square. To one side is the **Hôtel de Ville** (town hall), in the former Genoese governor's palace. Slip into the Middle Ages through the tunnel under the town hall to place du Maggiu and the ancient **Santa Anna** quarter, a warren of narrow, cobbled streets lined with granite houses. Scarcely 100 yards from the Hôtel de Ville, down a steep and winding street, is a 12th-century *tour de guet* (watchtower). Sartène is a key link to Corsica's prehistory, thanks to its proximity to Pianu de Levie's dolmens and megalithic statues.

★ **Musée Départemental de Préhistoire Corse** (*Regional Museum of Prehis-*
☾ *toric Corsica and Archaeology*). Some of the island's best prehistoric relics are in this renovated museum in what was once the town's prison. Explore this well-maintained depot of more than 250,000 items from Neolithic times to the 15th century. The galleries chronologically catalog the development of crafts, trade, culture, habitats, and demographics of ancient Corsica. ⊠ *Rue Croce* ☏ *04–95–77–01–09* ⊕ *www. prehistoire-corse.org* ☙ *€4* ☾ *Jun.–Sept., daily 10–6; Oct.–May, weekdays 9–noon and 1:30–5.*

BONIFACIO
52 km (31 miles) southeast of Sartène via N196.

Fodor's Choice The ancient fortress town of Bonifacio occupies a spectacular cliff-top
★ aerie above a harbor carved from limestone cliffs. It's 13 km (8 miles) from Sardinia, and the local speech is heavily influenced by the accent and idiom of that nearby Italian island. Established in the 12th century as Genoa's first Corsican stronghold, Bonifacio remained Genoese through centuries of battles and sieges. As you wander the narrow streets of the **Haute Ville** (Upper Village), inside the walls of the citadel, think of Homer's *Odyssey*. It's here, in the harbor, that scholars place the catastrophic encounter (Chapter X) between Ulysses's fleet and the Laestrygonians, who hurled lethal boulders down from the cliffs.

★ **Bastion de l'Étendard** (*Bastion of the Standard*). From place d'Armes at the city gate, enter the 13th century Bastion de l'Étendard, where you can still see the system of weights and levers used to pull up the drawbridge. The former garrison, the last remaining part of the original fortress, now houses life-size dioramas of Bonifacio's history, which describes the bombardment of the bastion in the 16th century Franco-Turkish war. A visit gives you access to the memorial and Vestiges garden. Climb the steep steps and be rewarded with an incredible panoramic view of the white-chalk cliffs and stunning coastline. ⊠ *Avenue Charles de Gaulle* ☙ *€2.5* ☾ *Mid-Jun.–mid-Sept., Mon.–Fri. 9–8; Sat.–Sun. 10–7.*

★ **Dragon Grottoes.** From Bonifacio hop on a number of boats that can
☾ bring you to see the blue Dragon Grottos, a spectacular geological site. Comprehensive tours typically venture to Venus's Bath (the trip

takes one hour on boats that set out every 15 minutes during July and August), sea caves at Sdragonatto and St-Angoine, and the Lavezzi Islands. ⊠ *Boats leave from Bonifacio marina* ⊕ *www.bonifacio.fr.*

★ **Eglise Sainte Marie Majeure.** The oldest structure in the city, the 12th-century church with buttresses attaching it to surrounding houses is located in the center of the citadel's maze of cobblestone streets. Inside the Pisan-Genoese church, look for the Renaissance baptismal font, carved in bas-relief, and the 3rd-century white-marble Roman sarcophagus. Walk around the back to see the loggia built above a huge cistern that stored water for use in times of siege, as did the circular stone silos seen throughout the town. The 14th-century bell tower rises 82 feet. Relics of the patron Saint Bonifacio reside in the central altar. ⊠ *Rue du Saint Sacrement* ☎ *04–95–73–11–88* ⊕ *www.bonifacio.fr.*

PORTO–LES CALANCHES
5 km (3 miles) west of Ota, 30 km (19 miles) south of Calvi.

The flashy resort town of Porto doesn't have much character, but its setting on the crystalline **Golfe de Porto** (Gulf of Porto), surrounded by massive pink-granite mountains, is superb. Activity focuses on the small port, where there is a boardwalk with restaurants and hotels. A short hike from the boardwalk will bring you to a 16th-century Genoese tower that overlooks the bay. Boat excursions leave daily for the **Réserve Naturel de Scandola.**

CALVI
92 km (58 miles) north of Piana, 159 km (100 miles) north of Ajaccio.

Calvi, Corsica's slice of the Riviera, has been described by author Dorothy Carrington as "an oasis of pleasure on an otherwise austere island." Calvi prospered by supplying products to Genoa; its citizens remained loyal supporters of Genoa long after the rest of the island declared independence. Calvi also claims to be the birthplace of Christopher Columbus. During the 18th century the town endured assaults from Corsican nationalists, including celebrated patriot Pasquale Paoli. Today Calvi sees a summertime invasion of tourists, drawn to the 6-km (4-mile) stretch of sandy white beach, the citadel, and the buzzing nightlife.

★ **Citadelle.** The Genoese citadel perched on a rocky promontory at the tip of the bay competes with the beach as a major attraction. An inscription above the drawbridge—*civitas calvi semper fidelis* (the citizens of Calvi always faithful)—reflects the town's unswerving allegiance to Genoa. At the welcome center, just inside the gates, watch the video on the city's history and arrange to take a guided tour given in English (three times a day) or follow the self-guided walking tour. ⊠ *Up hill off Ave. de l'Uruguay* ☎ *04–95–65–36–74* ⊕ *www.villedecalvi.fr* 🎫 *Guided tour and video show €9* ☉ *Tours Easter–early Oct., daily at 10, 4:30, and 6:30.*

St-Jean-Baptiste. The austere façade of the 13th-century church of John the Baptist is worth a visit to see its alabaster Renaissance baptismal font decorated with angel heads and rows of pews where the city's chaste upper-class women used to pray. ⊠ *Pl. d'Armes* ☎ *04–95–65–16–67.*

L'ILE ROUSSE

10 km (6 miles) northeast of Algajola, 37 km (22 miles) southwest of St-Florent.

L'Ile Rousse, famous for its market and named for the island of reddish rock now connected to the town by a causeway, is a favorite for vacationers who come to bask in its Riviera-like mise-en-scène. A small two-car train runs along the coast to Calvi, delivering sun-worshippers to beaches not accessible by road.

SHOPPING

Traditional handicrafts are found in abundance in the shopping streets of the major towns. Until the mid-20th century most Corsicans had to be relatively self-sufficient, and this has led to all manner of crafts from knives and walking sticks to warm winter sweaters. Look for pottery, for which the island is known. Corsican knives are a specialty item, and the finest examples have exquisite blades and handles. Also look for items carved from wood and bone, some practical, some ornate. Because food had to be put back for the winter, preserved foods became very important parts of the Corsican diet, and are now well known; the charcuterie is excellent—in addition to a range of hams and salamis, you'll find aromatic dried herbs, numerous cheeses, plus fragrant jams and honey. Don't forget to sample a bottle of Corsican wine.

The citadel of Bonifacio has excellent boutiques set in historic stone cottages and cellars. Both Ajaccio and L'Isle Rousse have excellent markets, and in Calvi the major shopping streets are rue Clemenceau and boulevard Wilson.

Art'Insula. A large selection of fabrics, leather, and knives crafted by local artisans is available here. Find beautiful jewelry, pottery, and Corsican batik to take home as souvenirs. For the gourmand, select an assortment of confitures, honeys, vinegars, and liqueurs. ☒ *57 rue Fesch, Ajaccio* ☎ *04–95–50–54–67* ⊕ *www.artisula.com.*

★ **Casa Napoléon.** Belonging to Charles Antona, a native Corsican producer of fine gastronomic goods for more than 30 years, Casa Napoléon is the well-stocked boutique selling organic jams, terrines, traditional dishes, olives oils, wine, sweets and other delicacies straight from his Campestra factory and plantations. A second store is in Porticcio's Espace Commercial La Viva. ☒ *3 rue Fesch, Ajaccio* ☎ *04–95–21–47–88* ⊕ *www.charlesantona.com.*

Paese Nostru. Spices and Corsican crafts of all kinds are for sale in this tiny souvenir shop. Of special interest is the cutlery, hand-forged with wrought-iron and wooden handles. ☒ *29 Rue Fesch, Ajaccio* ☎ *04–95–51–05–07* ☉ *Mon.–Fri., 10–7; Sat. 9–6.*

U Stazzu. Look for the big red awning and stone façade of this excellent source for high-quality Corsican charcuterie, cheese, and wine. The award-winning shop offers some of the best hams and saucisson on the island, including the waist-busting Coppa and Lonzu. Ask for tasting samples before purchase. ☒ *1 rue Bonaparte, Ajaccio* ☎ *04–95–51–10–80* ⊕ *www.ustazzu.com.*

ACTIVITIES

The area around Bonifacio is ideal for water sports, including wind-surfing and sea kayaking. The island also has several golf courses for those who can't bear to be away from the greens. In summer, sailing is a major pastime, with wealthy French and Italians plying a course to the chic harbors and the secluded rocky coves. Well-being is also taken very seriously, with several excellent spas.

SPAS

★ **Institut de Thalassothérapie.** Integrated into the Sofitel Hotel, the Institut de Thalassothérapie (Institute of Thalassotherapy) is part of an upscale complex in the luxurious beach resort town about a 30-minute drive from the capital. Notable for its seawater cures, hydrotherapies, and restorative massages and scrubs, the institute is the perfect place to unwind after a long day of sightseeing and sunbathing. ⊠ *Domaine de la Pointe Golfe d'Ajaccio, Porticcio* ☎ *04–95–29–40–00* ⊕ *www.accorthalassa.com.*

WATER SPORTS

Club Atoll. This PADI-endorsed club offers a variety of water sports for beginners or advanced, with equipment rental and training. ⊠ *Rte. de Porto-Vecchio, Cavallo Morto, Bonifacio* ☎ *04–95–73–02–83.*

BEACHES

There are fine Riviera-like strands north of Calvi reached by a little train service that runs around the bay to L'Isle Rousse. These do get busy between late July and the end of August, but can be delightfully peaceful early or late in the season. In summer there are numerous cafés and restaurants for refreshment. Note that topless sunbathing is acceptable here, and you will find bare breasts at every beach.

Plage d'Ostriconi. This long stretch of white-sand beach at the mouth of the Ostriconi River is a popular spot to swim and sunbathe, although strong winds keep waves high. ⊠ *20 km 13 miles north of L'Isle Rousse* ⊕ *www.ot-ile-rousse.fr.*

Plage Saleccia. This wild, undeveloped white-sand beach surrounded by rugged maquis and dunes is frequented by nude bathers and was used as a location for the 1960s film *The Longest Day.* No doubt you will be mesmerized by clear turquoise waters along the mile-long shore. ⊠ *St-Florent* ⊕ *www.corsica-saintflorent.com.*

WHERE TO EAT

$$$$ ✕ **20123.** Tables are full at this very popular Ajaccio establishment
FRENCH   known for its traditional homemade cuisine, fresh daily catches, and, in season, game specials such as *civet de sanglier* (wild boar stew) served in a bubbling earthenware casserole of cheese-infused polenta. The rustic interior invites with a "starry sky" in a mock French village, antique lanterns, music, and stone fountain where guests pour their own water into ceramic jugs. In keeping with the familial style of service and food presentation, cutting boards with fresh-baked loaves of wheat bread are provided to start your copious meal. Three-course fixed menus are

offered in two seatings at 7:30 and 9:30, and include an exquisite cheese platter with homemade fig confiture. ⑤ *Average main: €35* ⊠ *2 rue Roi-de-Rome, Ajaccio* ☎ *04–95–21–50–05* ⊕ *www.20123.fr* ☉ *Closed Mon. and Jan. 15–Feb. 15. No lunch June 15–Sept. 15.*

$$$
SEAFOOD
★

✕ **Le Voilier.** Chef Jean Paul Bartoli and his wife make this casual year-round restaurant at the port a popular dining spot. With warm smiles, chocolate-colored décor, and attentive service, the couple serves carefully selected and prepared seafood, along with fine Corsican sausage and traditional cuisine from *soupe corse* to *fiadone* (cheesecake). Try the affordably priced menus. Ordering a three-course meal a la carte will cost about 65€. ⑤ *Average main: €30* ⊠ *81 Quai Comparetti, Bonifacio* ☎ *04–95–73–07–06* ⊕ *n/a* ☉ *Closed Mon. No dinner Sun.*

BARCELONA, SPAIN

Updated by
Joanna Styles

Capital of Catalonia, 2,000-year-old Barcelona commanded a vast Mediterranean empire when Madrid was still a dusty Moorish outpost on the Spanish steppe. Relegated to second-city status only in 1561, Barcelona has long rivaled and often surpassed Madrid's supremacy. Catalans jealously guard their language and their culture. Barcelona has long had a frenetically active cultural life. It was the home of architect Antoni Gaudí, and the painters Joan Miró and Salvador Dalí. Pablo Picasso also spent his formative years in Barcelona. Native musicians include cellist Pablo (Pau, in Catalan) Casals, opera singers Montserrat Caballé and José (Josep) Carreras, and early-music master Jordi Savall. One of Europe's most visually stunning cities, Barcelona balances its many elements, from the medieval intimacy of its Gothic Quarter to the grace of the wide boulevards in the moderniste Eixample. In the 21st century innovative structures, such as the Ricardo Bofill *vela* (sail) hotel, demonstrate Barcelona's insatiable appetite for novelty and progress.

ESSENTIALS

CURRENCY
The euro.

HOURS
Museums are generally open from 9 until 7 or 8; many are closed on Monday and some close in the afternoon. Most stores are open Monday through Saturday 9 to 1:30 and 5 to 8, but a few remain open all afternoon. Virtually all close on Sunday.

SAFETY
Barcelona has a reputation for active pickpocketing and scamming, especially around La Rambla. The risk is much greater at night than during daylight hours, but it always pays to be vigilant to avoid becoming a victim. Keep bags and purses closed, and carry them across the front of your body (this includes backpacks); thieves tend to cut bag straps to steal your belongings. Be aware of any approach by a stranger; it's better to walk away from all such encounters. And certainly don't carry any cash or valuables that you do not need. The best way to avoid being targeted by scams and pickpockets is to act with confidence and don't dress like a tourist. People in Barcelona dress smartly and rarely wear shorts and T-shirts.

PRIVATE TOURS

Barcelona Guide Bureau (⊕ *www.barcelonaguidebureau.com*) offers thematic, general, or personalized tours of the city leaving daily from Plaça de Catalunya; personalized tours must be arranged in advance.

TELEPHONES

Spain has good land and mobile services. Public kiosks accept phone cards that support international calls (cards sold in press shops, bars, and telecom shops). Mobile services are GSM and 3G compatible. Major companies include Vodafone.

COMING ASHORE

Barcelona is one of Europe's busiest cruise ports. Vessels dock at the Port Vell facility, which has seven terminals catering to cruise-ship traffic. All terminals are equipped with duty-free shops, telephones, bar/restaurants, information desks, and currency-exchange booths. The ships docking closest to the terminal entrance are a 10-minute walk from the southern end of Las Ramblas (the Rambla), but those docked at the farthest end require passengers to catch a shuttle bus (the Autobús Azul, a distinctive blue bus) to the port entrance. The shuttle, which runs every 20 minutes, links all terminals with the public square at the bottom of the Rambla. If you walk up Las Ramblas, after about 10 minutes you'll reach Drassanes metro station for onward public transport around the city. The shuttle runs about every 30 minutes A single metro or bus ticket is €2; a day ticket (T-Dia) is €7.

If you intend to explore Barcelona, don't rent a car. Public transportation and taxis are by far the most sensible options. City buses run daily from 5:30 am to 11:30 pm. The FCG (Ferrocarril de la Generalitat) train is a comfortable commuter train that gets you to within walking distance of nearly everything in Barcelona; transfers to the regular city metro are free. The Barcelona Tourist Bus is another excellent way to tour the city. Three routes (Red, Blue, and Green) cover just about every place you might want to visit, and you can hop on and off whenever you want. Buses run from 9 am to 7 pm, and a one-day ticket costs €24; you can buy advance tickets online at ⊕ *www.barcelonabusturistic.cat*.

If you plan to explore the Spanish coast or countryside, a vehicle would be beneficial, but even an economy car (manual transmission) is expensive at approximately €50 per day. Allow for plenty of time to get back to your ship, as Barcelona traffic is always heavy.

GETTING TO THE AIRPORT

Barcelona's main airport is El Prat de Llobregat, 14 km (9 miles) south of Barcelona. If you choose not to purchase airport transfers from your cruise line, the simplest way to get from the airport to the cruise port is to take a taxi from the airport to the port (about €30). There are public transport options, but transfers between bus, metro, or rail stations do involve up to 10 minutes of walking, and this may be impractical with many pieces of luggage. If you only have light baggage, this will certainly be a less expensive option.

The RENFE airport train is inexpensive and efficient, but also runs only every 30 minutes. From the airport, the RENFE station is a 10- to 15-minute walk (with moving walkway) from the port gates. Trains

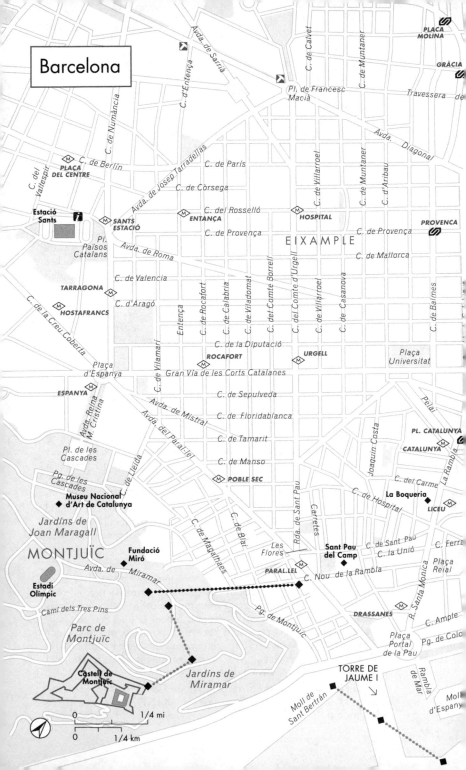

Barcelona

PLAÇA
MOLINA

GRÀCIA

Travessera de

Avda. Diagonal

Pl. de Francesc
Macià

C. de Calvet

C. de Muntaner

C. de París

C. de Còrsega

C. del Rosselló

C. de Provença

EIXAMPLE

C. de Villarroel

C. de Muntaner

C. d'Aribau

HOSPITAL

PROVENÇA

C. de Provença

C. de Mallorca

Avda. de Sarrià

C. d'Entença

Avda. de Josep Tarradellas

C. de Numància

C. de Berlín

C. del
Valtespir

PLAÇA
DEL CENTRE

Estació
Sants

SANTS
ESTACIÓ

ENTANÇA

Pl.
Països
Catalans

Avda. de Roma

C. de Valencia

TARRAGONA

C. d'Aragó

HOSTAFRANCS

C. de la Creu Coberta

C. de Rocafort

C. de Calàbria

C. de Viladomat

C. del Comte Borrell

C. del Comte d'Urgell

C. de Villarroel

C. de Casanova

C. de Balmes

Entença

C. de Vilamarí

C. de la Diputació

ROCAFORT

URGELL

Plaça
Universitat

Plaça
d'Espanya

Gran Vía de les Corts Catalanes

ESPANYA

Avda. Reina
M. Cristina

Avda. de Mistral

Avda. del Paral·lel

C. de Lleida

C. de Sepulveda

C. de Floridablanca

C. de Tamarit

C. de Manso

POBLE SEC

Pelai

PL. CATALUNYA

CATALUNYA

La Rambla

Joaquin Costa

C. del Carme

La Boqueria

LICEU

Pl. de les
Cascades

Pg. de les
Cascades

Museu Nacional
d'Art de Catalunya

Jardíns de
Joan Maragall

MONTJUÏC

Fundació
Miró

Avda. de Miramar

Estadi
Olímpic

Camí dels Tres Pins

Parc de
Montjuïc

Castell de
Montjuïc

Jardíns de
Miramar

C. de Magalhães

C. de Blai

C. de Hospital

Rda. de Sant Pau

Carretes

Les
Flores

Sant Pau
del Camp

C. de Sant Pau

C. la Unió

PARAL·LEL

C. Nou de la Rambla

Pg. de Montjuïc

DRASSANES

C. Ferra

Plaça
Reial

R. Santa Monica

C. Ample

Pg. de Colo

Plaça
Portal
de la Pau

TORRE DE
JAUME I

Moll de
Sant Bertrán

Rambla
de Mar

Moll
d'Espany

0   1/4 mi

0   1/4 km

run between 5:30 am and 12:45 am, stopping at the Estació de Sants. The one-way fare is €2.

Barcelona Guide Bureau (☎ 93/2682422 ⊕ *www.barcelonaguidebureau. com*) provides private transfers between El Prat and the cruise port. A round-trip costs around €45 per person.

EXPLORING BARCELONA

Barcelona's Old City includes **El Barri Gòtic** (the Gothic Quarter). Although this section of the city is being cleaned up, bag snatching is common here, so keep your wits about you, and if at all possible, carry nothing in your hands. Nearby is Sant Pere, which was once Barcelona's old textile neighborhood.

Barcelona's best-known promenade, **La Rambla,** is a constant and colorful flood of humanity with flower stalls, bird vendors, mimes, musicians, and outdoor cafés. Federico García Lorca called this street the only one in the world that he wished would never end; traffic plays second fiddle to the endless *paseo* (stroll) of locals and travelers alike. The whole avenue is referred to as Las Ramblas (Les Rambles, in Catalan) or La Rambla, but each section has its own name: Rambla Santa Monica is at the southeastern, or port, end; Rambla de les Flors is in the middle; and Rambla dels Estudis is at the top, near Plaça de Catalunya.

North of Plaça de Catalunya is the checkerboard known as the **Eixample.** With the dismantling of the city walls in 1860, Barcelona embarked upon an expansion scheme. The street grid was the work of urban planner Ildefons Cerdà; much of the building here was done at the height of Modernisme. The Eixample's principal thoroughfares are Rambla de Catalunya and Passeig de Gràcia, where the city's most elegant shops vie for space among its best art nouveau buildings.

Once Barcelona's pungent fishing port, **Barceloneta** retains much of its maritime flavor. Nearby is **La Ciutadella,** once a fortress but now the city's main downtown park. **Montjuïc,** a hill to the south of town, may have been named for the Jewish cemetery that was once on its slopes.

WHAT TO SEE

Fodor's Choice **La Boqueria.** Barcelona's most spectacular food market, also known as the
★   Mercat de Sant Josep, is an explosion of life and color sprinkled with delicious little bar-restaurants. A solid polychrome wall of fruits, herbs, wild mushrooms, vegetables, nuts, candied fruits, cheeses, hams, fish, poultry, and provender of every imaginable genus and strain greets you as you turn in from La Rambla and breathe air alive with the aromas of fresh produce and reverberating with the din of commerce. Within this steel hangar the market occupies a neoclassical square built in 1840 by architect Francesc Daniel Molina. Highlights include the sunny greengrocer's market outside (to the right if you've come in from the Rambla), along with **Pinotxo** (Pinocchio), just inside to the right, which has won international acclaim as a food sanctuary. The **Kiosko Universal,** over toward the port side of the market, or **Quim de la Boqueria** offer delicious alternatives. Don't miss the herb- and wild-mushroom stand at the back of the Boqueria. ⊠ *Rambla 91, Rambla* ⊕ *www.boqueria.info* ☉ *Mon.–Sat. 8–8* Ⓜ *Liceu.*

Fodor's Choice
★
Fundació Miró. The Miró Foundation, a gift from the artist Joan Miró to his native city, is one of Barcelona's most exciting showcases of contemporary art. The airy, white building, with panoramic views north over Barcelona, was designed by Josep Lluís Sert and opened in 1975; an extension was added by Sert's pupil Jaume Freixa in 1988. Miró's playful and colorful style, filled with Mediterranean light and humor, seems a perfect match for its surroundings, and the exhibits and retrospectives that open here tend to be progressive and provocative. Look for Alexander Calder's fountain of moving mercury. Miró himself rests in the cemetery on Montjuïc's southern slopes. During the Franco regime, which he strongly opposed, Miró first lived in self-imposed exile in Paris, then moved to Majorca in 1956. When he died in 1983, the Catalans gave him a send-off amounting to a state funeral. ⊠ *Av. Miramar 71, Montjuïc* ☎ *93/443–9470* ⊕ *www.bcn. fjmiro.es* 🖃 *€8.50* ☺ *Tues., Wed., Fri., and Sat. 10–7, Thurs. 10–9:30, Sun. 10–2:30.*

> **BARCELONA BEST BETS**
>
> **La Sagrada Família.** Gaudí's stalagmites, stalactites, and cylindrical towers add up to the city's most surprising architectural marvel.
>
> **Santa Maria del Mar.** Peerless Mediterranean Gothic style: a sweeping display of form and line. Hearing Renaissance polyphony in this architectural gem is the ultimate.
>
> **Stroll along the Rambla.** This fine avenue is the place to feel Barcelona's heartbeat with milling throngs of cool urbanites, families, and elderly city dwellers all out to see and be seen.

Fodor's Choice
★
Manzana de la Discòrdia. The name is a pun on the Spanish word *manzana*, which means both apple and city block, alluding to the three-way architectural counterpoint on this block and to the classical myth of the Apple of Discord (which played a part in that legendary tale about the Judgment of Paris and the subsequent Trojan War). The houses here are spectacular, and encompass three monuments of Modernisme—Casa Lleó Morera, Casa Amatller, and Casa Batlló. Of the three competing buildings (four if you count Sagnier i Villavecchia's comparatively tame 1910 Casa Mulleras at No. 37), Casa Batlló is clearly the star attraction, and the only one of the three offering visits to the interior.

Museu d'Història de Catalunya. Built into what used to be a port warehouse, this state-of-the-art interactive museum makes you part of Catalonian history from prehistoric times through more than 3,000 years and into the contemporary democratic era. After centuries of "official" Catalan history dictated from Madrid (from 1714 until the mid-19th century Renaixença, and from 1939 to 1975), this is an opportunity to revisit Catalonia's autobiography. Explanations of the exhibits appear in Catalan, Castilian, and English. Guided tours are available on Sunday at noon and 1 pm. The rooftop cafeteria has excellent views over the harbor and is open to the public (whether you visit the museum itself) during museum hours. ⊠ *Pl. Pau Vila 1, Barceloneta* ☎ *93/225–4700* ⊕ *www.mhcat.net* 🖃 *€5; free 1st Sun. of month* ☺ *Tues. and Thurs.– Sat. 10–7, Wed. 10–8, Sun. 10–2:30* Ⓜ *Barceloneta.*

Fodor's Choice   **Museu Nacional d'Art de Catalunya** (*MNAC, Catalonian National Museum*
★   *of Art*). Housed in the imposingly domed, towered, frescoed, and columned **Palau Nacional,** built in 1929 as the centerpiece of the International Exposition, this superb museum was renovated in 1995 by Gae
Aulenti, architect of the Musée d'Orsay in Paris. In 2004 the museum's
three collections—Romanesque, Gothic, and the Cambó Collection, an
eclectic trove, including a Goya, donated by Francesc Cambó—were
joined by the 19th- and 20th-century collection of Catalan impressionist
and moderniste painters. Also now on display is the Thyssen-Bornemisza
collection of early masters, with works by Zurbarán, Rubens, Tintoretto,
Velázquez, and others. ⊠ *Mirador del Palau 6, Montjuïc* ☎ *93/622–0360*
⊕ *www.mnac.es* ⊠ *€9 (valid for day of purchase and one other day in
same month)* ☉ *Tues.–Sat. 10–7, Sun. 10–2:30.*

Fodor's Choice   **Museu Picasso.** The Picasso Museum is housed in five adjoining pal-
★   aces on Carrer Montcada, a street known for Barcelona's most elegant
medieval palaces. Picasso spent his key formative years in Barcelona
(1895–1904), and this collection, while it does not include a significant
number of the artist's best paintings, is particularly strong on his early
work. The museum was begun in 1962 on the suggestion of Picasso's
crony Jaume Sabartés, and the initial donation was from the Sabartés collection. Later Picasso donated his early works, and in 1981 his
widow, Jaqueline Roque, added 141 pieces. ⊠ *Carrer Montcada 15–19,
Born-Ribera* ☎ *93/319–6310* ⊕ *www.museupicasso.bcn.cat* ⊠ *€9.50;
free 1st Sun. of month, free Sun. 3–8* ☉ *Tues.–Sun. 10–8* Ⓜ *Jaume I.*

★   **Palau de la Música Catalana.** One of the world's most extraordinary music
halls, with facades that are a riot of color and form, the Palau de la
Música (Music Palace) is a landmark of Carrer Amadeus Vives, set
just across Via Laietana, a five-minute walk from Plaça de Catalunya.
From its polychrome ceramic ticket windows on the Carrer de Sant
Pere Més Alt side to its overhead busts of (from left to right) Palestrina,
Bach, Beethoven, and (around the corner on Carrer Amadeus Vives)
Wagner, the Palau is a flamboyant tour de force designed in 1908 by
Lluís Domènech i Montaner. It is today considered the flagship of Bar-
celona's moderniste architecture. The exterior is remarkable in itself.
The Palau's interior is, well, a permanent uproar before the first note of
music is ever heard. ⊠ *Ticket office, Palau de la Musica 4–6(just off Via
Laietana, around corner from hall), Sant Pere* ☎ *93/295–7200* ⊕ *www.
palaumusica.org* ⊠ *Tour €12* ☉ *Sept.–June, tours daily 10–3:30; July
and Aug., tours daily 10–7* Ⓜ *Urquinaona.*

Fodor's Choice   **Santa Maria del Mar.** The most beautiful example of early Catalan Gothic
★   architecture, Santa Maria del Mar is extraordinary for its unbroken
lines and elegance. The lightness of the interior is especially surprising
considering the blocky exterior. Built by a mere stonemason who chose,
fitted, and carved each stone hauled down from the same Montjuïc
quarry that provided the sandstone for the 4th-century Roman walls,
Santa Maria del Mar is breathtakingly and nearly hypnotically symmetrical. The medieval numerological symbol for the Virgin Mary, the
number eight (or multiples thereof) runs through every element of the
basilica: The 16 octagonal pillars are 6.5 feet in diameter and spread
out into rib vaulting arches at a height of 52 feet. The painted keystones

at the apex of the arches are 105 feet from the floor. Furthermore, the central nave is twice as wide as the lateral naves (26 feet each), whose width equals the difference (26 feet) between their height and that of the main nave. The result of all this proportional balance and harmony is a sense of uplift that, especially in baroque and moderniste Barcelona, is both exhilarating and soothing. Set aside at least a half hour to see Santa Maria del Mar. ⊠ *Pl. de Santa Maria, Born-Ribera* ☎ *93/310–2390* ⊙ *Daily 9–1:30 and 4:30–8* Ⓜ *Jaume I.*

Fodor's Choice **Temple Expiatori de la Sagrada Família.** Barcelona's most emblematic archi-
★ tectural icon, Antoni Gaudí's Sagrada Família, is still under construction 130 years after it was begun. This striking and surreal creation was conceived as nothing short of a Bible in stone, a gigantic representation of the entire history of Christianity, and it continues to cause responses from surprise to consternation to wonder. No building in Barcelona and few in the world are more deserving of investing anywhere from a few hours to the better part of a day in getting to know it well. In fact, a quick visit can be more tiring than an extended one, as there are too many things to take in at once. However long your visit, it's a good idea to bring binoculars. For a €3 additional charge, you can take an elevator skyward to the top of the **bell towers** for some spectacular views. Back on the ground, visit the **museum**, which displays Gaudí's scale models. The architect is buried to the left of the altar in the **crypt**. ⊠ *Pl. de la Sagrada Família, Eixample* ☎ *93/207–3031* ⊕ *www.sagradafamilia.org* ▩ *€13, (17 with audioguide) bell-tower elevator €3* ⊙ *Oct.–Mar., daily 9–6; Apr.–Sept., daily 9–8* Ⓜ *Sagrada Família.*

SHOPPING

Between the surging fashion scene, a host of young clothing designers, clever home furnishings, delicious foodstuffs including wine and olive oil, and ceramics, art, and antiques, Barcelona is the best place in Spain to unload extra ballast from your wallet.

Barcelona's prime shopping districts are the Passeig de Gràcia, Rambla de Catalunya, Plaça de Catalunya, Porta de l'Àngel, and Avinguda Diagonal up to Carrer Ganduxer. For high fashion, browse along Passeig de Gràcia and the Diagonal between Plaça Joan Carles I and Plaça Francesc Macià. There are two-dozen antiques shops in the Gothic Quarter, another 70 shops off Passeig de Gràcia on Bulevard dels Antiquaris, and still more in Gràcia and Sarrià. For old-fashioned Spanish shops, prowl the Gothic Quarter, especially **Carrer Ferran.** The area around the church of Santa Maria del Mar, an artisans' quarter since medieval times, is full of cheerful design stores and art galleries. The area surrounding **Plaça del Pi,** from the Boqueria to Carrer Portaferrissa and Carrer de la Canuda, is thick with boutiques and jewelry and design shops. The **Barri de la Ribera,** around Santa Maria del Mar, especially the Born area, has a cluster of design, fashion, and and food shops. Design, jewelry, and knickknack shops cluster on Carrer Banys Vells and Carrer Flassaders, near Carrer Montcada.

★ **Art Escudellers.** Ceramic pieces from all over Spain converge here at both of these stores across the street from the restaurant Los Caracoles; more

than 140 different artisans are represented, with maps showing what part of Spain the work is from. There are wine, cheese, and ham tastings downstairs, and you can even throw a pot yourself in the display workshop. ⊠ *Carrer Escudellers 23–25, Barri Gòtic* ☎ *93/412–6801* ⊕ *www.escudellers-art.com* Ⓜ *Liceu, Drassanes.*

Galeria Joan Prats. "La Prats" has been one of the city's top galleries since the 1920s, showing international painters and sculptors from Henry Moore to Antoni Tàpies. Barcelona painter Joan Miró was a prime force in the founding of the gallery when he became friends with Joan Prats. The motifs of bonnets and derbies on the gallery's facade attest to the trade of Prats's father. José Maria Sicilia and Juan Ugalde have shown here, while Perejaume and Eulàlia Valldosera are regulars. ⊠ *Rambla de Catalunya 54, Eixample* ☎ *93/216–0284* ⊕ *www.galeriajoanprats. com* ☉ *Tues.–Sat. 11–8* Ⓜ *Passeig de Gràcia.*

WHERE TO EAT

$$
TAPAS
Fodor'sChoice
★

✕ **Cal Pep.** Cal Pep, a two-minute walk east from Santa Maria del Mar, is in a permanent feeding frenzy and has been this way for 30 years. Pep has Barcelona's best selection of tapas, cooked and served hot over the counter. For budget reasons, avoid ordering a fish dish (unless you're willing to part with an extra €35–€50), and stick with green peppers, fried artichokes, garbanzos and spinach, baby shrimp, the "trifasic" (mixed tiny fish fry), the nonpareil *tortilla de patatas* (potato omelet), and *botifarra trufada en reducción de Oporto* (truffled sausage in Port wine reduction sauce). The house wines are good, but the Torre la Moreira Albariño white perfectly complements Pep's offerings. Be prepared to wait for 20 minutes for a place at the counter; it's well worth it. ⑤ *Average main: €18* ⊠ *Pl. de les Olles 8, Born-Ribera* ☎ *93/319–6183* ⊕ *www.calpep. com* ☉ *Closed Sun. No lunch Mon. No dinner Sat.* Ⓜ *Jaume I.*

$$
ECLECTIC

✕ **Cuines Santa Caterina.** A lovingly restored market designed by the late Enric Miralles and completed by his widow Benedetta Tagliabue provides a spectacular setting for one of the city's most original dining operations. Under the undulating wooden superstructure of the market, the breakfast and tapas bar, open from dawn to midnight, offers a variety of culinary specialties cross-referenced by different cuisines (Mediterranean, Asian, vegetarian) and products (pasta, rice, fish, meat), all served on sleek counters and long wooden tables. ⑤ *Average main: €22* ⊠ *Av. Francesc Cambó 16, Barri Gòtic* ☎ *93/268–9918* ⊕ *www. cuinessantacaterina.com* Ⓜ *Catalunya, Liceu, Jaume I.*

WHERE TO STAY

$$$
HOTEL
Fodor'sChoice
★

⚐ **Duquesa de Cardona.** Inside a refurbished 16th-century town house, this hotel has contemporary facilities in soothing neutral tones all overlooking the port. **Pros:** great combination of traditional and contemporary; key spot over the port; roof terrace with live music in summer. **Cons:** rooms on the small side; roof terrace tiny; sea views restricted by Maremagnum complex on the port. ⑤ *Rooms from: €185* ⊠ *Passeig de Colom 12, Rambla* ☎ *93/301–2570* ⊕ *www.hduquesadecardona.com* ⤶ *44 rooms* ⍥ *No meals* Ⓜ *Drassanes.*

$$$$ 🔳 **Hotel Neri.** Built into a 17th-century palace over one of the Gothic
HOTEL Quarter's smallest and most charming squares, Plaça Sant Felip Neri,
Fodor's Choice the Neri marries ancient and avant-garde design. **Pros:** central location;
★ hip design; roof terrace for cocktails and breakfast. **Cons:** noise from the
echo-chamber square can be a problem on summer nights (and winter
morning school days); impractical design details such as the hanging bed
lights. ⑤ *Rooms from: €310* ✉ *St. Sever 5, Barri Gòtic* ☎ *93/304–0655*
⊕ *www.hotelneri.com* ⤵ *22 rooms* ⦿ *No meals* Ⓜ *Liceu, Catalunya.*

$$ 🔳 **Sant Agustí.** In a leafy square just off the Rambla, the Sant Agustí has
HOTEL long been popular with musicians performing at the Liceu opera house.
Fodor's Choice **Pros:** central location near the Boqueria market, the Rambla, and the
★ opera house; cozy, wood-beam, traditional design. **Cons:** noisy square
usually requiring closed windows; short on amenities and room service.
⑤ *Rooms from: €150* ✉ *Pl. Sant Agustí 3, El Raval* ☎ *93/318–2182*
⊕ *www.hotelsa.com* ⤵ *77 rooms* ⦿ *No meals* Ⓜ *Liceu.*

BARI, ITALY

Updated
by Bruce
Leimsidor

Puglia is one of three regions making up the heel and toe of Italy's boot,
and known collectively as the *mezzogiorno*. This is Italy's deep south,
where whitewashed buildings stand silently over the turquoise Mediter-
ranean, castles guard medieval alleyways, and grandmothers dry their
handmade orecchiette pasta in the midafternoon heat. At every turn,
Puglia boasts unspoiled scenery and a wonderful country food tradi-
tion. Beyond the cities, seaside resorts, and the few major sights, there's
a sparsely populated countryside with expanses of silvery olive trees,
vineyards of *primitivo* and *aglianico* grapes, and giant prickly-pear
cacti. Puglia is an increasingly popular tourist destination. Bari is at the
top of the heel of the boot, a lively, varied, and sometimes-seamy port
city on the Adriatic coast.

ESSENTIALS
CURRENCY
The euro.

HOURS
Shops are generally open from 8 am until noon or 1 pm, then again from 3 or
4 until 8, perhaps opening later in summer. Some museums and attractions stay
open throughout the day, while others close in the afternoon; it's best to plan to
visit such attractions in the morning, or check with the local tourist office or the
individual museum or church.

PRIVATE TOURS
Tour guides may be booked online on Viator, but the site lists only one
tour guide that has certification, Gianluca Guadagnino, who charges
€25 per hour per person for full 8-hour tour. Group tours from the port
can be arranged through the website Get your Guide; a 3-hour walking
tour of the city costs €17 per person and can be prebooked on line. The
company also offers half- and full-day tours to Alberobello and Lecce.

Contacts Get Your Guide. ⊕ *getyourguide.com.* **Viator.** ⊕ *viator.com.*

TELEPHONES

Tri-band GSM phones work in Italy. You can buy prepaid phone cards at telecom shops, news vendors, and tobacconists in all towns and cities. Phone cards can be used for local or international calls.

COMING ASHORE

Bari is a large port and has a dedicated cruise terminal; ships dock, giving passengers only a short walk to the port entrance. From here, it is a further short walk into the city, where you can explore on foot.

Bari is linked by rail to all the major towns in the region. Trani can be reached in 34 to 40 minutes; there are one or two trains per hour, depending on the time of day, and the single fare ranges from €2.60 to €7.50. Polignano a Mare is less than 30 minutes from Bari by train; there is a train almost hourly, and a single fare costs €2.10. Alberobello is a journey time of 80 to 100 minutes, and tickets cost €4. All train tickets—except those to Alberobello—can be bought online at ⊕ *www.trenilatia.com* and printed out at home, or retrieved from machines in Bari station. Buy tickets for Alberobello from the Ferrovie Sud-Est office at Bari railway station. Renting a vehicle would allow you to explore the Puglia countryside at your own pace. An economy manual vehicle costs from €34 to €75 per day, but delivery to the port may cost more.

EXPLORING BARI AND PUGLIA

BARI

Bari is a major port and a transit point for travelers catching ferries across the Adriatic to Greece and Croatia (Dubrovnik and other points along the Dalmatian coast), but it's also an exciting city with one of the most interesting historic centers in the region. Most of Bari is set out in a logical, 19th-century grid, following the designs of Joachim Murat (1767–1815), Napoléon's brother-in-law and King of the Two Sicilies. By day, explore the Old Town's winding alleyways, which offer glimpses into the daily routine of southern Italy—matrons hand-rolling pasta with their grandchildren home from school for the midday meal, and handymen perched on rickety ladders, patching up centuries-old arches and doorways. *Barivecchia,* or the Old City, used to be a "no go" area for tourists because of a high incidence of petty crime. Gentrification has allegedly improved the situation considerably, but caution is still advised.

★ **Basilica di San Nicola.** In the *città vecchia,* overlooking the sea and just off Via Venezia, is the Basilica di San Nicola, built in the 11th century to house the bones of Saint Nicholas, the inspiration for Santa Claus. His remains, buried in the crypt, are said to have been stolen by Bari sailors from Myra, where Saint Nicholas was bishop, in what is now Turkey. The basilica, of solid and powerful construction, was the only building to survive the otherwise wholesale destruction of Bari by the Normans in 1152. ⊠ *Piazza San Nicola* ☎ *080/5737111* ⊕ *www. basilicasannicola.it* ⊗ *Daily 7 am–8 pm.*

Castello Svevo. Looming over Bari's cathedral is the huge Castello Svevo. The current building dates from the time of Holy Roman Emperor Frederick II (1194–1250), who rebuilt an existing Norman-Byzantine castle to his own exacting specifications. Designed more for power than beauty, it looks out beyond the cathedral to the small Porto Vecchio (Old Port). Inside, a haphazard collection of medieval Puglian art is frequently enlivened by changing exhibitions featuring local, national, and international artists. ⊠ *Piazza Federico II di Svevia* ☎ *080/5286262* 🎟 *€2* ⊗ *Thurs.–Tues. 8:30–7:30. Last entrance at 7.*

Cattedrale di San Sabino. Bari's 12th-century Cattedrale di San Sabino is the seat of the local bishop and was the scene of many significant political marriages between important families in the Middle Ages. The cathedral's solid architecture reflects the Romanesque style favored by the Normans of that period. ⊠ *Piazza dell'Odegitria* ☎ *080/5210605* ⊗ *Mon.–Sat. 8–12:30 and 4–8, Sun. 8–12:30 and 4–10.*

TRANI

43 km (27 miles) northwest of Bari.

Smaller than the other ports along this coast, Trani has a picturesque Old Town with polished stone streets and buildings, medieval churches, and a harbor filled with fishing boats. Trani is also justly famous for its sweet dessert wine, Moscato di Trani.

Castello. The boxy, well-preserved Castello was built by Frederick II in 1233. ⊠ *Piazza Manfredi 16* ☎ *0883/506603* ⊕ *www.castelloditrani. beniculturali.it* 🎟 *€2* ⊗ *Daily 8:30–7:30.*

Cattedrale. The stunning, pinkish-white 11th-century Cattedrale, considered one of the finest in Puglia, is built on a spit of land jutting into the sea. ⊠ *Piazza Duomo* ☎ *0883/494210* ⊙ *Daily 9–noon and 3.30–6.*

Via Sinagoga (*Synagogue Street*). A Jewish community flourished here in medieval times, and on Via Sinagoga two of the four synagogues still stand. **Santa Maria Scolanova** and **Santa Anna,** both built in the 13th century, are now churches; the latter still bears a Hebrew inscription.

POLIGNANO A MARE

40 km (24 miles) southeast of Bari.

With a well-preserved whitewashed Old Town perched on limestone cliffs overlooking the Adriatic, Polignano a Mare is only a half-hour train ride down the coast from Bari. The town is virtually lifeless all winter, but becomes something of a weekend hot spot for city dwellers in summer.

CASTEL DEL MONTE

Fodor'sChoice **Castel del Monte.** Built by Frederick II in the first half of the 13th century,
★ Castel del Monte is an imposing octagonal castle with eight austere towers on an isolated hill. Little is known about the structure, since virtually no records exist. The ground-floor gift shop (closed in winter months) has many books that explore its mysterious past and posit theories based on its dimensions and Federico II's love of mathematics. It has none of the usual defense features associated with medieval castles, so it probably had little military significance. Some theories suggest it might have been built as a hunting lodge or may have served as an astronomical observatory, or even a stop for pilgrims on their quest for the Holy Grail. Most of the helpful information panels in the castle are translated into English. Note that if coming by car from April to September you have to park in designated areas about a mile away and then get a shuttle bus. ⊠ *On signposted minor road 18 mi (11 miles) south of Andria* ☎ *0883/569997, 0883/592283 tour reservations* ⊕ *www.casteldelmonte.beniculturali.it* ☎ *€5* ⊙ *Mar.–Sept., daily 10:15–7:15; Oct.–Feb., daily 9–5. Last entrance ½ hr before closing.*

ALBEROBELLO

59 km (37 miles) southeast of Bari.

Although Alberobello is frequently overrun by tourists, the amalgamation of more than 1,000 *trulli* (beehive-shape homes) huddled together along steep, narrow streets is nonetheless an unusual sight (as well as a national monument and a UNESCO World Heritage site). The origins of the beehive-shape trulli go back to the 13th century and maybe further. The trulli, found nowhere else in the world, are built of

BARI BEST BETS

Soaking in the atmosphere in Bari's Old Town. The dramas of life in Italy's deep south are not a show put on for tourists but a fascinating daily performance for lovers of people-watching.

Exploring Polignano a Mare. This whitewashed village's roots are well in sync with the Mediterranean heartbeat.

Touring Trulli country. These unique humble stone buildings surrounded by vines are one of Italy's most unusual architectural treasures.

2

local limestone, without mortar, and with a hole in the top for escaping smoke. As one of the most popular tourist destinations in Puglia, Alberobello has spawned some excellent restaurants (and some not-so-excellent trinket shops).

Trullo Sovrano. Alberobello's largest trullo, the Trullo Sovrano, is up the hill through the trulli zone (head up Corso Vittorio Emanuele past the obelisk and the basilica). Inside is a fairly conventional domestic dwelling: the real interest is the structure itself.

Alberobello–Martina Franca road. The trulli in Alberobello itself are impressive, but the most beautiful concentration of conical trulli is along a stretch of about 15 km (9 miles) on the Alberobello–Martina Franca road. Amid expanses of vineyards, you can see trulli put to all sorts of uses—including as wineries.

SHOPPING

Puglia is Italy's second most-productive wine region, so taste a few, including the famed dessert wine Moscato di Trani, and buy some bottles of your favorite. Olives are grown in great abundance, too. The virgin olive oil pressed here is of excellent quality. Other souvenirs include ceramics in a range of styles, from practical terra-cotta to beautiful glazed ornaments. Miniature trulli take on many forms, from faithfully finished stone copies to kitsch plastic fridge magnets. Italian styling is very much in evidence in the streets of Bari.

The main shopping streets in Bari are Via Argiro and Via Sparano. Souvenir shops are numerous in the narrow streets of the Old Town. Alberobello has many trulli that have been converted into souvenir shops.

WHERE TO EAT

$$$$

SEAFOOD

✗**Ristorante al Pescatore.** In the Old Town, opposite the castle and just around the corner from the cathedral, stands one of Bari's best seafood restaurants. In summer the fish is grilled outdoors, so you can enjoy the delicious aroma as you sit amid a cheerful clamor of quaffing and dining. Try a whole fish accompanied by a crisp salad and a carafe of invigorating local wine. Reservations are essential in July and August. Beware of bag snatchers if you sit outside. $ *Average main:* €45 ⊠ *Piazza Federico II di Svevia 6/8, Bari* ☎ 080/5237039 ⊕ *www. ristorantealpescatorebari.com* ☉ *Closed 2 wks mid-Jan.*

BORDEAUX, FRANCE

Updated by Jennifer Ladonne

Bordeaux as a whole, rather than any particular points within it, is what you'll want to visit in order to understand why Victor Hugo described it as Versailles plus Antwerp, and why, when he was exiled from his native Spain, the painter Francisco de Goya chose it as his last home (he died here in 1828). The capital of southwest France and the region's largest city, Bordeaux remains synonymous with the wine trade, and wine shippers have long maintained their headquarters along the banks of the River Garonne at the heart of town. As a whole, Bordeaux is a

less exuberant city than many others in France. The profits generated by centuries of fine vintages have been carefully invested in fine yet understated architecture, and an aura of 18th-century elegance permeates the downtown core. Conservative and refined, the city rewards visitors with its museums, shopping, and restaurants.

ESSENTIALS

CURRENCY
The euro.

HOURS
Museums are open 10–5, but most close on Monday or Tuesday. Stores are open Monday–Saturday 9–7, but some close for lunch (usually noon–2).

TELEPHONES
Tri-band GSM phones work in France. You can buy prepaid phone cards at telecom shops, news vendors, and tobacconists in all towns and cities. Phone cards can be used for local or international calls. Orange, SFR, Bouygues Telecom, and Virgin are leading telecom companies. If you have an unlocked GSM phone, LeFrenchMobile (⊕ *www. lefrenchmobile.com*) offers SIM cards (and micro SIM cards) with support in English, unlimited validity of credits, and prepurchase online.

COMING ASHORE
Cruise ships sail up the Gironde River and dock directly on the city waterfront within walking distance of all the major city attractions. Because of its proximity to the downtown core, there are no facilities specifically for cruise-ship passengers at the dock site.

Bordeaux is a compact city, and there will be no need to rent a vehicle unless you want to tour the many vineyards in the surrounding countryside independently. Cost of rental is approximately €70 per day for an economy manual vehicle. Taxis are plentiful and can provide tourist itineraries. For single-journey tariffs, rates are €2.30 for pick-up followed by €0.77 per km. There's an hourly rental fee of €29.90 (plus distance covered) if you should choose to take a taxi for a number of hours.

EXPLORING BORDEAUX

Cathédrale St-André. This may not be one of France's finer Gothic cathedrals but the intricate 14th-century chancel makes an interesting contrast with the earlier nave. Excellent stone carvings adorn the facade of this hefty edifice. You can climb the 15th-century, 160-foot **Tour Pey-Berland** for a stunning view of the city; it's open Tuesday–Sunday 10–noon and 2–5. ⊠ *Pl. Pey-Berland* ☎ *05–56–81–26–25* ⌐ *€5*.

★ **Grand Théâtre.** One block south of the Maison du Vin is the city's leading 18th-century monument: the Grand Théâtre, designed by Victor Louis and built between 1773 and 1780. It's the pride of the city, with an elegant exterior ringed by graceful Corinthian columns and a dazzling foyer with a two-winged staircase and a cupola. The theater hall has a frescoed ceiling with a shimmering chandelier composed of 14,000 Bohemian crystals. Contact the Bordeaux tourist office to learn about guided tours. ⊠ *Pl. de la Comédie* ☎ *05–56–00–85–95* ⊕ *www.opera-bordeaux.com* ⌐ *Tours €3*.

Haut-Brion. One of the region's most famous wine-producing châteaux is actually within the city limits: follow N250 southwest from central Bordeaux for 3 km (2 miles) to the district of Pessac, home to Haut-Brion, producer of the only non-Médoc wine to be ranked a *premier cru* (the most elite wine classification). It's claimed the very buildings surrounding the vineyards create their own microclimate, protecting the precious grapes and allowing them to ripen earlier. The white château looks out over the celebrated pebbly soil. The wines produced at **La Mission–Haut Brion (Domaine Clarence Dillon),** across the road, are almost as sought-after. ⊠ *135 av. Jean-Jaurès, Pessac* ☎ *05–56–00–29–30* ⊕ *www. haut-brion.com* ✉ *Free 1-hr visits by appointment, weekdays only, with tasting* ☉ *Closed mid-July–mid-Aug.*

★ **Maison du Vin.** Not far from the banks of the Garonne and the main artery of the Esplanade des Quinconces, tree-lined Cours du 30 Juillet is where you will find the important Maison du Vin (House of Wine), right across the street from the city tourist office. The Maison is run by the CIVB (Conseil Interprofessionnel des Vins de Bordeaux), the headquarters of the Bordeaux wine trade, and before you set out to explore the region's wine country, you should get some tips from the (English-speaking) person at the Tourisme de Viticole desk, who has helpful guides on all the various wine regions. More important, tasting a red

(like Pauillac or St-Émilion), a dry white (like an Entre-Deux-Mers, Graves, or Côtes de Blaye), and a sweet white (like Sauternes or Loupiac) will help you decide which of the 57 wine appellations to explore. You can also make purchases at the **Vinothèque** opposite. ✉ *8 cours du 30 Juillet* ☎ *05–56–52–32–05* ⊕ *www.la-vinotheque.com* 💳 *Free* 🕐 *Mon.–Sat. 10–7:30.*

★ **Musée d'Aquitaine.** Two blocks south of the Cathédrale St-André, this excellent museum takes you on a trip through Bordeaux's history, with emphases on Roman, medieval, Renaissance, port-harbor, colonial, and 20th-century daily life. The detailed prehistoric section almost saves you a trip to Lascaux II, which is reproduced here in part. ✉ *20 cours Pasteur* ☎ *05–56–01–51–00* 💳 *Free* 🕐 *Tues.–Sun. 11–6.*

> ### BORDEAUX BEST BETS
>
> **Opening a bottle of a fine wine.** Bordeaux is famed more for its wines than anything else, so indulge your olfactory sense and your taste buds with a vintage from an excellent château.
>
> **Touring the vineyards.** Not only is it wonderful to watch the grapes maturing on the vines, but to tour the historic châteaus and their extensive cellars is to understand the understated essence of this small region of France.

Musée d'Art Contemporain (*Contemporary Art Center*). Just north of the Esplanade des Quinconces, a sprawling square, this two-story museum is imaginatively housed in a converted 19th-century spice warehouse, the Entrepôt Lainé. Many shows here showcase cutting-edge artists who invariably festoon the huge expanse of the place with hanging ropes, ladders, and large video screens. ✉ *7 rue Ferrère* ☎ *05–56–00–81–50* 💳 *5€* 🕐 *Tues. and Thurs.–Sun. 11–6, Wed. 11–8.*

Musée des Beaux-Arts. Not far from the Cathédrale St-André, this museum adorns tidy gardens behind the ornate Hôtel de Ville (town hall). Inside is a fetching collection of works spanning the 15th to the 21st century, with important paintings by Paolo Veronese (*St. Dorothy*), Camille Corot (*Bath of Diana*), and Odilon Redon (*Apollo's Chariot*), and sculptures by Auguste Rodin. ✉ *20 cours d'Albret* ☎ *05–56–10–20–56* 💳 *Free* 🕐 *Wed.–Mon. 11–6.*

Pont de Pierre. For a view of the picturesque quayside, stroll across the Garonne on this bridge, built on the orders of Napoléon between 1810 and 1821, and until 1965 the only bridge across the river.

SHOPPING

Between the cathedral and the Grand Théâtre are numerous pedestrian streets where stylish shops and clothing boutiques abound—Bordeaux may favor understatement but there's no lack of elegance. Couture is well in evidence here for both women and men. Wines are of course a must if you haven't bought direct from the château, or indulge in France's other culinary obsession—cheese (perhaps for a picnic lunch).

Baillardran. With five stores in Bordeaux alone, Baillardran is going to be hard to walk by without at least looking in its windows at those

indigenous sweet delights, *Bordelais cannelés!* Much like a Doric column in miniature, these small indented, caramelized cakes, made with vanilla and a dash of rum, are a delicious regional specialty. ⊠ *55 cours de l'Intendance* ☎ *05–56–52–92–64* ⊕ *www.baillardran.com.*

Jean d'Alos Fromager-Affineur. For an exceptional selection of cheeses, go to Jean d'Alos Fromager-Affineur. ⊠ *4 rue Montesquieu* ☎ *05–56–44–29–66.*

Vinothèque. The Vinothèque sells top-ranked Bordeaux wines. ⊠ *8 cours du 30 Juillet* ☎ *05–56–52–32–05.*

WHERE TO EAT

$ ✕ **Café Français.** For more than 30 years, Madame Jouhanneau presided
BRASSERIE   over this venerable bistro in the heart of the Vieille Ville (Old Town), right by the Cathédrale St-André. Now Madame Mesnard has taken over and renovated the place but has kept the cuisine as it was: solidly based on fresh regional specialties. For solid sustenance at reasonable prices, it's hard to beat. Try for a table on the terrace: the view over Place Pey-Berland is never less than diverting. Ⓢ *Average main: €17* ⊠ *5–6 pl. Pey-Berland* ☎ *05–56–52–96–69.*

$ ✕ **l'Oiseau Cabosse.** This straight-up organic restaurant and coffee bar
FRENCH FUSION   is a good option for a snack or if you're on a tight budget, and with its warm and welcoming atmosphere and kind and spunky service, it's a welcome find in the city, even if it doesn't really compare with other bistro finds. It's popular for its tasty "homemade food"—not to be confused with "health food"—and options range from duck confit parmentier and lasagna to curry and leek quiche. Fresh baked desserts should not be missed, nor the organic and artisanal cola, lemonade or 100% pure cocoa hot chocolate. There's a nice outside terrace in the bourgeois bohemian *Quartier de la Grosse Cloche* (Big Clock neighborhood). Ⓢ *Average main: €12* ⊠ *30 rue Sainte Colombe* ☎ *05–57–14–02–07* ☺ *Closed Mon., no dinner Tues. or Sun.*

CÁDIZ, SPAIN (FOR SEVILLE AND JEREZ)

Updated by
Joanna Styles

Gypsies, bulls, flamenco, horses—Andalusia is the Spain of story and song, the one Washington Irving romanticized in the 18th century. Andalusia is, moreover, at once the least and most surprising part of Spain: Least surprising because it lives up to the hype and stereotype that long confused all of Spain with the Andalusian version, and most surprising because it is, at the same time, so much more. All the romantic images of Andalusia, and Spain in general, spring vividly to life in Seville. Spain's fourth-largest city is an olé cliché of matadors, flamenco, tapas bars, gypsies, geraniums, and strolling guitarists. The smaller cities of Cádiz—the Western world's oldest metropolis, founded by Phoenicians more than 3,000 years ago—and Jerez, with its sherry cellars and purebred horses, have much to explore as well.

ESSENTIALS
CURRENCY
The euro.

HOURS

Museums generally open 9 until 7 or 8, many are closed on Monday, and some close in the afternoon. Most stores are open Monday through Saturday 9 to 1:30 and 5 to 8, but a few stay open in the afternoon. Virtually all close on Sunday.

PRIVATE TOURS

Sights and Bikes. The tour company caters specifically to cruise visitors to Cádiz, organizing day trips with a cultural, natural, or sporting theme. ☎ *956/901108* ⊕ *www.sightsandbikes.com.*

TELEPHONES

Spain has good land and mobile services. Public kiosks accept phone cards that support international calls (cards sold in press shops, bars, and telecom shops). Mobile services support most tri-band GSM phones and are 3G compatible. Major companies include Vodafone.

COMING ASHORE

Vessels dock at the Alfonso XIII quay in the Cádiz Port, which is in the heart of the city. The passenger terminal has a restaurant, press outlet, phones, and taxi kiosk. From the port, the sights of downtown Cádiz are all within walking distance.

If you wish to travel independently, there is one train per hour from Cádiz to Seville. The journey takes between 1½ and 2 hours. Tickets cost €15 single. Taxi fare from Cádiz to Seville is currently €150 (€168 on weekends) each way—a vehicle takes four people. There is also one train per hour to Jerez. The journey takes 40 minutes, and the ticket price is €5.70 one-way. A car rental would open up much of the region to you, but parking and navigation in the cities is difficult. The price for an economy manual vehicle is approximately €50 per day.

EXPLORING CÁDIZ, SEVILLE, AND JEREZ DE LA FRONTERA

CÁDIZ

Founded as Gadir by Phoenician traders in 1100 BC, Cádiz claims to be the oldest continuously inhabited city in the Western world. Hannibal lived in Cádiz for a time, Julius Caesar first held public office here, and Columbus set out from here on his second voyage, after which the city became the home base of the Spanish fleet. During the 18th century Cádiz monopolized New World trade and became the wealthiest port in Western Europe. Most of its buildings—including the cathedral, built in part with gold and silver from the New World—date from this period. Today the Old City is African in appearance and immensely intriguing— a cluster of narrow streets opening onto charming small squares. The golden cupola of the cathedral looms above low white houses, and the whole place has a charming if slightly dilapidated air.

Ayuntamiento (*city hall*). The impressive *ayuntamiento* overlooks the Plaza San Juan de Diós, one of Cádiz's liveliest hubs. The building is attractively illuminated at night and open to visits on Saturday mornings. Just ring the bell next to the door. ⊠ *Pl. de San Juan de Dios* ☉ *Sat. 11–12:45.*

Cádiz

Bahía de Cádiz

Batería Candeleria

Alameda Marqués de Comillas

C. de Isabela la Católica
C. de A. López
C. de Isabela la Católica
Av. Ramón de Carranza
Av. del Puerto

Museo de Cádiz
Oratorio de la Santa Cueva
C. de San Francisco

Calderón de la Barca
Pl. de la Mina
C. de Buenos Aires
Pl. de Tinte

C. de Rosario
C. de Valverde
C. de Columela
C. de Feduchy
Pl. Candeleria
C. de Marqués de Cádiz

Pso. de Carlos III
C. de Gravina
C. de Benito Pérez Galdós
C. de Tetuán
C. de Enrique de las Marinas
Pl. San Antonio
C. de Cánovas del Castillo
C. de San José
C. de Ancha
C. de Novena
Pl. del Palillero
C. de Montañés
C. de Zapata
C. de Nicaragua

Ayuntamiento
Plaza San Francisco

Pl. del Mentidero
C. de Veedor
Murga de Cervantes
C. de Sagasta
Torre Tavira

Pl. San Felipe Neri
C. de Compañía
Pl. de Las Flores
C. de Obispo Urquinaona
C. de San Juan de Dios

Cádiz Cathedral

Parque Genovés

Av. Doctor Gómez Ulla
C. de Hércules
C. de Cebarros
C. de Santa Rosalía
C. de Benjumeda
Falla
Oratorio de San Felipe Neri
Museo de las Cortes
C. de Sacramento
Pl. Libertad
Mercado Central
C. de Desamparados

Gran Teatro Manuel de Falla

C. de Benito Pérez Galdós
C. de San Rafael
C. de la Rosa
C. de Hospital de Mujeres
C. de San José
C. de Sagasta
C. de Cardoso
C. de Cruz

C. de Doctor Marañón
C. de Patrocinio
C. de J. Cubiles
C. de Virgen de la Palma
C. de Pericón de Cádiz

Av. Duque de Nájera

Castillo de Santa Catalina

Balneario de la Palma

C. de Euber
C. de San Félix
C. de Venezuela
C. de Paraguay
C. de Campo del Sur

C. de Puerta de la Caleta

ATLANTIC OCEAN

0   1/8 mi
0   1/8 km

Seville

Adriano

Museo Flamenco
Palacio de Lebrija

Pl. Virgen de los Reyes
Mateos Gago
BARRIO DE SANTA CRUZ
Pl. Santa Cruz

Paseo de Colón
Vinuesa
Dos de Mayo
Cathedral
Archivo de las Indias
Pl. de los Venerables
Avda. Menéndez Pelayo

TRIANA
C. Rodrigo de Triana
Pagés del Corro
Guadalquivir
C. Betis
Alcázar

EL ARENAL
Santo Tomás
Agua

Almirante Lobo
P. de Jerez
C. San Fernando
Pl. D. Juan de Austria

Estación de Autobuses

Torre de Oro

Pte. de San Telmo
Avda. de Roma
Pso. de las Delicias
Palos de la Frontera
Avda. de Carlos V

Pl. de Cuba
Sebastián
Elcano
Avda. República Argentina

Gta. San Diego
Avda. Portugal

Avda. María Luisa

U.S. Consulate

Plaza de España

Pte. del Generalísimo
Gta. de los Marineros Voluntarios
Parque de María Luisa
Avda. Isabel la Católica
Gta. Covadonga

0   1/8 mi
0   1/8 km

KEY

 Tourist information

Cádiz Cathedral. Five blocks southeast of the Torre Tavira are the gold dome and baroque facade of Cádiz's cathedral, begun in 1722, when the city was at the height of its power. The Cádiz-born composer Manuel de Falla, who died in 1946 at the age of 70, is buried in the crypt. The cathedral museum, on Calle Acero, displays gold, silver, and jewels from the New World, as well as Enrique de Arfe's processional cross, which is carried in the annual Corpus Christi parades. The entrance price includes the crypt, museum, and church of Santa Cruz. The cathedral is accessible only during mass. ⊠ *Pl. Catedral* ☎ *956/286154* 💶 *€5* 🕙 *Museum, crypt and Santa Cruz: Mon.–Sat. 10–6:30, Sun. 1:30–6:30; Cathedral: mass Sun. at noon.*

Gran Teatro Manuel de Falla. Four blocks west of Santa Inés is the Plaza Manuel de Falla, overlooked by this amazing neo-Mudejar redbrick building. The classic interior is impressive as well; try to attend a performance. ⊠ *Pl. Manuel de Falla* ☎ *956/220828.*

Museo de Cádiz (*Provincial Museum*). On the east side of the Plaza de Mina is Cadiz's provincial museum. Notable pieces include works by Murillo and Alonso Cano as well as the *Four Evangelists* and a set of saints by Zurbarán. The archaeological section contains Phoenician sarcophagi from the time of this ancient city's birth. ⊠ *Pl. de Mina* ☎ *956/203368* 💶 *€1.50* 🕙 *Tues. 2:30–8:30, Wed.–Sat. 9–8:30, Sun. 9–2:30.*

Museo de las Cortes. Next door to the Oratorio de San Felipe Neri, the small but pleasant Museo de las Cortes has a 19th-century mural depicting the establishment of the Constitution of 1812. Its real showpiece, however, is a 1779 ivory-and-mahogany model of Cádiz, with all of the city's streets and buildings in minute detail, looking much as they do now. ⊠ *Santa Inés 9* ☎ *956/221788* 💶 *Free* 🕙 *Tues.–Fri. 9–6, weekends 9–2.*

Oratorio de la Santa Cueva. A few blocks east of the Plaza de Mina, next door to the Iglesia del Rosario, is this oval 18th-century chapel with three frescoes by Goya. ⊠ *Calle Rosario 10* ☎ *956/222262* 💶 *€3* 🕙 *Mid-June–mid-Sept., weekdays 11–1 and 5–8, weekends 10–1; mid-Sept.–mid-June, Tues.–Fri. 10–1:30 and 4:30–7:30, weekends 10–1.*

Oratorio de San Felipe Neri. A walk up Calle San José from the Plaza de la Mina will bring you to this church, where Spain's first liberal constitution (known affectionately as *La Pepa*) was declared in 1812. It was here, too, that the Cortes (Parliament) of Cádiz met when the rest of Spain was subjected to the rule of Napoléon's brother, Joseph

Bonaparte (more popularly known as Pepe Botella, for his love of the bottle). On the main altar is an *Immaculate Conception* by Murillo, the great Sevillian artist who in 1682 fell to his death from a scaffold while working on his *Mystic Marriage of St. Catherine* in Cádiz's Chapel of Santa Catalina. ⊠ *Calle Santa Inés 38* ☎ *956/229120* 🔾 *€3* 🕙 *Tues.– Sat. 10–1:45 and 5–7:45; Sun. 11–1:45.*

Plaza San Francisco. Near the *ayuntamiento* (town hall) is a pretty square surrounded by white-and-yellow houses and filled with orange trees and elegant streetlamps. It's especially lively during the evening *paseo* (promenade).

Fodor's Choice **Torre Tavira.** At 150 feet, this is the highest point in the Old City. More
★ than a hundred such watchtowers were used by Cádiz ship owners to
🔾 spot their arriving fleets. A camera obscura gives a good overview of the city and its monuments; the last show is a half hour before closing time. ⊠ *Calle Marqués del Real Tesoro 10* ☎ *956/212910* 🔾 *€5* 🕙 *Daily 10–6 (to 8 mid-June–mid-Sept.).*

SEVILLE
149 km (93 miles) northeast of Cádiz.

Seville's whitewashed houses bright with bougainvillea, its ocher-color palaces, and its baroque facades have long enchanted both Sevillanos and travelers. Lord Byron's well-known line, "Seville is a pleasant city famous for oranges and women," may be true, but is far too tame. Seville's color and vivacity are legendary but best seen during one of the traditional *fiestas,* when modern dress is swapped for vivid ruffled costume, and the streets come alive with song and dance.

Fodor's Choice **Alcázar.** The Plaza del Triunfo forms the entrance to the Mudejar palace
★ built by Pedro I (1350–69) on the site of Seville's former Moorish *alcázar* (fortress). Don't mistake the Alcázar for a genuine Moorish palace like Granada's Alhambra—it may look like one, and it was designed and built by Moorish workers brought in from Granada, but it was commissioned and paid for by a Christian king more than 100 years after the reconquest of Seville. The palace is the official residence of the king and queen when they're in town. ⊠ *Pl. del Triunfo, Santa Cruz* ☎ *954/502324* ⊕ *www.patronato-alcazarsevilla.es* 🔾 *€8.50* 🕙 *Apr.– Sept., daily 9:30–7; Oct.–Mar., daily 9:30–5.*

★ **Cathedral.** Seville's cathedral can be described only in superlatives: it's the largest and highest cathedral in Spain, the largest Gothic building in the world, and the world's third-largest church, after St. Peter's in Rome and St. Paul's in London. After Ferdinand III captured Seville from the Moors in 1248, the great mosque begun by Yusuf II in 1171 was reconsecrated to the Virgin Mary and used as a Christian cathedral. In 1401 the people of Seville decided to erect a new cathedral, one that would equal the glory of their great city. They pulled down the old mosque, leaving only its minaret and outer courtyard, and built the existing building in just over a century—a remarkable feat for the time. ⊠ *Pl. Virgen de los Reyes, Centro* ☎ *954/214971* 🔾 *Cathedral and Giralda €8* 🕙 *July and Aug., Mon.–Sat. 9:30–4:30, Sun. 2:30–6:30; Sept.–June, Mon.–Sat. 11–5:30, Sun. 2:30–6:30.*

Fodor's Choice **Museo del Baile Flamenco.** This private museum in the heart of Santa
★ Cruz (follow the signs) was opened in 2007 by the legendary flamenco
dancer Cristina Hoyos and includes audiovisual and multimedia displays explaining the history, culture, and soul of Spanish flamenco.
There are also regular classes and shows. ⊠ *Calle Manuel Rojas Mar-
cos 3, Santa Cruz* ☎ *954/340311* ⊕ *www.museoflamenco.com* ⊠ *€10*
⊙ *Daily 9:30–7.*

★ **Palacio de la Condesa de Lebrija.** This lovely palace has three ornate
patios, including a spectacular courtyard graced by a Roman mosaic
taken from the ruins in Itálica, surrounded by Moorish arches and fine
azulejos. The side rooms house a collection of archaeological items. The
second floor contains the family apartments and visits are by guided
tour only. ⊠ *Calle Cuna 8, Centro* ☎ *954/227802* ⊠ *€5 first floor only;
€8 with second floor tour* ⊙ *July and Aug., weekdays 9–3, Sat. 10–2;
Sept.–June, weekdays 10:30–7:30, Sat. 10–2 and 4–6, Sun. 10–2.*

Torre del Oro (*Tower of Gold*). Built by the Moors in 1220 to complete
the city's ramparts, this 12-sided tower on the banks of the Guadalquivir served to close off the harbor when a chain was stretched across the
river from its base to a tower on the opposite bank. In 1248, Admiral
Ramón de Bonifaz broke through the barrier, and Ferdinand III captured Seville. The tower houses a small naval museum. ⊠ *Paseo Alcalde
Marqués de Contadero s/n, El Arenal* ☎ *954/222419* ⊠ *€3; free Mon.*
⊙ *Mon.–Fri. 9:30–6:45, weekends 10:30–6:45.*

JEREZ DE LA FRONTERA
52 km (34 miles) northeast of Cádiz.

Jerez, world headquarters for sherry, is surrounded by vineyards of
chalky soil, whose Palomino grapes have funded a host of churches
and noble mansions. Names such as González Byass, Domecq, Harvey,
and Sandeman are inextricably linked with Jerez. At any given time
more than half a million barrels of sherry are maturing in Jerez's vast
aboveground wine cellars.

González Byass. If you have time for only one bodega, make it this one,
home of the famous Tío Pepe. The tour is well organized and includes
La Concha, an open-air aging cellar designed by Gustave Eiffel. ⊠ *Calle
Manuel María González* ☎ *902/440077* ⊕ *www.bodegastiopepe.com.*

Fodor's Choice **Real Escuela Andaluza del Arte Ecuestre** (*Royal Andalusian School of
★ Equestrian Art*). This prestigious school operates on the grounds of
Ͼ the Recreo de las Cadenas, a 19th-century palace. The school was mas-
terminded by Alvaro Domecq in the 1970s, and every Thursday (and
at various other times throughout the year) the Cartujana horses—a
cross between the native Andalusian workhorse and the Arabian—
and skilled riders in 18th-century riding costume demonstrate intricate dressage techniques and jumping in the spectacular show "Cómo
Bailan los Caballos Andaluces" (roughly, "The Dancing Horses of
Andalusia"). Reservations are essential. Admission price depends on
how close to the arena you sit; the first two rows are the priciest. At
certain other times you can visit the stables and tack room, and watch
the horses being schooled. ⊠ *Av. Duque de Abrantes* ☎ *956/319635
information, 956/318008 tickets* ⊕ *www.realescuela.org* ⊠ *Shows:*

€19–€25; stables tour and training sessions: €10 ☉ Shows: Mar.–mid-Dec., Tues. and Thurs. at noon (also Fri. at noon in Aug.); for Sat. shows check website. Tour and training sessions: Jan.–Feb., Mon. and Tues. 10–2; Mar.–Dec. Weds. and Fri. 10–2.

SHOPPING

The region abounds with colorful souvenirs, including fine flamenco costumes, classical guitars, ornate fans traditional to Andalusia. Look out also for copious choices in ceramics, porcelain, and textiles, including beautiful hand-stitched embroidery (be aware that machine-embroidered items have flooded the market). Don't forget a bottle or two of excellent Jerez sherry, or Spanish olives and olive oil to augment your larders back home.

Seville is the region's main shopping area and the place for archetypal Andalusian souvenirs, most of which are sold in the Barrio de Santa Cruz and around the cathedral and Giralda, especially on Calle Alemanes. The main shopping street for Sevillanos themselves is Calle Sierpes, along with its neighboring streets Cuna, Tetuan, Velázquez, Plaza Magdalena, and Plaza Duque—boutiques abound here. The streets of old Cádiz are the place to browse and buy.

Artesanía Textil. You can find blankets, shawls, and embroidered tablecloths woven by local artisans at the two shops of Artesanía Textil. ⊠ *Calle García de Vinuesa 33, El Arenal, Seville* ☎ *954/215088* ☉ *Weekends* ⊠ *Sierpes 70, Centro, Seville* ☎ *954/220125* ☉ *Weekends.*

WHERE TO EAT

$　✕**Casa Manteca.** Cádiz's most quintessentially Andalusian tavern is in
SPANISH　the neighborhood of La Viña (named for the vineyard that once grew
Fodor's Choice　here). *Chacina* (Iberian ham or sausage) served on waxed paper and
★　Manzanilla (sherry from Sanlúcar de Barrameda) are standard fare at this low wooden counter that has served bullfighters and flamenco singers, as well as dignitaries from around the world, since 1953. The walls are covered with colorful posters and other memorabilia from the annual carnival, flamenco shows, and ferias. No hot dishes are available. ⑤ *Average main: €8* ⊠ *Corralón de los Carros 66* ☎ *956/213603* ☉ *Closed Mon. No lunch Sun.*

$$　✕**Enrique Becerra.** Excellent tapas, a lively bar, and an extensive wine
SPANISH　list await at this restaurant run by the fifth generation of a family of
★　celebrated restaurateurs (Enrique's brother Jesús owns Becerrita). The menu focuses on traditional, home-cooked Andalusian dishes, such as *pez espada al amontillado* (swordfish cooked in dark sherry) and *cordero a la miel con espinacas y piñones* (honey-glazed lamb stuffed with spinach and pine nuts). Don't miss the fried eggplant stuffed with prawns. If you want a quiet meal, call to reserve a table in one of the small upstairs rooms. ⑤ *Average main: €21* ⊠ *Calle Gamazo 2, El Arenal, Seville* ☎ *954/213049* ☉ *Closed Sun. and Aug.*

CANNES, FRANCE (WITH THE ILES DE LÉRINS AND ANTIBES)

Updated
by Jennifer
Ladonne

A tasteful and expensive stomping ground for the upscale, Cannes is a sybaritic heaven for those who believe that life is short and sin has something to do with the absence of a tan. Backed by gentle hills and flanked to the southwest by the Estérel, warmed by dependable sun but kept bearable in summer by the cool Mediterranean breeze, Cannes is pampered with the luxurious climate that has made it one of the most popular and glamorous resorts in Europe. The cynosure of sun worshippers since the 1860s, it has been further glamorized by the modern success of its film festival. If you're a culture lover into art of the noncelluloid type you should look elsewhere. Come to Cannes for incomparable Continental panache and as a stepping-stone to attractions a little farther afield.

ESSENTIALS
CURRENCY
The euro.

HOURS
Most stores are open Monday–Saturday 9–7, but many close at lunchtime (usually noon–2 or 3) and some will open later and on Sunday during July and August. Museums are open 10–5, but most are closed on either Monday or Tuesday.

TELEPHONES
Tri-band GSM phones work in France. You can buy prepaid phone cards at telecom shops, news vendors, and tobacconists in all towns and cities. Phone cards can be used for local or international calls. Orange, SFR, Bouygues Telecom, and Virgin are leading telecom companies. If you have an unlocked GSM phone, LeFrenchMobile (⊕ *www. lefrenchmobile.com*) offers SIM cards (and micro SIM cards) with support in English, unlimited validity of credits, and prepurchase online.

COMING ASHORE
Cruise vessels anchor offshore in Cannes, and passengers are tendered ashore to the Old Port. From there it is walking distance to all the city attractions. Taxis are on hand, and it's a five-minute ride to the train or bus station.

There will be no need to rent a vehicle unless you want to tour the surrounding Provençal countryside. The rental cost is approximately €70 per day for an economy manual vehicle. Taxis are plentiful and can provide tourist itineraries. For single journeys, tariffs are €2.80 at flag fall, then €0.90 per km. If you want to rent by the hour, the daytime tariff is €28 plus the distance covered on the meter.

Local trains are frequent; you can reach Nice in 20 minutes (€7 or €9.50 by faster TGV), Antibes in 10 minutes (€3 or €4 by faster TGV), and almost all other coastal towns can also be reached on a local train in less than an hour. Both RCA and TAM bus lines have frequent service (RCA's 200 bus between Cannes and Antibes runs every 20 minutes).

EXPLORING CANNES

CANNES

La Croisette. Head to the famous mile-long waterfront promenade, La Croisette, which starts at the western end by the Palais des Festivals, and allow the *esprit de Cannes* to take over. This is precisely the sort of place for which the verb *flâner* (to dawdle, saunter) was invented, so stroll among the palm trees and flowers and crowds of poseurs (fur coats in tropical weather, cell phones on Rollerblades, and sunglasses at night). Head east past the broad expanse of private beaches, glamorous shops, and luxurious hotels (among them the wedding-cake Carlton, famed for its see-and-be-seen terrace-level brasserie). The beaches along here are almost all private, though open for a fee—each beach is marked with from one to four little life buoys, rating their quality and expense.

Le Suquet. Climb up Rue St-Antoine into the picturesque Vieille Ville neighborhood known as Le Suquet, on the site of the original Roman *castrum*. Shops proffer Provençal goods, and the atmospheric cafés provide a place to catch your breath; the pretty pastel shutters, Gothic stonework, and narrow passageways are lovely distractions.

Musée de la Castre. The hill is crowned by the 11th-century château, housing the Musée de la Castre, with its mismatched collection of

weaponry, ethnic artifacts, and ceramics amassed by a 19th century aristocrat. The imposing four-sided **Tour du Suquet** (Suquet Tower) was built in 1385 as a lookout against Saracen-led invasions. ⊠ *Pl. de la Castre, Le Suquet* ☎ *04–93–38–55–26* 🎫 *€6* ⊘ *Oct.–Mar., Tues.–Sun. 10–1 and 2–5; Apr.–June and Sept., Tues.–Sun. 10–1 and 2–6; July and Aug., daily 10–7.*

Palais des Festivals. Pick up a map at the tourist office in the Palais des Festivals, the scene of the famous Festival International du Film, otherwise known as the Cannes Film Festival. As you leave the information center, follow the Palais to your right to see the red-carpeted stairs where the stars ascend every year. Set into the surrounding pavement, the **Allée des Étoiles** (Stars' Walk) enshrines some 400 autographed imprints of film stars' hands—of Dépardieu, Streep, and Stallone, among others.

ÎLES LÉRINS

15–20 minutes by ferry off the coast of Cannes.

When you're glutted on glamour, you may want to make a day trip to the peaceful Iles de Lérins (Lérins Islands); boats depart from Cannes's Vieux Port. Allow at least a half day to enjoy either of the islands; you can fit both in only if you get an early start. Access to the ferry is across the large parking in front of the Sofitel hotel, southwest from the Palais des Festivals. You have two ferry options.

Tour Contacts Compagnie Planaria. Compagnie Planaria ⊠ *Quai Laubeuf (end of parking lot), port of Cannes, La Croisette, Cannes* ☎ *04–92–98–71–38* ⊕ *www.cannes-ilesdelerins.com.*

Trans Côte D'Azur. When it comes to transport to and from Isle St-Margueritte, the Trans Côte D'Azur is the way to go. ⊠ *Quai Laubeuf (end of parking lot), port of Cannes, La Croisette, Cannes* ☎ *04–92–98–71–30* ⊕ *www.trans-cote-azur.com.*

EXPLORING ILE ST-HONORAT

Ile St-Honorat. Ile St-Honorat can be reached in 20 minutes (€13 round-trip) from the Vieux Port. Smaller and wilder than Ste-Marguerite, it's home to an active monastery and the ruins of its 11th-century predecessor. The monks are more famous in the region for their nonreligious activity: manufacturing and selling a rather strong liqueur called Lérina. ⊕ *www.abbayedelerins.com.*

EXPLORING ILE STE-MARGUERITE

Ile Ste-Marguerite. Fron the Vieux Port it's a 15-minute, €12 round-trip to Ile Ste-Marguerite. Its **Fort Royal,** built by Richelieu and improved by Vauban, offers views over the ramparts to the rocky island coast and the open sea.

Musée de la Mer (*Marine Museum*). The complex includes the Musée de la Mer, with a Roman boat dating from the 1st century BC and a collection of amphorae and pottery recovered from ancient shipwrecks. It's more famous, however, for reputedly being the prison of the Man in the Iron Mask. Inside you can see his cell and hear his story, and although the truth of his captivity is not certain, it's true that many Huguenots were confined here during Louis XIV's religious scourges. ⊠ *Fort de l'île Sainte-Marguerite* ☎ *04–93–38–55–26* 🖭 *€6* ☾ *Oct.–Mar., Tues.–Sun. 10:30–1:15 and 2:15–4:45; Apr.–mid-June, Tues.–Sun. 10:30–1:15 and 2:15–5:45; mid-June–Sept., daily 10:30–5:45.*

ANTIBES

11 km (7 miles) northeast of Cannes, 15 km (9 miles) southeast of Nice.

Fodor's Choice
★

No wonder Picasso once called this home—Antibes (pronounced Awn-teeb) is a stunner. With its broad stone ramparts scalloping in and out over the waves and backed by blunt medieval towers and a skew of tile roofs, it remains one of the most romantic Old Towns on the Mediterranean coast. As gateway to the Cap d'Antibes, Antibes's Port Vauban harbor has some of the largest yachts in the world tied up at its berths—their millionaire owners won't find a more dramatic spot to anchor, with the tableau of the snowy Alps looming in the distance and the formidable medieval block towers of the Fort Carré guarding entry to the port. Stroll Promenade Amiral-de-Grasse along the crest of Vauban's seawalls, and you'll understand why the views inspired Picasso to paint on a panoramic scale. Yet a few steps inland you'll enter a souk-like maze of old streets that are relentlessly picturesque and joyously beautiful.

To visit Old Antibes, pass through the **Porte Marine,** an arched gateway in the rampart wall. Follow Rue Aubernon to **Cours Masséna,** where the little sheltered market sells lemons, olives, and hand-stuffed sausages, and the vendors take breaks in the shoebox cafés flanking one side.

Fodor's Choice
★

Commune Libre du Safranier (*Free Commune of Safranier*). A few blocks south of the Château Grimaldi is the Commune Libre du Safranier, a magical little neighborhood with a character all its own. Here, not far off the seaside promenade and focused around the Place du Safranier, tiny houses hang heavy with flowers and vines and neighbors carry on conversations from window to window across the stone-stepped Rue du Bas-Castelet. It's said that Place du Safranier was once a tiny fishing port; now it's the scene of festivals.

★ **Eglise de l'Immaculée-Conception.** From Cours Masséna head up to the Eglise de l'Immaculée-Conception, which served as the region's cathedral until the bishopric was transferred to Grasse in 1244. The church's 18th-century facade, a marvelously Latin mix of classical symmetry and fantasy, has been restored in stunning shades of ocher and cream. Its stout medieval watchtower was built in the 11th century with stones "mined" from Roman structures. Inside is a baroque altarpiece painted by the Niçois artist Louis Bréa in 1515. ⊠ *Rue St-Esprit.*

SHOPPING

Cannes caters to the upmarket crowd with a wealth of designer boutiques such as Chanel and Dior, and high-class jewelers. But if you don't want to max out your credit cards, there's a wealth of choice of less expensive ready-to-wear fashion. Boutiques also sell colorful crafts from the Provence region, including basketwork, bright fabrics, olive-wood items, plus delicious olives, olive oils, honey, dried herbs, and quaffable local wines. Film buffs may also want to stock up on official Cannes Film Festival merchandise.

Rue d'Antibes, running parallel with the Croisette but two blocks inland, is Cannes's main high-end shopping street. At its western end is **Rue Meynadier,** packed tight with trendy clothing boutiques and fine food shops. Not far away is the covered **Marché Forville,** the scene of the animated morning food market. The narrow alleyways of **Le Suquet,** are also a great place to browse. Film Festival merchandise can be bought at the **Palais du Festivals,** but the official Film Festival shop is found on La Croisette, close to the Majestic Hotel.

Vieil Antibes has an excellent shopping, though you'll find far fewer designer boutiques than in Cannes. Small shops sell an excellent range of local crafts and foodstuffs and there are several galleries selling work by local artists.

BEACHES

The pebble beach that fronts the full length of La Croisette has a chic atmosphere in summer. Most sections have been privatized and are owned by hotels and/or restaurants that rent out chaise longues, mats, and umbrellas to the public and hotel guests (who also have to pay). Public beaches are between the color-coordinated private beach umbrellas, and offer simple open showers and basic toilets. The restaurants here are some of the best places for lunch or refreshment, though you do pay extra for the location.

WHERE TO EAT

$ ✕ **La Pizza.** Sprawling up over two floors in front of the old port, this
PIZZA   busy restaurant (with two sister eateries, La Pizza and Le Quebec in Nice) serves steaks, fish, and salads every day of the year, but come here for gloriously good right-out-of-the-wood-fire-oven pizza in huge portions. ⑤ *Average main: €13* ✉ *3 quai St-Pierre* ☎ *04–93–39–22–56.*

CIVITAVECCHIA, ITALY (FOR ROME)

Updated
by Bruce
Leimsidor

Rome is a heady blend of artistic and architectural masterpieces, classical ruins, and opulent baroque churches and piazzas. The city's 2,700-year-old history is on display wherever you look; the ancient rubs shoulders with the medieval, the modern runs into the Renaissance, and the result is a bustling open-air museum. Julius Caesar and Nero, the Vandals and the Popes, Raphael and Caravaggio, Napoléon and Mussolini—these and countless other luminaries and villains have

left their mark on the city. Today Rome's formidable legacy is kept alive by its people, their history knit into the fabric of their everyday lives. Raphaelesque teenage girls zip through traffic on their *motorini*; priests in flowing robes talking on cell phones stride through medieval piazzas. Modern Rome has one foot in the past, one in the present—a fascinating stance that allows you to tip back an espresso while gazing at a Bernini fountain, then hop on the metro to your next attraction.

ESSENTIALS

CURRENCY

The euro.

HOURS

Stores are generally open from 9 or 9:30 to 1 and from 3:30 or 4 to 8. There's a tendency for shops in central districts to stay open all day. Many places close Sunday, and some also close Monday morning from September to mid-June and Saturday afternoon from mid-June through August.

PRIVATE TOURS

The most universally acclaimed private tour service in Rome is that offered by When in Rome Tours. The service offers a countless number of tour options. Booking a tour independently for one or two persons can be very expensive (€870 for the Shore excursions Rome option), but many cruise lines arrange group tours with this service, which should cost about €150/person, depending on the size of the group. The Shore Excursion Option includes pick-up at the port, a 3-hour transit to and from, and 7 hours of touring. You can also form your own group with other passengers before you book independently, but these tours must be arranged in advance, so if you are not traveling among a large group of cruise passengers, that can be logistically difficult.

Contacts **When in Rome Tours.** ☎ *(39)06/839–04705 in Rome* ⊕ *www.wheninrometours.com.*

TELEPHONES

Tri-band GSM phones work in Italy. You can buy prepaid phone cards at telecom shops, news vendors, and tobacconists in all towns and cities. Phone cards can be used for local or international calls.

COMING ASHORE

Civitavecchia is a large port, and you will be bused from the ship to the terminal area. There are passenger facilities such as cafés and information offices, but these are shared with commercial ferry traffic and can be crowded. A shuttle will take you to the railway station, where you can catch trains to Rome, or you can walk along the harborfront to the station in less than 10 minutes. Taxis charge around €20 for the journey to the train station. Train tickets to Rome cost approximately €5 to €10 one-way, depending on time of travel. If you prebook on the Trenitalia website ⊕ *www.trenitalia.com*, you can print out your tickets at the station. There are two or three trains per hour, and the journey time is 1 hour 15 minutes. The cost for a private car with driver to Rome is approximately €150 one-way.

Taxis in Rome are expensive, with extra charges when the taxi travels at less than 20 kph (12 mph), and with surcharges for busier times of the day, for every piece of luggage after the first, to order a taxi by phone, and for travel on holidays. You shouldn't rent a car if you want to explore only Rome, because both traffic and parking are difficult; however, if you want to explore the countryside around Civitavecchia a car would be useful. Rental costs are approximately €50 per day for a compact manual vehicle.

Rome's metro (subway) is somewhat limited, but it's quick if you are headed somewhere that it goes. The public bus and tram system is slow. Taking the compact electric buses of Lines 117 and 119 through the center of Rome can save a lot of walking. A ticket valid for 75 minutes on any combination of buses and trams and one entrance to the metro costs €1. Tickets for the public transit system are sold at tobacconists, newsstands, some coffee bars; you can also buy them in the green machines positioned in metro stations and some bus stops. A BIG ticket, valid for one day on all public transport, costs €4.

ROME BEST BETS

The Colosseum. Although jam-packed with tourists, this is still one of ancient Rome's most iconic relics and was the scene of some of its bloodiest contests.

Basilica di San Pietro. The mother church for all Catholics is redolent with spirit and filled with artistic masterpieces. Just remember that the Sistine Chapel can only be visited if you go to the Vatican Museums.

Join the throng at Piazza Navona. Visit this large square with its three fountains and immerse yourself in the energy that is modern Rome.

GETTING TO THE AIRPORT

If you do not purchase airport transfers from your cruise line, the most practical option is to take a taxi (with a set price of €120) or private transfer company (which costs around €150) to pick you up at the port and drop you at the airport. The private transfer vehicle will be larger than a taxi and can accommodate up to seven people. You can also take a train between Civitavecchia port railway station and Fiumicino airport (€11 one-way), but the trip involves changing trains in Rome and takes about 2 hours. It is not advised for travelers with lots of luggage (or little patience).

Contacts **ACS.** A somewhat less expensive limousine service in a modest car to Fiumicino airport through ACS (Airport Connection Service) costs €100 to €110 and takes 45 minutes. ☎ (39) 06/3383221 in Italy ⊕ www.airportconnection.it. **Dock Service.** This company can provide port to airport transfers (or vice versa) as well as guided land tours within Rome. ☎ 239/603–7469 in the U.S., 338/9139644 in Italy ⊕ www.limoservicesrome.net.

EXPLORING ROME

★ **Basilica di San Pietro.** The world's largest church, built over the tomb of St. Peter, is the most imposing and breathtaking architectural achievement of the Renaissance (although much of the lavish interior dates to the baroque). The physical statistics are impressive: it covers 18,000 square yards, runs 212 yards in length, and is surmounted by a dome

that rises 435 feet and measures 138 feet across its base. Its history is equally impressive. No fewer than five of Italy's greatest artists—Bramante, Raphael, Peruzzi, Antonio Sangallo the Younger, and Michelangelo—died while striving to erect this new St. Peter's.

The history of the original St. Peter's goes back to AD 349, when the emperor Constantine completed a basilica over the site of the tomb of St. Peter, the Church's first pope. The original church stood for more than 1,000 years. The current basilica was completed only in 1626 after more than 100 years of construction.

Under the Pope Pius V monument, the entrance to the sacristy also leads to the **Museo Storico-Artistico e Tesoro** (⌧ *Historical-Artistic Museum and Treasury* ☎ *06/69881840* 🎟 *€10 includes audio guide* ⊘ *Apr.–Sept., daily 8–7; Oct.–Mar., daily 8–6:20*), a small collection of Vatican treasures. Above, the vast sweep of the basilica's dome is the cynosure of all eyes. Proceed to the right side of the Basilica's vestibule; from here, you can either take the elevator or climb the long flight of shallow stairs to the roof (☎ *06/69883462* 🎟 *elevator €7, stairs €5* ⊘ *Apr.–Sept., daily 8–6; Oct.–Mar., daily 8–4; on a Papal Audience Wed., opens after the audience finishes, about noon; closed during ceremonies in piazza*). The entrance to the **Grotte Vaticane** (⌧ *Vatican Grottoes* 🎟 *Free* ⊘ *Weekdays and Sat. 9–4; Sun. 1:30–3:30; closed while the papal audience takes place in St. Peter's Square, until about noon on Wed.*) is to the right of the Basilica's main entrance. ⌧ *Piazza di San Pietro, Vatican* ⊘ *Apr.–Sept., daily 7–7; Oct.–Mar., daily 7–6; closed during the papal audience in St. Peter's Square Wed. mornings until about noon* Ⓜ *Ottaviano-San Pietro.*

Fodor's Choice **Cappella Sistina** (*Sistine Chapel*). In 1508, the redoubtable Pope Julius ★ II commissioned Michelangelo to fresco the more than 10,000 square feet of the Sistine Chapel's ceiling. (*Sistine,* by the way, is simply the adjective from *Sixtus,* in reference to Pope Sixtus IV, who commissioned the chapel itself.) The task took four years, and it's said that for many years afterward Michelangelo couldn't read anything without holding it over his head. The result, however, was the greatest artwork of the Renaissance. A pair of binoculars helps greatly, as does a small mirror—hold the mirror facing the ceiling and look down to study the reflection. More than 20 years later, Michelangelo was called on again, this time by the Farnese pope Paul III, to add to the chapel's decoration by painting the *Last Judgment* on the wall over the altar. The subject was well suited to the aging and embittered artist, who had been deeply moved by the horrendous Sack of Rome in 1527 and the confusions and disturbances of the Reformation. ⌧ *Vatican Palace; entry only through Musei Vaticani, Vatican.*

The Colosseum. The most spectacular extant edifice of ancient Rome, the Colosseo has a history that is half gore, half glory. Here, before 50,000 spectators, gladiators would salute the emperor and cry *Ave, imperator, morituri te salutant* ("Hail, emperor, men soon to die salute thee"). Designed by order of the Flavian emperor Vespasian in AD 72, the Colosseum was inaugurated by Titus eight years later with a program of games lasting 100 days. The arena has a circumference of

573 yards and was faced with travertine from nearby Tivoli. Its construction was a remarkable feat of engineering, for it stands on marshy terrain reclaimed by draining an artificial lake on the grounds of Nero's Domus Aurea. Originally known as the Flavian amphitheater, it came to be called the Colosseo because it stood on the site of the Colossus of Nero, a 115-foot-tall gilded bronze statue of the emperor that once towered here. The newly restored hypogeum, along with the third level of the Colosseum, reopened to much acclaim in fall 2010 (visitable only via a prebooked, guided tour). Since then, however, it's open and shut, depending on the season and recent rains. Check the Pierreci website for its current state.

If you go to the Roman Forum, a couple of hundred yards down Via dei Fori Imperiali on your left, or to the Palatine, down Via di San Gregorio, the €12 ticket you purchase there includes admission to the Colosseum and, even better, lets you jump to the head of the *loooooooong* line. Another way is to buy the Romapass (⊕ *www.romapass.it*) ticket—the Colosseo is covered and you get booted to the front of the line. Or you can book a ticket in advance through ⊕ *www.pierreci.it* (small surcharge)—the main ticket reservation service for many Italian cultural sights. ⊠ *Piazza del Colosseo* ☎ *06/39967700* ⊕ *www.pierreci. it* ⊟ *€12 (combined ticket with the Roman Forum, Palatine Hill, and Imperial Forums, if used within 2 days)* ☉ *Daily 8:30–1 hr before sunset* Ⓜ *Colosseo; Bus 117, 87, 186, 85, 850.*

Fodor'sChoice ★ **Musei Vaticani** (*Vatican Museums*). Other than the pope and his papal court, the occupants of the Vatican are some of the most famous artworks in the world. The museums that contain them are part of the **Vatican Palace**, residence of the popes since 1377. The palace consists of an estimated 1,400 rooms, chapels, and galleries. The pope and his household occupy only a small part of the palace; most of the rest is given over to the Vatican Library and Museums. Beyond the glories of the Sistine Chapel, the collection is so extraordinarily rich you may just wish to skim the surface, but few will want to miss out on the great antique sculptures, Raphael Rooms, and the old master paintings, such as Leonardo da Vinci's *St. Jerome.*

Rivaling the Sistine Chapel for artistic interest—and for the number of visitors—are the **Stanze di Raffaello** (Raphael Rooms). Pope Julius II moved into this suite in 1507, four years after his election. Reluctant to continue living in the Borgia apartments downstairs, with their memories of his ill-famed predecessor Alexander VI, he called in Raphael to decorate his new quarters. Downstairs, enter the recently restored **Borgia apartments,** where some of the Vatican's most fascinating historical figures are depicted on elaborately painted ceilings. Pinturicchio designed the frescoes at the end of the 15th century, though the paintings were greatly retouched in later centuries. It's generally believed that Cesare Borgia murdered his sister Lucrezia's husband, Alphonse of Aragon, in the Room of the Sibyl. Equally celebrated are the works on view in the **Pinacoteca** (Picture Gallery). These often world-famous paintings, almost exclusively of religious subjects, are arranged in chronological order, beginning with works of the 12th and 13th centuries.

To avoid the line into the museums, consider booking your ticket in advance online (⊕ *biglietteriamusei.vatican.va*); there is a €4 surcharge. Guided tours are €31 to €36, including entrance tickets, and can also be booked online. For information on tours, call *06/69883145* or *06/69884676*; visually impaired visitors can arrange tactile tours by calling *06/69884947*. Note: Ushers at the entrance of St. Peter's and sometimes the Vatican Museums will bar entry to people with bare knees or bare shoulders. ⊠ *Viale Vaticano (near intersection with Via Leone IV), Vatican* ⊕ *www.vatican.va* 🖃 *€15; free last Sun. of the month* ⊙ *Mon.–Sat. 9–6 (last entrance at 4), last Sun. of month 9–12:30* ⊙ *Closed Jan. 1 and 6, Feb. 11, Mar. 19, Easter and Easter Monday, May 1, June 29, Aug. 14 and 15, Nov. 1, and Dec. 8, 25, and 26* Ⓜ *Cipro–Musei Vaticani or Ottaviano–San Pietro. Bus 64, 40.*

★ **Trevi Fountain.** Alive with rushing waters commanded by an imperious Oceanus, the Fontana di Trevi (Trevi Fountain) earned full-fledged iconic status in 1954 when it starred in 20th-Century Fox's *Three Coins in the Fountain.* As the first color film in Cinemascope to be produced on location, it caused practically half of America to pack their bags for the Eternal City. The conceit of a fountain emerging full-force from a palace was first envisioned by Bernini and Pietro da Cortona for Pope Urban VIII's plan to rebuild the fountain (which marked the end-point of the ancient Acqua Vergine aqueduct, created in 18 BC by Agrippa). Only three popes later, under Pope Clement XIII, did Nicolo Salvi finally break ground with his winning design. ⊠ *Piazza di Trevi, accessed by Via Tritone, Via Poli, Via delle Muratte, Via del Lavatore, and Via di San Vincenzo, Trevi.*

Fodor's Choice **Musei Capitolini.** Surpassed in size and richness only by the Musei Vaticani, this immense collection was the first public museum in the world. A greatest-hits collection of Roman art through the ages, from the ancients to the baroque, it is housed in the twin Museo Capitolino and Palazzo dei Conservatori that bookend Michelangelo's famous piazza. Here, you'll find some of antiquity's most famous sculptures, such as the poignant *Dying Gaul,* the regal *Capitoline Venus,* the *Esquiline Venus* (identified as possibly another Mediterranean beauty, Cleopatra herself), and the *Lupa Capitolina,* the symbol of Rome. Although some pieces in the collection—which was first assembled by Sixtus IV (1414–84), one of the earliest of the Renaissance popes—may excite only archaeologists and art historians, others are unforgettable, including the original bronze statue of Marcus Aurelius whose copy sits in the piazza. ⊠ *Piazza del Campidoglio, Campidoglio* 🕾 *06/0608* ⊕ *www. museicapitolini.org* 🖃 *€12; audio guide €5* ⊙ *Tues.–Sun. 9–8* Ⓜ *Bus 44, 63, 64, 81, 95, 85, 492.*

Fodor's Choice **Pantheon.** One of the wonders of the ancient world, this onetime pagan temple, a marvel of architectural harmony and proportion, is the best-preserved ancient building in Rome. It was entirely rebuilt by the emperor Hadrian around AD 120 on the site of an earlier pantheon (from the Greek *pan,* all, and *theon,* gods) erected in 27 BC by Augustus's general Agrippa. The most striking thing about the Pantheon is not its size, immense though it is (until 1960 the dome was the largest ever built), nor even the phenomenal technical difficulties posed by so

vast a construction; rather, it's the remarkable unity of the building. You don't have to look far to find the reason for this harmony: the diameter described by the dome is exactly equal to its height. It's the use of such simple mathematical balance that gives classical architecture its characteristic sense of proportion and its nobility and why some call it the world's only architecturally perfect building. The great opening at the apex of the dome, the oculus, is nearly 30 feet in diameter and was the temple's only source of light. It was intended to symbolize the "all-seeing eye of heaven." One-hour tours (€8) are run regularly in English; check at the information desk on your right as you enter. ⊠ *Piazza della Rotonda, Navona* ☎ *06/68300230* 🔗 *Free; audio guides €5 suggested donation* ☉ *Mon.–Sat. 8:30–7:30, Sun. 9–6* Ⓜ *Closest bus hub: Argentina (buses 40, 85, 53, 46, 64, 87, 571, tram 8).*

Piazza Navona. Here, everything that makes Rome unique is compressed into one beautiful baroque piazza. Always camera-ready, Piazza Navona has Bernini sculptures, three gorgeous fountains, a magnificently baroque church (Sant'Agnese in Agone), and, best of all, the excitement of so many people strolling, admiring the fountains, and enjoying the view. The piazza has been an entertainment venue for Romans ever since being built over Domitian's circus (pieces of the arena are still visible near adjacent Piazza Sant'Apollinare). Although undoubtedly more touristy today, the square still has the carefree air of the days when it was the scene of medieval jousts and 17th-century carnivals. Today, it's the site of a lively Christmas "Befana" fair. At center stage is the Fontana dei Quattro Fiumi, created for Innocent X by Bernini in 1651. Bernini's powerful figures of the four rivers represent the four corners of the world: the Nile; the Ganges; the Danube; and the Plata, with its hand raised. ⊠ *Junction of Via della Cuccagna, Corsia Agonale, Via di Sant'Agnese, and Via Agonale.*

Fodor'sChoice
★
☺

The Spanish Steps. That icon of postcard Rome, the Spanish Steps (often called simply *la scalinata*—"the staircase"—by Italians) and the Piazza di Spagna from which they ascend both get their names from the Spanish Embassy to the Vatican on the piazza—even though the staircase was built with French funds in 1723. For centuries, the scalinata and its neighborhood have welcomed tourists, dukes, and writers in search of inspiration—among them Stendhal, Honoré de Balzac, William Makepeace Thackeray, and Byron, along with today's enthusiastic hordes. ⊠ *Junction of Via Condotti, Via del Babuino, and Via Due Macelli, Spagna* Ⓜ *Spagna.*

☺   **Pincio.** The Pincian gardens always have been a favorite spot for strolling. Grand Tourists, and even a pope or two, would head here to see and be seen among the beau monde of Rome. A stretch of ancient walls separates the Pincio from the southwest corner of Villa Borghese. From the balustraded terrace, you can look down at Piazza del Popolo and beyond, surveying much of Rome. Southeast of the Pincian terrace is the **Casina Valadier,** a magnificently decorated neoclassical building that was reopened to the public in 2007 after a decade-long renovation. It remains one of Rome's most historic restaurants (*06/69922090, casinavaladier.it*). ⊠ *Piazzale Napoleone I and Viale dell'Obelisco, Villa Borghese* Ⓜ *Flaminio (Piazza del Popolo).*

2

SHOPPING

Italian style is everywhere in Rome, from couture clothing to fashion accessories by all the best names. Specialties of the city include excellent silks, linens, lace, and other fabrics. Edibles include wines, olive oils, pasta, and sweet biscotti, small hard biscuits.

★ The city's most famous shopping district, **Piazza di Spagna,** is a galaxy of boutiques selling gorgeous wares with glamorous labels. **Via del Corso,** a main shopping avenue, has more than a mile of clothing, shoes, leather goods, and home furnishings from classic to cutting-edge. **Via Cola di Rienzo** is block after block of boutiques, shoe stores, department stores, and mid-level chain stores, as well as street stalls and upscale food shops. **Via dei Coronari** has quirky antiques and home furnishings. Via Giulia and other surrounding streets are good bets for decorative arts. Should your gift list include religious souvenirs, shop between Piazza San Pietro and **Borgo Pio.** Liturgical vestments and statues of saints make for good window-shopping on **Via dei Cestari.**

WHERE TO EAT

$$ ✕ **Da Baffetto.** Down a cobblestone street not far from Piazza Navona,
PIZZA this is Rome's most popular pizzeria and a summer favorite for street-
Fodor'sChoice side dining. The debate is constant whether or not this spot is mas-
★ sively overrated, but as with all the "great" pizzerias in Rome, it's hard to argue with the line that forms outside here on weekends. Happily, outdoor tables (enclosed and heated in winter) provide much-needed additional seating and turnover is fast (and lingering not encouraged). Baffetto 2, at Piazza del Teatro di Pompeo 18, is an extension of the pizzeria with the addition of pasta and *secondi*—and doesn't suffer from the overcrowding of the original location. ⑤ *Average main: €22* ⊠ *Via del Governo Vecchio 114, Navona* ☏ *06/6861617* ▭ *No credit cards* ⊗ *Closed Aug. and Tues. No lunch Mon.–Fri.*

$$$$ ✕ **Dal Bolognese.** The darling of the media, film, and fashion commu-
EMILIAN nities, this classic restaurant on Piazza del Popolo is not only an "in-crowd" dinner destination but makes a convenient shopping-spree lunch spot. As the name promises, the cooking adheres to the hearty tradition of Bologna. Start with a plate of sweet *San Daniele* prosciutto with melon, then move on to the traditional egg pastas of Emilia-Romagna. Second plates include the famous Bolognese *bollito misto,* a steaming tray of an assortment of boiled meats (some recognizable, some inde-cipherable) served with its classic accompaniment, a tangy, herby *salsa verde* (green sauce). During dessert, take in the passing parade of your fellow diners—they love to meet and greet with excessive air kisses. ⑤ *Average main: €75* ⊠ *Piazza del Popolo 1, Spagna* ☏ *06/3611426* ⌕ *Reservations essential* ⊗ *Closed Mon. and 3 wks in Aug.*

WHERE TO STAY

$$ ▦ **Albergo Santa Chiara.** If you're looking for a good location (right
HOTEL behind the Pantheon) and top-notch service at great prices—not to
Fodor'sChoice mention comfortable beds and a quiet stay—look no further than
★ this historic hotel, run by the same family for some 200 years. **Pros:**

great location in the historical center behind the Pantheon; the staff is both polite and helpful; there is a lovely terrace/sitting area in front of the hotel that overlooks the piazza. **Cons:** the rooms are small and could use some restyling. Some rooms don't have a window. Ⓢ *Rooms from: €250* ✉ *Via Santa Chiara 21, Pantheon* ☎ *06/6872979* ✉ *info@ albergosantachiara.com* ⊕ *www.albergosantachiara.com* ↪ *96 rooms, 3 suites, 3 apartments* ⦿ *Breakfast.*

$$$$
HOTEL
Fodor's Choice
★

🖳 **Hassler.** When it comes to million-dollar views, this exclusive hotel has the best seats in the house, which is why movie stars like Tom Cruise and Jennifer Lopez, money shakers, and the nouveaux riche are all willing to pay top dollar to stay at this top address of Rome, perched atop the Spanish Steps; they are indeed lucky, for while the Hassler's exterior is bland, the recently restyled guest rooms are among the world's most extravagant and lavishly decorated. **Pros:** charming old-world feel; prime location and panoramic views at the top of the Spanish Steps; just "steps" away from some of the best shopping in the world. **Cons:** VIP prices; many think the staff is too standoffish; the spa facilities are far from 5-star material. Ⓢ *Rooms from: €650* ✉ *Piazza Trinità dei Monti 6, Spagna* ☎ *06/69934755, 800/223–6800 Toll-free from the U.S.* ⊕ *www.hotelhasslerroma.com* ↪ *82 rooms, 13 suites* ⦿ *No meals.*

$$
B&B/INN
Fodor's Choice
★

🖳 **Scalinata di Spagna.** This tiny hotel's prime location at the top of the Spanish Steps, inconspicuous little entrance, and quiet, sunny charm all add to the character that guests fall in love with over and over again—which explains why it's often booked up for months, even years at a time—but if you're lucky enough to nab a spot here, you'll enjoy stylish rooms accentuated with floral fabrics and Empire-style sofas and the hotel's extravagant rooftop garden: gaze over Rome as you nibble cornetto and sip cappuccino. **Pros:** friendly and helpful concierge; fresh fruit in the rooms; free Wi-Fi throughout. **Cons:** it's a hike up the hill to the hotel; no porter and no elevator; service can be hit-or-miss. Ⓢ *Rooms from: €220* ✉ *Piazza Trinità dei Monti 17, Spagna* ☎ *06/6793006* ⊕ *www.hotelscalinata.com* ↪ *16 rooms* ⦿ *Breakfast.*

GENOA, ITALY

Updated
by Bruce
Leimsidor

Genoa (Genova, in Italian) claims that it was the birthplace of Christopher Columbus (one of several places that claim the explorer), but the city's proud history predates that explorer by several hundred years. Genoa was already an important trading station by the 3rd century BC, when the Romans conquered Liguria. Known as *La Superba* (The Proud), Genoa was a great maritime power in the 13th century, rivaling Venice and Pisa. But its luster eventually diminished, and the city was outshone by these and other formidable cities. By the 17th century it was no longer a great sea power. It has, however, continued to be a profitable port. Genoa is now a busy, sprawling, but nevertheless elegant city. But with more than two millennia of history under its belt, magnificent palaces and museums, and an elaborate network of ancient hilltop fortresses, Genoa is sure to satisfy your historic and aesthetic interests. Portofino can be visited on a day-trip from Genoa if your ship doesn't call there directly (⇨ *Portofino*).

2

ESSENTIALS

CURRENCY

The euro.

HOURS

Stores are generally open from 9 or 9:30 to 1 and from 3:30 or 4 to
8. Many shops close Sunday, though this is changing, too, especially
in the city center. Many national museums are closed on Monday and
may have shorter hours on Sunday.

PRIVATE TOURS

Benvenuto Tours offers full-day tours out of Genoa to the towns to
the east of the city: Portofino, the Cinque Terre, Lerici, and Portovenere. This is a pricey option (€450 per person) but an effortless way to
see some dramatic costal scenery and lovely historic villages, including
those beloved by the English romantic poets. Most of these places are
also served by rail out of Genoa.

Contacts **Benvenuto Tours.** ☎ *(39)081/007–2114 in Genoa*
⊕ *www.benvenutolimos.com.*

TELEPHONES

Tri-band GSM phones work in Italy. You can buy prepaid phone cards
at telecom shops, news vendors, and tobacconists in all towns and cities.
Phone cards can be used for local or international calls.

COMING ASHORE

Genoa is a massive port, and cruise ships usually dock at one of two
terminals, the Ponte dei Mille Maritime Station and Ponte Andrea
Doria Maritime Station. Ponte dei Mille is an impressive 1930s building (renovated 2001) with good passenger facilities that include shops,
restaurants, an information center, and a bank. Neighboring Ponte
Andrea Doria was refurbished in 2007 with similar facilities but on a
slightly smaller scale. From here it's a few minutes' walk to the port
entrance, from which you can also walk into the city; however, the
streets around the port are workaday and gritty, so you may want to
take a taxi rather than walk into the city proper. There is a "hop on/
hop off" tour bus (from April through October, €15) that starts at
Piazza Caricamento, right outside the entry to the cruise port. Buses
leave, with a few exceptions, every half-hour, and the complete circuit
takes about one hour.

With the occasional assistance of public transportation, the only way
to visit Genoa is on foot. Many of the more interesting districts are
either entirely closed to traffic, have roads so narrow that no car could
fit, or are, even at the best of times, blocked by gridlock. A vehicle
might be useful if you want to explore the Ligurian countryside and
coastline around Genoa. Rental costs are approximately €35 per day
for a compact manual vehicle. The most beautiful scenery is to the
east of Genoa, toward the Cinque Terre, but to appreciate it, you
will have to take local roads with numerous hairpin turns—not for
nervous drivers.

Within Liguria local trains make innumerable stops. Regular service
operates from Genoa's two stations: Stazione Principe travel to points

Granarolo funicular

Pza. del Principe

Pza. Acquaverde

Via Balbi

Cso. Dogali

Sal. Pietraminuta

Stazione Principe

Via A. Doria

V. Adua

Via Pte

Via Antonio Gramsci

Palazzo Reale

Via Balbi

NUOVA METROPOLITANA LEGGERA

Piazzale Staz. Marittima

Stazione Marittima

Galata Museo del Mare ◆

Darsena

V. delle Fontane

Ponte dei Mille

Ponte Parodi

Marina Porto Antico

Ponte Calvi

Ponte Spinola

Acquario di Genova ◆

Bacino Porto Vecchio

Ponte Embriaco

Il Bigo ◆

Molo Vecchio

V. del Molo

0 ——— 1/8 mi

0 ——— 1/8 km

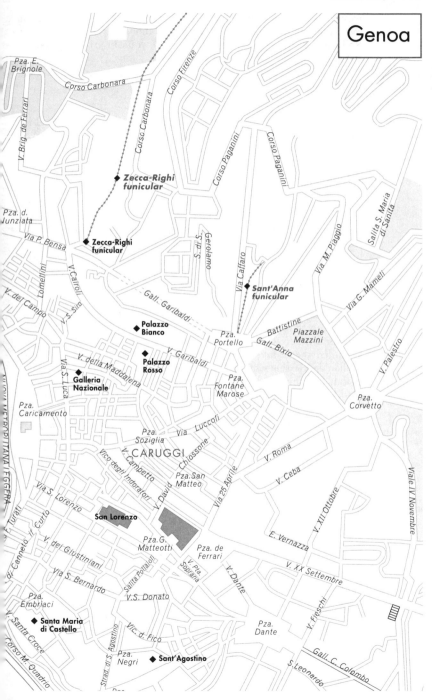

Genoa

2

west and Stazione Brignole to points east and south. All the coastal resorts are on this line. If you buy tickets though Trenitalia's (Italian Railway's) website (⊕ *www.trenitalia.com*), you can print them out at self-service machines in Genoa station.

EXPLORING GENOA

THE MEDIEVAL CORE

The medieval center of Genoa, threaded with tiny streets flanked by 11th-century portals, is roughly the area between the port and Piazza de Ferrari. This mazelike pedestrian zone is officially called the Caruggi District, but the Genovese, in their matter-of-fact way, simply refer to the area as the place of the *vicoli* (narrow alleys). In this warren of narrow, cobbled streets extending north from Piazza Caricamento the city's oldest churches sit among tiny shops selling antique furniture, coffee, cheese, rifles, wine, gilt picture frames, camping gear, and even live fish. The 500-year-old apartment buildings lean so precariously that penthouse balconies nearly touch those across the street, blocking what little sunlight would have shone down onto the cobblestones. Wealthy Genovese built their homes in this quarter in the 16th century, and prosperous guilds, such as the goldsmiths for whom Vico degli Indoratori and Via degli Orefici were named, set up shop here.

Galleria Nazionale. This gallery, housed in the richly adorned **Palazzo Spinola** north of Piazza Soziglia, contains masterpieces by Luca Giordano and Guido Reni. The *Ecce Homo,* by Antonello da Messina, is a hauntingly beautiful painting, of historical interest because it was the Sicilian da Messina who first brought Flemish oil paints and techniques to Italy from his sojourns in the Low Countries. ⊠ *Piazza Pellicceria 1, Maddalena* ☎ *010/2705300* ⊕ *www.palazzospinola.it* ☜ *€4, €6.50 with Palazzo Reale* ☾ *Tues.–Sat. 8:30–7:30, Sun. 1:30–7:30.*

Palazzo Bianco. It's difficult to miss the splendid white façade of this town palace as you walk down Via Garibaldi, once one of Genoa's most important streets. The building houses a fine collection of 17th-century art, with the Spanish and Flemish schools well represented. ⊠ *Via Garibaldi 11, Maddalena* ☎ *010/2759185* ⊕ *www.museidigenova.it* ☜ *€8, includes Palazzo Rosso and Palazzo Doria Tursi* ☾ *Tues.–Fri. 9–7, weekends 10–7.*

Fodor's Choice   **Palazzo Reale.** Lavish rococo rooms provide sumptuous display space for
★   paintings, sculptures, tapestries, and Asian ceramics. The 17th-century palace—also known as Palazzo Balbi Durazzo—was built by the Balbi family, enormously wealthy Genovese merchants. Its regal pretensions were not lost on the Savoy, who bought the palace and turned it into a royal residence in the early 19th century. The gallery of mirrors and the ballroom on the upper floor are particularly decadent. Look for works by Sir Anthony Van Dyck, who lived in Genoa for six years, beginning in 1621, and painted many portraits of the Genovese nobility. The formal gardens, which you can visit for €1, provide a welcome respite from the bustle of the city beyond the palace walls, as well as great views of the harbor. ⊠ *Via Balbi 10, Pré* ☎ *010/2710236* ⊕ *www.palazzorealegenova.it* ☜ *€4; €6.50 including Galleria Nazionale* ☾ *Tues. and Wed. 9–1:30, Thurs.–Sun. 9–7.*

2

Palazzo Rosso. This 17th-century baroque palace was named for the red stone used in its construction. It now contains, apart from a number of lavishly frescoed suites, works by Titian, Veronese, Reni, and Van Dyck. ⊠ *Via Garibaldi 18, Maddalena* ☎ *010/2759185* ⊕ *www.museidigenova.it* 🎟 *€8 including Palazzo Bianco and Palazzo Doria Tursi* ☉ *Tues.–Fri. 9–7, weekends 10–7.*

Zecca-Righi funicular. This is a seven-stop commuter funicular beginning at Piazza della Nunziata and ending at a high lookout on the fortified gates in the 17th-century city walls.

GENOA BEST BETS

Stroll the warren of narrow alleyways in medieval Genoa. This is a real slice of daily life, Ligurian style.

Taking in the views from Il Bigo. The panorama stretches across the city rooftops and out over the vast expanse of the harbor.

Visiting San Lorenzo Cathedral. The architecture is a fine example of the medieval northern Italian style.

Ringed around the circumference of the city are a number of huge fortresses; this gate was part of the city's system of defenses. From Righi you can undertake scenic all-day hikes from one fortress to the next. ⊠ *Piazza della Nunziata, Pré* ☎ *010/5582414* ⊕ *www.amt.genova.it* 🎟 *€2* ☉ *Daily 6 am–11:45 pm.*

SOUTHERN DISTRICTS AND THE AQUARIUM

Inhabited since the 6th century BC, the oldest section of Genoa lies on a hill to the southwest of the Caruggi District. Today, apart from a section of 9th-century wall near Porta Soprana, there is little to show that an imposing castle once stood here. Though the neighborhood is considerably run-down, some of Genoa's oldest churches make it a worthwhile excursion. No visit to Genoa is complete, however, without at least a stroll along the harborfront. The port was given a complete overhaul during Genoa's preparations for the Columbus quincentennial celebrations of 1992, and additional restorations in 2003 and 2004 have done much to revitalize the waterfront including a prehistoric Biosphere, Il Bigo panoramic lift *(mentioned later in this section)* with towering views over the town and port, and La Citta dei Bambino with over 90 interactive displays aimed especially at children. Combined tickets for these several attractions—marketed as Acquario Village and including entrance to the Aquarium and Galata Museo del Mare *(listed below)*— cost €39, but there are also several packages incorporating two or more of the individual attractions.

★ **Acquario di Genova.** Europe's biggest aquarium, second in the world
Ⓒ only to Osaka's in Japan, is the third-most-visited museum in Italy and a must for children. Fifty tanks of marine species, including sea turtles, dolphins, seals, eels, penguins, and sharks, share space with educational displays and re-creations of marine ecosystems, including a tank of coral from the Red Sea. An entire "Aquarium Village" has been created, which also includes a biosphere, hummingbird forest, and interactive submarine exhibit. If arriving by car, take the Genova Ovest exit from the autostrada. ⊠ *Ponte Spinola, Porto Vecchio* ☎ *0101/2345678* ⊕ *www.acquario.ge.it* 🎟 *€19 for adults, €13 for kids ages 4–12, free*

for children 0–3. Aquarium Village tickets (for entrance to all attractions): €39 for adults, €27 for children 4–12, free for children 0-3. ☼ *Mar.–June, weekdays 9–7:30, weekends 8:45–8:30; July and Aug., daily 8:30 am–10 pm; Nov.–Feb., weekdays 9:30–7:30, weekends 9:30–8:30. Entry permitted every ½ hr; last entry 1½ hrs before closing.*

Galata Museo del Mare. Devoted entirely to the city's seafaring history, this museum is probably the best way, at least on dry land, to get an idea of the changing shape of Genoa's busy port. Highlighting the displays is a full-size replica of a 17th-century Genovese galleon. ⊠ *Calata de Mari 1, Ponte dei Mille* ☎ *010/2345655* ⊕ *www.galatamuseodelmare.it* 🎟 *€11 for adults, €6 for kids 4–12, free for children 0–3* ☼ *Mar.–Oct., daily 10–7:30; Nov.–Feb., Tues.–Fri. 10–6, weekends 10–7:30. Last entry 1 hr. before closing.*

☾ **Il Bigo.** This spiderlike white structure, designed by world-renowned architect Renzo Piano, was erected in 1992 to celebrate the Columbus quincentenary. You can take its **Ascensore Panoramico Bigo** (Bigo Panoramic Elevator) up 650 feet for a 360-degree view of the harbor, city, and sea. In winter there's an ice-skating rink next to the elevator, in an area covered by sail-like awnings. ⊠ *Ponte Spinola, Porto Vecchio* ☎ *010/2345278 skating rink* 🎟 *Elevator €4 for adults, €3 for children 4–12 and children under 4 are free; skating rink €8* ☼ *Elevator: Jan. 7–Feb. and Nov.–Dec. 25, weekends 10–5; Mar.–May, Sept., and Oct., Mon. 2–6, Tues.–Sun. 10–6; June–Aug., Mon. 4–11 pm, Tues.–Sun. 10 am–11 pm; Dec. 26–Jan. 6, daily 10–5. Skating rink: Nov. or Dec.–Mar., weekdays 8 am–9:30 pm, Sat. 10 am–2 am, Sun. 10 am–midnight.*

San Lorenzo. Contrasting black slate and white marble, so common in Liguria, embellishes the cathedral at the heart of medieval Genoa—inside and out. Consecrated in 1118, the church honors Saint Lawrence, who passed through the city on his way to Rome in the 3rd century. For hundreds of years the building was used for religious and state purposes such as civic elections. Note the 13th-century Gothic portal, the fascinating twisted barbershop columns, and the 15th- to 17th-century frescoes inside. The last campanile dates from the early 16th century. The **Museo del Tesoro di San Lorenzo** (San Lorenzo Treasury Museum) housed inside has some stunning pieces from medieval goldsmiths and silversmiths, for which medieval Genoa was renowned. ⊠ *Piazza San Lorenzo, Molo* ☎ *010/2471831* 🎟 *Cathedral free, museum €4.50* ☼ *Cathedral daily 8–12 and 3–7. Museum Mon.–Sat. 9–12 and 3–6, and the first Sunday of the month 3–6.*

Sant'Agostino. This 13th-century Gothic church was damaged during World War II, but still has a fine campanile and two well-preserved cloisters that house an excellent museum displaying pieces of medieval architecture and fresco paintings. Highlights of the collection are the enigmatic fragments of a tomb sculpture by Giovanni Pisano (circa 1250–1315). ⊠ *Piazza Sarzano 35/R, Molo* ☎ *010/2511263* ⊕ *www. museidigenova.it* 🎟 *€4* ☼ *Tues.–Fri. 9–7, weekends 10–7.*

Santa Maria di Castello. One of Genoa's most significant religious buildings, an early Christian church, was rebuilt in the 12th century and finally completed in 1513. You can visit the adjacent cloisters and see

the fine artwork contained in the museum. Museum hours vary during religious services. ⊠ *Salita di Santa Maria di Castello 15, Molo* ☎ *010/25495-225* 🎟 *Free* ☉ *Daily 9–noon and 3:30–6:30.*

SHOPPING

2

In addition to the well-known Italian fine leather and haute couture, Liguria is famous for its fine lace, silver-and-gold filigree work, and ceramics. Look also for bargains in velvet, macramé, olive wood, and marble. Genoa is the best spot to find all these specialties. Don't forget the excellent wines, cheeses, dried meats, and olive oils.

In the heart of the medieval quarter, Via Soziglia is lined with shops selling handicrafts and tempting foods. Via XX Settembre is famous for its exclusive shops. High-end shops line Via Luccoli. The best shopping area for trendy but inexpensive Italian clothing is near San Siro, on Via San Luca.

WHERE TO EAT

$$$ ✗ **Bakari.** Hip styling and ambient lighting hint at this eatery's creative,
LIGURIAN   even daring, takes on Ligurian classics. Sure bets are the spinach-and-cheese gnocchi, any of several carpaccios, and the delicate beef dishes. Reserve ahead, request a table on the more imaginative ground floor or just stop by for an aperitivo and people-watching. ⑤ *Average main:* €25 ⊠ *Vico del Fieno 16/R, northwest of Piazza San Matteo, Maddalena* ☎ *010/291936* ⊕ *www.bakari.it* ☉ *Sat. lunch and Sun.*

$$ ✗ **Exultate.** When the weather permits, umbrella-shaded tables spread
LIGURIAN   out from this tiny eatery into the nearby square. Popular with locals, the restaurant's inexpensive daily menu is presented on a chalkboard for all to see; excellent pizza, meal-size salads, and delicious homemade desserts highlight the list. ⑤ *Average main:* €20 ⊠ *Piazza Lavagna 15/R, Maddalena* ☎ *010/2512605* ☉ *Closed Sun.*

GIBRALTAR

Updated by
Joanna Styles

The tiny British colony of Gibraltar—nicknamed Gib, or simply the Rock—whose impressive silhouette dominates the strait between Spain and Morocco, was one of the two Pillars of Hercules in ancient times, marking the western limits of the known world and in an ace position commanding the narrow pathway between the Mediterranean Sea and the Atlantic Ocean. Today the Rock is like Britain with a suntan. There are double-decker buses, policemen in helmets, and bright red mailboxes. Gibraltar was ceded to Great Britain in 1713 by the Treaty of Utrecht, and Spain has been trying to get it back ever since. Recently, Britain and Spain have been talking about joint Anglo-Spanish sovereignty, much to the ire of the majority of Gibraltarians, who remain fiercely patriotic to the crown. Millions of dollars have been spent in developing the Rock's tourist potential, and Gibraltar's economy is further boosted by its important status as an offshore financial center.

ESSENTIALS

CURRENCY
Gibraltar uses the British pound sterling but issues its own notes and coins, which are equivalent in value to British pounds. Euros can also be used in most of the shops, but the exchange rate may be unfavorable; U.S. currency is generally not accepted, but ATMs are common and credit cards are widely accepted.

HOURS
Shops are open weekdays from 9:30 to 7:30 pm, Saturday from 10 to 1. Some shops open Sunday when a ship is in port. Attractions have varied hours, but these are generally weekdays from 10 to 5, and some may open weekends.

PRIVATE TOURS
Gibraltar Rock Tours. The company offers several different tour options departing from the cruise port that take in the main sights. ☎ *350/5699–9000* ⊕ *www.gibraltartours.org.*

TELEPHONES
3G services are available on the island. GibTel is the main service provider. Public phones accept phonecards and credit cards.

VISITOR INFORMATION
Gibraltar Tourist Office ⊠ *Casement Sq.* ☎ *200/45000.*

COMING ASHORE
There is a dedicated cruise terminal within Gibraltar's commercial port. The passenger terminal has a range of facilities, including a bar-café, souvenir shop, tourist information center, bank and currency-exchange facilities, and an exhibition area. From here it is an easy walk into Gibraltar itself, where all the sites of town can be accessed on foot (or where you can take a bus to the attractions that are farther afield). You can also take a taxi; fares are £2.40 for pick-up and £0.20 per 200 meters or per minute of travel. On days when a number of cruise ships dock at the same time, taxis may be dfficult to find, and it would be wise to prebook a vehicle.

The town of Gibraltar is compact, and it's easy to walk around. Vehicles rented in Gibraltar can be taken over the border into Spain, so you could explore some of the southern Spanish coastline from here in a day. Vehicles are only rented to people between the ages of 25 and 75. The Official Rock Tour—conducted either by minibus or, at a greater cost, taxi—takes about 90 minutes and includes all the major sights, allowing you to choose which places to come back to and linger at later. Costs are around £18 to £25 per person (six-person max.).

The cable car to the top of the rock costs £8 round-trip.

EXPLORING GIBRALTAR

The colorful, congested library is where the dignified Regency architecture of Great Britain blends well with the shutters, balconies, and patios of southern Spain. Shops, restaurants, and pubs beckon on busy Main Street; at the Governor's Residence, the ceremonial Changing of the Guard takes place six times a year and the Ceremony of the Keys takes

Gibraltar

Marina Bay

Gibraltar Harbor

Gibraltar Town
see detail map

Devil's Tower Rd.

Queensway

Main St.

Willis's Rd.

Old Queen's Rd.

Queen's Rd.

Catalan Bay Rd.

Moorish Castle ◆

Great Siege Tunnels ◆

Sir Herbert Miles Rd.

Sandy Bay

Cable Car ◆

Apes' Den ◆

Botanical Gardens ◆

Wall of Charles V ◆

Europa Rd.

Queensway

Engineer Rd.

Queen's Rd.

St. Michael's Cave ◆

Dudley Ward Tunnel

Rosia Bay ◆

Rosia Bay

Upper Rock Nature Reserve ◆

Camp Bay

Governor's Beach

Europa Rd.

Europa Advance Rd.

Little Bay

Shrine of Our Lady of Europe ◆

Europa Point ◆

Bay of Gibraltar

Mediterranean Sea

| 0 | 1/2 mi |
| 0 | 1/2 km |

Gibraltar Town

Corral Rd.

Casemates Gate

Smith Dorrien Av.

Corral Rd.

Fish Market Rd.

Queensway

Casemates Sq. ◆

Crutchetts Ramp

Cooperage Ln.

American War Memorial

Parliament Ln.

Castle Ramp

Tuckey's Ln.

Irish Town

Main St.

Engineer Ln.

Bell Ln.

Castle St.

Market Ln.

Line Wall Rd.

John Mackintosh Sq. *i*

College Ln.

Cannon Ln.

Governor's St.

Hospital Ramp

Prince Edward's Rd.

King St.

Gunner's Ln.

Gibraltar Museum

Library St.

Governor's Pde.

Library Ramp

Bomb House Ln.

Cathedral of the Holy Trinity ◆

King's St.

Cathedral Sq.

George's Ln.

Town Range

Prince Edward's Rd.

Main Tourist Office ◆

Governor's Ln.

Queensway

Nefusot Yehudada Synagogue ◆

Convent Ramp

| 0 | 1/16 mi |
| 0 | 1/16 km |

place twice a year. Also, make sure you see the Law Courts, the Anglican Cathedral of the Holy Trinity, and the Catholic Cathedral of St. Mary the Crowned.

Apes' Den. The famous Barbary Apes are a breed of cinnamon-color, tailless monkeys (not apes, despite their name) native to Morocco's Atlas Mountains. Legend holds that as long as they remain in Gibraltar, the British will keep the Rock; Winston Churchill went so far as to issue an order for their preservation when their numbers began to dwindle during World War II. They are publicly fed twice daily, at 8 and 4, at Apes' Den, a rocky area down Old Queens Road near the Wall of Carlos V. Among the monkeys' talents are their grabbing of food, purses, and cameras, so be on guard.

GIBRALTAR BEST BETS

The town of Gibraltar. Immerse yourself in a little piece of Britain far south of the white cliffs of Dover.

Take in the panorama from the top of the Rock. Look south to the northern coast of Africa and north to the southern coastal plains of Spain.

Make friends with a Barbary ape. These cheeky primates inhabit the slopes of the Rock. They have a penchant for stealing bags and sunglasses—so you have been warned!

★ **Cable Car.** You can reach St. Michael's Cave—or ride all the way to the top of Gibraltar—on a cable car. The car doesn't go high off the ground, but the views of Spain and Africa from the Rock's pinnacle are superb. It leaves from a station at the southern end of Main Street, which is known as the Grand Parade. ✉ *Cable car £9 round-trip* ⊙ *Apr.–Oct., daily 9:30–6:45; Nov.–Mar., daily 9:30–5:45.*

Casemates Square. Gibraltar's social hub is on this pedestrian-only square in the northern part of town, where there are plenty of places to sit with a drink and watch the world go by. The Gibraltar Crystal company, where you can watch the glassblowers at work, is worth a visit.

Europa Point. From Europa Point, have a look across the straits to Morocco, 23 km (14 miles) away. You're now standing on one of the two ancient Pillars of Hercules. In front of you is the lighthouse that has dominated the meeting place of the Atlantic and the Mediterranean since 1841; sailors can see its light from a distance of 27 km (17 miles). ✉ *Continue along coast road to Rock's southern tip.*

Gibraltar Museum. Often overlooked by visitors heading to the Upper Rock Reserve, this museum houses a beautiful 14th-century Moorish bathhouse and an 1865 model of the Rock; the displays evoke the Great Siege and the Battle of Trafalgar. There's also a reproduction of the "Gibraltar Woman," the Neanderthal skull discovered here in 1848. ✉ *Bomb House La.* ☎ *200/74289* ⊕ *www.gibmuseum.gi* ✉ *£2* ⊙ *Weekdays 10–6, Sat. 10–2.*

Great Siege Tunnels. These tunnels, formerly known as the Upper Galleries, were carved out during the Great Siege of 1779–82 at the northern end of Old Queen's Road. You can plainly see the openings from which the guns were pointed at the Spanish invaders. They form part of what is arguably the most impressive defense system anywhere in the world.

The nearby and privately managed World War II Tunnels are also open to the public but are less dramatic.

Moorish Castle. The castle was built by the descendants of the Moorish general Tariq, who conquered the Rock in 711. The present Tower of Homage dates from 1333, and its besieged walls bear the scars of stones from medieval catapults (and later, cannonballs). Admiral George Rooke hoisted the British flag from its summit when he captured the Rock in 1704, and it has flown here ever since. The castle may be viewed from the outside only.

Nefusot Yehuda Synagogue. One of the oldest synagogues on the Iberian Peninsula, Nefusot Yehuda dates back to 1798. Guided tours, which include a short history of the Gibraltar Jewish community, can be reserved by phone. ☎ 200/78804.

Rosia Bay. There are fine views to be had if you drive up above Rosia Bay. The bay was where Nelson's flagship, HMS *Victory*, was towed after the Battle of Trafalgar in 1805. On board were the dead, who were buried in Trafalgar Cemetery on the southern edge of town—except for Admiral Nelson, whose body was returned to England, preserved in a barrel of rum. ⊠ *From Europa Flats, follow Queensway back along Rock's western slopes.*

Shrine of Our Lady of Europe. To the north of the lighthouse is the Shrine of Our Lady of Europe, venerated by seafarers since 1462. A former mosque, the small Catholic chapel has a small museum with a 1462 statue of the Virgin and some documents. ⊠ *Just north of Europa Point and lighthouse, along Rock's southern tip* 🖼 *Free* ☉ *Mon.–Thurs. 10–1 and 2:30–6, Fri. 10–1.*

St. Michael's Cave. This is the largest of Gibraltar's 150 caves; a visit here is part of the tour of the Upper Rock Nature Preserve. A series of underground chambers full of stalactites and stalagmites, it's an ideal performing-arts venue. The skull of a Neanderthal woman (now in the British Museum) was found at the nearby Forbes Quarry eight years before the world-famous discovery in Germany's Neander Valley in 1856; nobody paid much attention to it at the time, which is why the prehistoric species is called Neanderthal rather than *Homo calpensis* (literally, "Gibraltar Man," after the Romans' name for the Rock, *Calpe*). ⊠ *Queen's Rd..*

Upper Rock Nature Preserve. The preserve, accessible from Jews' Gate, includes St. Michael's Cave, the Apes' Den, the Great Siege Tunnels, the Moorish Castle, and the Military Heritage Center, which chronicles the British regiments that have served on the Rock. ⊠ *From Rosia Bay, drive along Queensway and Europa Rd. as far as Casino, above Alameda Gardens. Make a sharp right here, up Engineer Rd. to Jews' Gate, a lookout over docks and Bay of Gibraltar toward Algeciras* 🖼 *£10 for all attractions, plus £2 per vehicle* ☉ *Daily 9–6:15.*

SHOPPING

The quintessential Britishness of Gibraltar is reflected in its shopping. Many British main-street names can be found here, including Marks and Spencer, so you can stock up on marmalades, biscuits, and Cheddar cheese. Fine English china and glassware also make an appearance along with oodles of Royal memorabilia. Inexpensive items include Union Jack motifs and red double-decker buses printed on everything from T-shirts to coffee mugs. The island is tax-friendly so prices are cheaper than in Spain or the United Kingdom.

WHERE TO EAT

$ ✕ **Sacarello's.** Right off Main Street, this busy restaurant is as well
BRITISH known for its excellent coffee and cakes as it is for the rest of its food. There's a varied salad and quiche buffet, as well as filled baked potatoes and daily specials, which could include fresh sole, or stir-fried beef with green beans and chili sauce. Top your meal off with a specialty coffee with cream and vanilla. The restaurant has several warmly decorated rooms with cozy corners, dark-wood furnishings, and low-beamed ceilings, and the whole place has an old-fashioned English feel. $ *Average main: £8* ⊠ *57 Irish Town* ☎ *200/70625* ⊕ *www.sacarellosgibraltar. com* ⊘ *Closed Sun.*

$ ✕ **Waterfront.** Easily distinguished by its flags and appropriately located
INTERNATIONAL right at Queensway Quay, this restaurant is a favorite with locals, especially for the Sunday Carvery ($$). Navy and white are the colors that predominate among the cane furniture and the various Mediterranean touches. In addition to the upstairs and downstairs dining inside, there's also a generous terrace and several tables that sit perched on the quay, allowing for views over the marina and to the mountains in Spain. The menu is distinctly international, with specialties including steaks (they're aged on the premises), fish cakes with green curry sauce, and British staples such as bangers and mash (sausages with mashed potatoes in an onion gravy). Service is efficient and comes with a smile. $ *Average main: £15* ⊠ *4/5 Ragged Staff* ☎ *200/45666* ⊕ *www.gibwaterfront.com.*

IBIZA, SPAIN

Updated by
Joanna Styles

Sleepy from November to May, the capital of Ibiza is transformed in summer into Party Central for retro hippies and nonstop clubbers, but the town and the island have so much more to offer. Dalt Vila, the medieval quarter on the hill overlooking Ibiza Town, is a UNESCO World Heritage site with narrow alleyways brimming with atmosphere. Around the coastline the island has 50 sandy beaches. Ibiza was discovered by sun-seeking hippies in the late 1960s, eventually emerging as an icon of counter-culture chic. In the late 1980s and 1990s club culture took over. Young ravers flocked here from all over the world to dance all night and pack the sands of beach resorts all day. That Ibiza is still alive and well, but emblematic of the island's future are its growing numbers of luxury hotels, spas, and gourmet restaurants. Ibiza is toning down and scaling up.

ESSENTIALS

CURRENCY
The euro.

HOURS
Museums generally open 9 until 7 or 8, many are closed on Monday, and some close in the afternoon. Most stores are open Monday through Saturday 9 to 1:30 and 5 to 8, but tourist shops may open in the afternoon and also on Sundays between May and September.

PRIVATE TOURS
Ibiza Rutas. The company offers half-day and full-day trips exploring Ibiza and the neighboring island of Formentera. ☎ *626/633180* ⊕ *www.ibizarutas.com.*

TELEPHONES
Tri-band GSM phones should work in Spain, and mobile services are 3G compatible. Public kiosks accept phone cards that support international calls (cards sold in press shops, bars, and telecom shops). Major companies include Vodafone.

COMING ASHORE

Boats dock on the town pier at the edge of town. From here you can walk into the capital without problem, and for this reason, facilities at the terminal are limited. You won't need transport to enjoy Ibiza Town, however if you rent a car, you can explore much of this small but fascinating island in a day. An economy rental car for one day is €40 (from July through September, you'll really need to book ahead). Buses between Ibiza Town, Sant Rafael, and San Antonio leave every 30 minutes on weekdays (every hour on weekends). There are hourly buses between Ibiza, Sant Jordi, and Salinas. Ibiza and Santa Eulalia are connected by buses every 30 minutes. Fares start at €1.50, and all are under €2.60.

Taxis are also numerous and are metered. They can undertake tourist tours. Fares start at €0.98 per minute (min €3.25) and waiting time of €17.61 per hour. There is a small supplement (€1.65) for port pick-up.

EXPLORING IBIZA

IBIZA TOWN (EIVISSA)

Hedonistic and historical, Ibiza (Eivissa, in Catalan) is a city jam-packed with cafés and nightspots and trendy shops; looming over it are the massive stone walls of **Dalt Vila**—the medieval city was declared a UNESCO World Heritage site in 1999—and its Gothic cathedral. Squeezed between the north walls of the Old City and the harbor is **Sa Penya,** a long labyrinth of narrow stone-paved streets that offer the city's best exploring. What would the fishermen who used to live in this quarter have thought seeing so many of their little whitewashed houses transformed into bars and offbeat restaurants and boutiques with names like the Kabul Sutra Tantra Shop, and Good Times Jewelry, and Bitch?

One enters the Dalt Vila via a ramp through the **Portal de ses Taules,** the Old City's main gate. On each side stands a statue, Roman in origin and now headless: Juno on the right, an armless male on the left. Keep going up until you reach the sights.

Ibiza Island

Cala Xarraca
Portinatx
Caló d'Es Porcs
Sant Vicent
Puerto San Miguel
Cala San Vicente
San Miguel
Sant Joan
Sant Mateo
Balafi
Sant Carles
Santa Agnes
Sant Llorenç
Bahía de Sant Antoni
Santa Gertrudis de Fruitera
Santa Eulària des Riu
Sant Antoni
Sant Rafael
Ibiza Town
see detail map
Sant Josep
Sant Jordi
Playa d'En Bossa
Es Vedrà
Mitjorn
Es Cavallet
Ses Salines

Es Palmador

Trucadors
Estany Pudent
Puerto de La Sabina
Es Pujols
Sant Ferran
Sant Francesc Xavier
Cala Sahona
Playa de Mitjorn
El Pilar
Formentera
Cabo de Berbería

0 — 6 miles
0 — 9 km

Ibiza Town

Mediterranean Sea

Pl. de A. Riquer
C. Gallo
La Marina
C. Cruz
C. Castellar
SA PENYA
C. Virgen
Avda. Ramon y Tur
C. Obispo Cardona
C. Montgri
C. Carrer del Mar
Vista Alegre
Av. B. Roselló
Pl. Constitucio
C. Pedrera
C.B.V. y Ramón
Alfonso XII
Bastió de Sant Lucia
Pl. de Sa Font
Po. Vara de Rey
C. Cayetano Soler
C. Rosellon
C. Gral. Balanzat
Sant Domingo
C. Jaime I
C. San Luis
C. Sta. Maria
DALT VILA
V. Romana
C. Joan Roman
C. Obispo Torresd
Catedral
Centre d'Interpretació
Puig des Molins (Archeological Museum)
Bastió de Sant Bernat

0 — 1/16 mi
0 — 1/16 km

Catedral. On the site of religious structures from each of the cultures that have ruled Ibiza since the Phoenicians, the cathedral was built in the 13th and 14th centuries and renovated in the 18th century. It has a Gothic tower and a baroque nave. ⊠ *Carrer Major s/n* ☎ *971/312774* ☉ *Weekdays 10–1, Sun. 10:30–noon.*

Centre d'Interpretació Madina Yabisa. A few steps from the cathedral, the Centre d'Interpretació Madina Yabisa is a fascinating collection of audiovisual materials and exhibits on the period when the Moors ruled the island. ⊠ *Calle Mayor 2, Eivissa* ☎ *971/392390* 🎫 *€2* ☉ *Apr.–Jun., Sept. and Oct., Tues.–Sat. 10–3, Sun. 10–1; Jul. and Aug. Tues.–Sat. 10–2 and 6–9, Sun. 10–2; Nov.–Mar., Tues–Sat. 10–3, Sun. 10–2.*

Sant Domingo. The roof of the 16th-century church of Sant Domingo is an irregular landscape of tile domes. The nearby *ajuntament* (town hall) is housed in the church's former monastery. ⊠ *Carrer de Balanzat s/n.*

> ### IBIZA BEST BETS
>
> **Explore the narrow alleyways of Sa Penya.** Ibiza Town's most atmospheric quarter is great for browsing and shopping.
>
> **Bring your swimsuit.** Spend an afternoon on one of Ibiza's trendy beaches.
>
> **Stroll uphill in Dalt Vila.** The quarter's architecture has been designated a World Heritage site.

SANTA EULÀRIA DES RIU
15 km (9 miles) northeast of Eivissa.

At the edge of this town on the island's eastern coast, to the right below the road, a Roman bridge crosses what is claimed to be the only permanent river in the Balearics (hence "des Riu," or "of the river"). Ahead, on the hilltop, are the cubes and domes of the church—to reach it, look for a narrow lane to the left, signed "puig de missa," itself so named for the hill where regular mass was once held. A stoutly arched, cryptlike covered area guards the entrance; inside are a fine gold reredos and blue-tile Stations of the Cross. Santa Eulària itself follows the curve of a long sandy beach, a few blocks deep with restaurants, shops, and holiday apartments. From here it's a 10-minute drive to **Sant Carles** and the open-air **hippie market** held there every Saturday morning.

SANTA GERTRUDIS DE FRUITERA
15 km (9 miles) north of Eivissa.

Blink, and you miss it: that's true of most of the small towns in the island's interior—and especially so of Santa Gertrudis, not much more than a bend in the road from Eivissa to the north coast. But don't blink: Santa Gertrudis is strategic, and it's cute. From here you are only a few minutes' drive from some of the island's flat-out best resort hotels and spas. You are minutes from the most beautiful secluded north coves and beaches: **S'Illa des Bosc, Benirrás** (where they have drum circles to salute the setting sun), **S'Illot des Renclí, Portinatx, Caló d'En Serra.** Santa Gertrudis itself has offbeat shops, and laid-back sidewalk cafés, and good food. Artists and expats like it here: they've given it an appeal that now makes for listings of half a million dollars or more for a modest two-bedroom chalet.

SHOPPING

In the late 1960s and '70s Ibiza built a reputation for extremes of fashion. Little of this phenomenon survives, though the softer designs inspired by Smilja Mihailovich (under the Ad Lib label) still prosper. Clothing and beachwear plus fashion accessories of all kinds are the major buys here, including excellent leather goods, but there is also a community of artists working in glass, ceramics, and bronze. Along Carrer d'Enmig is an eclectic collection of shops and stalls selling fashion and crafts. Although the Sa Penya area of Eivissa still has a few designer boutiques, much of the area is now called the Mercat dels Hippies (hippie market), with more than 80 stalls of overpriced tourist ephemera.

Ibiza Republic. For trendy casual gear, sandals, belts, and bags, try Ibiza Republic. ⊠ *Carrer Antoni Mar 15, Eivissa* ☎ *971/314175.*

BEACHES

Immediately south of Ibiza Town is a long, sandy beach, the nearly 3-km (2-mile) **Playa d'en Bossa.** Farther on, a left turn at Sant Jordi on the way to the airport leads across the salt pans to **Es Cavallet** and **Ses Salines,** two of the best beaches on the island. Topless bathing is accepted all over Ibiza, but Es Cavallet is the official nudist beach. The remaining beaches on this part of the island are accessible from the Ibiza–Sant Josep–Sant Antoni highway, down side roads that often end in rough tracks. North of Sant Antoni there are no easily accessible beaches until you reach **Puerto San Miguel,** an almost rectangular cove with relatively restrained development. Next along the north coast, accessible via San Juan, is Portinatx, a series of small coves with sandy beaches, of which the first and last, **Cala Xarraca** and **Caló d'Es Porcs,** are the best. East of San Juan is the long, curved cove beach of **Cala San Vicente.** Popular with families, it has a more leisurely pace than Ibiza's other resorts. The beaches on the east coast have been developed, but **Santa Eulalia** remains attractive. The resort has a narrow, sloping beach in front of a pedestrian promenade that is much less frenetic than Sant Antoni.

WHERE TO EAT

$ ✕ **Can Caus.** Ibiza might pride itself on its seafood, but there comes a
SPANISH time for meat and potatoes. When that time comes, take the 20-minute drive to the outskirts of Santa Gertrudis to this family-style roadside restaurant. Feast on skewers of barbecued *sobrasada* (soft pork sausage), goat chops, lamb kebabs, or grilled sweetbreads with red peppers, onions, and eggplant. Most people eat at the long wooden tables on the terrace. ⑤ *Average main: €16* ⊠ *Ctra. Sant Miquel, Km 3.5* ☎ *971/197516* ⊙ *Closed Mon. Sept.–June.*

$$ ✕ **Mezzanotte.** This charming little port-side restaurant has just 12 tables,
ITALIAN softly lit with candles and track lighting. In summer, the seating expands to an interior patio and tables on the sidewalk. The kitchen prides itself on hard-to-find fresh ingredients flown in from Italy. The linguine with jumbo shrimp, saffron, and zucchini or with *bottarga* (dried and salted

mullet roe from Sardinia) is wonderful. The prix-fixe menu, served at dinner in summer and lunch in winter, is a bargain. ⑤ *Average main: €18* ⊠ *Paseo de s'Alamera 22, Santa Eulària* ☎ *971/319498* ⊘ *Closed Jan., Feb., and Sun. No lunch June–Aug.*

LE HAVRE, FRANCE (FOR NORMANDY AND PARIS)

2

Updated by Jennifer Ladonne

Le Havre, France's second-largest port (after Marseille), was destroyed in World War II. You may find the rebuilt city bleak and uninviting; on the other hand, you may admire Auguste Perret's audacious modern architecture, which earned the city UNESCO World Heritage status in 2005. The city is the perfect starting point for some of the highlights of Normandy, the French region of rolling verdant farmland and long, sandy beaches. Tiny fishing villages dot the coves around the city, a world away from the gritty urban feel of Le Havre itself. Normandy was also the location of the D-Day invasion of Europe by Allied forces during WWII, the largest wartime seaborne invasion of all time. You can visit the beach landing sites and evocative museums about the battle. From Le Havre it's also possible to visit Paris, one of the world's most famous cities.

ESSENTIALS

CURRENCY

The euro.

HOURS

Stores are generally open Monday through Saturday 9–7, but many close at lunchtime (usually noon–2 or 3) and some will open later and on Sunday during July and August. Museums open 10–5, but most are closed on either Monday or Tuesday.

TELEPHONES

Tri-band GSM phones work in France. You can buy prepaid phone cards at telecom shops, news vendors, and tobacconists in all towns and cities. Phone cards can be used for local or international calls. Orange, SFR, Bouygues Telecom, and Virgin are leading telecom companies. If you have an unlocked GSM phone, LeFrenchMobile (⊕ *www.lefrenchmobile.com*) offers SIM cards (and micro SIM cards) with support in English, unlimited validity of credits, and prepurchase online.

COMING ASHORE

Le Havre is a large port with vast amounts of freight traffic in addition to cruise ships. Disembarking passengers will find a small welcome center with practical information and multilingual staff, a small shop, plus taxi and tour services, including a shuttle service into the city, which stops at the railway station. If you intend to spend the day in Le Havre, it is only a few minutes' walk from the port entrance to the downtown area.

Le Havre is the main cruise port for visits to Paris (some ships do call in Honfleur); however, the city is a 2- to 2½-hour journey away depending on the service chosen. From the railway station there are hourly trains to Paris terminating at Gare St-Lazare. SNCF (⊕ *www.sncf.com*), the

French railway company, is reliable and efficient. Prices are cheaper if you buy tickets in advance, but a second-class round-trip should be around €66 if purchased on the day of travel.

We would advise against renting a car just to make the trip into Paris (traffic and parking are both very difficult); however, a rental car is an ideal way to explore the rolling countryside of Normandy. An economy manual car costs around €75 per day. Taxis wait outside the port gates and can provide tourist itineraries. For single journeys, fares are €1.80 at pick-up, then €0.89 per km.

Some smaller ships call directly in Honfleur, across the bay from Le Havre (and linked by a modern bridge). It is the most picturesque of the Côte Fleurie's little seaside towns. It was once an important departure point for maritime expeditions, including the first voyages to Canada in the 15th and 16th centuries.

EXPLORING NORMANDY AND PARIS

HONFLEUR
24 km (15 miles) southeast of Le Havre via A131 and the Pont de Normandie.

Fodor's Choice ★ The town of Honfleur, full of half-timber houses and cobbled streets, was once an important departure point for maritime expeditions, including the first voyages to Canada in the 15th and 16th centuries. The 17th-century harbor is fronted on one side by two-story stone houses with low, sloping roofs and on the other by tall, narrow houses whose wooden facades are topped by slate roofs. Note that parking can be a problem, so it's better to come by public transit. Some ships call here directly instead of in Le Havre.

★ **Ste-Catherine.** Soak up the seafaring atmosphere by strolling around the old harbor and paying a visit to the ravishing wooden church of Ste-Catherine, which dominates a tumbling square. The church and the ramshackle belfry across the way—note the many touches of marine engineering in their architecture—were built by townspeople to show their gratitude for the departure of the English at the end of the Hundred Years' War, in 1453. ⊠ *Rue des Logettes* ☎ *02–31–89–11–83.*

BAYEUX
10 km (6 miles) southwest of Arromanches via D516, 28 km (17 miles) northwest of Caen.

Bayeux, the first town to be liberated during the Battle of Normandy, was already steeped in history—as home to a Norman Gothic cathedral and the world's most celebrated piece of needlework: the Bayeux Tapestry.

Fodor's Choice ★ **Bayeux Tapestry.** Really a 225-foot-long embroidered scroll stitched in 1067, the Bayeux Tapestry, known in French as the *Tapisserie de la Reine Mathilde* (Queen Matilda's Tapestry), depicts, in 58 comic strip–type scenes, the epic story of William of Normandy's conquest of England in 1066, narrating Will's trials and victory over his cousin Harold, culminating in the Battle of Hastings on October 14, 1066. The tapestry was probably commissioned from Saxon embroiderers by the count of Kent—who was also the bishop of Bayeux—to be displayed in

his newly built cathedral, the Cathédrale Notre-Dame. Despite its age, the tapestry is in remarkably good condition; the extremely detailed, often homey scenes provide an unequaled record of the clothes, weapons, ships, and lifestyles of the day. It's showcased in the **Musée de la Tapisserie** (Tapestry Museum; free audioguides let you to listen to an English commentary about the tapestry). ⊠ *Centre Guillaume-le-Conquérant, 13 bis, rue de Nesmond, Bayeux* ☎ *02–31–51–25–50* ∰ *www. tapisserie-bayeux.fr* ⊠ *€7.80* ⊙ *May–Aug., daily 9–7; Sept.–Apr., daily 9:30–12:30 and 2–6.*

Cathédrale Notre-Dame. Bayeux's mightiest edifice, the Cathédrale Notre-Dame, is a harmonious mixture of Norman and Gothic architecture. Note the portal on the south side of the transept that depicts the assassination of English archbishop Thomas à Becket in Canterbury Cathedral in 1170, following his courageous opposition to King Henry II's attempts to control the church. ⊠ *Rue du Bienvenu, Bayeux* ☎ *02–31–92–01–85* ⊙ *Daily 9–6.*

THE D-DAY BEACHES
Omaha Beach is 16 km (10 miles) northwest of Bayeux.

History focused its sights along the coasts of Normandy at 6:30 am on June 6, 1944, as the 135,000 men and 20,000 vehicles of the Allied troops made landfall in their first incursion in Europe in World War II. The entire operation on this "Longest Day" was called Operation Overlord—the code name for the invasion of Normandy.

★ **Omaha Beach.** You won't be disappointed by the rugged terrain and windswept sand of Omaha Beach, 16 km (10 miles) northwest of Bayeux. Here you can find the **Monument du Débarquement** (Monument to the Normandy Landings) and the **Musée-Mémorial d'Omaha Beach,** a large shedlike structure packed with tanks, dioramas, and archival photographs that stand silent witness to "Bloody Omaha." Nearby, in Vierville-sur-Mer, is the **U.S. National Guard Monument.** Throughout June 6, Allied forces battled a hailstorm of German bullets and bombs, but by the end of the day they had taken the Omaha Beach sector, although they had suffered grievous losses. In Colleville-sur-Mer, overlooking Omaha Beach, is the hilltop **American Cemetery and Memorial,** designed by landscape architect Markley Stevenson. You can look out to sea across the landing beach from a platform on the north side of the cemetery. ⊠ *Musée-Mémorial d'Omaha Beach, Les Moulins, Av. de la Libération, Saint-Laurent-sur-Mer* ☎ *02–31–21–97–44* ∰ *www.musee-memorial-omaha.com* ⊠ *€5.90* ⊙ *Daily Feb. 15–Mar. 15, 10–noon and 2:30–6; Mar. 16–May 15, 9:30–6:30; May 16–Sept. 15, 9:30–7; Sept. 16–Nov. 15, 9:30–6:30. Closed mid-Nov. to mid-Feb.*

PARIS
A day trip to Paris of just a few hours can barely scratch the surface of what one of the world's greatest cities can offer, but that doesn't mean you won't find those few hours really worthwhile. Below are the highlights of the highlights.

Arc de Triomphe. Inspired by Rome's Arch of Titus, this colossal, 164-foot triumphal arch was ordered by Napoléon—who liked to consider himself the heir to the Roman emperors—to celebrate his military successes.

Normandy Coast

0 — 10 miles
0 — 15 km

English Channel (La Manche)

Barfleur
Étretat
St-Vaast-la-Hougue
Le Havre
Quinéville

D-Day Beaches

TO PARIS →

Omaha Beach
Honfleur
Utah Beach
Gold Beach
Juno Beach
Grandcamp-Maisy
Isigny-sur-Mer
Houlgate
D971 D514
D516
Bénouville D513
Bayeux N13
D513
St-Lô
Balleroy
Caen
Troarn
Lisieux
D972 D980 N174 D572
N175
N158
D579
LA SUISSE NORMANDE
St-Pierre-sur-Dives

---

bd. de Clichy
pl. Pigalle
bd. de Rochechouart
r. de Clichy

bd. Haussmann

Opéra Garnier

bd. des Italiens
bd. Montmartre
bd. Poissonnière
bd. St-Denis

bd. de Strasbourg
bd. de Magenta

r. Réaumur
av. de l'Opéra
bd. St-Martin
pl. de la République

r. de Châteaudun

Bibliothèque National
r. de Richelieu
r. Etienne Marcel
r. St-Denis
bd. de Sébastopol
r. de Turbigo
bd. Beaumarchais

r. du Louvre
Forum des Halles
r. Berger
r. St-Honoré
r. Rambuteau
r. du Temple

Louvre
r. St-Martin
Centre Pompidou
r. des Archives

quai du Louvre
r. de Rivoli
r. des Francs-Bourgeois

pont du Carrousel
pont des Arts
pont Neuf
bd. de Sébastopol
rue
pl. du Chatelet
MARAIS

r. Jacob
quai de l'Hôtel de Ville
r. de Rivoli
r. St-Antoine

Sainte-Chapelle

r. de Rennes
r. Bonaparte
bd. St-Germain
Ile de la Cité
pl. St-Michel
Notre-Dame
Ile St-Louis
bd. Henri IV

pl. Maubert
quai de la Tournelle
pont de Sully

Palais du Luxembourg
bd. St-Michel
r. St-Jacques
r. Monge

Jardin du Luxembourg

Seine

Unfortunately, Napoléon's strategic and architectural visions were not entirely on the same plane, and the Arc de Triomphe proved something of an embarrassment: although the emperor wanted the monument completed in time for an 1810 parade in honor of his new bride, Marie-Louise, the arch was still only a few feet high, and a dummy arch of painted canvas was strung up to save face. Empires come and go, but Napoléon's had been gone for more than 20 years before the Arc de Triomphe was finally finished, in 1836. ⊠ *Pl. Charles-de-Gaulle, Champs-Élysées* ☎ *01–55–37–73–77* ⊕ *www.arc-de-triomphe.monuments-nationaux.fr/* ✉ *€9, free under 18* ⊙ *Apr.–Sept., daily 10 am–11 pm; Oct.–Mar., daily 10 am–10:30 pm* Ⓜ *Métro or RER: Étoile.*

> ### LE HAVRE BEST BETS
>
> **Honfleur.** Wander the tangled knot of cobbled alleyways of the Old Town and enjoy an alfresco lunch in the picturesque harbor.
>
> **D-Day Beaches.** The battles that took place on these beaches on June 6, 1944, were the turning point of WWII.
>
> **Paris.** The city of romance, Paris is a must-see; it will be a quick tour, but you can see some highlights in a day.

Fodor's Choice
★

Hôtel des Invalides. Les Invalides (pronounced *lehz-ahn-vah-leed*), as this baroque complex is known, is the eternal home of Napoléon Bonaparte (1769–1821), or more specifically, the little dictator's tomb, which lies under the towering golden dome. There are two churches here: St-Louis des Invalides Church, built between 1677 and 1706, later subdivided into the Église du Dome and the Église des Soldats (Soldiers' Church). Louis XIV ordered this complex built in 1670 to house-disabled soldiers, and at one time 4,000 military men lived here. Today, a portion of it remains a veterans' residence and hospital. There's also the Musée de l'Armée, an exhaustive collection of military artifacts from antique armor to weapons. The World Wars Department, also housed here, chronicles the great wars that ravaged Europe. ■ TIP→ **The best entrance to use is at the southern end, on Place Vauban (Avenue de Tourville). The ticket office is here, as is Napoléon's Tomb. There are automatic ticket machines at the main entrance on the Place des Invalides.** ⊠ *Pl. des Invalides, Tour Eiffel* ☎ *01–44–42–38–77* ⊕ *www.invalides.org* ✉ *€9* ⊙ *Église du Dôme and museums Apr.–Sept., daily 10–6; Oct.–Mar., daily 10–5. Closed 1st Mon. of every month Oct–June* Ⓜ *La Tour-Maubourg/Invalides.*

Fodor's Choice
★

The Louvre. The most recognized symbol of Paris is the Tour Eiffel, but the ultimate traveler's prize is the Louvre. This is the world's greatest art museum—and the largest, with 675,000 square feet of works from almost every civilization on earth. The three most popular pieces of art here are, of course, the *Mona Lisa*, the *Venus de Milo*, and the *Winged Victory*. Beyond these must-sees, your best bet is to focus on whatever highlights interest you the most—and don't despair about getting lost, for you're bound to stumble on something interesting. Pick up an excellent color-coded map at the information desk. There are slick multimedia guides at the entrance to each wing; for €6 you get four self-guided tours and information about 250 works of art, plus a

function to help you find your bearings. There are 90-minute guided tours (€9) in English daily at 11 and 2. Thematic leaflets (including some for kids) and Louvre guided tours are available from the front desk. The Louvre is much more than a museum—it is a saga that started centuries ago, as a fortress at the turn of the 13th century, and later a royal residence. It was not until the 16th century, under François I, that today's Louvre began to take shape, and through the years Henry IV, Louis XIII, Louis XV, Napoléon I, and Napoléon III all contributed to its construction. Napoléon Bonaparte's military campaigns at the turn of the 19th century brought a new influx of holdings, as his soldiers carried off treasures from each invaded country. During World War II the most precious artworks were hidden, while the remainder was looted. Most of the stolen pieces were recovered after the liberation of Paris. No large-scale changes were made until François Mitterrand was elected president in 1981, when he kicked off the Grand Louvre project to expand and modernize the museum. ⊠ *Palais du Louvre, Louvre/Tuileries* ☎ *01–40–20–53–17 information* ⊕ *www.louvre.fr* ☜ *€10 (€10.50 projected); €11 for Napoléon Hall exhibitions; ticket allows same-day entry to Musée Eugène Delacroix; free 1st Sun. of month* ⊙ *Mon., Thurs., and weekends 9–6, Wed. and Fri. 9–9:30* Ⓜ *Palais-Royal–Musée du Louvre.*

Fodor's Choice ★ **Musée d'Orsay.** Opened in 1986, this gorgeous renovated Belle Époque train station has a world-famous collection of impressionist and post-impressionist paintings. There are three floors; to visit the exhibits in a roughly chronologic manner, start on the first floor, take the escalators to the top, and end on the second. If you came to see the biggest names on display here, head straight for the top floor and work your way down. Renovations are expected to be completed in 2015, so expect some gallery closings. Galleries off the main alley feature early works by Manet and Cézanne in addition to pieces by masters like Delacroix and Ingres. Impressionism gets going on the top floor, with iconic works by Degas, Pissarro, Sisley, and Renoir. Don't miss Monet's series on the cathedral at Rouen and, of course, samples of his waterlilies. The d'Orsay is closed Monday, unlike the Pompidou and the Louvre, which are closed on Tuesday. English audioguides are available just past the ticket booths; pick up a free color-coded map of the museum here, too. ⊠ *1 rue de la Légion d'Honneur, St-Germain-des-Prés* ☎ *01–40–49–48–14* ⊕ *www.musee-orsay.fr* ☜ *€9.50 (€8 without special exhibit); €7 (€5 without special exhibit) after 4:15 except Thurs. after 6* ⊙ *Tues.–Sun. 9:30–6, Thurs. 9:30 am–9:45 pm* Ⓜ *Solférino; RER: Musée d'Orsay.*

Fodor's Choice ★ **Notre-Dame.** Looming above Place du Parvis on the Ile de la Cité is the Cathédrale de Notre-Dame, the most enduring symbol of Paris. Begun in 1163, completed in 1345, badly damaged during the Revolution, and restored by the architect Eugène Viollet-le-Duc in the 19th century, Notre-Dame may not be France's oldest or largest cathedral, but in beauty and architectural harmony it has few peers—as you can see by studying the facade from the square in front. The most dramatic approach to Notre-Dame is from the Rive Gauche, crossing at the Pont au Double from Quai de Montebello, at the St-Michel métro or RER stop. This bridge will take you to the large square, Place du Parvis, in

front of the cathedral. This area is *kilomètre zéro*, the spot from which all distances to and from the city are officially measured. A polished brass circle set in the ground, about 20 yards from the cathedral's main entrance, marks the exact spot.

A separate entrance, to the left of the front facade if you're facing it, leads to the 387 stone steps of the south tower. These steps take you to the bell of Notre-Dame—as tolled by the fictional Quasimodo, in Victor Hugo's 1831 *Notre-Dame de Paris*. ■TIP→ **There are free guided tours in English on Wednesday and Thursday at 2 and Saturday at 2:30.** Down the stairs in front of the cathedral is the **Crypte Archéologique,** Notre-Dame's archaeological museum. ⊠ *Pl. du Parvis* ☎ *01–42–34–56–10* ⊕ *www.notredamedeparis.fr* ⊡ *Cathedral free, towers €8,crypt €4, treasury €3* ⊗ *Cathedral daily 7:45–6:45. Towers Apr.–June and Sept., daily 10 am–6:30; July and Aug., weekdays 10–6:30, weekends 10 am–11 pm; Oct.–Mar., daily 10–5:30. Note towers close early when overcrowded. Treasury weekdays 9:30–6 pm, Sat. 9:30–6:30, Sun. 1:30–6:30. Crypt Tues.–Sun. 10–6* Ⓜ *Cité.*

Fodor'sChoice **Sainte-Chapelle.** Built by the obsessively pious Louis IX (1226–70), this
★ Gothic jewel is home to the oldest stained-glass windows in Paris. The chapel was constructed over three years, at phenomenal expense, to house the king's collection of relics acquired from the impoverished emperor of Constantinople. These included Christ's Crown of Thorns, fragments of the Cross, and drops of Christ's blood—though even in Louis's time these were considered of questionable authenticity. Some of the relics have survived and can be seen in the treasury of Notre-Dame, but most were lost during the Revolution.

The upper chapel is where the famed beauty of Sainte-Chapelle comes alive: 6,458 square feet of stained glass is delicately supported by painted stonework that seems to disappear in the colorful light streaming through the windows. The lowest section of the windows was restored in the mid-1800s, and a painstaking five-year renovation should be completed by 2013. The lower chapel is a bit gloomy and plain, but notice the low, vaulted ceiling decorated with fleurs-de-lis and cleverly arranged *L*s for Louis. The dark spiral staircase near the entrance takes you upstairs. Come on a sunny day to appreciate the full effect of the light streaming in through all that beautiful stained glass. Free, guided tours in English are offered most days at 2:30. Call ahead to confirm. ⊠ *4 bd. du Palais* ☎ *01–53–40–60–97* ⊕ *www.sainte-chapelle.monuments-nationaux.fr* ⊡ *€8, joint ticket with Conciergerie €11* ⊗ *Mar.–Oct., daily 9:30–6; Nov.–Feb., daily 9–5* Ⓜ *Cité.*

Fodor'sChoice **Eiffel Tower.** If the Statue of Liberty is emblematic of New York, Big Ben
★ is London, and the Kremlin is Moscow, then the Eiffel Tower is the symbol of Paris. French engineer Gustave Eiffel—already famous for building viaducts and bridges—spent two years working to erect this monument, for the World Exhibition of 1889. You can stride up the stairs as far as the third floor, but if you want to go to the top you'll have to take the elevator. (Be sure to take a close look at the fantastic ironwork.) The view of the flat sweep of Paris at 1,000 feet may not beat the one from the Tour Montparnasse skyscraper, but the setting

makes it considerably more romantic, especially if you come in the late evening, after the crowds have dispersed. ■ **TIP→ Beat the crushing lines by reserving your ticket online. You can also book a guided tour.** ✉ *Quai Branly, Trocadéro/Tour Eiffel* ☎ *01–44–11–23–23* ⊕ *www.tour-eiffel. fr* ✉ *By elevator: 1st and 2nd levels €8.20, top €13.40. By stairs: 1st and 2nd levels only, €4.50.* ☉ *June–late Aug., daily 9 am–12:45 am (11:30 pm for summit); late Aug.–June, daily 9:30 am–11 pm. Stairs close at 6 pm in winter* Ⓜ *Bir-Hakeim, Trocadéro, École Militaire; RER: Champ de Mars.*

SHOPPING

The French practically created ready-to-wear fashion—think Cartier, Chanel, and Lacroix. The French love quality and style—and are willing to pay for it—so prices aren't cheap. The vast department stores **Galeries Lafayette** and **Printemps** on Boulevard Haussmann stock a vast range of clothing. The districts on the Left Bank and the Marais offer excellent boutiques selling one-of-a-kind accessories for the body and the home.

Normandy specialties include heavy cotton sailor's smocks, blue-and-white-stripe T-shirts, and chunky knits; popular choices in this traditional seafaring region. Calvados (distilled apple liqueur) is unique to the area, but other foodstuffs (pure butter and creamy cheeses) aren't really suitable to take home.

Honfleur has a huge choice of art galleries, craft shops, and boutiques with one-of-a-kind items.

WHERE TO EAT

$
CAFÉ
☕

✗ **La Ferme Opéra.** If your arm aches from flagging down café waiters, take a break at this bright, friendly, self-service spot near the Louvre that specializes in produce from the Ile-de-France region (around Paris). Inventive salads, sandwiches, and pastas are fresh and delicious, and for sweets there are wholesome fruit crumbles, tarts, and cheesecakes. Scones and freshly squeezed juices are served for breakfast every day, and there is brunch on Sunday from 11 am to 4 pm. There's free Wi-Fi in the spacious, barnlike dining room. ⑤ *Average main: €8* ✉ *55 rue St-Roch, 1er, Opéra/Grands Boulevards* ☎ *01–40–20–12–12* ⊕ *www. restolaferme.com* ☉ *Open 7 days a week* Ⓜ *Pyramides.*

$$
MODERN FRENCH
★

✗ **Le Fleur de Sel.** A low-beamed 16th-century fisherman's house provides the cozy atmosphere for chef Vincent's Guyon's locally influenced cuisine, centered on the daily catch. The ambitious menu usually includes at least five different fish dishes—presented with artistic panache—along with plenty of grilled meats, like salt-marsh lamb or pigeon. For starters, the oyster ravioli with a butternut mousse and chestnut foam, draws raves; it might be followed by a delicately crusted salmon with leeks in an almond vinaigrette and fromage blanc. Three fixed-price menus ($$$–$$$$) assure a splendid meal on any budget. Be sure to save room for one of the masterful desserts or an informed cheese course. ⑤ *Average main: €20* ✉ *17 rue Haute, Honfleur* ☎ *02–31–89–01–92* ⊕ *www.lafleurdesel-honfleur.com* ☉ *Closed Tues., Wed., and Jan.*

LEIXÕES, PORTUGAL (FOR PORTO)

Updated by
Joanna Styles

Lining the river that made it a trading center ever since pre-Roman times, vibrant and cosmopolitan Porto centers itself some 5 km (3 miles) inland from the Atlantic Ocean. The Moors never had the same strong foothold here that they did farther south, nor was the city substantially affected by the great earthquake of 1755; as a result, Porto's architecture shows off a baroque finery little seen in the south of Portugal. Its grandiose granite buildings were financed by the trade that made the city wealthy: wine from the upper valley of the Rio Douro (Douro River, or River of Gold) was transported to Porto, from where it was then exported around the world. Industrious Porto considers itself the north's capital and, more contentiously, the country's economic center. In the shopping centers, the stately stock exchange building, and the affluent port-wine industry, Porto oozes confidence, though the fashionable commercial heart of the city contrasts with the gritty workaday atmosphere in the Old Town.

ESSENTIALS

CURRENCY
The euro.

HOURS
Most shops are open weekdays 9–1 and 3–7 and Saturday 9–1; malls and supermarkets often remain open until at least 10. Some are also open on Sunday. Note that most museums are closed Monday, and that churches generally close for a couple of hours in the middle of the day.

PRIVATE TOURS
Diana Tours offers guided tours around Porto and day trips into the surrounding countryside and to famous cities such as Coimbra and Braga.

Contacts Diana Tours. ☎ 217/998540 ⊕ www.dianatours.pt.

TELEPHONES
Most quad- or tri-band GSM phones work in Portugal, which has a well-organized 3G compatible mobile network. You can buy prepaid phone cards at telecom shops, news vendors and tobacconists in all towns and cities. Phone cards can be used for local or international calls. Major companies include Vodafone and Optimus.

COMING ASHORE
Vessels dock at the quays of Leixões port, just north of the mouth of the River Douro. It's a two-minute walk or a short shuttle trip to the passenger terminal (depending on the exact quay), which has few facilities, but the restaurants and shops of Leixões town are within walking distance. Taxis wait at the port entrance.

From the port it is another 10-minute walk to the Matosinhos district, where the state-of-the-art metro will transfer you to central Porto in 30 minutes. Single tickets cost between €1.15 and €3.95. The single ticket from the port to downtown is €1.45. A 24-hour card is €13.10 for all zones. From the port to downtown the 24-hour ticket price is €3.80 (but this only entitles you to journey within three zones). Bus 76, which has a stop just outside the port, will also take you into Porto, but the journey time is longer.

EXPLORING PORTO

Avenida dos Aliados. This imposing boulevard is lined with bright flower beds and grand buildings and is essentially the heart of the central business district. In addition to corporate businesses and banks, you'll find clothing and shoe stores, plus restaurants and coffeehouses. At one end of it is the broad Câmara Municipal (town hall). A tall bell tower sprouts from the roof of this palacelike, early-20th-century building; inside is displayed an impressive Portuguese wall tapestry. Praça da Liberdade—the hub from which Porto radiates—is at the other end of the avenue. Two statues adorn the square: a cast of Dom Pedro IV sitting on a horse and a modern statue of the great 19th-century Portuguese poet and novelist Almeida Garrett.

Fodor'sChoice **Cais da Ribeira** (*Ribeira Pier*). A string of fish restaurants and *tascas*
★ (taverns) are built into the street-level arcade of timeworn buildings along this pier. In the Praça da Ribeira, people sit and chat around an odd, modern, cubelike sculpture; farther on, steps lead to a walkway above the river that's backed by tall houses. The pier also provides the easiest access to the lower level of the middle bridge across the Douro, the Ponte Dom Luis I. Boats docked at Cais da Ribeira and across the river in Vila Nova da Gaia offer various cruises around the bridges and up the river to Peso da Régua and Pinhão.

Casa-Museu de Guerra Junqueiro (*Guerra Junqueiro House and Museum*). This 18th-century white mansion, one of several buildings in Porto attributed by some to a pupil of Nicolau Nasoni and by others to Nicolau himself, was home to the poet Guerra Junqueiro (1850–1923). It's in the picturesque if shabby-in-parts Sé neighborhood, below the cathedral. Although furnishings, sculptures, and paintings are labeled in Portuguese, English, and French (and there are brochures in English), the short, guided tour of the elegant interior is less than enlightening if you don't speak Portuguese. ⊠ *Rua de Dom Hugo 32* ☎ *22/200–3689* 🖃 *Tues.–Fri. €2.10, free weekends* ☉ *Tues.–Sat. 10–12:30 and 2–5:30, Sun. 2–5:30.*

Fodor'sChoice **Estação de São Bento.** This train station was built in the early 20th century
★ (King D. Carlos I laid the first brick himself in 1900) and inaugurated in 1915. It sits precisely where the Convent of S. Bento de Avé-Maria was located, and therefore inherited the convent's name—Saint Bento. The atrium is covered with 20,000 azulejos painted by Jorge Colaço (1916) depicting scenes of Portugal's history as well as ethnographic images. It is one of the most magnificent artistic undertakings of the early 20th century. The building was designed by architect Marques da Silva. ⊠ *Praça Almeida Garret* ☎ *22/205–1714, 808/208208 national call center* ⊕ *www.cp.pt.*

Porto

R. do Bonjardim

R. Duque Saldanha

Campo 24 de Agosto

R. de Santos Pousada

R. de Fernandes Tomas

R. de Sto. Ildefonso

R. de Rodrigues Freitas

Praça da Alegria

R. Formosa

P. dos Poveiros

R. de Santa Catarina

R. de Sá da Bandeira

Mercado Bolhão

R. de Batalha

R. 31 de Janeiro

Estação de São Bento

Av. de Vimara Peres

Av. Gustavo Eiffel

Rio Douro

Avenida dos Aliados

Praça da Liberdade

R. do Almada

R. dos Clérigos

R. Dom Hugo

R. Mouzinho da Silveira

R. Infante D. Henrique

Praça da Ribeira

Cais da Ribeira

Torre dos Clérigos

R. de Oliveiras

P. de Carlos Alberto

R. de Cedofeita

R. de Miguel Bombarda

R. das Taipas

Rua da Vitória

Rua das Flores

Jardim de João Chagas

Palácio da Bolsa

Igreja de São Francisco

Hospital de S. António

R. do Rosário

R. do Breyner

R. de D. Manuel II

L. da Alfândega

R. Nova da Alfândega

Museu Nacional Soares dos Reis

R. da Torrinha

R. da Restauração

R. de Júlio Dinis

R. de Piedade

R. Alegre

R. de D. Pedro V

Jardim do Palácio de Cristal

R. de Monchique

Rio Douro

← TO MUSEU DE ARTE CONTEMPORÂNEA & LEIXÕES

| 0 | | 1/4 mi |
| 0 | | 1/4 km |

KEY

i Tourist information

Igreja da Misericórdia *(Mercy Church).* Today's building represents a compromise between the church first built during the late 16th century and its reconstruction between 1749 and 1755 by painter and architect Nicolau Nasoni. At the church museum next door you can see *Fons Vitae* (Fountain of Life), a vibrant, anonymous, Renaissance painting depicting the founder of the church, Dom Manuel I, his queen, and their eight children kneeling before a crucified Christ. ⊠ *Rua das Flores 5* ☎ *22/207–4710* 🖙 *Church free, museum €1.50* ☉ *Church Tues.– Fri. 8–12:30 and 2–5:30, museum weekdays 9–12:30 and 2–5:30.*

> ## PORTO BEST BETS
>
> **Sip some port.** You can try the country's famous after-dinner wine in the tasting rooms of port producers at Vila Nova de Gaia.
>
> **Climb the Torre dos Clérigos.** The panoramic views across the city are well worth the trip to the top.
>
> **Be dazzled by gold.** The exterior is undistinguished, but acres of gold leaf decorate the interior of Igreja de São Francisco.

Igreja de São Francisco *(Church of St. Francis).* During the last days of Porto's siege by the absolutist army (the *miguelistas*) in July 1842, there was gunfire by the nearby São Francisco Convent. These shootings caused a fire that destroyed most parts of the convent, sparing only this church. The church is an undistinguished, late 14th-century Gothic building on the outside, but inside is an astounding interior: gilded carving—added in the mid-18th century—runs up the pillars, over the altar, and across the ceiling. An adjacent museum (Museu de Arte Sacra) houses furnishings from the Franciscan convent. A guided tour (call the day before) includes a visit to the church, museum, and catacombs. Note that the riverside tram ride to Foz starts here. ⊠ *Rua do Infante Dom Henrique 93* ☎ *22/206–2100* 🖙 *€3.50* ☉ *Nov.–Feb., daily 9–5:30; Mar., Apr., and Oct., daily 9–6; May–Sept., daily 9–7.*

Fodor's Choice ★ **Museu de Arte Contemporânea.** Designed by Álvaro Siza Vieira, a winner of the Pritzker Prize and Portugal's best-known architect, the Contemporary Art Museum is part of the Serralves Foundation and is surrounded by lovely gardens. It has changing international exhibitions, as well as work from Portuguese painters, sculptors, and designers. Check with the tourist office for the latest information. The original art deco house and its small formal garden is also worth visiting; as well as housing the foundation, it hosts small exhibitions. Various joint tickets are available, including one to the museum and to the Sea Life aquarium in Foz. To get here, take a taxi or catch the metro to Casa da Música and then Bus 201, 203, 502, or 504 from the Rotunda da Boavista; or from downtown take Bus 201 from Avenida dos Aliados—about a 30-minute ride. ⊠ *Rua D. João de Castro 210* ☎ *22/615–6500 or 808/200–543* ⊕ *www.serralves.pt* 🖙 *Museum and garden Tues.–Sat. €7, garden €3; Sun. free to 1 pm* ☉ *Oct.–Mar. museum and house Tues.–Fri. 10–5, weekends 10–8; park Tues.–Sun. 10–7. Apr.–Sept. museum Tues.–Fri. 10–5, weekends 10–8; house Tues.–Fri. 10-5, weekends 10–7; park Tues.–Fri. 10–7, weekends 10–8.*

★ **Museu Nacional Soares dos Reis.** This art museum was the first in Portugal, founded in 1833 by King D. Pedro IV. In 1911 it was renamed after the 19th-century Portuguese sculptor whose works are contained within it. In 1940 it moved to this late-19th-century home, the Palácio dos Carrancas, which was once home to the royal family. The large art collection includes several Portuguese primitive works of the 16th century as well as superb collections of silver, ceramics, glassware, and costumes. ⊠ *Palácio dos Carrancas, Rua de Dom Manuel II* ☎ *22/339-3770* ⊕ *www.ipmuseus.pt* 🎫 *Tues.–Sat. €5, free Sun.* ☽ *Tues. 2–6, Wed.–Sun. 10–6.*

Palácio da Bolsa. Porto's neoclassical former stock exchange takes up much of the site of the former Franciscan convent at the Igreja de São Francisco. Guided tours (every half hour) are the only way to see the interior of this masterpiece of 19th-century Portuguese architecture. The Arab-style ballroom, in particular, is one of the most admired chambers and was designed by civil engineer Gustavo Adolfo Gonçalves e Sousa. ⊠ *Rua Ferreira Borges* ☎ *22/339-9013* ⊕ *www.palaciodabolsa.pt* 🎫 *Tours €6* ☽ *Apr.–Sept., daily 9–6:30; Oct.–Mar., daily 9–12:30 and 2–5:30.*

Ponte Dom Luís I *(Luís I Bridge).* Though it was intended to replace the Pênsil Bridge (also called Dona Maria Pia), this two-tier bridge was completed in 1886 at another site. Designed by Teófilo Seyrig with two tiers for both vehicles and pedestrians, it leads directly to the city of Vila Nova de Gaia. Its real glory, however, is the magnificent vistas it affords of downtown Porto. A jumble of red-tile roofs on pastel-color buildings mixes with gray-and-white Gothic and baroque church towers, and all is reflected in the majestic Douro River; if the sun is shining just right, everything appears to be washed in gold. Beside the foot of the bridge on the Porto riverbank is the lower station of the Funicular dos Guindais, the quaintest part of the city's public transportation system, which cranks uphill to the Batalha neighborhood, just to the east of the cathedral.

Sé do Porto *(Cathedral).* Originally constructed in the 12th century by the parents of Dom Afonso Henriques (Portugal's first king), Porto's granite cathedral has been rebuilt twice: first in the late 13th century and again in the 18th century, when the architect of the Torre dos Clérigos, Nicolau Nasoni, was among those commissioned to work on its expansion. Despite the renovations, it remains a fortresslike structure—an uncompromising testament to medieval wealth and power. Notice a low relief on the northern tower, depicting a 14th-century vessel and symbolizing the city's nautical vocation. Size is the only exceptional thing about the interior; when you enter the two-story, 14th-century cloisters, however, the building comes to life. Decorated with gleaming azulejos, a staircase added by Nasoni leads to the second level and into a richly furnished chapter house, from which there are fine views through narrow windows. Nasoni also designed the Paço dos Arcebispos (Archbishops' Palace) behind the cathedral. It has been converted to offices, so you can only admire its 197-foot-long facade. ⊠ *Terreiro da Sé* ☎ *22/205-9028* 🎫 *Cathedral free; cloisters €3* ☽ *Cathedral Nov.–Mar., Mon.–Sat. 8:45–12:30 and 2:30–6, Sun. 8:30–12:30 and 2:30–6; Apr.–Oct., Mon.–Sat.*

8:45–12:30 and 2:30–7, Sun. 8:30–12:30 and 2:30–7. Cloisters Nov.–Mar., Mon.–Sat. 9–12:15 and 2:30–5:30, Sun. 2:30–5:30; Apr.–Oct., Mon.–Sat. 9–12:15 and 2:30-6:30, Sun. 2:30–6:30.

Solar do Vinho do Porto *(Port Wine Institute).* On the ground floor of a 19th-century manor house called the Quinta da Macierinha, the institute offers relaxed tastings of Porto's famous wine in much the same fashion as its counterpart in Lisbon—but the wine has only had to travel across the river before being served. As well as 120 ports by the glass (and more by the bottle) table wines from the Douro are on sale, accompanied if you like by fine cheeses and hams. You can also buy crystal glasses and glossy books on local vineyards. There are lovely views of the river from the small formal garden, where chairs are often set out. The Quinta da Macierinha is also home to the **Museu Romântico da Quinta da Macierinha** (Romantic Museum), with displays of period furniture. Don't miss the leafy Palácio de Cristal gardens just uphill, which afford even more stunning river views. ⊠ *Quinta da Macierinha, Rua de Entre Quintas 220* ☎ *22/609–4749 Port Wine Institute, 22/605–7000 museum* ⊕ *www.ivp.pt Port Wine Institute* ✍ *dmpc@cm-porto.pt Museum* ✉ *Port Wine Institute free. Museum €2.10 Tues.–Fri., free weekends* ⊙ *Port Wine Institute Mon.–Sat. 4–midnight; museum Tues.–Sun. 10–12:30 and 2–5:30.*

Torre dos Clérigos. Designed by Italian architect Nicolau Nasoni and begun in 1754, the tower of the church Igreja dos Clérigos reaches an impressive height of 249 feet. There are 225 steep stone steps to the belfry, and the considerable effort required to climb them is rewarded by stunning views of the Old Town, the river, and beyond to the mouth of the Douro. The church itself, also built by Nasoni, predates the tower and is an elaborate example of Italianate baroque architecture. ⊠ *Rua S. Filipe Nery* ☎ *22/200–1729* ✉ *Tower €1.50, church free* ⊙ *Tower Sept.–May, daily 10–noon and 2–5; June and July, daily 9:30–1 and 2:30–7; Aug., daily 10–7. Church 8:45–12:30 and 3:30–7.*

☺ **Vila Nova de Gaia.** A city across the Rio Douro from central Porto, Vila Nova de Gaia has been the headquarters of the port-wine trade since the late 17th century, when import bans on French wine led British merchants to look for alternative sources. By the 18th century, the British had established companies and a regulatory association in Porto. The wine was transported from vineyards on the upper Douro to port-wine caves at Vila Nova de Gaia, where it was allowed to mature before being exported. Little has changed in the relationship between Porto and the Douro since those days, as wine is still transported to the city, matured in the warehouses, and bottled. Instead of traveling down the river on *barcos rabelos* (flat-bottom boats), however, the wine is now carried by truck. A couple of the traditional boats are moored at the quayside on the Vila Nova de Gaia side.

SHOPPING

The Portuguese specialize in a range of handicrafts collectively known as *artesanato*. The term includes bright *azulejos* (blue-and-white-glaze tiles), pottery and ceramics, colorful textiles, olive wood, cork items,

and basketwork. Gold and plated filigree is also a regional specialty, and the shoe trade is well established. You'll see port on sale throughout the city. But first taste the wine at either the Solar do Vinho do Porto or the caves at Vila Nova de Gaia. You may want to buy a bottle of the more unusual white port, drunk as an aperitif, as it's not commonly sold in North America.

The best shopping streets are those off the Praça da Liberdade, particularly Rua 31 de Janeiro, Rua dos Clérigos, Rua de Santa Catarina, Rua Sá da Bandeira, Rua Cedofeita, and Rua das Flores. Traditionally, Rua das Flores has been the street for silversmiths found along the same street and along Rua de Santa Catarina. On Rua 31 de Janeiro you'll find goldsmiths working.

Fodor's Choice
★
Livraria Lello e Irmão, This is one of the most special and important bookshops in Portugal. It opened in 1906, and shelters more than 60,000 books. But it's most famous for its neo-Gothic design and two-story interior with intricate wood-carved details—locals maintain that all this helped inspire J.K. Rowling, who dreamed up Harry Potter while living in Porto. ⊠ *Rua das Carmelitas 144* ☎ *22/200–2880.*

Via Catarina Shopping. Unlike most, this mall is in an old restored building. The top floor is occupied by little restaurants that re-create the Ribeira's architecture with small, medieval-style houses. ⊠ *Rua de Santa Catarina 312–350* ☎ *22/207–5600* ⊕ *www.viacatarina.pt.*

WHERE TO EAT

$
PORTUGUESE
Fodor's Choice
★
✕ **Abadia do Porto.** The cavernous interior, thick tablecloths, and well-heeled clientele tell you this is not just another *tasca*, but the food at this backstreet abbey downtown is ultratraditional. Although the decor has a monastic theme, meals here are far from austere, so come hungry to make the most of the huge servings of *cabrito assado* (roast kid), *rancho* (mixed grill), *bacalhau à Gomes Sá* (codfish with onions, potato, egg, and olives) and Porto *tripas*—tripe with beans, chouriço, and vegetables. It's all great value if you share a dish between two or even three people. The chocolate-flavor *paõ-de-ló* spongecake is divine, too. ⊠ *Rua Ateneu Comercial do Porto 22–24* ☎ *22/200–8757* ⊕ *www.abadiadoporto.com* ☯ *Closed Sun.*

$
PORTUGUESE
✕ **Chez Lapin.** At this Cais da Ribeira restaurant overlooking the river, the service may be slow and the folksy decor may be overdone, but the food is excellent. Grab a table on the attractive outdoor terrace and order generous portions of such traditional Portuguese dishes as bacalhau *à lagareiro* (baked salt cod with potatoes), sardines with rice and beans, and beef medallions with port wine. The restaurant is mainly patronized by foreign visitors, so if you're after authentic Porto cuisine in a less touristy setting, look elsewhere. The family-owned company that owns the restaurant (Douro Acima) offers river excursions on its six traditional boats docked at the quay. ⊠ *Rua dos Canastreiros 40–42* ☎ *22/200–6418* ⊕ *www.issimo.pt* ⚲ *Reservations essential.*

LISBON, PORTUGAL

Updated by
Joanna Styles

2

Lisbon bears the mark of an incredible heritage with laid-back pride. Spread over a string of seven hills north of the Rio Tejo (Tagus River) estuary, the city also presents an intriguing variety of faces to those who negotiate its switchback streets. In the oldest neighborhoods stepped alleys are lined with pastel-color houses and crossed by laundry hung out to dry; here and there *miradouros* (vantage points) afford spectacular river or city views. In the grand 18th-century center, black-and-white mosaic cobblestone sidewalks border wide boulevards. *Elétricos* (trams) clank through the streets, and blue-and-white azulejos (painted and glazed ceramic tiles) adorn churches, restaurants, and fountains. Some modernization has improved the city. To prepare for its role as host of the World Exposition in 1998, Lisbon spruced up its public buildings, overhauled its metro system, and completed an impressive bridge across the Rio Tejo, but Lisbon's intrinsic, slightly disorganized, one-of-a-kind charm hasn't vanished in the contemporary mix.

ESSENTIALS

CURRENCY
The euro.

HOURS
Most shops are open weekdays 9–1 and 3–7 and Saturday 9–1; malls and supermarkets often remain open until at least 10. Some are also open on Sunday. Note that most museums are closed Monday, and that churches generally close for a couple of hours in the middle of the day.

PRIVATE TOURS
Inside Lisbon offers guided walking tours around the city as well as daytrips to some of the most famous sights further afield.

Contacts Inside Lisbon. ☎ *968/412612* ⊕ *www.insidelisbon.com.*

TELEPHONES
You can use most tri- and quad-band GSM phones in Portugal, which has a well-organized 3G-compatible mobile network. You can buy prepaid phone cards at telecom shops, news vendors, and tobacconists in all towns and cities. Phone cards can be used for local or international calls. Major companies include Vodafone and Optimus.

COMING ASHORE
Facilities for cruise ships in Lisbon are undergoing major expansion at this writing with construction of the Lisbon Cruise Terminal (LCT) adjacent to the Santa Apolinia quay. The LCT will include a new quay, Jardim do Tabaco, able to berth larger ships and expected to be operational in 2013. Meanwhile, vessels dock at one of three quays along the River Tagus in a port area rebuilt for Expo '98 (the 1998 World's Fair). The main cruise port is the Cais de Alcântara, which has a terminal with shops, taxi ranks, and restrooms. Cais da Rocha Conde d'Óbidos also has a terminal with the same facilities. From both these terminals there are public transit routes into the city by bus (Buses 712, 728, 732, 760) or tram (Tram 15E, 18E). A suburban train also runs alongside the cruise terminal, and the Alcântara Mar station is the place to get on; the trip to Lisbon's main railway station takes about 10 minutes.

Fares for all these options are €1.75 per journey (bus) and €2.85 (tram). The walk into town from the cruise port takes around an hour, but is not unpleasant if you have the time. A one-day travel card for bus and metro costs €5.

Some small and midsize ships call at a smaller terminal in Santa Apolónia, which is closer to the center of the city and from where it's possible to walk to Alfalma and central Lisbon.

There are many companies running tours of the city. Don't rent a car if you are staying in Lisbon, where navigation and parking are almost impossible, but if you want to explore the countryside, you'll need one. An economy manual vehicle is about €40 per day.

AIRPORT TRANSFERS
Lisbon Airport Transfers offers airport to port transfers from €36 per person.

Contacts Lisbon Airport Transfers. ☎ *916/053420*
⊕ *www.lisbon-airport-transfer.com.*

EXPLORING LISBON

The center of Lisbon stretches north from the spacious Praça do Comércio—one of Europe's largest riverside squares—to the Rossío, a smaller square lined with shops and cafés. The district in between is known as the Baixa (lower town), an attractive grid of parallel streets built after the 1755 earthquake and tidal wave. The Alfama, the old Moorish quarter that survived the earthquake, lies east of the Baixa. In this part of town are the Sé (the city's cathedral) and, on the hill above, the Castelo de São Jorge (St. George's Castle).

West of the Baixa, sprawled across another of Lisbon's hills, is the Bairro Alto (Upper Town), an area of intricate 17th-century streets, peeling houses, and churches. Five kilometers (3 miles) farther west is Belém. A similar distance to the northeast is Lisbon's postmodernist Parque das Nações.

The modern city begins at Praça dos Restauradores, adjacent to the Rossío. From here the main Avenida da Liberdade stretches northwest to the landmark Praça Marquês de Pombal, dominated by a column and a towering statue of the man himself. The praça is bordered by the green expanse of the Parque Eduardo VII, named in honor of King Edward VII of Great Britain, who visited Lisbon in 1902.

Igreja e Museu de São Roque. Filippo Terzi, the architect who designed São Vicente on the outskirts of the Alfama, was also responsible for this Renaissance church. He was commissioned by Jesuits and completed the church in 1574. Curb your impatience with its plain facade and venture inside. Its eight-sides chapels have statuary and art dating from the early 17th century. The last chapel on the left before the altar is the extraordinary 18th-century Capela de São João Baptista (Chapel of St. John the Baptist): designed and built in Rome, with rare stones and mosaics that resemble oil paintings, the chapel was taken apart, shipped to Lisbon, and reassembled here in 1747. Adjoining the church, the Museu de São Roque displays a surprisingly engaging collection of clerical

vestments and liturgical objects. *⊠ Largo Trindade Coelho, Bairro Alto* ☎ *21/323–5421* ⊕ *www. museudesaoroque.com* ✉ *Church free; museum €2.50 Mon.–Sat., free Sun.* ☉ *Church Mon. 2–6 pm, Tues., Wed., Fri.– Sun. 9–6, Thurs. 9–9; museum Fri.–Wed. 10–6, Thurs. 2–9* Ⓜ *Baixa-Chiado or Restauradores (then Elevador da Glória).*

Fodor's Choice **Mosteiro dos Jerónimos.** Conceived
★ and commissioned by Dom Manuel I, who petitioned the Holy See for permission to build it in 1496, Belém's famous Jerónimos Monastery was financed largely by treasures brought back from Africa, Asia, and South America. Construction began in 1502 under the supervision of Diogo de Boitaca.

This UNESCO World Heritage site is a supreme example of the Manueline style of building (named after King Dom Manuel I), which represented a marked departure from the prevailing Gothic. Inside, the spacious interior contrasts with the riot of decoration on the six nave columns and complex latticework ceiling. This is the resting place of both explorer Vasco de Gama and national poet Luís de Camões. *⊠ Praça do Império, Belém* ☎ *21/362–0034* ⊕ *www.mosteirojeronimos.pt* ✉ *Church free, cloister €7, €10 combination ticket includes Torre de Belém, €13 includes Torre and Palacio de Ajuda* ☉ *May–Sept., Tues.–Sun. 10–6; Oct.–Apr., Tues.–Sun. 10–5.*

Fodor's Choice **Museu Calouste Gulbenkian.** On its own lush grounds, the museum of the
★ celebrated Calouste Gulbenkian Foundation, a cultural trust, houses treasures collected by Armenian oil magnate Calouste Gulbenkian (1869–1955) and donated to Portugal in return for tax concessions. The collection is split in two: one part is devoted to Egyptian, Greek, Roman, Islamic, and Asian art and the other to European acquisitions. Both holdings are relatively small, but the quality of the pieces is magnificent, and you should aim to spend at least two hours here. In the gardens outside the Fundação Calouste Gulbenkian at **Centro de Arte Moderna**, sculptures hide in every recess. You may want to spend a little time here before following signs to the Modern Art Center—the 20th-century art collection of the Calouste Gulbenkian Foundation, which has at its disposal the finest collection of contemporary and modern Portuguese art, as well as many British works from the same period—a legacy of the foothold the foundation retains in London. *⊠ Av. de Berna 45, Praça de Espanha* ☎ *21/782–3000* ⊕ *www.museu.gulbenkian.pt* ✉ *€4, temporary exhibitions €4–€5, combined ticket €5, combined ticket Museum with Modern Art Center €5, combined ticket for all €7; free Sun.* ☉ *Tues.–Sun. 10–5:45* Ⓜ *São Sebastião or Praça de Espanha.*

Fodor's Choice
★

Museu Nacional de Arte Antiga. On the route from the center of Lisbon to Belém is the Ancient Art Museum, the only institution in the city to approach the status of the Gulbenkian. Housed in a 17th-century palace once owned by the Counts of Alvor and vastly enlarged in 1940 when it took over the Convent of St. Albert, the museum has a beautifully displayed collection of Portuguese art—mainly from the 15th through 19th century. The religious works of the Flemish-influenced Portuguese school stand out, especially Nuno Gonçalves' masterpiece, the *St. Vincent Panels.* Painted between 1467 and 1470, the altarpiece has six panels believed to show the patron saint of Lisbon receiving the homage of king, court, and citizens (although there are other theories). Trams 15 and 18 from Praça do Comércio drop you at the foot of a steep flight of steps below the museum. Otherwise, Buses 727 from Praça Marquês de Pombal, 60 from Praça Martim Moniz, and 713 from Praça do Comércio run straight to Rua das Janelas Verdes; coming from Belém, you can pick the 727 up across from the Jerónimos monastery. ⊠ *Rua das Janelas Verdes, Lapa* ☏ 21/391–2800 ⊕ *www.mnarteantiga-ipmuseus. pt* 🎫 *€5, free Sun. to 2 pm* ☉ *Tues. 2–6, Wed.–Sun. 10–6.*

Fodor's Choice
★
☺

Oceanário de Lisboa. Europe's largest indoor aquarium wows children and adults alike with a vast saltwater tank featuring an array of fish, including several types of shark. Along the way you pass through habitats representing the North Atlantic, Pacific, and Indian oceans, where puffins and penguins dive into the water, sea otters roll and play, and tropical birds flit past you. You then descend to the bottom of the tank to watch rays float past gracefully and schools of silvery fish darting this way and that. ⊠ *Esplanada D. Carlos I (Doca dos Olivais), Parque das Nações* ☏ 21/891–7002 ⊕ *www.oceanario.pt* 🎫 *€12* ☉ *Apr.–Oct., daily 10–8; Nov.–Mar., daily 10–7; last entry 1 hr before closing* Ⓜ *Oriente.*

Padrão dos Descobrimentos. The white, monolithic Monument of the Discoveries was erected in 1960 to commemorate the 500th anniversary of the death of Prince Henry the Navigator. It was built on what was the departure point for many voyages of discovery, including those of Vasco da Gama for India and—during Spain's occupation of Portugal—of the Spanish Armada for England in 1588. Henry is at the prow of the monument, facing the water; lined up behind him are the Portuguese explorers of Brazil and Asia, as well as other national heroes, including Luís de Camões the poet, who can be recognized by the book in his hand. On the ground adjacent to the monument, an inlaid map shows the extent of the explorations undertaken by the 15th- and 16th-century Portuguese sailors. Walk inside and take the elevator to the top for river views. There are also 15- and 30-minute films about Lisbon's history. ⊠ *Av. de Brasília, Belém* ☏ 21/303–1950 🎫 *€2.50; 25-min movie €4, combined ticket monument and movie €5, €13 includes Torre de Belém* ☉ *Oct.–Apr., Tues.–Sun. 10–6; May–Sept., Tues.–Sun. 10–7.*

☺

Pavilhão do Conhecimento. The white, angular, structure designed by architect Carrilho de Graça for the Expo seems the perfect place to house the Knowledge Pavilion, or Living Science Centre, as it's also known. All of the permanent and temporary exhibits here are related to math, science, and technology; most are also labeled in English (a manual is available for the few that aren't), and all are interactive.

✉ *Alamada dos Oceanos, Lote 2.10.01, Parque das Nações* ☎ *21/891–9898* ⊕ *www.pavconhecimento.pt/home* 💷 *€7* ⊙ *Tues.–Fri. 10–6, weekends and holidays 11–7* Ⓜ *Oriente.*

Praça Marquês de Pombal. Dominating the center of Marquês de Pombal Square is a statue of the marquis himself, the man responsible for the design of the "new" Lisbon that emerged from the ruins of the 1755 earthquake. On the statue's base are representations of both the earthquake and the tidal wave that engulfed the city; a female figure with outstretched arms signifies the joy at the emergence of the refashioned city.

Praça dos Restauradores. This square, which is adjacent to Rossio train station, marks the beginning of modern Lisbon. Here the broad, tree-lined Avenida da Liberdade starts its northwesterly ascent. *Restauradores* means "restoration," and the square commemorates the 1640 uprising against Spanish rule that restored Portuguese independence. An obelisk (raised in 1886) commemorates the event. Note the elegant 18th-century Palácio Foz on the square's west side. Before World War I, it contained a casino; today it houses a national tourist office, the tourist police, and a shop selling reproductions from the country's state museums.

Torre de Belém. The openwork balconies and domed turrets of the fanciful Belém Tower make it perhaps the country's purest Manueline structure. It was built between 1514 and 1520 on what was an island in the middle of the Rio Tejo, to defend the port entrance, and dedicated to St. Vincent, the patron saint of Lisbon. Today the chalk-white tower stands near the north bank—evidence of the river's changing course. Cross the wood gangway and walk inside, not so much to see the plain interior but rather to climb the steps to the very top for a bird's-eye view of river and city. ✉ *Av. de Brasília, Belém* ☎ *21/362–0034* 💷 *€5* ⊙ *Oct.–Apr., Tues.–Sun. 10–5; May–Sept., Tues.–Sun. 10–6.30.*

SHOPPING

Although fire destroyed much of Chiado, Lisbon's smartest shopping district, in 1988, a good portion of the area has been restored. The neighborhood has a large new shopping complex as well as many small stores with considerable cachet, particularly on and around Rua Garrett. The Baixa's grid of streets from the Rossío to the Rio Tejo have many small shops selling jewelry, shoes, clothing, and foodstuffs. The Bairro Alto is full of little crafts shops with stylish, contemporary goods. Excellent stores continue to open in the residential districts north of the city, at Praça de Londres and Avenida de Roma. Most of Lisbon's antiques shops are in the Rato and Bairro Alto districts along one long street, which changes its name four times as it runs southward from Largo do Rato: Rua Escola Politécnica, Rua Dom Pedro V, Rua da Misericórdia, and Rua do Alecrim.

Handmade goods, such as leather handbags, shoes, gloves, embroidery, ceramics, linens, and basketwork, are sold throughout the city. Apart from top designer fashions and high-end antiques, prices are moderate.

Antiquália. This shop is packed with furniture, chandeliers, and porcelain. ✉ *Praça Luís de Camões 37, Chiado* ☎ *21/342–3260.*

Vista Alegre. Portugal's most famous porcelain producer, Vista Alegre, established its factory in 1824. A visit to the flagship store is a must even though you can buy perfect reproductions of their original table services and ornaments at dozens of shops. There are also seven other Vista Alegre–owned stores in the city, including those at the Colombo, Amoreiras, and Vasco da Gama malls. ⊠ *Largo do Chiado 20–23, Chiado* ☎ *21/346–1401* ⊕ *www.vistaalegreatlantis.com.*

WHERE TO EAT

$$$
SEAFOOD
Fodor's Choice
★

✕ **Aqui Há Peixe.** "There's fish here" is this restaurant's name, and make no mistake: it's one of the most fashionable places in town to eat seafood. Opened in 2009 by the proprietor of a well-known beachside restaurant at Comporta, south of Setúbal, it has a similarly informal vibe. At night it attracts a youngish crowd clearly intent on hitting the Bairro Alto's bars later. Popular dishes here include fish stews and tuna steak sautéed with peppercorns; don't forget to order a light *vinho verde* or a good white wine to wash them down. There are cheaper lunchtime specials, rustled up from whatever was in the market in the morning. ⊠ *Rua da Trindade 18A, Chiado* ☎ *21/343–2154* ⊕ *www.aquihapeixe. pt* ⊙ *Closed Mon. No lunch weekends.*

$
PORTUGUESE

✕ **Solar dos Bicos.** This charming restaurant, with its stone arches and beautiful *azulejos* offers typical Portuguese cuisine at very reasonable prices. It's right next to the Casa dos Bicos, which you can marvel at from a large shaded esplanade. Seafood is the main attraction: grilled sole, grouper, sea bass, bream or squid are all good options, or two diners could split a rich *caldeirada* (fish stew) or *arroz de marisco* (a sort of wet seafood risotto). There are plenty of no-nonsense meat dishes, too, such as mixed grill and barbecued pork chops, which come with fries and salad. Then choose between achingly sweet desserts and fresh fruit. ⊠ *Rua dos Bacalhoeiros, 8–A, Alfama* ☎ *21/886–9447* ⊕ *www. solardosbicos.pt* ⊙ *Closed Mon. Closed 2 wks late Dec. or early Jan.*

LIVORNO, ITALY (FOR FLORENCE AND PISA)

Updated
by Bruce
Leimsidor

One of the biggest and grittiest ports on the northwestern Italian coast, Livorno has little to attract visitors in itself. Nevertheless, the city is one of the most popular cruise ports of call in the western Mediterranean as the gateway to some of Italy's finest attractions, the cities of Florence and Pisa, not to mention the delightful landscapes of Tuscany. Florence gave birth to the Renaissance and changed the way we see the world. For centuries it has captured the imagination of travelers, who have come seeking rooms with views and phenomenal art. Pisa is famous for one of the world's most noted historical attractions: its leaning tower, but this structure is one part of a trio of attractions that offers one of the most dramatic architectural complexes in the country. It's unlikely you'll have time to see everything during this port stop, so plan your time wisely.

ESSENTIALS

CURRENCY
The euro.

HOURS
Shops are generally open 9 to 1 and 3:30 to 8 and are generally closed Sunday. Summer (June to September) hours are usually 9 to 1 and 4 to 8, and some shops close Saturday afternoon.

PRIVATE TOURS
For tours of Florence or Pisa, you are encouraged not to use the exorbitantly priced and unprofessional tours offered by taxi drivers in Livorno. The best course is to book your tour through a legitimate company based in either Florence or Pisa and travel to those cities by train from Livorno to meet your guide. Undoubtedly the best tours of Florence are offered by Walks Inside Florence (€60/ hour for groups of up to 4 persons), which also offers tours in Pisa and Lucca.

Contacts **Walks Inside Florence.** ☎ *055/488588 in Florence* ⊕ *www.walksinsideflorence.it.*

TELEPHONES
Tri-band GSM phones work in Italy. You can buy prepaid phone cards at telecom shops, news vendors, and tobacconists in all towns and cities. Phone cards can be used for local or international calls.

COMING ASHORE
The port of Livorno has good cruise facilities, including car-rental offices, ticket and information offices, a bar, and a garden. It is near the heart of the town, just a few blocks from Livorno's central area. The railway station is 3 km (2 miles) from the port, but there is no good public transport option there. One option is to take a taxi, but the price of about €20 is an exorbitant fare for just 3 km of travel. Better is to take a shuttle into the center of the city (Piazza del Municipio) and then bus #1 or #2 from nearby Piazza Grande (in front of the Cathedral) to the train station; this option costs €1.20. It's only a bit over 1 km to Piazza Grande from the port, so if your cruise line doesn't provide a shuttle, it's not a long walk.

Trains from Livorno to Florence currently run once per hour throughout the day. The journey time is about 90 minutes. Prices are about €14–€20 round-trip depending on time of departure. From Livorno it is just a 15-minute train journey to Pisa, at a price of about €2.90 depending on time of departure; from Pisa Central Station take a train to San Rossore, from where it is a five-minute walk to the Leaning Tower area. If you buy tickets on Trenitalia's (Italian railways') website (⊕ *www.trenitalia.com*), you can print them out at self-service machines in Livorno station.

Taxis are expensive, charging €3.20 initially, then an additional charge per km (½-mile) and a surcharge when traffic moves slowly or when you call for a taxi. Car rental would give you greater flexibility to explore Tuscany, but if you are going only to Florence, then a train will be better, since parking is difficult in Florence. Rentals are approximately €45 per day for a compact manual vehicle.

EXPLORING FLORENCE AND PISA

FLORENCE

95 km (60 miles) east of Livorno, 82 km (51 miles) east of Pisa.

The heart of Florence, stretching from the Piazza del Duomo south to the Arno, is as dense with artistic treasures as anyplace in the world. The churches, medieval towers, Renaissance palaces, and world-class museums and galleries contain some of the most outstanding aesthetic achievements of Western history.

★ **Bargello.** This building started out as the headquarters for the Capitano del Popolo (captain of the people) during the Middle Ages, and was later used as a prison. The exterior served as a "most wanted" billboard: effigies of notorious criminals and Medici enemies were painted on its walls. Today it houses the **Museo Nazionale,** home to what is probably the finest collection of Renaissance sculpture in Italy. For Renaissance art lovers, the Bargello is to sculpture what the Uffizi is to painting. ✉ *Via del Proconsolo 4, Bargello* ☎ *055/294883* ⊕ *www.polomuseale. firenze.it* 🎟 *€4* 🕑 *Daily 8:15–1:50; closed 2nd and 4th Mon. of month and 1st, 3rd, and 5th Sun. of month.*

Battistero (*Baptistery*). The octagonal Baptistery is one of the supreme monuments of the Italian Romanesque style and one of Florence's oldest structures. Local legend has it that it was once a Roman temple dedicated to Mars; modern excavations, however, suggest that its foundations date from the 1st century AD. The round Romanesque arches on the exterior date from the 11th century. The interior dome mosaics from the beginning of the 14th century are justly renowned, but—glittering beauties though they are—they could never outshine the building's famed bronze Renaissance doors decorated with panels crafted by Lorenzo Ghiberti. The doors—or at least copies of them—on which Ghiberti worked most of his adult life (1403–52) are on the north and east sides of the Baptistery, and the Gothic panels on the south door were designed by Andrea Pisano (circa 1290–1348) in 1330. The original Ghiberti doors were removed to protect them from the effects of pollution and acid rain and have been beautifully restored; they are now on display in the Museo dell'Opera del Duomo. ✉ *Piazza del Duomo* ☎ *055/2302885* ⊕ *www.operaduomo.firenze.it* 🎟 *€4* 🕑 *Mon.– Sat. 12:15–7; Sun. 8:30–2, 1st Sat. of month 8:30–2.*

Campanile. The Gothic bell tower designed by Giotto (circa 1266–1337) is a soaring structure of multicolor marble originally decorated with sculptures by Donatello and reliefs by Giotto, Andrea Pisano, and others (which are now in the Museo dell'Opera del Duomo). A climb of 414 steps rewards you with a close-up of Brunelleschi's cupola on the Duomo next door and a sweeping view of the city. ✉ *Piazza del Duomo* ☎ *055/2302885* ⊕ *www.operaduomo.firenze.it* 🎟 *€6* 🕑 *Daily 8:30–7:30.*

★ **Cappelle Medicee** (*Medici Chapels*). This magnificent complex includes the **Cappella dei Principi,** the Medici chapel and mausoleum that was begun in 1605 and kept marble workers busy for several hundred years, and the **Sagrestia Nuova** (New Sacristy), designed by Michelangelo and so called to distinguish it from Brunelleschi's Sagrestia Vecchia (Old

Florence

Stazione
Santa Maria
Novella

V. della Scala

V. S. Caterina da Siena

V. Valfonda

V. Fiume

V. Nazionale

V. Faenza

V. Panicale

V. dell'Ariento

Pza. Mercato Centrale

Borgo la N...

V. S. Antonio

Pza. dell' Unità Italiana

V. Faenza

Cappelle Medicee

V. del Melarancio

V. dei Panzani

V. del Giglio

V. dell'Attoro

V. Conti

Santa Maria Novella

V. dell'Albero

V. dei Canacci

V. Benedetta

V. M. Finiguerra

V. Palazzuolo

Pza. S. Maria Novella

V. d. Belle Donne

V. dei Banchi

Piza. S. Maria Maggiore

V. Cerretani

V. Rondinelli

V. Pecori

V. del Trebbio

Borgo Ognissanti

V. Montebello

Pza. Ognissanti

V. d. Porcellana

V. del Sole

Pza. Antinori

V. d. Corsi

V. dei Pescioni

V. Vecchietti

V. dei Tosingi

Lung. Amerigo Vespucci

V. dei Fossi

V. del Moro

Pza. San Pancrazio

V. Spada

V. Strozzi

Pza. della Republic

Arno

Pza. di Cestello

Lung. Soderini

Pza. Goldoni

V. Federighi

V. d. Vigna Nuova

V. del Purgatorio

V. Tornabuoni

Pza. Strozzi

V. dei Sassetti

V. Anselmi

V.

Lung. Corsini

V. Parioncino

V. dei Parione

Pza. Santa Trinita

V. Porta Rossa

V. delle Terme

C. de Manetti

C. Ricasoli

Borgo SS. Apostoli

Lung. Acciaioli

V. dell' Oro

V. Por S. Ma...

Pisa

V. Contessa Matilde

Campo dei Miracoli

SS12

V. Card. Maffi

V. S. Zeno

1/8 mi

Ponte Vecchio

Battistero

Duomo

Leaning Tower

Pza. Manin

Pza. Felice Cavallotti

0

0

1/8 km

V. Nicola Pisano

V. Salvi

V. Roma

V. Santa Maria

d. Mille

V. Paoli

V. Carducci

V. Oberdan

V. S. Lorenzo

V. S. Zeno

Valdaino

Borgo Sant' Jacopo

V. Risorgimento

Pza. F. Buonamici

V. Dini

Santo Stefano dei Cavalieri

Pza. S. Paolo

V. S. Francesco

V. di Simone

Pza. di S. Maria Soprarno

V. Trieste

Pza. Dante

V. S. Frediano

Borgo Stretto

Pza. Garibaldi

Lung. Mediceo

V. Guicciardini

Ramaglianti

V. Solferino

Lung. Pacinotti

Arno

Lung. Simonelli

Ponte Solferino

V. S. Paolo

V. Crispi

V. Mazzini

Lung. Galileo Galilei

V. S. Martino

Cso. Italia

Ponte alla fortezza

Palazzo Pitti

Ponte della Cittadella

Sacristy) in San Lorenzo. ✉ *Piazza di Madonna degli Aldobrandini, San Lorenzo* ☎ *055/294883 reservations* 💰 *€6; €9 during special exhibits* 🕐 *Mar.–Nov., daily 8:15–3:50; Dec.–Feb., daily 8:15–1:50. Closed 1st, 3rd, and 5th Mon. and 2nd and 4th Sun. of month.*

FodorsChoice ★ **Duomo** (*Cattedrale di Santa Maria del Fiore*). In 1296 Arnolfo di Cambio (circa 1245–circa 1310) was commissioned to build "the loftiest, most sumptuous edifice human invention could devise" in the Romanesque style on the site of the old church of Santa Reparata. The immense Duomo was not completed until 1436, the year it was consecrated. The imposing facade dates only from the 19th century; its neo-Gothic style somewhat complements Giotto's genuine Gothic 14th-century campanile. The real glory of the Duomo, however, is Filippo Brunelleschi's dome, presiding over the cathedral with a dignity and grace that few domes to this day can match. Brunelleschi's **cupola** was an ingenious engineering feat. The result was one of the great engineering breakthroughs of all time: most of Europe's later domes, including that of St. Peter's in Rome, were built employing Brunelleschi's methods, and today the Duomo has come to symbolize Florence in the same way that the Eiffel Tower symbolizes Paris. ✉ *Piazza del Duomo* ☎ *055/2302885* ⊕ *www.operaduomo.firenze.it* 💰 *Church free, crypt €3, cupola €8* 🕐 *Crypt and Duomo: Mon.–Wed. and Fri 10–5, Thurs. 10–4:30, Sat. 10–4:45, Sun. 1:30–4:45, 1st Sat. of month 10–3:30. Cupola: Weekdays 8:30–7, Sat. 8:30–5:40, 1st Sat. of month 8:30–4.*

FodorsChoice ★ **Galleria degli Uffizi.** The venerable Uffizi Gallery occupies the top floor of the U-shaped **Palazzo degli Uffizi**, designed by Giorgio Vasari (1511–74) in 1560 to hold the *uffizi* (administrative offices) of the Medici grand duke Cosimo I (1519–74). Later, the Medici installed their art collections here, creating what was Europe's first modern museum, open to the public (at first only by request) since 1591. It's probably the greatest collection of Renaissance paintings in the world. For a €4 fee, advance tickets can be reserved by phone, online, or, once in Florence, at the Uffizi reservation booth (*advance tickets* ✉ *Consorzio ITA, Piazza Pitti 1* ☎ *055/294883)* at least one day in advance of your visit. Keep the confirmation number and take it with you to the door at the museum marked "Reservations." Usually you're ushered in almost immediately. ✉ *Piazzale degli Uffizi 6, Piazza della Signoria* ☎ *055/23885* ⊕ *www. uffizi.firenze.it; reservations www.polomuseale.firenze.it* 💰 *€10, €11 during special exhibitions; reservation fee €4* 🕐 *Tues.–Sun. 8:15–6:50.*

LIVORNO BEST BETS

The Uffizi. The mother lode of Renaissance art offers priceless examples by artists including Michelangelo, Botticelli, and Raphael.

Galleria dell'Accademia. The number one draw in this museum is Michelangelo's *David*, a sculpture that has captured human imagination, but don't miss the rest of the collection.

Torre Pendente. Completed in 1173 Pisa's famous tower began to subside almost immediately. Intervention in the 1990s saved it from collapse and stabilized the structure.

★ **Galleria dell'Accademia** (*Accademia Gallery*). The collection of Florentine
ⓒ paintings, dating from the 13th to the 18th centuries, is largely unremarkable, but the sculptures by Michelangelo are worth the price of
admission. The unfinished *Slaves,* fighting their way out of their marble
prisons, were meant for the tomb of Michelangelo's overly demanding
patron Pope Julius II (1443–1513). But the focal point is the original
David, moved here from Piazza della Signoria in 1873. *David* was
commissioned in 1501 by the Opera del Duomo (Cathedral Works
Committee), which gave the 26-year-old sculptor a leftover block of
marble that had been ruined forty years earlier by two other sculptors.
Michelangelo's success with the block was so dramatic that the city
showered him with honors, and the Opera del Duomo voted to build
him a house and a studio in which to live and work. ⊠ *Via Ricasoli 60,
San Marco* ☎ *055/294883 reservations, 055/2388609 gallery* 🎫 *€11,
reservation fee €4* ☉ *Tues.–Sun. 8:15–6:50.*

Museo dell'Opera del Duomo (*Cathedral Museum*). Ghiberti's original Baptistery door panels (in restoration at press time) and the *cantorie* (choir
loft) reliefs by Donatello and Luca della Robbia (1400–82) keep company
with Donatello's *Mary Magdalene* and Michelangelo's *Pietà* (not to be
confused with his more famous *Pietà* in St. Peter's in Rome). Renaissance sculpture is in part defined by its revolutionary realism, but in its
palpable suffering Donatello's *Magdalene* goes beyond realism. Michelangelo's heart-wrenching *Pietà* was unfinished at his death; the female
figure supporting the body of Christ on the left was added by Tiberio Cal-
cagni (1532–65), and never has the difference between competence and
genius been manifested so clearly. ⊠ *Piazza del Duomo 9* ☎ *055/2302885*
⊕ *www.operaduomo.firenze.it* 🎫 *€6* ☉ *Mon.–Sat. 9–7:30, Sun. 9–1:45.*

Palazzo Vecchio (*Old Palace*). Florence's forbidding, fortresslike city hall
was begun in 1299, presumably designed by Arnolfo di Cambio, and its
massive bulk and towering campanile dominate Piazza della Signoria. It
was built as a meeting place for the guildsmen governing the city at the
time; today it is still City Hall. The interior courtyard is a good deal less
severe, having been remodeled by Michelozzo (1396–1472) in 1453; a
copy of Verrocchio's bronze *puttino* (cherub), topping the central fountain, softens the space. (The original is upstairs.) The main attraction is on
the second floor: two adjoining rooms that supply one of the most startling
contrasts in Florence. The first is the opulently vast **Sala dei Cinquecento**
(Room of the Five Hundred), named for the 500-member Great Council,
the people's assembly established after the death of Lorenzo the Magnificent, which met here. In comparison, the little **Studiolo,** just off the
Sala dei Cinquecento's entrance, was a private room meant for the duke
and those whom he invited in. Here's where the melancholy Francesco I
(1541–87), son of Cosimo I, stored his priceless treasures and conducted
scientific experiments. Designed by Vasari, it was decorated by him, Giam-
bologna, and many others. ⊠ *Piazza della Signoria* ☎ *055/2768465* 🎫 *€6*
☉ *Mon.–Wed. and Fri.–Sun. 9–7, Thurs. 9–2.*

★ **Ponte Vecchio** (*Old Bridge*). This charmingly simple bridge was built in
1345 to replace an earlier bridge swept away by flood. Its shops first
housed butchers, then grocers, blacksmiths, and other merchants. But
in 1593 the Medici grand duke Ferdinand I (1549–1609), whose private

corridor linking the Medici palace (Palazzo Pitti) with the Medici offices (the Uffizi) crossed the bridge atop the shops, decided that all this plebeian commerce under his feet was unseemly. So he threw out the butchers and blacksmiths and installed 41 goldsmiths and eight jewelers. The bridge has been devoted solely to these two trades ever since.

Fodor's Choice
★
Santa Croce. Like the Duomo, this church is Gothic, but also like the Duomo, its facade dates from the 19th century. As a burial place, the church probably contains more skeletons of Renaissance celebrities than any other in Italy, including those of Michelangelo, Galileo, Machiavelli, and the composer Rossini, as well as a monument to Dante Alighieri, who is buried in Ravenna. The most famous works are probably the Giotto frescoes in the two chapels immediately to the right of the high altar. ⊠ *Piazza Santa Croce 16* ☎ *055/2466105* 🖅 *€5 combined admission to church and museum* ☉ *Mon.–Sat. 9:30–5:30, Sun. 1–5.*

PISA
22 km (14 miles) north of Livorno, 82 km (51 miles) west of Florence.

All of Pisa's treasures date from a short period between the 11th and the 13th centuries, when Pisa was a leading power in the region. The three buildings set on Pisa's grassy Field of Miracles form one of the finest Romanesque ensembles in Italy.

Battistero. This lovely Gothic baptistery, which stands across from the Duomo's facade, is best known for the pulpit carved by Nicola Pisano (circa 1220–84; father of Giovanni Pisano) in 1260. Ask one of the ticket takers if he'll sing for you inside; the acoustics are remarkable. ⊠ *Piazza del Duomo* ☎ *050/835011* ⊕ *www.opapisa.it* 🖅 *€5, discounts available if bought in combination with tickets for other monuments* ☉ *Nov.–Feb., daily 10–5; Mar., daily 9–6; Apr.–Sept., daily 8–8; Oct., daily 9–7.*

Duomo. Pisa's cathedral brilliantly utilizes the horizontal marble-stripe motif (borrowed from Moorish architecture) that became common to Tuscan cathedrals. It is famous for the Romanesque panels on the transept door facing the tower that depict scenes from the life of Christ. The beautifully carved 14th-century pulpit is by Giovanni Pisano (son of Nicola). ⊠ *Piazza del Duomo* ☎ *050835011* ⊕ *www.opapisa.it* 🖅 *€5* ☉ *Nov.–Feb., daily 10–12:45 and 2–5; Mar., daily 10–6; Apr.–Sept., daily 10–8; Oct., daily 10–7.*

Fodor's Choice
★
Leaning Tower (Torre Pendente). Work on this tower, built as a campanile (bell tower) for the Duomo, started in 1173: the lopsided settling began when construction reached the third story. The tower's architects attempted to compensate through such methods as making the remaining floors slightly taller on the leaning side, but the extra weight only made the problem worse. The settling continued, and by the late 20th century it had accelerated to such a point that many feared the tower would simply topple over, despite all efforts to prop it up. The structure has since been firmly anchored to the earth. The final phase to restore the tower to its original tilt of 300 years ago was launched in early 2000 and finished two years later. The last phase removed some 100 tons of earth from beneath the foundation. Reservations, which are essential, can be made online or by calling the Museo dell'Opera del Duomo; it's also possible to arrive at the ticket office and book for the same day.

Note that children under eight years of age are not allowed to climb. ⊠ *Piazza del Duomo* ☎ *050/835011* ⊕ *www.opapisa.it* ⊠ *€17* ⊙ *Dec. and Jan., daily 10–4:30; Nov. and Feb., daily 9:30—5:30; Mar., daily 9–5:30; Apr.–Sept., daily 8:30–8; Oct., daily 9–7.*

SHOPPING

2

Window-shopping in Florence is like visiting an enormous contemporary-art gallery. Many of today's greatest Italian artists are fashion designers—Prada, Gucci, Versace, to name but a few—and most keep shops in Florence. Italian leather is famed for its quality and fashioned into clothing, shoes, and accessories. True art also makes a big impact on the souvenir market, with many street artists around the town and smarter galleries in the historic center. Terra-cotta pottery, straw goods, and handmade paper are all traditional handicrafts. Excellent olive oils and wines are also worthwhile buys in Florence.

The fanciest designer shops are mainly on **Via Tornabuoni** and **Via della Vigna Nuova.** The city's largest concentrations of antiques shops are on **Borgo Ognissanti** and the Oltrarno's **Via Maggio.** The **Ponte Vecchio** houses reputable but very expensive jewelry shops, as it has since the 16th century. The area near **Santa Croce** is the heart of the leather merchants' district.

Sbigoli Terrecotte. Traditional Tuscan terra-cotta and ceramic vases, pots, and cups and saucers are on offer at this shop in the Santa Croce neighborhood. ⊠ *Via Sant'Egidio 4/r, Santa Croce* ☎ *055/2479713.*

WHERE TO EAT

$$$$ ✕ **Frescobaldi Wine Bar.** The Frescobaldi family has run a vineyard for
TUSCAN more than 700 years, and this swanky establishment offers tasty and sumptuous fare to accompany the seriously fine wines. Warm terra-cotta-color walls with trompe-l'oeil tapestries provide a soothing atmosphere. The menu is typically Tuscan, but turned up a notch or two: the *faraona in umido con l'uva* (stewed guinea fowl with grapes) comes with a side of feather-light mashed potatoes. Save room for dessert, as well as one of the dessert wines. A separate, lovely little wine bar called Frescobaldino has a shorter—but equally good—menu and a delightful, multilingual barman called Primo. ⑤ *Average main: €35* ⊠ *Via de' Magazzini 2–4/r, Piazza della Signoria* ☎ *055/284724* ⊙ *Closed Sun. No lunch Mon.*

$$$$ ✕ **Il Latini.** It may be the noisiest, most crowded trattoria in Florence,
TUSCAN but it's also one of the most fun. The genial host, Torello ("little bull") Latini, presides over his four big dining rooms, and somehow it feels as if you're dining in his home. Ample portions of *ribollita* prepare the palate for the hearty meat dishes that follow. Both Florentines and tourists alike tuck into the *agnello fritto* (fried lamb) with aplomb. There's almost always a wait, even with a reservation. ⑤ *Average main: €32* ⊠ *Via dei Palchetti 6/r, Santa Maria Novella* ☎ *055/210916* ⊙ *Closed Mon. and 15 days at Christmas.*

MÁLAGA, SPAIN (WITH MARBELLA, NERJA, AND GRANADA)

Updated by
Joanna Styles

The city of Málaga and the surrounding region of eastern Andalusia creates the kind of contrast that makes travel in Spain so tantalizing. A Moorish legacy is a unifying theme and offers some of its most interesting and visually stunning historical attractions. Since the birth of mass tourism, Europeans have flocked here to the Costa del Sol or Sunshine Coast, a 70-km (43-miles) sprawl of hotels, vacation villas, golf courses, marinas, and nightclubs west of Málaga. Since the late 1950s this area has mushroomed from a group of impoverished fishing villages into an overdeveloped seaside playground and retirement haven. Despite the hubbub, you *can* unwind here. Málaga itself is a vibrant Spanish city, virtually untainted by tourism, and inland are quiet whitewashed villages just waiting to be explored.

ESSENTIALS

CURRENCY
The euro.

HOURS
Museums generally open 9 until 7 or 8, many are closed on Monday, and some close in the afternoon. Most stores are open Monday through Saturday 9 to 1:30 and 5 to 8, but a few tourist shops open in the afternoon and on Sunday.

PRIVATE TOURS
Julià Travel. Julià is one of the main companies offering day trips to Córdoba, Granada, Nerja, Seville, and even Tangier from Málaga. ☎ *902/024443* ⊕ *www.juliatravel.com.*

TELEPHONES
Most tri-band and quad-band GSM phones work in Spain, where mobile services are 3G-compatible. Public kiosks accept phone cards that support international calls (cards sold in press shops, bars, and telecom shops). Major companies include Vodafone.

COMING ASHORE
The cruise port at Málaga has just completed a major renovation. Along with a new cruise terminal, the port now incorporates shopping and eateries in the area known as Muelle Uno and an aquarium and park with over 400 palms. A spectacular undulating pergola runs the length of the park and provides a fine walkway into the city center. Facilities at the cruise terminals are comprehensive and shuttle buses carry passengers to the terminal areas.

The city of Málaga awaits just beyond the gates of the port, and you can explore the Old Town on foot. Granada is 1½ hours away to the north by road. Bus services to Granada are frequent, and buses are modern and air-conditioned; the fare at this writing is €10.62 for a single leg. The main bus station is next to the railway station in the city. Taking a taxi from the cruise port is the quickest and simplest transfer. Rail travel from Málaga to Granada is a much slower option, at 3 hours, and with few trains each day this is not a realistic option

for passengers in town for just a day. Renting a car would allow you to visit Granada or explore some of the resorts or countryside surrounding Málaga. The price for an economy manual vehicle is approximately €30 per day.

EXPLORING MÁLAGA AND VICINITY

MÁLAGA

Alcazaba. Just beyond the ruins of a Roman theater on Calle Alcazabilla stands Málaga's greatest monument. This fortress was begun in the 8th century, when Málaga was the principal port of the Moorish kingdom, though most of the present structure dates from the 11th century. The inner palace was built between 1057 and 1063, when the Moorish emirs took up residence; Ferdinand and Isabella lived here for a while after conquering the city in 1487. The ruins are dappled with orange trees and bougainvillea and include a small museum; from the highest point you can see over the park and port. ⊠ *Entrance on C. Alcazabilla* 🚌 *€2.20, €3.55 combined entry with Gibralfaro* ⊘ *Nov.–Mar., Tues.– Sun. 8:30–7; Apr.–Oct., Tues.–Sun. 9:30–8.*

Centro de Arte Contemporáneo (*Contemporary Arts Center*). This museum includes photographic studies and paintings, some of them immense. The 7,900 square feet of bright exhibition hall are used to showcase

ultramodern artistic trends—the four exhibitions are used for a changing show from the permanent collection, two temporary shows, and one show dedicated to up-and-coming Spanish artists. The gallery attracts world-class modern artists like the South African William Kentridge or the British Gilbert and George. The Victoria Lounge restaurant, which has a terrace overlooking the river, does a good lunch menu ($). ⊠ *Alemania s/n* ☎ *952/120055* ⊕ *www.cacmalaga.org* ✉ *Free* ☉ *Sept.–June, Tues.–Sun. 10–8; July–Aug., Tues.–Sun. 10–2 and 5–8.*

Fundación Picasso. Málaga's most famous native son, Pablo Picasso, was born here in 1881. Now the Fundación Picasso, the building has been painted and furnished in the style of the era and houses a permanent exhibition of the artist's early sketches and sculptures, as well as memorabilia, including his christening robe and family photos. ⊠ *Pl. de la Merced 15* ☎ *951/926060* ⊕ *www.fundacionpicasso.es* ✉ *€1* ☉ *Daily 9:30–8.*

Gibralfaro (*castle*). Surrounded by magnificent vistas, Málaga's Gibralfaro is floodlit at night. The fortifications were built for Yusuf I in the 14th century; the Moors called them Jebelfaro, from the Arab word for "mount" and the Greek word for "lighthouse," after a beacon that stood here to guide ships into the harbor and warn of pirates. The lighthouse has been succeeded by a small parador (*see Where to Stay*). You can drive here by way of Calle Victoria or take a minibus that leaves 10 times a day, between 11 and 7, roughly every 45 minutes, from the bus stop in the park near the Plaza de la Marina. ⊠ *Gibralfaro Mountain* ✉ *€2.20, €3.55 combined entry with Alcazaba* ☉ *Nov.–Mar., daily 9–6; Apr.–Oct., daily 9–8.*

Málaga's Cathedral. This cathedral, built between 1528 and 1782, is a triumph, although a generally unappreciated one, having been left unfinished when funds ran out. Because it lacks one of its two towers, the building is nicknamed *La Manquita* (the One-Armed Lady). The enclosed choir, which miraculously survived the burnings of the civil war, is the work of 17th-century artist Pedro de Mena, who carved the wood wafer-thin in some places to express the fold of a robe or shape of a finger. The choir also has a pair of massive 18th-century pipe organs, one of which is still used for the occasional concert. Adjoining the cathedral is a small museum of religious art and artifacts. A walk around the cathedral on Calle Cister will take you to the magnificent Gothic Puerta del Sagrario. ⊠ *C. de Molina Larios* ☎ *952/215917* ✉ *€5* ☉ *Weekdays 10–6, Sat. 10–5.*

Mercado de Atarazanas. From the Plaza Felix Saenz, at the southern end of Calle Nueva, turn onto Sagasta to reach the Mercado de Atarazanas.

The typical, 19th-century, iron structure incorporates the original **Puerta de Atarazanas,** the exquisitely crafted 14th-century Moorish gate that once connected the city with the port. Don't miss the magnificent, stained-glass window depicting highlights of this historical port city as you stroll round the stalls, filled with local produce. ⊙ *Mon.–Sat. 9–3.*

Museo Carmen Thyssen Málaga. Visitors who've been to Madrid are probably familiar with that city's Museo Carmen Thyssen, and in mid-2011 over 200 works from Baroness Thyssen's private collection went on display at Málaga's own branch. Shown in a renovated 16th-century palace, the collection features mainly Spanish paintings from the 19th century and includes some of Spain's greatest artists, like Joaquín Sorolla y Bastida and Francisco de Zurbarán. The museum also hosts regular talks and workshops on art. ⊠ *C. Compañia 10* ☎ *902/303131* ⊕ *www.carmenthyssenmalaga.org* ⊠ *€6 permanent exhibition, €4 temporary exhibition* ⊙ *Tues.–Sun. 10–8.*

Fodor's Choice **Museo Picasso.** Part of the charm of the Museo Picasso, one of the city's
★ most prestigious museums, is that it's such a family affair. These are the works that Pablo Picasso kept for himself or gave to his family, including the heartfelt *Paulo con gorro blanco* (*Paulo with a White Cap*), a portrait of his firstborn son painted in the early 1920s; and *Olga Kokhlova con mantilla* (*Olga Kokhlova with Mantilla*), a 1917 portrait of his certifiably insane first wife. The holdings were largely donated by two family members—Christine and Bernard Ruiz-Picasso, the artist's daughter-in-law and her son. The works are displayed in chronological order according to the periods that marked Picasso's development as an artist, from Blue and Rose to cubism and beyond. The museum is housed in a former palace where, during restoration work, Roman and Moorish remains were discovered. These are now on display, together with the permanent collection of Picassos and temporary exhibitions. Guided tours in English are held on Wednesdays at 11:30. ⊠ *C. de San Agustín* ☎ *952/127600* ⊕ *www.museopicassomalaga.org* ⊠ *Permanent exhibition €6, combined permanent and temporary exhibition €9, free entry Sun. 6–8* ⊙ *Tues.–Thurs. and Sun. 10–8, Fri. and Sat. 10–9.*

Palacio Episcopal (*Bishop's Palace*). Facing the cathedral's main entrance, this is a fine 18th-century mansion with one of the most stunning facades in the city, as well as interesting interior details. It's now a venue for temporary art exhibitions. ⊠ *Pl. Obispo 6* ☎ *951/294051* ⊠ *Free* ⊙ *Tues. 2.30–8, Wed.–Sat. 10–8, Sun. 10–2.*

Pasaje Chinitas. The narrow streets and alleys on each side of Calle Marqués de Larios have charms of their own. Wander the warren of passageways around Pasaje Chinitas, off Plaza de la Constitución, and peep into the dark, vaulted bodegas where old men down glasses of *seco añejo* or *Málaga Virgen,* local wines made from Málaga's muscatel grapes. Silversmiths and vendors of religious books and statues ply their trades in shops that have changed little since the early 1900s. Backtrack across Larios, and, in the streets leading to Calle Nueva, you can see shoeshine boys, lottery-ticket vendors, Gypsy guitarists, and tapas bars serving wine from huge barrels.

NERJA
52 km (32 miles) east of Málaga.

★ Nerja—the name comes from the Moorish word *narixa,* meaning "abundant springs." The village is on a headland above small beaches and rocky coves. In high season, Nerja is packed with tourists, but the rest of the year it's a pleasure to wander the Old Town's narrow streets.

★ **Balcón de Europa.** The highlight of Nerja is the Balcón de Europa, a
☺ tree-lined promenade on a promontory just off the central square, with magnificent views of the mountains and sea. You can gaze far off into the horizon using the strategically placed telescopes, or use this as a starting point for a horse and carriage clip-clop ride around town.

Cuevas de Nerja (*Nerja Caves*). The Nerja Caves lie between Almuñécar and Nerja on a road surrounded by giant cliffs and dramatic seascapes. Signs point to the cave entrance above the village of Maro, 4 km (2½ miles) east of Nerja. Its spires and turrets, created by millennia of dripping water, are now floodlit for better views. One suspended pinnacle, 200 feet long, is the world's largest known stalactite. The cave painting of seals discovered here may be the oldest example of art in existence—and the only ones known to have been painted by Neanderthals. The awesome subterranean chambers create an evocative setting for concerts and ballets during the Nerja Festival of Music and Dance, held annually during the second and third weeks of July. There is also a bar-restaurant near the entrance with a spacious dining room that has superb panoramic views.
☎ *952/529520* ⊕ *www.cuevadenerja.com* 🎫 *€8.50* ☾ *Daily 10–7:30.*

MARBELLA
52 km (32 miles) west of Málaga.

Playground of the rich and home of movie stars, rock musicians, and dispossessed royal families, Marbella has attained the top rung on Europe's social ladder. Dip into any Spanish gossip magazine and chances are the glittering parties that fill its pages are set in Marbella. However, much of this action takes place on the fringes—grand hotels and luxury restaurants line the waterfront for 20 km (12 miles) on each side of the town center.

Old Village. Marbella's appeal lies in the heart of the old village, which remains surprisingly intact. Here, a block or two back from the main highway, narrow alleys of whitewashed houses cluster around the central **Plaza de los Naranjos** (Orange Square), where colorful, albeit pricey, restaurants vie for space under the orange trees. Climb onto what remains of the old fortifications and stroll along the Calle Virgen de los Dolores to the Plaza de Santo Cristo.

Puerto Banús. Marbella's wealth glitters most brightly along the Golden Mile, a tiara of star-studded clubs, restaurants, and hotels west of town and stretching from Marbella to Puerto Banús. A mosque, an Arab bank, and the former residence of Saudi Arabia's late King Fahd betray the influence of oil money in this wealthy enclave. About 7 km (4½ miles) west of central Marbella (between Km 175 and Km 174), a sign indicates the turnoff leading down to Puerto Banús. Though now hemmed in by a belt of high-rises, Marbella's plush marina, with 915 berths, is a gem of ostentatious wealth, a Spanish answer to St. Tropez.

Huge yachts, beautiful people, and countless expensive stores and restaurants make up the glittering parade that marches long into the night. The backdrop is an Andalusian pueblo—built in the 1960s to resemble the fishing villages that once lined this coast.

GRANADA

128 km (80 miles) northeast of Málaga.

Granada rises majestically from a plain onto three hills, dwarfed—on a clear day—by the Sierra Nevada. Atop one of these hills perches the pink-gold Alhambra palace. The stunning view from its mount takes in the sprawling medieval Moorish quarter, the caves of the Sacromonte, and, in the distance, the fertile *vega* (plain), rich in orchards, tobacco fields, and poplar groves. These days much of the Alhambra and Albaicín areas are closed to cars, because of the difficult access, but starting from the Plaza Nueva there are now minibuses—Nos. 30, 31, and 34—that run frequently to these areas.

Fodor's Choice ★ **Alhambra.** With more than 2.3 million visitors a year, the Alhambra is Spain's most popular attraction. Simply take one of the minibuses, number 30 or 32, up from the Plaza Nueva. They run every few minutes; pay the fare of €1.20 on board. Just past the gate, take the path branching off to the left to the Puerta de la Justicia (Gate of Justice), one of the Alhambra's entrances. Yusuf I built the gate in 1348; its two arches have carvings depicting a key and a hand. The five fingers of the hand represent the five laws of the Koran. The complex has three main parts: the Alcazaba, the Palacios Nazaríes (Nasrid Palaces), and the Generalife, the ancient summer palace.

Construction of the Alhambra was begun in 1238 by Ibn el-Ahmar, the first king of the Nasrids. The great citadel once comprised a complex of houses, schools, baths, barracks, and gardens surrounded by defense towers and seemingly impregnable walls. Today, only the Alcazaba and the Palacios Nazaríes, built chiefly by Yusuf I (1334–54) and his son Mohammed V (1354–91), remain. The palace is an endless, intricate conglomeration of patios, arches, and cupolas made from wood, plaster, and tile; lavishly colored and adorned with marquetry and ceramics in geometric patterns and topped by delicate, frothy profusions of lacelike stucco and *mocárabes* (ornamental stalactites). Built of perishable materials, it was never intended to last but to be forever replenished and replaced by succeeding generations.

Across from the main entrance is the original fortress, the **Alcazaba.** Its ruins are dominated by the Torre de la Vela (Watchtower); from its summit you can see, to the north, the Albayzín; to the northeast, the Sacromonte; and to the west, the cathedral. The tower's great bell was once used, by both the Moors and the Christians, to announce the opening and closing of the irrigation system on Granada's great plain. ⊠ *Cuesta de Gomérez, Alhambra ⊕ www.alhambra-patronato.es ⊡ Alhambra and Generalife: €13; Generalife and Alcazaba: €7; Fine Arts Museum: €1.50; Museum of the Alhambra and Palace of Carlos V: free ⊙ Alhambra, Alcazaba, Generalife and Palace of Carlos V: daily 8:30–6 (to 8 pm Mar. 15–Oct. 14); Museum of the Alhambra: Tues.–Sun. 8:30–2; Museum of Fine Arts: Tues. 2:30–8, Wed.–Sat. 9–8, Sun. 9–2:30.*

SHOPPING

Málaga offers a full range of local specialties made throughout the region. Shoes and leather goods are of high quality. Handmade and mass-produced ceramics are produced in a range of colors and styles. Fans and silk shawls, along with other traditional Spanish clothing, range in price, depending on quality. Olives and olive oil will make gourmets happy, and olive oil is also used for a range of hair and beauty products. Other edibles include dried serrano ham, Manchego cheese, and *turrón* (an almond and honey sweet). *Seco añejo* sweet wine is also produced in the region.

In Málaga the main shopping street is Marqués de Larios, known locally as Larios, a traffic-free boulevard with excellent boutiques.

BEACHES

Lobster-pink sun worshippers from northern Europe pack these beaches in summer so heavily that there's little towel space on the sand. Beach chairs can be rented for around €5 a day. Beaches range from shingle and pebbles (Almuñecar, Nerja, Málaga) to fine, gritty sand (westward of Málaga). The best are those around Marbella. It's acceptable for women to go topless; if you want to take it *all* off, go to beaches designated *playa naturista*. The most popular nude beach is Maro (near Nerja).

WHERE TO EAT

$
SPANISH
Fodor's Choice
★

✕ **Lo Güeno.** This traditional tapas bar has two dining spaces: the original well-loved bar, shoehorned into a deceptively small space on a side street near Calle Larios, and a more recent expansion across the street. The original is especially appealing, with its L-shape wooden bar crammed with a choice of more than 75 tantalizing tapas, including many Loguéno originals such as grilled oyster mushrooms with garlic, parsley, and goat cheese. There's an excellent selection of Rioja and Ribera wines, and the service is fast and good, despite the lack of elbow room. $ *Average main: €8* ⊠ *Marin Garcia 9* ☎ *952/223048* ⊕ *www.loguéno.es.*

$
ECLECTIC

✕ **Vino Mio.** This Dutch-owned restaurant is well placed, just off Plaza de la Merced, and the menu is diverse and interesting, with dishes like "pasta rasta" (black tagliatelle with king prawns, arugula, and white wine) and the *boda Árabe* (Arab wedding) salad—warm couscous with fresh vegetables and raisins. Save room for the Guinness-and-chocolate cake. Monthly art exhibitions and flamenco music from Monday through Saturday help add to the chic atmosphere. The same menu, along with cocktails served after midnight, are featured at Vino Mio's sister restaurant nearby, at Plaza Jerónimo Cuervo 2. $ *Average main: €12* ⊠ *C. Alamos 11* ☎ *952/609093* ⊕ *www.restaurantevinomio.com.*

MALLORCA, SPAIN

Updated by
Joanna Styles

More than five times the size of its fellow Balearic Islands, Mallorca is shaped roughly like a saddle. The Sierra de Tramuntana, a dramatic mountain range soaring to nearly 5,000 feet, runs the length of its northwest coast, and a ridge of hills borders the southeast shores; between the two lies a great, flat plain that in early spring becomes a sea of almond blossoms, "the snow of Mallorca." The island draws more than 9 million visitors a year, many of them bound for summer vacation packages in the coastal resorts. The beaches are beautiful, but save time for the charms of the northwest and the interior: caves, bird sanctuaries, monasteries and medieval cities, local museums, outdoor cafés, and village markets.

ESSENTIALS

CURRENCY
The euro.

HOURS
Museums generally open 9 until 7 or 8, many are closed on Monday, and some close in the afternoon. Most stores are open Monday through Saturday 9 to 1:30 and 5 to 8, but tourist shops may open in the afternoon and also on Sunday between May and September.

PRIVATE TOURS
Autocares Comas. The company organizes a year-round program of trips to various locations on the island. ☎ *902/026424* ⊕ *www.autocarescomas.com.*

TELEPHONES
Most tri-band or quad-band GSM phones will work in Spain, where services are 3G-compatible. Public kiosks accept phone cards that support international calls (cards sold in press shops, bars, and telecom shops). Major companies include Vodafone.

COMING ASHORE
Vessels dock at the port directly in front of the Old Town of Palma. There is no shuttle, so passengers docking at the farthest berth (south side of the harbor) have a 20-minute walk to the terminal building and the port entrance. From the port entrance you can walk into Palma town. There are few facilities at the cruise terminal or in the port.

If you only want to enjoy Palma, you won't need to worry about transportation; however, Mallorca is a small island, and you can see a great deal of it in a day with a vehicle or on public transportion. Regular and reliable bus services link the major towns, though services are fewer on Sunday. Car rentals cost around €25 per day for an economy manual vehicle (book well in advance, especially in July and August), but it's much cheaper to explore by public transit.

EXPLORING MALLORCA

PALMA DE MALLORCA

If you look north of the cathedral (La Seu, or the "seat" of the Bishopric, to Mallorcans) on a map of the city of Palma, you can see the jumble of tiny streets around the Plaça Santa Eulalia that made up the early town. A stroll through these streets will bring you past many interesting neoclassical and moderniste buildings.

Ajuntament (*town hall*). Along Carrer Colom is the 17th-century Ajuntament. Stop in to see the collection of *gigantes*—the huge painted and costumed mannequins paraded through the streets during festivals—on display in the lobby. The olive tree on the right side of the square is one of Majorca's so-called *olivos milenarios*—purported to be more than 1,000 years old. ⊠ *Pl. Cort 1.*

Castell de Bellver (*Bellver Castle*). Overlooking the city and the bay from a hillside, the castle was built at the beginning of the 14th century, in Gothic style but with a circular design—the only one of its kind in Spain. It houses an archaeological museum of the history of Majorca, and a small collection of classical sculpture. ⊠ *Camilo José Cela s/n* ☎ *971/730657* 🎟 *€3, free Sun.* ☾ *Castle and museum open Oct.–Mar., Mon.–Sat. 8:30–6:45; Apr.–Sept., Mon.–Sat. 8:30–8:30. Museum is closed Sun., but castle is open 10–4:30.*

Fodor's Choice
★

Catedral de Majorca. Palma's cathedral is an architectural wonder that took almost 400 years to build. Begun in 1230, the wide expanse of the nave is supported by 14 70-foot-tall columns that fan out at the top like palm trees. The nave is dominated by an immense rose window, 40 feet in diameter, from 1370. Over the main altar (consecrated in 1346) is the surrealistic **baldoquí** by Antoni Gaudí, completed in 1912. This enormous canopy, with lamps suspended from it like elements of a mobile, rises to a Crucifixion scene at the top. To the right, in the Chapel of the Santísimo, is an equally remarkable 2007 work by the modern sculptor Miquel Barceló: a painted ceramic tableau covering the walls like a skin. Based on the New Testament account of the miracle of the loaves and fishes, it's a bizarre composition of rolling waves, gaping cracks, protruding fish heads, and human skulls. The **bell tower** above the cathedral's Plaça Almoina door holds nine bells, the largest of which is called N'Eloi, meaning "Praise." The five-ton N'Eloi, cast in 1389, requires six men to ring it and has shattered stained-glass windows with its sound. ■ TIP➔ **There's an organ concert in the basilica on the first Tuesday of every month, from noon–12:30.** ⊠ *Pl. Almoina s/n* ☎ *971/723130, 902/022445* ⊕ *www.catedraldemallorca.org* 🎟 *€6* ☾ *Apr. and May, weekdays 10–5:15, Sat. 10–2:15; June–Sept., weekdays 10–6:15, Sat. 10–2:15; Nov.–Mar., weekdays 10–3:15, Sat. 10–2:15; Sun. year-round for services only, 8:30–1:45 and 6:30–7:45.*

MALLORCA BEST BETS

The Cathedral. Palma's cathedral has a unique circular design as well as decorations by Gaudí.

Museu d'Es Baluard. The Museum of Modern and Contemporary Art is an exciting convergence of old and new.

Sóller. One of the most beautiful towns on the island, with a large collection of moderniste buildings.

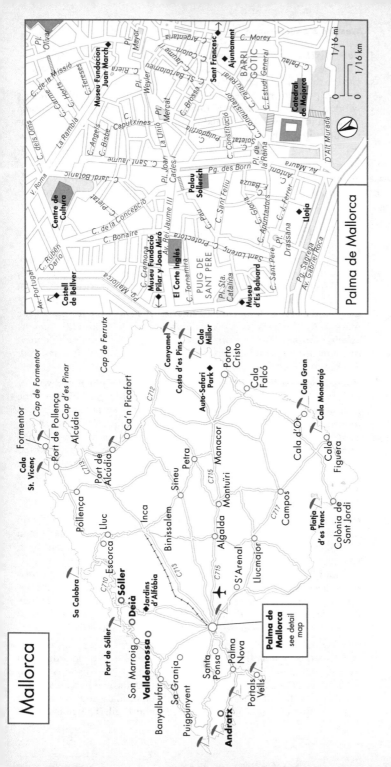

Mallorca

Cala St. Vicenç
Cap de Formentor
Formentor
Cap d'es Pinar
Port de Pollença
Cap de Ferrutx
Alcúdia
Ca'n Picafort
Port de Alcúdia
C713
Pollença
Lluc
Inca
Sineu
Petra
C712
Escorca
Sa Calobra
C710
Sóller
Deià
Jardins d'Alfàbia
Binissalem
Manacor
Port de Sóller
Son Marroig
Valldemossa
Sa Granja
Banyalbufar
Puigpunyent
Santa Ponsa
Palma Nova
Portals Vells
Andratx
Palma de Mallorca
see detail map
C713
C715
Algaida
Montuïri
S'Arenal
Llucmajor
C715
Campos
C717
C715
Colònia de Sant Jordi
Platja d'es Trenc
Cala Figuera
Cala d'Or
Cala Gran
Cala Mondrajó
Auto-Safari Park
Costa d'es Pins
Canyamel
Cala Millor
Porto Cristo
Cala Falcó

0   10 miles
0   15 km

Palma de Mallorca

Pl. Olivar
Av. de Portugal
C. Rubén Darío
Centre de Cultura
Castell de Bellver
Pg. Mallorca
Av. Roma
C. dels Oms
C. de la Missió
C. del Carme
C. Horts
C. Teresses
Museu Fundación Juan March
Pl. Riera
La Rambla
C. Angels
C. Bisbe
Caputxines
Pl. Weyler
Pl. Mayor
Pl. Mercat
La Unió
Pl. Joan Carles
Sant Jaume
C. de la Concepció
C. Bonaire
Jardí Botanic
C. Cremona
Museu Fundació Pilar y Joan Miró
El Corte Inglés
Av. Rei Jaume III
PUIG DE SANT PERE
C. Tornamira
Palau Sollerich
Pg. des Born
C. Sant Feliu
C. Pelleteria
Pl. Sta. Catalina
Museu d'Es Baluard
Sant Llorenç
C. de la Protectora
C. Sant Pere
Drassana
Av. Antoni Maura
Av. Gabriel Roca
Pg. Sagrera
C. Apuntadors
C. Bauza
C. Gloria
C. J. Ferrer
Llotja
Pl. de la Reina
Pl. Constitució
C. Soletat
Pg. des Born
Sant Bartolomeu
St. Jaume
C. Colom
Puigdorfila
C. Brossa
Conquistador
C. Constitució
C. Palau Reial
Pl. Cort
C. Estudi General
BARRI GÒTIC
Ajuntament
Sant Francesc
C. Morey
C. Palau
Catedral de Mallorca
D'Alt Murada

0   1/16 mi
0   1/16 km

Llotja (*Exchange*). On the seafront west of the Plaça de la Reina, the Llotja was built in the 15th century and connects via an interior court-yard to the **Consolat de Mar** (Maritime Consulate). With its decorative turrets, pointed battlements, fluted pillars, and Gothic stained-glass windows—part fortress, part church—it attests to the wealth Majorca achieved in its heyday as a Mediterranean trading power. The interior can be visited only during special exhibitions in the Merchants Chamber. ⊠ *Pl. de la Llotja 5* ☏ *971/711705* ⊙ *During exhibits, Tues.–Sat. 11–2 and 5–9, Sun. 11–2.*

Fodor's Choice **Museu d'Es Baluard** (*Museum of Modern and Contemporary Art of*
★ *Palma*). At the western end of the city, the Museu d'Es Baluard rises on a long-neglected archaeological site, parts of which date back to the 12th century. The building itself is an outstanding convergence of old and new: the exhibition space uses the surviving 16th-century perimeter walls of the fortified city, including a stone courtyard facing the sea and a promenade along the ramparts. There are three floors of galleries, and the collection includes work by Miró, Picasso, Henri Magritte, Tapiès, Alexander Calder, and other major artists. The courtyard café-terrace Restaurant del Museu (Nov.–May, Tuesday–Sunday 10–8; Jun.–Oct. 10-midnight) affords a fine view of the marina. ⊠ *Pl. Porta de Santa Catalina 10* ☏ *971/908200* ⊕ *www. esbaluard.org* ⊠ *Wed., Thurs. and weekends €6; Tues. €4.50; voluntary contributions on Fri.; free on some weekends in Feb.* ⊙ *Tues.–Sat. 10–8; Sun. 10–3.*

★ **Museu Fundación Juan March.** A few steps from the north archway of the Plaça Major is the Museu Fundación Juan March. This fine little museum was established to display what had been a private collection of modern Spanish art. The building itself was a sumptuous private home built in the 18th century. The second and third floors were redesigned to accommodate a series of small galleries, with one or two works at most—by Pablo Picasso, Joan Miró, Juan Gris, Salvador Dalí, Antoni Tàpies, and Miquel Barceló, among others—on each wall. ⊠ *Carrer Sant Miguel 11* ☏ *971/713515* ⊕ *www.march.es/museupalma* ⊠ *Free* ⊙ *Weekdays 10–6:30, Sat. 10:30–2.*

Museu Fundació Pilar y Joan Miró (*Pilar and Joan Miró Foundation Museum*). The permanent collection in the Museu Fundació Pilar y Joan Miró includes a great many drawings and studies by the Catalan artist, who spent his last years on Majorca, but shows far fewer finished paintings and sculptures than the Fundació Miró in Barcelona. Don't miss the adjacent studio, built for Miró by his friend the architect Josep Lluis Sert. The artist did most of his work here from 1957 on. ⊠ *Carrer Joan de Saridakis 29, Cala Major* ☏ *971/701420* ⊕ *miro.palmademallorca.es* ⊠ *€6* ⊙ *Tues.–Sat. 10–6 (to 7 May 16–Sept. 15), Sun. 10–3.*

Sant Francesc. The 13th-century monastery church of Sant Francesc was established by Jaume II when his eldest son took monastic orders and gave up rights to the throne. Fra Junípero Serra, the missionary who founded San Francisco, California, was later educated here; his statue stands to the left of the main entrance. The basilica houses the tomb of the eminent 13th-century scholar Ramón Llull. The cloisters are

especially beautiful and peaceful. ⊠ *Pl. Sant Francesc 7, Barrio Antiguo* 🕾 *€1.50* ◷ *Mon.–Sat. 9:30–12:30 and 3:30–6, Sun. 9:30–1.*

ANDRATX
16 km (10 miles) west of Palma.

Andratx is a charming cluster of white-and-ocher hillside houses, rather like cliff dwellings, with the 3,363-foot Mt. Galatzó behind it. Many of the towns on Majorca are at some distance from their seafronts; from Andratx you can take a 4-km (1½-mile) drive through S'Arracó to Sant Elm and on to the rocky shore opposite Sa Dragonera—an island shaped indeed like the long-armored back of a dragon. Local history has it that the tiny island of Pantaleu, just to the west of it, was where Jaume I chose to disembark in September 1200, on his campaign to retake Majorca from the Moors.

VALLDEMOSSA
18 km (11 miles) north of Palma.

Reial Cartuja (*Royal Carthusian Monastery*). It was founded in 1339, but when the monks were expelled in 1835, the Reial Cartuja became apartments for travelers. The most famous lodgers were Frédéric Chopin and his lover, the Baroness Amandine Dupin—a French novelist who used the pseudonym George Sand. The two spent three difficult months here in the cold, damp winter of 1838–39.

In the **church,** note the frescoes above the nave—the monk who painted them was Goya's brother-in-law. The **pharmacy,** made by the monks in 1723, is almost completely preserved. A long corridor leads to the apartments occupied by Chopin and Sand, furnished in period style. The piano is original. Nearby, another set of apartments houses the local **museum,** with mementos of Archduke Luis Salvador and a collection of old printing blocks. From here you return to the ornately furnished **King Sancho's palace,** a group of rooms originally built by King Jaume II for his son. The tourist office, in Valldemossa's main plaza, sells a ticket good for all of the monastery's attractions. ⊠ *Pl. de la Cartuja 11* 🕾 *971/612106* ⊕ *www.valldemossa.com* 🕾 *€7.50* ◷ *Dec. and Jan., Mon.–Sat. 9:30–3; Feb. and Nov., Mon.–Sat. 9:30–5, Sun. 10–1; Mar.–Oct., Mon.–Sat. 9:30–5:30, Sun. 10–1.*

JARDINS D'ALFÀBIA
17 km (10½ miles) north of Palma, 13 km (8½ miles) south of Sóller.

Jardins d'Alfàbia. Here's a sound you don't often hear in the Majorcan interior: the rush of falling water. The Moorish viceroy of the island developed the springs and hidden irrigation systems here sometime in the 12th century to create this remarkable oasis on the road to Sóller. Here you'll find 40-odd varieties of trees, climbers, and flowering shrubs. The 17th-century manor house, furnished with antiques and painted panels, has a collection of original documents that chronicles the history of the estate. ⊠ *Ctra. Palma–Sóller, Km 17* 🕾 *971/613123* ⊕ *www.jardinesdealfabia.com* 🕾 *€4.50* ◷ *Nov.–Mar., weekdays 9:30–5:30, Sat. 9:30–1; Apr.–Oct., Mon.–Sat. 9:30–6:30.*

SÓLLER

★ *13 km (8 ½ miles) north of Jardins d'Alfàbia, 30 km (19 miles) north of Palma.*

This is one of the most beautiful towns on the island, thick with palatial homes built in the 19th and early 20th centuries by the owners of agricultural estates in the Sierra de Tramuntana, and the merchants who thrived on the export of the region's oranges, lemons, and almonds. Many of the buildings here, like the **Church of Sant Bartomeu** and the **Bank of Sóller**, on the Plaça Constitució, and the nearby **Can Prunera**, are gems of the moderniste style, designed by contemporaries of Antoni Gaudí. The tourist information office in the **town hall,** next to Sant Bartomeu, has a walking tour map of the important sites.

Travel retro to Sóller from Palma on one of the six daily trains (round-trip: €20) from Plaça d'Espanya: a string of wooden coaches with leather-covered seats, dating from 1912.

Visit the Station Building Galleries before you set out on your exploration of the town—and if you're spending the night, book early: Sóller is not overly endowed with hotels.

Return to the station to catch the charming old blue-and-brass trolly (€4) that threads its way through town, down to Port de Sóller. Spend the day at the beach. Better yet: rent a car at the port for the spectacular drive over the Sierra de Tramontana to Deià and Son Marroig, or the Monestary of Lluc.

Station Building Galleries. Maintained by the Fundació Tren de l'Art, Sóller's Station Building Galleries have two small but remarkable collections, one of engravings by Miró, the other of ceramics by Picasso. ⊠ *Pl. Espanya 6* ☎ *971/630301* 🎟 *Free* ☉ *Daily 10:30–6:30.*

DEIÀ

9 km (5½ miles) southwest of Sóller.

★ Deià is perhaps best known as the adopted home of the English poet and writer Robert Graves, who lived here off and on from 1929 until his death in 1985. The village is still a favorite haunt of writers and artists, including Graves's son Tomás, author of *Pa amb oli (Bread and Olive Oil),* a guide to Majorcan cooking, and British painter David Templeton. The setting is unbeatable; all around Deià rise the steep cliffs of the Sierra de Tramuntana. On warm afternoons literati gather at the beach bar in the rocky cove at Cala de Deià, 2 km (1 mile) downhill from the village. Walk up the narrow street to the village church; the small **cemetery** behind it affords views of mountains terraced with olive trees and of the coves below. It's a fitting spot for Graves's final resting place, in a quiet corner beneath a simple slab.

Ca N'Alluny. The Fundació Robert Graves opened this museum dedicated to Deià's most famous resident in Ca N'Alluny, the house he built in 1932. The seaside house is something of a shrine: Graves's furniture and books, personal effects, and the press he used to print many of his works are all preserved. ⊠ *Ctra. Deià-Sóller s/n* ☎ *971/636185* ⊕ *www.lacasaderobertgraves.com* 🎟 *€7* ☉ *Apr.–Oct., weekdays 10–5, Sat. 10–3; Nov., Feb., and Mar., weekdays 9–4, Sat. 9–2; Dec. and Jan., weekdays 10–3.*

SHOPPING

Mallorca's specialties are leather shoes and clothing, porcelain, souvenirs carved from olive wood, handblown glass, artificial pearls, and espadrilles. Top-name fashion boutiques line **Avinguda Jaume III** and the nearby Plaça Joan Carles I. You can find several antiques shops on Plaça Almoina. Less-expensive shopping strips are **Carrer Sindicat** and **Carrer Sant Miquel**—both pedestrian streets running north from the Plaça Major—and the small streets south of the Plaça Major. The **Plaça Major** itself has a modest crafts market Monday, Thursday, Friday, and Saturday 10 to 2. In summer the market is open daily 10 to 2; January and February, it's open weekends only.

Gordiola. Glassmakers since 1719, visit Gordiola for a variety of original bowls, bottles, plates, and decorative objects. The company's factory is in Alguida, on the Palma–Manacor road, where you can watch the glass being blown and even try your hand at making a piece. ⊠ *Carrera Victoria 8, Centro, Palma* ☎ *971/711541.*

Las Columnas. Ceramics from all over the Balearic Islands are sold here. ⊠ *Carrer Sant Domingo 8, San Agustin, Palma* ☎ *971/712221.*

GOLF

Mallorca has more than a score of 18-hole golf courses, among them PGA championship venues of fiendish difficulty. Cruise passengers who want to play a round while in port should make arrangements through their cruise ship.

BEACHES

The closer a beach is to Palma, the more crowded it's likely to be. West of the city is **Palma Nova**; behind the lovely, narrow beach rises one of the most densely developed resorts on the island. **Paguera,** with several small beaches, is the only sizable local resort not overshadowed by highrises. **Camp de Mar,** with a good beach of fine white sand, is small and relatively undeveloped, but is sometimes overrun with day-trippers from other resorts. **Sant Elm,** at the end of this coast, has a pretty little bay and a tree-shaded parking lot. East of Palma, a 5-km (3-mile) stretch of sand runs along the main coastal road from C'an Pastilla to Arenal, forming a package-tour nexus also known collectively as **Playa de Palma**; the crowded beach is long with fine white sand.

WHERE TO EAT

$ ✕ **Café la Lonja.** A great spot for hot chocolate or a unique tea or cof-
TAPAS   fee, this classic establishment in the old fishermen's neighborhood has a young vibe that goes well with the style of the place. Both the sunny terrace in front of the Llotja—a privileged dining spot—and the dining room inside are excellent places for drinks and sandwiches. The seasonal menu might include a salad of tomato, avocado, and Manchego cheese; fluffy quiche; and tapas of squid or mushrooms. It's a good

rendezvous point and watering hole. ⑤ *Average main: €12* ⊠ *Carrer Llotja del Mar 2, Palma* ☎ *971/722799* ⊘ *Closed Sun.*

$ ✕ **La Bóveda.** Within hailing distance of the Llotja, this popular restau-
TAPAS   rant serves tapas and inexpensive platters such as chicken or ham cro-
quettes, grilled cod, garlic shrimp, and *revueltos de ajos con morcilla*
(scrambled eggs with garlic and black sausage). The tables in the back
are always at a premium (they're cooler on summer days), but there's
additional seating at the counter or on stools around upended wine
barrels. The huge portions of traditional tapas are nothing fancy but
very good. ⑤ *Average main: €12* ⊠ *Carrer de la Botería 3, La Llotja,
Palma* ☎ *971/714863* ⊘ *Closed Sun.*

MARSEILLE, FRANCE

Updated
by Jennifer
Ladonne

Marseille may sometimes be given a wide berth by travelers in search of
a Provençal idyll, but it's their loss. Miss it, and you miss one of the most
vibrant, exciting cities in France. With its cubist jumbles of white stone
rising up over a picture-book seaport, bathed in light of blinding clar-
ity and crowned by larger-than-life neo-Byzantine churches, the city's
neighborhoods teem with multiethnic life. Its souk-like African markets
reek deliciously of spices and coffees, and its labyrinthine Vieille Ville
is painted in broad strokes of saffron, cinnamon, and robin's-egg blue.
Feisty and fond of broad gestures, Marseille is a dynamic city, as cosmopolitan now as when the Phoenicians first founded it, and with all the
exoticism of the international shipping port it has been for 2,600 years.
Vital to the Crusades in the Middle Ages and crucial to Louis XIV as
a military port, Marseille flourished as France's market to the world—
and still does today. In 2013 Marseille will be the European Capital of
Culture and will host all manner of special events throughout the year.

ESSENTIALS

CURRENCY

The euro.

HOURS

Stores are open Monday through Saturday 9–7, but many close at
lunchtime (usually noon–2 or 3) and some will open later and on Sunday during July and August. Museums are open 10–5, but most are
closed on either Monday or Tuesday.

TELEPHONES

Tri-band GSM phones work in France. You can buy prepaid phone
cards at telecom shops, news vendors, and tobacconists in all towns
and cities. Phone cards can be used for local or international calls.
Orange, SFR, Bouygues Telecom, and Virgin are leading telecom companies. If you have an unlocked GSM phone, LeFrenchMobile (⊕ *www.
lefrenchmobile.com*) offers SIM cards (and micro SIM cards) with support in English, unlimited validity of credits, and prepurchase online.

COMING ASHORE

The Marseille Cruise Terminal is north of the Vieux Port historic area
and has benefited from a €90 million redevelopment. It now offers
three different docking areas depending on the size of the vessel and

a state-of-the-art welcome center with an ATM, shops, bars, and restaurants. Aside from this, the terminal is in an industrial area and is too distant to allow you to walk into the city. Most cruise lines offer shuttle service into town, but you should spring for a taxi if you don't take the shuttle.

A taxi from the cruise terminal into town is approximately €30 and takes around 20 minutes. Once in the Vieux Port area, most of the major attractions are reachable on foot. Taxis are plentiful and can provide tourist itineraries. Single journeys begin at €2.30 and are €0.80 per km thereafter.

Although there is no reason to drive if you're just staying in Marseille, renting a vehicle is the ideal way to explore the beautiful Provençal towns and landscapes around the city. Expect to pay around €75 per day for an economy manual vehicle.

MARSEILLE BEST BETS

Order bouillabaise. This aromatic fish stew is one of the world's most famous dishes, and originated here as a way for fishermen to use the leftover catch.

Stroll around Vieux Port and La Panier. The Vieux Port bustles with activity, but especially during the morning fish market. Neighboring Le Panier is a maze of narrow streets and picturesque corners with pretty boutiques and good museums.

Centre de la Vieille Charite. The museums here have important collections and artifacts from civilizations and societies from around the world.

EXPLORING MARSEILLE

★ **Abbaye St-Victor.** Founded in the fourth century by St. Cassien, who sailed into Marseille full of fresh ideas on monasticism that he acquired in Palestine and Egypt, this church grew to formidable proportions. With a Romanesque design, the structure would be as much at home in the Middle East as its founder was. The **crypt,** St. Cassien's original, is buried under the medieval church, and in the evocative nooks and crannies you can find the fifth-century sarcophagus that allegedly holds the martyr's remains. Upstairs, a reliquary contains what's left of St. Victor, who was ground to death between millstones, probably by Romans. There's also a passage into tiny **catacombs** where Early Christians worshipped St. Lazarus and Mary Magdalene, said to have washed ashore at Stes-Maries-de-la-Mer. The boat in which they landed is reproduced in canoe-shaped cookies called *navettes,* which are sold during the annual procession for Candelmas in February as well as year-round. ⊠ *3 rue de l'Abbaye, Rive Neuve* ☎ *04–96–11–22–60* ⊕ *www.saintvictor.net* 🖃 *Crypt €2* ☉ *Daily 9–7.*

Cathédrale de la Nouvelle Major. This gargantuan, neo-Byzantine 19th-century fantasy was built under Napoléon III—but not before he'd ordered the partial destruction of the lovely 11th-century original, once a perfect example of the Provençal Romanesque style. You can view the flashy decor—marble and rich red porphyry inlay—in the newer of the two churches; the medieval one is being restored. ⊠ *Pl. de la Major, Le Panier.*

★ **Centre de la Vieille Charité** (*Center of the Old Charity*). At the top of the Panier district you'll find this superb ensemble of 17th- and 18th-century architecture designed as a hospice for the homeless by Marseillais artist-architects Pierre and Jean Puget. Even if you don't enter the museums, walk around the inner court, studying the retreating perspective of triple arcades and admiring the baroque chapel with its novel egg-peaked dome. Of the complex's two museums, the larger is the **Musée d'Archéologie Méditerranéenne** (Museum of Mediterranean Archaeology), with a sizable collection of pottery and statuary from classical Mediterranean civilization, elementally labeled (for example, "pot"). There's also a display on the mysterious Celt-like Ligurians who first peopled the coast, cryptically presented with emphasis on the digs instead of the finds themselves. The best of the lot is the evocatively mounted Egyptian collection, the second largest in France after the Louvre's. There are mummies, hieroglyphs, and gorgeous sarcophagi in a tomblike setting. Upstairs, the **Musée d'Arts Africains, Océaniens, et Amérindiens** (Museum of African, Oceanic, and American Indian Art) creates a theatrical foil for the works' intrinsic drama: the spectacular masks and sculptures are mounted along a pure black wall, lighted indirectly, with labels across the aisle. ⊠ *2 rue de la Charité, Le Panier* ☎ *04–91–14–58–80* ☑ *€3 per museum* ☉ *May–Sept., Tues.–Sun. 10–6.*

★ **Château d'If.** François I, in the 16th century, recognized the strategic advantage of an island fortress surveying the mouth of Marseille's vast harbor and built this imposing edifice. Its effect as a deterrent was so successful that the fortress never saw combat, and was eventually converted into a prison. It was here that Alexandre Dumas locked up his most famous character, the Count of Monte Cristo. Though the count was fictional, the hole through which Dumas had him escape is real enough, on display in the cells. On the other hand, the real-life Man in the Iron Mask, whose cell is also erroneously on display, was not imprisoned here. The IF Frioul Express boat ride (from the Quai des Belges, €10; for information call ☎ *04–91–46–54–65*) and the views from the broad terrace are worth the trip. ☎ *08–26–50–05–00* ⊕ *if.monuments-nationaux.fr/en* ☑ *€5* ☉ *Mid-May–mid-Sept., daily 9:40–5:40; mid-Sept.–mid-May, daily 9–5:30. Closed Mon. mid-Sept.–Mar.*

Fodor's Choice
★ **Ferry Boat.** This Marseille treasure departs from the Quai below the Hôtel de Ville. For a pittance (although technically free, it is appropriate to tip the crew) you can file onto this little wooden barge and chug across the Vieux Port. ⊠ *Pl. des Huiles on Quai de Rive Neuve side and Hôtel de Ville on Quai du Port, Vieux Port* ☑ *Free.*

Fort St-Nicolas and Fort St-Jean. These twin forts guard the entrance to the Vieux Port. In order to keep the feisty, rebellious Marseillais under his thumb, Louis XIV had the fortresses built with the guns pointing *toward* the city. The Marseillais, whose identity has always been mixed with a healthy dose of irony, are quite proud of this display of the king's doubts about their allegiance. To view the guns, climb up to the Jardin du Pharo. In spring of 2013 Fort St-Jean will open under the banner of the Musée National des Civilisations de L'Europe et de la Mediterranée (National Museum of the Civilizations of Europe and the Mediterranean), housing in part the folk-art collection of the former Musée

des Arts et Traditions Populaires in Paris. ⊠ *Quai du Port, Vieux Port* ☎ *04–96–13–80–90* ⊕ *www.mucem.org.*

★ **Le Panier.** This is the old heart of Marseille, a maze of high-shuttered houses looming over narrow cobbled streets, *montées* (stone stairways), and tiny squares. Long decayed and neglected, the quarter is the principal focus of the city's efforts at urban renewal. Wander this neighborhood at will, making sure to stroll along Rue du Panier, the montée des Accoules, Rue du Petit-Puits, and Rue des Muettes.

★ **Musée d'Histoire de Marseille** (*Marseille Museum of History*). A modern and open space, this museum illuminates Massalia's history with a treasure of archaeological finds and miniature models of the city as it appeared in various stages of history. Best by far is the presentation of Marseille's Classical halcyon days. There's a recovered wreck of a Roman cargo boat, its third-century wood amazingly preserved, and the hull of a Greek boat dating from the fourth century BC. The model of the Greek city should be authentic—it's based on the eyewitness description of Aristotle. The museum is closed for renovation until late 2012. ⊠ *Centre Bourse, entrance on Rue de Bir-Hakeim, Vieux Port* ☎ *04–91–90–42–22* ⊠ *€3 joint ticket with Jardin des Vestiges* ⊙ *June–Sept., Mon.–Sat. noon–7; Oct.–May., Tues.–Sun. 10–5.*

Notre-Dame-de-la-Garde. Towering above the city and visible for miles around, this overscaled neo-Byzantine monument was erected in 1853 by Napoléon III. The interior is a Technicolor bonanza of red-and-beige stripes and glittering mosaics, and the gargantuan *Madonna and Child* on the steeple (almost 30 feet high) is covered in real gold leaf. While the panoply of naive ex-votos, mostly thanking the Virgin for deathbed interventions and shipwreck survivals, is a remarkable sight, most impressive are the views of the seaside city at your feet. ⊠ *Off bd. André Aune ✤ On foot, climb up Cours Pierre Puget, cross Jardin Pierre Puget, cross bridge to Rue Vauvenargues, and hike up to Pl. Edon. Or catch Bus 60 from Cours Jean-Ballard* ☎ *04–91–13–40–80* ⊙ *May–Sept., daily 7 am–8 pm; Oct.–Apr., daily 7–7.*

SHOPPING

Marseille offers contrasting shopping opportunities. For lovers of French haute couture there are many boutiques in the new town stocking the major designer labels—Christian Lacroix is a local boy—plus a thriving new fashion scene of young designers selling their own ready-to-wear collections from stylish galleries. Cours Julien is lined with stores, while Rue de la Tour in the Opera district is a center of modern design, known locally as "Fashion Street."

By contrast, the city, particularly Le Panier and rue St-Ferréol, also has numerous shops selling regional crafts and delicacies, including bright fabrics of blue and yellow, pottery, olive-wood items, plus delicious olives, olive oils, honey, tapenade (an olive paste), and dried herbs. **Savon de Marseille** (Marseille soap) is a household standard in France, often sold as a satisfyingly crude and hefty block in odorless olive-oil green. But its chichi offspring are dainty pastel guest soaps in almond, lemon, vanilla, and other scents.

Four des Navettes. The famous bakery Four des Navettes, up the street from Notre-Dame-de-la-Garde, makes orange-spice, shuttle-shape *navettes*. These cookies are modeled on the little boat in which it is said that Mary Magdalene and Lazarus washed up onto the nearby shores. ✉ *136 rue Sainte, Garde Hill* ☎ *04–91–33–32–12* ⊕ *www.fourdesnavettes.com.*

WHERE TO EAT

$$$$

SEAFOOD

✕ **Chez Fonfon.** Tucked into the film-like tiny fishing port Vallon des Auffes, this Marseillais landmark has one of the loveliest settings in greater Marseille. Once presided over by cult chef "Fonfon," it used to be a favorite movie-star hangout. A variety of fresh seafood, impeccably grilled, steamed, or roasted in salt crust are served in two pretty dining rooms with picture windows overlooking the fishing boats that supply your dinner. Try classic bouillabaisse served with all the bells and whistles—broth, hot-chili rouille, and flamboyant table-side filleting. ⑤ *Average main: €50* ✉ *140 rue du Vallon des Auffes* ☎ *04–91–52–14–38* ⊕ *www.chez-fonfon.com* ⌂ *Reservations essential* ⊗ *Closed Sun. and Mon. in winter; Sun. and Mon. lunch in summer. Closed first 2 wks in Jan.*

$$

PIZZA

✕ **Étienne.** A historic Le Panier hole-in-the-wall, this small pizzeria is filled with politicos and young professionals who enjoy the personality of chef Stéphane Cassero, who was once famous for announcing the price of the meal only after he'd had the chance to look you over. Remarkably little has changed over the years, except now there is a posted menu (with prices). Brace yourself for an epic meal, starting with a large anchovy pizza from the wood-burning oven, then fried squid, eggplant gratin, and a slab of rare grilled beef, all served with a background of laughter, rich patois, and abuse from the chef. ⑤ *Average main: €20* ✉ *43 rue de la Lorette, Le Panier* ⊟ *No credit cards.*

MENORCA, SPAIN (MAHÓN)

Updated by
Joanna Styles

Menorca, the northernmost Balearic Island, is a knobby, cliff-bound plateau with a single central hill—El Toro—from whose 1,100-foot summit you can see the whole island. Prehistoric monuments—*taulas* (huge stone T-shapes), *talayots* (spiral stone cones), and *navetes* (stone structures shaped like overturned boats)—left by the first Neolithic settlers are everywhere on the island, rising up out of a landscape of small, tidy fields bounded by hedgerows and drystone walls. Tourism came late to Menorca, but having sat out the early Balearic boom, Menorca has avoided many of the other islands' industrialization troubles: there are no high-rise hotels, and the herringbone road system, with a single central highway, means that each resort is small and separate.

ESSENTIALS
CURRENCY
The euro.

HOURS

Museums generally open 9 until 7 or 8, many are closed on Monday, and some close in the afternoon. Most stores are open Monday through Saturday 9 to 1:30 and 5 to 8, but a few tourist shops may open in the afternoon and also on Sunday between May and September.

PRIVATE TOURS

Rutas Menorca. The company organizes excursions and hiking trips round the island. ☎ *685/747308* ⊕ *rutasmenorca.com.*

TELEPHONES

Most tri-band or quad-band GSM phones will work in Spain, where services are 3G-compatible. Public kiosks accept phone cards that support international calls (cards sold in press shops, bars and telecom shops). Major companies include Vodafone.

COMING ASHORE

Vessels dock at the commercial port in Mahón, which sits directly below the Old Town. From here it is a short but steep walk up to the heart of the Old Town. There are few facilities at the port itself, but a selection of shops and cafés line the shady street outside. Taxis wait outside the port, and drivers can be hired for the day to do tourist itineraries.

Menorca is a small island, and you can travel across it in 40 minutes by vehicle. Public bus services are modern and reliable, but services to the smaller towns may not be frequent. The bus station is at the far side of Mahón and involves a steep climb from the port area. It might be advisable to take a taxi to the station. The journey time from Mahón to Ciutadella is 1 hour. Renting a car is the ideal way to get around; expect to pay as much as €80 per day for an economy manual vehicle (but rates can be much cheaper—from €25—if you pick up a car at the airport).

EXPLORING MENORCA

MAHÓN

Established as the island's capital in 1722, when the British began their nearly 80-year occupation, Mahón stills bears the stamp of its former rulers. The streets nearest the port are lined with four-story Georgian town houses in various states of repair; the Mahónese still nurse a craving for Chippendale furniture, and drink gin. You'll notice as you travel around the town and island that Menorcans use both Catalan and Castillian names in signage, Catalon most often by the people themselves. So you may hear Mahón called, simply, Maó by the locals, and will also see this on signs.

Ajuntament. From here, walk up Carrer Alfons III and turn right at the Ajuntament to Carrer Isabel II, a street lined with many Georgian homes. ✉ *Pl. de la Constitució 1* ☎ *971/369800.*

La Verge del Carme. This church has a fine painted and gilded altarpiece. Adjoining the church are the cloisters, now a **market,** with stalls selling fresh produce and a variety of local specialties such as cheeses and sausages. The central courtyard is a venue for a variety of cultural events throughout the year. ✉ *Pl. del Carme* ☎ *971/362402.*

2

Plaça de la Conquesta. Behind the church of Santa María, the Plaça de la Conquesta has a statue of Alfons III of Aragón, who wrested the island from the Moors in 1287.

Puerta de San Roque. At the end of Carrer Rector Mort, this massive gate is the only surviving portion of the 14th-century city walls. They were rebuilt in 1587 to protect the city from the pirate Barbarossa (Redbeard).

Santa María. Dating from the 13th century, this church was rebuilt during the British occupation and restored after being sacked during the civil war. The church's pride is its 3,200-pipe baroque organ, imported from Austria in 1810. From May or June through September, midday concerts are held here 11:30 to 12:30 every day except Sunday. ⊠ *Pl. de la Constitució* ☎ *971/363949.*

Teatre Principal. Built in 1824 as an opera house—the oldest in Spain—the Teatre Principal has five tiers of boxes, red plush seats, and gilded woodwork: a La Scala in miniature. Lovingly restored, it still hosts a brief opera season. If you're visiting in the first week of December or June, buy tickets well in advance. ⊠ *Carrer Costa Deià 40* ☎ *971/355603* ⊕ *www.teatremao.com.*

FORNELLS
35 km (21 miles) northwest of Mahón.

The first fortifications built here to defend the Bay of Fornells from pirates date to 1625. A little village (full-time population: 500) of whitewashed houses with red tile roofs. The bay—Menorca's second largest and its deepest—offers ideal conditions for windsurfing, sailing, and scuba diving. The real draw of Fornells is its restaurants. This is the best place on the island to try Menorca's specialty, *Es Pla caldereta de langosta* (lobster stew).

> **MENORCA BEST BETS**
>
> **Explore the Gothic and Renaissance core of Ciutadella.** The island's old capital was the religious and commercial heartbeat for several hundred years.
>
> **Tuck into a pot of** *Es Pla caldereta de langosta.* This lobster stew is always the most expensive item on the menu, but it's Menorca's pièce de résistance.
>
> **Take to the water.** The bay at Fornells is the perfect place to take up sailing or windsurfing.

CIUTADELLA
44 km (27 miles) west of Mahón.

Ciutadella was Menorca's capital before the British settled in Mahón, and its history is richer. As you arrive via the ME1, the main artery across the island from Mahón, turn left at the second roundabout and follow the ring road to the Passeig Maritim; at the end, near the **Castell de Sant Nicolau** watchtower (visits daily, June–October 10–1 and 5–10) is a **monument to David Glasgow Farragut**, the first admiral of the U.S. Navy, whose father emigrated from Ciutadella to the United States. From here, take Passeig de Sant Nicolau to the **Plaça de s'Esplanada,** and park near the Plaça d'es Born.

Ajuntament. From a passage on the left side of Ciutadella's columned and crenellated Ajuntament, on the west side of the Born, steps lead up to the **Mirador d'es Port,** a lookout from which you can survey the harbor. ⊠ *Pl. d'Es Born.*

Catedral. Carrer Major leads to the Gothic Catedral, which has some beautifully carved choir stalls. The side chapel has round Moorish arches, remnants of the mosque that once stood on this site; the bell tower is a converted minaret. ⊠ *Pl. de la Catedral at Pl. Píus XII, Ciutadella, Minorca.*

Convento de Santa Clara. Carrer del Seminari is lined on the west side with some of the city's most impressive historic buildings. Among them is the 17th-century Convento de Santa Clara, which hosts Ciutadella's summer festival of classical music. ⊠ *Carrer del Seminari at Carrer Obispo Vila.*

Museu Municipal. The museum houses artifacts of Minorca's prehistoric, Roman, and medieval past, including records of land grants made by Alfons III to the local nobility after defeating the Moors. It occupies an ancient defense tower, the Bastió de Sa Font (Bastion of the Fountain), at the east end of the harbor. ⊠ *Pl. de Sa Font s/n* ☎ 971/380297 💶 *€2.25, free Wed.* ☾ *May–Sept., Tues.–Sat. 10–2 and 6–9; Oct.–Apr., Tues.–Sat. 10–2.*

Palau Salort. On Carrer Major des Born, this is the only noble home open to the public—though at unpredictable times. The coats of arms on the ceiling are those of the families Salort (*sal* and *ort*, a salt pit and a garden) and Martorell (a marten). ⊠ *Carrer Major des Born* 🖼 *€2* 🕓 *May–Oct., Mon.–Sat. 10–2.*

Palau Torresaura. The blocklong 19th-century Palau Torresaura was built by the Baron of Torresaura, one of the noble families from Aragón and Catalonia that moved to Minorca after it was captured from the Moors in the 13th century. The interesting facade faces the plaza, though the entrance is on the side street. It is not open to the public. ⊠ *Carrer Major del Born 8.*

Port. Ciutadella's port is accessible from steps that lead down from Carrer Sant Sebastià. The waterfront here is lined with seafood restaurants, some of which burrow into caverns far under the Born.

SHOPPING

Menorca is known for shoes and leather, cheese, gin (introduced during British rule)—and recently, wine. The fine supple quality of the leather here serves high-class couturiers around the world, the surplus being sold in island factory shops. The streets of the compact center of Mahón are excellent for shopping.

Jaime Mascaro. The showroom here, on the main highway from Alaior to Cuitadella, features not only shoes and bags but fine leather coats and belts for men and women. ⊠ *Poligon Industrial s/n, Ferreries* ☎ *971/374500.*

Marks. In Mahón, buy leather goods at Marks. ⊠ *Sa Ravaleta 18, Mahón* ☎ *971/362660.*

Pons Quintana. In Alaior, this showroom has a full-length window overlooking the factory where its ultrachic women's shoes are made. It's closed weekends. ⊠ *Calle San Antonio 120, Alaior* ☎ *971/371050.*

Xoriguer. One gastronomic legacy of the British occupation was gin. Visit the distillery for Xoriguer, on Mahón's quayside near the ferry terminal, where you can take a guided tour, sample various types of gin, and buy some to take home. ⊠ *Anden de Poniente 91, Mahón* ☎ *971/362197.*

ACTIVITIES

Several miles long and a mile wide, but with a narrow entrance to the sea and virtually no waves, the Bay of Fornells gives the windsurfing and sailing beginner a feeling of security and the expert plenty of excitement.

Wind Fornells. Here you can rent boards, dinghies, and catamarans and take lessons. It's open May to October. ⊠ *Carrer Nou 33, Es Mercadal* ☎ *971/188150, 659/577760* ⊕ *www.windfornells.com.*

WHERE TO EAT

$$

SEAFOOD

✕ **El Jàgaro.** This simple waterfront restaurant, at the east end of the harbor promenade, is a local favorite. The lunchtime crowd comes for the platter of lightly fried mixed fish with potatoes, while in the evening you can enjoy grilled *pescado de roca* (rockfish) or *sepia* (cuttlefish). The *ortigues* (sea anemones) are a house specialty not to be missed. The menu takes a quantum leap in price for the €75 spiny lobster, a delicacy in its various forms. The prix-fixe lunch is a good value at €15.50. ⑤ *Average main: €22* ⊠ *Moll de Llevant 334–35* ☎ *971/362390* ⊘ *Closed Mon.; no dinner Sun. Nov.–Mar.*

$$$

SPANISH

Fodor's Choice

★

✕ **Es Moli de Foc.** Originally a flour mill—*de foc* means "of fire," signifying that the mill was operated by internal combustion—this is the oldest building in the village of Sant Climent, about 4 km (2½ miles) southwest of town. The interior, with paintings by local artists on the mellow yellow walls, is inviting and the food is exceptional. Don't miss the prawn carpaccio with cured Mahón cheese and artichoke oil or the black paella with monkfish and squid. Order off the menu for the *carrilleras de ternera* (boiled beef cheeks) with potato purée, or ask for the separate menu of *arrozes* (rice dishes)—the best on the island and arguably one of the best in Spain. End with Minorcan cheese ice cream and figs. In summer, book a table on the terrace. With a brewery now installed on the premises, and visible behind glass, you'll know what to drink. ⑤ *Average main: €24* ⊠ *Carrer Sant Llorenç 65, Sant Climent* ☎ *971/153222* ⊕ *www.esmolidefoc.es* ⊘ *Closed Jan. and Mon. Oct.–May. No dinner Sun.*

MESSINA, ITALY (FOR TAORMINA AND MT. ETNA)

Updated by Bruce Leimsidor

Sicily has beckoned seafaring wanderers since the trials of Odysseus were first sung in Homer's *Odyssey*. Strategically poised between Europe and Africa, this island has been an important center of every great civilization on the Mediterranean: Greek and Roman; then Arab and Norman; and finally French, Spanish, and Italian. Today Sicily offers the remains of sackings past: graceful Byzantine mosaics rubbing elbows with Greek temples, Roman amphitheaters, Byzantine and Romanesque churches, and baroque flights of fancy. Messina's ancient history lists a series of disasters, but the city nevertheless managed to develop a fine university and a thriving cultural environment. On December 28, 1908, Messina changed from a flourishing metropolis of 120,000 to a heap of rubble, shaken to pieces by an earthquake that produced a tidal wave and left 80,000 dead and the city almost completely leveled. For this reason Messina has few historic treasures, but the town makes a good jumping-off point for explorations of nearby wonders.

ESSENTIALS
CURRENCY
The euro.

HOURS

Shops are generally open 9 to 1 and 3:30 to 8, and are closed Sunday and Monday morning most of the year. Summer (June to September) hours are usually 9 to 1 and 4 to 8.

PRIVATE TOURS

Sicily Travel Net offers guided tours to Taormina and Etna from Messina. Prices depend on the number of travelers in the party, the season, and the qualifications and language of the tour guide.

Contacts Sicily Travel Net. ☏ *(39)360/397930 in Italy* ⊕ *www.sicilytourguides.net/.*

TELEPHONES

Tri-band GSM phones work in Italy. You can buy prepaid phone cards at telecom shops, news-vendors, and tobacconists in all towns and cities. Phone cards can be used for local or international calls.

COMING ASHORE

While some cruise ships do dock directly in Giardini-Naxos, the port far below Taormina, most ships dock in the main port of Messina. Passenger facilities cater to the many commercial ferry passengers who enter Sicily here, and though there are refreshment stands, they are often busy. There is no shuttle service, but it is possible to walk into Messina. Taxis wait at the port entrance, and it's a five-minute transfer to the train station.

It is possible to reach Taormina by train from Messina followed by the cable car from Giardini-Naxos up to Taormina proper. Most services take around an hour and cost €3.50 to €7.50 each way depending on the time of day; note, however, that while trains between Messina and Taormina run frequently in the afternoon and evening, there are no trains between 9:40 am and 12:10 pm. Taxis in Messina charge approximately €3.05 initially, then €0.80 per km with an increment of €0.13 per 140m when the taxi travels at less than 20 kph (12 mph). Mt. Etna is not easy to reach by public transport.

Taormina makes a good departure point for excursions around—but not always to the top of—Mt. Etna, with private companies offering a guiding service. A rental car would allow you to explore much of northern Sicily during your day in port. Rental costs are approximately €60 per day for a compact manual vehicle.

EXPLORING NORTHEASTERN SICILY

MESSINA

Duomo. The reconstruction of Messina's Norman and Romanesque Duomo, originally built by the Norman king Roger II and consecrated in 1197, has retained much of the original plan—including a handsome crown of Norman battlements, an enormous apse, and a splendid wood-beam ceiling. The adjoining bell tower contains one of the largest and most complex mechanical clocks in the world: constructed in 1933, it has a host of gilded automatons (a roaring lion among them), that spring into action every day at the stroke of noon. ⊠ *Piazza del Duomo* ☏ *090/774895* ⊙ *Daily 9–1 and 4–7.*

Taormina

Castello Saraceno

V. Luigi Prandello

Tunnel

Porta Messina

Palazzo Corvaja

Pza. Vittorio Emanuele

Teatro Comunale

V. Leonardo da Vinci

500 ft

Circonvallazione

Naumachia

V. Teatro Greco

San Domenico

Teatro Greco

Porta Catania

San Agostino

Pza. San Aprile

Archeological Area

Pza. San Antonio

Corso Umberto I

V. Roma

V. Bagnoli Croce

Duomo

V. Roma

Villa Comunale

Piazzale San Domenico

Taormina Mare

Parque Duchi di Cenaro

Tyrrhenian Sea

Golfo di Gioia

Mortelle

Capo d'Orlando

Milazzo

A20

Messina see detail map

Patti

S113

Reggio di Calabria

20 miles

30 km

Strait of Messina

Savoca

A18

Randazzo

Forzad'Aqro

S114

Taormina see detail map

Castelmola

Ionian Sea

Bronte

Mt. Etna

Riposto

Giardini-Naxos

Adrano

Giarre

Nicolosi

Acireale

Biancavilla

Paterno

A19

Messina

Ple. Don Blasco

V. Rizzi

V. Tom. Cannizzaro

Garibaldi

Duomo

S192

Lgo. Seggiola

Pza. Cairoli

Vle. S. Martino

Vle. la Farina

Catania

Golfo di Catania

S288

S114

Northeastern Sicily

1,000 ft

TAORMINA

43 km (27 miles) southwest of Messina.

The medieval cliff-hanging town of Taormina is overrun with tourists and trinket shops, but its natural beauty is still hard to argue with. The view of the sea and Mt. Etna from its jagged cactus-covered cliffs is as close to perfection as a panorama can get, especially on clear days, when the snow-capped volcano's white puffs of smoke rise against the blue sky. Writers have extolled Taormina's beauty almost since its founding in the 6th century BC by Greeks from Naples; Goethe and D. H. Lawrence were among its more recent well-known enthusiasts. The town's boutique-lined main streets become tiresome pretty quickly, but don't overlook the many hiking paths that wind through the beautiful hills surrounding Taormina. Nor should you miss the trip up to stunning Castelmola—whether on foot or by car.

Castello Saraceno. An unrelenting 20-minute walk up the Via Crucis footpath takes you to the church of the Madonna della Rocca, hollowed out of the limestone rock. Above it towers the medieval Castello Saraceno. Though the gate to the castle has been locked for decades, it's worth the climb just for the panoramic views. ⊠ *Monte Tauro.*

Palazzo Corvaja. Many of Taormina's 14th- and 15th-century palaces have been carefully preserved. Especially beautiful is the Palazzo Corvaja, with characteristic black-lava and white-limestone inlays. Today it houses the tourist office and the **Museo di Arte e Storia Popolare,** which has a collection of puppets and folk art, carts, and crèches. ⊠ *Largo Santa Caterina* ☎ *0942/23243* ✉ *Museum €2.60* ☻ *Museum Tues.–Sun. 9–1 and 4–8.*

Taormina Mare. Below the main city of Taormina is Taormina Mare, where summertime beachgoers jostle for space on a pebble beach against the scenic backdrop of the aptly named island of Isolabella.

Teatro Greco. The Greeks put a premium on finding impressive locations to stage their dramas, such as Taormina's hillside Teatro Greco. Beyond the columns you can see the town's rooftops spilling down the hillside, the arc of the coastline, and Mount Etna in the distance. The theater was built during the 3rd century BC and rebuilt by the Romans during the 2nd century AD. Its acoustics are exceptional: even today a stage whisper can be heard in the last rows. In summer Taormina hosts an arts festival of music and dance events and a film festival; many performances are held in the Teatro Greco. ⊠ *Via Teatro Greco* ☎ *0942/620198* ✉ *€6* ☻ *Daily 9–1 hr before sunset.*

★ **Villa Comunale.** Stroll down Via Bagnoli Croce from the main Corso Umberto to the Villa Comunale. Also known as the Parco Duca di

---

MESSINA BEST BETS

Get close up and personal with Mt. Etna. Europe's only active volcano continues to enchant with its regular fiery plumes.

Explore Taormina. This picturesque hilltop village hosts excellent Greek and Roman remains and has many good shops and galleries.

See the view from Castello Normanno. The views from the walls of this citadel at Castelmola are spectacular.

Cesarò, the lovely public gardens were designed by Florence Trevelyan Cacciola, a Scottish lady "invited" to leave England following a romantic liaison with the future Edward VII (1841–1910). Arriving in Taormina in 1889, she married a local professor and devoted herself to the gardens, filling them with native Mediterranean and exotic plants, ornamental pavilions (known as the beehives), and fountains. Stop by the panoramic bar, which has stunning views. ⊘ *Daily 9 am–sunset.*

CASTELMOLA
5 km (3 miles) west of Taormina.

You may think that Taormina has spectacular views, but tiny Castelmola, floating 1,800 feet above sea level, takes the word *scenic* to a whole new level. Along the cobblestone streets within the ancient walls, the 360-degree panoramas of mountain, sea, and sky are so ubiquitous that you almost get used to them (but not quite). Collect yourself with a sip of the sweet almond wine (best served cold) made in the local bars, or with lunch at one of the humble pizzerias or panino shops.

A 10-minute drive on a winding but well-paved road leads from Taormina to Castelmola; you must park in one of the public lots on the hillside below and climb a series of staircases to reach the center. On a nice day, hikers are in for a treat if they walk instead of driving. It's a serious uphill climb, but the 1½-km (¾-mile) path is extremely well maintained and not too challenging. You'll begin at Porta Catania in Taormina, with a walk along Via Apollo Arcageta past the Chiesa di San Francesco di Paolo on the left. The Strada Comunale della Chiusa then leads past Piazza Andromaco, revealing good views of the jagged promontory of Cocolanazzo di Mola to the north. Allow 45 minutes on the way up, a half-hour down. There's another, slightly longer—2-km (1-mile)—path that heads up from Porta Messina past the Roman aqueduct, Convento dei Cappuccini, and the northeastern side of Monte Tauro. You could take one path up and the other down.

Fodor's Choice **Castello Normanno.** The best place to savor Castelmola's views is from the ★ ruins of Castello Normanno, reached by a set of steep staircases rising out of the town center. In all of Sicily there may be no spot more scenic than atop it: you can gaze upon two coastlines, smoking Mount Etna, and the town spilling down the mountainside. Come during daylight hours to take full advantage of the vista.

MT. ETNA
64 km (40 miles) southwest of Taormina.

Fodor's Choice Mt. Etna is one of the world's major active volcanoes and is the largest ★ and highest in Europe—the cone of the crater rises to 10,902 feet above sea level. Plato sailed in just to catch a glimpse in 387 BC; in the 9th century AD the oldest gelato of all was shaved off of its snowy slopes; and in the 21st century the volcano still claims annual headlines. Etna has erupted 12 times in the past 30 or so years, most spectacularly in 1971, 1983, 2001, and 2002; many of these eruptions wiped out cable-car stations. There were two eruptions in 2008 and a sizeable one in 2009. The refuge at Sapienza, however, is currently operational. Although each eruption is predictably declared a "tragedy" by the media, owing to the economic losses, Etna almost never threatens human life. Travel

2

in the proximity of the crater depends on Mt. Etna's temperament, but you can walk up and down the enormous lava dunes and wander over its moonlike surface of dead craters. The rings of vegetation change markedly as you rise, with vineyards and pine trees gradually giving way to growths of broom and lichen. Taormina makes a good departure point for excursions around—but not always to the top of—Mt. Etna.

Circumetnea. Instead of climbing up Mount Etna, you can circle it on the Circumetnea, which runs near the volcano's base. The private railway almost circles the volcano, running 114 km (71 miles) between Catania and Riposto—the towns are just 30 km (19 miles) apart by the coast road. The line is small, slow, and only single-track, but has some dramatic vistas of the volcano and goes through lava fields. The trip takes about four hours, with about 10 departures a day. After you've made the trip one way, you can get back to where you started from on the much quicker, but less scenic, conventional state railway line between Catania and Riposto. ⊠ *Via Caronda 352, Catania* ☎ *095/541250* ⊕ *www.circumetnea.it* ✉ *€7.25 round-trip* ☉ *Mon.–Sat. 6 am–9 pm.*

SHOPPING

Taormina is the place in eastern Sicily for shopping, especially along Corso Umberto I and the surrounding alleyways, where chic boutiques sell lace and linen, including placemats and napkins. The island as a whole is famed for its ceramics, particularly its practical folk pottery from Caltagirone, close by along the north coast. Marble and wrought iron are also fashioned into souvenir pieces, and antique shops are numerous, though prices can be high.

Pasticceria Etna. A marzipan devotee should not leave Taormina without trying one of the almond sweets—maybe in the guise of the ubiquitous *fico d'India* (prickly pear) or in more unusual *frutta martorana* varieties—at Pasticceria Etna. A block of almond paste makes a good souvenir—you can bring it home to make an almond latte or granita. It's closed Monday. ⊠ *Corso Umberto 112, Taormina* ☎ *0942/24735.*

ACTIVITIES

Mount Etna is a natural magnet for adventure seekers, but because the volcano is active you should consult experts before tackling the peak. Hiking is certainly a popular choice on the lower slopes, while climbing Mt. Etna proves more challenging.

Club Alpino Italiano. Club Alpino Italiano in Catania is a great resource for Mount Etna climbing and hiking guides. If you have some experience and don't like a lot of hand holding, these are the guides for you. ⊠ *Via Messina 593/a, Catania* ☎ *095/7153515* ✉ *giorgiopace@ katamail.com* ⊕ *www.caicatania.it.*

Gruppo Guide Etna Nord. If you're a beginning climber, call the Gruppo Guide Etna Nord to arrange for a guide. Their service is a little more personalized—and expensive—than others. Reserve ahead. ⊠ *Via Roma 93, Linguaglossa* ☎ *095/7774502, 348/0125167* ⊕ *www.guidetnanord.com.*

WHERE TO EAT

$$ ✕ **Al Padrino.** The jovial owner of this stripped-down trattoria keeps
SICILIAN everything running smoothly. Meat and fish dishes are served with equal
verve in the white-wall dining room. Start with antipasti like eggplant
stuffed with ricotta; then move on to supremely Sicilian dishes such
as pasta with chickpeas or *polpette di alalunga* (albacore croquettes).
⑤ *Average main: €22* ⊠ *Via Santa Cecilia 54* ☎ *090/2921000* ⊕ *www.
alpadrino.it* ⊗ *Closed Sun. and Aug. No dinner Sat.*

$$$$ ✕ **La Piazzetta.** Sheltered from the city's hustle and bustle, this elegant little
SICILIAN eatery exudes a mood of relaxed sophistication. Classic dishes such as
risotto *alla marinara* (with seafood) are competently prepared, the grilled
fish is extremely fresh, and the service is informal and friendly. The modest
room has simple white walls—you're not paying for a view. ⑤ *Average
main: €32* ⊠ *Vico Francesco Paladini, off Corso Umberto* ☎ *0942/626317*
⊗ *Closed Nov., and 2 weeks in Feb. No lunch Mon.–Thurs., June–Sept.*

MONTE CARLO, MONACO

Updated
by Jennifer
Ladonne

In 1297 the Grimaldi family seized this fortified town and, except for a
short break under Napoléon, they have ruled here ever since. The Princi-
pality of Monaco covers 473 acres; it would fit comfortably inside New
York's Central Park while its 5,000 citizens would fill only a small frac-
tion of the seats in Yankee Stadium. The Grimaldis made money from
gambling and attracted a well-heeled, monied crowd, but the whole
world watched as Hollywood princess Grace Kelly wed Prince Rainier
ruler of Monaco to put this place on the map. It's the very favorable tax
system, not the gambling, that makes Monaco one of the most sought-
after addresses in the world, and the principality bristles with gleaming
high-rise apartment complexes owned by tax exiles. But at the town's
great 1864 landmark Hôtel de Paris—still a veritable crossroads of the
buffed and befurred Euro-gentry—at the Opéra, or the ballrooms of
the Casino, you'll still be able to conjure up Monaco's belle epoque.

ESSENTIALS
CURRENCY
The euro.

HOURS
Most stores open Monday through Saturday from 9 to 7, but many
close at lunchtime (usually noon to 2 or 3), and some will open later
and on Sunday during July and August. Museums are usually open 10
to 5, but most are closed on either Monday or Tuesday.

TELEPHONES
Tri-band GSM phones work in France (and Monaco). You can buy
prepaid phone cards at telecom shops, news vendors, and tobacconists
in all towns and cities. Phone cards can be used for local or interna-
tional calls. Orange, SFR, Bouygues Telecom, and Virgin are leading
telecom companies. If you have an unlocked GSM phone, LeFrench-
Mobile (⊕ *www.lefrenchmobile.com*) offers SIM cards (and micro SIM
cards) with support in English, unlimited validity of credits, and pre-
purchase online.

2

COMING ASHORE

Cruise ships dock at Port Hercule, just below Monaco-Ville, at a state-of-the-art cruise port within a $200-million breakwater that can accommodate several ships at a time. Even still, on busy days you may be tendered to the landing dock. There are few facilities at the port itself. An elevator about 500 yards away leads up to the town, where the attractions of old Monaco are located. It is approximately 1 mile from the port to the Monte Carlo district; this is a 15- to 30-minute walk depending on your level of fitness. Although the distance is not too great, there are many hills.

If you intend to confine your explorations to the principality, there is no need to hire a car. All the attractions of the Old Town are less than a 10-minute walk apart. Bus services 1 and 2 link Monaco-Ville with Monte Carlo; prices are €2 per journey. If you want to tour the stunning surrounding Provençal countryside, a vehicle would be useful. Expect to pay €85 for an economy manual vehicle for the day. Taxis wait outside the port gates and can provide tourist itineraries. For single journeys, tariffs are €3 initially, then €0.92 per km.

> ### MONTE CARLO BEST BETS
>
> **Watch the Changing of the Guard.** This short ceremony at exactly 11:55 am in the palace square has been taking place for centuries.
>
> **Place your bets.** The Casino de Monte Carlo is surely the most beautiful place in the world to lose your shirt. If you don't want to bet, buy a chip as a souvenir.
>
> **Have an aperitif at the café in the Place du Casino.** This is the place to watch the beautiful and megarich come and go and to enjoy the genteel atmosphere.

EXPLORING MONTE CARLO

Monte Carlo or Monaco? Many people use the names interchangeably, but officially, the Old Town or Vieille Ville is **Monaco-Ville** (or Le Rocher because it sits on a rocky plateau). This is where the Grimaldis live and the business of government is done. The "new" town, built in the 18th and 19th centuries and expanding upward rapidly even today, is called **Monte Carlo**, while the harbor area, or **La Condamine**, connects the two.

★ **Casino.** Place du Casino is the center of Monte Carlo, and is a must-see, even if you don't bet a sou. Into the gold-leaf splendor of the Casino, the hopeful traipse from tour buses to tempt fate beneath the gilt-edge rococo ceiling (but do remember the fate of Sarah Bernhardt, who lost her last 100,000 francs here). Jacket and tie are required in the back rooms, which open at 3 pm. Bring your passport (under-18s not admitted). Note that there are special admission fees to get into any of the period gaming rooms. ⊠ *Pl. du Casino* ☎ *377/98–06–20–12* ⊕ *www. sbm.mc* ☉ *Daily 2 pm–4 am.*

Monaco Cathedral. Follow the flow of crowds down the last remaining streets of medieval Monaco to the 19th-century Cathédrale de l'Immaculée-Conception, which has a magnificent altarpiece, painted

Monaco

Moyenne Corniche

Bretelle du Centre

av. de Vilaine

av. Maréchal

av. de Princesse Charlotte

bd. Princesse-Roqueville

bd. de Suisse

av. de la Costa

av. de l'Hermitage

av. de la Madone

av. des Spélugues

Noveau Musée ♦
National de Monaco

i

allée des
Boulingrins

Jardins
du Casino

pl. du
Casino

sq.
Beaumarchaise

Opéra de ♦
Monte-Carlo

Casino ♦

av. de
Monte Carlo

bd. Louis II

MONTE
CARLO

av. d'Ostende

bd. du Larvotto

av. John F. Kennedy

quai des Etats-Unis

pl. Ste-
Devote

LA CONDAMINE

bd. du Jardin

bd. Rainier III

r. Louis-Aureglia

r. Grimaldi

av. Princesse
Antoinette

r. Princesse

bd. Albert 1er

r. Louis

Pr. Florentine

r. S. Reymond

r. Grimaldi

r. Princesse Caroline

r. de Millo

r. Saige

quai Albert 1er

quai Albert 1er

quai Antoine 1er

av. de la Quarantaine

av. de la Porte Neuve

r. des Remparts Emile de Loth

av. des Pins

bd. de Belgique

av. Hector Otto

bd. du Jardin Exotique

Parc Princesse
Antoinette

av. Crovetto

av. prince Pierre

bd.
Charles III

bd. Rainier III

bd. du Bord de Mer

Train
Station

rampe
Major

THE
ROCK

av. du Port

pl.
d'Armes

Palais
Princier

pl. du
Palais

r. Col
de Castro

r. Basse

r. Emile de Loth

av. St-Martin

ch. des Pêcheurs

Musée
Oceanographiqu

Jardins
St-Martin

Monaco ♦
Cathedral

Jardin Exotique ♦
de Monaco

Jardin
Exotique

Collection des ♦
Voitures Anciennes

FONTVIEILLE

KEY

i *Tourist information*

0   1/8 mile

0   1/8 kilometer

in 1500 by Louis Bréa, and the tomb of Princess Grace. It's best to call ahead to check on the opening hours, which tend to vary. ✉ *Av. St-Martin* ☎ *377/93–30–87–70.*

🕐 **Collection des Voitures Anciennes** (*Collection of Vintage Cars*). In the impressive Collection des Voitures Anciennes, an assemblage of Prince Rainier's vintage cars, you'll find everything from a De Dion Bouton to a Lamborghini Countach. Also on the Terrasses de Fontvieille is the **Jardin Animalier** (Animal Garden), a mini-zoo housing the Grimaldi family's animal collection, an astonishing array of wild beasts that includes monkeys and exotic birds. ✉ *Terrasses de Fontvieille* ☎ *377/92–05–28–56, 377/93–25–18–31* ⊕ *www.mtcc.mc* 🎟 *€6 Voitures; €4 Animalier* ⊙ *Museum: Daily, 10–6; Garden: June–Sept., daily 9–noon and 2–7; Oct.–Feb., daily 10–noon and 2–5; Mar.–May, daily 10–noon and 2–6.*

Fodor'sChoice **Jardin Exotique de Monaco** (*Monaco Exotic Garden*). Carved out of the
★ rock face and one of Monte Carlo's most stunning escapes, the gardens are studded with thousands of succulents and cacti, all set along promenades and belvederes over the sea. There are rare plants from Mexico and Africa, and the hillside plot, threaded with bridges and grottoes and studded with faux boulders (actually hollow sculptures), can't be beat for coastal splendor. Prince Albert I established the gardens in the late 19th century. Also on the grounds, or actually under them, are the **Grottes de l'Observatoire**—spectacular grottoes and caves a-drip with stalagmites and spotlighted with fairy lights. The largest cavern is called "La Grande Salle" and looks like a Romanesque rock cathedral. Traces of Cro-Magnon civilization have been found here, so the grottoes now bear the official name of the **Musée d'Anthropologie Préhistorique.** ✉ *62 bd. du Jardin Exotique* ☎ *377/93–15–29–80* ⊕ *www.jardin-exotique.mc* 🎟 *€7* ⊙ *Mid-May–mid-Sept., daily 9–7; mid-Sept.–mid-May, daily 9–6.*

Nouveau Musée National de Monaco. Here you'll find a beguiling collection of 18th- and 19th-century dolls and automatons. The museum is housed in Villa Sauber, within a rose garden, in the Larvotto Beach complex—which is artfully created with imported sand. To get here, take the elevator down from Place des Moulins. The Villa Paloma (next door to the Jardin Exotique), recently restored with fabulous stained-glass windows, is also part of NMNM and hosts temporary exhibits. ✉ *Villa Sauber, 17 av. Princesse Grace* ☎ *377/98–98–91–26* ⊕ *www.nmnm.mc* 🎟 *€6* ⊙ *Daily 10–6.*

★ **Musée Océanographique** (*Oceanography Museum*). Perched dramatically
🕐 on a cliff, this museum is a splendid Edwardian structure, built under Prince Albert I to house specimens collected on amateur explorations. Jacques Cousteau (1910–97) led the missions from 1957 to 1988. The main floor displays skeletons and taxidermy of enormous sea creatures; early submarines and diving gear dating from the Middle Ages; and a few interactive science displays. The main draw is the famous **aquarium,** a vast complex of backlighted tanks containing every imaginable species of fish, crab, and eel. ✉ *Av. St-Martin* ☎ *377/93–15–36–00* ⊕ *www.oceano.mc* 🎟 *€14* ⊙ *July and Aug., daily 9:30–7:30; Apr.–June and Sept., daily 9:30–7; Oct.–Mar., daily 10–6.*

Opéra de Monte-Carlo. This grand theater was designed by Charles Garnier, who also built the Paris Opéra, and is graced with an 18-ton gilt-bronze chandelier and extravagant frescoes. Sarah Bernhardt inaugurated the main auditorium, the Salle Garnier, in 1879. ⊠ *Pl. du Casino* ☎ *377/98–06–28–00* ⊕ *www.opera.mc.*

Palais Princier. The famous Rock, crowned by this palace where the royal family resides, stands west of Monte Carlo. An audio guide leading you through this sumptuous chunk of history, first built in the 13th century and expanded and enhanced over the centuries, reveals an extravagance of 16th- and 17th-century frescoes, as well as tapestries, gilt furniture, and paintings on a grand scale. Note that the **Relève de la Garde** (Changing of the Guard) is held outside the front entrance of the palace most days at 11:55 am. ⊠ *Pl. du Palais* ☎ *377/93–25–18–31* ⊕ *www.palais.mc* 🖻 *€8 (includes audio guide)* ☉ *Apr.–Oct., daily 10–6.*

SHOPPING

The wealthy live in Monaco, and the wealthy visit Monaco, so it should not be a surprise that you can buy the finest designer clothing and accessories from very smart boutiques on the streets radiating out from the **Place du Casino. Monaco-Ville,** on the hill, has a range of souvenir emporia with a predominance of Princess Grace memorabilia, from the tacky to the tasteful. **La Condamine** has a range of shopping for those without sky-high credit card limits. Look out also for Formula 1 motor racing souvenirs; this race around the streets takes place in late May and is one of the highlights of the social season.

BEACHES

Larvotto is the public beach of the principality, but many people choose to buy a temporary membership in a private beach club, which also has facilities such as changing cabins, showers, and restaurants. If you want to spend a day at the beach, that is usually best arranged through your cruise ship.

WHERE TO EAT

$$$$
BRASSERIE

✕ **Café de Paris.** This landmark Belle Époque "La Brasserie 1900"—better known as Café de Paris—offers the usual classics (shellfish, steak tartare, matchstick frites, and fish boned table-side). Supercilious, superpro waiters fawn gracefully over titled preeners, jet setters, and tourists alike. Open daily from 8 am, there's good hot food until 2 am. Ⓢ *Average main: €32* ⊠ *Pl. du Casino* ☎ *377/98–06–76–23.*

$$$$
FRENCH
Fodor's Choice
★

✕ **Le Louis XV.** Louis Quinze to the initiated, this extravagantly showy restaurant stuns with neo-baroque details, yet it manages to be upstaged by its product: the superb cuisine of Alain Ducasse, one of Europe's most celebrated chefs. Ducasse leaves the Louis XV kitchen, for the most part, in the more-than-capable hands of chef Franck Cerutti, who draws much of his inspiration from the Cours Saleya market in Nice. Glamorous iced lobster with chestnuts and Alba white truffles slums happily with stockfish (stewed salt cod) and tripe. The decor is

magnificent—a surfeit of gilt, mirrors, and chandeliers—and the wait-staff seignorial as they proffer a footstool for madame's handbag. In Ducasse fashion, the baroque clock on the wall is stopped just before 12. Cinderella should have no fears. If your wallet is a chubby one, this is a must. The 400,000 bottles in the wine cellar should offer you enough of a choice. $ *Average main: €100* ✉ *Hôtel de Paris, Pl. du Casino* ☎ *377/98–06–88–64* ⊕ *www.alain-ducasse.com* ⚓ *Reservations essential Jacket required* ☉ *Closed Dec. (but open for New Year's Eve) and Tues. and Wed. (but open Wed. dinner mid-June–Aug.).*

NAPLES, ITALY (WITH HERCULANEUM, POMPEII, AND CAPRI)

Updated by Bruce Leimsidor

Campania is a region of evocative names—Capri, Sorrento, Pompeii, Herculaneum—that conjure up visions of cliff-shaded coves, sun-dappled waters, and mighty ruins. The area's unique geology is responsible for its gorgeous landscape. A languid coastline stretches out along a deep blue sea, punctuated by rocky islands. Heading inland, the hills at first roll gently, then transform into mountains. Campania's complex identity is most intensely felt in its major city, Naples, which sprawls around its bay as though attempting to embrace the island of Capri, while behind it Mt. Vesuvius glowers. It's one of those few cities in the world that is instantly recognizable: lush, chaotic, scary, funny, confounding, intoxicating, and very beautiful. Few who visit remain ambivalent. You needn't participate in the mad whirl of the city, however. The best pastime in Campania is simply finding a spot with a stunning view and indulging in *il dolce far niente* (the sweetness of doing nothing).

ESSENTIALS

CURRENCY
The euro.

HOURS
Shops are open 9:30 until 1, then 4:30 until 8. Most are closed on Sunday and also on Monday morning.

PRIVATE TOURS
Siteseeings.com offers half-day tours of Naples and Pompeii to small groups in a minibus with an English-speaking guide for €80 per person, exclusive of entry fees. You can reserve and book on the Internet, and you can arrange for a pick-up at the port. This is one of the few services operating out of Naples for a guaranteed fixed price.

Contacts Sightseeings.com. ☎ *415/332–7916 in the U.S.* ⊕ *www.siteseeings.it.*

SAFETY
Naples has a reputation for active pickpocketing and bag snatching, especially in the historic Old Town and on public transportation. It always pays to be vigilant to avoid becoming a victim. Thieves do cut bag straps to steal your belongings. Bag-snatchers often ride on scooters, grabbing your bag on the streetside as they whiz by. The best advice is to do as Neopolitan women do and simply don't carry a bag; keep a

wallet with anything essential in an inside pocket. Crowded trams and trains are popular with pickpockets. Certainly never carry any cash or valuables that you don't need.

Generally, you can avoid problems by acting with confidence; thieves are more likely to target travelers who seem confused or lost. And you should try to blend in by dressing smartly. Locals in Naples rarely wear shorts and T-shirts.

TELEPHONES

Tri-band GSM phones work in Italy. You can buy prepaid phone cards at telecom shops, news vendors, and tobacconists in all towns and cities. Phone cards can be used for local or international calls.

COMING ASHORE

The Stazione Maritima is on the city's seafront; passenger facilities include a tourist information office, shops, and cafés.

Buses 3S, 152, Sepsa, and CTP run to the train station, Piazza Garibaldi, along with tram routes 1 to 4. By the Circumvesuviana line from Piazza Garibaldi, you can reach Pompeii, Ercolano (Herculanium), and Castellammare (for the funicular to Mount Vesuvius). There are at least three hourly trains, and fares begin at €2.30 to Pompeii (one way, 40 minutes); a single ticket within Naples is €1.20, a day-pass is €3.60 (€3 on weekends).

The EAVBUS route also links central Naples with Vesuvius and Pompeii with Vesuvius. Departing from Piazza Piedigrotta in Naples at 9 am or 10:15. A one-day ticket costs €12.30.

Ferries to Capri depart from the same port where cruise ships disembark; fast ferries leave from the Clata Porta di Massa, and hydrofoils leave from Molo Beverello. Hydrofoils (which are more frequent) make the trip in 40 minutes, other ferries 50 minutes. You can just walk on the ferry after buying a ticket. Fast-ferry prices are €17.80, and hydrofoils are €18.80–€20.20. Once on the island, the funicular railway from the port up to Capri Town is €1.40 round-trip.

Taxis charge approximately €3 initially (more on Sundays and holidays), then €0.05 per 65 meters or 10 seconds of idling. A car rental could be useful if you want to explore the Amalfi coast, but it imperative that you return to Naples with time to spare, because traffic along the coast can be very heavy and slow-moving. Expect to pay €55 per day for a compact manual vehicle.

EXPLORING NAPLES AND VICINITY

NAPLES

★ **Castel Nuovo.** Known to locals as Maschio Angioino, in reference to its Angevin builders, this imposing castle is now used more for marital than military purposes—a portion of it serves as a government registry office. Its looming Angevin stonework is upstaged by a white four-tiered triumphal entrance arch, ordered by Alfonso of Aragon after he entered the city in 1443 to seize power from the increasingly beleaguered Angevin Giovanna II. You can visit the Sala dell'Armeria, where a glass floor reveals recent excavations of Roman baths from the Augustan period.

The castle's first floor holds a small gallery that includes a beautiful early Renaissance *Adoration of the Magi* by Marco Cardisco, with the roles of the three Magi played by the three Aragonese kings: Ferrante I, Ferrante II, and Charles V. ⊠ *Piazza Municipio, Toledo* ☎ *081/7955877* 🎫 *€5* ⊙ *Mon.–Sat. 9–7* Ⓜ *Montesanto (in construction: Piazza Municipio).*

Castel Sant'Elmo. Perched on the Vomero, this massive castle is almost the size of a small town. It was built by the Angevins in the 14th century to dominate the port and the Old City; then remodeled by the Spanish in 1537. The parapets, configured in the form of a six-pointed star, provide fabulous views. Its prison, the Carcere alto di Castel Sant'Elmo, is the site of the **Museo del Novecento Napoli,** which traces Naples's 20th-century artistic output, from the futurist period through the 1980s. You get in the castle free if you have a ticket to the adjoining Certosa di San Martino. ⊠ *Largo San Martino, Vomero* ☎ *081/2294401* ⊕ *www. polomusealenapoli.beniculturali.it* 🎫 *€5; Museo del Novecento Napoli, €5* ⊙ *Wed.–Mon. 8:30–7:30; Museo del Novecento Napoli, Wed.–Mon. 9–7* Ⓜ *Vanvitelli.*

Duomo di San Gennaro. The Duomo was established in the 1200s, but the building you see was erected a century later and has since undergone radical changes—especially during the baroque period. Inside, 110 ancient columns salvaged from pagan buildings are set into the piers that support the 350-year-old wooden ceiling. Off the left aisle you step down into the 4th-century church of **Santa Restituta,** which was incorporated into the cathedral. Though Santa Restituta was redecorated in the late 1600s in the prevalent baroque style, a few very old mosaics remain in the **Battistero** (Baptistery).

On the right aisle of the cathedral, in the **Cappella di San Gennaro,** are multicolor marbles and frescoes honoring Saint Januarius, the miracle-working patron saint of Naples, whose altar and relics are encased in silver. Three times a year—on September 19 (his feast day); on the Saturday preceding the first Sunday in May, which commemorates the transfer of his relics to Naples; and on December 16—his dried blood, contained in two sealed vials, is believed to liquefy during rites in his honor. On these days large numbers of devout Neapolitans offer up prayers in his memory. The **Museo del Tesoro di San Gennaro** houses a rich collection of treasures associated with the saint. Paintings by Solimena and Luca Giordano hang alongside statues, busts, candelabras, and tabernacles in gold, silver, and marble by Cosimo Fanzago and other 18th-century baroque masters. ⊠ *Via Duomo, 149, Spaccanapoli* ☎ *081/449097 Duomo, 081/294764 museum* ⊕ *www. museosangennaro.com* 🎫 *€7, €1.50 for Baptistery* ⊙ *Daily 9–6; Baptistery, 8:30–1, 3:30–6:30.*

Fodor's Choice
★
Museo Archeologico Nazionale (*National Museum of Archaeology*). Those who know and love this legendary museum—now restyled as MANN (Museo Archeologico Nazionale Napoli)—also know that the museum, which holds one of the world's greatest collections of Greek and Roman antiquities, is undergoing a long-term renovation, the fruits of which are starting to become visible. Some of the "newer" rooms, covering archaeological discoveries in the Greco-Roman settlements and

Naples

Bay of Naples

KEY

- Funicular
- **M** Metro stop

10 mi
10 km

1/4 mi
1/4 km

Stazione Marittima

Molo Beverello

Bacino Angioino

Via Colombo

Castel Nuovo

Galleria Umberto

Palazzo Reale

Teatro San Carlo

Piazza del Plebiscito

Funicolare Centrale

SANTA LUCIA

Via C. Console

Via N. Sauro

Via Gen. Orsini

Via Santa Lucia

Santa Lucia

V. Nardones

Via Chiaia

V. Solitaria

V. Monte di Dio

V. Chiatamone

Via Partenope

Tunnel Vittoria

Castell dell'Ovo

Porto S. Lucia

CHIAIA

Pza. dei Martii

V. Moretti

V. Carlo Poerio

Pza. Vittoria

V. Sta. Teresa

V. del Mille

V. S. Pasquale a Chiaia

V. Carducci

Riviera di Chiaia

Via Caracciolo

Villa Comunale

V. Colon

V.G. Basan

V. del Parco Margherita

V. Ascensione

Pza. Amedeo

Yca mangitore G. Manucci

V. F. Crispi

Via C. Manucci

TO EDENLANDIA

Golfo di Napoli

Bay of Naples

Marano di Nápoli

Mirano

Casória

Pozzuoli-Solfatara

Marechiaro

Marano

Palma

A10

A16

TO CASERTA

S. Anastasia

Pomigliano

Ottaviano

Cércola

S. Giuseppe

S. Antonio

Terzigno

Vesuvius

Boscotrecase

Oplontis

E45

18

Portici

Herculaneum

Torre del Greco

Naples

Pompeii

A3

Circum-vesuviana Rail Line

Castellammare di Stábia

145

Vico Equense

Gragnana

Marina di Equa

Positano

145

Alimuri

Marina di Puolo

Sorrento

Meta

Sant'Agata sui Due Golfi

Massa Lubrense

Métrano

Términi

Anacapri

Capri

Capri

necropolises in and around Naples, have helpful informational panels in English. The core of the museum is nucleus of world-renowned archaeological finds that puts most other museums to shame, with over 13,500 items on display (and a further 300,000 in storage). It includes the legendary Farnese collection of ancient sculpture, together with local sculptural finds, and almost all the good stuff—the best mosaics and paintings—from Pompeii and Herculaneum. The quality of these collections is unmatched and, as far as the mosaic, painting, and bronze sections are concerned,

> ### NAPLES BEST BETS
>
> **Pompeii.** The finest and largest Roman site in the world is less than an hour from Naples.
>
> **Herculaneum.** Pompeii's sibling is smaller, but it's more manageable and better preserved.
>
> **Museo Archeologico Nazionale.** The daily lives of Roman citizens at Pompeii and Herculaneum are brought to life with monumental statues and a wealth of personal and domestic items.

unique in the world. ⊠ *Piazza Museo 19, Spaccanapoli* ☎ *081/440166* ⊕ *sbanap.campaniabeniculturali.it* ☒ *€6.50, more for special exhibits* ☯ *Wed.–Mon. 9–7* Ⓜ *Museo.*

★ **Museo di Capodimonte.** The grandiose 18th-century neoclassical Bourbon royal palace houses an impressive assortment of fine and decorative art. Capodimonte's greatest treasure is the excellent collection of paintings well displayed in the **Galleria Nazionale,** on the palace's first and second floors. Aside from the artworks, part of the royal apartments still has a complement of beautiful antique furniture (most of it on the splashy scale so dear to the Bourbons), and a staggering range of porcelain and majolica from the various royal residences. Most rooms have fairly comprehensive information cards in English, whereas the audio guide is overly selective and somewhat quirky. ⊠ *Via Miano 2, Porta Piccola, Via Capodimonte, Capodimonte* ☎ *199/199100 for information and tickets for special exhibitions* ☒ *€8* ☯ *Daily 10–7:30; ticket office closes at 7.*

Fodor's Choice
★ **Palazzo Reale.** Dominating Piazza del Plebiscito, this huge palace— perhaps best described as overblown imperial—dates from the early 1600s. It was renovated and redecorated by successive rulers, including Napoléon's sister Caroline and her ill-fated husband, Joachim Murat (1767–1815), who reigned briefly in Naples after the French emperor sent the Bourbons packing and before they returned to reclaim their kingdom. Don't miss seeing the **royal apartments,** sumptuously furnished and full of precious paintings, tapestries, porcelains, and other objets d'art. The monumental marble staircase gives you an idea of the scale on which Neapolitan rulers lived. ⊠ *Piazza del Plebiscito, 1, Toledo* ☎ *081/400547, 848/800288 schools and guided tours* ⊕ *www. palazzorealenapoli.it* ☒ *€4* ☯ *Thurs.–Tues. 9–7* Ⓜ *Dante (in construction: Piazza Municipio).*

Santa Chiara. This monastery church is a Neapolitan landmark and the subject of a famous old song. It was built in the 1300s in Provençal Gothic style, and it's best known for the quiet charm of its cloister garden, where columns and benches are sheathed in 18th-century ceramic

tiles painted with delicate floral motifs and vivid landscapes. An adjoining museum traces the history of the convent; the entrance is off the courtyard at the left of the church. ⊠ *Piazza Ges³ Nuovo, Spaccanapoli* ☎ *081/7971224* ⊕ *www.monasterodisantachiara.eu* ⊠ *Museum and cloister €5* ⊙ *Church: daily 7–13 and 4:30–8. Museum and cloister: Mon.–Sat. 9:30–5, Sun. 10–2* Ⓜ *Dante, Università.*

HERCULANEUM

★ **Herculaneum Ruins.** About 5,000 people lived here when it was destroyed in AD 79 by the gigantic eruption of Vesuvius (which also destroyed Pompeii). The semiliquid volcanic mass seeped into the crevices and niches of every building, covering household objects, enveloping textiles and wood—and sealing all in a compact, airtight tomb. Today less than half of Herculaneum has been excavated.

Decorations are especially delicate in the **Casa del Nettuno ed Anfitrite** (House of Neptune and Amphitrite), named for the subjects of a still-bright mosaic on the wall of the *nymphaeum* (a recessed grotto with a fountain), and in the **Terme Femminili** (Women's Baths), where several delicate black-and-white mosaics embellished the rooms. Annexed to the former house is a remarkably preserved wineshop, where amphorae still rest on carbonized wood shelves. On the other side of the house is the **Casa del Bel Cortile** (House of the Beautiful Courtyard). One of its inner rooms displays a cast taken of three skeletons found in the storerooms down at the old seafront, where almost 300 inhabitants sought refuge from the eruption and were ultimately encapsulated for posterity. The **Casa dei Cervi** (House of the Stags), with an elegant garden open to the sea breezes, evokes a lively, luxurious way of life. ⊠ *Corso Resina 6, Ercolano* ☎ *081/8575347* ⊕ *www.pompeiisites.org* ⊠ *€11 for Herculaneum only; €20 for biglietto cumulativo ticket to 5 sites (Pompeii, Herculaneum, Boscoreale, Oplontis, and Stabiae) valid for 3 days* ⊙ *Nov.–Mar., daily 8:30–5, ticket office closes at 3:30; Apr.–Oct., daily 8:30–7:30, ticket office closes at 6.*

POMPEII

★ **Pompeii.** The site of Pompeii, petrified memorial to Vesuvius's eruption on August 24, AD 79, is the largest, most accessible, and probably most famous excavation anywhere. A busy commercial center with a population of 12,000–15,000, ancient Pompeii covered about 160 acres on the seaward end of the fertile Sarno Plain.

As you enter the ruins at Porta Marina, the first buildings to the left after you've gone through the ticket turnstiles are the **Terme Suburbane** (Suburban Baths), built right up against the city walls. These have eyebrow-raising frescoes in the *apodyterium* (changing room) that strongly suggest more than just bathing and massaging went on here. On the walls are scenes of erotic games clients could "play" in the second-floor **Lupanare** (brothel).

Several homes were captured in various states by the eruption of Vesuvius, each representing a different slice of Pompeiian life. The **Casa del Poeta Tragico** (House of the Tragic Poet) is a typical middle-class residence. On the floor is a mosaic of a chained dog and the inscription *cave canem* ("Beware of the dog").

There's no more magnificently memorable evidence of Pompeii's devotion to the pleasures of the flesh than the frescoes on view at the **Villa dei Misteri** (Villa of the Mysteries), a palatial abode built at the far northwestern fringe of Pompeii. Unearthed in 1909 this villa had many rooms, all adorned with frescoes—the finest of which are in the *triclinium*. Painted in the most glowing Pompeiian red, the panels relate the saga of a young bride and her initiation into the mysteries of the cult of Dionysus, who was a god imported to Italy from Greece and then given the Latin name of Bacchus. ☎ *081/8575347* ⊕ *www.pompeiisites.org* 🎫 *€11, tickets are valid for one full day* ۞ *Apr.–Oct., daily 8:30–7:30 (last admission at 6), and Nov.–Mar., daily 8:30–5 (last admission at 3:30)* Ⓜ *Pompei-Villa dei Misteri.*

CAPRI
75 min by boat, 40 min by hydrofoil from Naples.

Once a pleasure dome to Roman emperors and now Italy's most glamorous seaside getaway, Capri (pronounced with an accent on the first syllable) is a craggy island at the southern end to the bay of Naples.

CAPRI TOWN
The town is perched some 450 feet above the harbor. Piazza Umberto I, much better known as the Piazzetta, is the island's social hub.

Certosa di San Giacomo. You can window-shop in expensive boutiques and browse in souvenir shops along Via Vittorio Emanuele, which leads south toward the many-domed Certosa di San Giacomo. You'll be able to visit the church and cloister of this much-restored monastery and also pause long enough to enjoy the breathtaking sight of Punta Tragara and the Faraglioni, three towering crags, from the viewing point at the edge of the cliff. ⊠ *Via Certosa* ☎ *081/8376218* ⊕ *www.polomusealenapoli. beniculturali.it* 🎫 *Free* ۞ *Tues.–Sun. 9–2.*

Giardini di Augusto (*Gardens of Augustus*). From the terraces of Giardini di Augusto, a beautiful public garden, you can see the village of Marina Piccola below—restaurants, cabanas, and swimming platforms huddle among the shoals—and admire the steep, winding Via Krupp, actually a staircase cut into the rock. Friedrich Krupp, the German arms manufacturer, loved Capri and became one of the island's most generous benefactors. If you find the path too challenging you can reach the beach by taking a bus from the Via Roma terminus down to Marina Piccola. ⊠ *Via Matteotti, beyond monastery of San Giacomo* 🎫 *€1* ۞ *Daily dawn–dusk.*

ANACAPRI
A tortuous road leads up to Anacapri, the island's "second city," about 3 km (2 miles) from Capri Town. Crowds are thick down Via Capodimonte leading to Villa San Michele and around the square, Piazza Vittoria, which is the starting point of the chairlift to the top of Monte Solaro. Elsewhere, Anacapri is quietly appealing.

Monte Solaro. An impressive limestone formation and the highest point on Capri (1,932 feet), Monte Solaro affords gasp-inducing views toward the bays of both Naples and Salerno. A 12-minute chairlift ride will take you right to the top (refreshments available at the bar), where you can launch out on a number of scenic trails on the western side of the

island. Picnickers should note that even in summer it can get windy at this height, and there are few trees to provide shade or refuge. ⊠ *Piazza Vittoria, Anacapri* ☎ *081/8371428* 🕾 *€7.50 one-way, €10 round-trip* ⊙ *Daily 9:30–1 hr before sunset. Closed in adverse weather conditions.*

San Michele. In the heart of Anacapri, the octagonal baroque church of San Michele, finished in 1719, is best known for its exquisite majolica pavement designed by Solimena and executed by the *mastro-riggiolaro* (master tiler) Chiaiese from Abruzzo. A walkway skirts the depiction of Adam and a duly contrite Eve being expelled from the Garden of Eden, but you can get a fine overview from the organ loft, reached by a winding staircase near the ticket booth (a privileged perch you have to pay for). Outside the church is the Via Finestrale, which leads to Anacapri's noted **Le Boffe quarter.** This section of town, centered on the Piazza Ficacciate, owes its name to the distinctive domestic architecture prevalent here, which uses vaults and sculpted groins instead of crossbeams. ⊠ *Piazza San Nicola, Anacapri* ☎ *081/8372396* ⊕ *www.chiesa-san-michele.com* 🕾 *€2* ⊙ *Apr.–Oct., daily 9–7; Nov and Mar., daily 10–2.*

ELSEWHERE ON THE ISLAND

★ **Grotta Azzurra.** Only when the Grotta Azzurra was "discovered" in 1826 by the Polish poet August Kopisch and Swiss artist Ernest Fries, did Capri become a tourist haven. The water's extraordinary sapphire color is caused by a hidden opening in the rock that refracts the light. At highest illumination the very air inside seems tinted blue. The Grotta Azzurra can be reached from Marina Grande or from the small embarkation point below Anacapri on the northwest side of the island, accessible by bus from Anacapri. ⊠ *Grotta Azzurra* 🕾 *€24.50 from Marina Grande, €12.50 by rowboat from Grotta Azzurra near Anacapri* ⊙ *9–1 hr before sunset closed if sea is even minimally rough.*

SHOPPING

Leather goods, jewelry, and cameos are some of the best items to buy in Campania. In Naples you'll generally find good deals on handbags, shoes, and clothing. If you want the real thing, make your purchases in shops, but if you don't mind imitations, rummage around at the various street-vendor *bancherelle* (stalls).

In Naples the immediate area around **Piazza dei Martiri,** in the center of Chiaia, has the densest concentration of luxury shopping, with perfume shops, fashion outlets, and antiques on display. **Via dei Mille** and **Via Filangieri,** which lead off Piazza dei Martiri, are home to Bulgari, Mont Blanc, and Hermès stores. The small, pedestrian-only **Via Calabritto,** which leads down from Piazza dei Martiri toward the sea, is where you'll find high-end retailers such as Prada, Gucci, Versace, Vuitton, Cacharel, Damiani, and Cartier. **Via Chiaia** and **Via Toledo** are the two busiest shopping streets for most Neapolitans; there you'll find reasonably priced clothes and shoes. The **Vomero** district yields more shops, especially along Via Scarlatti and Via Luca Giordano. **Via Santa Maria di Costantinopoli,** which runs from Piazza Bellini to the Archaeological Museum, is the street for antiques shops.

Nel Regno di Pulcinella. Nel Regno di Pulcinella is the workshop of Lello Esposito, a Neapolitan artist renowned for his renderings of a popular puppet named Pulcinella. ⊠ *Vico San Domenico Maggiore 9, Spaccanapoli* ☎ *081/5514171.*

WHERE TO EAT

$$$$
SOUTHERN
ITALIAN

✕ **Al Grottino.** This small and friendly family-run restaurant, which is in a 14th-century building handy to the Piazzetta, has arched ceilings and lots of atmosphere; autographed photos of famous customers cover the walls. House specialties are *scialatielli ai fiori di zucchine e gambaretti* (homemade pasta with zucchini flowers and shrimps) and linguine *ai scampi*, but the owner delights in taking his guests through the menu. ⑤ *Average main: €40* ⊠ *Via Longano 27, Capri Town* ☎ *081/8370584* ⊕ *www.ristorantealgrottino.net* ⊘ *Closed Nov.–mid-Mar.*

$
PIZZA
Fodor's Choice
★

✕ **Da Michele.** You may recognize this from the movie "Eat, Pray, Love," but for more than 140 years before Julia Roberts arrived this place has been a culinary reference point in Naples. Despite offering only two types of pizza—marinara (with tomato, garlic, and oregano) and *margherita* (with tomato, mozzarella, and basil)—plus a small selection of drinks, it still manages to attract long lines. The prices have something to do with it. But the pizza itself suffers no rivals, so even those waiting in line are good-humored: the boisterous, joyous atmosphere wafts out with the smell of yeast and wood smoke onto the street. Step right up to get a number at the door and then hang outside until it's called. Note: The restaurant is off Corso Umberto, between Piazza Garibaldi and Piazza Nicola Amore. ⑤ *Average main: €7* ⊠ *Via Sersale 1/3, Piazza Garibaldi* ☎ *081/5539204* ⊕ *www.damichele.net* ▭ *No credit cards* ⊘ *Jun.-Nov. closed Sun. and 2 wks in Aug.*

NICE, FRANCE

Updated
by Jennifer
Ladonne

The fifth-largest city in France, Nice is also one of the noblest. The city is capped by a dramatic hilltop château, at whose base a bewitching warren of ancient Mediterranean streets unfolds. Although now French to the core, the town was allied with a Latin Duchy until 1860, and this almost 500 years of history adds a rich Italian flavor to the city's culture, architecture, and dialect. In the late 19th century, Nice saw the birth of tourism, as English and Russian aristocrats began to winter in the temperate climate along the famed waterfront, Promenade des Anglais, which is now lined with grand hotels, a part of their legacy. Nowadays Nice strikes an engaging balance between historic Provençal grace, port-town exotica, urban energy, whimsy, and high culture. Its museums—particularly its art collections—are excellent, and the atmosphere is langourous yet urbane.

ESSENTIALS
CURRENCY
The euro.

HOURS

Most stores open Monday through Saturday from 9 to 7, but many close at lunchtime (usually noon to 2 or 3), and some will open later and on Sunday during July and August. Museums are usually open 10 to 5, but most are closed on either Monday or Tuesday.

TELEPHONES

Tri-band GSM phones work in France. You can buy prepaid phone cards at telecom shops, news vendors, and tobacconists in all towns and cities. Phone cards can be used for local or international calls. Orange, SFR, Bouygues Telecom, and Virgin are leading telecom companies. If you have an unlocked GSM phone, LeFrenchMobile (⊕ *www. lefrenchmobile.com*) offers SIM cards (and micro SIM cards) with support in English, unlimited validity of credits, and prepurchase online.

COMING ASHORE

Ships dock at Nice Port, east of the city center and a 30- to 40-minute walk from the city's attractions. The port facilities include a tourist office and currency-exchange desk. There is a free shuttle service into the downtown core in high season, and taxis are also available.

Don't rent a car if you intend to explore in the city, but it is a sensible option if you want to tour the spectacular Provençal countryside. Expect to pay approximately €75 per day for an economy manual vehicle. Taxis are plentiful and can provide tourist itineraries. For single journeys, fares begin at €3 and then €0.90 per km.

Public transport is reliable and comprehensive,, with Ligne d'Azur (⊕ *www.lignedazur.com*) providing services within the city and suburbs. Route 15 heads to Cimiez and offers a free transfer between the Chagall and Matisse museums. Single tickets are €1 at this writing, and allow you to ride for for 74 minutes. A one-day pass is €4. There is fast and reliable train service between Nice and Cannes, Monte Carlo, Antibes, and other coastal towns if you want to explore farther afield without a car.

EXPLORING NICE

VIEUX NICE

Framed by the "château"—really a rocky promontory—and Cours Saleya, Nice's Vieille Ville is its strongest drawing point and the best place to capture the city's historic atmosphere. Its grid of narrow streets, darkened by houses five and six stories high with bright splashes of laundry fluttering overhead and jewel-box baroque churches on every other corner, creates a magic that seems utterly removed from the French Riviera fast lane.

Colline de Château (*Château Hill*). This hilltop park, acceesible by elevator from the east end of the Promenade des Anglais, commands the site of a once-massive medieval stronghold of which only a few ruins remain. From here take in extraordinary views of the Baie des Anges, the length of the Promenade des Anglais, and the red-ocher roofs of the Vieille Ville. ⊙ *Daily 7–7.*

Nice

CARABACEL

♦ Monastère de Cimiez
♦ Musée Matisse
♦ Musée Archéologique
♦ Musée National Marc-Chagall

av. des Arènes de Cimiez

av. Galliéni
bd. Risso
av. de la République

r. Barberis
r. Beaumont
r. Smolett
r. Auguste Gal
r. Scaliero
r. Arson
bd. de Riquier
bd. Carnot

r. Barla
r. Bonaparte
r. Lascaris
r. Fodéré
Lech Walesa
bd. de Stallingrad
bd. Fr. Platte

r. Penchienatti
r. Defly
bd. Carabacel
r. Delfille
r. Tonduit de l'Escarène
r. des Postes
av. St-Jean Baptiste

pl. Garibaldi
r. C. Ségurane
r. Cassini
r. Guizot
r. F.F.
quai Lunel
r. de Foresta
quai Rauba Capeu

Prom. du Paillon
Espace Masséna
av. Félix Faure
bd. Jean Jaurès
r. de la Préfecture
r. A. Mari

Musée d'Art Moderne

pl. St-François

VIEUX NICE

r. Droite
r. Rossetti
Cimetière

Colline de Château

av. Notre Dame
r. de Lépante
bd. Dubouchage
r. de l'Hôtel des Postes
r. Gioffredo
r. de l'Opéra
Cours Saleya

r. de Paris
r. Maréchal Foch
r. Biscarra
av. Jean-Médecin

CAMP LONG

r. Pastorelli
r. de la Liberté
r. Masséna
av. de Verdun

r. de l'Angleterre
r. Paul Déroulède
r. Alph. Karr
r. Maccarani
r. Massenet
r. du Congrès

quai des États-Unis
r. de la Préfecture

Baie des Anges

Train Station

av. Thiers
av. Georges Clemenceau
r. Paganini
r. Rossini
r. Paul
r. Gounod
r. Berlioz
r. Verdi
r. Guigla
av. Auber
bd. Victor Hugo
bd. du Maréchal Joffre
r. de Rivoli
r. de la Buffa
r. de France
r. Dalpozzo
r. Meyerbeer
promenade des Anglais

r. de Cronstadt
r. de France
bd. Gambetta
av. des Fleurs
av. des Baumettes
bd. François Grosso

LA BUFFA

r. Dante
r. F.F. Passel
r. Caffarelli
Autoroute Urbaine Sud
r. du Tzarewitch
r. de Châteauneuf
r. Schuman
av. d'Estienne d'Orves
av. Gay

Musée de Beaux-Arts Jules-Chéret

0 — 1/8 mi
0 — 1/8 km

★ **Cours Saleya.** This long pedestrian thoroughfare, half street, half square, is the nerve center of Old Nice, the heart of the Vieille Ville and the stage set for the daily dramas of marketplace and café life. Framed with 18th-century houses and shaded by plane trees, the long, narrow square bursts into a fireworks-show of color Tuesday through Sunday, when flower-market vendors roll armloads of mimosas, irises, roses, and orange blossoms into *cornets* (paper cones) and thrust them into the arms of shoppers. Cafés and restaurants, all more or less touristy, fill outdoor tables with onlookers who bask in the sun. At the far-eastern end, antiques and *brocantes* (collectibles) draw avid junk-hounds every Monday morning. At this end you can also find Place Félix. Little wonder the great painter Matisse lived (from 1921 to 1938) in the imposing yellow stone building at 1 Place Charles Félix that looms over the square. Indeed, you don't need to visit the city's famous Musée Matisse to understand this great artist: simply stand in the doorway of his former home and study the Place de l'Ancien Senat 10 feet away—the scene is a golden Matisse pumped up to the nth power.

Musée d'Art Moderne. The assertive contemporary architecture of the Modern Art Museum makes a bold and emphatic statement regarding Nice's presence in the modern world. The art collection inside focuses intently and thoroughly on contemporary art from the late 1950s onward, but pride of place is given to sculptor Nikki de Saint Phalle's recent donation of more than 170 exceptional pieces. The rooftop terrace, sprinkled with minimalist sculptures, has stunning views over the city. Guided tours are offered Wednesdays at 3 pm. €5 ⊠ *Promenade des Arts, Vieux Nice* ☎ *04–97–13–42–01* ⊕ *www.mamac-nice.org* ✉ *Free; guide tours €5* ☉ *Tues.–Sun. 10–6.*

★ **Musée des Beaux-Arts Jules-Chéret** (*Jules-Chéret Fine Arts Museum*). Originally built for a member of Nice's Old Russian community, the Princess Kotschoubey, this Italianate mansion is a Belle Époque wedding cake and is replete with one of the grandest staircases on the coast. After the *richissime* American James Thompson took over and the last glittering ball was held here, the villa was bought by the municipality as a museum in the 1920s. Unfortunately, much of the period decor was sold but in its place are paintings by Degas, Boudin, Monet, Sisley, Dufy, and Jules Chéret, whose posters of winking *damselles* distill all the *joie* of the Belle Époque. From the Negresco Hotel area the museum is about a 15-minute walk up a gentle hill. ⊠ *33 av. des Baumettes, Centre Ville* ☎ *04–92–15–28–28* ⊕ *www.musee-beaux-arts-nice.org* ✉ *Free; guided tours €5* ☉ *Daily 10–6.*

NICE BEST BETS

Musée Matisse. Nice, where the artist made his home from 1917 until his death in 1954, has the finest collection of his work.

Musée National Marc Chagall. Specially designed galleries house the 17 canvases making up *Message Biblique,* "Biblical Message," one of the postimpressionist's most charismatic works.

Strolling through the alleyways of Vieux Nice. The pastel facades of the lively Old Town have inspired generations of artists. Enjoy the cafés, the quaint boutiques, and the flower market on Cours Saleya.

2

CIMIEZ

Once the site of the powerful Roman settlement Cemenelum, the hilltop neighborhood of Cimiez—4 km (2½ miles) north of Cours Saleya—is Nice's most luxurious quarter (use Bus 15 from Place Masséna or Avenue Jean-Médecin to visit its sights).

Monastère de Cimiez. This fully functioning monastery is worth the pilgrimage. You can find a lovely **garden,** replanted along the lines of the original 16th-century layout; the **Musée Franciscain,** a didactic museum tracing the history of the Franciscan order; and a 15th-century **church** containing three works of remarkable power and elegance by Bréa. ⊠ *Pl. du Monastère, Cimiez* ☎ *04–93–81–00–04* ⌨ *Free* ⊙ *Church Thurs.–Tues. 9–6 and Sun. 2:30–8:30. Museum Mon.–Sat. 10–noon and 2–5:30.*

Musée Archéologique (*Archaeology Museum*). This museum, next to the Matisse Museum, has a dense and intriguing collection of objects extracted from the digs around the Roman city of Cemenelum, which flourished from the 1st to the 5th century. Among the fascinating ruins are an amphitheatre, frigidarium, gymnasium, baths, and sewage trenches, some dating back to the 3rd century are fascinating; it's best to avoid midday visits on warm days. ⊠ *160 av. des Arènes-de-Cimiez, Cimiez* ☎ *04–93–81–59–57* ⊕ *www.musee-archeologique-nice. org* ⌨ *Free; €5 guided tour* ⊙ *Wed.–Mon. 10–6.*

★ **Musée National Marc Chagall** (National Museum *Marc Chagall*). This museum has one of the finest permanent collections of Chagall's (1887–1985) late works. Superbly displayed, 17 vast canvases depict biblical themes, each in emphatic, joyous colors. The museum also hosts chamber music and classical concert series, admission may apply. ⊠ *Av. du Dr-Ménard, head up Av. Thiers, then take left onto Av. Malausséna, cross railway tracks, and take first right up Av. de l'Olivetto, Cimiez* ☎ *04–93–53–87–20* ⊕ *www.musee-chagall.fr* ⌨ *€7.50* ⊙ *May–Oct., Wed.–Mon. 10–6; Nov.–Apr., Wed.–Mon. 10–5.*

Fodor'sChoice **Musée Matisse.** In the '60s the city of Nice bought this lovely, light-bathed
★ 17th-century villa, surrounded by the ruins of Roman civilization, and restored it to house a large collection of Henri Matisse's works. Matisse settled along Nice's waterfront in 1917, seeking a sun cure after a bout with pneumonia, and remained here until his death in 1954. During his years on the French Riviera, Matisse maintained intense friendships and artistic liaisons with Renoir, who lived in Cagnes, and with Picasso, who lived in Mougins and Antibes. He eventually moved up to the rarefied isolation of Cimiez and took an apartment in the Hôtel Regina (now an apartment building, just across from the museum), where he lived out the rest of his life. Matisse walked often in the parklands around the Roman remains and was buried in an olive grove outside the Cimiez cemetery. The collection of artworks includes several pieces the artist donated to the city before his death; the rest were donated by his family. In every medium and context—paintings, gouache cutouts, engravings, and book illustrations—the collection represents the evolution of his art, from Cézanne-like still lifes to exuberant dancing paper dolls. Even the furniture and accessories speak of Matisse, from the Chinese

vases to the bold-printed fabrics with which he surrounded himself. A series of black-and-white photographs captures the artist at work, surrounded by personal—and telling—details. ✉ *164 av. des Arènes-de-Cimiez, Cimiez* ☎ *04–93–81–08–08* ⊕ *www.musee-matisse-nice.org* 🎟 *Free* ⊘ *Wed.–Mon. 10–6.*

BEACHES

Nice's pebble beaches extend all along the Baie des Anges, backed full-length by the Promenade des Anglais. Public stretches alternate with posh private beaches that have restaurants—and bar service, mattresses and parasols, waterskiing, parasailing, windsurfing, and Jet Skiing.

Beau Rivage. One of the handiest private beaches is the Beau Rivage, set across from the Opéra and next to the Jardin Albert Ier. The €20 daily rental fee for a lounger is a good investment (book the night before) as it allows access to the toilets and shade of a parasol. The beach restaurant is excellent, but you can bring your own beach bag of goodies. ✉ *24 rue Saint François de Paule* ☎ *04–92–47–82–82* ⊕ *www. plagenicebeaurivage.com.*

Florida Beach. One of the new private beaches making a splash on the Prom, Florida is très hip nd has an excellent restaurant and bar service. ✉ *71 Promenade des Anglais* ☎ *04–93–44–72–86* ⊕ *www.florida-beach.fr.*

SHOPPING

As the largest city in Provence, Nice is a trove of regional crafts and delicacies, including basketwork, bright fabrics, perfumes, lavender soaps, olive-wood items, plus delicious olives, olive oils, honey, dried herbs, and quaffable local wines. The city is particularly renowned for its delicious crystallized fruit. The best place to find crafts is in the Old Town, while French couture can be found on the elegant boulevards of the new town.

Confiserie Florian du Vieux Nice. A good source for crystallized fruit, a Nice specialty, is the Confiserie Florian du Vieux Nice, on the west side of the port. ✉ *14 quai Papacino, Vieux Nice* ⊕ *www.confiserieflorian.com.*

Henri Auer. The venerable Henri Auer has sold crystallized fruit since 1820. ✉ *7 rue St-François-de-Paule, Vieux Nice* ⊕ *www.maison-auer.com.*

WHERE TO EAT

$ ✕**Chez René Socca.** This back-alley landmark is the most popular dive FRENCH in town for *socca,* the chickpea-pancake snack food unique to Nice. Rustic olive-wood tables line the street, and curt waiters splash down your drink order. Then you get in line, choose your plate, and carry it steaming to the table yourself. It's off Place Garibaldi on the edge of the Vieille Ville, across from the old *Gare Routière* (bus station). ⑤ *Average main: €3* ✉ *2 rue Miralheti, Vieux Nice* ☎ *04–93–92–05–73* ⊟ *No credit cards* ⊘ *Closed Mon. and Jan.*

$$$
SEAFOOD

✕ **Grand Café de Turin.** Whether you squeeze onto a banquette in the dark, low-ceiling bar or win a coveted table under the arcaded porticoes on Place Garibaldi, this is *the* place to go for shellfish in Nice: sea snails, clams, plump *fines de claires,* and salty *bleues* oysters, and urchins by the dozen. It's packed noon and night (and has been since it opened in 1908), so don't be too put off by the sometimes brusque reception of the waiters. ⑤ *Average main: €30* ⊠ *5 pl. Garibaldi, Vieux Nice* ☎ *04–93–62–29–52* ⊕ *www.cafedeturin.fr.*

PALERMO, ITALY

Updated
by Bruce
Leimsidor

Once the intellectual capital of southern Europe, Palermo has always been at the crossroads of civilization. Favorably situated on a crescent-shaped bay at the foot of Monte Pellegrino, it has attracted almost every culture touching the Mediterranean world. To Palermo's credit, it has absorbed these diverse cultures into a unique personality that is at once Arab and Christian, Byzantine and Roman, Norman and Italian. The city's heritage encompasses all of Sicily's varied ages, but its distinctive aspect is its Arab-Norman identity, an improbable marriage that, mixed in with Byzantine and Jewish elements, created some resplendent works of art. No less noteworthy than the architecture is Palermo's chaotic vitality, on display at some of Italy's most vibrant outdoor markets, public squares, street bazaars, and food vendors, and above all in its grand climax of Italy's most spectacular *passeggiata* (the leisurely social stroll along the principal thoroughfare).

ESSENTIALS
CURRENCY
The euro.

HOURS
Most shops are open 9 to 1 and 4 or 4:30 to 7:30 or 8 and closed Sunday; in addition, most food shops close Wednesday afternoon, and other shops normally close Monday morning. Most museums/attractions open throughout the day, though some, particularly churches, close in the afternoon. Because of budget cutbacks and increasing number of museums have cutback their hours, most often in the afternoon, so mornings are almost uniformly best for touring.

PRIVATE TOURS
Siteseeings.com offers half-day tours of Palermo and Monreale to small groups in a minibus with an English-speaking guide for €35 per person. You can reserve and book on the Internet. On Thursdays the company conducts full-day tours in small groups to Agrigento and Piazza Amerina. Tours cost €70 to €80.

Get your guide conducts one day tours of Palermo, Monreale, and Cefalu with an English-speaking guide, generally on weekends, for €95 per person. Tours should be booked in advance.

Contacts Get Your Guide. ☎ *(49)30/540–45944 in Italy* ⊕ *www.getyourguide.com/.* **Sightseeings.com.** ☎ *415/332–7916 in the U.S.* ⊕ *www.siteseeings.it.*

TELEPHONES

Tri-band GSM phones work in Italy. You can buy prepaid phone cards at telecom shops, news vendors, and tobacconists in all towns and cities. Phone cards can be used for local or international calls.

COMING ASHORE

Palermo's cruise port has recently been expanded to accommodate larger vessels. The terminal building has a café and a shop. Just outside the gates are taxis and horse-drawn carriages. It is possible to walk directly from the ship into the city; however, the port area has a reputation for pickpockets and scam artists, so be aware.

Three bus routes (Gialla, Rossa, and Verde) ply the streets of the Old Town, but none links with the port; tickets cost €1. Taxis begin at €3.05, then add €2.25 for the first km and €0.80 per km (½-mile) thereafter, with supplments for slow traffic, luggage, and holidays. Tourists are almost uniform in reporting serious overcharging by taxis in Palermo; it's best to ask at the cruise pier or at a restaurant or shop what the fare should be before you head out. Renting a car would open up much of the island to you, but heavy traffic in Palermo may play havoc with your nerves. Expect to pay about €60 per day for a compact manual vehicle.

EXPLORING PALERMO

Catacombe dei Cappuccini. The spookiest sight in all of Sicily, this 16th-century catacomb houses nearly 9,000 corpses of men, women, and young children—some in tombs but many mummified and preserved—hanging in rows on the walls, divided by social caste, age, or gender. Most wear signs indicating their names and the years they lived. The Capuchins were founders and proprietors of the bizarre establishment (many of the corpses are Capuchin friars) from 1599 to 1911, and it's still under the auspices of the nearby Capuchin church. ⊠ *Piazza Cappuccini 1, off Via Cappuccini, near Palazzo Reale* ☎ *091/212633* ⊠ *€3* ☉ *Daily 9–12 and 3–5:30.*

★ **Cattedrale.** This church is a lesson in Palermitan eclecticism—originally Norman (1182), then Catalan Gothic (14th to 15th century), then fitted out with a baroque and neoclassical interior (18th century). Its turrets, towers, dome, and arches come together in the kind of meeting of diverse elements that King Roger II (1095–1154), whose tomb is inside along with that of Frederick II, fostered during his reign. The back of the apse is gracefully decorated with interlacing Arab arches inlaid with limestone and black volcanic tufa. ⊠ *Corso Vittorio Emanuele, Capo* ☎ *091/334373* ⊠ *€3* ☉ *Mar.–Oct., Mon.–Sat. 9:30–5:30; Nov.–Feb., Mon.–Sat. 9:30–1:30.*

La Martorana. Distinguished by an elegant Norman campanile, this church was erected in 1143 but had its interior altered considerably during the baroque period. High along the western wall, however, is some of the oldest and best-preserved mosaic artwork of the Norman period. Near the entrance is an interesting mosaic of King Roger II being crowned by Christ. ⊠ *Piazza Bellini 3, Quattro Canti* ☎ *091/6161692* ☉ *Mon.–Sat. 8:30–1 and 3:30–5:30, Sun. 8:30–1.*

Palermo

Museo delle Marionette

V. Butera

Foro Italico

Pza. Kalsa

V. Torremazza

Palazzo Abatellis

V. N. Cervello

Villa Giulia

Villa Giardino Garibaldi

Vlo Cala

La Cala

V. Scopari

V. della Vetreria

V. Rao

LA KALSA

V. Spasimo

Orto Botanico

V. Archirafi

V. Barilai

V. Cassari

Pza. Marina

V. Bottai

V. Alloro

V. Castrofilippo

V. Scavuzzo

V. Lincoln

V. Bendazzo

VUCCIRIA

V. Tavola Tonda

Vittorio Emanuele

V. Paternostrio

V. Garibaldi

V. Milano

Cso. dei Mille

TO POLITEAMA & LIBERTÀ

Museo Archeologico Regionale Salinas

Pza. San Domenico

Cso.

Via Roma

La Martorana

V. Calderai

V. Divisi

V. Torino

V. Mura di S. Agata

Train Station

V. S.Basilio

V. Bari

V. Napoli

S.S. Antonio

San Cataldo

Via Maqueda

Cso. Tukory

V. Venezia

Piazza Pretoria

V. Puglia

V. d. Alessi

V. Ponticello

V. d. Bosco

Teatro Mássimo

Pza. Verdi

V. Favara

Pza. S. Onofrio

V. Candelai

V. del Celso

V. Ragusi

V. Forcalla

V. Ballarò

ALBERGHERIA

V. Nasso

V. Majali

V. Volturno

V. Mura di V. S. Vito

V. S-Gregorio

V. S. Agostina

V. Judica

V. Groniti

Corso Vittorio Emanuele

V. Porto di Castro

V. Cristina

V. Alberghetia

CAPO

V. Porta Carini

V. dei Cartellieri

V. Maria E.lesu

Cattedrale

Pza. d. Vittoria

V. del Bastione

V. d. Mongitore

V. d. Benedettini

San Giovanni degli Eremiti

TO UNIVERSITY

Pza. Vitt. Emanuele Orlando

V. Papireto

Villa Bonanno

Pza. d. Parlamento

Palazzo Reale

C. Re Ruggero

Corso Alberto Amadeo

Colonna Rotta

Corso Vittorio Emanuele

Pza. Indipendenza

TO MONREALE

V. Giuffredi

V. Ranzano

V. C. Lascaris

V. d'Ossuna

V. G. Mosca

Cso. F. Aprile

V. Imera

Pza. Danisinni

V. dei Cappuccini

Catacombe dei Cappuccini

V. Marco Polo

V. Zisa

V. Cipressi

V. G. il Buono

0   1/8 mi

0   1/8 km

2

Museo Archeologico Regionale Salinas (*Salinas Regional Museum of Archaeology*). Especially interesting pieces in this small but excellent collection are the examples of prehistoric cave drawings and a marvelously reconstructed Doric frieze from the Greek temple at Selinunte, which reveals the high level of artistic culture attained by the Greek colonists in Sicily some 2,500 years ago. (To enter, use the door around the corner on Via Roma.) Extensive renovations at the museum are scheduled to continue through 2012. ⊠ *Piazza Olivella 24, Via Roma, Olivella* ☎ *091/6116806* 🎫 *€4* ⊘ *Tues.–Fri. 8:30–1:30 and 2:30–6:30, weekends 8:30–1; last entry ½ hr before closing.*

PALERMO BEST BETS

Marvel at the Duomo in Monreale. The finest example of Norman fusion architecture in Sicily blends Eastern and Western influences.

Take a peek at Palazzo Real. Once home to Bourbon royalty and their particular taste in home decor it now houses the Sicilian Parliament.

Stroll the Old Town. A genuine slice of life southern Italian style will play out before your eyes as you kick the dust off your shoes by walking through these streets.

Palazzo Abatellis. Housed in this late-15th-century Catalan Gothic palace with Renaissance elements is the **Galleria Regionale.** Among its treasures are the *Annunciation* (1474), a painting by Sicily's prominent Renaissance master Antonello da Messina (1430–79), and an arresting fresco by an unknown 15th-century painter, titled *The Triumph of Death,* a macabre depiction of the plague years. Two new rooms were opened in early 2010 after years of work. ⊠ *Via Alloro 4, Kalsa* ☎ *091/6230011* 🎫 *€8* ⊘ *Tues.–Fri. 9–5:30, weekends 9–1.*

Palazzo Reale (*Royal Palace*). This historic palace, also called Palazzo dei Normanni (Norman Palace), was the seat of Sicily's semiautonomous rulers for centuries. The building is a fascinating mesh of abutting 10th-century Norman and 17th-century Spanish structures. Because it now houses the Sicilian Parliament, parts of the palace are closed to the public from Tuesday to Thursday when the regional Parliament is sitting. The **Cappella Palatina** (Palatine Chapel) remains open. Built by Roger II in 1132, it's a dazzling example of the harmony of artistic elements produced under the Normans. Here the skill of French and Sicilian masons was brought to bear on the decorative purity of Arab ornamentation and the splendor of 11th-century Greek Byzantine mosaics. The interior is covered with glittering mosaics and capped by a splendid 10th-century Arab honeycomb stalactite wooden ceiling. Biblical stories blend happily with scenes of Arab life—look for one showing a picnic in a harem—and Norman court pageantry.

Upstairs are the royal apartments, including the **Sala di Re Ruggero** (King Roger's Hall), decorated with medieval murals of hunting scenes—an earlier (1120) secular counterpoint to the religious themes seen elsewhere. French, Latin, and Arabic were spoken here, and Arab astronomers and poets exchanged ideas with Latin and Greek scholars in one of the most interesting marriages of culture in the Western world. The Sala is always included with entry to the palace or chapel. ⊠ *Piazza*

Indipendenza, Albergheria ☎ *091/6262833* ⊕ *www.federicosecondo. org* ▣ *Palazzo Reale or Cappella Palatina €7, entry to both €8.50* ☯ *Palazzo Reale: Mon. and Fri. 8:15–5, Sun. 8:15–12:30. Cappella Palatina: Mon.–Sat. 8:15–5, Sun. 8:15–12:30, but closed for Sun. services 9:45–11:15. Last entry ½ hr before closing.*

Piazza Pretoria. The square's centerpiece, a lavishly decorated fountain with 500 separate pieces of sculpture and an abundance of nude figures, so shocked some Palermitans when it was unveiled in 1575 that it got the nickname "Fountain of Shame." It's even more of a sight when illuminated at night.

★ **San Cataldo.** Three striking Saracenic scarlet domes mark this church, built in 1154 during the Norman occupation of Palermo. The church now belongs to the Knights of the Holy Sepulchre and has a spare but intense stone interior. If closed, inquire next door at La Martorana. ⊠ *Piazza Bellini 3, Kalsa* ☎ *091/7827390* ▣ *€2.50* ☯ *Daily 9:30–12:30 and 3–6.*

San Giovanni degli Eremiti. Distinguished by its five reddish-orange domes and stripped-clean interior, this 12th-century church was built by the Normans on the site of an earlier mosque—one of 200 that once stood in Palermo. The emirs ruled Palermo for nearly two centuries and brought to it their passion for lush gardens and fountains. One is reminded of this while sitting in San Giovanni's delightful cloister of twin half columns, surrounded by palm trees, jasmine, oleander, and citrus trees. ⊠ *Via dei Benedettini 14, Albergheria* ☎ *091/6515019* ▣ *€6* ☯ *Tues.–Sat. 9–7; Mon. and Sun. 9–1:30; last entry ½ hr before closing.*

Teatro Massimo. Construction of this formidable neoclassical theater, the largest in Italy, was started in 1875 by Giovanni Battista Basile and completed by his son Ernesto in 1897. A reconstruction project started in 1974 ran into gross delays, and the facility remained closed until just before its centenary in 1997. Its interior is as glorious as ever. *The Godfather: Part III* ended with a famous shooting scene on the theater's steps. Visits, by 25-minute guided tour only, are available in six languages, including English. ⊠ *Piazza Verdi 9, at top of Via Maqueda, Olivella* ☎ *091/6053521* ⊕ *www.teatromassimo.it* ▣ *€7* ☯ *Tues.–Sun. 10–3.*

MONREALE
10 km (6 miles) southwest of Palermo.

Cloister. The lovely cloister of the abbey adjacent to the Duomo was built at the same time as the church but enlarged in the 14th century. The beautiful enclosure is surrounded by 216 intricately carved double columns, every other one decorated in a unique glass mosaic pattern. Afterward, don't forget to walk behind the cloister to the belvedere, with stunning panoramic views over the Conca d'Oro (Golden Conch) valley toward Palermo. ⊠ *Piazza del Duomo* ☎ *091/6404403* ▣ *€6* ☯ *Tues.–Sat. 9–6:30; Mon. and Sun. 9–1; last entry ½ hr before closing.*

Fodor'sChoice **Duomo.** Monreale's splendid Duomo is lavishly executed with mosaics
★ depicting events from the Old and New Testaments. After the Norman conquest of Sicily the new princes showcased their ambitions through

monumental building projects. William II (1154–89) built the church complex with a cloister and palace between 1174 and 1185, employing Byzantine craftsmen. The result was a glorious fusion of Eastern and Western influences, widely regarded as the finest example of Norman architecture in Sicily.

The major attraction is the 68,220 square feet of glittering gold mosaics decorating the cathedral interior. *Christ Pantocrator* dominates the apse area; the nave contains narratives of the Creation; and scenes from the life of Christ adorn the walls of the aisles and the transept. The painted wooden ceiling dates from 1816–37. The roof commands a great view (a reward for climbing 172 stairs).

Bonnano Pisano's bronze doors, completed in 1186, depict 42 biblical scenes and are considered among the most important of medieval artifacts. Barisano da Trani's 42 panels on the north door, dating from 1179, present saints and evangelists. ⊠ *Piazza del Duomo* ☏ *091/6402424* ⊙ *Mar.–Oct., daily 8:30–1 and 3–6:30; Nov.–Feb., daily 8:30–12:45 and 3–5.*

SHOPPING

Sicilian specialties include lace and linen, including place mats and napkins, and ceramics, particularly its practical folk pottery from Caltagirone, on the north coast. Marble and wrought iron are also fashioned into souvenir pieces and antiques shops are numerous, though prices can be high. Edibles include an excellent range of wines and olive oils, jams, and tasty sweets.

In Palermo, north of Piazza Castelnuovo, **Via della Libertà** and the streets around it represent the luxury end of the shopping scale, with some of Palermo's best-known stores. A second nerve center for shoppers is the pair of parallel streets connecting modern Palermo with the train station, **Via Roma,** and **Via Maqueda,** where boutiques and shoe shops become increasingly upmarket as you move from the Quattro Canti past Teatro Massimo to Via Ruggero Settimo, but are still a serious notch below their counterparts in the Libertà area.

If you're interested in truly connecting with local life while searching for souvenirs, a visit to one of Palermo's many bustling markets is essential. Between Via Roma and Via Maqueda the many *bancherelle (market stalls)* on Via Bandiera sell everything from socks to imitation designer handbags.

Enoteca Picone. Enoteca Picone is the best wineshop in town, with a fantastic selection of Sicilian and national wines. Though the service can be curt, you can taste a selection of wines by the glass in the front of the store. There are tables in the back, where meats and cheeses are also served. The branch on Viale Strasburgo offers full meals. Both branches are closed Sunday. ⊠ *Via Marconi 36, Libertà* ☏ *091/331300* ⊕ *www.enotecapicone.it* ⊠ *Viale Strasburgo 235, Resuttana* ☏ *091/6880357.*

WHERE TO EAT

$ ✕ **Pizzeria Ai Comparucci.** One of Palermo's best pizzerias doubles as a
PIZZA   modern art gallery. The colorful paintings give the place a fun, casual vibe. Better yet are the delicious Neapolitan pizzas coming out of the big oven in the open kitchen—the genius is in the crust, which is seared in a matter of seconds. The owners make their money on a quick turnover (so don't expect a long, leisurely meal). But the pizza is delicious, and the place often serves until midnight—later than almost any other restaurant in the neighborhood. ⓢ *Average main: €12* ✉ *Via Garzilli 1, Libertà* ☎ *091/6090467* ⊘ *Closed Mon. and lunchtime.*

$$$ ✕ **Trattoria Altri Tempi.** This small and friendly "retro" restaurant is a
SICILIAN   favorite among locals who pine for the rustic dishes served by their
★   ancestors. A meal begins when the server plunks down a carafe of the house red and a superb spread of traditional antipasti on your table. Dishes have old-fashioned names: *fave a cunigghiu* is fava beans prepared with olive oil, garlic, and remarkably flavorful oregano; and *vampaciucia c'anciova* is a lasagna-like dish with a concentrated sauce of tomatoes, anchovies, and grapes. The meal ends well, too, with free house-made herb or fruit liquors and excellent cannoli. ⓢ *Average main: €25* ✉ *Via Sammartino 65/67, Libertà* ☎ *091/323480* ⊘ *Closed 2 weeks late Aug. and Sun. June–Aug. No dinner Sun.*

PORTO CERVO, SARDINIA, ITALY

Updated by
Victoria Tang

An uncut jewel of an island, Sardinia remains unique and enigmatic. Would-be conquerors have left their marks, but inland, a proud Sard culture and language flourish. Sardinia has some of Europe's most expensive resort destinations, but it's also home to areas as rugged and undeveloped as anywhere on the continent. Fine sand and clean waters draw sun seekers to beaches that are unquestionably among the best in the Mediterranean. Best known are those along the Costa Smeralda (Emerald Coast), where the superrich have anchored their yachts since the 1960s. But most of the coast is unsettled, a jagged series of wildly beautiful inlets accessible only by sea. And inland, Sardinia remains shepherd's country, silent and stark. Spaghetti Westerns were once filmed here, and it's not hard to imagine why: the desolate mountainous terrain seems the perfect frontier set. Against this landscape are the striking and mysterious stone *nuraghi* (ancient defensive structures), which provide clues to the lifestyles of the island's prehistoric peoples.

ESSENTIALS
CURRENCY
The euro.

HOURS
Shops are generally open 9 to 1 and 3:30 to 8 and are generally closed Sunday. Summer (June to September) hours are usually 9 to 1 and 4 to 8, and some shops close Saturday afternoon.

TELEPHONES

Tri-band GSM phones work in Italy. You can buy prepaid phone cards at telecom shops, news vendors, and tobacconists in all towns and cities. Phone cards can be used for local or international calls.

COMING ASHORE

Poltu Quatu means "hidden port" in the Sardinian dialect, and it is hidden at the head of a narrow inlet. Small cruise ships can dock at the port, but larger ships dock beyond the mouth of the inlet and tender passengers ashore. The port is one element in an extended tourist "village"; other facilities include a selection of cafés, sports outfitters, and shops. You can rent a boat for the day directly from the harbor to cruise the coast. There is no public transport to the port.

Renting a car gives you a great opportunity to explore the northern half of the island and still have time to relax. Europcar has an office in the port. Other car-rental companies will deliver to the port for an extra charge. Rental prices for a compact manual vehicle start at €80 per day. There is a taxi stand within the resort village. Taxis will meet boats at the port but must be prebooked. Taxi fares are €20 into Puerto Cervo, which is just around the headland.

EXPLORING NORTHERN SARDINIA

PORTO CERVO

35 km (22 miles) southeast of La Maddalena, 30 km (19 miles) north of Olbia.

★ Sardinia's northeastern coast is fringed with low cliffs, inlets, and small bays. This has become an upscale vacationland, with glossy resorts such as Baia Sardinia and Porto Rotondo just outside the confines of the famed Costa Smeralda, developed by the Aga Khan (born 1936), who in 1965 accidentally discovered the coast's charms—and potential—when his yacht took shelter here from a storm. In the late 1960s and '70s the Costa Smeralda, with its heart in Porto Cervo, was *the* place to summer. The attractions remain geared to those who can measure themselves by the yardstick of Khan's fabled riches. Italy's most expensive hotels are here, and the world's most magnificent yachts anchor in the waters of Porto Cervo. Golf courses, yacht clubs, and numerous alfresco restaurants and bars cater to those who want to see and be seen. All along the coast, carefully tended lush vegetation surrounds vacation villages and discreet villas that have sprung up over the past decade in spurious architectural styles best described as "bogus Mediterranean." The trend has been to keep this an enclave of the very rich. Outside the peak season, however, prices plunge and the majesty of the natural surroundings shines through, justifying all the hype and the Emerald Coast's fame as one of the truly romantic corners of the Mediterranean.

Northern Sardinia

0 — 20 miles
0 — 30 km

Isola Asinara

Golfo dell' Asinara

COSTA SMERALDA

Santa Teresa di Gallura
La Maddalena
Caprera
Palau
Poltu Quatu
Arzachena
Porto Cervo
Porto Rotondo
Golfo Aranci
Olbia

Stintino
Porto Torres
Castelsardo
SS200
SS133

Anghelu Ruiu
Sassari
Oschiri
SS127
SS199
SS125

Capo Caccia
Alghero
Ozieri

SARDINIA

Grotta di Nettuno

Siniscola

SS131

SS129
Macomer
Nuoro
Cala Gonone
Oliena

Lago Omodeo

Golfo di Orosei

Yacht Club
Baia di Porto Cervo
Vecchio Molo

MARINA

Porto Cervo
VILLAGE

LA MADDALENA

30 km (19 miles) east of Santa Teresa di Gallura, 45 km (20 miles) northwest of Olbia.

From the port of Palau you can visit the archipelago of La Maddalena, seven granite islands embellished with lush green scrub and wind-bent pines that belong to the Olbia-Tempio province. Car ferries make the 3-km (2-mile) trip about every half hour. A handful of sites to see include ancient Roman ruins and squares. Explore the village then head to one of several picture-postcard coves, the perfect spot to pack a picnic and rejuvenate after your journey to the region.

Tomb of Giuseppe Garibaldi's. Pilgrims pay homage to the 19th century national hero and military leader who is buried on the grounds of his farm on Isola Caprera. The patriot, who laid the groundwork for the first unification of Italy, lived from 1807 to 1882, and at one point owned half of Isola Caprera. Take the ferry to Isola Maddalena and then the bridge to Isola Caprera. Currently the site is closed to the public. In 2012, upon the request of descendants, authorities are currently exhuming the body and conducting DNA tests to verify the body's authenticity. Garibaldi continues to make history. ✉ *7 km (4½ miles) east of Isola Maddalena* ☎ *0789/727162* ⊕ *www.compendiogaribaldino.it* 🎟 *€4* ⏱ *Oct.–Apr., Tues.–Sun. 9–1:30; May–Sept., Tues.–Sun. 9–6:30.*

SANTA TERESA DI GALLURA

55 km (34 miles) west of Porto Cervo.

At the northern tip of Sardinia, Santa Teresa di Gallura retains the relaxed, carefree air of a former fishing village. Nearby beaches rival those farther down the coast, but manage not to seem overcrowded with tourists.

GOLFO ARANCI

47 km (29 miles) southeast of Puerto Cervo.

At the mouth of the Gulf of Olbia, Golfo Aranci is a small-scale resort and major arrival point for ferries from the mainland. Tour the village to relax on an outdoor terrace or shop in one of many quaint shops. There is a large selection of restaurants, cafés, and bars. On August 15, the annual fish festival promises excellent seafood. The craggy headland west of town has been left undeveloped as a nature reserve. Drive a few miles along the panoramic road to Olbia. You will reach the enchanting waters of Cala Moresca, Cala Greca, Cala Sabina, and White Beach, perfect for swimming, diving, and any other water sport imaginable.

SARDINIA BEST BETS

Take an espresso in the harbor at Porto Cervo. Most of Europe's royalty spends at least some time here every summer, as does a sprinkling of celebrities. This is a prime place for people-watching.

Take a dip on the Costa Smeralda. The setting of golden sand, russet rocks, and limpid waters is sublime.

Take a stroll around Alghero. Built by the Spanish as their capital in medievel times, Alghero is still a little piece of Spain in modern Italy.

OLBIA

30 km (19 miles) south of Porto Cervo, 19 km (12 miles) southwest of Golfo Aranci, 65 km (41 miles) southeast of Santa Teresa di Gallura.

Amid the resorts of Sardinia's northeastern coast, Olbia, a town of about 60,000, is a lively little seaport and port of call for mainland ferries at the head of a long, wide bay.

★ **San Simplicio.** The little Catholic basilica, a short walk behind the main Corso Umberto and past the train station, is worth searching out if you have any spare time in Olbia. The simple granite structure dates from the 11th century, part of the great Pisan church-building program, using pillars and columns recycled from Roman buildings. Playing an important role in the island's evangelical progress, the basilica has three naves separated by a series of arches. ⊠ *Via San Simplicio* ☎ *0789/23358* ⊕ *www.monumentiaperti.com* ☉ *Sat. and Sun. 9–1 and 3–6.*

SASSARI

100 km (62 miles) southwest of Santa Teresa di Gallura.

The island's second largest city and relatively chaotic with cars, Sassari is an important university town and administrative center, notable for its history of intellectualism and bohemian student culture, an ornate old cathedral, and a good archaeological museum. Look for downtown vendors of *fainè,* a pizzalike chickpea-flour pancake glistening with olive oil, which is a Genoese and Sassarese specialty. Sassari is the hub

of several highways and secondary roads leading to various coastal resorts, among them Stintino and Castelsardo.

Duomo. A must-see in Sassari, the elegant stone structure of the city's Duomo dedicated to Saint Nicolas of Bari took just under 600 years to build. The foundations were laid in the 12th century and the facade, in Spanish colonial style, was finished in the 18th. Of particular interest in the interior are the ribbed Gothic vaults, the 14th-century painting of the Maddona del Bosco on the high alter, and the early-19th-century tomb of Placido Benedetto di Savoia, the uncle of united Italy's first king. ⊠ *Piazza Duomo 3* ☏ *079/233185* ⊕ *www.ilportalesardo.it* ⌨ *Free* ☉ *Apr.–Oct., daily 9–noon and 5–7; Nov.–Mar., daily 9–12:30 and 4–6.*

Ⓒ **Museo Sanna.** Sassari's excellent cultural museum has the best archaeological collection outside Cagliari, spanning nuraghic, Carthaginian, and Roman histories, including well-preserved bronze statues and household objects from the 2nd millennium BC. Summer hours vary from year to year. ⊠ *Via Roma 64* ☏ *079/272203* ⊕ *www.museosannasassari. it* ⌨ *€4* ☉ *Tue.–Sun. 9–8; closed Mon.*

ALGHERO
34 km (21 miles) southwest of Sassari, 137 km (85 miles) southwest of Olbia.

A tourist-friendly town of about 45,000 inhabitants with a distinctly Spanish flavor, Alghero is also known as "Barcelonetta" (little Barcelona). Rich wrought-iron scrollwork decorates balconies and screened windows; a Spanish motif appears in stone portals and bell towers. The town was built and inhabited in the 14th century by the Aragonese and Catalans, who constructed seaside ramparts and sturdy towers encompassing an inviting nucleus of narrow, winding streets with whitewashed palazzi. The native language spoken here is a version of Catalan, not Italian, although you probably have to attend one of the Masses conducted in Algherese (or listen in on stories swapped by older fishermen) to hear it. To reach Alghero, head into the Sassari province in the northwestern region of Sardinia. Besides its historic architectural gems such as the Alghero Cathedral and Palazzo d'Albis, the fortified city is well worth a visit to simply stroll and discover local culture on narrow cobblestone streets. The city also has a reputation to serve great food at reasonable prices.

Capo Caccia. Head northwest of Alghero for broad sandy beaches and the spectacular heights of an imposing limestone headland. The rugged promontory, blanketed by lush maquis, is close to the Porto Ferro marina, popular Lampianu beach, and remote coves and caves such as the Grotte di Nettuno.

Fodor's Choice **Grotta di Nettuno** (*Neptune's Caves*). At the base of a sheer cliff, the
★ pounding sea has carved an entrance to the vast fantastic cavern filled
Ⓒ with stunning water pools, stalactites, and stalagmites. You must visit with a guide; tours start on the hour. It's possible to reach the caves by boat or by land. Boat trips depart at regular intervals from the port of Alghero for €10 (price of admission to Grotto extra). The dramatic cave and coves, discovered by fishermen in the 18th century, are

considered one of the most popular tourist attractions on the island for their sheer natural beauty. ⊠ *13 km (8 miles) west of Alghero* ☎ *079/946540* 🎫 *€12* 🕐 *Apr.–Sept., daily 9–7; Oct., daily 9–5; Nov.–Mar., daily 9–4.*

Escala del Cabirol (*Mountain Goat's Stairway*). By land, you can reach the entrance to the Grotta di Nettuno by descending the 654 dizzying "goat steps" of the aptly named zigzagging stairway cut into the steep cliff. By public bus, the trip to the top of the stairway takes about 50 minutes. Allow 15 minutes for the descent by foot. ⊠ *Via Catalogna* ☎ *079/950179* 🎫 *€12 round-trip* 🕐 *From Alghero: 9:15 year-round and 3:10 and 5:10 June–Sept. From Capo Caccia: noon year-round and 4:05 and 6:05 June–Sept.*

Museo Diocesano d'Arte Sacra (*Diocesan Museum of Sacred Art*). This cathedral museum is housed in a 13th-century church designed with Catalan Gothic architecture. The usual assortment of religious treasures—paintings, wooden sculptures, and bronze statues—is on display; look for the masterful 16th-century Catalan silverware, intricately forged with ancient motifs. ⊠ *Via Maiorca 1* ☎ *079/9733041* ⊕ *www. diocesialghero-bosa.it/* 🎫 *€3* 🕐 *Jan.–Mar., Thurs.–Tues. by appointment; Apr., May, and Oct., Thurs.–Tues. 10–1 and 5–8; June and Sept., Thurs.–Tues. 10–1 and 5–9; July and Aug., Thurs.–Tues. 10–1 and 6–11; Dec., Thurs.–Tues. 10–1 by appointment and 4–7; the museum is closed Nov.*

Torre San Giovanni. This old stone tower fortress can be climbed for good views from the terrace. Stop at the interesting city history display on the computer terminals inside the tower. There's also a rotating set of exhibits and a miniature model of Alghero's Old Town. ⊠ *Via Mateotti 12* ☎ *079/973–1605* 🎫 *€2* 🕐 *Apr.–Jun., Tue.–Sun. 10–1 and 5–8; Jul.–Aug., Tue.–Sat., 10–1 and 6:30–10, Sun.–Mon. 6:30–10.*

CASTELSARDO
32 km (20 miles) northeast of Sassari.

The walled seaside citadel of Castelsardo is a delight for craft lovers, with tiny shops crammed with all kinds of souvenirs, particularly woven baskets. The appropriately shaped **Roccia dell'Elefante** (Elephant Rock) on the road into Castelsardo was hollowed out by primitive man to become a *domus de janas* (literally, "fairy house," in fact a Neolithic burial chamber).

SHOPPING

The Sard are very adept craftsmen and -women. For many generations the people in the mountains had to be self-sufficient and worked with bone, wood, and clay to produce practical yet beautiful items, including fine knives, the must-have tool of the shepherd. The women were traditionally weavers—in wool and straw—or lace-makers. Red coral and filigree jewelry also have a long tradition here. If you are looking for some comestibles to take home, Sardinian wine and honey are highly prized. The narrow streets of Alghero and Castelsardo are the best places to shop for locally made crafts. Porto Cervo has fewer craft

shops, but designer names line the shopping streets with top-quality haute couture and jewelry stores plus independent boutiques selling gifts and collectibles.

The walled seaside citadel of **Castelsardo,** 32 km (20 miles) northeast of Sassari, is a delight for basket lovers. Roadside stands and shops in the Old Town sell woven baskets, as well as rugs and wrought iron.

ISOLA. ISOLA is state-sponsored cooperative set up to promote Sardinian crafts. Sassari has Sardinia's main craft exhibition center in the public gardens next to Viale Mancini, built specifically as a showcase for handcrafted gifts and souvenirs in wood, precious metal, ceramic, and fabrics. ⊠ *Giardini Pubblici, Sassari* ☎ *079/230101* ⊕ *www.regione. sardegna.it/isola.*

BEACHES

The beaches around the Costa Smeralda are some of the most exclusive in Europe, but they don't disappoint, with fine golden sand sheltered by red cliffs and fronting azure waters. Most can only be reached by boat, and there are regular small ferries from Porto Cervo. Rentals of sunbeds and towels are reassuringly expensive.

WHERE TO EAT

$$$ ✕ **Da Pietro.** The pleasing menu at Da Pietro includes *bucatini*
ITALIAN   *all'algherese* (hollow, spaghetti-like pasta with a sauce of clams, capers, tomatoes, and olives) and baked fish with a white-wine sauce keeps this seafood restaurant bustling below its vaulted ceilings. Sample *sebadas*, ravioli stuffed with mascarpone cheese and topped with honey. Look for Da Pietro in the Old Town near Largo San Francesco. ⑤ *Average main: €30* ⊠ *Via Ambrogio Machin 20, Sassari* ☎ *079/979645* ⊘ *Closed Wed. and 2 wks in Dec.*

$$$ ✕ **L'Assassino.** Get a true taste of great local Sassarese cooking—and
ITALIAN   many of the other obscure Sardinian specialties for which you may be searching—in a cozy vaulted room with terra-cotta tiling. Horse, donkey, and roast pig figure prominently on the menu; best of all is a *cena sarda,* a 10-dish tasting menu with *porcetto* (roast suckling pig), also spelled porcheddu. The service is friendly, and the room is warm and cozy. Food is served throughout the afternoon. ⑤ *Average main: €25* ⊠ *Via pettenadu 19, Sassari* ☎ *079/235041* ⊕ *www.trattorialassassino. it* ⊘ *Closed Sun.*

PORTOFERRAIO, ITALY (ELBA)

Updated
by Bruce
Leimsidor

Elba is the Tuscan archipelago's largest island, but it resembles nearby verdant Corsica more than it does its rocky Italian sisters, thanks to a network of underground springs that keep the island lush and green. It's this combination of semitropical vegetation and dramatic mountain scenery—unusual in the Mediterranean—that has made Elba so prized for so long, and the island's uniqueness continues to draw boatloads

of visitors throughout the warm months. Lively Portoferraio, the main port, makes a good base for exploring the island.

ESSENTIALS

CURRENCY
The euro.

HOURS
Many shops are open 9–1 and 3:30–7:30 Monday through Saturday. Banks are open weekdays 8:30–1:30 and 2:45–3:45.

PRIVATE TOURS
Taxis offer special prices to see the main sights on the island from July through September.

TELEPHONES
Tri-band GSM phones work in Italy. You can buy prepaid phone cards at telecom shops, news vendors, and tobacconists in all towns and cities. Phone cards can be used for local or international calls.

COMING ASHORE
The cruise-ship dock is just a stone's throw from the historic center of Portoferraio, so most passengers just walk to town. If you want to get around the island, public buses operated by ATL (⊕ *www.atl.livorno.it*) stop at most towns several times a day; the tourist office on viale Elba has timetables. Day tickets cost €8.50. There are numerous places to rent bikes, scooters, motorcycles, or cars. Expect to pay around €45 for a compact manual car in low season and €75 in high season.

EXPLORING ELBA

PORTOFERRAIO
Especially enjoyable in Portoferraio is a stroll around the *centro storico*, fortified in the 16th century by the Medici grand duke Cosimo I. Most of the pretty, multicolor buildings that line the old harbor date from the 18th and 19th centuries, when the boats in the port were full of mineral exports rather than tourists.

Marina di Campo. On the south side of Elba, this small town with a long sandy beach and protected cove is a classic summer vacationer's spot. The laid-back marina is full of bars, boutiques, and restaurants. ⊠ *Elba*.

Monte Capanne. The highest point on Elba, Monte Capanna is crossed by a twisting road that provides magnificent vistas at every turn; the tiny towns of **Poggio** and **Marciana** have enchanting little piazzas full of flowers and trees. You can hike to the top of the mountain, or take an unusual open-basket cable car from just above Poggio. ⊠ *Elba*.

Museo Archeologico. Exhibits at this museum reconstruct the island's ancient history through a display of Etruscan and Roman artifacts recovered from shipwrecks. ⊠ *Località Linguella, Calata Buccari* ☎ *0565/937111* ⊠ *€2* ☉ *June 15–Sept. 15, daily 9:30–2:30 and 5–midnight; Sept. 16–June 14, Thurs. 10:30–1:30 and 4–8.*

Palazzina dei Mulini. During Napoléon's famous exile on Elba in 1814–15, he built this residence out of two windmills. It still contains furniture from the period and Napoléon's impressive library, with the more than

2,000 volumes that he brought here from France. ⊠ *Piazzale Napoleone 1* ☎ *0565/915846* 💶 *€7, €13 with admission to Villa San Martino* 🕙 *Mon. and Wed.–Sat. 9–7, Sun. 9–1.*

Porto Azzurro. The waters of the port at Elba's eastern end are noticeably *azzurro* (sky-blue). It's worth a stop for a walk and a gelato along the rows of yachts harbored here. ⊠ *Elba.*

Rio Marina. Elba's quietest town is an old-fashioned port on the northeastern edge of the island. Here you'll find a pebble beach, an old mine, a leafy public park, and ferry service to Piombino. ⊠ *Elba.*

Villa San Martino. A couple of miles outside Portoferraio, this splendid villa was Napoléon's summer home during his 10-month exile on Elba. Temporary exhibitions are held in a gallery attached to the main building. The Egyptian Room, decorated with idealized scenes of the Egyptian campaign, may have provided Napoléon the consolation of glories past. The villa's classical facade was added by a Russian prince, Anatolia Demidoff, after he bought the house in 1852. ⊠ *Località San Martino, Elba* ☎ *0565/914688* 💶 *€7, €13 with admission to Palazzina dei Mulini* 🕙 *Tues.–Sat. 9–7 and Sun. 9–1.*

BEACHES

Elba's most celebrated beaches are the sandy stretches at **Biodola, Procchio,** and **Marina di Campo,** but the entire island—and particularly the westernmost section, encircling Monte Capanne—is ringed with beautiful coastline. Indeed, it seems that every sleepy town has its own perfect tiny beach. Try **Cavoli** and **Fetovaia** anytime but July and August, when all the car-accessible beaches on the island are packed (there are also some accessible only by boat, such as the black-sand beach of **Punta Nera**).

ACTIVITIES

WATER SPORTS

Il Viottolo. Adventurous types can rent sea kayaks and mountain bikes from this tour operator, or participate in three-day guided excursions on land or by sea. ⊠ *Via Fucini 279, Marina di Campo* ☎ *0565/978005* ⊕ *www.ilviottolo.it.*

Spaziomare. If you are hoping to rent a motorboat for a half- or full-day, this is the place. Sailboats to rent by the week are also available. ⊠ *Via Vittorio Veneto 13, Porto Azzurro* ☎ *0565/95112, 348/6017862* ⊕ *www.spaziomare.it.*

Subnow. Contact this group of experienced divers for information on diving excursions in the waters of Elba's National Marine Park. ⊠ *Via della Foce 89, Località La Foce, Marina di Campo* ☎ *0565/979051* ⊕ *www.subnow.it.*

WHERE TO EAT

$ ✕ **Il Mare.** Homemade pastas and fresh seafood are served here with a
ITALIAN   dash of style. The young chef puts a creative spin on the classics, coming
★   up with such delights as homemade vegetable gnocchi with scampi in a
butter and saffron sauce. The *semifreddi* (literally, "half cold"; frozen
desserts made with ice cream and eggs) are particularly good. Just a
few steps from Rio Marina's pretty port, this is an easy stop on your
way to or from the ferry. ⑤ *Average main: €9* ⊠ *Via del Pozzo 16, Rio
Marina* ☎ *0565/962117.*

$$ ✕ **Trattoria da Lido.** Come here for commendable *gnocchetti di pesce*
ITALIAN   (bite-size potato-and-fish dumplings) with a white cream sauce and
fresh *pesce all'elbana* (whitefish baked with vegetables and potatoes).
The bustling, casual trattoria is in the old center of Portoferraio, at the
beginning of the road to the old Medici walls. ⑤ *Average main: €22*
⊠ *Salita del Falcone 2* ☎ *0565/914650* ⊙ *Closed mid-Dec.–mid-Feb.*

PORTOFINO, ITALY

Updated
by Bruce
Leimsidor

Like the family jewels that bedeck its habitual visitors, the Italian Riv-
iera is glamorous, but in an old-fashioned way. The rustic and ele-
gant, the provincial and chic, the cosmopolitan and the small-town are
blended together here in a sun-drenched pastiche that defines the Ital-
ian side of the Riviera. Although the region bearing the name Liguria
extends inland, its greatest charms are found on the coast, which has
inspired poets and artists for centuries. One of the most photographed
villages along the Ligurian coast, with a decidedly romantic and afflu-
ent aura, Portofino has long been a popular destination for foreigners.
Once an ancient Roman colony and taken by the Republic of Genoa
in 1229, it has also been ruled by the French, English, Spanish, and
Austrians, as well as by marauding bands of 16th-century pirates. Elite
British tourists first flocked to the lush harbor in the mid-1800s, and
today some of Europe's wealthiest lay anchor in Portofino in summer.

ESSENTIALS
CURRENCY
The euro.

HOURS
Stores are generally open from 9 or 9:30 to 1 and from 3:30 or 4 to 7
or 7:30. Many shops close Sunday. Many national museums are closed
Monday and may have shorter hours on Sunday.

PRIVATE TOURS
Benvenuto Tours offers full-day tours out of Portofino to the towns
to the east, the Cinque Terre, Lerici, and Portovenere. This is a pricey
option (€450 per person) but an effortless way to see some dramatic
costal scenery and lovely historic villages, including those beloved by
the English romantic poets.

Contacts Benvenuto Tours. ☎ *(39)081/007–2114 in Genoa*
⊕ *www.benvenutolimos.com.*

TELEPHONES

Tri-band GSM phones work in Italy. You can buy prepaid phone cards at telecom shops, news vendors, and tobacconists in all towns and cities. Phone cards can be used for local or international calls.

COMING ASHORE

Ships must tender passengers ashore in the heart of the picturesque port. There is no train station in Portofino: You must take the bus to Santa Margherita Ligure (€1) and pick up train services from there. An alternative is a ferry, Sirvizio Marittimo di Tigullio, which connects Santa Margherita Ligure to all of the towns along the cost at convenient hours.

A rental car is useful to explore the Ligurian coast, but allow plenty of time to return your rental car as roads become extremely busy during the summer, and journey times may be longer than the distance suggests. Expect to pay about €45 for a compact manual vehicle. Delivery to the portside is an additional cost. Drivers should be warned, however, that while the scenery is spectacular, the drive is very taxing, with constant hairpin turns.

EXPLORING PORTOFINO AND VICINITY

PORTOFINO

Abbazia di San Fruttuoso (*Abbey of San Fruttuoso*). On the sea at the foot of Monte Portofino, the medieval Abbazia di San Fruttuoso, built by the Benedictines of Monte Cassino, protects a minuscule fishing village that can be reached only on foot or by water—a 20-minute boat ride from Portofino and also reachable from Camogli, Santa Margherita Ligure, and Rapallo. The restored abbey is now the property of a national conservation fund (FAI) and occasionally hosts temporary exhibitions. The church contains the tombs of some illustrious members of the Doria family. The old abbey and its grounds are delightful places to spend a few hours, perhaps lunching at one of the modest beachfront trattorias nearby (open only in summer). Boatloads of visitors can make it very crowded very fast; you might appreciate it most off-season. ⊠ *15-min boat ride or 2-hr walk northwest of Portofino* ☎ *0185/772703* 🖼 *€7 Apr.–Sept., €5 Oct.–Mar.* ۞ *June–Sept. 15, daily 10–5:45; May & Sept. 16-30, daily 10–4:45; Oct.–Mar., Tues.–Sun. 10–3:45. Last entry 1 hr before closing.*

Castello Brown. From the harbor, follow the signs for the climb to Castello Brown—the most worthwhile sight in Portofino—with its medieval relics, impeccable gardens, and sweeping views. The castle was founded in the Middle Ages but restored in the 16th through 18th centuries. In true Portofino form, it was owned by Genoa's English consul from 1870 until it opened to the public in 1961. ⊠ *Above harbor* ☎ *0185/269046* ⊕ *www.castellobrown.it* 🖼 *€3* ۞ *Apr.–Sept., Wed.–Mon. 10–6; Oct.–Mar., Wed.–Mon. 10–5.*

Paraggi. The only sand beach near Portofino is at Paraggi, a cove on the road between Santa Margherita and Portofino. The bus will stop here on request.

Italian Riviera

A15

A12

SS1

SS523

SS586

SS586

SS45

SS226

SS35

Genoa

Nervi

Zoagli

Rapallo

Chiavari

Lavagna

Cavi di Lavagna

Sestri Levante

Moneglia

Levanto

Monterosso al Mare

Vernazza

Corniglia

Manarola

Riomaggiore

Portovenere

La Spezia

San Terenzo

Lerici

Tellaro

Parco Nazionale delle Cinque Terre

Golfo di Genova

Ligurian Sea

Portofino Area
see detail maps

10 miles

15 km

Portofino Promontory

A12

Camogli

Ruta

Punta Chiappa

Monte Portofino

Pietre Strette

Santa Margherita Ligure

Paraggi

Olmi

Abbazia di San Fruttuoso

Portofino
see detail map

Portofino

P.N. Regionale di Portofino

Pza. d. Libertà

V. Duca degli Abruzzi

Senno Carone

Pza. Martiri dall'Olivetti

V. Roma

San Giorgio

Castello Brown

l'Isoletto

Golfo di Tigullio

Porto

Punta Portofino

Punta del Capo

Ligurian Sea

1/8 mi

1/8 km

Punta Portofino. Pristine views can be had from the deteriorating *faro* (lighthouse) at Punta Portofino, a 15-minute walk along the point that begins at the southern end of the port. Along the seaside path you can see numerous impressive, sprawling private residences behind high iron gates.

San Giorgio. The small church San Giorgio, sitting on a ridge, was rebuilt four times during World War II. It is said to contain the relics of its namesake, brought back from the Holy Land by the Crusaders. Portofino enthusiastically celebrates Saint George's Day every April 23. ⊠ *Above harbor* ☎ *0185/269337* ☉ *Daily 7–6.*

> ## PORTOFINO BEST BETS
>
> **Linger over an espresso at a waterfront café.** Portofino is a place to see and be seen, so relax and survey your surroundings.
>
> **Walk the hillside paths above the town.** The views along the Riviera are delightful.
>
> **Visit Camogli.** You'll get a touch of gritty reality contrasting with the glitz of Portofino itself.

SANTA MARGHERITA LIGURE
5 km (3 miles) from Portofino.

A beautiful old resort town favored by well-to-do Italians, Santa Margherita Ligure has everything a Riviera playground should have—plenty of palm trees and attractive hotels, cafés, and a marina packed with yachts. Some of the older buildings here are still decorated on the outside with the trompe-l'oeil frescoes typical of this part of the Riviera. This is a pleasant, convenient base, which for many represents a perfect balance on the Italian Riviera: bigger and less Americanized than the Cinque Terre; less glitzy than San Remo; more relaxing than Genoa and environs; and ideally situated for day trips, such as an excursion to Portofino.

CAMOGLI
15 km (9 miles) northwest of Portofino, 20 km (12 miles) east of Genoa.

★ Camogli, at the edge of the large promontory and nature reserve known as the Portofino Peninsula, has always been a town of sailors. By the 19th century it was leasing its ships throughout the continent. Today multicolor houses, remarkably deceptive trompe-l'oeil frescoes, and a massive 17th-century seawall mark this appealing harbor community, perhaps as beautiful as Portofino but without the glamour. When exploring on foot, don't miss the boat-filled second harbor, which is reached by ducking under a narrow archway at the northern end of the first one.

Acquario (*Aquarium*). The Castello Dragone, built onto the sheer rock face near the harbor, is home to the Acquario, which has tanks filled with local marine life built into the ramparts. ⊠ *Via Isola* ☎ *0185/773375* 🎟 *€3* ☉ *Summer: 10–12 and 3–7; Winter: 10–11:45 and 2–5:45.*

RAPALLO
8 km (5 miles) north of Portofino, 3 km (2 miles) north of Santa Margherita, 28 km (17 miles) east of Genoa.

Rapallo was once one of Europe's most fashionable resorts, but it passed its heyday before World War II and has suffered from the building boom brought on by tourism. Ezra Pound and D. H. Lawrence lived here, and many other writers, poets, and artists have been drawn to it. Today the town's harbor is filled with yachts. A single-span bridge on the eastern side of the bay is named after Hannibal, who is said to have passed through the area after crossing the Alps.

SHOPPING

In addition to the fine leather and haute couture for which Italy is known, Liguria is famous for its fine laces, silver-and-gold filigree work, and ceramics. Look for bargains in velvet, macramé, olive wood, and marble. Don't forget the excellent wines, cheeses, dried meats, and olive oils.

Portofino is awash with small boutiques selling fashion and gift items, but it's also one of the most expensive places to shop along the coast, catering to the wealthy yacht owners who call in during the summer. However, all the coastal villages have pretty shops to explore.

The attractive coastal village of Zoagli on the S1, 4 km (2½ miles) east of Rapallo, has been famous for silk, velvet, and damask since the Middle Ages.

ACTIVITIES

If you have the stamina, you can hike to the **Abbazia di San Fruttuoso** from Portofino. It's a steep climb at first, and the walk takes about 2½ hours one way. Much more modest hikes from Portofino include a 1-hour uphill walk to Cappella delle Gave, a bit inland in the hills, from where you can continue downhill to Santa Margherita Ligure (another 1½ hours) and a gently undulating paved trail leading to the beach at Paraggi (½ hour). Finally, there's a 2½-hour hike from Portofino that heads farther inland to Ruta, through Olmi and Pietre Strette. The trails are well marked, and maps are available at the tourist information offices in Rapallo, Santa Margherita, Portofino, and Camogli.

BEACHES

The Ligurian coast is known for its rocky vistas, but the Portofino promontory has one sandy beach, on the east side, at **Paraggi.**

WHERE TO EAT

$ ✕ **Canale.** If the staggering prices of virtually all of Portofino's restaurants put you off, the long line outside this family-run bakery indicates that you're not alone and that something special is in store. Here all the focaccia Genovese is baked on the spot and served fresh from the oven, along with all kinds of sandwiches, pastries, and other refreshments.

BAKERY

The only problem is there's nowhere to sit—time for a picnic! $ *Average main: €10* ⊠ *Via Roma 30* ☎ *0185/269248* ⊟ *No credit cards* ⊗ *Closed Nov.–Feb.*

$$$$ ✕**Vento Ariel.** This small, friendly restaurant serves some of the best
SEAFOOD   seafood in town. Dine on the shaded terrace in summer and watch
the bustling activity in the nearby port. Only the freshest seafood is
served; try the spaghetti *alle vongole* (with clams) or the mixed grilled
fish. $ *Average main: €40* ⊠ *Calata Porto, Camogli* ☎ *0185/771080*
⊗ *Closed Wed., 1st half of Dec., and Jan.*

ST-TROPEZ, FRANCE

Updated   Brigitte Bardot kick-started the rush in the early 1960s, and she was fol-
by Jennifer   lowed by the likes of Liz Taylor and Sophia Loren. People still flock to
Ladonne   St-Tropez for the sun, the sea, and, the celebrities. The new generation
includes Elton, Barbra, Oprah, Jack, and Uma, though they stay hidden
in villas, and the people you'll see on the streets are mere mortals, lots
of them, many intent on displaying the best—and often the most—of
their youth, beauty, and wealth. Still, if you take an early-morning stroll
around the pretty port or down the narrow medieval streets with their
candied-almond hues, you'll see just how charming St-Tropez can be.
There's a weekend's worth of boutiques to explore and many cute cafés
where you can sit under colored awnings and watch the spectacle that
is St-Trop (*trop* in French means "too much") saunter by. Or head to
the beaches, which are some of the most fashionable in Europe.

ESSENTIALS
CURRENCY
The euro.

HOURS
Most stores are open Monday–Saturday 9–7, but many close at lunchtime (usually from noon to 2 or 3), and some open on Sunday during
July and August. Museums are generally open 10–5, but most are closed
either Monday or Tuesday.

TELEPHONES
Tri-band GSM phones work in France. You can buy prepaid phone
cards at telecom shops, news vendors, and tobacconists in all towns
and cities. Phone cards can be used for local or international calls.
Orange, SFR, Bouygues Telecom, and Virgin are leading telecom companies. If you have an unlocked GSM phone, LeFrenchMobile (⊕ *www.
lefrenchmobile.com*) offers SIM cards (and micro SIM cards) with support in English, unlimited validity of credits, and prepurchase online.

COMING ASHORE
The port at St-Tropez is too small to accept commercial cruise vessels, so
passengers are tendered to a landing dock, which is about a five-minute
walk from town. There are no passenger facilities portside. Taxis and
tour buses are not allowed into the staging area, which means a walk
from the landing stage to transport connections is unavoidable.

Car-rental offices can be found in the town; expect to pay about €75
for an economy manual vehicle. Taxis are available at the port entrance

Golfe de St-Tropez

and can provide tourist itineraries or transfers to the beaches. For single journeys, prices are €3.20 then €0.85 per km (½-mile). Be aware that, especially during the summer, traffic heading into St-Tropez builds up, and you can spend more than an hour just traveling the last two or three miles to the port and town. Always allow plenty of time to return any rental car or make the return taxi journey.

EXPLORING ST-TROPEZ

Citadelle. Head up Rue de la Citadelle to these 16th-century ramparts, which stand in a lovely hilltop park offering a fantastic view of the town and the sea. Amid today's bikini-clad sun worshippers it's hard to imagine St-Tropez as a military outpost, but inside the Citadelle's donjon the **Musée Naval** (Naval Museum) displays ship models, cannons, maps, and pictures of St-Tropez from its days as a naval port (closed for renovation through 2012). ⊠ _Rue de la Citadelle_ ☎ _04–94–97–59–43_ 🎫 _Citadelle €2.50_ ⊘ _Oct.–Mar., daily 10–noon and 1:30–5; Apr.–Sept., daily 10–6:30._

★ **Musée de l'Annonciade** (_Annunciation Museum_). The legacy of the artists who loved St-Tropez has been lovingly preserved in this extraordinary museum, housed in a 14th-century chapel just inland from the southwest corner of the Vieux Port. Cutting-edge temporary exhibitions

keep visitors on their toes while works stretching from pointillists to fauvists to cubists line the walls. Signac, Matisse, Signard, Braque, Dufy, Vuillard, and Rouault are all here, and their work traces the evolution of painting from impressionism to expressionism. The museum also hosts temporary exhibitions every summer, from local talent to up-and-coming international artists. ⊠ *Quai de l'Épi/Pl., Georges Grammont* ☎ *04–94–17–84–10* 🛒 *€5* ☺ *Jan.–Oct. and Dec., Wed.–Mon. 10–noon and 2–6.*

Place des Lices. Enjoy a time-out in the the social center of the Old Town, also called the Place Carnot, just off the Montée Guy Ringrave as you descend from the Citadelle.

A symmetrical forest of plane trees provides shade to rows of cafés and restaurants, skateboarders, children, and grandfatherly pétanque players. The square becomes a moveable feast (for both eyes and palate) on market days—Tuesday and Saturday—while at night a café seat is as hotly contested as a quayside seat during the day. Just as Deborah Kerr and David Niven once did in *Bonjour Tristesse,* watch the boule players under the glow of hundreds of electric bulbs. Heading back to the Vieux Port area, take in the boutiques lining Rues Sibilli, Clemenceau, or Gambetta to help accessorize your evening look—you never know when that photographer from *Elle* will be snapping away at the trendoisie.

Quartier de la Ponche. This Old Town maze of backstreets and ramparts is daubed in shades of gold, pink, ocher, and sky blue. Trellised jasmine and wrought-iron birdcages hang from the shuttered windows, and many of the tiny streets dead-end at the sea. Here you can find the **Port des Pécheurs** (Fishermen's Port), on whose beach Bardot did a star turn in *And God Created Woman.* Twisting, narrow streets, designed to break the impact of the mistral, open to tiny squares with fountains. The main drag here, Rue de la Ponche, leads into Place l'Hôtel de Ville, landmarked by a *mairie* (town hall) marked out in typical Tropezienne hues of pink and green.

Vieux Port. Bordered by Quai de l'Épi, Quai Bouchard, Quai Peri, Quai Suffren, and Quai Jean-Jaurès, Vieux Port is a place for strolling and looking over the shoulders of artists daubing their versions of the view on easels set up along the water's edge. Meanwhile, folding director's chairs at the famous port-side cafés Le Gorille (named for its late exceptionally hirsute manager), Café de Paris, and Sénéquier's are well placed for observing the cast of St-Tropez's living theater play out its colorful roles.

RAMATUELLE
12 km (7 miles) southwest of St-Tropez.

A typical hilltop whorl of red-clay roofs and dense inner streets topped with arches and lined with arcades, this ancient market town was destroyed in the Wars of Religion and rebuilt as a harmonious whole in 1620, complete with venerable archways and vaulted passages. Now its souvenir shops and galleries attract day-trippers out of St-Tropez, who enjoy the pretty drive through the vineyards as much as the village itself. At the top of the village you can visit the Moulin de Paillas, on Route du Moulin de Paillas, a windmill recently restored in the old style with a mechanism made entirely of wood; the site offers a panoramic view of the coastline. Free, guided tours of the windmill are held every Tuesday from 10 to noon. Ramatuelle is also just a heartbeat away from the **Plage de Pamplonne**—a destination location among hippies and starlets alike.

SHOPPING

Designer boutiques may be spreading like wild mushrooms all over St-Tropez, but the main fashionista strutting platform is along **Rue Gambetta** or **Rue Allard.** For those who balk at spending a small fortune on the latest strappy sandal, **Rue Sibilli,** behind the Quai Suffren, is lined with all kinds of trendy, more affordable boutiques. The **Place des Lices** overflows with produce, regional foods, clothing, and *brocantes* (collectibles) on Tuesday and Saturday mornings. Don't miss the picturesque little fish market that fills up **Place aux Herbes** every morning.

BEACHES

The famous beaches of St-Tropez lie southeast of the town on a small peninsula.

Plage de Pamplonne. A typical hilltop whorl of red-clay roofs and dense inner streets topped with arches and lined with arcades, this ancient market town was destroyed in the Wars of Religion and rebuilt as a harmonious whole in 1620, complete with venerable archways and vaulted passages. Now its souvenir shops and galleries attract day-trippers out of St-Tropez, who enjoy the pretty drive through the vineyards as much as the village itself. Plage de Pamplonne is home to the ever-famous **Club 55**, where the rich and famous are known to play. ✉ *Plage de Pamplonne* ☎ *04–94–55–55–55* ⊕ *www.leclub55.com.*

WHERE TO EAT

$$$ ✕ **La Table du Marché.** This charming bistro, tearoom, and boutique from
BISTRO celebrity chef Christophe Leroy offers up a mouthwatering spread of regional specialties in a surprisingly casual atmosphere. The service is warm, and the homey fare includes cheese and macaroni made chic with lobster, tomato *pistou* tart, and whipped potatoes with truffles. Lunchtime visitors can dive into a nicely balanced set menu or choose from a selection of goods seductively on display. ⑤ *Average main: €30* ✉ *21*

bis rue Allard, St-Tropez ☎ *04–94–97–91–91* ⊕ *www.christophe-leroy. com* ☾ *Nov.–end of Mar.*

$$ ✕ **Le Café.** The busy terrace here often doubles as a stadium for differ-
BISTRO ent factions cheering on favorite local pétanque players in the Place des
Lices. You, too, can play—borrow some boules from the friendly bar
staff (and get your pastis bottle at the ready: you'll need it to properly
appreciate the full pétanque experience). Hilarious "beginner" pétanque
soirees are on tap Saturday nights in spring and summer. The food is
as good as the setting: Try the Provençal beef stew and traditional fish
soup; there's a well-priced lunch menu. It's always busy, so reservations
are strongly recommended. ⑤ *Average main: €22* ⊠ *5 pl. des Lices, St-
Tropez* ☎ *04–94–97–44–69* ⊕ *www.lecafe.fr.*

VALENCIA, SPAIN

Updated by   Despite its proximity to the Mediterranean, Valencia's history and geog-
Joanna Styles raphy have been defined most significantly by the River Turia and the
fertile floodplain (*huerta*) that surrounds it. Modern Valencia was best
known for its flooding disasters until the River Turia was diverted to the
south in the late 1950s. Since then, the city has been on a steady course
of urban beautification. The lovely *puentes* (bridges) that once spanned
the Turia look equally graceful spanning a wandering municipal park,
and the spectacular futuristic Ciudad de las Artes y de las Sciencias
(City of Arts and Sciences), designed by Valencian-born architect San-
taigo Clalatrava, has at long last created an exciting architectural link
between this river town and the Mediterranean. Valencia's port, and
parts of the city itself, underwent major structural refurbishment for
the America's Cup sailing classic held here in 2007 and 2010. A new
cruise terminal is planned for 2014–15.

ESSENTIALS
CURRENCY
The euro.

HOURS
Museums are generally open from 9 until 7 or 8, but many are closed
on Monday and some close in the afternoon. Most stores are open
Monday–Saturday 9–1:30 and 5–8, but tourist shops may open in the
afternoon and also on Sunday between May and September.

PRIVATE TOURS
Valencia Tourist Board. The Valencia tourist board organizes a number of
guided tours and trips, known as "Experiences," around the city and
further afield. Online discounts are available. ☎ *900/701818* ⊕ *www.
turisvalencia.es.*

TELEPHONES
Most tri-band and quad-band GSM phones will work in Spain, where
mobile services are 3G-compatible. Public kiosks accept phone cards
that support international calls (cards sold in press shops, bars, and
telecom shops). Major companies include Vodafone.

COMING ASHORE

Valencia's port area received a face-lift to coincide with the arrival of the America's Cup competition in June 2007. Though the terminal itself has limited facilities, the public interface areas, where the port and waterfront meet the city, have lots of restaurants, cafés, and shops.

It is a long walk from the port to the historic downtown district, but the trip is enjoyable if you want to take the time. You may be interested in the Valencia Cruise Card available from the tourist office in the port. Costing €10, the card includes a shuttle bus from the port stopping at L'Oceanogràphic, Ciudad de las Artes, and the city center, as well as discounts on local attractions and sights. The city has an excellent public transport system (⊕ *www.emtvalencia.es*), so reaching all parts of the city by bus, metro, or tram is a cinch. A single journey is €1.50, and a one-day ticket is €3.90 within the downtown zone, €9.60 for all three zones.

Renting a car won't be an advantage when exploring the city, but it will allow you to head out along the coast or inland to explore the countryside. For an economy manual vehicle, expect to pay about €45 per day.

EXPLORING VALENCIA

Casa Museo José Benlliure. The modern Valencian painter and sculptor José Benlliure is known for his intimate portraits and massive historical and religious paintings, many of which hang in Valencia's Museo de Bellas Artes (Museum of Fine Arts). Here in his elegant house and studio are 50 of his works, including paintings, ceramics, sculptures, and drawings. On display are also works by his son, Pepino, who painted in the small, flower-filled garden in the back of the house, and iconographic sculptures by Benlliure's brother, the well-known sculptor Mariano Benlliure. ⊠ *Calle Blanquerías 23* ☎ *963/919103* ⊡ *€2; free weekends and holidays* ⊙ *Tues.–Sat. 10–2 and 4:30–8:30, Sun. 10–3.*

Cathedral. Valencia's 13th- to 15th-century cathedral is the heart of the city. The building has three portals—Romanesque, Gothic, and rococo. Inside, Renaissance and baroque marble was removed to restore the original Gothic style, as is now the trend in Spanish churches. The Capilla del Santo Cáliz (Chapel of the Holy Chalice) displays a purple agate vessel purported to be the Holy Grail (Christ's cup at the Last Supper) and thought to have been brought to Spain in the 4th century. Behind the altar you can see the left arm of **St. Vincent,** who was martyred in Valencia in 304. Stars of the cathedral **museum** are Goya's two famous paintings of St. Francis de Borja, duke of Gandia. To the left of the cathedral entrance is the octagonal tower **El Miguelete,** which you can climb: the roofs of the Old Town create a kaleidoscope of orange and brown terra-cotta, and the sea appears in the background. It's said that you can see 300 belfries from here, including bright-blue cupolas made of ceramic tiles from nearby Manises. The tower was built in 1381 and the final spire added in 1736. ⊠ *Pl. de la Reina* ☎ *963/918127* ⊕ *www.catedraldevalencia.es* ⊡ *Cathedral and museum €4.50, tower €2* ⊙ *Nov.–mid-Mar., Mon.–Sat. 10–5:30; mid-Mar.–Oct., Mon.–Sat. 10–6:30, Sun. 2–6:30.*

Valencia

2

- Plaza Portal Nuevo
- C. Blanquerias
- ◆ Casa Museo José Benlliure
- ◆ Institut Valencià d'Art Modern (IVAM)
- C. Conde Trenor
- Puente de Serranos
- Puente de la Trinidad
- ◆ Museo de Bellas Artes
- Jardines del Real
- C. San Pio V
- Turia
- C. Serranos
- C. Pintor López
- C. Trinitarios
- Puente del Real
- C. Abadía (San Nicolás)
- ◆ San Nicolás
- **Plaza de la Virgen** ◆
- C. Caballeros
- Plaza Tetuán
- Plaza San Jaime
- Plaza del Mercado
- **Cathedral** ◆
- Plaza de la Reina
- C. de la Paz
- ◆ **Lonja de la Seda**
- ◆ **Real Colegio del Patriarca**
- C. de la Nave
- Plaza Patriarca
- Plaza Porta de la Mar
- **Palacio del Marqués de Dos Aguas** ◆
- C. Poeta Querol
- Avda. Barón de Carcer
- TO AMERICA'S CUP PARK/MARINA →
- C. Barcas
- C. Pintor Sorolla
- C. Sorni
- **Plaza del Ayuntamiento** ◆
- C. Pascual y Genís
- C. Colón
- C. Hernán Cortés
- C. Isabel la Católica
- C. Jorge Juan
- Avda. Marqués de Sotelo
- Paseo Russafa
- Plaza San Agustín
- C. Játiva
- C. Cirilo
- **Estación del Norte**
- Pasaje Dr. Serra
- Gran Vía Marqués del Turia
- Gran Vía Marqués del Turia
- **Plaza de Toros** ◆
- C. Pelayo
- C. de Bailén
- **Palau de la Música** ◆
- **Ciutat de les Arts i les Ciències** ◆

0   1/8 mi

0   1/8 km

Fodor's Choice   **Ciutat de les Arts i les Ciències.** Designed by native son Santiago Calatrava,
★   this sprawling futuristic complex is the home of Valencia's **Museu de les**
☺   **Ciències Príncipe Felipe** (Prince Philip Science Museum), **L'Hemisfèric**
(Hemispheric Planetarium), **L'Oceanogràfic** (Oceanographic Park),
and **Palau de les Arts** (Palace of the Arts). With resplendent buildings
resembling combs and crustaceans, the Ciutat is a favorite of architecture buffs and curious kids. The Science Museum has soaring platforms filled with lasers, holograms, simulators, hands-on experiments,
and a swell "zero gravity" exhibition on space exploration. The eye-
shaped planetarium projects 3-D virtual voyages on its huge IMAX
screen. At the Oceanographic Park you can take a submarine ride
through a coastal marine habitat. Recent additions include an amphitheater, an indoor theater, and a chamber-music hall. ⊠ *Av. Autovía del
Saler 7* ☎ *902/100031* ⊕ *www.cac.es* ✉ *Museu de les Ciències €7.70,
L'Hemisfèric €7.70, L'Oceanogràfic €24.50; combination ticket €32.40*
☉ *Museum mid-Sept.–June, Sun.–Fri. 10–8, Sat. 10–9; July–mid-Sept.,
daily 10–9. L'Oceanogràfic mid-Sept.–June, Sun.–Fri. 10–6, Sat. 10–8;
July–mid-Sept. 10–midnight. L'Hemisfèric daily shows generally every
hr on hr 11–8; Fri. and Sat., additional show at 9.*

Estación del Norte. Designed by Demetrio Ribes Mano in 1917, the
train station is a splendid moderniste structure decorated with motifs
of Valencia oranges. The tops of the two towers seem to sprout like
palm trees. ⊠ *Calle Játiva s/n* ☎ *902/240202.*

Institut Valencià d'Art Modern (IVAM). Dedicated to modern and contemporary art, this blocky, uninspired building on the edge of the Old
City—where the riverbed makes a loop—houses a permanent collection of 20th-century avant-garde painting, European Informalism
(including the Spanish artists Antonio Saura, Antoni Tàpies, and Eduardo Chillida), pop art, and photography. ⊠ *Guillem de Castro 118*
☎ *963/863000* ⊕ *www.ivam.es* ✉ *€2, free Sun.* ☉ *July and Aug., Tues.–
Sun. 10–10; Sept.–June, Tues.–Sun. 10–8.*

Lonja de la Seda (*Silk Exchange*). On the Plaza del Mercado sits the 15th-
century Lonja de la Seda, a product of Valencia's golden age, when the
city's prosperity as one of the capitals of the Corona de Aragón made
it a leading European commercial and artistic center. The Lonja was
constructed as an expression of this splendor. Widely regarded as one of
Spain's finest civil Gothic buildings, its facade is decorated with ghoul-
ish gargoyles, complemented inside by high vaulting and slender heli-
coidal (twisted) columns. Opposite the Lonja stands the **Iglesia de los
Santos Juanes** (Church of the St. Johns), whose interior was destroyed
during the 1936–39 Spanish Civil War, and, next door, the moderniste **Mercado Central** (Central Market), with its wrought-iron girders
and stained-glass windows. The bustling food market is open Monday
through Saturday 8 to 2; local shoppers and visitors alike queue up at
the colorful stalls filled with fruit, vegetables, meat, fish, and confection-
ary. ⊠ *Pl. del Mercado s/n* ☎ *963/917395* ⊕ *www.lonjadevalencia.com*
✉ *Free* ☉ *Tues.–Sat. 10–2 and 4:30–8:30, Sun. 10–3.*

★   **Museo de Bellas Artes** (*Museum of Fine Arts*). Valencia was a thriving
center of artistic activity in the 15th century, one reason that the city's

Museum of Fine Arts is among the best in Spain. To get here, cross the old riverbed by the Puente de la Trinidad (Trinity Bridge) to the north bank; the museum is at the edge of the **Jardines del Real** (Royal Gardens), with its fountains, rose gardens, tree-lined avenues, and small zoo. The Royal Gardens are open daily 8–dusk. The permanent collection of the museum, with its lovely palm-shaded cloister, includes many of the finest paintings by Jacomart and Juan Reixach, two of several artists known as the Valencian Primitives, as well as work by Hieronymus Bosch—or

> ### VALENCIA BEST BETS
>
> **Go straight to the top.** The view of Valencia from the Miguelete Tower is magnficient.
>
> **Cast an eye over Ciutat de les Arts i les Ciències.** One of Spain's most imaginative modern-iste developments is in Valencia.
>
> **Leave the bull at home.** Tread carefully in the Museo Nacional de Cerámica, which showcases porcelain, one of the city's most famous exports.

El Bosco, as they call him here. The ground floor has a number of the brooding, 17th-century Tenebrist masterpieces of Francisco Ribalta and his pupil José Ribera, a Diego Velázquez self-portrait, and a room devoted to Goya. Upstairs, look for Joaquín Sorolla (Gallery 66), the Valencian painter of everyday Spanish life in the 19th century. ✉ *Calle San Pío V 9* ☎ *963/870300* ⊕ *www.museobellasartesvalencia.gva.es* 🎫 *Free* ⊙ *Tues.–Sun. 10–8.*

★ **Palacio del Marqués de Dos Aguas** (*Ceramics Museum*). This building near Plaza Patriarca has gone through many additions over the years and now has elements of several architectural styles, including a fascinating baroque alabaster facade. Embellished with carvings of fruits and vegetables, the rococo facade was designed in 1740 by Ignacio Vergara. It centers on the two voluptuous male figures representing the Dos Aguas (Two Waters), a reference to Valencia's two main rivers and the origin of the noble title of the Marqués de Dos Aguas. Since 1954, the palace has housed the **Museo Nacional de Cerámica,** with a magnificent collection of local and artisanal ceramics. Look for the Valencian kitchen on the second floor. ✉ *C. Poeta Querol 2* ☎ *963/516392* 🎫 *Palace and museum €3, free Sat. afternoon and Sun. morning* ⊙ *Tues.–Sat. 10–2 and 4–8, Sun. 10–2.*

Palau de la Música (*Music Palace*). On one of the nicest stretches of the Turia riverbed is this huge glass vault, Valencia's main concert venue. Supported by 10 arcaded pillars, the dome gives the illusion of a greenhouse, both from the street and from within its sun-filled, tree-landscaped interior. Home of the Orquesta de Valencia, the main hall also hosts performers on tour from around the world, including chamber and youth orchestras, opera, and an excellent concert series featuring early, baroque, and classical music. For concert schedules, pick up a Turia guide or one of the local newspapers at any newsstand. To see the building without concert tickets, pop into the **art gallery,** which hosts free changing exhibits. ✉ *Paseo de la Alameda 30* ☎ *963/375020* ⊕ *www.palauvalencia.com* ⊙ *Gallery daily 10:30–1:30 and 5:30–9.*

Plaza del Ayuntamiento. With the massive baroque facades of the *ayuntamiento* (city hall) and the central post office facing each other across the park, this plaza is the hub of city life. City hall itself houses the municipal tourist office and a museum of paleontology. ⊙ *Ayuntamiento weekdays 8:30–2:30.*

Plaza de Toros. Adjacent to the train station is the bullring, one of the oldest in Spain. The best bullfighters are featured during Las Fallas in March, particularly March 18 and 19.

Museo Taurino (*Bullfighting Museum*). Down Pasaje Doctor Serra, the Museo Taurino has bullfighting memorabilia, including bulls' heads and matador swords. ⊠ *Pasaje Doctor Serra 10* ☎ *963/883738* ⚏ *Free* ⊙ *Bullring and museum Tues.–Sun. 10–6*

Real Colegio del Patriarca (*Royal Seminary of the Patriarch*). This seminary, with its church, cloister, and library, is the crown jewel of Valencia's Renaissance architecture and one of the city's finest sites. Founded by San Juan de Ribera in the 16th century, it has a lovely Renaissance patio and an ornate church, and its museum holds works by Juan de Juanes, Francisco Ribalta, and El Greco. ⊠ *C. de la Nave 1* ☎ *963/514176* ⚏ *€2* ⊙ *Daily 11–1:30.*

San Nicolás. A small plaza contains Valencia's oldest church, once the parish of the Borgia Pope Calixtus III. The first portal you come to, with a tacked-on, rococo bas-relief of the Virgin Mary with cherubs, hints at what's inside: every inch of the originally Gothic church is covered with exuberant early-baroque ornamentation. ⊠ *C. Caballeros 35* ☎ *963/913317* ⚏ *Free* ⊙ *Open for mass weekdays 8–9 am and 7–8 pm; Sat. 6:30–8:30 pm; Sun. various masses 8–1:15.*

SHOPPING

Shoes and leather goods are among Valencia's main products. Both handmade and mass-produced ceramics are created in a range of colors and styles. Fans and silk shawls, along with other traditional Spanish dress, are priced according to quality. Olives and olive oil will make gourmets happy, and olive oil is also used for a range of hair and beauty products. A flea market is held every Sunday morning by the cathedral. Another market takes place on Sunday morning in Plaza Luis Casanova, near Valencia's soccer stadium. If it's great local designer wear you're after, then head straight to the Barrio Carmen.

The town of Manises, 9 km (5 ½ miles) west of Valencia, is a center for Valencian ceramics, known particularly for its azulejos.

WHERE TO EAT

$ ✗ **La Riuà.** A favorite with Valencia's well connected and well-to-do
SPANISH   since 1982, this family-run restaurant a few steps from the Plaza de la Reina specializes in seafood dishes like *anguilas* (eels) prepared with *all i pebre* (garlic and pepper), *pulpitos guisados* (stewed baby octopus), and traditional paellas. Lunch begins at 2 and not a moment before. The walls are covered with decorative ceramics and the gastronomic awards the restaurant has won over the years. ⚏ *Average main: €13*

✉ *C. del Mar 27* ☎ *963/914571* ✍ *lariua@lariua.com* ⊕ *www.lariua. com* ⚒ *Reservations essential* ⊘ *Closed Sun., Easter wk, and Aug. No dinner Mon.*

$$
SEAFOOD
✕ **El Timonel.** Decorated like the inside of a yacht, this restaurant two blocks east of the bullring serves outstanding shellfish. The cooking is simple but makes use of the freshest ingredients; try the grilled *lenguado* (sole) or *lubina* (sea bass). Also top-notch are the eight different kinds of rice dishes, including paella with lobster and *arroz a banda,* with peeled shrimp, prawns, mussels, and clams. For a sweet finale, try the house special *naranjas a la reina,* oranges spiced with rum and topped with *salsa de fresa* (strawberry sauce). Lunch attracts businesspeople, and dinner brings in a crowd of locals and foreigners. ⑤ *Average main: €18* ✉ *Félix Pizcueta 13* ☎ *963/526300* ✍ *restaurante@eltimonel.com* ⊕ *www.eltimonel.com* ⊘ *Closed Mon.*

VALLETTA, MALTA

Updated by Lindsay Bennett

Hulking megalithic temples, ornate baroque churches, narrow old-world streets, and hilltop citadels are Malta's human legacy. Dizzying limestone cliffs, sparkling seas, and charming rural landscapes make up its natural beauty. In its 7,000 years of human habitation, Malta has been overrun by every major Mediterranean power: Phoenicians, Carthaginians, Romans, Byzantines, and Arabs; Normans, Swabians, Angevins, Aragonese, and the Knights of the Order of St. John of Jerusalem; the French, the British, and now tourists. The Germans and Italians tried to take it in World War II—their air raids were devastating—but could not. The islands' history with the Knights of the Order of St. John has given them their lasting character. In 1565, when the forces of Süleyman the Magnificent laid siege here, it was the Knights' turn, with the faithful backing of the Maltese, to send the Turks packing. The handsome limestone buildings and fortifications that the wealthy Knights left behind are all around the islands. Valletta will be the European capital of culture for 2018.

ESSENTIALS
CURRENCY
The euro.

HOURS
Government museums are open daily 10–4 and are closed on Thursday. All sites are closed on January 1, Good Friday, December 24, 25, and 31. Some archaeological sites are open by appointment only. Shops are open Monday–Saturday 9–1 and 4–7.

TOURS
Darrell Azzopardi is a registered guide who can offer bespoke tours around Malta in English.

Beware of cheap tours: officially licensed guides should wear an identification tag.

Contacts Darrell Azzopardi ☎ *9942–2580* ✍ *dazman@onvol.net.*

TELEPHONES
Malta's mobile services operate on a single GSM-band system. The system supports text and data but not 3G technology. Public phones operate by means of telecards with smartchip technology. They can be used to make international calls. GO and Vodafone are the main providers.

COMING ASHORE
Cruise ships dock at the Valletta Waterfront Facility in the heart of the historic Grand Harbour. The facility is extensive, and houses modern, high-quality shops, eight restaurants, and exhibition spaces. Taxi fare to the town of Valetta is €10 and the trip takes only five minutes. It's a steep walk up to the Valletta citadel on foot, but a new elevator (€1) makes the trip much easier. Malta has a well-organized public bus service, but there are also car rentals and taxis. Ferries can also whisk passengers from the port across the Great Harbour to the Three Cities in a few minutes.

Most bus routes across the island start at Valletta Terminal just outside the entrance to the Citadel, and run daily from 5:30 am to 11 pm depending on the route (service ends earlier outside the main towns). Some night routes run in the main tourist areas from midnight until around 4 am. A day ticket is available for €2.60. Bus routes are marked on the maps distributed by the tourist office.

Renting a car would allow you to visit many of Malta's attractions during a day. Prices for a compact manual vehicle are about €35 per day. Driving is on the left. Void of highways, Malta is traversed by country roads with speed limits ranging between 24 and 40 mph. Seatbelt laws are strictly enforced.

Taxis operate on a fixed-fee basis from the port and airport to Valletta and can be extravagantly expensive. Sample fares are (€20) to Marsaxlokk and (€23) to Mdina. Taxi tours can be organized on a per-hour basis; for example, the fare for five hours is about €70. Some taxis have meters, but it is best to ask approximate rates before the ride begins.

EXPLORING MALTA

VALLETTA
Malta's capital, the minicity of Valletta, has ornate palaces and museums protected by massive fortifications of honey-color limestone. Houses along the narrow streets have overhanging wooden balconies for people-watching from indoors. The main entrance to town is through the City Gate (where all bus routes end), which leads onto Triq Repubblika (Republic Street), the spine of the grid-pattern city and the main shopping street. Triq Mercante (Merchant Street) parallels Repubblika to the east and is also good for strolling. From these two streets, cross streets descend toward the water; some are stepped. Valletta's compactness makes it ideal to explore on foot. Before setting out along Republic Street, stop at the tourist information office (just inside the city gate) for maps and brochures.

★ **Casa Rocca Piccola.** The exquisitely cultured current owners, Nicolas and Frances de Piro d'Amico Inguanez, host tours of the last of the

Malta

Gozo
Comino

Mediterranean Sea

Mellieha Bay

Mosta

Valletta
see detail map

Senglea

Birgu Cospicua

Mdina

Hal Saflieni Hypogeum

Marsaxlokk

Rabat

Tarxien Temples

0   3 mi

0   3 km

Dingli Cliffs

Wied-iz-Zurrieq

Mnajdra

Ghar Dalam

Mediterranean Sea

Ball's Bastion

Abercrombie's Bastion

St. Gregory Bastion

Fort St.Elmo

St. Lazarus Bastion

0   1/8 mi

0   1/8 km

Sebastion Bastion

St.

Sebastian St.

Fountain St.

St. Joseph St.

North St.

West St.

Bull St.

St. Dominic St.

Casa Rocca Piccola

Old Hospital St.

Sacra Infermeria

Marsamxett Harbour

St. Salvatore Bastion

Marsamxett St.

St. Christopher St.

St. Nicholas St.

Republic St.

St. Frederick St.

Merchants St.

St. Paul St.

Old Wells St.

Archbishop St.

St. Andrew's Bastion

St. Patrick St.

Old Mint St.

St. Lucia St.

Bakery

Old Theatre St.

Strait St.

Great Seige of Malta and the Knights of St. John

Grand Masters' Palace

Queen's Sq.

Market

St. Ursula St.

Lower Baracca Gardens

St. Mark St.

St. John St.

Great Siege Sq.

National Museum of Archaeology

St. John's Co-Cathedral

St. Paul's Shipwreck Church

East St. Ino Mediteran

Grand Harbour

St. Michael's Bastion

Melita St.

Vassalli St.

South St.

St. Zachary St.

St. Barbara Bastion

Windmill St.

Republic St.

St. John's Cavalier

St. Barbara

Battery St.

St. Anthony St.

Hastings Garden

Ordnance St.

Victory St.

i

St. James Cavalier

Upper Baracca Gardens

Triq l-assedju l-Kbir

Pope Pious V. St.

St. James Bastion

Tritons Fountain

Valletta

patrician houses still occupied. The treasures inside chart the history of the house, from a portable baroque chapel for baptisms to a painting of "Miss Electricity," commissioned to mark the local contribution of an ambitious ancestor. New exhibits include a costume gallery and an underground bomb shelter, used by Valletta residents during the war. ✉ *74 Triq Repubblika* ☎ *2122–1499* ∰ *www.casaroccapiccola.com* 🎟 *€9* ⊗ *Guided tours Mon.–Sat. 10–4 on the hour.*

★ **Grand Masters' Palace.** The palace houses the president's office; Malta's Parliament meets here until the new parliament building is completed. The palace, completed in 1574, has a unique collection of Gobelin tapestries; the main hall is

MALTA BEST BETS

The Grand Harbour. Best viewed from the ship when you arrive and depart, the Grand Harbour is one of Europe's finest natural anchorages. Generations of European power brokers have fortified it to create the vista you see today.

Sacra Infermeria. The former medieval Hospital of the Knights Hospitallers of St. John, a crusader force, now hosts the "Malta Experience" multimedia presentation.

St. John's Co-Cathedral. Caravaggio's masterpiece *The Beheading of St. John the Baptist* is the main attraction here.

decorated with frescoes depicting the history of the Knights and the Great Siege. On view are works by Ribera, Van Loo, and Batoni. At the back of the building is the **Armoury of the Knights,** with exhibits of arms and armor through the ages. ✉ *Palace Sq., Triq Repubblika* ☎ *2124–9349 Palace Armoury* ∰ *www.heritagemalta.org* 🎟 *€10 (joint admission Palace and Armoury), €6 for Palace Armoury* ⊗ *Daily 9–5* ⊗ *The Palace is closed to the public when Parliament is in session.*

Great Siege of Malta and the Knights of St. John. A walk-through presentation traces the order's history from its founding in 1099 in the Holy Land and its journeys from Jerusalem to Cyprus, Rhodes, and Malta. Also depicted are epic scenes from the Great Siege of 1565, the naval Battle of Lepanto, and the order's eviction from Malta by the French. ✉ *Cafe Premier Complex, Treasury St.* ☎ *2124–7300* ∰ *www.greatsiege.com.mt* 🎟 *€7.50* ⊗ *Weekdays 10–4:30, Sat. 10–3* ⊗ *Closed Sun.*

★ **National Museum of Archaeology.** Housed in the Auberge de Provence (the hostel of the Knights from Provence), the museum has an excellent collection of finds from Malta's many prehistoric sites—Tarxien, Haġar Qim, and the Hypogeum at Paola. ✉ *Triq Repubblika* ☎ *2122–1623* ∰ *www.heritagemalta.org* 🎟 *€5* ⊗ *Daily 9–7.*

★ **Sacra Infermeria** (*Hospital of the Knights*). This gracious building, the ancient hospital of the Knights of St. John or Knights Hospillaters, near the seawall has been converted into the Mediterranean Conference Center. For an introduction to the island, see the *Malta Experience,* a multimedia presentation on the history of Malta that is given here daily on the hour. ✉ *St. Elmo's Bastions, Mediterranean St.* ☎ *2124–3776* ∰ *www.themaltaexperience.com* ⊗ *Shows weekdays hourly 11–4, weekends hourly 11–2; no show Sun. at 2 July–Sept.*

Fodor's Choice **St. John's co-Cathedral.** Functional in design but lavishly decorated, the
★ Order of St. John's own church (1578) is Malta's most important trea-
sure. The Knights' colored-marble tombstones on the floor are gorgeous. Each of the side chapels was decorated by a national hostel of
the Knights. Many of the paintings and the decoration scheme are by
the island's beloved 17th-century painter Mattia Preti (b. 1613). In
the Oratory, Caravaggio's only signed work, the dramatic *Beheading of John the Baptist* (1607), is the collection's masterpiece. The
cathedral museum has illuminated manuscripts and a rich collection
of Flemish tapestries. The entrance fee includes an audio guide. Public
access (main ticket office) is on Republic Street. ■ TIP➔ **Narrow heeled
shoes such as stilettos are not allowed, but slippers can be purchased at
reception.** ⊠ *Pjazza San Gwann, St. John St.* ☏ *2123–9628* ⊕ *www.
stjohnscocathedral.com* ◱ *€6* ⊗ *Weekdays 9:30–4:30, Sat. 9:30–12:30
(last admittance 30 min before).*

★ **St. Paul's Shipwreck Church.** The importance of St. Paul to the Maltese
explains the work lavished on this baroque marvel—its raised central
vault, oval dome, and marble columns. The *os brachii* (arm bone) relic
of the saint is housed in a chapel on the right, a splendid gated chapel
is on the left, and a baptismal font stands by the entrance. ⊠ *Triq San
Pawl* ☏ *2123–6013* ⊕ *www.maltadiocese.org.*

THE THREE CITIES
Birgu is 8 km (5 miles) east of Valletta.

East across the Grand Harbor from Valletta, the three cities of **Vittoriosa,
Senglea,** and **Cospicua** are where the Knights of the Order of St. John first
settled—and where crucial fighting took place in the Great Siege of the
Turks in 1565. Vittoriosa, also called Birgu, is named for the victory
over the Turks. The 5 km (3 miles) of great walls around the cities are
the Cottonera Lines, built in the 1670s.

In **Vittoriosa/Birgu** in early October, hundreds of actors stage a Grand
Master's crossing of the harbor, and monastery doors on Triq San Lawrenz open to the public for the **Birgu Festa.** On the narrow streets north
of the main square you can loop from the Triq La Vallette to the Triq
Majjistral on the right. Triq It-Tramuntana takes you past baroque
doorways, the Knights' Auberge d'Angleterre (Inn of England), and a
Saracen-style house that is thought to date from the 1200s.

Church of St. Lawrenz. Below Birgu's main square, the Church of St.
Lawrenz is the city's finest church, with the 17th-century painter Mattia Preti's *Martyrdom of San Lawrenz.* ⊠ *Triq San Lawrenz, Birgu*
☏ *2182–7057* ⊕ *www.maltadiocese.org.*

Gardjola Gardens. At the tip of Senglea, Gardjola Gardens, once a guard
post, has great views across Grand Harbour to Valletta, and a turret
carved with a vigilant eye and ear. ⊠ *Triq Portu Salvu, Senglea.*

Inquisitor's Palace. The displays in Birgu's Inquisitor's Palace reveal less-
discussed aspects of less-tolerant times in Malta. The palace dates from
the 1530s and the first Inquistor General and Apostolic delegate to
Malta arrived here in 1547. ⊠ *Triq Il-Mina Il Kbira, Birgu* ☏ *2182–
7006* ⊕ *www.heritagemalta.org* ◱ *€6* ⊗ *Daily 9–5.*

PAOLA AND TARXIEN
Paola is 4.8 km (3 miles) south of Valletta.

★ **Ħal Saflieni Hypogeum.** This massive labyrinth of underground chambers was used for burials more than 4,000 years ago. Many chambers are decorated with red ocher or fine carvings. ■**TIP→** Book tickets for tours at least a month in advance. ⊠ *Burial St., on road to Santa Lucija, Paola* ☎ *2180–5018* ⊕ *www.heritagemalta.org* ⊠ *€20* ⊙ *Daily 9–4. Tour times must be prebooked.*

Tarxien Temples. The three interconnecting Tarxien Temples have curious carvings, oracular chambers, and altars, all dating from about 2800 BC. Nearby are remains of an earlier temple from about 4000 BC. ⊠ *Neolithic Temples St., behind Paola's Church of Christ the King, Tarxien* ☎ *2169–5578* ⊕ *www.heritagemalta.org* ⊠ *€6* ⊙ *Daily 9–5.*

MARSAXLOKK
8 km (5 miles) southeast of Valletta.

Malta's main fishing fleet bobs on the water in the wide sheltered bay. The unique colorful fishing boats (luzzu), with their vertical prow and protective "eye of Osiris" symbol, are descendents of Phoenician craft that plied these waters in ancient times. Most afternoons you'll find the fishermen and their families mending nets and preparing for the next sailing. Old honey-colored stone cottages once lived in by these families line the waterfront, though many have now been converted to seafood restaurants and bars. There's a craft market each morning along the waterfront promenade. Sunday hosts a traditional fish market alongside the craft stalls.

GĦAR DALAM
9 km (6 miles) southeast of Valletta.

cave. The semifossilized remains of long-extinct species of dwarf elephants and hippopotamuses that roamed the island some 125,000 years ago were found in a cave here. The fossils are now on display in the small **museum.** The earliest evidence of human occupation on Malta dating from 7,000 years ago was found in the excavated upper layer on the cave floor. ⊠ *Zejtun Rd.* ☎ *2165–7419* ⊕ *www.heritagemalta. org* ⊠ *€5* ⊙ *Daily 9–5.*

ZURRIEQ
11 km (7 miles) south of Valletta.

On the way to Zurrieq and Qrendi from Valletta you will pass limestone quarries, where orchards are planted, protected from the wind, after the limestone is exhausted.

★ **Blue Grotto.** The turnoff for the Blue Grotto is 1 km (½ mile) beyond the lookout. A steep road takes you to the rocky inlet where noisy boats (€7.50) leave for the grottoes (there are many) and the stained-glass-blue waters that splash their walls. ■**TIP→** Bring a bathing suit in case the water is calm enough for swimming. ⊠ *Coast Rd.*

Mnajdra. From the temple of Mnajdra ("mna-ee-dra"), on the edge of a hill by the sea, views are superb. The temple is encircled by hard coralline limestone walls and has the typical, cloverlike trefoil plan. A visitor center adds useful information about the temple builders and

their lifestyle. ⊠ *Triq Ħaġar Qim, Coast Rd., Qrendi* ☎ *2142–4231* ⊕ *www.heritagemalta.org* 🎟 *€9 (combined ticket with Ħaġar Qim)* ⊙ *Mid-Oct.–mid-Apr. daily 9–5, mid-Apr.–mid-Oct. daily 9–7.*

Wied-iz-Zurrieq (*Zurrieq Valley*). On the far side of town, Zurrieq Valley runs along the road to a lookout over the towering walls of the Blue Grotto's bay. There's a lookout point with parking that offers views of the grotto and surrounding cliffs.

MDINA

★ *12 km (7 miles) southwest of Valletta.*

In Malta's ancient, walled capital—the longtime stronghold of Malta's nobility—traffic is limited to residents' cars, and the noise of the world outside doesn't penetrate the thick, golden walls. The quiet streets are lined with sometimes block-long, still-occupied noble palaces.

★ **Mdina Cathedral.** The serene, baroque Mdina Cathedral (dedicated to St. Peter and St. Paul) contains Mattia Preti's 17th-century painting *The Shipwreck of St. Paul.* In the cathedral museum are Dürer woodcuts and illuminated manuscripts. ⊠ *Archbishop Sq.* ☎ *2145–4679* ⊕ *www. mdinacathedral.com* 🎟 *€2.50* ⊙ *Weekdays 9–4:30, Sat. 9–3:30.*

Palazzo Falson. A medieval Patrician stone mansion, dating from between the 13th and 15th centuries, reveals a wealth of original architectural features. The mansion's rooms display more than 45 collections of objects including art works by Anthony Van Dyck, Nicolas Poussin, and Mattia Preti. ⊠ *Villegaignon St.* ☎ *2145–4512* ⊕ *www.palazzofalson. com* 🎟 *€10* ⊙ *Tues.–Sun. 10–5.*

RABAT

The town's name means "suburb"—of Mdina, in this case.

Catacombs. Catacombs run under much of Rabat. Up Triq Santa Agatha from Parish Square, the **Catacombs of St. Paul** are clean of bones but full of carved-out burial troughs. Don't forget the way out when you set off to explore. **St. Agatha's Crypt and Catacombs,** farther up the street, were beautifully frescoed between 1200 and 1480, then defaced by Turks in 1551. ⊠ *St. Agatha St.* ☎ *2145–4562* ⊕ *www.heritagemalta. org* 🎟 *€5* ⊙ *Daily 9–5.*

St. Paul's Church. Completed in 1683, this beautiful church stands above a grotto where St. Paul reputedly took refuge after his shipwreck on Malta. ⊠ *Parish Sq.* ☎ *2145–4467 Parish Office* ⊕ *www.maltadiocese.org.*

MOSTA

10 km (6 miles) west of Valletta.

Rotunda. The Rotunda (Church of St. Mary) has the third-largest unsupported dome in Europe, after St. Peter's in Rome and Hagia Sophia in Istanbul. A German bomb fell through the roof during World War II—without detonating. ⊠ *Rotunda Sq.* ☎ *2143–3826* ⊕ *www. maltadiocese.org* ⊙ *Daily 9–noon and 3–6.*

SHOPPING

Most shops in Malta are open from 9 to 7, except in commercial areas where they stay open until 10 pm. Generally stores are closed on Sunday and public holidays. Malta has several crafts that make excellent souvenirs. Blown glass is a modern phenomenon, but is now a signature gift of the island. More traditional are bizzilla (hand-woven lace), silver filigree, globigerina limestone, and coralline limestone. Valletta's main shopping street, **Triq Repubblika,** is lined with touristy shops—pick up postcards and film here, and then venture onto side streets for a look at everyday Maltese wares. At the **open-air market** *(Triq Mercante)*, with some haggling you may snap up a good bargain.

Joseph Busuttil. This tiny shop sells a range of quality Maltese crafts including silver and gold filigree jewelry, blown glass, handmade lace, and limestone carvings. ⊠ *222 Merchants St., Valletta* ☎ *2124–3241* ⊘ *Closed Sun.*

BEACHES

Malta has many lovely beaches, which range from small rock-flanked coves to vast strands. Many beaches see lots of European (mainly British) tourists during the summer season, so they may be busy.

☾ **Ghajn Tuffieha Bay.** Malta's prettiest beach, also known as Golden Bay, is also it's wind and kite surfing center, with onshore breezes being particularly advantageous outside the main summer season. Between May and the end of September the beach is very popular with visitors, many of whom stay at the nearby Radisson Blu hotel. Weekends can be crowded with Maltese families who come to spend the day. The soft fine sand is some of the best on an island that has more rocky bays and inlets than sandy beaches. Shade is provided by rented sun umbrellas (summer only). **Best for:** swimming; wind surfing. **Amenities:** food and drink; lifeguards (summer only); parking (no fee); showers; toilets. ⊠ *Southwest of Mellieha town, Mellieha.*

WHERE TO EAT

$ ✕ **Caffe Cordina.** On the ground floor of the original treasury of the
CAFÉ Knights is Valletta's oldest café. Since 1837, this ornate, vaulted confectionery has produced hot, savory breakfast pastries and *qaghaq ta' l-ghasel* (honey rings). The lunch menu also includes sandwiches, salads, and a choice of daily specials. The interior air-conditioned café attracts Valletta movers and shakers, because of its close proximity to Parliament and the law courts. The shaded outside tables in Victoria Square are the city's prime people-watching spots. Enjoy a coffee, beer, or glass of wine and relax. ⑤ *Average main: €7* ⊠ *244–45 Triq Repubblika, Valletta* ☎ *2123–4385* ⊕ *www.caffecordina.com.*

$ ✕ **Guzé.** This young and dynamic team is reinventing the traditional
MODERN Maltese trattoria with a vibrant contemporary menu using traditional
EUROPEAN local ingredients. Set in a 400-year-old vaulted stone building, the series
Fodor's Choice of small simply furnished and elegantly lit dining spaces are intimate.
★ ⚠ **When the restaurant is full, space can be a little tight.** Guzé is known

for its monthly menu—a choice of chef-inspired dishes made with fresh seasonal ingredients—but there's also a good range of staple Maltese dishes on the à la carte menu. ⑤ *Average main: €16* ✉ *22 Old Bakery St., Valletta* ☎ *2123–9686* ⊕ *www.guze.com.mt* ⊘ *Closed Sun.; no lunch Mon.–Thurs.*

VENICE, ITALY

Updated by Bruce Leimsidor

It's called La Serenissima, "the most serene," a reference to the majesty, wisdom, and immense power of this city that was for centuries the mistress of trade between Europe and the Orient. Built largely on water by men who both defied and loved the sea, Venice is unlike any other town. No matter how many times you've seen it in movies or on TV, the real thing is more startlingly beautiful than you could ever imagine. Its landmarks, the Basilica di San Marco and the Palazzo Ducale, are exotic mixes of Byzantine, Gothic, and Renaissance styles. Shimmering sunlight and silvery mist soften every perspective here, and you understand how the city became renowned in the Renaissance for its artists' rendering of color. It's full of secrets, inexpressibly romantic, and at times given over to pleasure.

ESSENTIALS
CURRENCY
The euro.

HOURS
Shops are generally open 9–1 and 3:30–7:30 and are closed Sunday and Monday morning most of the year, however, tourist shops in the city will remain open throughout the day and into the evening and on Sundays.

PRIVATE TOURS
Walks inside Venice provides full- and half-day tours by academically trained, English-speaking professional tour guides who will lead you through Venice's dazzling labyrinth. There are several types of small group tours, depending upon your interests, or you can book a tour specially geared to your passions.

Contacts **Walks Inside Venice.** ☎ *(39)41/275–0687 for Sara, (39)41/524–1706 for Roberta, (39)41/520–2434 for Cristina* ⊕ *www.walksinsidevenice.com.*

TELEPHONES
Tri-band GSM phones work in Italy. You can buy prepaid phone cards at telecom shops, news vendors, and tobacconists in all towns and cities. Phone cards can be used for local or international calls.

COMING ASHORE
Venice is a huge port handling vast numbers of cruise ships and much of commercial traffic as well. The cruise terminal sits at the southwestern corner of city, and has two main docking areas, the Marittima area for large ships and the San Basilio for smaller ones.

Marittima has duty-free shops, information desks, and refreshment facilities. From here there is a shuttle bus to Piazzale Roma at the western edge of the city, just outside the port, or you can take Bus 6 from the port entrance. You can also take a boat. Among the seafaring options

Canale delle Sacche

Canale Cannaregio

CANNAREGIO

Rio del Battello

Rio di S. Girolamo

Rio di S. Sensa

Rio d. Madonna dell'Orto

Campo del Ghetto Nuovo

C. Riello

Ponte Guglie

R. t. S. Leonardo

R. di Noale

C. Racchetta

Bridge to Mainland

Stazione Ferroviaria Santa Lucia

Lista di Spagna

Ponte degli Scalzi

Grand Canal (Canalazzo)

Lista d. Barì

Strada Nuova

R. di S. Zan Degolà

C. d. Tintor

Nuova Isola del Tronchetto

F. d. S. Simeon Piccolo

C. della Lana

Corte Canal

C. Larga

Canale di S. Chiara

C. d. S. Andrea

Piazzale Roma

C. d. Lacca

SANTA CROCE

R. di S. Cassiano

C. dei Botteri

Ponte di Rialto

Bacino Stazione Marittima

Canale Scomenzera

Rio d. S. Maria Maggiore

F. d. S. Foscari

C. d. Fonderia

C. d. Chiovere

SAN POLO

Campo S. Polo

R. Terrà

Riva del Vin

Me

Santa Maria Gloriosa dei Frari

F. Minotto

Rio Nuovo

Scuola Grande di San Rocco

R. della Frescada

R. d.

S. Luca

Grand Canal (Canalazzo)

Fond. dei Cereri

Fond. Rossa

Rio Foscari

C. d. Carrozze

Campo S. Angelo

Rio S. Margherita

Campo di S. Margherita

Rio d. S. Barnaba

Campo Santo Stefano

SAN MARCO

Frezze

Rio di S. Nicola

Calle Avogaria

Campo S. Barnaba

Ponte dell'Accademia

C. d. Traghetto

Saliz. San Baségio

Calle della Toletta

Gallerie dell'Accademia

Peggy Guggenheim Collection

Fond. Soranzo della Fornace

Rio d. Fornace

Fondamenta delle Zattere

Rio d. Ognissanti

Rio Terà A. Foscarini

Rio d. S. Vio

Santa Maria della Salute

DORSODURO

Canale della Giudecca

C. della Scuola

Sacca Fisola

Rio d. S. Biagio

Fond. S. Biagio

R. d. Convertire

Fond. S. Eufemia

GIUDECCA

Chiesa del Redentore

Laguna Veneta

are the Alilaguna M Line (Linea M) boat, which travels direct from Marittima to Piazza San Marco. You could also take Linea Blu or Linea Rosso from Tronchetto to San Marco, though this service has more stops enroute. Vaporetto services 41, 42, 51, 52, 61, 62 operate along the same route. The journey takes around 20 minutes.

At San Basilio there are fewer passenger facilities, but the quay has a vaporetto stop, from which services 61, 62, and 82 take you into the heart of Venice. The current fare is €6.50.

Vaporetto services take you right to St. Mark's Square. Cars aren't allowed into Venice proper, so there is no point to renting a car unless you want to explore the Veneto region. Expect to pay about €45 for a compact manual vehicle.

VENICE BEST BETS
Take a gondola ride along the canals. Despite the high cost, the views are sublime, and the minor waterways take you to quiet backwaters that are little visited by most tourists.
Explore Basilica San Marco. The mother lode of Byzantine treasure and art lies within the walls of this great church.
Sip an espresso in St. Mark's Square. From here you can admire the architecture and watch the world go by.

GETTING TO THE AIRPORT

If you do not purchase airport transfers from your cruise line, the simplest transfer is to take a vaporetto to Piazzalle Roma and then city bus #5 to Marco Polo Airport, the main airport of Venice. If you are traveling from Treviso airport, there are private buses (€5) from Piazzale Roma that will take to the airport there.

A private *motoscafo* (water taxi) transfer direct from the airport dock to the cruise port will cost around €90 for up to four people but may be a necessary expense for very early departures.

The quickest transfer on public transport is to take the city Bus 5 overland to Piazzale Roma and then transfer from Piazzale Roma to the cruise port. Blue buses run by **ATVO** (☎ *0421/383672* ⊕ *www.atvo.it*) also make a 20-minute trip from the airport to Piazzale Roma (tickets €5). Tickets are sold from machines and at the airport booth in Ground Transportation (open daily 9–7:30), and on the bus when tickets are otherwise unavailable. The ATVO buses are more comfortable, but not any quicker, than the cheaper city busses. A land taxi to Piazzale Roma costs about €30. From Piazzale Roma there are shuttle buses to the cruise terminal.

EXPLORING VENICE

There's no better introduction to Venice than a trip down the Grand Canal. It is, without a doubt, one of the world's great "avenues." For 4 km (2½ miles) it winds its way in a backward "S," past 12th- to 18th-century palaces built by the city's richest families. There is a definite theatrical quality to the Grand Canal; it's as if each facade had been designed to steal your attention from its rival across the way. The most

romantic—albeit expensive—way to see the canal is from a gondola (approximately €60 for up to 4 persons). The next best thing—at a fraction of the cost—is to take in the view from vaporetto Line 1.

PIAZZA SAN MARCO

One of the world's most evocative squares, Piazza San Marco (St. Mark's Square) is the heart of Venice, a vast open space bordered by an orderly procession of arcades marching toward the fairy-tale cupolas and marble lacework of the Basilica di San Marco.

Piazzetta San Marco, the "little square" leading from Piazza San Marco to the waters of Bacino San Marco (St. Mark's Basin), is a *molo* (landing) that was once the grand entryway to the republic. It's distinguished by two columns towering above the waterfront. One is topped by the winged lion, a traditional emblem of St. Mark that became the symbol of Venice itself; the other supports St. Theodore, the city's first patron, along with his dragon.

Fodor's Choice
★

Basilica di San Marco. An opulent synthesis of Byzantine and Romanesque styles, Venice's gem is laid out in a Greek-cross floor plan and topped with five plump domes. It didn't become the cathedral of Venice until 1807, but its original role as the Chiesa Ducale (the doge's private chapel) gave it immense power and wealth. The original church was built in 828 to house the body of Saint Mark the Evangelist. His remains, filched from Alexandria by the doge's agents, were supposedly hidden in a barrel under layers of pickled pork to sneak them past Muslim guards.

A 976 fire destroyed most of the original church. It was rebuilt and reopened in 1094, and for centuries it would serve as a symbol of Venetian wealth and power, endowed with all the riches admirals and merchants could carry off from the Orient, to the point where it earned the nickname "Chiesa d'Oro" (Golden Church). The four bronze horses that prance and snort over the doorway are copies of sculptures that victorious Venetians took from Constantinople in 1204 after the fourth crusade (the originals are upstairs in the Museo di San Marco). The rich, colorful exterior decorations, including the numerous different marble columns, all came from the same source.

The basilica is famous for its 43,055 square feet of mosaics, which run from floor to ceiling thanks to an innovative roof of brick vaulting. Climb the steep stairway to the **Galleria** and the **Museo di San Marco** for the best overview of the basilica's interior. From here you can step outdoors for a sweeping panorama of Piazza San Marco and out over the lagoon to San Giorgio.

Be aware that guards at the basilica door turn away anyone with bare shoulders, midriff, or knees: no shorts, short skirts, or tank tops are allowed. To skip the line at the basilica entrance, reserve your arrival—at no extra cost—on the basilica website. You can also skip the line if you check a bag at the nearby bag-check facility (find it on the map at the basilica entrance)—just show your bag-check ticket to the entrance guard and he'll wave you in. ✉ *Piazza San Marco, San Marco 328, San Marco* ☎ *041/2708311 basilica, 041/2413817 tour info 10–noon weekdays* ⊕ *www.basilicasanmarco.it* ✉ *Basilica free, Tesoro €2, Santuario*

and Pala d'Oro €1.50, Galleria and Museo di San Marco €3 ⊗ May–Sept., Mon.–Sat. 9:45–5, Sun. 2–5; Oct.–Apr., Mon.–Sat. 9:45–5, Sun. 2–4. Last entry 1 hr before closing; interior illuminated Mon.–Sat. 11:30–12:30, Sun. 2–5 Ⓜ *Vallaresso/San Zaccaria.*

Campanile. Construction of Venice's famous brick bell tower (325 feet tall, plus the angel) began in the 9th century, and took on its present form in 1514. In 1902, the tower unexpectedly collapsed, taking with it Jacopo Sansovino's 16th-century marble loggia at its base. The largest original bell, called the *marangona*, survived. The crushed loggia was promptly reconstructed, and the new tower, rebuilt to the old plan, reopened in 1912. Today, on a clear day the stunning view includes the Lido, the lagoon, and the mainland as far as the Alps, but, strangely enough, none of the myriad canals that snake through the city. ⊠ *Piazza San Marco* ☎ *041/5224064* 🖃 *€8* ⊗ *Easter–June, Oct., and Nov., daily 9–7; July–Sept., daily 9–9; Nov.–Easter, daily 9–3:45. Last entry 1 hr before closing* Ⓜ *Vaporetto: Vallaresso, San Zaccaria.*

Fodor's Choice
★
Palazzo Ducale (*Doge's Palace*). Rising above the Piazzetta San Marco, this Gothic fantasia of pink-and-white marble is a majestic expression of Venetian prosperity and power. It served not only as the doge's residence, but also as the central administrative center of the Venetian Republic. The palace's sumptuous chambers have walls and ceilings covered with works by Venice's greatest artists. The ceiling of the **Sala del Senato** (Senate Chamber), featuring *The Triumph of Venice* by Tintoretto, is magnificent, but it's dwarfed by his masterpiece *Paradise* in the **Sala del Maggiore Consiglio** (Great Council Hall). ⊠ *Piazzetta San Marco, Piazza San Marco* ☎ *041/2715911, 041/5209070 Secret Itineraries tour* ⊕ *www.museicivicveneziani.it* 🖃 *Museums of San Marco Pass €14 (or €16.50 if there is a special exhibition), Musei Civici Pass €18.50.* ⊗ *Apr.–Oct., daily 9–7; Nov.–Mar., daily 9–5. Last entry 1 hr before closing* Ⓜ *Vaporetto: San Zaccaria, Vallaresso.*

ELSEWHERE IN VENICE

Fodor's Choice
★
Gallerie dell'Accademia. Napoleon founded these galleries in 1807 on the site of a religious complex he had suppressed. They were carefully and subtly restructured between 1945 and 1959 by the renowned architect Carlo Scarpa. In them you'll find the world's most extensive collection of Venetian paintings. Booking is necessary to see the **Quadreria,** where additional works cover every inch of a wide hallway. A free map notes art and artists, and the bookshop sells a more informative English-language booklet. In the main galleries a €4 audio guide saves reading, but adds little to each room's excellent annotation. ⊠ *Dorsoduro 1050, Campo della Carità just off the Accademia Bridge* ☎ *041/5222247 Quadreria reservations, 041/5200345 reservations* ⊕ *www.gallerieaccademia.org* 🖃 *€6.50, €11 includes Ca' d'Oro and Museo Orientale* ⊗ *Galleria: Tues.–Sun. 8:15 am–7:15 pm, Mon. 8:15–2. Quadreria: Fri. 11 am–1 pm, Sat. 11–noon* Ⓜ *Vaporetto: Accademia.*

Madonna dell'Orto. Though built toward the middle of the 14th century, this church takes its character from its beautiful late-Gothic façade, added between 1460 and 1464; it's one of the most beautiful

Gothic churches in Venice. Tintoretto lived nearby, and this, his parish church, contains some of his most powerful work. Lining the chancel are two huge (45 feet by 20 feet) canvases, *Adoration of the Golden Calf* and *Last Judgment*. In glowing contrast to this awesome spectacle is Tintoretto's *Presentation of the Virgin at the Temple* and the simple chapel where he and his children, Marietta and Domenico, are buried. Paintings by Domenico, Cima da Coneglano, Palma il Giovane, Palma il Vecchio, and Titian also hang in the church. A chapel displays a photographic reproduction of a precious *Madonna with Child* by Giovanni Bellini. The original was stolen one night in 1993. ⊠ *Campo della Madonna dell'Orto, Cannaregio* ☎ *041/2750462 Chorus Foundation* ⊕ *www.chorusvenezia.org* ⊠ *€3, Chorus Pass €10* ☉ *Mon.–Sat. 10–5, Sun. 1–5* Ⓜ *Vaporetto: Orto.*

☾ **Peggy Guggenheim Collection.** A small selection of 20th-century painting and sculpture is on display at this gallery in the late heiress Peggy Guggenheim's Grand Canal home. The collection represents the eccentric lady's generally excellent taste. Through wealth and social connections, Guggenheim (1898–1979) became an important art dealer and collector from the 1930s through the 1950s, and her personal collection here in Palazzo Venier dei Leoni includes works by Picasso, Kandinsky, Pollock, Motherwell, and Ernst (at one time her husband). ⊠ *Fondamenta Venier dei Leoni, Dorsoduro 701* ☎ *041/2405411* ⊕ *www.guggenheim-venice. it* ⊠ *€12* ☉ *Wed.–Mon. 10–6* Ⓜ *Vaporetto: Accademia.*

FodorśChoice **Ponte di Rialto** (*Rialto Bridge*). The competition to design a stone bridge
★ across the Grand Canal attracted the best architects of the late 16th century, including Michelangelo, Palladio, and Sansovino, but the job went to the less-famous (but appropriately named) Antonio da Ponte (1512–95). His pragmatic design, completed in 1591, featured shop space and was high enough for galleys to pass beneath. Along the railing you'll enjoy one of the city's most famous views: the Grand Canal vibrant with boat traffic. Ⓜ *Vaporetto: Rialto.*

★ **Santa Maria dei Miracoli.** Tiny yet harmoniously proportioned, this Renaissance gem, built between 1481 and 1489, is sheathed in marble and decorated inside with exquisite marble reliefs. Architect Pietro Lombardo (circa 1435–1515) miraculously compressed the building into its confined space, then created the illusion of greater size by varying the color of the exterior, adding extra pilasters on the building's canal side, and offsetting the arcade windows to make the arches appear deeper. The church was built to house *I Miracoli,* an image of the Virgin Mary by Niccolò di Pietro (1394-1440) that is said to have performed miracles—look for it on the high altar. ⊠ *Campo Santa Maria Nova, Cannaregio* ☎ *041/2750462 Chorus Foundation* ⊕ *www.chorusvenezia.org* ⊠ *€3, Chorus Pass €10* ☉ *Mon.–Sat. 10–5* Ⓜ *Vaporetto: Rialto.*

★ **Santa Maria della Salute.** En route to becoming Venice's most important baroque architect, 32-year-old Baldassare Longhena won a competition in 1631 to design a shrine honoring the Virgin Mary for saving Venice from a plague that in the space of two years (1629–30) killed 47,000 residents, or one-third of the city's population. It was

not completed, however, until 1687—five years after Longhena's death. Outside, this ornate, white Istrian stone octagon is topped by a colossal cupola with snail-like ornamental buttresses and a baroque facade; inside are a polychrome marble floor and six chapels. The Byzantine icon above the main altar has been venerated as the Madonna della Salute (Madonna of Health) since 1670, when Francesco Morosini brought it here from Crete. Do not leave the church without visiting the **Sacrestia Maggiore**, which contains a dozen works by Titian, including his *San Marco Enthroned with Saints* altarpiece. ⊠ *Punta della Dogana, Dorsoduro* ☎ *041/2743928* 🖼 *Church free, sacristy €2* ⊙ *Apr.–Sept., daily 9–noon and 3–6:30; Oct.–Mar., daily 9–noon and 3–5:30* Ⓜ *Vaporetto: Salute.*

Fodor'sChoice **Santa Maria Gloriosa dei Frari.** This immense Gothic church of russet-
★ color brick was completed in 1442 after more than a century of work. *I Frari* (as it's known locally) contains some of the most brilliant paintings in any Venetian church. Inside you'll see works by Giovanni Bellini, Bartolomeo Vivarini, Conatello, and Titian. The Frari also holds a Sansovino sculpture of St. John the Baptist, and Longhena's impressive baroque tomb designed for Doge Giovanni Pesaro. ⊠ *Campo dei Frari, San Polo* ☎ *041/2728618, 041/2750462 Chorus Foundation* ⊕ *www. chorusvenezia.org* 🖼 *€3, Chorus Pass €10* ⊙ *Mon.–Sat. 9–6, Sun. 1–6* Ⓜ *Vaporetto: San Tomà.*

★ **Scuola Grande di San Rocco.** Saint Rocco's popularity stemmed from his miraculous recovery from the plague and his care for fellow sufferers. Throughout the plague-filled Middle Ages, followers and donations abounded, and this elegant example of Venetian Renaissance architecture, built between 1517 and 1560 and including the work of at least four architects, was the result. Although it is bold and dramatic outside, its contents are even more stunning—a series of more than 60 paintings by Tintoretto. ⊠ *Campo San Rocco, San Polo 3052* ☎ *041/5234864* ⊕ *www.scuolagrandesanrocco.it* 🖼 *€8 (includes audio guide)* ⊙ *Daily 9:30–5:30. Last entry ½ hr before closing* Ⓜ *Vaporetto: San Tomà.*

SHOPPING

Glass, most of it made on the separate island of Murano, is Venice's number-one product, and you'll be confronted by mind-boggling displays of traditional and contemporary glassware, much of it kitsch. Carnival masks also make a unique souvenir. The finest ones are handcrafted to fit the wearer, but inexpensive alternatives abound. The city also has a long history of supplying lace and luxury materials, though many of the cheaper items on sale are now imported. Don't forget classic Italian design in clothing, shoes, and leather accessories such as purses and belts. All these can be found in the streets radiating out from St Mark's Square.

Il Merletto. The best of Burano's renowned lace-making tradition is rarely represented by the examples you'll see on display. However, at Il Merletto, you can ask for the authentic, handmade lace safeguarded in drawers behind the counter. This is the only place in Venice connected with the students of the Scuola del Merletto in Burano, who, officially,

do not sell to the public. Hours of operation are daily 10 to 5. ✉ *Sotoportego del Cavalletto under the Procuratie Vecchie, Piazza San Marco 95* ☎ *041/5208406.*

L'Isola. L'Isola has chic, contemporary glassware signed by Carlo Moretti. ✉ *Campo San Moisè, San Marco 1468* ☎ *041/5231973* ⊕ *www.carlomoretti.com.*

Lorenzo Rubelli. Lorenzo Rubelli, founded in1858, offers the same sumptuous brocades, damasks, and cut velvets used by the world's most prestigious decorators. ✉ *Campiello del Teatro, San Marco 3877* ☎ *041/5236110* ⊕ *www.rubelli.com.*

WHERE TO EAT

$$$$
VENETIAN
✕**Alla Madonna.** "The Madonna" used to be world-famous as "the" classic Venetian trattoria, but in the past decades, has settled down to middle age. Owned and run by the Rado family since 1954, this Venetian institution looks like one, with its wood-beams, stained glass windows, and panoply of paintings on white walls. Folks still head here to savor the classic Venetian repertoire and, as most dishes are properly prepared (for the stiff prices, they should be), the rooms here are usually bustling so get ready to enjoy a festive and lively meal. $ *Average main:* €60 ✉ *Calle della Madonna, San Polo 594* ☎ *041/5223824* ⊕ *www.ristoranteallamadonna.com* ⚖ *Reservations essential* ⊙ *Closed Wed., Jan., and 2 wks in Aug.* Ⓜ *Vaporetto: San Silvestro.*

$$$$
VENETIAN
★
✕**Vini da Gigio.** Paolo and Laura, a brother-sister team, run this refined trattoria as if they've invited you to dinner in their home, while keeping the service professional. Deservedly popular with Venetians and visitors alike, it's one of the best values in the city. Indulge in pastas such as rigatoni with duck sauce and arugula-stuffed ravioli. Fish is well represented—try the sesame-encrusted tuna—but the meat dishes steal the show. The steak with red-pepper sauce and the *tagliata di agnello* (sautéed lamb fillet with a light, crusty coating) are both superb, and you'll never enjoy a better *fegato alla veneziana* (Venetian-style liver with onions). This is a place for wine connoisseurs, as the cellar is one of the best in the city. Come at lunch or for the second sitting in the evening, to avoid being rushed. $ *Average main: €40* ✉ *Fondamenta San Felice, Cannaregio 3628/A* ☎ *041/5285140* ⊕ *www.vinidagigio.com* ⚖ *Reservations essential* ⊙ *Closed Mon. and Tues., 2 wks in Jan., and 3 wks in Aug.* Ⓜ *Vaporetto: Ca' d'Oro.*

WHERE TO STAY

$
HOTEL
Fodor's Choice
★
Locanda Orseolo. This cozy, elegant hotel offers a welcome respite from the throngs churning around Piazza San Marco. **Pros:** intimate and romantic; friendly staff; Wi-Fi is free. **Cons:** no elevator; canalside rooms can be noisy (think singing gondoliers); its reputation and price bracket, mean guests should book as early as possible. $ *Rooms from: €180* ✉ *Corte Zorzi off Campo San Gallo, San Marco 1083* ☎ *041/5204827* ⊕ *www.locandaorseolo.com* ➷ *12 rooms* ⊙ *Closed Jan.* ❢❂ *Breakfast* Ⓜ *Vaporetto: Rialto or Vallaresso.*

$$ **Palazzo Sant'Angelo sul Canal Grande.** There's a distinguished yet
HOTEL comfortable feel to this elegant palazzo, which is large enough to
deliver expected facilities and services but small enough to pamper its
guests. **Pros:** convenient to vaporetto stop. **Cons:** modest breakfast;
fee for Wi-Fi, and Internet available only in common areas, not in
rooms. $ *Rooms from: €420* ✉ *Campo Sant'Angelo, San Marco 3488*
☎ *041/2411452* ⊕ *www.palazzosantangelo.com* ⇝ *14 rooms* ⦿ *Breakfast* Ⓜ *Vaporetto: Sant'Angelo.*

$$ **Palazzo Stern.** The gracious terrace that overlooks the Grand Canal
HOTEL is almost reason alone to stay here. **Pros:** excellent service; lovely views
★ from many rooms; modern renovation retains historic ambience; steps
from vaporetto stop. **Cons:** multiple renovations may turn off some
Venetian architectural purists; rooms with a Grand Canal view are
much more expensive. $ *Rooms from: €340* ✉ *Calle del Traghetto,
Dorsoduro 2792* ☎ *041/2770869* ⊕ *www.palazzostern.com* ⇝ *18
rooms, 5 junior suites, 1 suite* ⦿ *Breakfast* Ⓜ *Vaporetto: Ca' Rezzonico.*

VIGO, SPAIN (FOR SANTIAGO DE COMPOSTELA)

Updated by   Spain's most Atlantic region is en route to nowhere, an end in itself.
Joanna Styles Northwestern Spain is a series of rainy landscapes, stretching from
your feet to the horizon and the country's wildest mountains, the
Picos de Europa. Ancient granite buildings wear a blanket of moss,
and even the stone *horreos* (granaries) are built on stilts above the
damp ground.

Santiago de Compostela, where a cathedral holds the remains of the
apostle James, has drawn pilgrims over the same roads for 900 years,
leaving northwestern Spain covered with churches, shrines, and former
hospitals. Asturias, north of the main pilgrim trail, has always maintained a separate identity, isolated by the rocky Picos de Europa. This
and the Basque Country are the only parts of Spain never conquered
by the Moors, so regional architecture shows little Moorish influence.

ESSENTIALS
CURRENCY
The euro.

HOURS
Museums generally open from 9 until 7 or 8; many are closed on Mondays and some close in the afternoons. Most stores are open Monday–Saturday 9–1:30 and 5–8, but tourist shops may open in the afternoon
and also on Sunday between May and September.

PRIVATE TOURS
SECCHI. The company organizes half and full-day tours exploring Galician towns, cities, coastline and countryside. ☎ *981/554176* ⊕ *www.
turismosecchi.com.*

TELEPHONES

Spain has good land and mobile services. Public kiosks accept phone cards that support international calls (cards sold in press shops, bars, and telecom shops). Mobile services are 3G compatible. Major companies include Vodafone.

COMING ASHORE

The cruise terminal, which sits on the waterfront directly off the Old Town, was expanded in 2011 to handle larger ships. It's possible to walk from the ship and explore on foot with shops and restaurants close by. Facilities in the terminal include a spa and leisure area within the A Laxe commercial center in the port.

In Vigo a tourist bus operates a continuous hop-on, hop-off service during Easter week and the summer (June 15–Sept. 15) and on cruise-ship days during the rest of the year. Tickets cost €7.50. The bus passes the port when cruise ships are in dock.

There is at least one train per hour to Santiago de Compostela. Journey time is around 1½ hours, and tickets cost approximately €10.40 one-way. It's a 30-minute walk from the port to the railway station or a 10-minute taxi trip.

Renting a vehicle would allow you to explore Santiago de Compostela and the rugged countryside of this wild corner of Spain. Rental price for an economy manual vehicle is approximately €45.

> ### SANTIAGO DE CAMPOSTELA BEST BETS
>
> **Santiago's Cathedral.** One of the holiest places in Christendom; the quality of the Romanesque stonework is exquisite.
>
> **The Museo de las Peregrinaciones.** Learn about the triumphs, trials, and tribulations of the medieval pilgrims who journeyed across Europe to worship at the cathedral.
>
> **The atmosphere of Santiago's medieval quarter.** These narrow streets have been serving the needs of travelers since the cathedral was completed in the 12th century.

EXPLORING VIGO AND SANTIAGO DE COMPOSTELA

VIGO

Vigo's formidable port is choked with trawlers and fishing boats and lined with clanging shipbuilding yards. Its sights (or lack thereof) fall far short of its commercial swagger. The city's casual appeal lies a few blocks inland, where the port commotion gives way to the narrow, dilapidated streets of the Old Town. From 8:30 to 3:30 daily on **Rúa Pescadería,** in the barrio called La Piedra, Vigo's famed *ostreras*—a group of rubber-glove fisherwomen who have been peddling fresh oysters to passersby for more than 50 years.

Parque del Castro. South of Vigo's Old Town is the hilltop Parque del Castro, a quiet, stately park with sandy paths, palm trees, mossy embankments, and stone benches. Atop a series of steps are the remains of an old fort and a *mirador* (lookout) with fetching views of Vigo's coastline and the Islas Cíes. ⊠ *Between Praza de España and Praza do Rei, beside Av. Marqués de Alcedo.*

SANTIAGO DE COMPOSTELA

80 km (50 miles) north of Vigo, 77 km (48 miles) southwest of À Coruña.

A large, lively university makes Santiago one of the most exciting cities in Spain, but its cathedral makes it one of the most impressive. The building is opulent and awesome, yet its towers create a sense of harmony as a benign St. James, dressed in pilgrim's costume, looks down from his perch.

Casco Antiguo (*Old Town*). The best way to spend your time in Santiago de Compostela is to simply to walk around the *casco antiguo*, losing yourself in its maze of stone-paved narrow streets and little plazas. The streets hold many old *pazos* (manor houses), convents, and churches. The most beautiful pedestrian thoroughfares are Rúa do Vilar, Rúa do Franco, and Rúa Nova—portions of which are covered by arcaded walkways called *soportales,* designed to keep walkers out of the rain.

Cathedral. From the Praza do Obradoiro, climb the two flights of stairs to the main entrance of Santiago's cathedral. Although the facade is baroque, the interior holds one of the finest Romanesque sculptures in the world, the **Pórtico de la Gloria.** Completed in 1188 by Maestro Mateo, this is the cathedral's original entrance, its three arches carved with figures from the Apocalypse, the Last Judgment, and purgatory. Below Jesus is a serene St. James, poised on a carved column. Look carefully and you can see five smooth grooves, formed by the millions of pilgrims who have placed their hands here over the centuries. On the back of the pillar, people, especially students preparing for exams, lean forward to touch foreheads with the likeness of Maestro Mateo in the hope that his genius can be shared. In his bejeweled cloak, St. James presides over the **high altar.** The stairs behind it are the cathedral's focal point, surrounded by dazzling baroque decoration, sculpture, and drapery. Here, as the grand finale of their spiritual journey, pilgrims embrace St. James and kiss his cloak. In the crypt beneath the altar lie the remains of James and his disciples St. Theodore and St. Athenasius.

A Pilgrims' Mass is celebrated every day at noon. On special, somewhat unpredictable occasions, the *botafumeiro* (huge incense burner) is attached to the thick ropes hanging from the ceiling and prepared for a ritual at the end of the Pilgrims' Mass: as small flames burn inside, eight strong laymen move the ropes to swing the vessel in a massive semicircle across the apse. In earlier centuries, this rite served as an air freshener—by the time pilgrims reached Santiago, they smelled a bit, well, you can imagine. A botafumeiro and other cathedral treasures are on display in the **museums** downstairs and next door. On the right (south) side of the nave is the **Porta das Praterías** (Silversmiths' Door), the only purely Romanesque part of the cathedral's facade. The statues on the portal were cobbled together from parts of the cathedral. The double doorway opens onto the **Praza das Praterías,** named for the silversmiths' shops that used to line it. ⊠ *Praza do Obradoiro* ☎ *981/581155 cathedral, 981/569327 museum* ⊕ *www. catedraldesantiago.es* ⊠ *Cathedral free, combined museum ticket €5* ☉ *Cathedral daily 7 am–9 pm; museums June–Sept., Mon.–Sat. 10–2 and 4–8, Sun. 10–2; Oct.–May, Mon.–Sat. 10–1:30 and 4–8, Sun. 10–1:30.*

Cathedral Roofs. For excellent views of the city, join one of the tours arranged by Xelmírez Palace that takes you across the *cubiertas*, the granite steps of the cathedral roofs. Pilgrims made the same 100-foot climb in medieval times to burn their travel-worn clothes below the Cruz dos Farrapos (Cross of Rags). ⊠ *Pazo de Xelmírez, Praza do Obradoiro* ☎ *981/552985* ⊕ *www.catedraldesantiago.es* 🖼 *€10* ☉ *Tues.–Sun. 10–2 and 4–8.*

Centro Galego de Arte Contemporánea (*Galician Center for Contemporary Art*). On the north side of town, off the Porta do Camino, the CGAC is a stark but elegant modern building that contrasts with the ancient feel of most other places in Santiago. Portuguese designer Álvaro Siza built the museum of smooth, angled granite, which mirrors the medieval convent of San Domingos de Bonaval next door. Inside, a gleaming lobby of white Italian marble gives way to white-walled, high-ceiling exhibition halls flooded with light from massive windows and skylights. The museum has a good permanent collection and even better changing exhibits. ⊠ *Rúa de Valle Inclán s/n* ☎ *981/546619* ⊕ *www.cgac.org* 🖼 *Free* ☉ *Tues.–Sun. 11–8.*

Hostal dos Reis Católicos (*Hostel of the Catholic Monarchs*). The Hostal dos Reis Católicos, facing the cathedral from the left, was built in 1499 by Ferdinand and Isabella to house the pilgrims who slept on Santiago's streets every night. Having lodged and revived travelers for over 500 years, it's the oldest refuge in the world; it was converted from a hospital to a parador in 1954. The facade bears a Castilian coat of arms along with Adam, Eve, and various saints; inside, the four arcaded patios have gargoyle rainspouts said to be caricatures of 16th-century townsfolk. Behind the lobby is the building's focal point, a Renaissance chapel in the shape of a cross. ⊠ *Praza do Obradoiro 1* ☎ *981/582200* ⊕ *www.parador.es* 🖼 *€3* ☉ *Daily noon–2 and 4–6.*

Museo das Peregrinacións (*Pilgrimage Museum*). North of Acibechería (follow Ruela de Xerusalén) is the Museo das Peregrinacións, with Camino de Santiago iconography from sculptures and carvings to *azabache* (compact black coal, or jet) items. For an overview of the history of St. James, the cathedral, and the pilgrimage, as well as the Camino's role in the development of the city itself, this is a key visit. ⊠ *Rúa de San Miguel 4* ☎ *981/581558* ⊕ *www.mdperegrinacions.com* 🖼 *€2.40* ☉ *Tues.–Fri. 10–8, Sat. 10:30–1:30 and 5–8, Sun. 10:30–1:30.*

Museo do Pobo Galego (*Galician Folk Museum*). Next door to the CGAC stands the Museo do Pobo Galego, in the medieval convent of San Domingos de Bonaval. Photos, farm implements, traditional costumes, and other items illustrate aspects of traditional Galician life. The star attraction is the 13th-century self-supporting spiral granite staircase that still connects three floors. ⊠ *C. San Domingos de Bonaval s/n* ☎ *981/583620* ⊕ *www.museodopobo.es* 🖼 *€3* ☉ *Tues.–Sat. 10–2 and 4–8, Sun. 11–2.*

Pazo de Xelmírez (*Palace of Archbishop Xelmírez*). Step into the rich 12th-century Pazo de Xelmírez, an unusual example of Romanesque civic architecture with a cool, clean, vaulted dining hall. The little figures carved on the corbels in this graceful, 100-foot-long space are

drinking, eating, and listening to music with great medieval gusto. Each is different, so stroll around for a tableau of mealtime merriment. ⊠ *Praza do Obradoiro* ☎ *981/569327* ⊕ *www.catedraldesantiago.es* ▥ *Combined ticket for Pazo and cathedral €5* ⊙ *June–Sept., Mon.–Sat. 10–2 and 4–8, Sun. 10–2; Oct.–May, Mon.–Sat. 10–1:30 and 4–8, Sun. 10–1:30.*

SHOPPING

Souvenirs of Galicia include authentic *zuecos* (hand-painted wooden clogs) still worn in some villages to navigate mud, jewelry and trinkets carved from azabache (jet, or compact black coal), ceramics, and excellent leatherwear of all kinds. Santiago has an excellent selection of religious items in all price ranges.

Sargadelos. Galicia is known throughout Spain for its distinctive blue-and-white ceramics with bold modern designs, made in Sargadelos and O Castro. There is a wide selection at Sargadelos. ⊠ *Rúa Nova 16* ☎ *981/581905.*

WHERE TO EAT

$$ ✕ **A Barrola.** With polished wooden floors and a lively terrace, this sea-
SPANISH food-heavy restaurant is a favorite with the university faculty. The *caldo gallego*, *santiaguiños* (slipper lobsters), *arroz con bogavante* (rice with lobster), and seafood empanadas are superb, and local delicacies like *angulas* (elvers) and lamprey are served seasonally. If options overwhelm you and you can't decide, you might opt for the *parrillada de pescados* (mixed seafood grill). A Barrola is one of a chain of three restaurants in the area; Casa Elisa and Xantares are both equally popular and within a stone's throw, on Rúa do Franco. ⑤ *Average main: €20* ⊠ *Rúa do Franco 29* ☎ *981/577999* ⊕ *www.restaurantesgrupobarrola. com* ⊙ *Closed Dec.–Apr.; closed Mon. May–Nov.*

$$ ✕ **Carretas.** This casual spot for fresh Galician seafood is around the
SEAFOOD corner from the Hostal dos Reis Católicos. Fish dishes abound, but the specialty here is shellfish. Start with a plate of melt-in-your-mouth battered mini-scallops, then, for the full experience, order the labor-intensive *variado de mariscos,* a comprehensive platter of langostinos, king prawns, crab, and "goose" barnacles, a white or gray crustacean found in deep waters. *Salpicón de mariscos* presents the same creatures shelled. For dessert, there's the tastier-than-it-sounds fried milk pudding. ⑤ *Average main: €20* ⊠ *Rúa das Carretas 21* ☎ *981/563111* ⊕ *www.restaurantesanclemente.com* ⊙ *Closed Sun. and Mon.*

VILLEFRANCHE-SUR-MER, FRANCE

Updated by Jennifer Ladonne

Nestled discreetly along the deep scoop of harbor between Nice and Cap Ferrat, this pretty watercolor of a fishing port is a stage set of brightly colored houses—the sort of place where Pagnol's *Fanny* could have been filmed. Genuine fishermen actually skim up to the docks here in weathered blue *barques,* and the streets of the Vieille Ville flow

Villefranche-sur-Mer and Vicinity

St-Martin-du-Var

L'Escarène

Sospel

Var

Castagniers

N202

D2204

Castillon

D21

Peillon

St-Agnes

A8

MONACO

A8

ITALY

N7

Villefranche-sur-Mer

N7

Menton

Nice

Èze

N98

Monte Carlo

Roquebrune

Beaulieu-sur-Mer

St-Jean-Cap-Ferrat

Golfe de St-Hospice

Cap-Martin

Baie des Anges

Mediterranean Sea

0   5 miles

0   5 kilometers

directly to the waterfront, much as they did in the 13th century. The deep harbor, in the caldera of a volcano, was once preferred by the likes of Onassis and Niarchos and royals on their yachts. The character of Villefranche was subtly shaped by the artists and authors who gathered at the Hôtel Welcome, and above all, Jean Cocteau, who came here to recover from the excesses of Paris life. Villefranche is also the gateway to other treasures along this most select part of the Riviera.

ESSENTIALS

CURRENCY
The euro.

HOURS
Stores open Monday–Saturday 9–7, but many close at lunchtime (usually noon to 2 or 3) and some will open later and on Sunday during July and August. Museums open 10–5, but most are closed on either Monday or Tuesday.

TELEPHONES
Tri-band GSM phones work in France. You can buy prepaid phone cards at telecom shops, news vendors, and tobacconists in all towns and cities. Phone cards can be used for local or international calls. Orange, SFR, Bouygues Telecom, and Virgin are leading telecom companies. If you have an unlocked GSM phone, LeFrenchMobile (⊕ *www.*

lefrenchmobile.com) offers SIM cards (and micro SIM cards) with support in English, unlimited validity of credits, and prepurchase online.

COMING ASHORE

Cruise ships dock offshore in the bay of Villefranche-sur-Mer and passengers are tendered to the quayside in the heart of the town. The terminal is small, but has an information center, restrooms, and car-rental kiosks. You can tour Villefranche-sur-Mer itself on foot from here, but to visit surrounding attractions you'll need transport. The train station is a five-minute walk from the cruise port and the service along the coast to Beaulieu and Èze-sur-Mer is frequent (at least two trains per hour), fast (less than 10 minutes travel time), and reliable. Tickets cost around €2 for the short hop between Villefranche-sur-Mer and Beaulieu-sur-Mer. From the train station at Èze-sur-Mer there are frequent shuttle buses to Èze village (15 minutes, Route 83). By train both Nice and Monte Carlo are also within 15-minutes journey time. Frequent bus services by Ligne d'Azur (⊕ *www.lignedazur.com*) link Villefranche-sur-Mer with Beaulieu-sur-Mer, Cap Ferrat, Èze, Nice, and Monte Carlo. One ride is €1.10, and a day pass is €4. Route 81 links Villefranche-sur-Mer with Beaulieu-sur-Mer and St-Jean-Cap-Ferrat (also with Nice). Line 100 links Villefranche-sur-Mer with Nice and Èze-sur-Mer (and on to Monte Carlo).

The cost of car rental is approximately €75 for an economy manual vehicle. However, there are no car-rental options in town so vehicles have to be prebooked and there are fees for delivery and return.

Taxis are plentiful, and can provide tourist itineraries. For a single journey, fares are €3 for pick-up followed by a day fare of €0.90 per km (½-mile) plus a fee for any waiting time. Taxis can be prebooked for return journeys, making them a good option for transfer to local attractions.

EXPLORING VILLEFRANCHE-SUR-MER AND VICINITY

VILLEFRANCHE-SUR-MER

Chapelle St-Pierre. So enamored was Jean Cocteau of this painterly fishing port that he decorated the 14th-century Chapelle St-Pierre with images from the life of St. Peter and dedicated it to the village's fishermen. ⊠ *Pl. Pollanai Quai Courbet* ☎ *04–93–76–90–70* ⊠ *€2.50* ☉ *May–mid-Sept., Tues–Sun. 10–noon and 3–7; mid-Sept.–mid-Nov. and mid-Dec.–Apr., Tues.–Sun. 10–noon and 2–6.*

Citadelle St-Elme. Open year round, the stalwart 16th-century Citadelle St-Elme, restored to perfect condition, anchors the harbor with its broad, sloping stone walls. Beyond its drawbridge lie the city's administrative offices and a group of minor gallery-museums, with a scattering of works by Picasso and Miró. Whether or not you stop into these private collections of local art (all free of charge), you're welcome to stroll around the inner grounds and to circle the imposing exterior. ⊠ *Harbor* ☎ *Free* ☉ *Museums: June–Sept., Tues.–Sat. 10–noon and 3–6:30, Sun. 3–6:30; Oct–May, Tues.–Sat. 10–noon and 2–5:30, Sun 2–5:30.*

Rue Obscure. Running parallel to the waterfront, the extraordinary 13th-century Rue Obscure (literally, "Dark Street") is entirely covered by

vaulted arcades; it sheltered the people of Villefranche when the Germans fired their parting shots—an artillery bombardment—near the end of World War II.

BEAULIEU-SUR-MER
4 km (2½ miles) east of Villefranche.

With its back pressed hard against the cliffs of the corniche and sheltered between the peninsulas of Cap Ferrat and Cap Roux, this once-grand resort basks in a tropical microclimate that earned its central neighborhood the name *Petite Afrique* (little Africa). The town was the pet of 19th-century society, and its grand hotels welcomed Empress Eugénie, the Prince of Wales, and Russian nobility. Today it's still a posh address.

Fodor's Choice
★   **Villa Kerylos.** One manifestation of Beaulieu's Belle Époque excess is the eye-knocking Villa Kerylos, a mansion built in 1902 in the style of classical Greece (to be exact, of the villas that existed on the island of Delos in the 2nd century BC). It was the dream house of the amateur archaeologist Théodore Reinach, who hailed from a wealthy family from Frankfurt, helped the French in their excavations at Delphi, and became an authority on ancient Greek music. He commissioned an Italian architect from Nice, Emmanuel Pontremoli, to surround him with Grecian delights: cool Carrara marble, rare fruitwoods, and a dining salon where guests reclined to eat *à la grecque.* Don't miss this—it's one of the most unusual houses in the south of France. ⊠ *Rue Gustave-Eiffel* ☎ *04–93–01–01–44* ⊕ *www.villa-kerylos.com* ☒ *€9; €17 for both villas* ☯ *Mid-Feb–June and Sept.–Oct., daily 10–6; July and Aug., daily 10–7; Nov.–Feb., weekdays 2–6, weekends 10–6.*

ST-JEAN-CAP-FERRAT
2 km (1 mile) south of Beaulieu on D25.

This luxuriously sited pleasure port moors the peninsula of Cap Ferrat; from its port-side walkways and crescent of beach you can look over the sparkling blue harbor to the graceful green bulk of the corniches. Yachts purr in and out of port, and their passengers scuttle into cafés for take-out drinks to enjoy on their private decks. Unfortunately, Cap Ferrat is a vast peninsula and hides its secrets—except for the Villa Ephrussi, most fabled estates are hidden behind iron gates and towering hedges—particularly well.

★   **Villa Ephrussi de Rothschild.** Between the port and the mainland, the floridly beautiful Villa Ephrussi de Rothschild stands as witness to the wealth and worldly flair of the baroness who had it built. Constructed in 1905 in neo-Venetian style (its flamingo-pink facade was thought not to be in the best of taste by the local gentry), the house was baptized "Ile-de-France" in homage to the Baroness Bétrice de Rothschild's favorite ocean liner (her staff used to wear sailing costumes and her ship travel kit is on view in her bedroom). Precious artworks, tapestries, and furniture adorn the salons—in typical Rothschildian fashion, each room is given over to a different 18th-century "époque." Upstairs are the private apartments of Madame la Baronne, which can only be seen on a guided tour offered around noon. The grounds are landscaped with no fewer than seven theme gardens and topped off with a Temple

of Diana; be sure to allow yourself time to wander here, as this is one of the few places on the coast where you'll be allowed to experience the lavish pleasures characteristic of the Belle Époque Côte d'Azur. Tea and light lunches are served in a glassed-in porch overlooking the grounds and spectacular views of the coastline. A combination ticket allows you to also visit Villa Kerylos in nearby Beaulieu in the same week. ✉ *Av. Ephrussi, St-Jean-Cap-Ferrat* ☎ *04–93–01–33–09* ⊕ *www.villa-ephrussi.com* 🎫 *€12; €17 for both villas* ⊙ *Mar.–June and Sept.–Oct., daily 10–6; July and Aug., daily 10–7; Nov.–Feb., weekdays 2–6, weekends 10–6.*

ÈZE
2 km (1 mile) east of Beaulieu.

Fodor'sChoice
★

> ## VILLEFRANCHE-SUR-MER BEST BETS
>
> **Èze.** One of the most charming of France's *villages perchés*, or perched villages, is built high on a rocky parapet. Views down the Riviera coast are spectacular.
>
> **Villa Kerylos.** The splendors of ancient Greek art and architecture are beautifully re-created here in the south of France at the home of a wealthy amateur archaeologist.
>
> **Villa Ephrussi de Rothschild.** This magnificent century-old mansion surrounded by glorious gardens is stuffed with the finest furniture and decoration its baroness owner could afford.

Towering like an eagle's nest above the coast and crowned with ramparts and the ruins of a medieval château, preposterously beautiful Èze (pronounced *ehz*) is the most accessible of all the perched villages—this means crowds, many of whom head here to shop in the boutique-lined staircase-streets. (Happily, most shops here are quite stylish, and there is a nice preponderance of bric-a-brac and vintage fabric dealers.) But most come here to drink in the views, for no one can deny that this is the most spectacularly sited of all coastal promontories; if you can manage to shake the crowds and duck off to a quiet overlook, the village commands splendid views up and down the coast, one of the draws that once lured fabled visitors—lots of crowned heads, Georges Sand, Friedrich Nietzsche—and residents: Consuelo Vanderbilt, when she was tired of being duchess of Marlborough, traded in Blenheim Palace for a custom-built house here.

Jardin Exotique (*Tropical Garden*). From the crest-top Jardin Exotique, full of rare succulents, you can pan your videocam all the way around the hills and waterfront. But if you want a prayer of a chance at enjoying the magnificence of Eze's arched passages, stone alleyways, and ancient fountains, come at dawn or after sunset—or (if you have the means) stay the night—but spend the midday elsewhere. The church of **Notre-Dame,** consecrated in 1772, glitters inside with baroque altarpieces. Èze's tourist office, on Place du Général-de-Gaulle, can direct you to the numerous footpaths—the most famous being the **Sentier Friedrich Nietzsche**—that thread Èze with the coast's three corniche highways. ✉ *Moyenne Corniche* 🎫 *€6* ⊙ *Nov.–Jan., daily 9–4:30; Feb. and Mar., daily 9–5; Apr. and May, daily 9–6; June and Sept., daily 9–7; July and Aug., daily 9–7:30; Oct., daily 9–5:30.*

SHOPPING

This part of the Riviera coastline has some of the most expensive addresses, and thus some of the finest shopping, with excusive boutiques selling very high-class fashion and decorative goods. In the shops of Cap Ferrat and Beaulieu you'll shop among France's more mature lunching ladies, while Villefranche-sur-Mer has a good selection of characterful boutiques with more down-to-earth prices. The streets of Èze are replete with artists' studios selling excellent art and ceramics, plus cute collectibles. In every town you'll find local Provençal specialties such as excellent olive oil, soaps, dried herbs, colorful fabrics, pottery, and basketwork.

WHERE TO EAT

$$$ ✕ **La Grignotière.** Tucked down a narrow side street just a few steps away
FRENCH from the marketplace, this small and friendly local restaurant offers up generous portions of top-quality, inexpensive dishes. The homemade lasagne is excellent, as is the spaghetti pistou. ⑤ *Average main: €25* ✉ *3 rue du Poilu* ☎ *04–93–76–79–83* ⊘ *Closed Wed.*

$$$ ✕ **Troubadour.** Amid the clutter and clatter of the nearby coast, this is
FRENCH a wonderful find (and has been for more than 30 years!): comfortably relaxed, this old family house proffers pleasant service and excellent dishes like roasted scallops with chicken broth and squab with citrus zest and beef broth. ⑤ *Average main: €30* ✉ *4 rue du Brec* ☎ *04–93–41–19–03* ⊘ *Closed Sun. and Mon., mid-Nov.–mid-Dec., and 1st wk of Mar. and July.*

Eastern Mediterranean and Aegean

PORTS IN CROATIA, CYPRUS, EGYPT, GREECE, ISRAEL, MONTENEGRO, AND TURKEY

Dubrovnik, Croatia

WORD OF MOUTH

"Ephesus is probably one of the most incredible sights you will ever see. Even better than Pompeii, IMHO! You will enjoy it more if you're not in a group of 50 or 100. If you stop in Istanbul, you're in for a treat. . . . There is no place like Istanbul."

—zwho

Eastern Mediterranean cruises are especially good for travelers who want to see the archaeological ruins of Europe's two great classical civilizations, Rome and Greece. These ports are rich in history, and some are even rich in natural beauty. There are few ports of call more breathtaking than Santorini or the island of Hvar.

Many Eastern Mediterranean itineraries begin in Piraeus, the seaport of Athens, or Istanbul, and visit ports in Greece and Turkey. Some may cross the Mediterranean to call in Alexandria or Port Said (for an exhausting, daylong visit to Cairo). Other cruises begin in Italy, often in Rome or Venice. These cruises may take in ports in Sicily and southern Italy (if they leave from Rome) or even Malta before heading toward Greece. Cruises beginning in Venice may call at one or more ports along Croatia's breathtaking Adriatic coast, and these port calls are highlights of any voyage.

ABOUT THE RESTAURANTS
All the restaurants we recommend serve lunch; they may also serve dinner if your cruise ship stays late in port and you choose to dine off the ship. Cuisine in Europe is varied, but Europeans tend to eat a leisurely meal at lunch, but in most ports there are quicker and simpler alternatives for those who just want to grab a quick bite before returning to the ship. Note that several Eastern Mediterranean countries do not use the euro, including Croatia, Cyprus, Egypt, and Turkey. Price categories in those countries are based on the euro-equivalent costs of eating in restaurants. All price categories are based on the average cost of a main course at dinner, so in some cases lunch may be cheaper.

ALEXANDRIA, EGYPT

Ancient Egypt's gateway to the Mediterranean was founded by Alexander the Great in 331 BC, but its name is inextricably linked with Cleopatra. She inhabited vast palaces and worshipped at monumental temples. The city's great library was also under her control, and her city was protected by one of the Seven Wonders of the Ancient World, the great Pharos of Alexandria, a lighthouse. Sadly, all of these great treasures are lost or buried underneath the modernity. That doesn't mean Alexandria is bereft of history; in a second incarnation it became a decadent, early-20th-century mercantile and colonial enclave with a multicultural mix. It seduced novelist E. M. Forster during World War I and gave birth to Lawrence Durrell's *Alexandria Quartet*, which captivated a generation of American readers in the late 1950s. At the same time, its reputation as an Arabic seat of learning has stayed in the ascendant. With lively streets and graceful cafés, Alexandria is still a great city and remains an utterly charming place to visit.

ESSENTIALS

CURRENCY
The Egyptian pound.

HOURS
Museums are usually open from 9 to 5. Many museums are closed on Monday. Shops open from 8 until 7. During Ramadan (the Muslim month of fasting) opening times vary; during this period shops close during the day but stay open late into the evening.

TELEPHONES
GSM phones work in Egypt, where mobile systems are single-band and are not 3G-compatible. Telecom Egypt runs the fixed line system. Public phones accept calling cards available from retail outlets; however, connections are not always smooth. Major companies are MobiNil and Vodafone.

COMING ASHORE
Alexandria's cruise terminal is in the commercial port in the western harbor, and ships dock right alongside busy commercial ships; it's a frenetic environment. The terminal has shopping facilities and a taxi stand.

From the port, it is an easy 20-minute walk along the corniche to the heart of town, but navigating your way to the various attractions can be a challenge, and taxis are the best way to get around. They are inexpensive, and you can flag them down almost anywhere. The driver might try to pick up another passenger en route—it's standard practice, so don't be surprised. Drivers don't use their meters, so you have to guess at the appropriate fare or try to negotiate one in advance. A ride from the cruise port to downtown should be around £E10–£E15. If you look wealthy, expect to pay a bit more.

Though they're picturesque and cheap, trams are likely to take four to five times longer to get where you're going than a taxi would. The main tram station is Raml, near Maydan Sa'd Zaghlul. Buy tickets on board. Horse-drawn *caleches* (carriages) offer an alternative way to tour the town, but agree on a price before you get aboard.

Contacts Avis ✉ *Cecil Hotel, Maydan Sa'd Zaghlul, Raml Station* ☎ *03/485–7400* ⊕ *www.avis.com.*

EXPLORING ALEXANDRIA

Abu al-Abbas al-Mursi Mosque. This attractive mosque was built during World War II over the tomb of a 13th-century holy man, who is the patron saint of the city's fishermen. The area surrounding it has been turned into Egypt's largest and most bizarre religious/retail complex, with a cluster of mosques sharing a terrace that hides an underground shopping center. Intruding on the space is a horrific modernism-on-the-cheap office building (with yet more shops) that is as pointed and angular as the mosques are smooth and curved. If you are dressed modestly and the mosque is open, you should be able to get inside. If so, remove your shoes and refrain from taking photos. ✉ *Corniche, al-Anfushi, El Anfushi.*

Alexandria

Eastern Harbour

1/8 mi
1/8 km

Mediterranean Sea

Fort Qayt Bey

Eastern Harbour

Abu al-Abbas al-Mursi Mosque

El ANFUSHI

El Saiyala
Sidi Yakout
El Haggary

Ras el-Tin Sabiy
Safar Pasha
Ras el-Tim

GOMROK

El Gomrok

Western Harbour

Kasr Ras el-Tim
Gouda
El Tarsana
El Tarsana

## Main map labels:

Port Said

Bibliotheca Alexandrina

Dr. Ali Mostafa Mosharrafa

AL AZARITA
Abdel Hamid Badawy
El Akbar
El Eskandar
El Akbar

Champollion

Mohammed M. Motawei
Reyad Pasha

El Shallalat Garden

Alexandria National Museum

Nouh Afandi
El batalesa
El fawatem
Dr. Ibrahim Abdel Sayed
El Damamini
EL SHALLALAT

Victor Basily

Fouad

Batris Lumumba

Geranfil

GOMROK

El Soltan Hussein Kamel

KOUM EL-DEKKA

Solaiman Yousry

Kolyet El Teb

Grand Trianon

Zaghloul

Safia

• Kom al-Dikka

Masr Train Station

RAML STATION Ⓜ

Midan Saad Zaghloul

MHATET EL RAMEL

Istanboul

The Cavafy Museum

El Nabi Daniel

Midan El Gumhorriya

El Mohatza

Midan El Mohatza

Saad Zaghloul
Ibn Zenki
El Shohadaa
El Ghoria El Togareya
Adib Bek Ishak
Kennisei El Akbal
Bek Ali Talak
Mahmoud
Salah Salem
Ahmed Orabi

Ahmed Mursy Badr

Masged El Attarin

Masged El Attarin

Sidi El Metwally

Ismail Mehana (El Mohatza)

El Courniche (26th of July St.)
El Ghoria El
El MANSHIYA
Midan Orabi
Midan Tahrir
Noubar
Gohar

Salah El Din

Abu El Dardaa

ABU EL DARDAA

Masged El Oskufeia

El Courniche (26th of July St.)

Faransa

El Ka'ed
El Sabaa Banat
Banat
El Hamamil (El Essias)
Masged El Fatham
El Gazayer
El Halawany
Ishak Sanad
Sidi Eskandar
El Nadim
El Baidawy

Bahary Bey
El Kadi Sanad
Karasta
Sahet Bakir

El Farahda

Abdel Moneim

El Kobli El Kadeem
El Bab El Akhbar
Bab El Akhbar

◆ Catacombs of Kom al-Shaqafa

◆ Pompey's Pillar

Alexandria National Museum. A small but high-quality collection of artifacts includes items found under the waters of the Western Harbor during recent marine archaeological projects. The display galleries cover every era of the city's long history and include Christian pieces, Islamic arts and crafts, and more recent information about Alexandria's colonial era. The early-20th-century Italianate palace that houses the museum, designed by a French architect, is a prime example of this colonial past. ⊠ *110 Shar'a el Horreya, El Shallalat* ☎ *03/483–5519* 🖃 *E30* ☾ *Daily 9–4.*

Bibliotheca Alexandrina. This monumental, $190 million, UNESCO-sponsored project began with an instinctively appealing idea: to resurrect the Great Library of ancient

Alexandria, once one of the world's major centers of learning. Its location near the Silsileh Peninsula on the edge of the Eastern Harbor has tremendous symbolic resonance, having been the royal quarters in ancient times and one of several possible locations of the original library. The modernist Norwegian-designed building is in the form of an enormous multitiered cylinder tilted to face the sea, with a roof of diamond-shaped windows that allow controlled light into the seven cascading interior floors. The most impressive feature, however, is the curving exterior wall covered in rough-hewn granite blocks from Aswan that have been engraved with letters from ancient languages.

Once you've enjoyed the view of the vast interior from the mezzanine gallery, there's little to hold you in the main hall, but the library has several small museums and exhibitions that are of more interest. The **Manuscripts Museum** has a large collection of rare documents, parchments, and early printed books. The **Impressions of Alexandria** exhibition features paintings and sketches of the city dating from the 15th to the 19th centuries and photographs taken in the late 19th and early 20th centuries. The **Antiquities Museum** on the basement level has a collection of finds from Pharaonic, Roman, and Islamic Alexandria. Examples of monumental Roman statuary include *Huge Forearm Holding a Ball* (nothing else remains of the immense piece), and a finely chiseled bust of the Emperor Octavian (Augustus). Egypto-Roman artifacts include the mummy of Anhk Hor, governor of Upper Egypt, and several 2nd-century funerary masks showing the prevalent cross-styling between the classical Egyptian and Roman Egyptian styles. A planetarium and IMAX theater are the latest additions to the complex. ⊠ *63 Shar'a Soter, Chatby* ☎ *03/483–9999* ⊕ *www.bibalex. org* 🖃 *Library E10, Antiquities Museum E20, Manuscripts Museum E20 Planetarium and IMAX shows E25* ☾ *Sat.–Thurs. 11–7, Fri. 3–7.*

★ **Catacombs of Kom al-Shoqafa.** This is the most impressive of Alexandria's ancient remains, dating from the 2nd century AD. Excavation started in 1892, and the catacombs were discovered accidentally eight years later when a donkey fell through a chamber ceiling. A long spiral staircase leads to the main hall. The stairs run down the outside of a shaft, which excavators used to transport the bodies of the dead. The staircase leads to the rotunda, which, like all but the lowest chamber, is undecorated but striking for the sheer scale of the underground space, supported by giant columns carved out of the bedrock.

A few rooms branch off from the rotunda: the Triclinium was a banquet hall where relatives and friends toasted the deceased, and the Caracalla Hall has four lightly painted tombs and a case of bones. The next level down contains a labyrinth of smaller nooks for storing bodies and leads to the lowest excavated room, which is framed by columns and sculpted snakes. Casts of two statues stand here—the originals are in the Greco-Roman Museum—and three tombs are of interest for their mix of pharaonic and Greek imagery. ⊠ *Shar' El Shenity Abu Mandour, Karmouz* ☎ *03/482–5800* 🎟 *E35* ⊙ *Daily 9–4:30.*

The Cavafy Museum. The writer Constantine Cavafy was ignored during his lifetime but has received international recognition since his death in 1933. His poetry, which focused on such themes as one's moral dilemmas and uncertainty about the future, spoke to the Greek-speaking community around the Eastern Mediterranean and has been translated into all major languages. The small flat where Cavafy spent the last years of his life has been turned into a museum. Half of it is given over to a re-creation of his home. The other half of the museum houses newspaper clippings about the poet's life and a library of his works. ⊠ *4 Shar'a CP Cavafy(formerly Shar'a Sharm El-Sheikh), Mahatet El Raml* ☎ *03/468–1598* 🎟 *E20* ⊙ *Tues.–Sun. 10–3.*

Fort Qayt Bay. This sandstone fort lies on the very tip of the Corniche, dominating the view of the Eastern Harbor. It was built on the site of Alexandria's Pharos lighthouse, one of the seven wonders of the ancient world and incorporates its remains—much of which are still visible—into the foundation. A Greek named Sostratus in the 3rd century BC constructed the lighthouse under the Ptolemies. Standing about 400 feet high and capable of projecting a light that could be seen 53 km (35 miles) out to sea, it was one of the most awesome structures created by ancients. The base of the four-tiered Pharos was thought to have contained some 300 rooms, as well as a hydraulic system for lifting fuel to the top of the tower.

In the centuries that followed, the Pharos was damaged and rebuilt several times, until it was finally destroyed in the great earthquake of 1307. It lay in ruins for two centuries until the Mamluk Sultan Qayt Bay had the current fortress constructed in 1479. Recently, a French team found what are thought to be parts of the Pharos in shallow waters just offshore, rekindling local interest in the ancient monument—there is even talk of an underwater museum, although that is unlikely to materialize anytime soon. ⊠ *Corniche (far western end), El Anfushi* ☎ *03/480–9144* 🎟 *E25* ⊙ *Daily 9–5:30.*

Kom al-Dikka (*Roman Theater*). The focal point of this excavated section of the ancient city is a well-preserved amphitheater—the only one of its kind in Egypt—originally constructed in the 4th century AD, then rebuilt in the 6th century, following an earthquake. At that time a large dome was added (only its supporting columns still stand), and the theater went from being a cultural venue to a forum for public meetings of the City Council—a change deduced from ancient graffiti promoting various political parties. The other half of the site is the ancient baths and living quarters, although much of this area is, in fact, best seen through the fence from the side near Pastroudis Café, where the cisterns and walls are clearly visible. The red bricks mark the location of the heated baths—warmed by an elaborate underground system—which complemented the adjacent cold and steam baths. The whole area fell into disuse after the 7th-century Persian conquest of Egypt. One noteworthy site in the residential section is a Roman house known as the **Villa of the Birds,** so named for its colorful floor mosaics depicting birds in several forms. The colorful and detailed craftsmanship shows a high level of sophistication. The mosaics, now restored, are protected by a modern structure. ⊠ *Off Maydan El Shohada, opposite the Misr train station, Kon al-Dikka* ☎ *03/490–2904* ▣ *E20, E15 for Villa of the Birds* ☉ *Daily 9–4:30.*

Pompey's Pillar (*Serapium Oracle*). Despite being Alexandria's most famous tourist sight, Pompey's Pillar is a disappointment. After all, it's just a granite pillar—albeit at 88 feet, a very tall one—placed on a hill surrounded by ruins. Known in Arabic as *al-'Amud al-Sawiri* (Column of the Horseman), the pillar was misnamed after Pompeius (106–48 BC) by the Crusaders. In fact, it dates to the 3rd century AD, when it was erected in honor of the emperor Diocletian on the site of a Ptolemaic temple to Serapis. The late-model sphinxes lying around on pedestals add a little character. The most interesting element, ironically, is that from the hill you can get a glimpse inside the walled cemetery next door, as well as a view of a long and busy market street. ⊠ *Corner of Amoud El Sawary and El Shenity Abou Mandour, Karmouz* ☎ *03/482–5800* ▣ *E20* ☉ *Daily 9–4.*

SHOPPING

Egyptians are shrewd businessmen and retailers, and Alexandria has long been a trading city. You'll find an amazing array of crafts, but quality varies from first-class to dreadful, so do check items carefully.

Egyptians specialize in worked brass and copper articles, wood inlay on jewelry boxes and chess sets, and leather. The hookah or hubble-bubble pipe is also an interesting remembrance of the country. Egyptian cotton is a byword for quality, and the shops of Alexandria are the place to buy items like bedding and towels. The long flowing *jellabas* worn by the men are cool and comfortable, and there's a never-ending supply of cut-price T-shirts.

If you want to purchase genuine antiques and antiquities, you'll need to have a certificate of approval from the Egyptian authorities to export your purchase, but copies are on sale everywhere. These items

needn't be expensive: you can buy a lucky alabaster scarab beetle for a few Egyptian pounds (it's almost a compulsory souvenir of your trip to Egypt).

Whatever you buy, you'll need to haggle. In Egypt very few items have a set price. Some visitors find this stressful, but try to remember that bartering isn't meant to be a argument; it's a discussion to reach a mutually suitable price. Start at around 40% of the first asking price and rise little by little, but walk away if the offer price seems too high. Once you've agreed on a price, it's very bad form to walk away from a transaction.

For cottons, visit the shops on the streets radiating from Sa'd Zaghlul Square. The new cruise terminal promises upmarket shopping opportunities just a short distance from the ship.

Attarine Market. This area acquired its reputation in the 1960s as the place where the high-quality antiques sold by fleeing foreigners resurfaced. Those days are long gone. There are now only a few true antiques stores left in the area, but it's fascinating nonetheless to see the tiny workshops where the reproduction French-style furniture so popular in Egypt originates. Almost all the workshops will be happy to sell direct if you find a piece that appeals to you, but consider the challenge of shipping it back home before you give in to temptation. The market actually consists of a series of alleyways, the sum of which feels less established—and far less touristy—than Cairo's Khan al-Khalili. ✛ *To find the market, walk one block west of the Attarine Mosque and cross Shar'a al-Horreya to the alley between the café and the parts store, El Attarine.*

WHERE TO EAT

★ **Grand Trianon.** One of Alexandria's most stylish institutions since it opened in the 1920s, the Grand Trianon remains a forum for courtship, gossip, and rediscovery. Its most popular area is the café, which has a certain old-world grandeur, despite being the least decorated part of the place. The adjacent restaurant is an extravagant art nouveau jewel, with colorful murals on the wall and a spectacular stained-glass window over the entrance to the kitchen. But the pièce de résistance is in the patisserie around the corner. There, behind elaborately carved wooden cabinets, a series of Venetian wood-panel paintings of sensual water nymphs will take your breath away. The colors are muted, but as your eyes adjust the images will start to shimmer like a Gustav Klimt kiss. The café and restaurant close at midnight, the patisserie at 8 pm. ✉ *Maydan Sa'd Zaghlul, Mahatet El Raml* ☎ *03/486–8539.*

ASHDOD, ISRAEL

Updated by Jessica Steinberg

Busy Ashdod is not only one of Israel's fastest-growing cities, it's also the country's largest port. Perched on the Mediterranean, it processes more than 60% of the goods imported into Israel. Home to many ancient peoples over the centuries, Ashdod today is a modern, planned city. It's also a convenient jumping-off point for exploring several of Israel's most interesting cities, including Jerusalem, Tel Aviv, and Bethlehem.

ESSENTIALS

CURRENCY

The shekel.

HOURS

Shops are generally open Sunday through Thursday from 9 to 7, though some close in the afternoons. Museums vary in hours, being open Monday through Thursday from around 10 to 6, but most have shorter hours from Friday through Sunday (often open only from 10 to 2 or 3). Some museums close on Fridays.

PRIVATE TOURS

Several companies can provide private tours for cruise passengers calling Ashdod.

Contacts Elana Dascal. ☎ 054/621–6209 ✉ edascal@gmail.com. **Eshcolot Tours** ☎ 02/566-5555 ✉ advantag@netmedia.net.il. **Ryan Friedland.** ☎ 052/674–7911. **Philip J. Gordon Lavine.** ☎ 050/812–8842 ✉ philtheguide@gmail.com.

TELEPHONES

Most multiband mobile phones will work in Israel, and GSM and 3G systems are well established in the urban areas. Major providers are Cellcom Israel, Parner Communication (Orange), and Pelephone.

COMING ASHORE

Ashdod, 43 miles west of Jerusalem, is Israel's largest port, and is therefore always busy with commercial traffic. The modern passenger terminal has a café, currency-exchange desk, and duty-free shops. Taxi drivers who wait at the terminal building have been security-cleared to work there; reports suggest that they charge a premium above other taxis, about $75. Other taxi drivers may not be allowed access into the port if they have not been approved, so for a cheaper alternative you can try outside the port entrance. Security is tight, so always carry ID and boarding passes.

Route 448 is a direct bus service from Ashdod Central Station to Jerusalem. Buses depart every 30 minutes at peak times, but are less frequent in the middle of the day. The journey takes around 90 minutes, and one-way fare is NIS18. To get to the central station in Ashdod, you'll need to take a taxi from the port if your ship doesn't provide a shuttle bus into town.

Currently it is possible to travel by bus between Jerusalem and Bethlehem, but your journey may be interrupted by security checks, which can be lengthy and may cause havoc with your scheduling. It's probably better to visit Bethlehem on a guided tour if you have limited time.

ASHDOD BEST BETS

Dome of the Rock, Jeruslaem. Holy to both Jews and Muslims, it is here that the lost Jewish Temple constructed by Solomon stood and also the place from where Mohammed was carried up to heaven to receive the wisdom of God.

Church of the Holy Sepulchre, Jersualem. The holiest Christian site in Jerusalem is the supposed site of the crucifixion.

The Dead Sea. The lowest place on Earth is famous for its salty waters and mud with (supposedly) healing properties.

3

Old City Jerusalem

MOUNT OF OLIVES

0 — 1/8 mi
0 — 1/8 km

Jericho Rd.

Sultan Suleiman Rd.

Ophel Rd.

Lions' (St. Stephen's) Gate

Golden Gate

Dome of the Rock

Al-Aqsa Mosque

KIDRON VALLEY

OPHEL

Ophel Rd.

CITY OF DAVID

Western (Wailing) Wall Plaza

Western Wall Tunnel

Dung Gate

Melchizedek Rd.

Herod's Gate

MUSLIM QUARTER

El-Wad Rd.

El-Wad Rd.

Bab el-Silsila St.

Via Dolorosa St.

St. Francis Rd.

Suq Khan e-Zeit

Suq el-Qattanin St.

Church of the Holy Sepulcher

Suq el-Lahhamin

JEWISH QUARTER

Hurva Square

Habad St.

Ma'aleh Hashalom

MT. ZION

Saladin St.

Nablus Rd.

Damascus Gate

Hatzanhanim St.

CHRISTIAN QUARTER

Greek Orthodox Patriarchate Rd.

Omar ibn el-Khattab Square

St. George St.

Christian Quarter Rd.

Muristan Rd.

David St.

ARMENIAN QUARTER

Armenian Orthodox Patriarchate Rd.

Citadel

Jaffa Gate

Zion Gate

MT. ZION

Hativat Etzioni

Hativat Yerushalayim

Hutzot Hayotzer

Mishkenot Sha'ananim

Mamilla Rd.

Jaffa Rd.

New Gate

Notre Dame de France

Rd. 1

Jerusalem Archaeological Park

Central Israel

Mediterranean Sea

Netanya

Tulkarm

Shekhem

WEST BANK

Ramallah

Jericho

Dead Sea

Qalqiliya

Jerusalem

Bethlehem

Masada

Ein Bokek

Arad

Hebron

Ramla

Rehovot

Tel Aviv–Jaffa

Ashdod

Ashkelon

Kiryat Gat

Beit Qama

Qfaqim

Beersheba

10 mi
10 km

There are no car-rental offices at the cruise terminal, so you'll be charged a premium for delivery—or have to take a taxi ride to the rental office. Prices start around $70 for a compact vehicle, but mileage is usually charged on top of that. If you want to combine Jerusalem and Bethlehem with the Dead Sea (doable, albeit as a rather long day of touring), it may be worth engaging a tour company that knows the routes and locations, because this will save you time.

As the security situation in Israel is subject to change, always check whether independent travel is advised before you decide not to book your excursions through your ship, particularly if you wish to visit Bethlehem.

3

EXPLORING ISRAEL FROM ASHDOD

BETHLEHEM

Today the great majority of Bethlehem's residents, as elsewhere in the West Bank, are Muslim. But for Christians the world over, the city is synonymous with the birth of Jesus, and the many shrines that celebrate that event. As well, Bethlehem is the site of the Tomb of Rachel, the only one of the biblical patriarchs and matriarchs not buried in Hebron.

★ **Church of the Nativity.** At this church marking the traditional site of the birth of Jesus, the stone exterior is crowned by the crosses of the three denominations sharing it: the Greek Orthodox, the Latins (Roman Catholic, represented by the Franciscan order), and the Armenian Orthodox. This is the oldest standing church in the country. From the right transept at the front of the church, descend to the **Grotto of the Nativity,** encased in white marble. Long lines can form at the entrance to the grotto, making the suggestion of spending just an hour to see the church an impossibility. Once a cave—precisely the kind of place that might have been used as a barn—the grotto has been reamed, plastered, and decorated beyond recognition. Immediately on the right is a small altar, and on the floor below it is the focal point of the entire site, a 14-point **silver star** with the Latin inscription: *hic de virgine maria jesus christus natus est* ("Here of the Virgin Mary, Jesus Christ was born"). ✉ *Manger Sq.* ☎ *02/274–1020* 🎟 *Free* 🕙 *Church: Apr.–Sept., daily 6:30 am–7:30 pm; Oct.–Mar., daily 5:30–5:30. Grotto: Apr.–Sept., Mon.–Sat. 9–7:30, Sun. noon–7:30; Oct.–Mar., Mon.–Sat. 9–5:30, Sun. noon–5:30.*

Church of St. Catherine. Adjacent to the Church of the Nativity, and accessible by a passage from its Armenian chapel, is Bethlehem's Roman Catholic parish church. From this church, the midnight Catholic Christmas mass is broadcast around the world. Steps descend from within the church to a series of dim grottoes, clearly once used as living quarters. A small wooden door (kept locked) connects the complex with the Grotto of the Nativity. ✉ *Manger Sq.* ☎ *02/274–2425* 🕙 *Apr.–Sept., daily 6–noon and 2–7; Oct.–Mar., daily 5:30–5:30.*

Manger Square. Bethlehem's central plaza and the site of the Church of the Nativity, Manger Square is built over the grotto thought to be the birthplace of Jesus. The end of the square opposite the church is the Mosque of Omar, the city's largest Muslim house of worship. The square occupies the center of Bethlehem's old city. It has a tourist-information office, a few restaurants, and several good souvenir shops.

Visiting Bethlehem

Although Bethlehem (approximately 70 km [43 miles] from Ashdod) is within the boundaries of the Palestinian Authority, tourists with a foreign passport will have no difficulty visiting; allow 90 minutes for travel. Although security may seem daunting at the heavily fortified border post, you simply show the cover of your passport to be whisked through. Israeli guides are not allowed to take you to the sights, but Israeli tour companies can help arrange for Palestinian guides to meet you at the border. If you're a more independent traveler, you can take one of the Palestinian taxis at the border. If taking a taxi, *sherut* (shared taxi), or bus from East Jerusalem, you must take a local bus or taxi from the Bethlehem side of the terminal to Manger Square. Driving is not recommended. Taxis will offer day-tour services, and this could be a sensible way to link the sites you want to see. Prices run around NIS 200 per hour, but may be inflated by taxi drivers with approval to wait at the cruise pier; you'll have to arrange to have your Israeli taxi driver wait while you visit the sights in Bethlehem and then return you to the pier; be sure to negotiate the price for this waiting time in advance.

Rachel's Tomb. This Israeli enclave in a Palestinian area is on the right shortly after passing through the border. The Bible relates that the matriarch Rachel, second and favorite wife of Jacob, died in childbirth on the outskirts of Bethlehem, "and Jacob set up a pillar upon her grave" (Genesis 35:19–20). There is no vestige of Jacob's original pillar, but observant Jews for centuries have hallowed the velvet-draped cenotaph inside the building as the site of Rachel's tomb. Islam as well venerates Rachel. Next to the tomb is a Muslim cemetery, reflecting the Middle Eastern tradition that it is a special privilege to be buried near a great personage. ⊠ *Rte. 60* 🎫 *Free* 🕐 *Sun.–Thurs., open 24 hrs.*

Shepherds' Fields. As you approach Bethlehem, you'll see the fields of the adjacent town of Beit Sahour, to the east of the city, traditionally identified with the biblical story of Ruth the Moabite, daughter-in-law of Naomi, who "gleaned in the field" (Ruth 2:2) of Boaz, Naomi's kinsman. The same fields are identified by Christian tradition as those where bewildered shepherds "keeping watch over their flock by night" received "tidings of great joy"—word of the birth of Jesus in Bethlehem (Luke 2). Two chapels—the Greek Orthodox Der El Rawat and the Catholic El Ghanem—commemorate the event.

DEAD SEA

The sudden and startling sight, in this bare landscape, of gleaming, ultramodern hotels surrounded by waving palm trees signals your arrival at the spa-resort area of Ein Bokek, near the southern tip of the Dead Sea. According to the Bible, it was along these shores that the Lord rained fire and brimstone on the people of Sodom and Gomorrah (Genesis 19:24) and turned Lot's wife into a pillar of salt (Genesis 26). Here, at the lowest point on Earth—the bottom of the world: 1,292 feet

below sea level—the hot, sulfur-pungent air hangs heavy, and a haze often shimmers over the water. You can float, but you cannot sink, in the warm, salty water.

MASADA

Fodor's Choice **Masada.** A symbol of the ancient kingdom of Israel, Masada (Hebrew
★ for "fortress") towers majestically over the western shore of the Dead Sea. Its unusual natural form—a plateau set off on all sides by towering cliffs—attracted Herod the Great, who built an opulent desert palace here. In recognition of its historical significance, this was the first site in Israel to be added to the UNESCO World Heritage List in 2001. To reach the top, most visitors make use of the speedy **cable car.** Starting at 8 am, it runs every half hour, with intermediate runs depending on demand. Maps, a detailed brochure, and a very useful audio guide are available at the top entrance.

3

The **Northern Palace,** Masada's most impressive structure, is an extraordinary three-tiered structure that seems to hang off the highest and most northerly point of the mountain. The **bathhouse** (upon return from the upper terrace) was a state-of-the-art facility in Herod's time, with its *apodyterium* (changing room), *frigidarium, tepidarium,* and *caldarium* (cold, lukewarm, and hot rooms, respectively). The **synagogue,** one of only four that have been uncovered from the Second Temple period, can be seen in the western casemate. It was likely here, in the community's spiritual center, that the leaders of the revolt against Rome made their fateful decision. In the summer of 2005, the rear genizah was renovated to house a permanent Torah scroll, which is used for bar and bat mitz-vah (coming-of-age) ceremonies. Adjoining the lower cable-car station is the **Masada Museum,** with hundreds of artifacts from the site. Especially moving is a set of 12 pottery shards, each bearing a single name. Archeologists believe these might have been lots drawn to decide the order in which the last remaining rebels would die. ⊠ *Off Rte. 3199, Ein Gedi* 🕾 *08/658–4207/8* ⊕ *www.parks.org.il* 🖃 *Site NIS 27; site and cable car NIS 72* ☯ *Apr.–Sept., Sat.–Thurs. 8–5, Fri. and Jewish holiday eves 8–3; Oct.–Mar., Sat.–Thurs. 8–4, Fri. and Jewish holiday eves 8–2.*

MOUNT OF OLIVES AND EAST JERUSALEM

The sights in this area are for the most part distinctly Christian. A few are a little off the beaten path, and the best way to explore them is on foot. **Garden of Gethsemane.** After the Last Supper, the New Testament relates, Jesus and his disciples came to a "place" called Gethsemane. There he agonized and prayed, and there, in the end, he was betrayed and arrested. The **Church of All Nations,** with its brilliantly colorful, landmark mosaic facade, was built in the garden in 1924 on the scanty remains of its Byzantine predecessor. At the altar is the so-called Rock of the Agony, where Jesus is said to have endured his Passion; this is the source of the older name of the church, the **Basilica of the Agony.** ⊠ *Jericho Rd., Kidron Valley, Jerusalem* 🕾 *02/626–6444* 🖃 *Free* ☯ *Apr.–Sept., daily 8–12 and 2–6; Oct.–Mar., daily 8–12 and 2–5.*

★ **Mt. of Olives Observation Point.** This is the classic panoramic view of the Old City: looking across the Kidron Valley over the gold Dome of the Rock. It's best in the early morning, with the sun at your back, or at

sunset on days with some clouds, when the golden glow can compensate for the glare. The Mt. of Olives has been bathed in sanctity for millennia. On the slope beneath you, and off to your left, is the vast **Jewish cemetery,** reputedly the oldest still in use anywhere in the world. Camel and donkey drivers (usually one of each) are always pushing to give you a short ride (not cheap!), and the vendors can be persistent, but a polite "no thank you" is sometimes enough for them to go bother someone else. The frequent police presence has made the locals less aggressive, but still beware of pickpockets here and on the road down to Gethsemane. Fairly good bathrooms are a welcome addition. ⊠ *E-Sheikh St., opposite Seven Arches Hotel, Mt. of Olives, Jerusalem.*

OLD CITY JERUSALEM

Drink in the very essence of Jerusalem as you explore the city's primary religious sites in the Muslim and Christian quarters, and at the Western Wall, and touch the different cultures that share it.

★ **Church of the Holy Sepulcher.** Vast numbers of Christians, especially adherents of the older "mainstream" churches, believe this to be the place where Jesus was crucified by the Romans, was buried, and rose from the dead. On the floor just inside the entrance of the church is the rectangular pink **Stone of Unction,** where, it is said, the body of Jesus was cleansed and prepared for burial. Steep steps take you up to **Golgotha,** or Calvary, meaning "the place of the skull," as the site is described in the New Testament. The tomb itself (**Station XIV**), encased in a pink marble edifice, is in the rotunda to the left of the main entrance of the church, under the great dome that dominates the Christian Quarter. An astonishing peculiarity of the Holy Sepulcher is that it is shared, albeit unequally and uncomfortably, by six Christian denominations (Catholic, Greek Orthodox, Armenian Orthodox, Syrian Orthodox, Egyptian Coptic, and Ethiopian). ⊠ *Between Suq Khan e-Zeit and Christian Quarter Rd., Christian Quarter, Jerusalem* ☏ *02/627-3314* ▢ *Free* ☽ *Apr.–Sept., daily 5 am–9 pm; Oct.–Mar., daily 4 am–7 pm.*

★ **Dome of the Rock and Temple Mount.** The magnificent golden **Dome of the Rock** dominates the vast 35-acre Temple Mount, the area known to Muslims as *Haram esh-Sharif* (the Noble Sanctuary). At its southern end, immediately in front of you as you enter the area from the Western Wall plaza (the only gate for non-Muslims), is the large, black-domed **al-Aqsa Mosque,** the third in holiness for Muslims everywhere. At the center of the plaza stood Herod's splendidly rebuilt Second Temple, the one Jesus knew, renowned as an architectural wonder of its day. The Romans reduced it to smoldering ruins in the summer of AD 70. Jewish tradition identifies the great **rock** at the summit of the hill—now under the gold dome—as the foundation stone of the world, and the place where Abraham bound and almost sacrificed his son Isaac (Genesis 22). Awakened by the archangel Gabriel, Muhammad was taken on the fabulous winged horse el-Burak to the *masjid al-aqsa,* the "farthermost place" (hence the name "al-Aqsa" Mosque). From there he rose to heaven, met God face to face, received the teachings of Islam, and returned to Mecca the same night. Tradition has it that the masjid al-aqsa was none other than Jerusalem, and the great rock the very

spot from which the prophet ascended. At the time of this writing, the Muslim shrines were closed to non-Muslims for an indefinite period, leaving the faithful alone to enjoy the wondrous interiors of stained-glass windows, granite columns, green-and-gold mosaics, arabesques, and superb medieval masonry. Security check lines to enter the area are often long; it's best to come early. Note: the Muslim attendants prohibit Bibles in the area. ⊠ *Access between the Western Wall and Dung Gate, Temple Mount, Jerusalem* ☎ *02/622–6250* ☉ *Apr.–Sept., Sun.–Thurs. 7:30 am–11 am and 1:30 pm–2:30 pm; Oct.–Mar., Sun.–Thurs. 7:30 am–10 am and 12:30 pm–1:30 pm, subject to change.*

Jerusalem Archaeological Park. Overlooked by many casual visitors, the site still often referred to as the Western and Southern Wall Excavations, or the Ophel, was a historical gold mine for Israeli archaeologists in the 1970s and '80s. Interesting Byzantine and early Arab structures came to light, but by far the most dramatic and monumental finds were from the Herodian period, the late 1st century BC. Exposed to the left of the corner is the white pavement of an impressive main street and commercial area from the Second Temple period. The protrusion left of the corner and high above your head is known as **Robinson's Arch.** Named for a 19th-century American explorer, it is a remnant of a monumental bridge to the Temple Mount which was reached by a staircase from the street where you now stand: look for the ancient steps. ⊠ *Dung Gate, Western Wall, Jerusalem* ☎ *02/627–7550* ⊕ *www.archpark.org.il* ☜ *NIS 30* ☉ *Sun.–Thurs. 8–5, Fri. and Jewish holiday eves 8–2.*

Via Dolorosa. The Way of Suffering—or Way of the Cross, as it's more commonly called in English—is venerated as the route Jesus walked, carrying his cross, from the place of his trial and condemnation by Pontius Pilate to the site of his crucifixion and burial. There are the 14 stations on the Via Dolorosa that mark the route that Jesus took, from trial and condemnation to crucifixion and burial. ⊠ *Muslim and Christian Quarters, Jerusalem.*

★ **Western Wall.** Historically, the Jewish faith has tended to place greater emphasis on the significance of an event than on the place where it may have occurred. Among the exceptions to that rule, the 2,000-year-old Western Wall is in a class of its own. Its status as the most important *existing* Jewish shrine derives from its connection with the ancient Temple, the House of God. It was not itself part of the Temple edifice, but of the massive retaining wall King Herod built to create the vast plaza now known as the Temple Mount. After the destruction of Jerusalem by the Romans in AD 70, and especially after the dedication of a pagan town in its place 65 years later, the city was off-limits to Jews for generations. The memory of the precise location of the Temple—in the vicinity of today's Dome of the Rock—was lost. Even when access was eventually regained, Jews avoided entering the Temple Mount for fear of unwittingly trespassing on the most sacred, and thus forbidden, areas of the ancient sanctuary. With time, the closest remnant of the period took on the aura of the Temple itself, making the Western Wall a kind of holy place by proxy. (Expect a routine check of your bags—smaller is better—by security personnel at the plaza entrance.) ⊠ *Near Dung Gate, Western Wall, Jerusalem* ⊕ *english.thekotel.org* ☉ *Daily 24 hrs.*

Western Wall Tunnel. The long tunnel beyond the men's side (north of the plaza) of the Western Wall is not a rediscovered ancient thoroughfare but was deliberately dug in recent years with the purpose of exposing a strip of the Western Wall along its entire length. One course of the massive wall revealed two building stones estimated to weigh an incredible 400 tons and 570 tons, respectively. Local guided tours are available and are recommended—you can visit the site only as part of an organized tour—but the times change from week to week (some include evening hours). The ticket office is under the arches at the northern end of the Western Wall plaza. ⊠ *Western Wall, Jerusalem* ☎ *02/627–1333* ⊕ *english.thekotel.org* ☒ *NIS 25* ⊙ *Sun.–Thurs. 7 am–late evening (changing schedules), Fri. and Jewish holiday eves 7–noon. Call ahead for exact times.*

WEST JERUSALEM

Visitors tend to focus, naturally enough, on the historic and religious sights on the eastern side of town, especially in the Old City; but West Jerusalem houses the nation's institutions, is the repository for its collective memory, and—together with the downtown—gives more insight into contemporary life in Israel's largest city. The world-class Israel Museum and Yad Vashem are located here.

Fodor's Choice   **Israel Museum.** In 2010, this eclectic treasure trove and world-class don't-
★   miss museum emerged like a butterfly from a lengthy renewal of its
🖑   entire main complex. The three main specialties of art, archaeology, and Judaica have been much enhanced by new or rearranged exhibits, fresh ideas, and state-of-the-art presentations. The **Dead Sea Scrolls** are certainly the Israel Museum's most famous—and most important—collection. A Bedouin boy discovered the first of the 2,000-year-old scrolls in 1947 in a Judean Desert cave, overlooking the Dead Sea. All in all, nine main scrolls (one engraved on copper) and bags full of small fragments surfaced over the years: the Israel Museum possesses some of the most important and most complete of these ancient texts. The white dome of the Shrine of the Book, the separate building in which the scrolls are housed, was inspired by the lids of the clay jars in which the first ones were found. ⊠ *Ruppin Rd., Givat Ram, Jerusalem* ☎ *02/670–8811* ⊕ *www.imj.org.il* ☒ *NIS 50 (includes audio guide); half price for return visit within 3 months (keep your ticket)* ⊙ *Sun., Mon., Wed., Thurs., Sat., and Jewish holidays 10–5, Tues. 4–9, Fri. and Jewish holiday eves 10–2.*

★   **Yad Vashem.** The experience of the Holocaust—the annihilation of 6 million Jews by the Nazis during World War II—is so deeply seared into the Jewish national psyche that understanding it goes a long way toward understanding Israelis themselves. The institution of Yad Vashem, created in 1953 by an act of the Knesset, was charged with preserving a record of those times. The name *Yad Vashem*—"a memorial and a name (a memory)"—comes from the biblical book of Isaiah (56:5). The Israeli government has made a tradition of bringing almost all high-ranking official foreign guests to visit the place.

The riveting **Holocaust History Museum**—a well-lit, 200-yard-long triangular concrete "prism"—is the centerpiece of the site. Powerful

visual and audiovisual techniques in a series of galleries document Jewish life in Europe before the catastrophe and follow the escalation of persecution and internment to the hideous climax of the Nazi's "Final Solution." Video interviews and personal artifacts individualize the experience. ⊠ *Hazikaron St., near Herzl Blvd., Mt. Herzl, Jerusalem* ☎ *02/644–3565* ⊕ *www.yadvashem.org* 🖾 *Free* ☉ *Sun.–Wed. 9–5, Thurs. 9–8 (late closing for History Museum only), Fri. and Jewish holiday eves 9–2. Last entrance 1 hr before closing.*

3

WHERE TO EAT

$ ✕ **Abu Shukri.** In the heart of the Old City, at Station V on the Via Dolo-
MIDDLE EASTERN   rosa, this place has an extraordinary and well-deserved reputation for the best hummus in town. Don't expect much in the way of decor. This is a neighborhood eatery, and a look at the clientele—Palestinian Arabs and Jewish Israeli insiders—confirms that you have gone local. Enjoy the excellent fresh falafel balls, baba ghanoush, tahini, and *labaneh* (a slightly sour cheese served with olive oil and *za'atar* [spice mixture]); no meat is served. Eat family style, and don't over-order: you can get additional portions on the spot. ⑤ *Average main: $8* ⊠ *63 El-Wad Rd. (Hagai St.), Muslim Quarter, Jerusalem* ☎ *02/627–1538* ⚞ *Reservations not accepted* ▭ *No credit cards* ☉ *No dinner.*

$ ✕ **Nafoura.** Just inside the Jaffa Gate (up the first street on the left),
MIDDLE EASTERN   Nafoura offers a tranquil courtyard for alfresco lunchtime dining. Your
☾   table might lean against the Old City's 16th-century wall. The pleasant if unremarkable interior is a comfortable refuge in inclement weather. Start with the traditional meze, an array of salads: the smaller version is enough for two people. Insist on the excellent local dishes only (hummus, eggplant dip, tahini, carrots, and so on) and skip the mushrooms and corn. Ask for the *kibbeh,* delicacies of cracked wheat and ground beef, or the *lahmajun,* the meat-topped "Armenian pizza." From the typical selection of entrées, try the lamb cutlets or the sea bream. The NIS 50 buffet (chicken, kebab, side dishes, and fruit) is an excellent value. ⑤ *Average main: $15* ⊠ *18 Latin Patriarch Rd., Christian Quarter, Jerusalem* ☎ *02/626–0034* ☉ *No dinner.*

CORFU, GREECE

Updated by
Adrian Vrettos
and Alexia
Amvrazi

Kerkyra (Corfu) is the greenest and, quite possibly, the prettiest of all Greek islands—emerald mountains, ocher-and-pink buildings, shimmering silver olive leaves. The turquoise waters lap rocky coves and bougainvillea, scarlet roses, and wisteria spread over cottages. This northernmost of the major Ionian Islands has, through the centuries, inspired artists, conquerors, royalty, and, of course, tourists. Indeed, when you look at Corfu in total, it's hard to believe that any island so small could generate a history so large. Classical remains vie with architecture from the centuries of Venetian, French, and British rule, leaving Corfu with a pleasant combination of contrasting design elements. The town of Corfu remains one of the loveliest in all of Greece, every nook and cranny tells a story, every street meanders to a myth,

even during the busiest summer day. Corfu today is a vivid tapestry of cultures, a sophisticated weave, where charm, history, and natural beauty blend.

ESSENTIALS

CURRENCY
The euro.

HOURS
Store hours are typically 9 to 9 on weekdays and 9 to 6 on Saturday. Museums are generally from open 9 to 5, but many are closed on Monday. Some shops, restaurants, and museums close between October and April.

TELEPHONES
Tri-band GSM phones work in Greece. You can buy prepaid phone cards at telecom shops, news vendors, and tobacconists in all towns and cities. Phone cards can be used for local or international calls. Vodafone is the leading mobile telecom company. OTE is the national domestic provider. Calls can be made at OTE offices and paid for after completion.

COMING ASHORE
Boats dock at Corfu's purpose-built cruise port, which has a welcome center with an information desk, car-rental desks, and a taxi stand. A 10-minute ride into the Old Town costs around €17. Alternatively, you can walk along the seafront in about 30 minutes.

You can explore the town on foot, but you need a car to get to some of the island's loveliest places. Prices can range from €35 a day for a compact vehicle (where you pay an additional fee for each km driving) to €80 a day for a four-wheel-drive Jeep with extras. Expect additional charges of around €15 for insurance, delivery, and so forth.

EXPLORING CORFU

CORFU TOWN

★ **Byzantine Museum.** Panagia Antivouniotissa, an ornate church dating from the late 15th century, houses an outstanding collection of Byzantine religious art. More than 50 icons from the 13th to the 17th century hang on the walls. Look for works by the celebrated icon painters Tzanes and Damaskinos; they are perhaps the best-known artists of the Cretan style of icon painting, with unusually muscular, active depictions of saints. Their paintings more closely resemble Renaissance art—another Venetian legacy—than traditional, flat orthodox icons. ⊠ *3rd Parados Arseniou St.* ☎ *26610/38313* ☜ *€2* ☉ *Apr.–Oct., Tues.–Sun. 9–4; Nov.–Mar., Tues.–Sun. 8–3.*

Fodor's Choice **Campiello.** This medieval quarter, part of a UNESCO-designated World
★ Heritage site, is an atmospheric labyrinth of narrow, winding streets, steep stairways, and secretive little squares. Laundry lines connect balconied Venetian palazzi engraved with the original occupant's coat of arms to neoclassic 19th-century buildings constructed by the British. Small cobbled squares with central wells and watched over by old churches add to the quiet, mysterious, and utterly charming urban space. If you enter, you're almost sure to get lost, but the area is small

Corfu

← TO DIAPONTIA ISLANDS

TO ITALY

Avliotes
Sidari
Roda
Pelekito
Agios Stefanos
Karoussades
Acharavi
Kassiopi
Kavadades
Episkepsi
Mt. Pantokrator
Kalami
Kouloura
Ano Korakiana
Barbati
Agni
Makrades
Skripero
Pirgi
Nissaki
Lakones
Ipsos
Paleokastritsa
Sgombou
Liapades
Dassia
Gouvia
Kondokali Bay
Ptihia
Gianades
Agios Ioannis
Corfu Town see detail map
Ermones
Vatos
Pelekas
Mon Repos
Myrtiotissa
Kanoni
Moni Viahernes
Glyfada
Perama
Pontikonisi
Kinopiastes
Gastouri
Sinarades
Achilleion
Ayios Gordis
Benitses
Pendati
TO IGOUMENITSA
Agios Ioannis Peristeron
Strongili
Moraitika
Ayios Matheos
Mesonghi
Ionian Sea
Adriatic Sea
Lake Korisia
Hlomos
Boukari
TO PATRAS
Argirades
Perivoli
Lefkimmi
Paleohori
Neohori
Dragotina
Kavos

0 — 4 miles
0 — 6 km

Corfu Town

New Port
Old Port
Arseniou
Byzantine Museum
TO BUTRINT ARCHEOLOGICAL PARK
Palace of St. Michael and St. George
Ayios Nikolaos Bay
New Fortress
Zavitsianou
Campiello
N. Theotoki
Church of St. Spyridon
Velissariou
Liston
Canal
Pl. San Rocco
Theotoki Sq.
Old Fortress
Arraniou
P. Konstanda
Guilford
The Esplanade
Maitland Rotunda
Lefkimis
G. Theotoki
Dessila
Kapodistriou
Marasti
Alexandras
Vraila
Dimokratias

Archaeological Museum

0 — 1/8 mi
0 — 1/8 km

KEY
✈ Airport
⛱ Beach
🚢 Ferry lines

enough so that eventually you'll come out on one of Corfu town's major streets, or on the sea wall. ⊠ *West of the Esplanade, northeast of New Fortress.*

Fodor's Choice ★ **Church of St. Spyridon.** Built in 1596, this church is the tallest on the island, thanks to its distinctive red-dome bell tower, and is filled with silver treasures. The patron saint's remains—smuggled here after the fall of Constantinople—are contained in a silver reliquary in a small chapel; devout Corfiots visit to kiss the reliquary and pray to the saint. The silver casket is carried in procession through the town four times a year. Spyridon was not a Corfiot but a shepherd from Cyprus, who became a bishop before his death in AD 350. His miracles are said to have saved the island four times: once from famine, twice from the plague, and once from the hated Turks. During World War II, a bomb fell on this holiest place on the island but didn't explode. Maybe these events explain why it seems every other man on Corfu is named Spiros. If you keep the church tower in sight you can wander as you wish without getting lost around this fascinating section of town. Agiou Spyridonos, the street in front of the church, is crammed with shops selling religious trinkets and souvenirs. ⊠ *Agiou Spyridonos.*

Fodor's Choice ★ **The Esplanade.** Central to the life of the town, this huge, open parade ground and park just west of the Old Fortress is, many say, the most beautiful *spianada* (esplanade) in Greece. It is bordered on the west by a street lined with Venetian and English Georgian houses and a famous arcaded building called the **Liston,** built by the French under Napoleon and meant to resemble the Rue du Rivoli in Paris. Cafés spill out onto the passing scene, and Corfiot celebrations, games, and concerts take place here; at night, lovers promenade and children play in this festive public space. Sunday cricket matches, a holdover from British rule, are sometimes played on the northern half of the Esplanade, which was once a Venetian firing range. Standing in the center is an ornate **Victorian bandstand** and, just south of it, the **Maitland Rotunda,** a circular Ionic memorial built in honor of Sir Thomas Maitland, the not-much-loved first British lord high commissioner who was appointed in 1814 when the island became a protectorate of Britain. At the southernmost tip of the Esplanade a **statue of Ioannis Kapodistrias,** a Corfu resident and the first president of modern Greece, looks out over Garitsa bay. Kapodistrias was also, unfortunately, the first Greek president to be assassinated, in 1831. ⊠ *Between Old Fortress and Old Town.*

CORFU BEST BETS

Relax over a coffee at the Liston. This is a wonderful place to immerse yourself in modern Greek life.

Take pictures of Pontikonisi. Mouse Island, as this tiny islet is also known, is one of the iconic Greek landscape views. Shimmering waters and verdant foliage contrast dramatically with the modest whitewashed chapel.

Explore Paleokastritsa. A breathtaking landscape of tiny rocky coves, azure waters, and fragrant woodland offers exceptional vistas surrounded by the sound of buzzing cicadas.

New Fortress. Built in 1577–78 by the Venetians, the New Fortress was constructed to strengthen town defenses—only three decades after the construction of Venetian fortifications on the "Old" Fortress. The French and the British subsequently expanded the complex to protect Corfu town from a possible Turkish invasion. You can wander through the maze of tunnels and fortifications; the dry moat is the site of the town's fish-and-vegetable marketplace. A classic British citadel stands at its heart. At the top, there is an exhibition center. ⊠ *Solomou on promontory overlooking New Port* ☎ *26610–44444* ✉ *€3* ☉ *May–Oct., daily 8:30–8.*

★ **Old Fortress.** Corfu's entire population once lived within the walls of the Old Fortress, or Citadel, built by the Venetians in 1546 on the site of a Byzantine castle. Separated from the rest of the town by a moat, the fort is on a promontory mentioned by Thucydides. Its two heights, or *korypha* ("peaks"), gave the island its name. Standing on the peaks, you have a gorgeous view west over the town and east to the mountainous coast of Albania. A statue of Count Schulenburg, an Austrian mercenary who became a local hero in 1716 when he helped to defeat the invading Turks, stands at the fort's entrance; just inside, there is an exhibition that tells Schulenburg's story. Most of the old Venetian fortifications inside the fortress were destroyed by the British, who replaced them with their own structures. The most notable of these is the **Church of St. George,** built to look like an ancient Doric temple. Near it, overlooking Garitsa bay, there is a shaded café where you can sit and enjoy the splendid view. ⊠ *On eastern point of Corfu town peninsula* ☎ *26610/48310* ✉ *€4* ☉ *Apr.–Oct., Tues.–Sun. 8–4; Nov.–Mar., Tues.–Sun. 7–3.*

Fodor's Choice **Palace of St. Michael and St. George (Museum of Asian Art).** It may seem a
★ bit incongruous to admire Ming pottery in an ornate British colonial palace as the Ionian Sea shimmers outside the windows. But this elegant, colonnaded, 19th-century Regency structure houses the **Museum of Asian Art,** a notable collection of Asian porcelains, Japanese *ukiyo-e* prints, Indian sculpture, and Tibetan temple art. ⊠ *Palaia Anaktora, at north end of Esplanade* ☎ *26610/30443* ✉ *€3* ☉ *Tues.–Sun. 8:30–4.*

KANONI

5 km (3 miles) southwest of Corfu Town.

At Kanoni, 5 km (3 miles) south of Corfu town, the site of the ancient capital, you may behold Corfu's most famous view, which looks out over two beautiful islets.

Fodor's Choice **Mon Repos.** The compact neoclassic palace (really a villa) was built
★ in 1831 by Sir Frederic Adam for his wife, and it was later the summer residence of the British lord high commissioners; the architect, Sir George Whitmore, also designed the Palace of St. Michael and St. George in Corfu town. After Greece won independence from Britain in 1864, Mon Repos was used as a summer palace for the royal family of Greece. Queen Elizabeth II's husband, Prince Philip, was born here in 1921 (he was a royal prince of Greece and Denmark; the Corfiots, who have no love of royalty, call him "the penniless Greek who married a queen"). When King Constantine fled the country in 1967, the

Greek government expropriated Mon Repos. Throughout the 1990s, the estate was entangled in an international legal battle over ownership; the Greek government finally paid Constantine a settlement and opened the fully restored palace as a museum dedicated to the area's archaeological history. After touring the palace, wander around the extensive grounds (entrance is free, so you can do this even if you don't visit the palace), which include the elusive remains of a Doric temple from the 7th and 6th centuries BC and the small but beautiful beach that was once used exclusively by the Greek royal family and is now open to the public. Bring your suit and join the locals on the long pier jutting out into the crystal-clear waters of the Ionian Sea. Opposite Mon Repos are ruins of Ayia Kerkyra, the 5th-century church of the Old City. ✛ *1 km (½ mile) south of Old Fortress, following oceanfront walk* ☎ *26610/41369* ▧ *€3, gardens free* ☼ *Apr.–Oct., Tues.–Sun. 9–4; Nov.–Mar., Tues.–Sun. 8–3.*

GASTOURI
19 km (12 miles) southwest of Corfu Town.

Fodor's Choice
★
Achilleion. This Teutonic palace, built in the late 19th century for Empress Elizabeth of Austria, is perhaps the most popular tourist attraction in Corfu and remains a monument of 19th-century historicism. The empress used the place as a retreat to escape court life and to ease her heartbreak over husband Franz Josef's numerous affairs and her son Archduke Rudolph's mysterious murder or suicide at Mayerling in 1889. Elizabeth named the palace after her favorite hero, Achilles, whom she inexplicably identified with Rudolph. After Elizabeth was assassinated in 1898, Kaiser Wilhelm II bought the villa and lived in it until the outbreak of World War I, during which time the Achilleion was used by French and Serbian troops as a military hospital. After the armistice, the Greek government received it as a spoil of war. During World War II, it was appropriated and used as a headquarters by the occupying Italian and German forces. In 1962 the palace was restored, leased as a gambling casino, and later used as the set for the casino scene in the James Bond film *For Your Eyes Only.* (The casino has since moved to the Corfu Holiday Palace.)

Today it's a museum, but not a terribly inspiring one. The interior is a series of rather ungainly, uninteresting rooms done in various styles (a pseudo-Byzantine chapel, a pseudo-Pompeian room, a pseudo-Renaissance dining hall), with a smattering of period furniture scattered about; the vulgar fresco called *Achilles in His Chariot,* on the ceiling of the entrance hall, tells you all you need to know about the empress's taste in pseudo-classical art. More appealing is the terrace, laid out like an Ionic peristyle with a number of 19th-century statues, the best of which is *The Dying Achilles.* The gardens, surrounded by olive groves and with a distant view of the sea, are pretty but, all in all, the whole place looks a bit vacuous and forlorn. Still and all, lovers of period style won't want to miss this. For a website on the estate, go to the Wikipedia entry (the easiest way to access it) and then hit the link to the Achilleion site. ✉ *Main street, The Achilleion* ☎ *26610/56210* ▧ *€6* ☼ *Apr.–Oct., daily 8–7; Nov.–Mar., daily 8:30–3:30.*

PALEOKASTRITSA

25 km (16 miles) northwest of Corfu Town.

This spectacular territory of grottoes, cliffs, and turquoise waters is breathtaking.

Lakones. The village of Lakones, built on the steep mountain behind the Paleokastritsa Monastery, looks rather forbidding, but tourists flock there for the view. Kaiser Wilhelm was among many famous people who would make the ascent to enjoy the magnificent panorama of Paleokastritsa's coves from the cafés at Bella Vista, just beyond the village. From nearby Krini you can climb up to the ruins of the 13th-century **Angelokastro**, a fortress built by a despot of Epirus during his brief rule over Corfu. On many occasions during the medieval period the fort sheltered Corfiots from attack by Turkish invaders. Look for the chapel and caves, which served as sanctuaries and hiding places. ✉ *5 km (3 miles) northeast of Paleokastritsa.*

Paleokastritsa Monastery. Paleokastritsa Monastery, a 17th-century structure, is built on the site of an earlier monastery, among terraced gardens overlooking the Ionian sea. Its treasure is a 12th-century icon of the Virgin Mary, and there's a small museum with some other early icons. Note the Tree of Life motif on the ceiling. Be sure to visit the inner courtyard (go through the church), built on the edge of the cliff and looking down a precipitous cliff to the placid green coves and coastline to the south. There's a small gift shop on the premises. ✉ *On northern headland* 🖾 *Donations accepted* ☉ *Daily 7–1 and 3–8.*

SHOPPING

Corfu Town has myriad tiny shops. For traditional goods, head for the narrow streets of the Campiello where olive wood, ceramics, lace, jewelry, and wine shops abound. Kumquat liqueur is a specialty of the island.

Mironis Olive Wood. Bowls, sculptures, wooden jewelry, and much more are crammed into two tiny family-run shops. Smaller items are made as you watch. ✉ *Filarmonikis 27, Corfu Town* ☎ *26610/40621* 🖾 *Agiou Spyridon 65, Corfu Town* ☎ *26610/20731.*

Nikos Sculpture and Jewellery. Corfu-born Nikos Michalopoulos creates original gold and silver jewelry and sculptures in cast bronze; they're expensive, but worth it. ✉ *Paleologou 50, Corfu Town* ☎ *26610/31107* ⊕ *www.nikosjewellery.gr* 🖾 *N. Theotoki 54, Corfu Town* ☎ *26610/ 32009.*

Rolandos. Visit the talented artist Rolando and watch him at work on his paintings and handmade pottery. ✉ *N. Theotoki 99, Corfu Town* ☎ *26610/45004.*

BEACHES

Glyfada. The large, golden beaches at Glyfada are the most famous on the island. Though the sands are inevitably packed with sunbathers, it remains one of the hottest hot spots in Corfu. Sun beds, umbrellas,

and water-sports equipment is available for rent and there are several tourist resorts. ⊠ *2 km [1 mile] south of Pelekas, Pelekas.*

Myrtiotissa. The isolated Myrtiotissa beach, between sheer cliffs, is known for its good snorkeling—and its nude sunbathing. Backed by olive and cypress trees, this sandy stretch was called by Lawrence Durrell in *Prospero's Cell* (with debatable overenthusiasm) "perhaps the loveliest beach in the world." ⊠ *3 km (2 miles) north of Pelekas.*

Pelekas. The beach at Pelekas has soft, golden sand and clear water but is developed and tends to be crowded. The huge Aquis Pelekas Beach Hotel resort complex rises up behind it, and Pelekas village is popular with summer tourists. Depending on time of year and demand, there is sometimes a free shuttle service between Pelekas Village and the beach (which is a long and steep walk otherwise).

WHERE TO EAT

$ ✕ **Gerekos.** One of the island's most famous seafood tavernas, Gerekos's
SEAFOOD   raw materials are supplied daily by the family's own fishing boats. The menu varies according to the catch and the season, but the friendly staff will guide your choice. For a light meze, opt for a table on the terrace and try the whitefish *me ladi* (cooked in olive oil, garlic, and pepper) with a salad and some crisp white wine. Too bad this place is located on a dusty resort street with cars going past by diners' toes. $ *Average main: €14* ⊠ *Kontokali bay, 6 km (4 miles) north of Corfu town, Corfu Town* ☏ *26610/91281* ⌖ *Reservations essential.*

$ ✕ **Rex.** A friendly Corfiot restaurant in a 19th-century town house, Rex
GREEK   has been a favorite for nearly 100 years, and with good reason. Classic
Fodor's Choice   local specialties such as a hearty and meaty *pastitsada* (layers of beef and
★   pasta, called *macaronia* in Greek, cooked in a rich and spicy tomato sauce and topped off with béchamel sauce), *stifado* (meat stewed with sweet onions, white wine, garlic, cinnamon, and spices), and *stamna* (lamb baked with potatoes, rice, beans, and cheese) are reliably delicious. Dishes such as rabbit stewed with fresh figs and chicken with kumquats are successful twists on the regional fare. Look on the menu for the "specials of the day," which might include some other unusual dishes. Outside tables are perfect for people-watching. $ *Average main: €16* ⊠ *Kapodistriou 66, 1 street west of Liston, Corfu Town* ☏ *26610/39649.*

DUBROVNIK, CROATIA

Updated by
Jane Foster

Commanding a splendid coastal location, Dubrovnik is one of the world's most beautiful fortified cities. Its massive stone ramparts and splendid fortress towers curve around a tiny harbor, enclosing graduated ridges of sun-bleached orange-tiled roofs, copper domes, and elegant bell towers. In the 7th century AD, residents of the Roman city Epidaurum (now Cavtat) fled the Avars and Slavs of the north and founded a new settlement on a small rocky island, which they named Laus, and later Ragusa. On the mainland hillside opposite the island, the Slav settlement called Dubrovnik grew up. In the 12th century the narrow channel separating the two settlements was filled in, and Ragusa and Dubrovnik became

one. The city was surrounded by defensive walls during the 13th century, and these were reinforced with towers and bastions during the late 15th century. The city became a UNESCO World Heritage site in 1979. During the war for independence, it came under heavy siege, though thanks to careful restoration work few traces of damage remain. Today Dubrovnik is once again a fashionable, high-class destination; Eva Longoria Parker, Beyoncé, John Malkovich, and Sir Roger Moore have been recent visitors. New in July 2010 is a cable car, which takes visitors up to the top of Mount Srdj for fantastic views down onto the Old Town and out to sea.

DUBROVNIK BEST BETS

Walk the city walls. The Old Town's massive Gradske Zidine were begun in the 13th century and reinforced over the years.

Strolling along the harbor front. Dubrovnik's picturesque harbor has a promenade perfect for a stroll.

Relaxing in a café. All summer long, Dubrovnik's many cafés and restaurants have tables outside (many within the walls of the Old Town), where you can sit under an umbrella and enjoy a seafood lunch or a drink.

ESSENTIALS
CURRENCY
The Croatian kuna.

HOURS
Offices are open weekdays from 8:30 to 4. Shops often close for lunch around 1, and may close for as long as three hours; banks also sometimes close for lunch. Post offices are open on Saturday during the main summer season, from June through September.

TELEPHONES
Most tri- and quad-band GSM phones will work in Croatia. Public phones use calling cards, which can be purchased at the post office, newsstands, and hotels. Major mobile phone companies include TMobile and VIPNet.

COMING ASHORE
In Dubrovnik almost all ships dock at Gruž Harbor, which is 4 km (2½ miles) from Stari Grad (Old Town). Some ships will provide a free shuttle. The trip to Dubrovnik's Old Town takes about 10 minutes by taxi or 30 to 40 minutes on foot. You can also take a public bus. There's a taxi stand at the harbor.

A few smaller ships might still tender passengers ashore in the Old Town, where you're just steps from everything that Dubrovnik has to offer.

Since the Old Town is compact and pedestrian-friendly, we recommend that you not rent a car in Dubrovnik. It's easy to reach Cavtat by bus or ferry, and unless you want to explore the countryside away from Dubrovnik, a car will not help you. If you choose to rent, expect to pay about €55 for a manual compact vehicle, though you can rent a semiautomatic Smart car at some outlets for about €50. Note, however, that during high season it can be very difficult to find a company that is willing to rent just for one day.

EXPLORING DUBROVNIK

All the main sites lie in Stari Grad (Old Town) within the city walls, an area that is compact and car-free.

Akvarij (*Aquarium*). This dark, cavernous space houses several small pools and 27 well-lit tanks containing a variety of fish from rays to small sharks, as well as other underwater denizens such as sponges and sea urchins. Children will find the octopus in his glass tank either very amusing or horribly scary. ⊠ *Damjana Jude 2, Stari Grad* ☎ *020/323–125* 🎫 *40 Kn* ⏲ *June–Sept., daily 9–9; Apr., May, Oct., and Nov., daily 9–6; Dec.–Mar., Mon.–Sat. 9–1.*

Crkva Svetog Vlaha (*Church of St. Blaise*). This 18th-century baroque church replaced an earlier one destroyed by fire. Of particular note is the silver statue on the high altar of St. Blaise holding a model of Dubrovnik, which is paraded around town each year on February 3, the Day of St. Blaise. ⊠ *Luža, Stari Grad* 🎫 *Free* ⏲ *Daily 8–noon and 4:30–7.*

Dominikanski samostan (*Dominican monastery*). With a splendid, late-15th-century floral Gothic cloister as its centerpiece, the monastery is best known for its museum, which houses a rich collection of religious paintings by the so-called Dubrovnik School from the 15th and 16th

centuries. Look out for works by Božidarević, Hamzić, and Dobričević, as well as gold and silver ecclesiastical artifacts crafted by local goldsmiths. ☒ *Sv Domina 4, Stari Grad* 🕾 *020/321–423* 🖃 *20 Kn* ☾ *May–Oct., daily 9–6; Nov.–Apr., daily 9–5.*

Franjevačka samostan (*Franciscan monastery*). The monastery's chief claim to fame is its pharmacy, which was founded in 1318 and is still in existence today; it's said to be the oldest in Europe. There's also a delightful cloistered garden, framed by Romanesque arcades supported by double columns, each crowned with a set of grotesque figures. In the Treasury a painting shows what Dubrovnik looked like before the disastrous earthquake of 1667. ☒ *Placa 2, Stari Grad* 🕾 *020/321–410* 🖃 *30 Kn* ☾ *May–Oct., daily 9–6; Nov.–Apr., daily 9–5.*

FodorśChoice
★
Gradske Zidine (*city walls*). Most of the original construction took place during the 13th century, though the walls were further reinforced with towers and bastions over the following 400 years. On average they are 80 feet high and up to 10 feet thick on the seaward side, 20 feet thick on the inland side. ☒ *Placa, Stari Grad* 🕾 *020/324–641* 🖃 *70 Kn* ☾ *June–July 8 am–7:30 pm; Aug.–mid-Sept. 8 am–7 pm; May and mid-Sept.–Oct. 8 am–6 pm; Nov.–Apr. 10 am–3 pm.*

Katedrala Velika Gospa (*Cathedral of Our Lady*). The present structure was built in baroque style after the original was destroyed in the 1667 earthquake. The interior contains a number of notable paintings, including a large polyptych above the main altar depicting the *Assumption of Our Lady,* attributed to Titian. The Treasury displays 138 gold and silver reliquaries, including the skull of St. Blaise in the form of a bejeweled Byzantine crown and also an arm and a leg of the saint, likewise encased in decorated gold plating. ☒ *Držićeva Poljana, Stari Grad* 🕾 *020/323–459* 🖃 *Cathedral free, Treasury 15 Kn* ☾ *May–Oct., Mon.–Sat. 9–5, Sun. 11:30–5; Nov.–Apr., daily 9–noon and 3–5.*

Knežev Dvor (*Bishop's Palace*). Originally created in the 15th century but reconstructed several times through the following years, this exquisite building with an arcaded loggia and an internal courtyard shows a combination of late-Gothic and early Renaissance styles. On the ground floor there are large rooms where, in the days of the republic, the Great Council and Senate held their meetings. Over the entrance to the meeting halls a plaque reads: *obliti privatorum publica curate* ("Forget private affairs, and get on with public matters"). Upstairs, the rector's living quarters now accommodate the Gradski Muzej (City Museum), containing exhibits that give a picture of life in Dubrovnik from early days until the fall of the republic. ☒ *Pred Dvorom 3, Stari Grad* 🕾 *020/321–497* 🖃 *40 Kn* ☾ *May–Oct., daily 9–6; Nov.–Apr., daily 9–4.*

Muzej Pravoslavne Crkve (*Orthodox Church Museum*). Next door to the Orthodox church, this small museum displays religious icons from the Balkan region and Russia, as well as several portraits of eminent early-20th-century Dubrovnik personalities by local artist Vlaho Bukovac. ☒ *Od Puca 8, Stari Grad* 🕾 *020/323–283* 🖃 *10 Kn* ☾ *May–Oct., Tues.–Sun. 9–2; Nov.–Apr., Mon.–Fri. 9–2.*

Placa (*Stradun*). This was once the shallow sea channel separating the island of Laus from the mainland. Although it was filled in during the 12th century, it continued to divide the city socially for several centuries, the nobility living in the area south of Placa and the commoners living on the hillside to the north. Today it forms the venue for the *korzo*, an evening promenade where locals meet to chat, maybe have a drink at one of the numerous open-air cafés, and generally size one another up. ⊠ *Stari Grad.*

Pomorski Muzej (*Maritime Museum*). Above the aquarium, on the first floor of St. John's Fortress, this museum's exhibits illustrate how rich and powerful Dubrovnik became one of the world's most important seafaring nations. On display are intricately detailed models of ships as well as engine-room equipment, sailors' uniforms, paintings, and maps. ⊠ *Damjana Jude 2, Stari Grad* ☎ *020/323–904* 🖃 *40 Kn* ⊗ *May–Oct., Tues.–Sun. 9–6; Nov.–Apr., Tues.–Sun. 9–2.*

Sinagoga (*Synagogue*). This tiny 15th-century synagogue, the second-oldest in Europe (after Prague's) bears testament to Dubrovnik's once thriving Jewish community, made up largely of Jews who were expelled from Spain and Italy during the medieval period. ⊠ *Žudioska 5, Stari Grad* ☎ *020/321–028* 🖃 *20 Kn* ⊗ *May–Sept., daily 10–8; Oct.–Apr., weekdays 10–3.*

Vrata od Pila (*Pile Gate*). Built in 1537 and combining a Renaissance arch with a wooden drawbridge on chains, this has always been the main entrance to the city walls. A niche above the portal contains a statue of Sveti Vlah (St. Blaise), the city's patron saint, holding a replica of Dubrovnik in his left hand. From May to October, guards in deep-red period-costume uniforms stand vigilant by the gate through daylight hours, just as they would have done when the city was a republic. ⊠ *Pile, Stari Grad.*

Vrata od Ploča (*Ploče Gate*). One of two gates in the town walls, Ploče comprises a stone bridge and wooden drawbridge plus a 15th-century stone arch bearing a statue of Sveti Vlah (St. Blaise). As at Pile Gate, guards in period costume stand vigilant here through the summer season. ⊠ *Ploče, Stari Grad.*

Fodor'sChoice ★ **War Photo Limited.** Shocking but impressive, this modern gallery devotes two entire floors to war photojournalism. Past exhibitions include images from conflicts in Afghanistan, Iraq, the former Yugoslavia, Israel, Palestine, and Lebanon. Refreshingly impartial by Croatian standards, the message—that war is physically and emotionally destructive whichever side you are on—comes through loudly and clearly. You'll find it in a narrow side street running between Placa and Prijeko. ⊠ *Antuninska 6, Stari Grad* ☎ *020/322–166* ⊕ *www.warphotoltd.com* 🖃 *30 Kn* ⊗ *May and Oct., Tues.–Sun. 10–4; June–Sept., daily 9–9.*

BEACHES

Eastwest Beach. Eastwest Beach Club is on Banje beach, just a short distance from Ploče Gate, with views across the sea to the tiny island of Lokrum. It's a fashionable spot, with a curving stretch of golden sand, complete with chaise longues and parasols for rent, and a chic bar-restaurant. **Amenities:** food and drink; showers; toilets. **Best for:** partiers; swimming. ⊠ *Frana Supila, Banje Beach* ☎ *020/412–220.*

The more upmarket hotels, such as the Excelsior and Villa Dubrovnik, have their own beaches that are exclusively for the use of hotel guests. The most natural and peaceful beaches lie on the tiny island of **Lokrum**, a short distance south of the Old Town. Through high season, boats leave from the Old Harbor, ferrying visitors back and forth from morning to early evening (9 am to 8 pm, every 30 minutes). Return tickets cost 40 Kn.

SHOPPING

Despite its role as an important tourist destination, Dubrovnik offers little in the way of shopping or souvenir hunting. If you're in search of gifts, your best bet is a bottle of good Dalmatian wine or *rakija* (a fruit brandy popular throughout much of eastern Europe).

Croata. This small boutique close to the Rector's Palace in the Old Town specializes in "original Croatian ties" in presentation boxes. ⊠ *Pred dvorom 2, Stari Grad* ☎ *020/638–330* ⊕ *www.croata.hr.*

Dubrovačka Kuća. Tastefully decorated, the wineshop stocks a fine selection of regional Croatian wines, *rakija,* olive oil, and truffle products, plus works of art by contemporary local artists on the upper two levels; it's close to Ploče Gate. ⊠ *Svetog Dominika bb, Stari Grad* ☎ *020/322–092.*

WHERE TO EAT

$$$$ ✕ **Lokanda Peškarija.** Just outside the town walls—and affording unfor-
SEAFOOD gettable views over the old harbor—this seafood restaurant is a par-
Fodor's Choice ticularly good value. The seafood on offer is guaranteed fresh each
★ day, not least because the restaurant stands next door to Dubrovnik's covered fish market. It has a beautifully designed, split-level interior with exposed stone walls and wooden beams, plus romantic outdoor candlelit tables by the water. ■ **TIP→ Definitely not only for tourists, locals love eating here as well, so reservations are recommended, especially for dinner.** ⑤ *Average main: 90 Kn* ⊠ *Na Ponti, Stari Grad* ☎ *020/324–750* ⊕ *www.mea-culpa.hr* ⊙ *Closed Jan.–Mar.*

$$$$ ✕ **Proto.** A reliable choice for dinner, Proto is on a side street off Stra-
SEAFOOD dun, with tables arranged on a vine-covered, upper-level, open-air terrace. The menu features a good selection of traditional Dalmatian seafood dishes—including oysters from nearby Ston—and barbecued meats, notably succulent steaks. The restaurant dates back to 1886. Recent celebrity guests have included actor Richard Gere and Bono. ■ **TIP→ Reservations are recommended.** ⑤ *Average main: 140 Kn* ⊠ *Široka 1, Stari Grad* ☎ *020/323–234* ⊕ *www.esculaprestaurants.com.*

HAIFA, ISRAEL

Updated
by Jessica
Steinberg

Israel's largest port city (and third-largest city overall), Haifa was ruled for four centuries by the Ottomans and gradually grew up the mountainside into a cosmopolitan city whose port served the entire Middle East. In 1902 Theodor Herzl enthusiastically dubbed it "the city of the future." The city is the world center for the Baha'i faith, and the most striking landmark on the city's mountainside is the gleaming golden dome of the Baha'i Shrine, set amid utterly beautiful circular grass terraces that fill the slope from top to bottom.

ESSENTIALS

CURRENCY

The shekel.

HOURS

Shops are generally open Sunday through Thursday from 9 to 7, though some close in the afternoon. Museums vary in hours, but most are open Monday through Thursday from 10 to 6 with shorter hours on Friday through Sunday, often from 10 to 2 or 3. Some museums close on Friday.

TELEPHONES

Most multiband mobile phones work in Israel, and GSM and 3G systems are well established in the urban areas. Major providers are Cellcom Israel, Parner Communication (Orange), and Pelephone.

COMING ASHORE

The cruise port sits directly on the Haifa waterfront. The cruise terminal has some shops, a café, currency exchange desk, and a tax-refund kiosk, and the waterfront area is slowly being improved with new restaurants and shops opening their doors. From the port it's an easy walk into downtown, but the city is built on hills, so if you intend to explore on foot, wear comfortable shoes.

The Egged bus cooperative provides regular service from Haifa to Nazareth, and to Tiberias on the Sea of Galilee. To get from Haifa to Tiberias, take the slow Bus 430 (about an hour), which leaves hourly from Merkazit Hamifratz.

Driving is the best way to explore the Lower Galilee, and you can easily link several excursions and take your time enjoying the panoramic views, since Nazareth is only 56 km (35 miles) east of Haifa and the Golan Heights around two hours' drive away. Some newer four-lane highways are excellent, but some secondary roads may be in need of repair. Signposting is clear (and usually in English), with route numbers clearly marked. Prices for a subcompact car are around $80 a day and a compact $100 per day, though many companies charge for mileage.

Haifa

0 _____ 1/4 mile
0 _____ 1/4 kilometer

Northern Israel

Rosh Hanikra
Achziv National Park
Shelomi
Montfort
Ma Alot-Tarshiha
Mediterranean Sea
Lochamei Hageta'ot
Nahariya
Yehiam
Baha'i Founder's Shrine and Garden
Abu Sinan
Shagor
Akko
Karmi'el
Mifraz Bay
Haifa
Kiryat Motzkin
Kiryat Bialik
Sakhnin
Tamra
Arraba
Kafar Manda
Tirat Carmel
Carmel National Park
Kiryat Ata
Nesher
Shefar'am
ISRAEL
Isfiya
0   4 mi
0   4 km
Nazareth

Mediterranean Sea

BAT GALIM

Hasharon
Ha'aliya   Hashnia

Train Station
Bus Station

KIRYAT ELIEZER
Zahal St.
Allenby Rd.
Derekh Stella Maris
Sderot Hahagana
Heyl Hayam St.
Tel Aviv St.

Harbor

KIRYAT ELIAHU

FRENCH CARMEL
Shaul Tschernikhovski
Yeshayahu

Deror
Sderot James
Yitzhaq Sade St.
Sderot Hameginim
Sderot Rothschild
Haganim St.
Ben Gurion Blvd.
Allenby Rd.
Hagefen Blvd.

DOWNTOWN

GERMAN COLONY

Khouri St.
Yaffo
Sderot Ha'atzma'ut
Shivat Zion St.
Nathanson

RAMAT HATISHBI
Shomrom

Vista of Peace Sculpture Garden
Baha'i Shrine & Gardens

Yefe Nof

Hanassi Avenue

Sderot Hatziyonut

Gid'on St.
Shabbetai Levy St.
I. L. Perez St.
Hassan Shukri
Bialik

WESTERN CARMEL
Hacarmel St.
Hayam
birim St.
Hayam
Kadima St.

MERKAZ CARMEL
(the top of the mountain)

Tikotin Museum of Japanese Art

Eliyahu Golumb St.
Hahashmona'im St.

Balfour St.
Herzl St.
Pevsner St.
Arlosoroff St.
Spinoza
Hapoel St.
Geula

HADAR

Sderot Wedgewood
Sderot Wingale
Sderot Rish

EXPLORING ISRAEL FROM HAIFA

HAIFA

The metropolis is divided into three main levels, each crisscrossed by parks and gardens: the port down below; Hadar HaCarmel, a commercial shopping area in the middle; and Merkaz HaCarmel, with the posher hotels and many restaurants, on top.

Fodor'sChoice **Baha'i Shrine and Gardens.** The most striking feature of the stunning gar-
★   dens that form the centerpiece of Haifa is the Shrine of the Bab, whose brilliantly gilded dome dominates—and illuminates—the city's skyline. The renovated shrine of the Bab, unveiled in April 2011, gleams magnificently with 11,790 gold-glazed porcelain tiles. The Persian authorities martyred Bab in 1850. Baha'u'llah's son and successor built the gardens and shrine and had the Bab's remains reburied here in 1909. The building, made of Italian stone and rising 128 feet, gracefully combines the canons of classical European architecture with elements of Eastern design and also houses the remains of Baha'u'llah's son. The dome glistens with some 12,000 gilded tiles imported from the Netherlands. Note: the Shrine of the Bab is a pilgrimage site for the worldwide Baha'i community; visitors to the shrine are asked to dress modestly (no shorts). ⊠ *16 Golomb St., Merkaz Carmel* ☎ *04/831–3131* ⊕ *www.ganbahai. org.il/en/haifa/* ⊠ *Free* ⊙ *Shrine daily 9–noon; gardens daily 9–5.*

Fodor'sChoice **German Colony.** It is only one street—actually a broad boulevard—but
★   "The Colony" packs in history (with explanatory placards), interesting architecture, great restaurants, and wonderful spots for people-watching. Ben Gurion Boulevard was the heart of a late-19th-century colony established by the German Templer religious reform movement. Along either side are robust one- and two-story stone houses with pointed red-tile roofs. Many bear German names, dates from the 1800s, biblical inscriptions above the doors, and old wooden shutters framing narrow windows. Neglected for years, the German Colony is now one of the city's loveliest (and flattest) strolls. ⊠ *German Colony.*

★   **Tikotin Museum of Japanese Art.** Established in 1957 by Felix Tikotin, this graceful venue adheres to the Japanese tradition of displaying beautiful objects that are in harmony with the season, so exhibits change frequently. The Japanese atmosphere, created in part by sliding doors and partitions made of wood and paper, enhances a display of scrolls, screens, pottery and porcelain, lacquer and metalwork, paintings from several schools, and fresh-flower arrangements. ⊠ *88 Hanassi Blvd., Merkaz Carmel* ☎ *04/838–3554* ⊕ *www.tmja.org.il/* ⊠ *NIS 50* ⊙ *Sun.– Wed. 10–4, Thurs. 10–7, Fri. 10–1, Sat. and Jewish holidays 10–5.*

NAZARETH

The Nazareth where Jesus grew up was an insignificant village nestled in a hollow in the Galilean hills. Today's city of 65,000 is pulsing with energy. Apart from the occasional donkey plying traffic-clogged Paulus VI Street, there's little that evokes the Bible in contemporary Nazareth.
Baptist Church. Christianity speaks with many voices in Nazareth. The Baptist Church, a few hundred yards north of the Church of St. Gabriel, is affiliated with the Southern Baptist Convention of the United States. Sunday services (10:30 am) are conducted in Arabic with an English

translation of the sermon; the Baptist school next door also offers services, with more English speakers, at the same time. The year 2011 marked 100 years of Baptist presence in the Holy Land. ⊠ *Paulus VI St.* ☎ *04/657–6946, 04/657–4370* ⊕ *www.lbc-nazareth.org.*

★ **Basilica of the Annunciation.** Casa Nova Street climbs steeply to the entrance of the Roman Catholic Basilica of the Annunciation, the largest church in the Middle East, consecrated in 1969. It enshrines a small ancient cave dwelling or grotto, identified by many Catholics as the home of Mary. Here, they believe, the angel Gabriel appeared to her and announced (hence, Annunciation) that she would conceive "and bear a son" and "call his name Jesus" (Luke 1). Pilgrim devotions suffuse the site throughout the day. Crusader-era walls and some restored Byzantine mosaics near the grotto bear witness to the antiquity of the tradition. The grotto is in the so-called lower church. Look up through the "well," or opening over the grotto, that connects with the upper church to the grand cupola, soaring 195 feet above you.

> **HAIFA BEST BETS**
>
> **Basilica of the Annunciation.** Built on a spot thought to be central to the life of Jesus and his family.
>
> **Baha'i Shrine and Gardens.** A stunning World Heritage site with terraced gardens cascading down a hillside.
>
> **The Golan Heights.** Israel's Little Tuscany has breathtaking countryside.

A spiral staircase leads to the vast upper church, the parish church of Nazareth's Roman Catholic community. The artwork of the site, donated by Catholic communities around the world, is eclectic in the extreme but the more interesting for it. The portico around the courtyard just inside the main gate is decorated with striking contemporary mosaics, many depicting the Madonna and Child in styles and with facial features reflecting the donor nation. The massive main doors leading to the lower church relate, in bronze relief, the central events of Jesus' life; abstract stained-glass windows brilliantly counterpoint the dim lighting here. The large panels on the walls of the upper church, again on the theme of mother and child, include a vivid offering from the United States, a fine Canadian terra-cotta, and mosaics from England and Australia. Particularly interesting are the gifts from Japan (with gold leaf and pearls), Venezuela (a carved-wood statue), and Cameroon (a stylized painting in black, white, and red).

In the exit courtyard, a glass-enclosed baptistery is built over what is thought to have been an ancient mikvah, a Jewish ritual bath. The adjacent small Church of St. Joseph, just past Terra Sancta College, is built over a complex of rock-hewn chambers traditionally identified as the workshop of Joseph the Carpenter. Note that parking is hard to find; try Paulus VI Street or the side streets below it. ⊠ *Casa Nova St.* ☎ *04/657–2501* ▭ *Free* ⊙ *Hours vary by section. Grotto, 6 am–9 pm, Upper Basilica, 8–6, St. Joseph's Church, 7–6. Masses daily at 6:30 am (Italian) and 7:15 am (Arabic), and Sun. at 7, 8:30, 10, 5 pm, and 6 (all Arabic). Programs: Silent Prayer, daily 6–9 am, Nazareth's Rosary, Tues. 8:30 am, Eucharistic Adoration, Thurs. 8:30 am, Candlelight Procession, Sat. 8:30 am.*

Church of St. Gabriel. The Greek Orthodox Church of St. Gabriel, about 1 km (¾ mile) north of the junction of Paulus VI and Casa Nova streets, is built over Nazareth's only natural water source, a spring dubbed Mary's Well. The Greek Orthodox, citing the noncanonical Gospel of St. James, believe it to be the place where the angel Gabriel appeared to Mary to announce the coming birth of Jesus. (On Paulus VI Street, at the bottom of the short approach to the church, is a round, white, stone structure marked "Mary's Well," but this is merely a modern outlet.)

The ornate church was built in 1750 and contains a stunning carved-wood pulpit and iconostasis (chancel screen), with painted New Testament scenes and silver-haloed saints. The walls are adorned with frescoes of figures from the Bible and the Greek Orthodox hagiography. A tiny "well" stands over the running water, and a modern aluminum cup gives a satisfying plop as it drops in. (The water is clean; the cup is more suspect.) ⊠ *Off Paulus VI St.* ☎ *04/657–6437* 🖃 *Donation expected* ⊙ *Mon.–Sat. 8–5, Sun. after services–5.*

⟳ **Nazareth Village.** The shepherds, weavers, and other characters in this reconstructed Jesus-era community will delight children and adults alike. Using information gained from archaeological work done in the area, this attraction aims to reconstruct Jewish rural life as Jesus would have known it more than 2,000 years ago. Workshops, farms, and houses have been created with techniques that would have been used at the time. Interpreters in period costume cook and work at wine-presses and looms, giving a sense of daily life. The village is geared toward Christian travelers but may also be of interest to others; there is a re-created synagogue and *mikvah* (ritual bath). Guided tours with different themes are offered; check in advance about these, as reservations are required. ⊠ *Nazareth YMCA, 2nd floor, 5105 St., opposite the French hospital* ☎ *04/645–6042* ⊕ *www.nazarethvillage.com* 🖃 *NIS 50* ⊙ *Mon.–Sat. 9–5 (last tour at 3).*

Souk. Full of the aroma of fresh spices, Nazareth's market, in the Old City, has something for everyone, from coffee sets to pastries to T-shirts and antiques. The old lanes are narrow and shops are tiny, with goods spilling into the street, but this souk is more orderly than those in many other Israeli cities. If it does get overwhelming, take a coffee break. ⊠ *Casa Nova St. and vicinity.*

THE GOLAN HEIGHTS

Considered the most fertile land in Israel, the Golan Heights is known for its many fine wineries. As you drive through these verdant hills, covered with wildflowers in the spring, you'll also see abundant olive groves and apple and cherry orchards. The whole region was once volcanic, and many symmetrical volcanic cones and pronounced reliefs still dominate the landscape, particularly in the upper Golan. The gentle terrain and climate of the rest of the region have historically attracted far more settlement than the less hospitable northern Upper Galilee. Today it's home to Jewish, Druze, and Alawite communities.

★ **Hermon River (Banias) Nature Reserve.** One of the most stunning parts of Israel, this reserve contains gushing waterfalls, dense foliage along river-banks, and the remains of a temple dedicated to the god Pan. There

are two entrances, each with a parking lot: the sign for the first reads Banias Waterfall; the other is 1 km (½ mile) farther along the same road and is marked Banias.

The **Banias Spring** emerges at the foot of mostly limestone Mt. Hermon, just where it meets the basalt layers of the Golan Heights. The most popular short route in the reserve is up to the **Banias Cave**, via the path that crosses the spring. Excavations have revealed the five niches hewed out of the rock to the right of the cave; these are what remain of Hellenistic and Roman temples, depicted in interesting artist's renderings. Three of the niches bear inscriptions in Greek, mentioning Pan, the lover of tunes, Echo, the mountain nymph, and Galerius, one of Pan's priests. ⊠ *Off Rte. 99, Kiryat Shmona* ☎ *04/695–0272* 🏛 *NIS 27* ⊙ *Apr.–Sept., Sat.–Thurs. 8–5, Fri. 8–4; Oct.–Mar., Sat.–Thurs. 8–4, Fri. 8–3; last entrance 1 hr before closing.*

★ **Nimrod's Fortress.** The dramatic views of this towering, burly fortress
☺ perched above Banias, appearing and disappearing behind each curve of the narrow road that leads to it, are part of the treat of a visit to Nimrod's Fortress (Kal'at Namrud). And once you're there, the fortress commands superb vistas, especially through the frames of its arched windows and the narrow archers' slits in its walls. In 1218 the Mameluke warlord al-Malik al-Aziz Othman built this fortress to guard the vital route from Damascus via the Golan and Banias, to Lebanon and to the Mediterranean coast, against a Crusader *reconquista* after their 1187 defeat. Nimrod's Fortress is a highlight for kids, with a ladder down to a vaulted cistern, a shadowy spiral staircase, and unexpected nooks and crannies. A path leads up to the fortress's central tower, or keep, where the feudal lord would have lived. ⊠ *Nimrod's Fortress National Park, Rte. 989, Kiryat Shmona* ☎ *04/694–9277* 🏛 *NIS 21* ⊙ *Apr.–Sept., daily 8–5; Oct.–Mar. 8–4; last entrance 1 hr before closing.*

SEA OF GALILEE

The Sea of Galilee is, in fact, a freshwater lake, measuring 21 km (13 miles) long from north to south and 11 km (7 miles) wide from east to west. Almost completely ringed by cliffs and steep hills, the lake lies in a hollow about 700 feet below sea level, which accounts for its warm climate and subtropical vegetation. This is Israel's Riviera-on-a-lake, filled with beaches and outdoor recreation facilities. Its shores are also dotted with sites hallowed by Christian tradition (note that several of these sites demand modest dress) as well as some important ancient synagogues. Tiberias itself is one of Judaism's four holy cities, along with Jerusalem, Hebron, and Tzfat (Safed).

BEACHES

Haifa's coastline is one fine, sandy public beach after another.

Hof HaShaket. North of the Leonardo Hotel, Hof HaShaket offers separate gender days: Sunday, Tuesday, and Thursday for women; Monday, Wednesday, and Friday for men; Saturday for whomever. ⊠ *David Elazar St., South Haifa.*

WHERE TO EAT

$$ ✕ **Douzan.** Inside this old German Templer building with a pleasant
MEDITERRANEAN   outdoor terrace, a huge metal lamp studded with colored glass casts
lacy designs on the walls. The food, much of it prepared by the owner's
mother, is an intriguing combination of French and local Arabic cuisines. Her specialty is *kibbeh,* deep-fried torpedoes of cracked wheat
kneaded with minced beef, pine nuts, onions, and exotic spices. A variation on it is *sfeeha,* puff pastry topped with delicately spiced beef,
onions, and pine nuts. ⑤ *Average main: $17* ✉ *35 Ben Gurion Blvd.,
German Colony* ☎ *04/852–5444* ⊕ *www.rest.co.il.*

$ ✕ **Nadima Sabithi Eatery.** A somewhat typical one-woman show, Nadima
ISRAELI   has been running her home kitchen–style eatery for some 40 years, serving up the day's offerings on a row of gas burners. There's always a
seasoned rice, *majadera* (rice with lentils), and vegetables stuffed with
meat, while the vegetables themselves are a veritable menu of wild herbs
and roots, including okra, spinach, mallow, and chicory. ⑤ *Average
main: $5* ✉ *35 Yohanan Hakadosh, Wadi Nisnas, Netanya* ▭ *No credit
cards* ☉ *Closed Sun. No dinner.*

HVAR, CROATIA

Updated by
Jane Foster

The island of Hvar bills itself as the "sunniest island in the Adriatic."
Not only does it have the figures to back up this claim—an annual average of 2,724 hours of sunshine with a maximum of two foggy days a
year—but it also makes visitors a sporting proposition, offering them a
money-back guarantee if there is ever a foggy day. While fog has been
known to happen, hotels don't ordinarily have to give much of their
income back. All this sun is good for the island's fields of lavender,
rosemary, and grapes. Hvar is also probably Croatia's hippest island,
attracting gossip column–worthy celebrities, would-be artists, politicians, and nudists. Visitors have included King Abdullah and Queen
Rania of Jordan, Nicky Hilton (Paris's sister), and local tennis champion
Goran Ivaniševiæ.

ESSENTIALS

CURRENCY
The Croatian kuna. ATMs are easy to find.

HOURS
Offices are open weekdays from 8:30 to 4. Shops often close for lunch
around 1 and may close for as long as three hours; banks also sometimes
close for lunch. Post offices are open Saturday during the main summer
season, from June through September.

TELEPHONES
Most tri- and quad-band GSM phones will work in Croatia. Public
phones use calling cards, which can be purchased at the post office,
newsstands, and hotels. Major mobile phone companies include TMobile and VIPNet.

COMING ASHORE

Ships can't dock in Hvar, so you'll be brought into Hvar Town from the ship by tender, which docks right in town. Most of the town is closed to cars, so the town is best seen on foot, and since many ships make Hvar a short port call (sometimes staying as few as four hours), it doesn't make much sense to set out to do too much. If you are in port long enough, you'll need to rent a car to see more of the island. Expect to pay at least €55 for a manual economy vehicle. The island also has bus service, particularly to Stari Grad and Jelsa, several times a day.

EXPLORING HVAR

HVAR TOWN

Hvar is both the name of the island and the name of the capital, near the island's western tip. Little **Hvar Town** rises like an amphitheater from its harbor, backed by a hilltop fortress and protected from the open sea by a scattering of small islands known as Pakleni Otoci. Along the palm-lined quay, a string of cafés and restaurants is shaded by colorful awnings and umbrellas. A few steps away, the magnificent main square, **Trg Sveti Stjepan**, the largest piazza in Dalmatia, is backed by the 16th-century **Katedrala Sveti Stjepan** (Cathedral of St. Stephen). Other notable sights include the *kazalište* (a theater) and the *Franjevački Samostan* (Franciscan

monastery). Hvar Town is currently a very "in" spot, so expect it to be crowded and expensive through peak season. Recent visitors have included Tom Cruise, Beyoncé, Italian clothing entrepreneur Luciano Benetton, and local tennis champion Goran Ivanišević.

Franjevački samostan (*Franciscan monastery*). East of town, along the quay past the Arsenal, lies the Franjevački samostan. Within its walls, a pretty 15th-century Renaissance cloister leads to the former refectory, now housing a small museum with several notable artworks. ⊠ *Križa bb* ☏ *25 Kn* ⏰ *May–Oct., daily 9–1 and 5–7.*

> ### HVAR BEST BETS
>
> **See the Tvrdalj.** This oddly interesting house in Stari Grad is worth a trip.
>
> **Visit the Pakleni Otoci.** The small islands off Hvar's southwest coast have Hvar's best beaches, and are scenic enough to be worth a trip in their own right.
>
> **Wander the pedestrian-only alleys of Hvar Town.** If you have just a few hours in port, spend them wandering the car-free streets of Hvar's picturesque Old Town, stopping at a café or two.

PAKLENI OTOCI

Sveti Klement is approximately 20 minutes by boat from Hvar Town.

The 20 small islets that make up the Pakleni Islands are directly southwest of Hvar Town's harbor. Their name derives from the Croatian word *paklina,* which is what melted pine resin is called (the resin from the island's many pine trees was melted down to make ships watertight). The largest of the islands, Sveti Klement, is where Hvar's main yacht harbor is located; a church here is dedicated to the saint. Summer restaurants and beach bars are built on many of the islands, some of which have excellent beaches that are reachable only by boat. Jerolim, the closest of the islands to Hvar Town, has a famous nude beach.

JELSA

10 km (6 miles) east of Stari Grad, 27 km (17 miles) east of Hvar Town.

In this village on the northern coast of the island you'll see many structures from the Renaissance and baroque periods, though St. Mary's Church dates back to the early 1300s. A tower built by the ancient Greeks overlooks the harbor; it dates to the 3rd or 4th century BC. About 1 km (½ mile) east of the modern town is the older Grad, the original fortified area that was protected by the fortress called Galesink, which now stands in ruins. The small town is an alternative to the busier Hvar Town and is surrounded by swimmable beaches—including the island's most popular nude beaches—and some resorts. It's surrounded by thick forests of pine trees.

STARI GRAD

17 km (11 miles) east of Hvar Town.

Stari Grad. The site of the original Greek settlement on Hvar, called Pharos by the Greeks, Stari Grad is a conglomeration of smaller communities; it's also the entry-point to the island for bus transportation from the mainland, as well as passenger ferries. The town is 10 km (6 miles) east of Hvar Town.

Tvrdalj. The main sight is the Tvrdalj, the fortified Renaissance villa of the 16th-century poet Petar Hektorović. The home has been renovated twice over the centuries, first in the 18th-century baroque style; a partial restoration was also done in the 19th century. Hektorović attempted to create a "model universe" to be embodied in his home. To that end, a large fishpond is stocked with gray mullet, as they were in the poet's own time, representing the sea; above the fish pond in a tower is a dovecote, representing the air. Ivy was allowed to cover the walls to tie the home to the land. Quotations from his poetry are inscribed on many walls. ⊠ *Trg Tvrdalj bb, Stari Grad* ☎ *021/765–068* ✉ *10 Kn* ☾ *May, June, Sept., and Oct., daily 10–1; July and Aug. daily 10–1 and 5–8*

BEACHES

There are several decent beaches within walking distance of town—the best-equipped being the Hotel Amfora's **Bonj les Bains** beach, a pebbled cove rimmed by a 1930s stone colonnade housing private stone cabanas, 10 minutes west of the main square. However, sun worshippers in search of a more back-to-nature experience head for the nearby Pakleni Otoci (Pakleni Islands), which can be reached by taxi boats that depart regularly (in peak season, every hour, from 8 to 8) from in front of the Arsenal in the town harbor. The best-known and best-served are **Sveti Jerolim** (on the island of the same name, predominantly a nudist beach), **Stipanska** (on the island of Marinkovac, home to trendy Carpe Diem Stipanska, complete with a restaurant, lounge-bar, pool, and two beaches with palapas and wooden sun beds for hire), and **Palmižana** (on the island of Sveti Klement, also clothing-optional).

WHERE TO EAT

$$ ✗ **Konoba Menego.** On the steps between the main square and the castle,
MEDITERRANEAN this authentic stone-walled konoba has candlelit tables and whole *pršut* (prosciutto) hanging from the wooden beamed ceiling. Come here to snack on small platters of locally produced, cold Dalmatian specialties such as *kožji sir* (goat cheese), pršut, *salata od hobotnice* (octopus salad) and *masline* (olives), accompanied by a carafe of homemade wine. Before leaving, round off your meal with *pijane smokve* (figs marinated in brandy), and be sure to check out the world atlas where guests sign on the pages of their hometowns. ⑤ *Average main: 60 Kn* ⊠ *Groda bb, Hvar Town* ☎ *021/742–036* ⊕ *www.menego.hr* ⊟ *No credit cards* ☾ *Closed Dec.–Mar.*

$$$$ ✗ **Restoran Palmižana.** On the tiny island of Sveti Klement, a 20-minute
SEAFOOD taxi-boat ride from Hvar Town, this terrace restaurant is backed by a
★ romantic wilderness of Mediterranean flora and offers stunning views over the open sea. The walls are decorated with contemporary Croatian art, and there are classical-music recitals on Sunday morning. Besides fresh seafood, goodies include *kožji sir sa rukolom* (goat cheese with arugula), and *pašticada* (beef stewed in sweet wine and prunes). ⑤ *Average main: 110 Kn* ⊠ *Vinogradišće Uvala, Sveti Klement* ☎ *021/717–270* ☾ *Closed Nov.–Mar.*

ISTANBUL, TURKEY

Though it is often remarked that Turkey straddles Europe and Asia, it's really the city of Istanbul that does the straddling. European Istanbul is separated from its Asian suburbs by the Bosphorus, the narrow channel of water that connects the Black Sea, north of the city, to the Sea of Marmara in the south. What will strike you more than the meeting of East and West in Istanbul, though, is the juxtaposition of the old and the new, of tradition and modernity. Office towers creep up behind historic old palaces; women in jeans or elegant designer outfits pass others wearing long skirts and head coverings; donkey-drawn carts vie with shiny BMWs for dominance of the streets; and the Grand Bazaar competes with Western-style boutiques and shopping malls. At dawn, when the muezzin's call to prayer rebounds from ancient minarets, there are inevitably a few hearty revelers still making their way home from nightclubs while other residents kneel in prayer.

ESSENTIALS

CURRENCY
The Turkish lira.

HOURS
Shops open daily from 9 to 9, though some will close for an hour or so on Friday lunchtime for prayers. Attractions are usually open daily from 8 until 5 or 6, though some are closed on Monday.

PRIVATE TOURS
Private tours with a guide are useful and popular. Guides will also help you shop at the Grand Bazaar. The Turkish Tour Guides organization can assure that yours is licensed and knowledgeable.

Contact **Turkish Tour Guides.** ⊕ *www.turkishguides.org.*

TELEPHONES
If you have a multiband cell phone (some countries use frequencies other than those used in the United States) and your service provider uses the world-standard GSM network (as do T-Mobile, AT&T, and Verizon), you can probably use your phone in Turkey. Roaming fees can be steep, though—99¢ a minute is considered reasonable—and you will probably pay the toll charges for incoming calls. It's almost always cheaper to send a text message than to make a call since text messages have a very low set fee (often less than 5¢). Public phones accept tokens or telephone cards (which can be purchased at newsstands and telecom shops); phones accepting cards will also accept credit cards in payment for calls. Turk Telekom, Turkcell, and Telcim are the major telecom companies.

COMING ASHORE
Ships dock at Karakoy, in the shadow of the famous Galata Tower. It's possible to walk from the pier to the Sultanahmet (the historic quarter) in about 45 minutes, but the immediate and pervasive bustle of the city might be off-putting (though it's not intrinsically dangerous). Taxis wait at the pier for the 10-minute ride into Sultanahmet.

We strongly advise against renting a car in Istanbul. The public transport system is also quite chaotic, so we recommend you take taxis. Once you reach Sultanahmet, many of the most important sights are all within walking distance of each other.

GETTING TO THE AIRPORT

If you do not purchase airport transfers from your cruise line, there are several inexpensive possibilities for your transfer from airport to cruise terminal.

Ataturk International Airport is 28 km (17½ miles) outside the city. The light metro line links the airport with downtown at Koça Mustafa Pasha station. Trains run from around 6 am to midnight, but the service is not high-speed and trains can be crowded. From the metro station a 10-minute taxi ride takes you to the cruise quayside.

Airport shuttle buses operated by Havaş leave the arrivals terminal for the Turkish Airlines office in Taksim Square. Departures are every 30 minutes during the day, and prices are currently TL 10 per ticket. A taxi from Taksim Square to the cruise quay takes around 15 minutes.

Taxi fares are about .90 TL for 1 km (about ½ mile); 50% higher between midnight and 6 am. Fares from the airport to downtown are around TL 25–TL 35, and the trip from the airport to the cruise pier takes around 40 minutes depending on traffic (which can be heavy at peak times).

Commercial companies also offer inexpensive door-to-door services. Istanbul Airport Shuttle runs a transfer every couple of hours between 6 am and 9 pm, and prices for airport to cruise port (or downtown hotel) transfers are €10 per person.

Contacts Istanbul Airport Shuttle. ☎ *212/518–0354*
🌐 *www.istanbulairportshuttle.com.*

EXPLORING ISTANBUL

Fodor's Choice **Arkeoloji Müzeleri** (*Istanbul Archaeology Museums*). Step into this vast
★ repository of spectacular finds, housed in a three-building complex in
♺ a forecourt of Topkapı Palace, to get a head-spinning look at the civilizations that have thrived for thousands of years in and around Turkey. The most stunning pieces are tombs that include the so-called Alexander Sarcophagus, found in Lebanon, carved with scenes from Alexander the Great's battles, and once believed, wrongly, to be his final resting place. Don't miss a visit to the **Çinili Köşk** (Tiled Pavilion), one of the most visually pleasing sights in all of Istanbul—a bright profusion of colored tiles covers this one-time hunting lodge of Mehmet the Conqueror, built in 1472. The **Eski Şark Eserleri Müzesi** (Museum of the Ancient Orient) transports visitors to even earlier times: The vast majority of the panels, mosaics, obelisks, and other artifacts here, from Anatolia, Mesopotamia, and elsewhere in the Arab world, date from the pre-Christian centuries. One of the most significant pieces in the collection is a 13th-century BC tablet on which is recorded the Treaty of Kadesh, perhaps the world's earliest known peace treaty, an accord between the Hittite king Hattusili III and the Egyptian pharaoh Ramses II. ⊠ *Gülhane Park, next to Topkapı Sarayı* ☎ *212/520–7740* 🖾 *10 TL (total) for*

Kemankeş Cad.

...esi

ÖY

Rih Tim Cad.

Galata Bridge

• Deniz Otobüsü İskelesi

Karaköy
Vapur İskelesi

Bosphorus (Boğaziçi)

• Şehirhattı İskelesi

REŞADİYE

Reşadiye Caddesi

• Eminönü İskelesi

• Sirkeci Feribot İskelesi

SERAGLIO POINT

SIRKECI

SİRKECİ

Hamidiye Cad.

Şah Pehlevi Cad.

Aşir Efendi Cad.

Cemal Nadir Sok.

Ankara Caddesi

Hüdavendigar Cad.

İbni Kemal Cad.

**Sirkeci Rail
Station**

Taya Hatun Sok.

Ebussuut Cad.

*Gülhane
Parkı*

Gotlar Sütunu

CAGALOGLU

Türkocağı Cad.

Ankara Cad.

Kazım Gürkan
Cad.

Alay Köşkü Cad.

Alemdar Cad.

**Topkapı
Sarayı**

**Arkeoloji Müzesi
(Archaeological
Museum)**

Nuruosmaniye Cad.

Babıali Caddesi

İsmail Yerebatan Cad.

GÜLHANE

...daftar Sokak

Çatal Çeşme Sok.

Soğukçeşme Sok.

**Aya İrini
Kilisesi**

Caferiye Sok.

SULTANAHMET

Divan Yolu Caddesi

**Aya
Sofya**

**Ibrahim Paşa Sarayi
(and Museum
of Turkish and
Islamic Arts)**

Atmeydanı Sok.

Atmeydanı Sok.

Babıhümayun Cad.

İshak Paşa Cad.

SULTANAHMET

*Sultanahmet
Parkı*

Kütlüğün Sok.

Kennedy Caddesi (Sahil Yolu)

Tavukhane Sok.

**Blue
Mosque**

Kabasakal Cad.

Akbıyık Cad.

**Cankurtaran
Rail Station**

Feneri Kapı Sok.

Cankurtaran Cad.

Ahırkapı Sok.

...Sok.

Aksakal Sok.

Kennedy Caddesi (Sahil Yolu)

0 — 1/4 mi

0 — 1/4 km

KEY	
🚢	Ferry Stops
	Ferry Lines
Ⓜ	Metro Stops
ℹ	Information
•	Tramway

the 3 museums ☉ *Tues.–Sun. 9–7 in summer, 9–5 in winter; ticket sales until an hr before closing.*

Fodor'sChoice
★   **Aya Sofya** (*Hagia Sophia, Church of the Holy Wisdom*). This soaring edifice is perhaps the greatest work of Byzantine architecture and for almost a thousand years, starting from its completion in 537, it was the world's largest and most important religious monument. As Justinian may well have intended, the impression that will stay with you longest, years after a visit, is the sight of the dome. As you enter, the half domes trick you before the great space opens up with the immense dome, almost 18 stories high and more than 30 meters (100 feet) across, towering above—look

up into it and you'll see the spectacle of thousands of gold tiles glittering in the light of 40 windows. Only Saint Peter's in Rome, not completed until the 17th century, surpassed Aya Sofya in size and grandeur. It was the cathedral of Constantinople, the heart of the city's spiritual life, and the scene of imperial coronations. It was also the third church on this site: the second, the foundations of which you can see at the entrance, was burned down in the antigovernment Nika riots of 532.

Mehmet II famously sprinkled dirt on his head before entering the church after the conquest as a sign of humility. His first order was for Aya Sofya to be turned into a mosque and, in keeping with the Islamic proscription against figural images, mosaics were plastered over. Successive sultans added the four minarets, *mihrab* (prayer niche), and *minbar* (pulpit for the *imam*) that visitors see today, as well as the large black medallions inscribed in Arabic with the names of Allah, Muhammad, and the early caliphs. In 1935, Atatürk turned Aya Sofya into a museum and a project of restoration, including the uncovering of mosaics, began. ✉ *Aya Sofya Sq.* ☎ *212/522–1750* 💵 *20 TL* ☉ *Tues.–Sun. 9–7 in summer, 9–5 in winter (last entry 1 hr before closing time).*

Fodor'sChoice
★   **Blue Mosque** (*Sultanahmet Camii*). Only after you enter the Blue Mosque do you understand the name: the inside is covered with 20,000 shimmering blue-green İznik tiles interspersed with 260 stained-glass windows; calligraphy and intricate floral patterns are painted on the ceiling. After the dark corners and stern faces of the Byzantine mosaics in Aya Sofya, this mosque feels gloriously airy and full of light. Indeed, this favorable comparison was the intention of architect Mehmet Ağa (a former student of the famous Ottoman architect Sinan), whose goal was to surpass Justinian's crowning achievement (Aya Sofya). At the behest of Sultan Ahmet I (ruled 1603–17), he created this masterpiece of Ottoman craftsmanship, starting in 1609 and completing it in just eight years, and many believe he indeed succeeded in outdoing the

splendor of Aya Sofya. ⊠ *Sultanahmet Sq., Sultanahmet* ☉ *Mosque: Daily 9–6:30 in summer, 9–5 in winter; closed to tourists during prayer times. Mausoleum: Tues.–Sun. 9–4:30.*

★ **Grand Bazaar** (*Kapalı Çarşı*). It's said that this early version of a shopping mall is the largest concentration of stores under one roof anywhere in the world, and that's easy to believe. ⊠ *Yeniçeriler Cad. and Çadırcılar Cad.* ☎ *212/519–1248* ☉ *Mon.–Sat. 8:30–7.*

Fodor's Choice **Süleymaniye Camii** (*Mosque of Süleyman*). Perched on a hilltop opposite
★ Istanbul University, Süleymaniye Camii is perhaps the most magnificent mosque in Istanbul and is considered one of the architect Sinan's masterpieces. Thanks to a three-year, multimillion-dollar restoration project completed in late 2010, the Süleymaniye can now be seen in its full glory. The tomb of Sinan is just outside the walls, on the northern corner, while those of his patron, Süleyman the Magnificent, and the sultan's wife, Roxelana, are housed in the cemetery adjacent to the mosque. The *külliye*, or mosque complex, still includes a hospital, library, hamam, several schools, and other charitable institutions that mosques traditionally operate, so take a stroll around the beautiful grounds—and don't miss the wonderful views of the Golden Horn. ⊠ *Süleymaniye Cad., near Istanbul University's north gate* ☉ *Daily sunrise–sunset except during prayer times.*

Fodor's Choice **Topkapı Sarayı** (*Topkapı Palace*). This vast palace on Seraglio Point,
★ above the confluence of the Bosphorus and the Golden Horn, was the residence of sultans and their harems, in addition to being the seat of Ottoman rule from the 1460s until the middle of the 19th century. Few other royal residences match this hilltop compound when it comes to mystery, intrigue, and the lavishly exotic intricacies of court life. Sultan Mehmet II built the original Topkapı Palace, known simply as the New Palace, between 1459 and 1465, shortly after his conquest of Constantinople. Over the centuries, sultan after sultan added ever more elaborate architectural frills and fantasies, until the palace had acquired four courtyards and quarters for some 5,000 full-time residents, including slaves, concubines, and eunuchs.

The main entrance, or Imperial Gate, leads to the **Court of the Janissaries,** also known as the First Courtyard—it is, and has always been, freely accessible to the general public. Today, the courtyard where these members of the sultan's guard once assembled is a tranquil green park full of tourist groups, and there is little to evoke the splendors and tragedies of the palace's extraordinary history. You will begin to experience the grandeur of the palace when you pass through the **Bab-üs Selam** (Gate of Salutation). Süleyman the Magnificent built the gate in 1524 and was the only person allowed to pass through it on horseback; others had to dismount and enter on foot. Prisoners were kept in the towers on either side of the gate before they were executed next to the nearby fountain, a handy arrangement that made it easy for executioners to wash the blood off their hands after carrying out their orders.

The **Second Courtyard,** once the administrative hub of the Ottoman Empire, is planted with rose gardens and ornamental trees, and filled with a series of ornate *köşks,* pavilions once used for the business of

state as well as for more mundane matters, like feeding the hordes of servants. The **Harem,** a maze of 400 halls, terraces, rooms, wings, and apartments grouped around the sultan's private quarters, evokes all the exoticism and mysterious ways of the Ottoman Empire. Seeing the 40 or so Harem rooms that have been restored and open to the public, though, brings to mind not just luxury but the regimentation, and even barbarity, of life in this enclosed enclave. A separate ticket must be purchased to visit the Harem.

Beyond the Harem is the **Third Courtyard,** shaded by regal old trees and dotted by some of the most ornate of the palace's pavilions. (From the Harem, you enter to the side of the courtyard, but to see this beautiful space to best advantage, make your way to its main gate, the **Bab-üs Saadet,** or Gate of Felicity, exit and reenter—and consider yourself privileged to do so, because for centuries only the sultan and grand vizier were allowed to pass through the gate.) Foreign ambassadors once groveled in the Arz Odası (Audience Chamber), but access to the courtyard was highly restricted, in part because it housed the **Treasury,** four rooms filled with imperial thrones and lavish gifts bestowed upon generations of sultans, and spoils garnered from centuries of war and invasions. The glittering prizes here are the jewels. The most famous pieces are the 86-carat Spoonmaker's Diamond and the emerald-studded Topkapı Dagger.

The **Fourth Courtyard,** more of an open terrace, was the private realm of the sultan, and the small, elegant pavilions, mosques, fountains, and reflecting pools are scattered amid the gardens that overlook the Golden Horn and Bosphorus. The octagonal **Revan Köşkü,** built by Murat IV in 1636 to commemorate a military victory in eastern Anatolia and the Caucasus, is often referred to in Ottoman histories as the Turban Room (Sarık Odası) because it is where the sultan used to keep his turbans. In the İftariye (Golden Cage), also known as the Sofa Köşkü, the closest relatives of the reigning sultan lived in strict confinement under what amounted to house arrest—superseding an older practice of murdering all possible rivals to the throne. Just off the open terrace with the wishing well is the lavishly tiled **Sünnet Odası** (Circumcision Room), where little princes would be taken for ritual circumcision during their ninth or 10th year. ✉ *Babıhümayun Cad., Gülhane Park, near Sultanahmet Sq.* ☎ *212/512–0480* ⊕ *www.topkapisarayi.gov.tr* ✉ *Palace: 20 TL; Harem: 15 TL* ⊘ *Palace: Wed.–Mon. 9–7 in summer, 9–5 in winter (last entry 1 hr before closing time). Harem: Wed.–Mon. 9–5 in summer, 9–4 in winter.*

SHOPPING

Istanbul has been a shopper's town for, well, centuries—the sprawling Grand Bazaar could easily be called the world's oldest shopping mall—but this is not to say that the city is stuck in the past. Along with its colorful bazaars and outdoor markets, Istanbul also has a wide range of modern options. Whether you're looking for trinkets and souvenirs, kilims and carpets, brass and silverware, leather goods, old books, prints and maps, or furnishings and clothes (Turkish textiles are among

the best in the world), you can find them here. **Nuruosmaniye Caddesi,** one of the major streets leading to the Grand Bazaar, is lined with some of Istanbul's most stylish shops, with an emphasis on fine carpets, jewelry, and antiques.

The Arasta Bazaar. Just behind the Blue Mosque, the Arasta Bazaar is a walkway lined with shops selling items similar to those you'll find at the Grand Bazaar (primarily carpets and ceramics), but often at lower prices. The atmosphere is also considerably calmer and, unlike the Grand Bazaar, the Arasta is open on Sunday. ⊠ *Sultanahmet.*

The Egyptian Bazaar. The Egyptian Bazaar is also known as the Spice Market, and has stall after enticing stall filled with mounds of exotic spices and dried fruits. ⊠ *near Yeni Cami Meydanı, Eminönü.*

Sahaflar Çarşısı. The Sahaflar Çarşısı, reached through a doorway just outside the western end of the Grand Bazaar, is home to a bustling book market, with both old and new editions. Most are in Turkish, but English and other languages are also represented. The market is open daily, though Sunday has the most vendors. ⊠ *Grand Bazaar.*

WHERE TO EAT

$ ✕ **Doy-Doy.** *Doy-doy* is a Turkish expression for "full" and, unlike many
TURKISH other places in tourist-filled Sultanahmet, you can indeed fill up for a reasonable sum at this no-frills spot frequented by locals. A variety of kebabs and *pide*, a type of Turkish pizza baked in a wood-burning oven, with different toppings are served, and the lunchtime specials, including vegetable stew, meatballs, and eggplant and meat moussaka, are a particularly good deal. The two-level rooftop terrace, open in summer, has fine views of the Blue Mosque and Sea of Marmara—but don't expect to savor the view with a drink in hand, as no alcohol is served. ⑤ *Average main: 12 TL* ⊠ *Şifa Hamamı Sok. 13, Sultanahmet* ☎ *212/517–1588* ⊕ *www.doydoy-restaurant.com.*

$ ✕ **Khorasani.** One of Sultanahmet's most popular restaurants empha-
TURKISH sizes the Arab- and Kurdish-influenced cuisine of southeastern Turkey,
Fodor's Choice from where the restaurant's owners hail. This translates to delicious
★ mezes like hummus, *muhammara* (hot pepper and walnut spread), and thyme salad, as well as unusual mains that include quail kebab and a pistachio kebab made with both lamb and beef. Diners can sit outdoors on the cobblestoned sidewalk or get a table inside to watch the chefs prepare kebabs over the large charcoal grill. ⑤ *Average main: 26 TL* ⊠ *Ticarethane Sok. 39/41, Sultanahmet* ☎ *212/519–5959* ⊕ *www. khorasanirestaurant.com.*

WHERE TO STAY

$$$ ▥ **Ayasofya Konakları.** Nine charming, pastel-color wooden mansions from the late 19th century have been restored by Turkey's Touring and Automobile Club and turned into a row of elegant guest houses, where smallish rooms are furnished in period Ottoman style, with brass beds and chandeliers, wooden floors and furniture, and plush upholstery, and have either half-size tubs or showers. **Pros:** unique, historic buildings;

location adjacent to Aya Sofya. **Cons:** high room rates because of location; some accommodations far from reception and dining area; most rooms lack TV and Wi-Fi. ⑤ *Rooms from: 410 TL* ✉ *Soğukçeşme Sok., Sultanahmet* ☎ *212/513–3660* ⊕ *www.ayasofyakonaklari.com* ⌑ *57 rooms, 10 suites* ⦿|*Breakfast.*

$$$$
Fodor's Choice
★

⚞ **Çırağan Palace Kempinski Istanbul.** Once a residence for the Ottoman sultans, the late 19th-century Çırağan Palace (pronounced chi-rahn) is Istanbul's most luxurious hotel, with ornate public spaces that feel absolutely decadent and a breathtaking setting right on the Bosphorus—the outdoor infinity pool seems to hover on the water's edge and most rooms, full of Ottoman-inspired wood furnishings and textiles in warm colors, have balconies overlooking the Bosphorus as well. **Pros:** grand setting in incredible location; over-the-top feeling of luxury; free Wi-Fi. **Cons:** exorbitant price of food and drinks; high rates, especially for rooms that have no Bosphorus view. ⑤ *Rooms from: 1300 TL* ✉ *Çırağan Cad. 32, Beşiktaş* ☎ *212/326–4646* ⊕ *www.kempinski. com/istanbul* ⌑ *282 rooms, 31 suites.*

$$
HOTEL
Fodor's Choice
★

⚞ **Dersaadet Hotel.** *Dersaadet* means "place of happiness" in Ottoman Turkish and this small, cozy hotel lives up to its name—rooms have an elegant, even plush, feel, with colorful rugs on the floor, antique furniture, and ceilings hand-painted with Ottoman ornamental motifs. **Pros:** extraordinary level of service; lovely terrace; good value. **Cons:** some rooms modest in size; no view from rooms on lower floors. ⑤ *Rooms from: 276 TL* ✉ *Küçükayasofya Cad. Kapıağası Sok. 5, Sultanahmet* ☎ *212/458–0760* ⊕ *www.dersaadethotel.com* ⌑ *14 rooms, 3 suites* ⦿|*Breakfast.*

KATAKOLON, GREECE (FOR OLYMPIA)

Updated by
Adrian Vrettos
and Alexia
Amvrazi

Katakolon could not seem less of a cruise port if it tried. A tiny enclave clinging to the western Peloponnese coast, it's a sleepy place except when ships dock. But it's a popular cruise destination because of its proximity to Olympia. Ancient Olympia was one of the most important cities in classical Greece. The Sanctuary of Zeus was the city's raison d'être, and attracted pilgrims from around the eastern Mediterranean, and later the city played host to Olympic Games, the original athletic games that were the inspiration for today's modern sporting panplanetary meet. At the foot of the tree-covered Kronion hill, in a valley near two rivers, Katakolon is today one of the most popular ancient sites in Greece. If you don't want to make the trip to Olympia, then Katakolon is an ideal place for a leisurely Greek lunch while you watch the fishermen mend their nets, but there's just not much else to do there.

ESSENTIALS
CURRENCY
The euro.

HOURS
Stores are generally open from 9 to 9 on weekdays and 9 to 6 on Saturday. Museums are generally open from 9 to 5, but many are closed on Monday.

TELEPHONES

Tri-band GSM phones work in Greece. You can buy prepaid phone cards at telecom shops, news vendors, and tobacconists in all towns and cities. Phone cards can be used for local or international calls. Vodafone is the leading mobile telecom company. OTE is the national domestic provider. Calls can be made at OTE offices and paid for after completion.

COMING ASHORE

Katakolon is a very small port. Ships dock at the jetty, from where it is a short walk (five minutes) into Katakolon Town. It's a small Greek town with a lot of character; most residents still make their living from fishing; a few restaurants are along the waterfront, as well as shops selling souvenirs to cruise-ship passengers. There are no passenger facilities at the jetty itself. Though there are refreshment stands, telephones, currency exchange offices, and an ATM in the town.

Taxis are available at the dock to meet ships. However, cabs charge an overinflated fixed fare for the journey to Olympia, so it's often better to go on a ship-sponsored excursion.

Contacts **Katakolon Car Rental.** Diplas Dionysios runs this agency, but it has a limited number of vehicles, so it's vital to book in advance if you want to drive yourself to Olympia. Prices for a compact manual vehicle are approx €40 per day. ☎ 26210/41727.

EXPLORING OLYMPIA

★ **Ancient Olympia.** Located at the foot of the pine-covered Kronion hill,
☾ and set in a valley where the Kladeos and Alpheios rivers join, Ancient Olympia is one of the most celebrated archaeological sites in Greece. Home to a sacred sanctuary dedicated to Zeus, Olympia also became famed as the host of the Olympic Games. Just as athletes from city-states throughout ancient Greece made the journey to compete in the ancient Olympics—the first sports competition—visitors from all over the world today make their way to the small modern Arcadian town that appears to have been already been a legend as long ago as the 10th century BC. The Olympic Games, first staged around the 8th century BC, were played here in the stadium, hippodrome, and other venues for some 1,100 years. Today, the venerable ruins of these structures attest to the majesty and importance of the first Olympiads. Modern Olympia, an attractive mountain town surrounded by pleasant hilly countryside, has hotels and tavernas, convenient for visitors to the ancient site.

As famous as the Olympic Games were—and still are—Olympia was first and foremost a sacred place, a sanctuary honoring Zeus, king of the gods, and Hera, his wife and older sister. The sacred quarter was known as the Altis, or the Sacred Grove of Zeus, and was enclosed by a wall on three sides and the Kronion Hill on the other. Inside the Altis were temples, altars, and twelve treasuries of various city-states.

To honor the cult of Zeus established at Olympia as early as the 10th century BC, altars were first constructed outdoors, among the pine forests that encroach upon the site. But around the turn of the 6th century BC, the earliest building at Olympia was constructed, the Temple

Ancient Olympia

Kronion Hill

Stadium

Treasuries

Nymphaion

Heraion

Metroon

Stoa of Echo

House of Nero

Prytaneion

Philippeion

Altis

Temple of Zeus

Roman bath

Entrance

Palaestra

Pheidias's Workshop

Leonidaion

Gymnasion

River Kladeos

0 — 1/16 mi

0 — 1/16 km

Northern Peloponnese

Halandritsa

A C H A I A

E L I S

Olympia

Ancient Olympia
see detail map

Pirgos

Alfíos

Amalias

Spiantza

Lehena

Gastouni

Katakolon

Kastro

Chlemoutsi
Castle

Loutra
Killinis

Ionian Sea

0 — 6 miles

0 — 9 km

of Hera, which originally honored Zeus and Hera jointly, until the Temple of Zeus was constructed around 470 BC. The Temple of Zeus was one of the finest temples in all of Greece. Thirteen columns flanked the sides, and its interior housed the most famous work of ancient Greece—a gold and ivory statue of Zeus. Earthquakes in 551 and 552 finished off the temple.

After the Treasuries, the Bouleuterion, and the Pelopeion were built, the 5th and 4th centuries BC, the Golden Age of the ancient games, saw a virtual building boom. The monumental Temple of Zeus, the Prytaneion, and the Metroon went up at this time. The enormous Leonidaion was built around 300 BC, and as the games continued to thrive, the Palaestra and Gymnasion were added to the complex.

> ## OLYMPIA BEST BETS
>
> **The Twelve Labors of Hercules.** This series now in the archaeological museum is regarded as a high point in classical Greek sculpture.
>
> **Statue of Hermes by Praxiteles.** Also in the museum, this is one of the most complete classical statues to have been unearthed.
>
> **Remains of the Temple of Zeus.** The above-mentioned treasures once adorned this vast temple, which was one of the largest and finest in ancient Greece. Today only the platform remains.

The history of the Olympic Games is long and fabled. For almost eleven centuries, freeborn Greeks from the various city-states gathered to participate in the games, held every four years in August or September. These games became so much a part of the culture that the four-year interval between the games became a standard unit of time, an Olympiad. An Olympic truce—the Ekecheiria—allowed safe passage for athletes from the different city-states traveling to the games, and participation in them meant allegiance to a "Panhellenic" ideal of a united Greece. The exact date of the first games is not known, but the first recorded event is a footrace, a *stade,* run in 776 BC. A longer race, a *diaulos,* was added in 724 BC, and wrestling and a pentathlon—consisting of the long jump, the javelin throw, the discus throw, a footrace, and wrestling—in 708 BC. Boxing and chariot racing were 7th-century BC additions, as was the *pankration,* a no-holds-barred match (broken limbs were frequent and strangulation sometimes the end)—Plato, the great philosopher, was a big wrestling fan. By the 5th century BC, the games featured nine events, held over four days, with the fifth day reserved for the ceremonies. Most of the participants were professional athletes, for whom winning a laurel wreath at Olympia ensured wealth and glory from the city-states that sponsored them.

Today's tranquil pine-forested valley at Olympia, set with weathered stones of peaceful dignity, belies the sweaty drama of the first sporting festivals. Stadium foot-races run in the nude; *pankration* wrestling so violent today's Ultimate Fighting matches look tame; week-long bacchanals—serviced by an army of *pornoi* and prostitutes—held in the Olympic Village: Little wonder this ancient event is now called the "Woodstock of its day" by modern scholars (wrestlers, boxers, and discus-throwers being the rock stars of ancient Greece).

For today's sightseer, the ruins of many of Olympia's main structures are still visible. The **Altis** was the sacred quarter was also known as the Sacred Grove of Zeus. In the **Bouleuterion**, the seat of the organizers of the games, the Elean senate, athletes swore an oath of fair play. In the **Gymnasion**, athletes practiced for track and field events in an open field surrounded by porticoes. In the **Hippodrome**, horse and chariot races were run on a vast racecourse. The **House of Nero** was a lavish villa built for the emperor's visit to the games of AD 67, in which he competed. The **Leonidaion** was a luxurious hostel for distinguished visitors to the games; it later housed Roman governors. The **Metroon** was a small Doric temple dedicated to Rhea (also known as Cybele), Mother of the Gods. The **Nymphaion**, a semicircular reservoir, stored water from a spring to the east that was distributed throughout the site by a network of pipes. The **Palaestra** was a section of the gymnasium complex used for athletic training; athletes bathed and socialized in rooms around the square field. The **Pelopeion**, a shrine to Pelops, legendary king of the region now known as the Peloponnese, housed an altar in a sacred grove. **Pheidas's Workshop** was the studio of the great ancient sculptor famed for his enormous statue of Zeus, sculpted for the site's Temple of Zeus. The **Prytaneion** was a banquet room where magistrates feted the winners and a perpetual flame burned in the hearth. The **Stadium** held as many as 50,000 spectators, who crowded onto earthen embankments to watch running events. The starting and finishing lines are still in place. The **Temple of Hera** was one of the earliest monumental Greek temples was built in the 7th century BC. The **Temple of Zeus,** a great temple and fine example of Doric architecture, housed an enormous statue of Zeus that was one of the seven wonders of the ancient world. The famous **Treasuries** were temple-like buildings that housed valuables and equipment of twelve of the most powerful of the city-states competing in the games.

You'll need at least two hours to fully see the ruins and the Archaeological Museum of Olympia (to the north of the ancient site), and three or four hours would be better. ⊠ *Off Ethnikos Odos 74, ½ km (¼ mile) outside modern Olympia* ☎ *26240/22517* ⊕ *www.culture.gr* ⊠ *€6, combined ticket with Archaeological Museum €9* ☉ *Sun.–Mon. 9–4; Tues.–Sat. 8–5.*

Archaeological Museum of Olympia. Of all the sights in ancient Olympia, some say the modern Archaeological Museum of Olympia gets the gold. Housed in a handsome glass and marble pavilion at the edge of the ancient site, the magnificent collections include the sculptures from the Temple of Zeus and the *Hermes Carrying the Infant Dionysus*, sculpted by the great Praxiteles, which was discovered in the Temple of Hera in the place noted by Pausanias. The central gallery of the museum holds one of the greatest sculptural achievements of classical antiquity: the pedimental sculptures and metopes from the Temple of Zeus, depicting Hercules's Twelve Labors. The *Hermes* was buried under the fallen clay of the temple's upper walls and is one of the best-preserved classical statues. Also on display is the famous *Nike of Paionios*. Other treasures include notable terra-cottas of Zeus and Ganymede; the head of the cult statue of Hera; sculptures of the family and imperial patrons of Herodes

Atticus; and bronzes found at the site, including votive figurines, cauldrons, and armor. Of great historic interest are a helmet dedicated by Miltiades, the Athenian general who defeated the Persians at Marathon, and a cup owned by the sculptor Pheidias, which was found in his workshop on the Olympia grounds. ⊠ *Off Ethnikos Odos 74, ½ km (¼ mile) outside modern Olympia* ☎ *26240/22742* ⊕ *www.culture.gr* ⊠ *€6, combined ticket with Ancient Olympia €9* ⊙ *May–Oct., Mon. 11–7:30, Tues.–Sun. 8–7:30; Nov.–Apr., daily 8:30–3.*

SHOPPING

Lovers of handicrafts will really enjoy shopping in Greece. There's an abundance of ceramics, both traditional and modern, wooden bowls, reproductions of ancient statuary, woven rugs, jewelry, lace, and edibles such as delicious honey and olive oil. Cotton clothing is perfect for the summer temperatures, along with strong handcrafted sandals and leather goods that have always been popular purchases here. Around Olympus other popular souvenirs are reproductions of ancient artifacts found at the ancient site. Shop in modern Olympia or in Katakalon before reboarding your ship. There are just a few shops in Kalakon, but they sell a full range of souvenirs.

★ **Archaeological Museum.** The shop of the Archaeological Museum carries an appealing line of figurines, bronzes, votives, and other replicas of objects found in the ruins. ⊠ *Off Ethnikos Odos 74, north of Ancient Olympia site* ☎ *26240/22742.*

★ **Atelier Exekias.** At Atelier Exekias Sakis Doylas sells exquisite handmade and hand-painted ceramic bowls and urns, fashioned after finds in Ancient Olympia; the glazes and colors are beautiful. ⊠ *Kondoli, Olympia* ☎ *6936/314054 or 26240/23816.*

WHERE TO EAT

$ ✕ **Aegean.** Don't let the garish signs depicting the menu put you off: the far-ranging offerings are excellent. You can eat lightly—a gyro or pizza—but do venture into some of the more-serious fare, especially such local dishes as the fish that's been oven-baked with onion, garlic, green peppers, and parsley. The house's barrel wine is a nice accompaniment to any meal. ⑤ *Average main: €7* ⊠ *Douma, near Hotel New Olympia, Olympia* ☎ *26240/22540.*

GREEK

$ ✕ **Taverna Bacchus.** The best restaurants in Greece are often in small villages, and this appealing family-run taverna and inn, a favorite among Olympians, is one such example. Locals start to trek in around 10:30 pm for dishes that include a delicious chicken with oregano. ⑤ *Average main: €8* ⊠ *Ancient Pissa (Mirika), Olympia* ☎ *26240/22298* ⊙ *Closed Dec.–Feb.*

GREEK

KOPER, SLOVENIA

Updated
by Bruce
Leimsidor

Just half the size of Switzerland, Slovenia is often bypassed in favor of more well-known countries such as Croatia and Italy. The country's relative obscurity owes much to its history. From Roman times to nearly the present day, Slovenian territory was incorporated into far-larger empires, relegating Slovenia through the ages to the role of rustic, if charming, hinterland. Backed by hills planted with olive groves and vineyards, Slovenia's small strip of Adriatic coastline is only 47 km (29 miles) long and dominated by the towns of Koper, Izola, Piran, and Portorož. Following centuries of Venetian rule, the coast remains culturally and spiritually connected to Italy, and Italian is still widely spoken. Koper, Slovenia's largest port, and Izola, its biggest fishery, are workaday towns that nevertheless retain a lot of historical charm. The medieval port of Piran is a gem and a must-see. Its Venetian core is nearly perfectly preserved. The most unspoiled stretch of coast is at the Strunjan Nature Reserve—which also has an area reserved for nudists—between Piran and Izola.

ESSENTIALS

CURRENCY

The euro. In major cities banks and ATMs are easy to find, but not all ATMs readily accept international cards.

HOURS

Most banks are open weekdays 9 to noon and 2 to 4:30, Saturday 9 to 11. The main museums are open Tuesday through Sunday from 10 to 6. Larger shops are open Monday through Saturday from 10 to 6, although smaller ones may open mornings only from 10 to 2. Most stores are closed Sunday. Some restaurants close one day a week—usually Sunday, but sometimes Monday.

TELEPHONES

The country code for Slovenia is 386. When dialing from outside the country, drop any initial "0" from the area code. Pay phones (although they are becoming rare) take magnetic telephone cards, available from post offices and kiosks. Most tri-band GSM mobile phones will work in Slovenia provided you enable international service.

COMING ASHORE

Cruise ships dock immediately below Koper's Old Town, at a recently renovated modern passenger terminal. From here, it's 300 meters to Titov trg, the main square, in the pedestrian-only Old Town, where you'll find the city's main sights, plus a useful Tourist Information Center. The Old Town can be explored on foot, so there is no need to rent a car if you decide to stay in Koper. But some people will choose to go into Ljubljana (77 miles [124 km] away, which is about three hours by bus or a little more than two hours by car). Most cruise lines offer tours that include time in Ljubljana. Other popular excursions include the nearby seaside towns of Izola and Piran, the Lipica Stud Farm, and Postojna Cave. There's a taxi stand in the port.

If you choose to rent a car, expect to pay about €55 for a manual compact vehicle, though you can rent a semiautomatic Smart car at some outlets for about €50.

EXPLORING SLOVENIA FROM KOPER

KOPER

Today a port town surrounded by industrial suburbs, Koper nevertheless warrants some exploration. The Republic of Venice made Koper the regional capital during the 15th and 16th centuries, and the magnificent architecture of the Old Town bears witness to the spirit of those times. The most important buildings are clustered around **Titov trg,** the central town square. Here stands the **Cathedral,** which can be visited daily from 7 to noon and 3 to 7, with its fine Venetian Gothic facade and bell tower dating back to 1664. Across the square the splendid **Praetor's Palace,** formerly the seat of the Venetian Grand Council, combines Gothic and Renaissance styles. From the west side of Titov trg, the narrow, cobbled **Kidriceva ulica** brings you down to the seafront.

> ### KOPER BEST BETS
>
> **Koper Old Town.** Wander through Koper's lovely medieval car-free streets to arrive on Titov trg, the main square.
>
> **Postojna Cave.** Explore the underground depths of this vast and impressive show cave.
>
> **Ljubljana Castle.** See the Slovenian capital at its best, from the ramparts of the hilltop castle.

3

IZOLA

Izola is a normally placid fishing town that lets its hair down in summer. DJs decamp from Ljubljana for parties on the coast, artists set up their studios, and the city adopts the relaxed persona of a shaggy beach town. Less industrial than Koper and less self-consciously pretty than Piran, Izola makes a perfect day outing. It's also a great place to eat. The fish is fresh and the customers—many of them local Slovenians— are demanding.

Like that of its immediate neighbor, Koper, the city's history goes back hundreds of years. Izola rose to prominence in the Middle Ages and then declined in the 16th and 17th centuries with the rise of the port of Trieste in present-day Italy. The name "Izola" comes from the Italian word for "island" and describes a time when the walled city in fact was an island. The city walls were knocked down by the French occupation at the start of the 19th century. The bricks were then used to connect the city to the mainland.

LIPICA

Kobilarna Lipica (*Lipica Stud Farm*). The Kobilarna Lipica was founded in 1580 by the Austrian archduke Karl II. It's where the white Lipizzaners—the majestic horses of the famed Spanish Riding School in Vienna—originated. Today the farm no longer sends its horses to Vienna, but breeds them for its own performances and riding instruction. The impressive stables and grounds are open to the public. Riding classes are available, but lessons are geared toward experienced riders and must be booked in advance. ⊠ *Lipica 5, Sežana* ☎ *05/739–1708* ⊕ *www.lipica.org* ⊘ *Dressage performances June–Oct., Tues., Fri., and Sun. at 3. Stable tours July and Aug., daily 9–6; Apr.–June and Sept. and Oct., daily 10–5; Nov.–Mar., daily 11–3.*

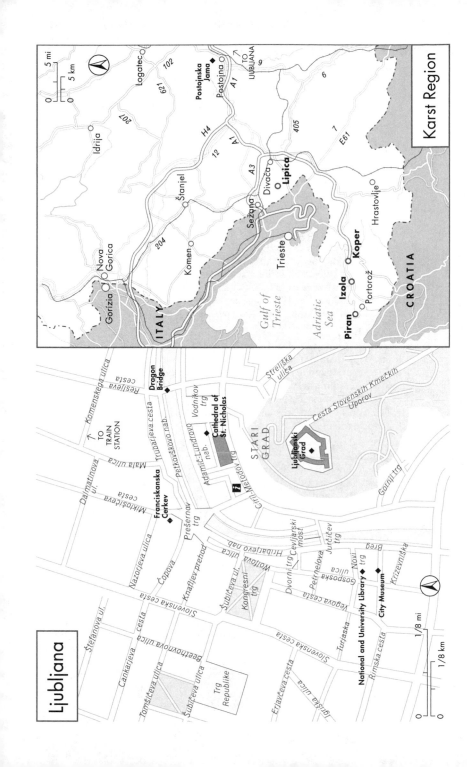

Karst Region

Logatec

102

621

207

Idrija

Postojnska Jama ◆

Postojna

A1

TO LJUBLJANA

9

6

H4

12

A1

A3

Štanjel

204

Komen

Sežana

Divača

Lipica ◆

Lipica

405

7

E61

Hrastovlje

Nova Gorica

Gorizia

ITALY

Gulf of Trieste

Trieste

Adriatic Sea

Koper

Izola

Portorož

Piran

CROATIA

5 mi

5 km

Ljubljana

Komenskega ulica

Resljeva cesta

Dragon Bridge ◆

Vodnikov trg

Trubarjeva cesta

Petkovškovo nab.

Cathedral of St. Nicholas ◆

Streliška ulica

Cesta Slovenskih Kmečkih Uporov

TO TRAIN STATION

Mala ulica

Adamič-Lundrovo nab.

Ciril-Metodov trg

S T A R I G R A D

Dalmatinova ul.

Miklošičeva cesta

Franciskanska Cerkev ◆

Prešernov trg

Nazorjeva ulica

Čopova

Slovenska cesta

Wolfova ulica

Hribarjevo nab.

Subičeva ulica

Dvorni trg

Ljubljanski Grad ◆

Gornji trg

Knafljev prehod

Kongresni trg

Cevljarski most

Vegova cesta

Petnelova

Jurčičev trg

Breg

Štefanova ul.

Cankarjeva cesta

Beethovnova ulica

Tomšičeva ulica

Subičeva ulica

Trg Republike

Slovenska cesta

Gosposka ulica

Novi trg

National and University Library ◆

City Museum ◆

Turjaška

Zoisova cesta

Emonska cesta

Igriška ulica

Rimska cesta

Križevniška

1/8 mi

1/8 km

POSTOJNSKA JAMA

Postojnska Jama (*Postojna Cave*). Postojnska Jama conceals one of the largest networks of caves in the world, with 23 km (14 miles) of underground passageways. A miniature train takes you through the first 7 km (4½ miles), to reveal a succession of well-lighted rock formations. This strange underground world is home of the snakelike "human fish" on view in an aquarium in the Great Hall. Eyeless and colorless because of countless millennia of life in total darkness, these amphibians can live for up to 60 years. Temperatures average 8°C (46°F) year-round, so bring a sweater, even in summer. Tours leave every hour on the hour throughout the year. ⊠ *Jamska 30, Postojna* ☎ *05/700–0163* ⊕ *www. postojna-cave.com* ⊠ *€22.90* ⊙ *May–Sept., daily 8:30–6; Apr. and Oct., daily 8:30–5; Nov.–Mar., weekdays 9:30–1:30, weekends 9:30–3.*

LJUBLJANA

Slovenia's small but exceedingly charming capital is enjoying a tourism renaissance. The tiny city center is captivating. Part of the charm is doubtless the emerald green Llubljanica River that winds its way slowly through the Old Town, providing a focal point and the perfect backdrop to the cafés and restaurants that line the banks. Partly, too, it's the aesthetic tension between the stately baroque houses along the river and the white neoclassical, modern, and Secessionist set pieces that dot the streets and bridges everywhere.

Cathedral of St. Nicholas. This proud baroque cathedral overlooking the daily market on Vodnikov trg is dedicated to St. Nicholas, the patron saint of fisherman and boatmen who created a powerful guild in medieval Ljubljana. Building took place between 1701 and 1708, under the Italian architect Andrea Pozzo, who modeled it after the church of Il Gesù in Rome. The magnificent frescos on the ceiling of the nave are by the Lombard painter Giulio Qualglio and depict the transfiguration of St. Nicholas and the persecution of Christians under Diocletian and Nero. In 1996, in honor of Pope John Paul II's visit, new bronze doors were added to the church. The main door tells the story of Christianity in Slovenia, whereas the side door shows the history of the Ljubljana diocese. ⊠ *Dolničarjeva 1, Ljubljana* ☎ *01/234–2690* ⊕ *lj-stolnica.rkc. si* ⊠ *Free* ⊙ *Daily 7–noon and 3–7.*

Čevljarski most (*Cobblers' Bridge*). The most southerly of the historic bridges linking the old and new sides of town, this romantic pedestrian bridge was built in 1931 according to plans by the architect Jože Plečnik. The name (cobbler's bridge) refers to a wooden structure lined with shoemakers' huts that once stood here. ⊠ *Ljubljana.*

★ **City Museum of Ljubljana.** Situated in the grand Auersberg Palace, this museum and its beautifully designed exhibits trace the history of the city from pre-Roman times through the Austrian domination, the World Wars, the Tito years, and finally the establishment of independent Slovenia. In the basement, you can walk on a piece of the ancient Roman road and see a cross-sectioned excavation that shows the burning of Emona by Attila the Hun through a black, charred stratum. If you're interested, you can arrange for a museum guide to take you to other ancient Roman sites around the city. The city museum also houses

the world's oldest wooden wheel, dating from 4000 BC. ⊠ *Gosposka ulitca 15, Ljubljana* ☎ *01/241 2500* ⊕ *www.mgml.si* 🎫 *€4* ☉ *Tues.– Sun. 10–6, Thurs. 10–9.*

Dragon Bridge. Four fire-breathing winged dragons crown the corners of this locally cherished concrete-and-iron structure. The dragons refer to the mythological origins of the city, when Jason, returning home from winning the Golden Fleece, killed a monster in a swamp on the present site of Ljubljana. ⊠ *Ljubljana.*

Franciskanska cerkev (*Franciscan Church*). This imposing, pink, high-baroque church was built between 1646 and 1660 for Augustinian priests; the Franciscans took it over in the 18th century and painted it red, the color of their order (although the outside facade has now faded to pink). The main altar, by Francesco Robba (1698–1757), dates from 1736. The three sets of stairs in front are a 19th century addition added after the ground was leveled in the plaza and now serve as a popular meeting place for students. ⊠ *Prešernov trg 4, Ljubljana* ☎ *01/4253007* ☉ *Daily 8–12:30, 1:30–8.*

Ljubljanski grad (*Ljubljana Castle*). Ljubljana's hilltop castle affords views over the river and the Old Town's terra-cotta rooftops, spires, and green cupolas. On a clear day, the distant Julian Alps are a dramatic backdrop. The castle walls date from the early 16th century, although the tower was added in the mid-19th century. The surrounding park was landscaped by Plečnik in the 1930s. The castle also houses a virtual museum showcasing Slovenian history through digital technology. ⊠ *Studentovska ul, uphill from Vodnikov trg, Grajska planota 1, Ljubljana* ☎ *01/306–4293* ⊕ *www.ljubljanskigrad.si* 🎫 *€8 (including cable car)* ☉ *Apr.–Oct., daily 9–9; Nov.–Mar., daily 10–7.*

★ **National and University Library.** Built from 1936 to 1941, the National Library is architect Jože Plečnik's secular masterpiece. The external facades present a modernist version of an Italian reanaissance palazzo, using brick, stone, and even archeological remains from excavations around Ljubljana. Inside, there is a beautiful collonaded black marble staircase and a reading room with huge windows at either end to let in light. The austere furniture in the reading room was also designed by Plečnik. Don't miss the beautiful horsehead door handles on the main entrance. ⊠ *Turjaška ultica 1, Ljubljana* ☎ *01/2001121* ⊕ *www.nuk. uni-lj.si* ☉ *Reading Room open weekdays 9–8, Sat. 9–2.*

SHOPPING

Although you wouldn't come to Slovenia to do much serious shopping, fashionable shoe stores abound in Ljubljana; for the latest selection head to shops on Stari trg in the Old Town.

Ljubljana Flea Market. You can pick up antiques and memorabilia at the Ljubljana Flea Market, held on the Breg Embankment each Sunday morning. ⊠ *Breg Embankment, Ljubljana.*

Open-Air Market. The most interesting shopping experience is undoubtedly a visit to the open-air market, where you can find fresh fruit and vegetables as well as dried herbs and locally produced honey. ⊠ *Vodnikov trg, Ljubljana.*

WHERE TO EAT

$$$ ✗ **Skipper.** Noted for its vast summer terrace overlooking the marina,
SEAFOOD   Skipper is popular with the yachting fraternity. The menu includes
pasta dishes, risottos, grilled meats, and fish. ⑤ *Average main: €30*
✉ *Kopališko nab 3, Koper* ☎ *05/626–1810.*

$ ✗ **Trta.** In a country filled with pizza joints, this may be Slovenia's best.
PIZZA   It offers supersize pies, fresh and inventive ingredients, and a small
garden for warm evenings. Walk south along the river (on the same
side as the Old Town), cross over busy Zoisova cesta, and continue
along Grudnovo nabrežje. ⑤ *Average main: €8* ✉ *Grudnovo nabrezje
21, Ljubljana* ☎ *01/426–5066* ⊕ *www.trta.si* ☽ *Closed Sun.*

KORČULA, CROATIA

Updated by
Jane Foster

Southern Dalmatia's largest, most sophisticated, and most visited
island, Korčula was known to the ancient Greeks, who named it *Ker-
kyra Melaina,* or "Black Corfu." Between the 10th and 18th centuries
it spent several periods under Venetian rule. Today most Croatians
know it for its traditional sword dances and its excellent white wines.
Korčula is also the name of the capital, which is near the island's eastern
tip. Eight centuries under Venetian rule bequeathed the town a trove of
Gothic and Renaissance churches, palaces, and piazzas, all built from
fine local stone. Korčula's main claim to fame, though one still disputed
by historians, is that it was the birthplace of Marco Polo (1254–1324).
The approach by sea is breathtaking; if the hour isn't too early, make
sure you're on deck for this one.

ESSENTIALS

CURRENCY
The Croatian kuna. ATMs are easy to find.

HOURS
Offices are open weekdays from 8:30 to 4. Shops often close for lunch
around 1, and may close for as long as three hours; banks also some-
times close for lunch. Post offices are open on Saturday during the main
summer season, from June through September.

TELEPHONES
Most tri- and quad-band GSM phones will work in Croatia. Public
phones use calling cards, which can be purchased at the post office,
newsstands, and hotels.

COMING ASHORE
Smaller ships may be able to dock at two cruise-ship docks in Korčula
Town, but larger vessels will have to anchor and tender passengers
ashore at the same dock. The dock area is lined with stores, cafés, and
tourism offices. If you are staying in town, there's no advantage to hav-
ing a car for your day in port. If you'd like to explore the island, you
can rent a car, scooter, or even a bicycle. Expect to pay about €55 per
day for a compact manual vehicle. Guided tours can also be arranged,
including visits to local vineyards.

Korčula Island

Neretvanski kanal

PELJEŠAC

Orebić
Kučište
Žrnovo
Lumbarda

Korčula Town
see detail
map

Korčulanski kanal

Prigradica
Babina
Račišće
Pupnat

KORČULA

Čara
Zavalatica

Vela Luka
Blato
Brna

Scedro

Lastovski kanal

Lastovo
Lastovo

Ublji

4 miles

6 km

0

0

Korčula Town

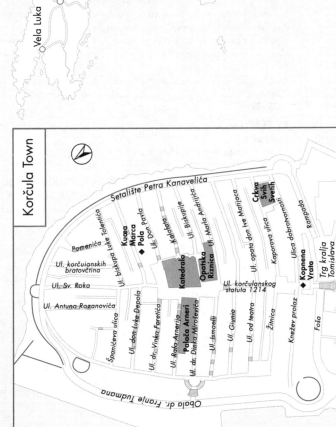

Šetalište Petra Kanavelića

Pomenića
Ul. biskupa Luke Tolentića
Ul. korčulanskih bratovčtina
Ul. Sv. Roka
Ul. Antuna Rozanovića

Španićeva ulica
Ul. don Luke Depola
Ul. dra Vinka Foretića
Ul. Rafa Arneri

Palača Arneri
Ul. dr. Dinka Mirošević

Obala dr. Franje Tuđmana

Kuca Marca Pola
♦ Pola Pavla

Ul. Don Pavla
Kaldata
Ul. Biskupie
Ul. Marka Andrijica

Katedrala

Opatska Riznica

Ul. Ismoelli
Ul. Giunio
Ul. od teatra

Ul. korčulanskog
statuta 1214

Ul. opata don Ive Matijaca
Kaporova ulica
Ulica dobrovrnosti

Crkva Svih Svetih

Rampada

Žrnica

Knežev prolaz

♦ **Kopnena Vrata**

Foša

Trg kralja
Tomislava

EXPLORING KORČULA TOWN

At first view, Korčula may seem like a much smaller version of Dubrovnik: the same high walls, the circular corner fortresses, and the church tower projecting from within an expanse of red roofs. The main difference lies in the town plan, as narrow side streets run off the main thoroughfare at odd angles to form a herringbone pattern, preventing cold winter winds from whistling unimpeded through town. The center is small and compact, and can be explored in an hour.

Katedrala (*Cathedral*). On the main square, the splendid Gothic-Renaissance cathedral is built from a wheat-colored stone that turns pale gold in sunlight, amber at sunset. Enter through the beautifully carved Romanesque main portal, which is guarded by Adam and Eve standing upon twin lions. Inside, check out the elegant 15th-century ciborium; within, two paintings are attributed to the Venetian master Tintoretto. ⊠ *Trg Sv Marka* 🕮 *15 Kn* ⊙ *May.–Sept., Mon.–Sat. 9 am–7 pm; Nov.–Apr., by appointment.*

Kopnena Vrata (*Land Gate*). The main entrance into the Old Town is topped by the 15th-century Revelin Tower, housing an exhibition connected with the *Moreška* sword dance, and offering panoramic views over the Old Town. ⊠ *Kopnena Vrata* 🕮 *15 Kn* ⊙ *July and Aug., daily 9–9; May, June, and Sept., daily 10–2 and 4–8; Nov.–Apr., by appointment only.*

Kuća Marca Pola (*Marco Polo House*). A couple of blocks east of the main square is the place where the legendary 13th-century discoverer is said to have been born, when Korčula was part of the Venetian Empire. At present only the tower is open, with a modest exhibition about Polo's life on the first floor and a belvedere up top offering panoramic views. There are plans to restore the entire house and garden to form an educational museum, though this project is unlikely to be realized in the near future. ⊠ *Ul Marka Pola* 🕮 *020/716–529* 🕮 *20 Kn* ⊙ *Apr.–June and Sept.–Oct., daily 9 am–3 pm; July–Aug., daily 9–9* ⊙ *Closed Nov.–Mar.*

Opatska Riznica (*Abbot's Treasury*). Next to the cathedral, the treasury museum occupies the 17th-century Renaissance bishop's palace. This collection of sacred art includes Italian and Croatian Renaissance paintings, the most precious being a 15th-centruy triptych, *Our Lady with Saints*, by the Dalmatian master Blaž Jurjev Trogiranin, plus gold and silver ecclesiastical artifacts and ceremonial vestments. ⊠ *Trg Sv Marka* 🕮 *25 Kn* ⊙ *May.–Sept., Mon.–Sat. 9 am–7 pm; Nov.–Apr., by appointment.*

KORČULA BEST BETS

Search for Marco Polo. The explorer's purported birthplace is right in the Old Town.

Sip some wine. Korčula is a major wine-producing region in Dalmatia; have a glass or buy a bottle of one of the local vintages.

Watch the Dance of the Moors. If your ship remains in port on one of the nights the island's famous dance is offered, this is a must-do.

SHOPPING

Cukarin. This family-run store is renowned for its five different types of delicious handmade biscuits, as well as roasted almonds and home-made *rakija* flavored with local herbs. ⊠ *Hrvatska Bratske Zajednice* ☎ *020/711–055* ⊕ *www.cukarin.hr.*

SPORTS AND ACTIVITIES

DIVING

MM Sub. MM Sub is a diving center based in Lumbarda offering diving instruction and trips for those with some experience. Nearby diving destinations include an underwater archaeological site, as well as several sea caves and shipwrecks. ⊠ *Lumbarda* ☎ *020/712–321* ⊕ *www. mm-sub.hr.*

MOREŠKA DANCES

The Moreška is a colorful sword dance originally performed each year on July 29 (the feast day of the town's protector, St. Theodore). Now it's performed at 9 pm each Monday and Thursday evening from May to October just outside the city walls (tickets 100 Kn), next to the Kopnena Vrata (Land Gate). The word *Moreška* means "Moorish." The dance is said to celebrate the victory of the Christians over the Moors in Spain, but the dance's real roots are conjecture. The dance itself is not native to Croatia, and was performed in many different Mediterranean countries, including Spain, Italy, and Malta. The story of the dance is a clash between the Black (Moorish) king and the White (Christian) king over a young maiden. The dance is done with real swords.

BEACHES

The closest spot for a quick swim is Banje, a small pebble beach about 10 minutes on foot east of the town walls, close to Hotel Liburnija. For more leisurely bathing, the best beaches lie near the village of **Lumbarda,** which is 6 km (4 miles) southeast of Korčula Town. The most popular of these is the sandy south-facing Przina, 2 km (1 mile) south of Lumbarda, while the smooth-white-stoned Bili Žal lies a short distance east of Lumbarda.

WHERE TO EAT

$$$$
EASTERN
EUROPEAN
Fodor's Choice
★

✕ **Adio Mare.** A long-standing favorite with locals and visitors alike, Adio Mare occupies a Gothic-Renaissance building in the Old Town, close to Kuća Marca Pola. There's a high-ceiling dining room, an open-plan kitchen so you can watch the cooks while they work, plus an open-air terrace. The menu has not changed since the restaurant opened in 1974: expect Dalmatian classics such as *pašta-fažol* (beans with pasta) and *pašticada* (beef stewed in wine and prunes), as well as fresh fish and seafood. The local wine, *pošip,* is excellent. ■ **TIP→ This restaurant is particularly popular, so reservations are strongly recommended, especially in August.** ⑤ *Average main: 120 Kn* ⊠ *Sv. Roka 2* ☎ *020/711–253* ☉ *Closed Nov.–Mar.*

$$$$
MEDITERRANEAN
$$$$ ✕ **Konoba Mate.** In the courtyard of an old stone cottage in the village of
MEDITERRANEAN Pupnat (21 miles west of Korčula Town, so you'll need to hire a car or
take a taxi), this welcoming eatery serves gourmet fare prepared from
the family's own farm. The menu changes with the seasons, but look
out for the house specialty, a platter of *pršut* (prosciutto), goat's cheese,
olives, and eggplant pâté, which you might follow with *pašticada* (beef
stewed in sweet wine and prunes, served with gnocchi) as a main.
There's also an excellent wine list, though the house wine, served by
the carafe, is a better value and is extremely palatable. $ *Average main:
110 Kn* ✉ *Pupnat bb* ☎ *020/717–109* ◷ *Closed Sun. lunch.*

KOTOR, MONTENEGRO

Updated by
Jane Foster

Located in Bokor Kotorska (Kotor Bay), Europe's most southerly fjord,
Kotor lies 50 miles (80 km) west of Podgorica, the capital of Montenegro, from which it is separated by a belt of dramatic, rugged mountains. Listed as a UNESCO World Heritage site, Kotor's medieval Stari
Grad (Old Town) is enclosed within well-preserved defensive walls built
between the 9th and 18th centuries and presided over by a proud hilltop
fortress. In the Middle Ages, as Serbia's chief port, Kotor was an important economic and cultural center with its own highl -regarded schools
of stone-masonry and iconography. Later, it spent periods under the
control of Venice, Austria, and France, though it was undoubtedly the
Venetians who left the strongest impression on the city's architecture.
Since the breakup of Yugoslavia, some 70% of the stone buildings in the
romantic Old Town have been snapped up by foreigners. Fast becoming
a celebrity destination, it's been visited recently by such celebrities as
Catherine Zeta-Jones and Michael Douglas.

ESSENTIALS
CURRENCY
The euro (despite the fact that Montenegro has not yet entered the
European Union).

HOURS
Offices are open weekdays from 8 to 4. Shops are generally open weekdays from 9 to 9, Saturday from 8 to 1, though some shut for lunch
around 2 and may close for as long as three hours. Banks stay open
weekdays from 9 to 7, Saturday from 9 to 1.

PRIVATE TOURS
Many private travel agencies offer tours, with hiking in the mountains
and rafting on the Tara River being the most popular. Meridian DMC
runs rafting trips on the Tara River as well as sightseeing excursions to
points of interest like Kotor Bay and Dubrovnik.

Contacts Meridian DMC ✉ *Stari Grad 436* ☎ *032/323–448*
⊕ *www.meridiandmc.me.*

TELEPHONES
The country code for Montenegro is 382.

Kotor Old Town

River Škuda

Citadella

Zgrada Napoleonovog pozorišta

Kneževa palata

Glavna Gradska Vrata

Gradske Zidine

Boka Kotorska

Trg. Bla_ene Ozane

Tvrdjava Sv Ivana

Crkva Sv Nikole

Trg. Bratsva Jedinstva

Crkva Sv Luke

Narodni Odbor

Toranj za sat

Trg od Oržja

Palata Bisanti

Pomorski Muzej Crne Gore

Trg. Bokeljske Mornarice

Trg. Pubune Mornara

Katedrala Sv Tripuna

Skaljarski Trg.

BOSNIA-HERZEGOVINA

Zabljak

Mojkovac

N.P. Biogradsko

Niksic

MONTENEGRO

Dubrovnik

Perast

CROATIA

Kotor

Cetinje

Podgorica

ALBANIA

Boka Kotrsko

Skadarsko Jezero

Adriatic Sea

Shkodër

Ulcinj

0   20 miles
0   30 km

COMING ASHORE

Arriving at Kotor from the water is an impressive experience in itself, so be sure to be up on the deck in advance. Your ship will sail up a 28-km (18-mile) long bay (often referred to as a fjord), with rugged mountains rising in the background. Cruise ships dock on the quay, immediately in front of Kotor's medieval walled Old Town. Since the Old Town is compact and pedestrian-friendly, you do not need to rent a car in Kotor. It's easy to reach nearby Perast by bus or taxi.

EXPLORING KOTOR

Kotor's Old Town takes approximately half a day to explore. Plan your visit for the morning, when the main sights are open to the public and the afternoon sun has yet to reach peak force.

Crkva Sveti Luke (*St. Luke's Church*). Built in 1195, this delightful Romanesque church is the only building in the Old Town to have withstood all five major earthquakes that affected Kotor. Originally a Catholic church, the building later became an Orthodox place of worship. Today there are two altars, one for each faith. ■ TIP→ **The church is generally closed but you can ask at the nearby Crkva Sveti Nikole, which is open daily 8–1 and 5–7, and someone will open it for you.** ⊠ *Trg bratstvo i jedinstva.*

Crkva Sveti Nikole (*St. Nicholas' Church*). Designed by a Russian architect and built in pseudo-Byzantine style between 1902 and 1909, this is Kotor's most important Orthodox church (the Cathedral, by definition, is Catholic). The gold used to gild the spires was a gift from Russia. ⊠ *Trg bratstvo i jedinstva* ⊗ *Daily 8–1 and 5–7.*

Glavna Gradska Vrata. The Main Town Gate (also known as the Sea Gate because of its position on the coast), which accesses the Stari Grad (Old Town) via the western facade of the city walls, dates back to the 16th century, and comprises Renaissance and baroque details.

KOTORS BEST BETS

Kotor Old Town. Roam the car-free streets of this centuries-old fortified town, now a UNESCO World Heritage site.

St John's Fortress. Follow Kotor's medieval walls uphill to arrive at this small fort, affording magnificent views of the Old Town and the bay below.

Our Lady of the Rock. Take a boat ride across the bay from Perast to visit a tiny islet, capped by a church.

Originally, the outer gate bore a relief of the Venetian Lion, but in Tito's time this was replaced by the socialist star and dates recording the liberation of Kotor on November 21, 1944, at the end of WWII. There are two other entrances to the Stari Grad: the Južna Vrata (South Gate) and the Sjeverna Vrata (North Gate). ⊠ *Jadranski put.*

Gradske Zidine (*Town Walls*). Especially beautiful at night, when they are illuminated, the well-preserved town walls were built between the 9th and 18th centuries. They measure almost 5 km (3 miles) in length, and reach up to 66 feet in height and 52 feet in width. They form a triangular defense system around the Old Town, then rise up the hill behind it to Tvrdjava Sveti Ivana (St. John's Fortress), 853 feet above sea level. You can walk up to the fortress along the walls. Allow at least one hour to get up and back down. Wear good hiking shoes and don't forget to bring some water. ⊠ *Old Town, Stari Grad.*

Katedrala Sveti Tripuna (*St. Tryphon's Cathedral*). Undoubtedly Kotor's finest building, the Romanesque cathedral dates back to 1166, though excavation work shows that there was already a smaller church here in the 9th century. Due to damage caused by a succession of disastrous earthquakes, the cathedral has been rebuilt several times—the twin baroque bell towers were added in the late 17th century. Inside, the most important feature is the 14th-century Romanesque Gothic ciborium above the main altar. Also look out for fragments of 14th-century frescoes, which would once have covered the entire interior. A collection of gold and silver reliquaries, encasing body parts of various saints and crafted by local masters between the 14th and 18th century, is on display in the treasury. ⊠ *Trg Ustanka Mornara* ☏ *032/322–315* 🖃 *€1 (treasury)* ⊗ *May–Oct., daily 7–7; Nov.–Apr., daily 9–2.*

Pomorski Muzej Crne Gore (*Montenegrin Naval Museum*). Housed within the 18th-century baroque Grgurina Palace, this museum traces Montenegro's cultural and economic ties to the sea. In the 18th century, tiny Kotor had some 400 ships sailing the world's oceans. The exhibition

extends over three floors, and includes model ships; paintings of ships, ship owners, and local naval commanders; navigation equipment; and uniforms worn by Montenegrin admirals and captains. ⊠ *Trg Grgu-rina, Stari Grad* ☎ *032/304–720* ⊕ *www.museummaritimum.com* 🖾 *€4* ⊙ *Jul.–Aug., Mon.–Sat. 8 am–11 pm, Sun. 10 am–4 pm; May–June and Sept., Mon.–Sat. 8 am–6 pm, Sun. 9 am–1 pm; Oct.–Apr., weekdays 9 am–5 pm, weekends 9 am–noon.*

Toranj za sat (*Clock Tower*). Built in the 17th century and considered a symbol of Kotor, the Clock Tower stands directly opposite the Main City Gate. You'll still find a watchmaker's shop at ground level (locals claim that the same family of watchmakers have worked here since the 17th century). In front of the Clock Tower, the "Pillar of Shame" was used to subject local criminals to public humiliation. ⊠ *Trg od Oržja, Stari Grad.*

Trg od Oržja (*Square of Arms*). The Main Town Gate leads directly into the Square of Arms, Kotor's main square, today a large paved space animated by popular open-air cafés. Under Venice, arms were repaired and stored here, hence the name. Notable buildings on the square include the 17th-century **Toranj za Sat** (Clock Tower), the 19th-century **Napoleonovog Pozorišta** (Napoléon Theater), and the 18th-century **Kneževa Palata** (Duke's Palace), the latter two now forming part of the upmarket Hotel Cattaro. ⊠ *Trg od Oržja, Stari Grad.*

★ **Tvrdjava Sveti Ivana** (*St. John's Fortress*). On the hill behind Kotor, 853 feet above sea level, this fortress is approached via a series of serpentines and some 1,300 steps. The fantastic view from the top makes the climb worthwhile: the terra-cotta-tile rooftops of the Old Town, the meandering fjord, and the pine-clad mountains beyond. On the way up, you will pass the tiny Crkva Gospe od Zdravlja (Church of Our Lady of Health), built in the 16th century to protect Kotor against the plague. Be sure to wear good walking shoes and take plenty of water. The route up starts from behind the east side of the city walls. ⊠ *Above Old Town.*

PERAST

Lying 8 miles (13 km) northwest of Kotor, the peaceful little town of Perast is made up of semiabandoned stone houses built by local sea captains during the 17th and 18th centuries. In the bay in front of Perast lie two charming islets, each with a church.

★ **Gospa od Skrpjela** (*Our Lady of the Rock*). Unlike its sibling island, St. George, this island is man-made. Folklore has it that in 1452, local sailors found an icon depicting the Virgin and Child cast upon a rock jutting up from the water. Taking this as a sign from God, they began placing stones on and around the rock, slowly building an island over it. By 1630 they had erected a church upon the new island. The original icon (which has been attributed to the 15th-century local artist Lovro Dobričević) is displayed on the altar. Over the centuries, locals have paid their respects to it by donating silver votive offerings, some 2,500 of which are now on display. To get here, hop a boat taxi from the waterfront (a five-minute trip). ⊠ *Kotor Bay, Perast* ☎ *032/373–753 for Kotor tourist office information* ⊕ *www.gospa-od-skrpjela.me* 🖾 *€1* ⊙ *May–mid-Nov., daily 9–7; mid-Nov.–Apr. by appointment.*

Muzej Grad Perasta. In the 17th-century Renaissance-baroque Bujović Palace, on the water's edge, Muzej Grad Perasta (Perast Town Museum) displays paintings of local sea captains and their ships, plus a horde of objects connected to Perast's maritime past. ⊠ *Obala Marka Martinovića bb, Perast* ☎ *032/373–519* ⊕ *www.muzejperast.me* ⊠ *€2.50* ⊘ *July–Aug., Mon.–Sat. 9–7, Sun. 9–2; May–June and Sept., Mon.–Sat. 9–5, Sun. 9–2; Oct.–Apr., daily 8–2.*

Sveti Djordje (*St. George*). This natural islet is one of Perast's famous pair of islands. It's ringed by a dozen elegant cypress trees and crowned by the Monastery of St. George, dating back to the 12th century and still inhabited by monks. In the 18th century the island became a favorite burial place for local sea captains, whose crypts remain today. ■ TIP➔ The island is closed to the public, but you can snap photos from shore or neighboring Our Lady of the Rock to your heart's content. ⊠ *Kotor Bay, Perast.*

SHOPPING

Market. This market that sells fruit and vegetables is just outside the city walls, on the main coastal road, and is filled with colorful, local, seasonal produce: artichokes, asparagus, and cherries in spring; tomatoes, eggplants, and peaches in summer. It takes place every morning but Sunday. ⊠ *E65 runs all the way down the coast. The market is on the road side, immediately outside the old town walls.*

BEACHES

The small, pebble **town beach,** which is close to the center, is fine for a quick swim; however, for really decent swimming, locals recommend either **Jaz Beach** or **Plavi Horizonti,** both of which are some 14 miles (23 km) south of Kotor, between Tivat and Budva.

WHERE TO EAT

$$$$
SEAFOOD
✕ **Galion.** A five-minute walk along the coast from the Old Town, this sophisticated seafood restaurant occupies an old stone building with a glass-and-steel extension overlooking the bay, offering views of Kotor's medieval walls. Expect funky modern furniture and chill-out music, and a menu featuring favorites such as octopus salad, homemade gnocchi, and barbecued fresh fish. ⑤ *Average main: €24* ⊠ *Šuranj bb* ☎ *032/325–054* ⊕ *www.hotelvardar.com* ⊘ *Closed Nov.–Mar.*

$
EASTERN
EUROPEAN
✕ **Kantun.** Locals swear by this friendly, down-to-earth eatery in the Old Town, on a small piazza near the Montenegrin Naval Museum. The menu features a choice of seafood and meat dishes, but ask the waiter to recommend the day's special, which could be anything from *gulaš* (Hungarian goulash) to *sarma* (cabbage leaves stuffed with rice and minced meat). Get a table outside in summer and soak in the Old Town atmosphere, though note that service can be slow when they're busy. The restaurant is open year-round. ⑤ *Average main: €8* ⊠ *Trg od Muzeja bb* ☎ *032/325–757* ▭ *No credit cards.*

KUŞADASI, TURKEY (FOR EPHESUS)

The central and southern Aegean is probably the most developed area of Turkey, and the rolling hills, mountains surrounded by clear blue seas, and glorious white-sand beaches are just a few of the reasons why. Wandering through historic ruins, boating, scuba diving, basking in the Anatolian sun, and eating fresh fish are just some of the ways you can fill your day. Kuşadası itself is the most developed resort along the coast. Surrounding the tiny, atmospheric Old Town, a brash, very touristy development replete with tacky pubs and fish-and-chips restaurants has mushroomed in the last 20 years. On a positive note, Kuşadası is the stepping-stone to some of Turkey's most important ancient sites, including Ephesus and the early Christian site of Meryemana. Kuşadası also offers excellent shopping in high-class goods.

ESSENTIALS

CURRENCY
The Turkish lira.

HOURS
Most shops are open daily from 9 until 9. Attractions are open daily from 8 to 5 or 6, though some are closed on Monday.

PRIVATE TOURS
Having a private guide in Ephesus can be useful, and there are local companies that can arrange this in advance. Unlicensed guides will be available at the sight, but they may not be very helpful or accurate.

Contacts Kuşadası Tours. ⊠ *Candan Turhan Bulvarı, 104/1–2* ☎ *256/614–1282, 1–866/921–0299 toll-free from U.S.* ⊕ *www.kusadasitours.com.*

TELEPHONES
Most tri- and quad-band GSM phones will work in Turkey, but the Turkish mobile system is not 3G-compatible, and handsets are single band. Public phones accept tokens or telephone cards, phones accepting cards will also accept credit cards in payment for calls. Tokens and cards can be purchased at newsstands and telepcom shops. Turk Telekom, Turkcell, and Telcim are the major telecom companies.

COMING ASHORE
Boats dock at the Ephesus town port. The passenger cruise terminal, Scala Nuova, has international shops such as Body Shop, plus a Starbucks and a Burger King. There is also a duty-free shop for reboarding passengers. From the dock it's a short walk of a few minutes to the port gate and into the town directly beyond, with immediate access to taxis, car rental offices, shops, and restaurants.

The public bus service from Kuşadası to the site at Ephesus and into Selçuk (the town near to Ephesus) is cheap and quick. *Dolmuş* (15-seat minivans) are the bulk of the fleet, and they depart from the bus terminus at Süeyman Demirel Boulevard, a 20-minute walk from the port. There are several services every hour except in mid-afternoon, when services drop to a couple per hour. Journey time is around 15 minutes. Most services stop at the end of the entry road to the archaeological site, leaving passengers with a 10-minute walk to the site entrance.

Ephesus

Selçuk-Ephesus Rd.

St. John Basilica

TO İZMİR

Atatürk Cad.

Cengiz Topel Cad.

Train Station

Isa Bey Cami

St. Jean Sok.

Turgut Reis Cad.

Agora Çarşısı

SELÇUK

Temple of Artemis

Gymnasium of Vedius

Ephesus Müzesi [i]

1 Spor Sahası Sok.

2 Spor Sahası Sok.

3 Spor Sahası Sok.

Stadium

Byzantine Wall

TO ANCIENT HARBOR

P

Graves of the Seven Sleepers

E-87

▲ Mt. Pion

Gymnasium

EPHESUS

Byzantine Wall

Arcadian Way

Theater

Byzantine Wall

Marble Ave.

Agora

Temple of Serapis

Street of Kuretes

Brothel

Library of Celsus

Temple of Hadrian

1/4 mi

1/4 km

Temple of Domitian

Nymphaion

Prytaneion

Odeon

State Agora

E-87

Upper Entrance & Ticket Office

Magnesian Gate

Bülbül Dağ

▲ Mt. Koressos

Meryemana

KEY	
[i]	Tourist Information
P	Parking

Kuşadasi

Atatürk Bul.

TO EPHESUS AND SELÇUK

Ünlü S.

K. Arıkan C.

Sevinç S.

Liman C.

Kışla S.

Bahçearası S.

Güvercinada C.

[i]

Barbaros Hayrettin Paşa Bul.

Bazkurt S.

İsmet İnönü Blvd.

50 YIL C.

Bezirgan S.

Kıbrıs C.

Genoese Castle

Sağlık C.

Sabucalı S.

Burç Sokak

Rıfat Arın S.

Zeki Aydınlı S.

Kervansaray

Aydınlık S.

Aslanlar C.

Kahramanlar C.

Mülgen S.

Candan Tarhan Bul.

Tepe S.

İmam S.

Güzel S.

Anıl S.

Altın S.

Yıldırım C.

Barlar S.

Zafer S.

Sarı S.

Adnan Menderes Blvd.

Özgür S.

Öztürk S.

Sülün S.

Taxis are plentiful, and they are metered with prices fixed by the municipality. Check that the meter is set to the day (lower) tariff. There are also numerous tour companies that can provide day tours to surrounding attractions. You can make these arrangements in travel agencies in Kuşadası.

Renting a car would allow you to have a full day of sightseeing and to tailor a schedule to your own desires. Car-rental companies are plentiful. Car rental is approximately $70 per day for a compact manual vehicle. You will be quoted a rate in dollars and can pay in dollars.

> ## KUŞADASI BEST BETS
>
> **Kuretes Street, Ephesus.** Follow in the footsteps of millions of Roman citizens and celebrity visitors, including St. Paul of Tarsus.
>
> **The Terrace House, Ephesus.** Venture inside this house to catch a glimpse of high-class interior design, circa the 2nd century AD.
>
> **Ephesus Museum, Selçuk.** Monumental archaeological treasures vie with personal items for prize of best artifact.

EXPLORING KUŞADASI, SELÇUK, AND EPHESUS

KUŞADASI

One of the most popular resort towns in the southern Aegean, Kuşadası is an ideal base, geographically, from which to explore the surrounding area. Unfortunately, being popular isn't always easy, and Kuşadası long ago lost its local charm. The huge yacht marina, the largest in the region, has only exacerbated the situation. What was a small fishing village up until the 1970s is now a sprawling, hyperactive town packed with curio shops and a year-round population of around 60,000, which swells several times over in summer with the influx of tourists and Turks with vacation homes.

Genoese castle. There aren't many sights in Kuşadası proper, but the causeway off Kadınlar Plajı (Women's Beach), just south of the harbor, connects the town to an old Genoese castle on Güvercin Adası (Pigeon Island). Today the site of a popular disco and several teahouses with gardens and sea views, the fortress was home to three Turkish brothers in the 16th century. These infamous pirates—Barbarossa, Oruc, and Hayrettin—pillaged the coasts of Spain and Italy and sold passengers and crews from captured ships into slavery in Algiers and Constantinople. Rather than fight them, Süleyman the Magnificent (ruled 1520–66) hired Hayrettin as his grand admiral and set him loose on enemies in the Mediterranean. The strategy worked: Hayrettin won victory after victory and was heaped with honors and riches.

Kervansaray. Kuşadası's 300-year-old kervansaray, now the Hotel Club Kervansaray, is loaded with Ottoman atmosphere. Its public areas are worth a look even if you're not staying here. ⌧ *Atatürk Bulvarı 1.*

SELÇUK

20 km (12 miles) northeast of Kuşadasý on Rte. 515.

Selçuk, the closest city to the archaelogical site of Ephesus, lies beneath an ancient fortress, and is, unfortunately, often overlooked. The former

farming town has interesting sights of its own to offer—St. John the Evangelist was purportedly buried here, and the city has one of the oldest mosques in Turkey.

İsa Bey Cami (*İsa Bey Mosque*). İsa Bey Cami is one of the oldest mosques in Turkey, dating from 1375. The jumble of architectural styles suggests a transition between Seljuk and Ottoman design: like later-day Ottoman mosques, this one has a courtyard, not found in Seljuk mosques. The structure is built out of "borrowed" stone: marble blocks with Latin inscriptions, Corinthian columns, black-granite columns from the baths at Ephesus, and pieces from the altar of the Temple of Artemis. ⊠ *St. John Sok.* ⊙ *Daily 9–6.*

St. John Basilica. The emperor Justinian built the St. John Basilica over a 2nd-century tomb on Ayasoluk Hill, believed by many to have once held the body of St. John the Evangelist. Eleven domes formerly topped the basilica, which rivaled Istanbul's Aya Sofya (Haghia Sophia) in scale. The barrel-vaulted roof collapsed after a long-ago earthquake, but the church is still an incredible sight, with its labyrinth of halls and marble courtyards. It provides beautiful views both of Selçuk's castle and the Plain of Ephesus. ⊠ *Entrance off St. John Sok., just east of İsa Bey Cami* ⊙ *Daily 8–5.*

EPHESUS

Ephesus Archaelogical Site. The ruins of Ephesus, once the most important Greco-Roman city of the Eastern Mediterranean, is one of the best preserved ancient sites in the world. Today, modern travelers can trace the fault lines of ancient civilization in Ephesus's spectacular landscape of ruined temples, theaters, and colonnaded streets. There are two entrances to the site, which is on a hill, one at the top of the site and one at the bottom. The main avenue is about a mile long but there are a number of intriguing detours, so a minimum visit of two hours can easily stretch to four, not including an hour in the museum in town.

The road leading to the upper entrance of the site passes a 1st-century AD **stadium,** where chariot and horse races were held on a track 712 feet long, and where gladiators and wild beasts met in combat before 70,000 spectators. On the left-hand side after you enter the site from the upper entrance is a 25,000-seat **theater,** backed by the western slope of Mt. Pion. Construction on this huge semicircle, with row upon row of curved benches, was begun by Alexander's general, Lysimachus, and completed by emperors Claudius and Trajan in the 2nd century AD. There is a fine view from the top of the steps. Higher still, near the top of Mt. Pion, are vestiges of the city's Byzantine walls. The theater is used for music and dance performances each May during the Selçuk Ephesus Festival of Culture and Art. Leading away from the theater toward the ancient port, now a marsh, is the **Arcadian Way.** This 1,710-foot-long street was once lined with shops and covered archways. Only a long line of slender marble columns remains.

In front of the theater is Marble Avenue. Follow it to the beautiful, two-story **Library of Celsus.** The courtyard of this much-photographed building is backed by wide steps that climb to the reading room, where you can still see rolls of papyrus. The library is near Marble Avenue's intersection

with the **Curetes Street,** a still-impressive thoroughfare named for the college of priests once located there. At this corner is a large house believed to have been a **brothel.** Look for the floor mosaics of three women. To the right along the street are the **terrace houses** the multistoried houses of the nobility, with terraces and courtyards—there is a separate entrance fee to the terrace houses but the elaborate housing complexes of the Ephesian bourgeoisie are very interesting. A block from the brothel is the facade of the **Temple of Hadrian,** with four Corinthian columns and a serpent-headed hydra above the door to keep out evil spirits; beyond is a partially restored fountain dedicated to the emperor Trajan. The street then forks and opens into a central square that once held the **Prytaneion,** or town hall; the Nymphaion, a small temple decked with fountains; and the **Temple of Domitian,** on the south side of the square, which was once a vast sanctuary with a colossal statue of the emperor for whom it was named. All are now a jumble of collapsed walls and columns.

Returning to the Street of Kuretes, turn right to reach the **odeon,** an intimate semicircle with just a few rows of seats, where spectators would listen to poetry readings and music. Columns mark the northern edge of the state agora (market). Beyond, the Magnesian Gate (also known as the Manisa Gate), at the end of the street, was the starting point for a caravan trail and a colonnaded road to the Temple of Artemis. ⊠ *Site entry 4 km (2½ miles) west of Selçuk on Selçuk–Ephesus Rd.* ☎ *232/892–6010* ⊘ *mid-Apr.–mid-Oct., daily 8:30–7; mid-Oct.–mid-Apr., daily 8:30–5:30.*

Graves of the Seven Sleepers. According to the legend attached to the Graves of the Seven Sleepers, seven young Christian men hid in a cave to avoid persecution by the Romans in the 3rd century AD. They fell into a sleep that lasted 200 years, waking only after the Byzantine Empire had made Christianity the official state religion. When they died, they were buried here, and a church was built over them. The tombs in the large cemetery are largely from the Byzantine era. ⊠ *South of Sor Sahasi Sok. 3* 🎫 *Free.*

SHOPPING

The downtown cores of Kuşadası and Selçuk offer excellent shopping opportunities, though prices and quality vary enormously. Generally, Turkey offers an exceptional range of handicrafts in all price ranges, but is most famed for its hand-woven carpets and kilims in a range of sizes and patterns. The finest are made of silk threads, but more common is cotton or wool. Other traditional wares include items with worked brass and copper articles such as large pots and ornate tables, ceramics, marble items, inlaid wooden articles including jewelry boxes and chess sets, or leatherwear fashioned into bags, shoes, or clothing. For a truly exotic gift, take home a genuine *nargile* (hubble-bubble pipe), or a blue glass *boncuk,* a talisman said to ward off the evil eye.

Kuşadası also has several excellent jewelry shops selling gold, precious stones, and modern jewelry and designer watches at competitive prices. Don't forget to haggle over the price of your souvenirs; never pay the first price asked, whatever you want to buy.

BEACHES

There are many fine beaches around Kuşadası, and these are also served by dolmuş buses.

WHERE TO EAT

$ ✗ **Ejder Restaurant.** This popular spot overlooking the Selçuk aqueduct
TURKISH is run by Mehmet and his wife, the sole cook. It may sometimes take a while to get your food, but the traditional kebabs and Turkish specialties are well worth the wait. Mehmet takes pride in his guestbook filled with customers' comments, so make sure to add a few lines. ⓢ *Average main: 7 TL* ✉ *Cengiz Topel Cad. 9/E, Selçuk* ☎ *232/892–3296.*

$ ✗ **Öz Urfa.** The focus at this causal, 50-year-old spot is on kebabs and
TURKISH other Turkish fast food. The modest surroundings, including a pleasant terrace, are just off Barbaros Hayrettin Caddesi, the main thoroughfare. Alcohol is not served. ⓢ *Average main: 10 TL* ✉ *Cephane Sokak 7/A, Kuşadası* ☎ *256/612–9881* ⊕ *www.ozurfakebabs.com.*

LIMASSOL, CYPRUS

Updated by
Liz Humphreys

Cyprus, once a center for the cult of the Greek goddess Aphrodite, is a modern island nation that retains an essentially Mediterranean character. Its 3,572 square miles (about the size of Connecticut) encompass citrus and olive groves, pine-forested mountains, and some of Europe's cleanest beaches. Cyprus's strategic position as the easternmost island in the Mediterranean Sea has made it subject to regular invasions by powerful empires. Greeks, Phoenicians, Assyrians, Egyptians, Persians, Romans, Byzantines, the Knights Templar, Venetians, Ottomans and the British—all have either ruled or breezed through here. Vestiges of the diverse cultures that have ruled here dot the island, from remnants of Neolithic settlements and ancient Greek and Roman temple sites, to early Christian basilicas and painted Byzantine churches. But Cyprus isn't limited to its architecture and history; there's also a vibrant lifestyle to be explored.

ESSENTIALS
CURRENCY
The euro.

HOURS
Museum hours vary, so it pays to check ahead. Generally, museums tend to close on the early side, around 4 or 5 pm. Most ancient monuments are open from dawn to dusk, which means earlier closing times in the winter months. Many shops close at 2 pm on Wednesdays and Saturdays and are not open at all on Sundays.

PRIVATE TOURS
Licensed guides can be hired for half-day or evening (starting at €82.95) and full-day (€130.52) tours, with a 50% surcharge on Sundays; a list of licensed guides is available from the Cyprus Tourist Guides Association.

For more organized guided tours, Argonaftis (based in Limassol) leads day tours including an excursion from Limassol to Kourion, Kolossi

Castle, and Aphrodite's Rock; a "luxury grand tour" that visits the Troodos Mountains, Lefkara, the Kykkos Monastery, and a winery; and a day-trip to Nicosia and Lefkara. The company also offers such specialized tours as an Akamas jeep safari.

For wine lovers, Paphos Wine Tours offers half- or full-day trips in a comfortable air-conditioned van from Limassol to wineries in the Troodos Mountains, with optional stops at the Cyprus Wine Museum, Kolossi Castle, and Omodos; winery tours leaving from Paphos are also available (€50–€60 per person, including morning coffee and picnic lunch, from September to May).

Contacts Argonaftis Tours ☎ *25/586333* ⊕ *www.argonaftis.com.*
Cyprus Tourist Guides Association ☎ *22/765755* 🖷 *22766872*
⊕ *www.cytouristguides.com.* **Paphos Wine Tours** ☎ *99/158312, 99/158324*
⊕ *www.paphoswinetours.com.*

TELEPHONES
The country code for Cyprus is 357. GSM-based mobile phones work in Cyprus provided that they can operate at 900 or 1800 MHz. Some public phones accept Telecards, which can be purchased at post offices, banks, souvenir shops, and kiosks; others accept coins.

COMING ASHORE
Most cruise ships dock at the main port in Limassol, which is about 4 km (2½ miles) southwest of the downtown. This is a vast commercial enterprise, but has dedicated cruise berths and offers a shuttle to the passenger terminal. Here you'll find refreshments, tourist information, currency exchange, and a taxi station. Some cruise ships also call at Larnaca, but at this writing Limassol is the major cruise port.

If you want to explore independently, take a taxi or bus from the port into the downtown. Bus 30 takes about 15 minutes to reach downtown Limassol. Urban taxis have an initial charge of €3.42 (€4.36 at night) and then €0.73 per km in the daytime, €0.85 at night. The waiting time day-rate is €13.66 per hour. Urban taxi drivers are bound by law to run their meter, rural taxis are not, but if you engage a taxi in town it will be classed as an urban taxi.

To travel farther afield, consider taking a service taxi (four- to eight-seat minibus) run by Travel & Express. Service taxis link all major towns for a fixed fee; for instance, Limassol to Larnaca costs €9.90 Monday to Saturday and €11.80 on Sunday. Urban taxis are generally very cheap for local travel, but far more expensive than service taxis between towns. Buses are cheaper, with Limassol to Larnaca a single fare of €3, but they are slower than service taxis.

You can reach many interesting and ancient attractions in the surrounding Cypriot countryside if you rent a vehicle for the day. Car rentals are about €50 for a subcompact manual vehicle. There will be an extra charge for delivery to the port or pick-up in central Limassol.

Cyprus

Mediterranean Sea

Cape Andreas

KARPASIA PENINSULA

Famagusta Bay

Famagusta
Varosha
Cape Greco
Ayia Napa

Range

NORTHERN CYPRUS

Kyrenia

UN Buffer Zone

Larnaca
Kition
Kition

Nicosia

Dhali
Phikardou
Lefkara
Zygi

Lefkara

Kyrenia
Lapithos
Karavostasi
Lefkara
Kakopetria
Olympus

Pitsilia Foothills
A1

Cape Kormakiti

Morphou Bay

Cape Gata

Akrotiri Bay

Limassol
see detail map

Kolossi Castle
Cyprus Wine Museum
Kourion Archaeological site
Apollo Hylates

THE REPUBLIC OF CYPRUS

B9

Olympus
Pano Platres
Troodos Mts.
Laneia
Omodos

TROODOS

Ayios Neophytos Monastery

B7

Kathikas
Paphos
Tombs of the Kings
Petra tou Romiou

Episkopi Bay

AKAMAS PENINSULA

Khrysokhou Bay

Polis
Latchi
Kokkina

20 miles

30 km

Limassol

Limassol Zoo
Limassol
Zinas Kanther
Archaeological Museum
Folk Art Museum
Androu
Sp. Araouzou
Zinonos
Chr. Sozou
El. Palaiologinas
Vasileos Makedonos

Kariskaki
Agapinoros
Mesolongiou
Kolokotroni
Kapodistria
G. Malekidi
Ipeirou
Gladstonos
Ayias Zonis
Anexartisias

Leontiou Machaira
Agias Fylaxeos
Victoros Hugo
Naftliou

Gladstonos
Navarinou
Navarinou

Megalou Alexandrou
Vraxonisidon
Thermopylon
Trenis
Eleftherias

Athinon
Themidos
Sariipolou
Kitiou Kyprianou
Ellados
Enosis

Thessalonikis
Kanari
Eleftherias
Ay. Theklis

Limassol Castle
Tosifsa
Chr. Chatzipaulou
Spyrou Araouzou

Akrotiri Bay

1/8 mi
1/8 km

EXPLORING CYPRUS FROM LIMASSOL

LIMASSOL AND VICINITY

A major commercial port, cruise-ship port of call, and wine-making center on the south coast, Limassol, 75 km (47 miles) from Nicosia, is a bustling, cosmopolitan town. Luxury hotels, apartments, and guesthouses stretch along 12 km (7 miles) of seafront. In the center, the elegant, modern shops of Makarios Avenue contrast with those of the old part of town, where local handicrafts prevail.

Apollo Hylates. The Apollo Hylates (Sanctuary of Apollo of the Woodlands), an impressive archaeological site, stands 3 km (2 miles) west of the Temple of Kourion. It includes a partially restored main sanctuary with enormous Roman columns. ⊠ *Main Paphos Rd.* ☎ *25/991049* 🖾 *€1.70* ☉ *June–Aug., daily 8–7:30; Apr.–May and Sept.–Oct., daily 8–6; Nov.–Mar., daily 8–5.*

Fodor's Choice **Cyprus Wine Museum.** Located about 10 minutes west of Limassol in
★ the village of Erimi, this comprehensive museum succeeds at explaining the history of the grape in Cyprus, one of the oldest winemaking regions in the world. You'll get to view ancient wine jugs and vessels on a short guided tour of the museum and watch a film before heading downstairs for a sampling of Cyprus wines, including the island's famous sweet Commandaria, accompanied by tasty halloumi cheese. ⊠ *42 Paphou St., Erimi* ☎ *25/873808* ⊕ *www.cypruswinemuseum.com* 🖾 *€7* ☉ *Daily 9–5.*

★ **Kolossi Castle.** Kolossi Castle, a Crusader fortress of the Knights of St. John, was constructed in the 13th century and rebuilt in the 15th. Though there's not much left of the castle to see, it's worth a visit for the views from the rooftop of the surrounding vineyards, many of which produce Commandaria, the famous sweet wine of Cyprus. ⊠ *11 km (7 miles) west of Limassol, on the road to Paphos* ☎ *25/934907* 🖾 *€1.70* ☉ *June–Aug., daily 8–7:30; Apr.–May and Sept.–Oct., daily 8–6; Nov.–Mar., daily 8–5.*

Fodor's Choice **Kourion Archaeological Site.** The Kourion (Curium) Archaeological Site,
★ west of Limassol, has Greek and Roman ruins. Classical and Shakespearean plays are sometimes staged in the impressive amphitheater. Next to the theater is the Villa of Eustolios, a summerhouse built by a wealthy Christian with interesting mosaic floors from the 5th century AD; nearby is the partially rebuilt Roman stadium. ⊠ *19 km (12 miles) west of Limassol, Main Paphos Rd.* ☎ *25/934250* 🖾 *€1.70* ☉ *Jun.–Aug., daily 8–7:30; Apr.–May and Sept.–Oct., daily 8–6; Nov.–Mar., daily 8–5.*

★ **Limassol Castle.** The 14th-century Limassol Castle was built on the site of a Byzantine fortification. Richard the Lionheart married Berengaria of Navarre and crowned her Queen of England here in 1191. The **Cyprus Medieval Museum** in the castle displays medieval armor and relics. ⊠ *Richard and Berengaria Sts.* ☎ *25/305419* ⊕ *www.limassolmunicipal. com.cy* 🖾 *€3.40* ☉ *Tues.–Sat. 9–5, Sun. 10–1.*

Limassol District Archaeological Museum. Browse interesting archaeological finds from the Limassol area, including pottery, coins, jewelry, tools, and sculptures, from the Prehistoric period (10,000 BC)

up to the Late Roman period (AD 327). The collection also contains many items related to Aphrodite, including ancient terra-cotta figures. ⊠ *5 Anastasi Sioukri & Vyronos* ☎ *25/305157* ⊕ *www.limassolmunicipal.com.cy* 🖂 *€1.70* ⊘ *Mon. 8–2:30; Tues., Wed., Fri. 8–3; Thurs. 8–5; Sat. 9–3.*

🐣 **Limassol Zoo.** Reopened in the summer of 2012 after an extensive renovation, the zoo has modern enclosures that use only stone, glass, wood, and rope. Both kids and adults will enjoy the Asian otters, Cyprus oxes, Egyptian geese, and Cuban boa constrictors, among a good variety of other mammals, birds, and reptiles (though no lions, tigers, or elephants here). To see the animals in action, check the website for specific feeding times. ⊠ *Municipal Gardens* ☎ *25/581012* ⊕ *www.limassolzoo.com* 🖂 *€5* ⊘ *Jun.–Aug., daily 9–7; Apr.–May and Sept., daily 9–6; March and Oct., daily 9–5; Nov.–Dec., daily 9–4:30; Jan., daily 9–4.*

Municipal Folk Art Museum. For a glimpse of Cypriot folklore, visit the Municipal Folk Art Museum. The collection includes national costumes and fine examples of weaving and other crafts. ⊠ *Agiou Andreou 253* ☎ *25/362303* 🖂 *€2* ⊘ *Weekdays 8:30–3.*

LARNACA

51 km (32 miles) southeast of Nicosia, 66 km (41 miles) east of Limassol.

The seaside resort with its own airport has a flamboyant Whitsuntide celebration, called Cataklysmos, as well as fine beaches, a palm-fringed seaside promenade, and a modern harbor.

Fodor's Choice ★ **Ayios Lazarus.** In the town center stands one of the island's more important churches, Ayios Lazarus (Church of Lazarus), resplendent with gold icons and unique woodcarvings. Constructed in AD 890 by Byzantine Emperor Leo VI and restored to its glory in the 17th century, it is a beautiful example of Byzantine architecture. The church includes a fascinating crypt containing the sarcophagus of the Biblical Lazarus mentioned in Luke; Jesus is said to have resurrected Lazarus four days after his death, after which time Lazarus traveled to Kition (Larnaca's ancient city), where he became a bishop for 30 years. ⊠ *Plateia Agiou Lazarou* ☎ *24/652498* 🖂 *Free* ⊘ *Weekdays 8–12:30 and 2:30–5:30; weekends 8–5:30.*

★ **Hala Sultan Tekke.** On the edge of Salt Lake a mosque stands in an oasis of palm trees guarding the Hala Sultan Tekke—burial place of the prophet Muhammad's aunt Umm Haram, and an important Muslim shrine. ⊠ *Salt Lake* 🖂 *Free* ⊘ *Jun.–Aug., daily 8–7:30; Apr.–May and Sept.–Oct., daily 8–6; Nov.–Mar., daily 8–5.*

CYPRUS BEST BETS

Visit the mosaics of Paphos. Some of the finest Roman workmanship yet uncovered, they are an awe-inspiring sight.

Enjoy the galleries at Larnaca Museum. The museum is stuffed with ancient Greek and Roman artifacts, from monumental statues to precious jewelry to mundane kitchen utensils.

Browse for souvenirs at Lefkara. This whitewashed village has a vibrant Greek heartbeat.

3

Kition. Kition, the old Larnaca of biblical times, was one of the most important ancient city-kingdoms. Though most of the ruins are still buried beneath the modern city, you can see architectural remains of temples that date from the 13th century BC. ⊠ *Kyman St., north of Larnaca Museum* ☎ *24/304115* 🖃 *€1.70* ⊗ *Mon., Tues., Thurs., and Fri 8–2:30; Wed. 8–5.*

☉ **Larnaca Fort.** The Larnaca Fort was originally built in the late 1300s and then rebuilt in 1625; during British colonial rule, it was used as a prison. Today it's mainly worth visiting for the lovely views of the sea. The small **Medieval Museum** is inside the fort and has finds from Hala Sultan Tekke and Kition. ⊠ *Leoforos Athinon, within sight of marina on seafront* ☎ *24/304576* 🖃 *€1.70* ⊗ *Jun.–Aug., weekdays 9–7:30; Sept.–May, weekdays 9–5.*

Larnaca District Archaeological Museum. The Larnaca District Archaeological Museum displays treasures, including outstanding sculptures, pottery, and other architectural fragments from prehistoric times through to the Roman period. ⊠ *Plateia Kalograion* ☎ *24/304169* 🖃 *€1.70* ⊗ *Mon. 8–2:30; Tue., Thurs., and Fri. 8–3; Wed. 8–5; Sat. 9–3.*

☉ **Municipal Museum of Natural History.** If you'd like to learn more about the natural history of Cyprus, this small museum inside the Municipal Gardens is a must-see. Exhibits on geology, animals, birds, fossils, marine life, insects, plants, and more provide a worthy introduction to the vast array of island life, from the ancient past to the present day. ⊠ *Leoforos Grigori Afxentiou, inside the Municipal Gardens* ☎ *24/652569* 🖃 *€.50* ⊗ *Weekdays 9–4, Sat. 10–1.*

★ **Panayia Angeloktistos.** The 11th-century Panayia Angeloktistos church, 11 km (7 miles) south of Larnaca, has extraordinary Byzantine wall mosaics that date from the 6th and 7th centuries. ⊠ *Rte. B4, Kiti* ☎ *24/424646* 🖃 *Free* ⊗ *Sept.–May, daily 8–noon and 2–4; Jun.–Aug., daily 2–5:30.*

Pierides-Marfin Laiki Bank Museum. The Pierides–Marfin Laiki Bank Museum is a private assemblage of more than 3,000 pieces distinguished by its Bronze Age terra-cotta figures as well as Roman and Byzantine-era art. ⊠ *4 Zinonos Kitieos St., near Lord Byron St.* ☎ *24/814555* ⊕ *www.pieridesfoundation.com.cy* 🖃 *€2* ⊗ *Mon.–Thurs. 9–4, weekends 9–1.*

☉ **Salt Lake.** About 7 km (4 miles) southwest of Larnaca, near the airport, is the 6½-square-km (2½-square-mile) Salt Lake. In winter it's a refuge for migrating birds, especially flamingoes, and in summer it dries up with salt deposits. Though you can't walk on the lake itself, there are plenty of nature trails and picnic spots around it. ⊠ *Just off the airport road, 7 km (4 miles).*

Stavrovouni Monastery. On a mountain 40 km (25 miles) west of Larnaca stands the Stavrovouni (Mountain of the Cross) Monastery. It was founded by St. Helena in AD 326; the present buildings date from the 19th century. The views from here are splendid. Ideally, you should visit the monastery in a spirit of pilgrimage rather than sightseeing, out of respect for the monks. Only male visitors (no women) are allowed inside the monastery daily. ⊠ *Stavrovouni* ☎ *22/533630* 🖃 *Free* ⊗ *Apr.–Aug., 8–noon and 3–6; Sept.–Mar., 7–11 and 2–5.*

LEFKARA

40 km (25 miles) northwest of Larnaca, 64 km (40 miles) north of Limassol.

Some 40 km (25 miles) west of Larnaca, this picturesque village—one of the prettiest in Cyprus—is best known for its lace: Lefkaritika has been woven by hand here for centuries. Much of it is indeed beautiful, and most shopkeepers are willing to bargain. But considerably more evocative is the village itself, clustered on two hills and split between an upper portion, Kato Lefkara, and lower portion, Pano Lefkara. The tiny streets open up to a small plaza in front of the Church of the Holy Cross in Pano Lefkara, with a stupendous view of the surrounding sun-drenched hills.

TROODOS MOUNTAINS

20 km (25 miles) north of Limassol.

North of Limassol, these mountains, which rise to 6,500 feet, have shady cedar and pine forests and cool springs. Small, painted Byzantine churches in the Troodos and Pitsilia foothills are rich examples of a rare indigenous art form. Asinou Church, a UNESCO World Heritage site near the village of Nikitari, and Agios Nikolaos tis Stegis (St. Nicholas of the Roof), south of Kakopetria, are especially noteworthy.

Kykkos Monastery. At the Kykkos monastery, founded in 1100, the prized icon of the Virgin is reputed to have been painted by St. Luke; you can view the icon enclosed in a shrine, and the museum also includes other icons, woodcarvings, and embroidery. The monastery has been repeatedly destroyed by fire, and the current structure dates from 1831. ⊠ *20 km west of Pedoulas* ☎ *22/942435* ⊕ *www.kykkos-museum.cy.net* 🎫 *€5* ☽ *June–Oct., daily 10–6; Nov.–May, daily 10–4.*

PETRA TOU ROMIOU

20 km (12 miles) west of Limassol.

Fodor's Choice ★ **Petra tou Romiou.** The legendary birthplace of Aphrodite—Greek goddess of love and beauty—is a large offshore rock just off the main road between Limassol and Paphos. Swimming around Petra tou Romiou (Aphrodite's Rock) three times is purported to bring you eternal love. Whether or not you believe the legend, it's a dramatic place to stop for a snack or picnic lunch and a look at the unquestionably romantic views. Park in the lot and take the passageway under the highway to the large pebble beach, where you may be tempted to swim or stay for sunset. **Amenities:** food and drink; parking (no fee); toilets; water sports. **Best for:** sunset; swimming. ⊠ *Between Limassol and Paphos.*

PAPHOS

68 km (42 miles) west of Limassol.

In the west of the island and 142 km (88 miles) southwest of Nicosia, Paphos combines a seaside with stellar archaeological sites and a buzzing nightlife. Since the late 1990s it has attracted some of the most lavish resorts on the island (as well as the largest influx of British travelers). It's also the most pedestrian-friendly town in Cyprus, with a long beachside path running alongside most of the hotels all the way down to the pleasant leisure harbor, anchored by a medieval fortress. The surrounding

area is one of the most scenic in Cyprus, especially the untrammeled Akamas Peninsula—still accessible only to off-road vehicles. In short, if you want to combine easy accessibility to the beach with interesting historic attractions, this is the place you'll want to make your base.

Ayios Neophytos Monastery. The hermit and scholar Neophytos settled at what's now referred to as the Ayios Neophytos Monastery in 1159, carving a home for himself out of the rock. Known in his time as the leading critic of Richard the Lionheart and the Byzantine tax collectors, today he is best known for what became a series of grottoes hewn from the hillside rock and the evocative religious frescoes—some actually painted by Neophytos—they contain. The monastery itself, with no more than a half dozen or so monks, is situated below the grottoes. ⊠ *6 miles north of town* ⊡ *€1.70* ⊙ *Nov.–Mar., daily 9–4; Apr.–Oct., daily 9–1 and 2–6.*

★ **Byzantine Museum.** The Byzantine Museum houses notable mosaics, icons, and sacred books and artifacts collected from churches and monasteries throughout Paphos and dating from the 7th through the 18th centuries. The collection includes one of the oldest icons discovered in Cyprus, the Agia Marina, thought to be from the 8th or 9th century. Though it's on the small side, the museum provides a good introduction to the rich Byzantine history of the Paphos region and is well worth a stop. ⊠ *5 Andrea Ioannou St.* ☎ *26/931393* ⊡ *€2* ⊙ *Weekdays 9–4, Sat. 9–1.*

Paphos District Archaeological Museum. The Paphos District Archaeological Museum displays pottery, jewelry, and statuettes from Cyprus's Roman villas. ⊠ *43 Griva Digheni Ave., Ktima* ☎ *26/306215* ⊡ *€1.70* ⊙ *Mon. 8–2:30; Tues., Thurs., Fri. 8–3; Wed. 8–5; Sat. 9–3.*

Paphos Fort. The squat 16th-century Paphos Fort—a UNESCO World Heritage site—guards the entrance to the harbor; from the rooftop there's a lovely view. ⊠ *Paphos Harbour* ⊡ *€1.70* ⊙ *Daily Nov.–Mar. 8–5; Apr.–May and Sept.–Oct. 8–6; June–Aug. 8–7:30.*

Fodor's Choice ★ **Roman Mosaics.** Don't miss the elaborate 3rd- to 5th-century AD Roman mosaics in the Roman Villa of Theseus, the House of Dionysos, and the House of Aion—all part of a UNESCO World Heritage protected site. The impressive mosaics are an easy walk from the harbor. ⊠ *Kato Phaphos, near the habor* ☎ *26/306217* ⊡ *€3.40* ⊙ *June–Aug., daily 8–7:30; Apr.–May and Sept.–Oct., daily 8–6; Nov.–Mar., daily 8–5.*

Tombs of the Kings. The Tombs of the Kings, an early necropolis, date from 300 BC. The coffin niches are empty, but a powerful sense of mystery remains. There are lovely views from here over the Mediterranean Sea. ⊠ *Kato Paphos* ☎ *26/306295* ⊡ *€1.70* ⊙ *June–Aug., daily 8–7:30; Apr.–May and Sept.–Oct., daily 8–6; Nov.–Mar., daily 8–5.*

SHOPPING

Cyprus has a great range of handicrafts. Lace and embroidery from Lefkara are still handmade and are widely available. Other items to look for are basketware, ceramics, blown glass, carved wood (the best being olive wood), hand-tied cotton rugs, silverware, and copperware, including beautiful decorative urns. Leather and shoes are excellent

value. Museums sell copies of ancient artifacts, and the Orthodox monasteries offer Byzantine icons. Edibles include superb olive oil, honey, and delicious wine.

Shopping in the villages of Lefkara, Omodos, and Laneia is a pleasure, with numerous galleries and shops set along the whitewashed alleyways. In Limassol the main shopping street, Makarios Avenue, has a range of modern boutiques.

BEACHES

Cyprus has numerous excellent beaches, but they get busy between June and September with vacationers from across Europe.

☾ **Lady's Mile Beach.** The closest beach to Limassol's cruise ship port, Lady's Mile is a 7-km (4-mile) hard sand and pebble beach about a 15-minute drive from the center of town. Its shallow waters are popular with locals, especially on the weekends. Bring your own umbrella if you'd like some shade, as well as insect repellent in the evenings. **Amenities:** food and drink; lifeguards; water sports. **Best for:** swimming. ⊠ *Near New Port, Limassol.*

WHERE TO EAT

$$
MEDITERRANEAN
Fodor's Choice
★
✕**Limanaki.** Chef Sam Kazzaz truly bucks the Cyprus meze trend by using touches of Indian and Moroccan flare at his simple yet elegant restaurant just a block from the beach in Pissouri (though he also offers Mediterranean fish and meat mezes with eight hours' advance notice); though not located in Limassol proper, it's certainly worth the short drive. He masterfully uses curry in such dishes as Curried Away Calamari and Lamb Jalfrazi, while catering to non-meat eaters with his weekly changing vegetarian special, such as a subtly spiced tagine with chickpeas, eggplant, celery, peppers, and other fresh veggies. Whether you're seated inside surrounded by stone walls or outside on the pleasant terrace, you'll agree this is a Cyprus meal that's different from the rest—and one to remember. ⑤ *Average main: €15* ⊠ *Pissouri Jetty, Pissouri* ☎ *25/221288* ⊕ *www.limanakipissouri.com* ⚱ *Reservations essential* ⊘ *Closed Mon.*

$
MEDITERRANEAN
✕**Militzis.** This meat-centric restaurant is popular with locals for both lunch and dinner; it's well known for its homemade meze and other Cypriot specialties. If you're daring, opt for the liver and intestines of lamb, the salted pork, or the lamb's head. To play it safe, you can't go wrong with the *tavas*—pieces of lamb and beef cooked with potatoes, onions, tomatoes, and spices; the *souvla* (roasted pork in wine); or the moussaka. But best of all for those with hearty appetites is the meze—plate after plate of salad, olives, cheese, seafood, and meats, all for a reasonable fixed price. Sit on the terrace for lovely views of the sea. ⑤ *Average main: €10* ⊠ *42 Piale Pasha St., Larnaca* ☎ *24/655867.*

MYKONOS, GREECE

Updated by
Adrian Vrettos
and Alexia
Amvrazi

Put firmly on the map by Jackie O, Mykonos has become one of the most popular of the Aegean islands. Although the dry, rugged island is one of the smallest of the Cyclades—16 km (10 miles) by 11 km (7 miles)—travelers from all over the world are drawn to its sandy beaches, its thatched windmills, and its picturesque, whitewashed port town of Mykonos, whose cubical two-story houses and churches have been long celebrated as some of the best examples of classic Cycladic architecture. Here backpackers rub elbows with millionaires, and the atmosphere is decidedly cosmopolitan. Happily, the islanders seem to have been able to fit cosmopolitan New Yorkers or Londoners gracefully into their way of life. For almost 1,000 years, neighboring Delos Island was the religious and political center of the Aegean and host every four years to the Delian games, the region's greatest festival. This is a must-visit site for anyone interested in ancient history.

ESSENTIALS

CURRENCY
The euro.

HOURS
Museums are generally open from 9 to 5, but many are closed on Monday. Shops are open daily in the summer (9 to noon or 1, reopening at 4 or 5 until 9 on weekdays and 9 to 6 on Saturday).

PRIVATE TOURS
Windmills Travel takes a group every morning for a day tour of Delos. The company also has half-day guided tours of the Mykonos beach towns, with a stop in Ano Mera for the Panayia Tourliani Monastery. Windmills also provides excursions to nearby Tinos; arranges private tours of Delos and Mykonos and off-road jeep trips; charters yachts; and, in fact, handles all tourist services. John van Lerberghe's office, the Mykonos Accommodations Center, is small, but he can plan your trip from soup to nuts.

Contacts Windmills Travel. ⊠ *Fabrica, Mykonos* ☎ *22890/26555, 22890/23877* ✐ *info@windmills-travel.com* ⊕ *www.windmillstravel.com.*

TELEPHONES
Tri-band GSM phones work in Greece. You can buy prepaid phone cards at telecom shops, news vendors, and tobacconists in all towns and cities for local or international calls. Vodafone is the leading mobile telecom company. OTE is the national domestic provider. Calls can be made at OTE offices and paid for after completion.

COMING ASHORE
The main cruise port is about a mile north of Mykonos Town (on the other side of a very steep hill). Shuttle buses transport passengers to town, where you can catch buses or take a taxi to the beaches. If you anchor offshore and are tendered to the island, you'll alight at the old port in the town itself.

Because the island is so small, journey times anywhere are short. There is a cheap (fares between €1.40 and €1.70) and reliable bus service from

the town to all the main beaches, but services can get crowded in July and August. Small boats called *caïques* also act as taxis, taking people from the old port to the various beaches. These are reliable and popular services. Commercial taxis operate on fixed fare routes, but the taxi system is easily over-burdened when a large ship is in port. These are posted at the taxi rank in Mavro Square, just inland from the old harbor.

Most travel offices in Mykonos Town run guided tours to Delos that cost about €40, including boat transportation and entry fee. Alternatively, take one of the caïques that visit Delos daily from the old port: the round-trip costs about €17, and entry to the site (with no guide) is €5. They leave between 8:30 am and 3 pm, and return noon to 4 pm.

> ## MYKONOS BEST BETS
>
> **Explore Ancient Delos.** Delos was the religious center of the Aegean. Large sections of the city have been excavated, revealing treasures magnificent and humble.
>
> **Stroll the streets of Mykonos Town.** Cosmopolitan and bohemian, Mykonos is one of the most fashionable places to be during the European summer, yet the alluring narrow streets retain a vibrant Greek character.
>
> **Spend some time at the beach.** The town sleeps during the heat of the afternoon, so choose one of the island's famous beaches—from fun to hedonism—there's something for every taste.

With reliable transport services, a car rental isn't absolutely necessary, but if you want to do some exploring on your own you can rent an ATV or scooter for two people in town for about €15 to €30, depending on time of the season; motor scooters are not recommended for inexperienced riders (each year people are seriously injured because they don't know how to ride the many hills and narrow roads of Mykonos). A rental car costs about €40 to €50 per day for a subcompact or Smartcar.

EXPLORING MYKONOS

MYKONOS TOWN

If your ship remains in port late (often the case in Mykonos), the best time to visit the central harbor is in the cool of the evening, when the islanders promenade along the esplanade to meet friends and visit the numerous cafés. By the open-air fish market, Petros the Pelican preens and cadges eats. In the 1950s a group of migrating pelicans passed over Mykonos, leaving behind a single exhausted bird; Vassilis the fisherman nursed it back to health, and locals say that the pelican in the harbor is the original Petros, though you'll see several lurking around the fish tavernas right off the esplanade.

Archaeological Museum. Before setting out on the mandatory boat excursion to the isle of Delos, check out the Archaeological Museum, set at the northern edge of town. It affords insight into the intriguing history of its ancient shrines. The museum houses Delian funerary sculptures, many with scenes of mourning; most were moved to Rhenea when the Athenians cleansed Delos in the 6th century, during the sixth year of the Peloponnesian war, and, under instruction from the Delphic Oracle,

the entire island was purged of all dead bodies. The most significant work from Mykonos is a 7th-century BC *pithos* (storage jar), showing the Greeks in the Trojan horse and the sack of the city. ✉ *Ayios Stefanos, between boat dock and town* ☎ 22890/22325 💶 *€3* 🕑 *Wed.–Mon. 8:30–2:30.*

Fodor's Choice
★ **Church of Paraportiani** (*Our Lady of the Postern Gate*). Mykonians claim that exactly 365 churches and chapels dot their landscape, one for each day of the year. The most famous of these is the Church of Paraportiani. The sloping, whitewashed conglomeration of four chapels, mixing Byzantine and vernacular idioms, looks fantastic. It is solid and ultimately sober, and its position on a promontory facing the sea sets off the unique architecture. ✉ *Ayion Anargyron, near folk museum.*

★ **Little Venice.** Many of the early ship's captains built distinguished houses directly on the sea here, with wooden balconies overlooking the water. Today this neighborhood, at the southwest end of the port, is called Little Venice. This area, architecturally unique and one of the most attractive in all the islands, is so called because its handsome houses, which once belonged to shipowners and aristocrats, rise from the edge of the sea, and their elaborate buttressed wooden balconies hang over the water—these are no Venetian marble palazzi reflected in still canals. Many of these fine old houses are now elegant bars specializing in sunset drinks, or cabarets, or shops, and crowds head to the cafés and clubs, many found a block inland from Little Venice. These are sometimes soundproofed. ✉ *Mitropoleos Georgouli.*

Mando Mavrogenous Square. Start a tour of Mykonos Town (Hora) on the main square, Mando Mavrogenous Square (sometimes called Taxi Square). Pride of place goes to a bust of Mando Mavrogenous, the island heroine, standing on a pedestal. In the 1821 War of Independence the Mykonians, known for their seafaring skills, volunteered an armada of 24 ships, and in 1822, when the Ottomans landed a force on the island, Mando and her soldiers forced them back to their ships. After independence, a scandalous love affair caused the heroine's exile to Paros, where she died. An aristocratic beauty who becomes a great revolutionary war leader and then dies for love may seem unbelievably Hollywoodish, but it is true.

★ **Mykonos windmills.** Across the water from Little Venice, set on a high hill, are the famous Mykonos windmills, echoes of a time when wind power was used to grind the island's grain. The area from Little Venice to the windmills is called **Alefkandra,** which means "whitening": women once hung their laundry here. A little farther toward the windmills the bars chockablock on shoreside decks are barely above sea level, and when the north wind is up (often) surf splashes the tables. Farther on, the shore spreads into an unprepossessing beach, and tables are placed on sand or pebbles. After dinner (there are plenty of little tavernas here), the bars turn up their music, and knowing the beat thumps into the night, older tourists seek solace elsewhere.

ANO MERA

8 km (5 miles) east of Mykonos Town.

Interesting little tavernas line the central square of Ano Mera, which is the "second city" of Mykonos, in the hills near the center of the island.

Monastery of the Panayia Tourliani. Monastery buffs should head to Ano Mera, a village in the central part of the island, where the Monastery of the Panayia Tourliani, founded in 1580 and dedicated to the protectress of Mykonos, stands in the central square. Its massive baroque iconostasis (altar screen), made in 1775 by Florentine artists, has small icons carefully placed amid the wooden structure's painted green, red, and gold-leaf flowers. At the top are carved figures of the apostles and large icons depicting New Testament scenes. The hanging incense holders with silver molded dragons holding red eggs in their mouths show an Eastern influence. In the hall of the monastery, an interesting **museum** displays embroideries, liturgical vestments, and wood carvings. A good taverna is across the street. The monastery's big festival—hundreds attend—is on August 15. ⊠ *On central square* ☎ *22890/71296* ⊗ *By appointment only; call in advance.*

DELOS

Fodor's Choice **Delos.** Arrive at the mythical, magical, and magnificent site of Delos and
★ you might wonder how this barren islet, which has virtually no natural resources, became the religious and political center of the Aegean. One answer is that Dhílos—to use the Modern Greek transliteration—provided the safest anchorage for vessels sailing between the mainland and the shores of Asia; another answer is that it had no other use. A third is provided if you climb Mt. Kynthos to see that the isle is shielded on three sides by other islands. Indeed, this is how the Cyclades—the word means "circling ones"—got their name: they circle around the sacred island.

On the left from the harbor is the **Agora of the Competialists** (circa 150 BC), members of Roman guilds, mostly freedmen and slaves from Sicily who worked for Italian traders. They worshipped the *Lares Competales,* the Roman "crossroads" gods; in Greek they were known as Hermaistai, after the god Hermes, protector of merchants and the crossroads. The **Sacred Way,** east of the agora, was the route, during the holy Delian festival, of the procession to the Sanctuary of Apollo. The **Propylaea,** at the end of the Sacred Way, were once a monumental white marble gateway with three portals framed by four Doric columns. Beyond the Propylaea is the **Sanctuary of Apollo**; though little remains today, when the Propylaea were built in the mid-2nd century BC, the sanctuary was crowded with altars, statues, and temples—three of them to Apollo. Inside the sanctuary and to the right is the **House of the Naxians,** a 7th- to 6th-century BC structure with a central colonnade. Dedications to Apollo were stored in this shrine.

One of the most evocative sights of Delos is the 164-foot-long **avenue of the Lions.** These are replicas; the originals are in the museum. The five Naxian marble beasts crouch on their haunches, their forelegs stiffly upright, vigilant guardians of the Sacred Lake. They are the survivors of a line of at least nine lions, erected in the second half of the 7th century BC by the Naxians. One, removed in the 17th century,

now guards the Arsenal of Venice (though with a later head). The **Archaeological Museum** is also on the road south of the gymnasium; it contains most of the antiquities found in excavations on the island: monumental statues of young men and women, stelae, reliefs, masks, and ancient jewelry. Immediately to the right of the museum is a small **Sanctuary of Dionysus,** erected about 300 BC; outside it is one of the more-boggling sights of ancient Greece: several monuments dedicated to Apollo by the winners of the choral competitions of the Delian festivals, each decorated with a huge phallus, emblematic of the orgiastic rites that took place during the Dionysian festivals. Around the base of one of them is carved a lighthearted representation of a bride being carried to her new husband's home.

Beyond the path that leads to the southern part of the island is the **ancient theater,** built in the early 3rd century BC in the elegant residential quarter inhabited by Roman bankers and Egyptian and Phoenician merchants. Their one- and two-story houses were typically built around a central courtyard, sometimes with columns on all sides. Floor mosaics of snakes, panthers, birds, dolphins, and Dionysus channeled rainwater into cisterns below; the best preserved can be seen in the **House of the Dolphins,** the **House of the Masks,** and the **House of the Trident.** A dirt path leads east to the base of Mt. Kynthos, where there are remains from many **Middle Eastern shrines,** including the **Sanctuary of the Syrian Gods,** built in 100 BC. A flight of steps goes up 368 feet to the summit of **Mt. Kynthos** (after which all Cynthias are named), on whose slope Apollo was born. ⊠ *Delos island and historic site, take a small passenger boat from Mykonos Town* ☎ *22890/22259* ⊕ *www. culture.gr* ⊠ *€7* ☉ *Tues.–Sun. 9–3.*

SHOPPING

Mykonos Town has excellent shopping, with many high-class boutiques aimed at the well-heeled sitting side by side with moderately priced shops selling Greek crafts and fashionable clothing. It's a real pleasure for retail junkies, with a seemingly limitless array of choices. Almost every surface of the narrow alleyways is festooned with cotton clothing or cheerful ceramics, leather shoes, or bars of olive-oil soap. Artists are drawn here as much by the clientele as by the beauty and light of the Aegean, so galleries are numerous. The town is especially famed for its jewelry, from simple strings of colourful beads to precious stones in designer settings. Upscale duty-free jewelry shops also abound.

White Shop Mykonos. Anna Gelou's shop, started by her mother 50 years ago, carries authentic copies of traditional handmade embroideries, all using white Greek cotton, in clothing, tablecloths, curtains, and such. ⊠ *Kouzi Gewrgouli 50, Mykonos Town* ☎ *22890/26825.*

★ **Ilias Lalaounis.** Known internationally, Ilias Lalaounis is for fine jewelry based on ancient Greek and other designs, reinterpreted for the modern woman. With many of their earrings and necklaces as lovingly worked as art pieces, the shop is as elegant as a museum. New collections are introduced every year. Stop by at the right hour and you'll get a glass of fine wine. The salespeople all live here and know everything about their

island. ✉ *Polykandrioti 14, near taxis, Mykonos Town* ☎ *22890/22444* ⊕ *www.iliaslalaounis.com.*

Nikoletta. Mykonos used to be a weaver's island, where 500 looms clacked away. Only Nikoletta remains, where Nikoletta Xidakis sells her skirts, shawls, and bedspreads made of local wool, as she has for 50 years. ✉ *Little Venice, Mykonos Town* ☎ *22890/27503.*

ACTIVITIES

There's a full range of water sports on offer in Mykonos, and many concessions operate directly on the beach (from May through September). Windsurfing is particularly popular because of the prevailing *meltemi* winds that blow across the island throughout the summer. The windy northern beaches on Ornos Bay are best for this.

Aphrodite Beach Hotel. This hotel is known for its water sports facilities. ✉ *Kalafati beach, Mykonos Town* ☎ *28890/71367.*

BEACHES

There is a beach for every taste in Mykonos. Beaches near Mykonos Town, within walking distance, are **Tourlos** and **Ayios Ioannis. Ayios Stefanos**, about a 45-minute walk from Mykonos Town, has a minigolf course, water sports, restaurants, and umbrellas and lounge chairs for rent. The south coast's **Psarou,** protected from wind by hills and surrounded by restaurants, offers a wide selection of water sports and is often called the finest beach. Nearby **Platys Yialos,** popular with families, is also lined with restaurants and dotted with umbrellas for rent. **Ornos** is also perfect for families.

Paranga, Paradise, Super Paradise, and **Elia** are all on the southern coast of the island, and are famously nude, though getting less so. **Super Paradise** is half-gay, half-straight, and swings at night. All have tavernas on the beach. At the easternmost end of the south shores is **Kalafatis,** known for package tours, and between Elia and Kalafatis there's a remote beach at **Kato Livadhi,** which can be reached by road.

WHERE TO EAT

$$ ✕ **Kounelas.** This long-established fresh-fish taverna is where many fish-
GREEK ermen themselves eat, for solid, no-frills food. The menu depends on the weather—low winds means lots of fish. Note: even in simple places such as Kounelas, fresh fish can be expensive. Ⓢ *Average main: €12* ✉ *Off port near Delos boats, Mykonos Town* ☎ *22890/28220.*

$$$ ✕ **Sea Satin Market–Caprice.** If the wind is up, the waves will sing at this
SEAFOOD magical spot, set on a far tip of land below the famous windmills of
★ Mykonos. The preferred place for Greek shipowners, Sea Satin Market sprawls out onto a seaside terrace and even onto the sand of the beach bordering Little Venice. When it comes to fish, prices vary according to weight. Shellfish is a specialty, and everything is beautifully presented. In summer, live music and dancing add to the liveliness. Ⓢ *Average main: €25* ✉ *On seaside under windmills, Mykonos Town* ☎ *22890/24676.*

PIRAEUS, GREECE (FOR ATHENS)

Updated by
Adrian Vrettos
and Alexia
Amvrazi

If you come to Athens in search of gleaming white temples, you may be aghast to find that much of the city has melded into what appears to be a viscous concrete mass. Amid the sprawl and squalor, though, the ancient city gives up its treasures. Lift your eyes 200 feet above the city to the Parthenon, and you behold architectural perfection that has not been surpassed in 2,500 years. Today this shrine of classical form, this symbol of Western civilization and political thought, dominates a 21st-century boomtown. To experience Athens fully is to understand the essence of Greece: tradition juxtaposed with a modernity that the ancients would strain to recognize but would heartily endorse. Ancient Athens is certainly the lure for the millions of visitors to the city, but since the late 1990s, inspired by the 2004 Olympics, the people have gone far toward transforming Athens into a sparkling modern metropolis.

ESSENTIALS

CURRENCY
The euro.

HOURS
Most stores are open from 9 to 9 on weekdays, from 9 to 6 on Saturday. Museums are generally open from 9 to 5, but many are closed on Monday.

TELEPHONES
Tri-band GSM phones work in Greece. You can buy prepaid phone cards at telecom shops, news vendors, and tobacconists in all towns and cities. Phone cards can be used for local or international calls. Vodafone is the leading mobile telecom company. OTE is the national domestic provider. Calls can be made at OTE offices and paid for after completion.

COMING ASHORE
Piraeus is the port of Athens, 11 km (7 miles) southwest of the city center, and is itself the third-largest city in Greece, with a population of about 500,000. In anticipation of a flood of visitors during the 2004 Olympics, the harbor district was given a general sprucing up. The cruise port has 12 berths, and the terminal has duty-free shops, information, and refreshments.

The fastest and cheapest way to get to Athens from Piraeus is to take the metro. Line 1 (Green Line) reaches the downtown Athens stops most handy to tourists, including Platia Victorias, near the National Archaeological Museum; Omonia Square; Monastiraki, in the old Turkish bazaar; and Thission, near the ancient Agora. The trip takes 25 to 30 minutes. The Piraeus metro station is off Akti Kallimasioti on the main harbor, a 20-minute walk from the cruise port.

A flat fare covering all forms of public transport within central Athens and valid for 1 hour 30 minutes is €1.40. A day pass valid on all buses, trams, metro, and suburban railway is €4. Passes should be validated when first used, and are then valid for 24 hours from that time.

Taxis wait outside the terminal entrance. Taxis into the city are not necessarily quicker than public transport. Taxis rates begin at €1,

then €0.48 per km (½ miles), and there are numerous surcharges. A taxi takes longer than the metro because of traffic, and costs around €12–€15. Athens taxi drivers have a reputation for overcharging passengers, so make sure the meter is switched on. It is common practice for drivers to pick up other passengers if there is room in the cab. These extra passengers will also pay the full fare for the trip. Radio taxis also have an additional charge of €3 to €5 for the pick-up.

GETTING TO THE AIRPORT

If you choose not to purchase airport transfers from your cruise line, there are inexpensive options available.

The best way to get to the airport from downtown Athens is by metro or light-rail. Single tickets cost €8, and include transfers within 90 minutes of the ticket's initial validation to bus, trolley, or tram. Combined tickets for two (€14) and three (€20) passengers are also available. Five express buses connect the airport with the metro (Ethniki Amyna and Dafni station), Syntagma Square, Kifissia, Kifissos Bus Station, and Piraeus (from which it is a short taxi ride to the port). Express buses leave the arrivals level of the airport every 10 minutes and operate 24 hours a day. Bus X95 will take you to Syntagma Square (Amalias Avenue); X94 goes to the bus terminus at the Ethniki Amyna metro stop (Line 3), which will get you into Syntagma within 10 minutes. Bus X97 goes to the Dafni metro stop; X93 brings voyagers to the dusty Kifissos intercity bus station. Bus X96 goes directly to Piraeus. The Attiki Odos and the expansion of the city's network of bus lanes has made travel times more predictable, and on a good day the X94 can get you to Ethniki Amyna in 40 minutes. Tickets cost €5 for any of these buses. Once in the city, pick up Metro line 1 for Piraeus and a 20-minute walk or short taxi transfer to the port.

Taxis are readily available at the arrivals level of the Athens airport; it costs an average of €45 to get to the port. Private limousine service starts at €120 for one-way transfer from the airport to the port.

Contacts Limousine Service Travel ☎ *210/970–6416*
⊕ *www.limousine-service.gr.* **Royal Prestige Limousine Service** ☎ *210/988–3221* ☎🖶 *210/983–0378* ⊕ *www.limousine-services.gr.*

ATHENS BEST BETS

The Parthenon. Regarded as the pinnacle of ancient architectural achievement, this classical temple has inspired poets, artists, and architects.

The National Archaeological Museum. A wide-ranging collection covers Greece's ancient history, from the splendid finds Schliemann excavated at Mycenae to the monumental statues that graced the cities of Attica.

New Acropolis Museum. This dazzling new museum at the base of the Acropolis is a welcome development for both Athens and Greece.

EXPLORING ATHENS

Fodor's Choice **Acropolis.** You don't have to look far in Athens to encounter perfection.
★ Towering above all—both physically and spiritually—is the Acropolis,
the ancient city of upper Athens. The Greek term *Akropolis* means
"High City," and today's traveler who climbs this table-like hill is paying tribute to the prime source of Western civilization. Most of the
notable structures on this flat-top limestone outcrop, 512 feet high,
were built from 461 to 429 BC, when the intellectual and artistic life
of Athens flowered under the influence of the Athenian statesman Pericles. With most of the major restoration work now completed, a visit
to the Acropolis evokes the spirit of the ancient heroes and gods who
were once worshiped here. The sight of the Parthenon—the Panathenaic
temple at the crest of this *ieros vrachos* (sacred rock) —has the power
to stir the heart as few other ancient relics do.

At the loftiest point of the Acropolis stands the **Parthenon,** the architectural masterpiece conceived by Pericles and executed between 447
and 438 BC. It not only raised the bar in terms of sheer size, but also
in the perfection of its proportions. Dedicated to the goddess Athena
(the name Parthenon comes from the Athena Parthenos, or the virgin Athena), the Parthenon served primarily as the treasury of the
Delian League, an ancient alliance of cities formed to defeat the Persian incursion.

Once you pass through the Beulé Gate you will find the **Temple of
Athena Nike.** Designed by Kallikrates, the mini-temple was built in
427–424 BC to celebrate peace with Persia. The bas-reliefs on the surrounding parapet depict the Victories leading heifers to be sacrificed.
In 1998, Greek archaeologists began dismantling the entire temple for
conservation. After laser-cleaning the marble, the team will reconstruct
the temple on its original site.

If the Parthenon is the masterpiece of Doric architecture, the **Erechtheion** is undoubtedly the prime exemplar of the more graceful Ionic
order. A considerably smaller structure than the Parthenon, it out-
matches, for sheer elegance and refinement of design, all other buildings of the Greco-Roman world. For the populace, the Erechtheion,
completed in 406 BC, remained Athena's holiest shrine, for legend has
it that Poseidon plunged his trident into the rock on this spot, dramatically producing a spring of water, while Athena created a simple
olive tree, whose produce remains a main staple of Greek society.
A panel of judges declared the goddess the winner, and the city was
named Athena.

Most people take the metro to the Acropolis station, where the New
Acropolis Museum is just across the main exit. Another entrance is
along the rock's northern face via the Peripatos, a paved path from the
Plaka district. ⊠ *Dionyssiou Areopagitou, Acropolis* ☎ *210/321–4172,
210/321–0219* ⊕ *www.culture.gr* ✉ *€12 joint ticket for all Unification
of Archaeological Sites* ☾ *Apr.–Oct., daily 8–6:30 (last entry); Nov.–
Mar., daily 8–3* Ⓜ *Acropolis.*

Fodor's Choice **Ancient Agora.** The commercial hub of ancient Athens, the Agora was
★ once lined with statues and expensive shops, the favorite strolling
ground of fashionable Athenians as well as a mecca for merchants and
students. The long colonnades offered shade in summer and protection
from rain in winter to the throng of people who transacted the day-
to-day business of the city, and, under their arches, Socrates discussed
matters with Plato and Zeno expounded the philosophy of the Stoics
(whose name comes from the six *stoa,* or colonnades of the Agora).
Besides administrative buildings, it was surrounded by the schools, theaters, workshops, houses, stores, and market stalls of a thriving town.
The foundations of some of the main buildings, which may be most
easily distinguished include the circular Tholos, the principal seat of
executive power in the city; the Mitroon, shrine to Rhea, the mother of
gods, which included the vast state archives and registry office (*mitroon*
is still used today to mean registry); the Boulerterion, where the council
met; the Monument of Eponymous Heroes, the Agora's information
center, where announcements such as the list of military recruits were
hung; and the Sanctuary of the Twelve Gods, a shelter for refugees and
the point from which all distances were measured.

The Agora's showpiece was the **Stoa of Attalos II,** where Socrates once
lectured and incited the youth of Athens to adopt his progressive ideas
on mortality and morality. Today the Museum of Agora Excavations,
this two-story building was first designed as a retail complex and erected
in the 2nd century BC by Attalos, a king of Pergamum. The reconstruction in 1953–56 used Pendelic marble and creamy limestone from
the original structure. On the low hill called Kolonos Agoraios in the
Agora's northwest corner stands the best-preserved Doric temple in all
Greece, the **Hephaistion,** sometimes called the Thission because of its
friezes showing the exploits of Theseus. Like the other monuments, it
is roped off, but you can walk around it to admire its preservation. A
little older than the Parthenon, it is surrounded by 34 columns and is
104 feet in length, and was once filled with sculptures (the only remnant
of which is the mutilated frieze, once brightly colored). ⊠ *3 entrances:
from Monastiraki on Adrianou; from Thission on Apostolou Pav-
lou; and descending from Acropolis on Ayios Apostoloi, Monastiraki*
☎ *210/321–0185* ⊕ *www.culture.gr* ☜ *€4; €12 joint ticket for holders
of the Acropolis (Unification of Archaeological Sites) ticket* ☉ *Daily
8–3; museum closes ½ hr before site* Ⓜ *Thiseio.*

Fodor's Choice **Benaki Museum.** Just in time for the 2004 Olympics, Greece's oldest
★ private museum received a spectacular face-lift. Established in 1926
by an illustrious Athenian family, the Benaki was one of the first to
place emphasis on Greece's later heritage at a time when many archaeologists were destroying Byzantine artifacts to access ancient objects.
The permanent collection (more than 20,000 items are on display in
36 rooms, and that's only a sample of the holdings) moves chronologically from the ground floor upward, from prehistory to the formation
of the modern Greek state. ⊠ *Koumbari 1, Kolonaki* ☎ *210/367–1000*
⊕ *www.benaki.gr* ☜ *€7, free Thurs.* ☉ *Wed., Fri., and Sat. 9–5, Thurs.
9 am–midnight, Sun. 9–3* Ⓜ *Syntagma or Evangelismos.*

★ **Byzantine and Christian Museum.** One of the few museums in Europe focusing exclusively on Byzantine art displays an outstanding collection of icons, mosaics, tapestries, and sculptural fragments (the latter provides an excellent introduction to Byzantine architecture). The permanent collection is divided in two main parts: the first is devoted to Byzantium (4th–15th c. AD) and contains 1,200 artifacts while the second is entitled "From Byzantium to the Modern Era" and presents 1,500 artworks dating from the 15th to the 21st century. ✉ *Vasilissis Sofias 22, Kolonaki* ☎ *213/213–9572, 213/723–9511* ⊕ *www.byzantinemuseum.gr* 🎫 *€4* ⊙ *Nov.–Mar., Tues.–Sun. 8; Apr.–Oct., Tues.–Sun. 9–4* Ⓜ *Evangelismos.*

Fodor's Choice **Museum of Cycladic Art.** Also known as the Nicholas P. Goulandris Foundation, and funded by one of Greece's richest families, this museum has an outstanding collection of 350 Cycladic artifacts dating from the Bronze Age, including many of the enigmatic marble figurines whose slender shapes fascinated such artists as Picasso, Modigliani, and Brancusi. ✉ *Neofitou Douka 4, Kolonaki* ☎ *210/722–8321 through 210/722–8323* ⊕ *www.cycladic.gr* 🎫 *€7* ⊙ *Mon., Wed., Fri., and Sat. 10–5, Thurs. 10–8, Sun. 11–5* Ⓜ *Evangelismos.*
★
☉

Fodor's Choice **National Archaeological Museum.** Many of the greatest achievements in ancient Greek sculpture and painting are housed here in the most important museum in Greece. Artistic highlights from every period of its ancient civilization, from Neolithic to Roman times, make this a treasure trove beyond compare. With a massive renovation completed, works that have languished in storage for decades are now on view, reorganized displays are accompanied by enriched English-language information, and the panoply of ancient Greek art appears more spectacular than ever.
★

The museum's most celebrated display is the **Mycenaean Antiquities.** Here are the stunning gold treasures from Heinrich Schliemann's 1876 excavations of Mycenae's royal tombs: the funeral mask of a bearded king, once thought to be the image of Agamemnon but now believed to be much older, from about the 15th century BC; a splendid silver bull's-head libation cup; and the 15th-century BC Vaphio Goblets, masterworks in embossed gold.

Withheld from the public since they were damaged in the 1999 earthquakes, but not to be missed, are the beautifully restored **frescoes from Santorini,** delightful murals depicting daily life in Minoan Santorini. Along with the treasures from Mycenae, these wall paintings are part of the museum's Prehistoric Collection.

Other stars of the museum include the works of Geometric and Archaic art (10th to 6th century BC), and kouroi and funerary stelae (8th to 5th century BC), among them the stelae of the warrior Aristion signed by Aristokles, and the unusual *Running Hoplite* (a hoplite was a Greek infantry soldier). The collection of classical art (5th to 3rd century BC) contains some of the most renowned surviving ancient statues: the bareback *Jockey of Artemision,* a 2nd-century BC Hellenistic bronze salvaged from the sea; from the same excavation, the bronze *Artemision Poseidon* (some say Zeus), poised and ready to

fling a trident (or thunderbolt?); and the *Varvakios Athena,* a half-size marble version of the gigantic gold-and-ivory cult statue that Pheidias erected in the Parthenon.

Light refreshments are served in a lower ground-floor café, which opens out to a patio and sculpture garden. During the summer months, concerts are often organized in the front garden (check the museum's website). ⊠ *28 Oktovriou (Patission) 44, Exarchia* ☎ *210/821–7717, 210/821–7724* ⊕ *www.namuseum.gr* ✉ *€7* ⊘ *Apr.–Oct., Mon. 1:30–8, Tues.–Sun. 9–4; Nov.–Mar., Mon. 1:30–8, Tues.–Sun. 8–3* Ⓜ *Victoria, then 10-min walk.*

Fodor's Choice
★
New Acropolis Museum. Designed by the celebrated Swiss architect Bernard Tschumi in collaboration with Greek Architect Michalis Fotiadis, the New Acropolis Museum made world headlines when it opened in June 2009. If some buildings define an entire city in a particular era, Athens's newest museum boldly sets the tone of Greece's modern era. Occupying a large plot of the city's most prized real estate, the New Acropolis Museum nods to the fabled ancient hill above it but speaks—thanks to a spectacular building—in a contemporary architectural language.

Regal glass walkways, very high ceilings, and panoramic views are all part of the experience. In the five-level museum, every shade of marble is on display and bathed in abundant, UV-safe natural light. Visitors pass into the museum through a broad entrance and move ever upwards. Delicate ancient craftsmanship is contrasted throughout with industrial modern accents (massive columns and symmetrical wall apertures); abundant glass on floors and balcony spaces allow the exhibition levels to gracefully communicate with each other.

The ground floor exhibit, The Acropolis Slopes, features objects found in the sanctuaries and settlements around the Acropolis—a highlight is the collection of theatrical masks and vases from the Sanctuary of the matrimonial deity Nymphe. The next floor is devoted to the Archaic period (650 BC–480 BC), with rows of precious statues mounted for 360-degree viewing. The second floor is devoted to the terrace and small restaurant/bar, which serves mezedes (a more ambitious restaurant is rumored to be in the works). Drifting into the top-floor atrium, the visitor can watch a video on the Parthenon before entering the star gallery devoted to the temple's Pentelic marble decorations, many of which depict a grand procession in the goddess Athena's honor. Frieze pieces (originals and copies), metopes, and pediments are all laid out in their original orientation. With all the ancient and fabled riches now gloriously on view here, a visit of at least two hours to this grand new museum is highly recommended. ⊠ *Dionyssiou Areopagitou 15, Makriyianni, Acropolis* ☎ *210/900–0900* ⊕ *www. theacropolismuseum.gr* ✉ *€5* ⊘ *Tues.–Thurs., Sat.–Sun., 8–8; Fri. 8–10; closed Mon.* Ⓜ *Acropolis.*

★
Roman Agora. The city's commercial center from the 1st century BC to the 4th century AD, the Roman Market was a large rectangular courtyard with a peristyle that provided shade for the arcades of shops. Its most notable feature is the west entrance's Bazaar Gate, or **Gate of**

Athena Archegetis, completed around AD 2; the inscription records that it was erected with funds from Julius Caesar and Augustus. Halfway up one solitary square pillar behind the gate's north side, an edict inscribed by Hadrian regulates the sale of oil, a reminder that this was the site of the annual bazaar where wheat, salt, and oil were sold. On the north side of the Roman Agora stands one of the few remains of the Turkish occupation, the **Fethiye (Victory) Mosque.** The eerily beautiful mosque was built in the late 15th century on the site of a Christian church to celebrate the Turkish conquest of Athens and to honor Mehmet II (the Conqueror). During the few months of Venetian rule in the 17th century, the mosque was converted to a Roman Catholic church; now used as a storehouse, it is closed to the public. Three steps in the right-hand corner of the porch lead to the base of the minaret, the rest of which no longer exists. ⊠ *Pelopidas and Aiolou, Plaka* ☎ *210/324–5220* ⊕ *www. culture.gr* ⊒ *€2; €12 joint ticket for all Unification of Archaeological Sites* ☉ *Daily 8–3* Ⓜ *Monastiraki.*

★ **Syntagma (Constitution) Square.** At the top of the city's main square stands the Greek **Parliament,** formerly King Otto's royal palace, completed in 1838 for the new monarchy. It seems a bit austere and heavy for a southern landscape, but it was proof of progress, the symbol of the new ruling power. The building's saving grace is the stone's magical change of color from off-white to gold to rosy mauve as the day progresses. In recent years the square has become the new frontline of mass protests against harsh austerity measures and the ongoing economic crisis in Greece, as well as the base for the citizen movement of the "Indignants." ⊠ *Vasilissis Amalias and Vasilissis Sofias, Syntagma Sq.* Ⓜ *Syntagma.*

SHOPPING

Athens has great gifts, particularly handmade crafts. Shops stock copies of traditional Greek jewelry, silver filigree, Skyrian pottery, onyx ashtrays and dishes, woven bags, attractive rugs (including *flokati,* or shaggy goat-wool rugs), wool sweaters, and little blue-and-white pendants designed as amulets to ward off the *mati* (evil eye). Greece is also known for its well-made shoes (most shops are clustered around the Ermou pedestrian zone and in Kolonaki), its furs (Mitropoleos near Syntagma), and its durable leather items (Pandrossou in Monastiraki).

Shops on Pandrossou sell small antiques and icons, but keep in mind that many of these are fakes. You must have government permission to export genuine objects from the ancient Greek, Roman, and Byzantine periods. Many museums sell good-quality reproductions or miniatures of their best pieces.

Fodor's Choice **Center of Hellenic Tradition.** The Center is an outlet for quality handi-
★ crafts—ceramics, weavings, sheep bells, wood carvings, prints, and old paintings. Take a break from shopping in the center's quiet and quaint I Oraia Ellas café, to enjoy a salad or mezedes in clear view of the Parthenon. Upstairs is an art gallery hosting temporary exhibitions of Greek art. ⊠ *Mitropoleos 59 and Pandrossou 36, Monastiraki* ☎ *210/321–3023, 210/321–0517.*

Fodor's Choice
★
Korres. Natural beauty products blended in traditional recipes using Greek herbs and flowers have graced the bathroom shelves of celebrities like Rihanna and Angelina Jolie but in Athens they are available at most pharmacies for regular-folk prices. For the largest selection of basil-lemon shower gel, coriander body lotion, olive-stone face scrub, and wild-rose eye cream, go to the original Korres pharmacy (behind the Panathenaic Stadium). Not surprisingly, Korres also maintains a traditional laboratory for herbal preparations such as tinctures, oils, capsules, and teas. ⊠ *Eratosthenous 8 and Ivikou, Pangrati* ☎ *210/722–2744* ⊕ *www.korres.com.*

Thiamis. Iconographer Aristides Makos creates beautiful hand-painted, gold-leaf icons on wood and stone. His slightly cluttered shop also sells beautiful handmade model ships and made-to-order items. ⊠ *Asklipiou 71, Kolonaki* ☎ *210/363–7993* ⊕ *www.thiamis.com.*

WHERE TO EAT

On Mitropoleos off Monastiraki Square are a handful of counterfront places selling *souvlaki*—grilled meat rolled in a pita with onions, *tzatziki* (yogurt-garlic dip), and tomatoes—the best bargain in Athens. Make sure you specify whether you want a souvlaki sandwich or a souvlaki plate, which is an entire meal.

$$$$
GREEK
Fodor's Choice
★
✕ **Daphne's.** Discreet service and refined Mediterranean and Greek dishes (such as pork with celery and egg lemon sauce, fricassee of melt-off-the-bone lamb with greens, beef with olives, rabbit in mavrodaphne wine sauce and the traditional *moussaka*) help make Daphne's one of the most exclusive (and at times pricey) destinations in Plaka. The Pompeian frescoes on the walls, the fragments of an ancient Greek building in the garden, and the tasteful restoration of the neoclassic building in terra-cotta and ochre hues also contribute to a pleasant and romantic evening. ⑤ *Average main: €40* ⊠ *Lysikratous 4, Plaka* ☎ *210/322–7971* ⊕ *www.daphnesrestaurant.gr.*

$
GREEK
Fodor's Choice
★
✕ **O Platanos.** Set on a picturesque pedestrianized square, this is one of the oldest tavernas in Plaka (established 1932)—a welcome sight compared with the many overpriced tourist traps in the area. A district landmark—it is set midway between the Tower of the Winds and the Museum of Greek Popular Musical Instruments—it warms the eye with its pink-hue house, nicely color-coordinated with the bougainvillea-covered courtyard. Although the rooms here are cozily adorned with old paintings and photos, most of the crowd opts to relax under the courtyard's plane trees (which give the place its name). Platanos is packed with locals, who flock here because the food is good Greek home cooking and the waiters fast and polite. Don't miss the oven-baked potatoes, lamp or veal casserole with spinach or eggplant, fresh green beans in savory olive oil, fresh grilled fish, and the exceptionally cheap but delicious barrel retsina. Open for lunch. ⑤ *Average main: €15* ⊠ *Diogenous 4, Plaka* ☎ *210/322–0666* ▭ *No credit cards* ◯ *Closed June–Aug.*

WHERE TO STAY

$ **Acropolis Select.** For only €10 more than many basic budget options,
HOTEL you get to stay in a slick-looking hotel with a lobby full of designer
Fodor's Choice furniture in the residential neighborhood of Koukaki, south of Filo-
★ pappou Hill, a 15-minute walk from the Acropolis, so not quite in the
center of things. **Pros:** comfortable rooms; friendly staff; located in a
pretty, low-key neighborhood; great value for money. **Cons:** no free
Wi-Fi; small elevator. $ *Rooms from: €75 ⊠ Falirou 37–39, Koukaki*
☎ 210/921–1610 ⊕ www.acropoliselect.gr ⬏ 72 rooms.

$$$$ **Electra Palace.** If you want simple elegance, excellent service, and
Fodor's Choice a great location, this is the hotel for you—rooms from the fifth floor
★ up have a view of the Acropolis and in summer you can bask in the
sunshine at the outdoor swimming pool as you take in the view of
Athens's greatest monument or catch the sunset from the rooftop garden. **Pros:** gorgeous rooms; great location; outstanding service: early
check-in available. **Cons:** pricey! $ *Rooms from: €330 ⊠ Nikodimou*
18–20, Plaka ☎ 210/337–0000 ⊕ www.electrahotels.gr ⬏ 135 rooms,
20 suites ⫾○⫾ Breakfast.

PORT SAID, EGYPT (FOR CAIRO)

One of the world's great cosmopolitan cities for well over a thousand
years, Cairo is infinite and inexhaustible. Different religions, different
cultures—sometimes, it seems, even different eras—coexist amid the
jostling crowds and aging monuments gathered here at the start of the
Nile delta. But if you come expecting a city frozen in time, you're in for
a shock: Cairo's current vitality is as seductive as its rich past. Like so
much else in Egypt, Cairo's charm is a product of its history, the physical remains of a thousand years of being conquered and reconquered by
different groups. Cairo gradually reveals its treasures, not with pizzazz
and bells and whistles, but with a self-assured understatement. On a
one-day visit you'll only be able to take in the tip of a vast iceberg of
treasures here.

ESSENTIALS
CURRENCY
The Egyptian pound. U.S. currency is accepted for high-value items in
shops but not in restaurants and markets. ATMs are not common. You'll
need small local bills for tips in Egypt, particularly to use the restroom.

HOURS
Museums are usually open from 9 to 5. Many museums are closed on
Monday. Shops are open from 8 am until 7 pm. During Ramadan (the
Muslim month of fasting), opening times vary; shops close during the
day but stay open late into the evening.

TELEPHONES
Mobile phone coverage is limited to Cairo, the Nile Valley and delta, and
the Red Sea coast. The mobile system in Egypt is 3G-supportive. Vodafone, Etisalat Egypt, and Mobinil are the major providers in the country.

Cairo

ZAHIR

ISLAMIC CAIRO

S. al-Mu'iz li Din Allah

S. al-Baggala

S. al-Siyargi

Maydan Ahmad Maher

S. Ahmad Maher

S. Bur Sa'id

S. Ramsis

GAMRA

S. al-Ahyili

S. al-Mustafa

S. Ahmad Hilmi

S. S. Muhmisa Sari

S. Gamra

S. al-Tahir

MUSKI

S. al-Azhar

S. Abd al-Aziz

ABIDIN

S. Kamil Sidqi

S. Bab al-Bahr

HUSNI MUBARAK

Maydan Ramses

S. al-Gala

S. Clot Bay

S. Gomhouriya

S. al-Gais

S. Bur Sa'id

S. Subra

S. al-Tur S. al-Bulaqia

S. al-Mustafa

S. Ahmad Badawi

S. Gazirat Badran

S. Ibn al-Kurani

S. Sa'im al-Dahr

S. Ibn al-Rasid

AHMAD I'RABI

S.Muhammad Farid

S. Sherif

S. Nil

Khan al-Khalili Souk

S. al-Bustan

S. Talaat Harb

S. Qasr al-Nil

GAMAL 'ABD AL-NASIR

S. 26 Yulyu

S. Ramsis

S. al-Gala

DOWNTOWN

Maydan Tahrir

ANWAR AL-SADAT

S. al-Saih Rihan

S. Sanan

S. Buraq al-Gadid Pipe being laid

BOULAQ

Pyramids at Giza

Ticket Office

TO CAIRO

NAZLAT AL-SAMMAN VILLAGE

Pyramid of Khufu

MASTABAS (DYNASTIES IV & V)

Boat Pits

Pyramids of Queens

Causeway

MASTABAS (DYNASTIES IV & V)

Boat Museum

Mortuary Temple

Causeway

Great Sphinx

Sphinx Temple

Sound and Light

Valley Temple

Tomb of Queen Khentawes

MASTABAS AND ROCK-CUT TOMBS

Pyramid of Khafre

Valley Temple

TO ABU SIR & SAQQARA

Kubri 6 Uktubat

S. al-Tahir

DOQQI

S. al-Saqa al-

S. Wizarat al-Zira'a

S. al-Taura

S. Nadi el-Sid

Pyramid of Menkaure

Mortuary Temple

Causeway

Pyramids of Queens

S. Muhiy al-Din Abu

N

0   1/8 mi
0   1/8 km

COMING ASHORE

Ships with passengers bound for Cairo generally dock at Port Said, Egypt's premier commercial port. The town was founded at the southern outlet of the Suez Canal as a camp for engineers and workers building the waterway in the mid-19th century. From the port it is a short walk into this unprepossessing town, but there is little to hold the visitor. Most passengers will choose to take a ship-sponsored shore excursion into Cairo.

Taxis wait at the dock entrance, and can offer transfers to Cairo for a day rate, but this is a port where we strongly recommend a ship-sponsored excursion because of the distance and schedule issues. If you decide to travel independently, it's important to agree on a price and to assess the condition of the vehicle first. The journey is long, and a breakdown would be a major inconvenience. We caution strongly against trying to rent a car to visit Cairo. There are too many security issues, and driving in Cairo traffic is not an experience the average cruise passenger is prepared for.

CAIRO BEST BETS
The Cairo Museum. The most comprehensive collection of ancient Egyptian artifacts in the world, this museum is a must for serious history buffs or curious amateurs keen to catch sight of a mummy.
The Pyramids. When you view the Pyramids (and the Sphinx), you are sure to be awed. The mystery of their origin remains, and that's part of the allure.
Khan al-Khalili souk. One of the world's oldest and most authentic markets, Khan al-Khalili is a cornucopia of crafts ranging from the mundane to the magnificent.

EXPLORING CAIRO

Fodor's Choice ★ **The Egyptian Antiquities Museum.** On the north end of Maydan Tahrir, this huge neoclassical building is home to the world's largest collection of ancient Egyptian artifacts. With more than 100,000 items in total, it is said that if you were to spend just one minute on each item, it would take over nine months to complete the tour. Needless to say, you need to be selective here.

Some of the museum's finest pieces are in the center of the ground floor, below the atrium and rotunda. The area makes a good place to start, acting as a preview for the rest of the museum. Among the prized possessions here are three colossi of the legendary New Kingdom pharaoh Ramses II (1290–1224 BC); a limestone statue of Djoser (around 2600 BC), the 2nd Dynasty pharaoh who built the Step Pyramid in Saqqara; several sarcophagi; and a floor from the destroyed palace of Akhenaton (1353–1335 BC), the heretic monotheist king. The Narmer Palette, a piece from about 3000 BC, is thought to document the first unification of northern and southern Egypt.

On the museum's upper floor is the famous Tutankhamun collection. Look for its beautiful gold funerary mask and sarcophagus (Room 3), ancient trumpet (Room 30), thrones (rooms 20 and 25), the four huge gilded boxes that fit one inside the other (exhibits 7 and 8, located

in the hallway just outside Room 30), and a royal toilet seat to boot (outside Room 30); it is one of the few air-conditioned rooms in the museum. (The collection is scheduled to be relocated to the new Grand Egyptian Museum in Giza as early as 2010.) Also upstairs is the royal Mummy Room, which houses 11 pharaonic dignitaries, including the body of Ramses II (Room 52). If you are discouraged by the Mummy Room's steep entrance fee, don't miss the assortment of mummified animals and birds in the adjacent room (Room 53), which has no additional charge. Also on the upper floor is a series of specialized exhibits, including a collection of papyri and Middle Kingdom wooden models of daily life (rooms 24 and 27).

In 2003, the museum unveiled Hidden Treasures of the Egyptian Museum, more than 150 of the best objects that form part of the museum's vast stock of artifacts kept in storage. Fittingly, the new galleries sit in the museum basement, where the catalogued items used to lie on dark dusty shelves. In 2009, a permanent Children's Museum was opened and aimed specifically at younger visitors. These galleries combine authentic artifacts with Lego models (donated by the Danish State) to explain aspects of life and customs in ancient Egypt. Children are free to use Lego bricks to construct their own models. ⊠ *al-Mathaf al-Masri, Maydan Tahrir, Downtown* ☎ *02/2579–6948* 🖃 *Museum £E80, Mummy Room £E100* ☉ *Daily 9–6:30.*

GIZA
12 km (8 miles) southwest of Cairo.

The three pyramids of Khufu (Greek name: Cheops), Khafre (Chephren), and Menkaure (Mycerinus) dominate the Giza Plateau. Surrounding the father-son-grandson trio are smaller pyramids belonging to their female dependents, and the *mastabas* (large, trapezoid-shape tombs) of their courtiers and relatives. The word *mastaba* comes from the Arabic word for bench, which these tombs resemble in shape, if not in scale, and the mastabas were often painted and/or decorated with reliefs inside, with the actual burial sites placed in shafts cut into the bedrock. The great Sphinx crouches at the eastern edge of the plateau, guarding the necropolis. A museum south of the Great Pyramid contains one of the most extraordinary artifacts from ancient Egypt, Khufu's own royal boat. The pyramids, Sphinx, and some of the mastabas date from the Fourth Dynasty, while other mastabas date to the Fifth and Sixth Dynasties. South of the Sphinx and its adjacent temples, archaeologists have recently found the living and eating areas of the workmen who built the pyramids, as well as the cemeteries where they were buried.

Great Sphinx. Carved from the living rock of the pyramids plateau during the 4th Dynasty, the enigmatic limestone Sphinx is attached Pharaoh Khafre's funerary complex. The figure of a recumbent lion with a man's face wearing a *nemes* (traditional headdress of the pharaoh) was thought to be Khafre in the guise of Ra-Harakhte, a manifestation of the Sun God. The role of the Sphinx was to guard the vast royal necropolis that incorporated the pyramids and *mastabas* (large trapezoidal tombs) on the Giza plateau, and it's visited as part of the longer

visit incorporating these other monuments at the site. It's possible to get close to the Sphinx along a wide viewing platform that has been built around it, but climbing is forbidden and there's no entry into the small interior chambers (most of the Sphinx, however, is solid rock). ⊠ *Fayyum Rd.* ▦ *Sphinx £E60 (includes both Pyramids and Sphinx), Sound & Light Show £E75* ⊙ *Daily 8–6:30; Sound & Light Show (in English) Oct.–Apr., Mon.–Wed. and Fri.–Sat. 6:30 pm, Thurs. 7:30 pm, Sun. 9:30 pm; May–Sept., Mon.–Wed. and Fri.–Sat. 8:30 pm, Thurs. 9:30 pm, Sun. 11:30 pm.*

Fodor'sChoice
★
Pyramid Plateau. Three 4th-Dynasty pyramids dominate the skyline of the desert plateau to the southwest of Cairo. The largest is that of Pharaoh Khufu (Greek name: Cheops) also known as "The Great Pyramid." The second was built by his son Khafre (Greek name: Chephren). The smallest of pyramids was built by Menkaure (Greek name: Mycerinus), the grandson of Khufu who reigned from 2490 to 2472 BC. These are surrounded by smaller pyramids belonging to their respective female dependents, as well as numerous *mastabas* (large trapezoidal tombs) of their lesser relatives and courtiers. The site is "guarded" by the monumental carved-limestone Sphinx. A small museum in the shadow of Khufu's Pyramid contains the Pharaoh's Royal Solar Boat, by tradition the boat used to transport the Pharaoh on his final journey to the afterlife after his mummy was entombed. The pyramid interiors are open on a rotating basis, and ticket numbers are limited to 150 per morning and another 150 per afternoon. A range of *mastabas* will be open to view on any given day. The ticket office will give you current information when you buy your ticket. Buses and cars are no longer allowed on the plateau; electric trams link the ticket office with the plateau, from where you'll be able to explore the site on foot. ⊠ *Pyramids Rd.* ▦ *General admission £E60 (includes both Pyramids and Sphinx), Great Pyramid £E100, Khafre's Pyramid £E30, Mankaure's Pyramid £E25, Solar Boat Museum £E50* ⊙ *Site daily 8–6:30, pyramid and tomb interiors daily 9–4 (but the openings are staggered, so not all pyramid interiors are open every day).*

SHOPPING

Cairo has always been a mercantile and trading town. The hundreds of magnificent mosques and palaces scattered around the city are a testament to Cairo's highly skilled craftspeople. The artisans of Egypt continue this tradition of detailed workmanship, offering a tremendous array of handmade items.

Egyptians specialize in worked brass and copper articles, wood inlay on jewelry boxes and chess sets, and leatherwear. The hookah is also an interesting regional specialty. Egyptian cotton is a byword for quality, and the shops of Cairo are a great place to buy items like bedding and towels. If you want to purchase genuine antiques and antiquities you'll need to have a certificate of approval from the Egyptian authorities to export your purchase, but reproductions are on sale everywhere. These items needn't be expensive: you can buy a lucky alabaster scarab beetle for a few Egyptian pounds—in fact, this small item is almost a compulsory souvenir of your trip to Egypt.

Khan al-Khalili. Cairo shopping starts at this great medieval souk. Although it has been on every tourist's itinerary for centuries, and some of its more visible wares can seem awfully tacky, the Khan is where everyone—newcomer and age-old Cairene alike—goes to find traditional items: jewelry, lamps, spices, clothes, textiles, handicrafts, water pipes, metalwork, you name it. Whatever it is, you can find it somewhere in this skein of alleys or the streets around them. Every Khan veteran has the shops he or she swears by—usually because of the fact (or illusion) she or he is known there personally and is thus less likely to be overcharged. Go, browse, and bargain hard. Once you buy something, don't ask how much it costs at the next shop; you'll be happier that way. Many shops close Sunday. ⊠ *Islamic Cairo North, Cairo.*

> ## GRAND EGYPTIAN MUSEUM
>
> The Grand Egyptian Museum will be a fitting home for the mother lode of ancient artifacts excavated in the country in the last 150 years. When opened it will be the world's biggest museum dedicated to ancient Egypt, covering 123 acres (50 hectares) on the Giza Plateau less than 2 miles from the Pyramids. The foundation stone of the museum was laid in 2002, and at this writing only the research labs of the complex are complete. Current estimates are that the museum will open to the public in 2013.

WHERE TO EAT

$$
SEAFOOD
✗ **The Fish Market.** On the upper deck of a boat permanently moored on the west bank of the Nile, the scene here is decidedly simple: there's no menu, just a display of unbelievably fresh fish, shrimp, crabs, calamari, and shellfish on ice. Pick what appeals, pay by weight, and the kitchen will prepare it however you like, with a slew of Middle Eastern salads on the side. The delicious bread is baked on the premises in a *baladi* (country) oven. ⑤ *Average main: £E330* ⊠ *26 Shar'a al-Nil, Giza, Cairo* ☎ *02/3570–9694* ⟀ *Reservations essential.*

$$
MIDDLE EASTERN
✗ **Naguib Mahfouz Café.** Named after Egypt's most famous novelist and run by the Oberoi Hotel Group, this is a haven of air-conditioned tranquility in the midst of the sometimes-chaotic Khan al-Khalili. The restaurant serves variations on the usual Egyptian dishes, dressed up in historically resonant names to justify what, by the standards of the area, constitute exorbitant prices. That being said, the food and service are also of higher quality than you'll find in most of the nearby restaurants. The adjoining café serves lighter fare, consisting mostly of sandwiches, at a fraction of the price of the main dishes. ⑤ *Average main: £E330* ⊠ *5 al-Badestan La., Khan al-Khalili, Islamic Cairo North, Cairo* ☎ *02/2590–3788.*

RHODES, GREECE

Updated by
Adrian Vrettos
and Alexia
Amvrazi

The island of Rhodes (1,400 square km [540 square miles]) is one of the great islands of the Mediterranean. It was long considered a bridge between Europe and the East, and has seen many waves of settlement throughout recorded history. Ancient Rhodes was a powerful city and its political organization became the model for the city of Alexandria in Egypt. When Rome took the city in 42 BC, it was fabled for its beauty and for the sanctuary of Lindos, which drew pilgrims from around the region. Rhodes was a crucial stop on the road to the Holy Land during the Crusades. It came briefly under Venetian influence, then Byzantine, then Genoese, but in 1309, when the Knights of St. John took the city from its Genoese masters, its most glorious modern era began. Today Rhodes is a popular holiday island for Europeans who come for the sun and the beaches.

ESSENTIALS

CURRENCY

The euro.

HOURS

Shops are open from 9 to 9 on weekdays and from 9 to 6 on Saturday. Museums are generally open from 9 to 5, but many are closed on Monday.

TELEPHONES

Tri-band GSM phones work in Greece. You can buy prepaid phone cards at telecom shops, news vendors, and tobacconists in all towns and cities. Phone cards can be used for local or international calls. Vodafone is the leading mobile telecom company. OTE is the national domestic provider. Calls can be made at OTE offices and paid for after completion.

COMING ASHORE

Ships dock at the commercial port directly outside the city walls of Rhodes Town. It is a short walk from the port to all the attractions of the walled citadel. For this reason, there are few facilities in the port itself.

The bus station for services down the east coast is found by turning right outside the port and walking for 10 minutes to Rimini Square. There are several services to Lindos each day. Journey time is about one hour, and ticket prices are €5.

Taxis wait outside the port gates but can also be found at Rimini Square. For a journey to Lindos, prices are fixed at a fare of €35 one-way. Journey time is approximately 30 minutes. You could enjoy a full day touring Rhodes island if you rent a car, though both Rhodes's Old Town and Lindos are pedestrian-only or have very limited vehicular access. Costs are €45 per day for a subcompact vehicle, and the major companies can bring a car to the port for you.

Rhodes

Ialyssos (Trianda)
Ixia
Koskinou
Ialyssos
Bay of Kallitheas
Petaloudes
Faliraki
Kameiros
Mount Profitis Ilias
Afandou
Alimia
Kritinia
Epta Piges
Halki
Embonas
Arhangelos
Nimborio
Mount Ataviros
Laerma
Vliha Bay
Siana
Monolithos
Fournoi
Lardos
Lindos
Bay of Apolakia
Apolakkia
Pefki
Messanagros
Gennadi
Katavia
Ayios Pavlos
Plimiri
Prasonisi
Agios Georgios

Rhodes Town see detail map

0   8 miles
0   12 km

Rhodes Town

Koundourioti Sq.
Akti Bouboulli
Mandraki
Harbor
Promitheou
Kisthiniou
Pl. Eleftherias
Makariou
Alexandrias Sq.
Simis Sq.
Aktisahtouri
Pindarou
Alhadef
Vas. Georgiou Sq.
Amerikis
25 Martiou
Kiprou Sq.
Rimini Sq.
Papagou
Museum of Decorative Arts
Aristotelous
Perikleous
28 Oktovriou
Sofia Venizelou
Lambraki
Makariou
Ippoton
Archaeological Museum
Lahitos
Byzantine Museum
Pithagora
Sokratous
Tipotemou
Attas
Amphostou
Palace of the Grand Masters
Sokratous
Athinas Sq.
Solotkeos
Omirou
Alexandrou Diakou
Inn of France
Loggia of St. John
Kleovoulou Sq.
Orfeous
Mosque of Süleyman
Agiou Fanouriou
Erithrou Stavrou
El. Venizelou
Turkish Library
Arionos Sq.
Riga Ferrou
Navarinou
Dimokratias
Walls of Rhodes
Ipodemou
Tradatou
Fileimon
Dimokratias

0   1/8 mi
0   1/8 km

EXPLORING RHODES

RHODES TOWN

Rhodes Town is still a city of two parts: the Old Town, a UNESCO World Heritage site, contains exceptional medieval architecture, Orthodox and Catholic churches, and an alluring old Turkish quarter. Spreading away from the walls that encircle the Old Town is the modern metropolis, or new town.

Archaeological Museum. The Hospital of the Knights, completed in 1489, houses the town's Archaeological Museum. In the courtyard just beyond the imposing facade are cannonballs from the Ottoman siege of 1522, and, in surrounding halls, are two well-known representations of Aphrodite: the *Aphrodite of Rhodes,* who, while bathing, pushes aside her hair as if she's listening; and a standing figure, known as *Aphrodite Thalassia,* or "of the sea," as she was discovered in the water off the northern city beach. Other important works include two 6th-century BC *kouros* (statues of idealized male youth) found in the nearby ancient city of Kameiros, and the beautiful 5th-century BC funerary stela of Timarista bidding farewell to her mother, Crito. ⊠ *Mouseou Sq.* ☎ *22413/65200* 🖾 *€6* ☾ *Apr.–Oct., daily 8–8; Nov.– Mar., Tues.–Sun. 9–4.*

Byzantine Museum. Icons and frescoes from churches throughout Rhodes Town (most of them long since destroyed) are displayed within the 11th-century Lady of the Castle church, once the Byzantine cathedral and, under the Turks, a mosque. ⊠ *Off Mouseou Sq.* ☎ *22413/65200* 🖾 *€6* ☾ *Apr.–Oct., daily 8–8; Nov.–Mar., Tues.–Sun. 9–4.*

Inn of France. The Inn of France, the most elaborate of the striking inns on this famously historic street, today houses a French language institute (appropriately enough). The facade is ornately carved with the fleur-de-lis and heraldic patterns and bears an inscription that dates the building between 1492 and 1509. ⊠ *About halfway down street of Knights from Loggia of St. John.*

Loggia of St. John. Before the court of the Palace of the Grand Masters is the Loggia of St. John. This 19th-century neo-Gothic structure stands on the site of the 14th-century church of St. John, patron of the Knights of St. John and the final resting place of many members of the order. Used as an ammunition storehouse during Turkish occupation, the church was reduced to rubble in an explosion sparked by lightning in 1856.

Mosque of Süleyman. The Mosque of Süleyman was built circa 1522 to commemorate Sultan Süleyman's conquest of Rhodes and rebuilt in 1808, with a graceful minaret and distinctive pink and white stripes. ⊠ *At top of Sokratous* ☎ *22413/65200* 🖾 *Closed for renovation.*

Museum of Decorative Arts. Housed in a stone-vaulted warehouse of the Knights, the town's museum of decorative arts, which is closed for a renovation through much of 2013, exhibits finely made ceramics, wooden tools and utensils, and costumes and textiles from the various regions of the Dodecanese. ⊠ *Argyrokastrou Sq.* ☎ *22413/65200* 🖾 *€3* ☾ *Apr.–Oct., Tues.–Sun. 8:30–7; Nov.–Mar., Tues.–Sun. 8:30–3.*

Palace of the Grand Masters. The Knights of St. John built most of their monuments along a street known as the **Street of the Knights** (Ippoton), which descends from the Palace of the Grand Masters, at the highest spot of the medieval city, toward the commercial port. This cobbled lane is a little more than a third of a mile long and follows the route that once connected the ancient acropolis to the harbor. This medieval assemblage is bordered on both sides by the **Inns of the Tongues**, where the Knights supped and held their meetings. **The Palace of the Grand Masters of the Knights of Rhodes** (to use its official name) is a massive affair with fairy-tale towers, crenellated ramparts, and more than 150 rooms. Situated at the top of

> ### RHODES BEST BETS
>
> **Walk down the Street of the Knights.** This medieval street is one of the most complete of its kind in the world. Imagine the Crusader knights going about their business here.
>
> **Explore the Turkish Quarter.** These narrow alleyways now play host to boutiques and cafés, but it's still a living district with real Aegean character.
>
> **Survey Lindos Town from the Acropolis above.** The splendid vista includes a tangle of narrow streets, whitewashed walls, and terra-cotta roofs down to the horseshoe bay with azure waters.

the Street of the Knights, it is the place to begin a tour. Unscathed during the Turkish siege of Rhodes in 1522, the palace was destroyed in 1856 by an explosion of ammunition stored nearby in the cellars of the Church of St. John; the present structure—a Mussolini-era Italian reconstruction—was rebuilt in a storybook, pseudo-medieval style then all the rage in the early 20th century and was later used as a holiday abode for King Vittorio Emmanuele III of Italy. Today, the palace's collection of antiques and antiquities includes Hellenistic and Roman mosaic floors from Italian excavations in Kos, and in the permanent exhibition downstairs, extensive displays, maps, and plans showing the layout of the city will help you get oriented before wandering through the labyrinthine Old Town. ⊠ *Ippoton, Old Town* ☎ *22413/65270* 💶 *€6* 🕙 *May–Oct., Mon. 9–4, Tues.–Sun. 8–8; Nov.– Apr., Tues.–Sun. 9–4.*

★ **Turkish Library.** The Turkish Library dates to the late 18th century and houses a rare collection of Turkish, Persian, and Arab manuscripts, including many rare Korans. Striking reminders of the Ottoman presence, the library and the Mosque of Suleyman are still used by those members of Rhodes's Turkish community who stayed in Rhodes after the 1923 population exchange, a mass repatriation of Greek and Turkish migrants. ⊠ *Sokratous, opposite Mosque of Süleyman* ☎ *2241/7400* 💶 *Free* 🕙 *Mon.–Sat. 9:30–3.*

Walls of Rhodes. One of the great medieval monuments in the Mediterranean, the walls of Rhodes are wonderfully restored and illustrate the engineering capabilities as well as the financial and human resources available to the Knights of St. John. For 200 years the Knights strengthened the walls by thickening them, up to 40 feet in places, and curving them so as to deflect cannonballs. The moat between the inner and outer

walls never contained water; it was a device to prevent invaders from constructing siege towers. You can also get a sense of the enclosed city's massive scale by walking inside the moat. ⊠ *Old Town* ☎ *22413/65270* 🖼 *Moat free; tours €2* ☉ *Tours Tues. and Sat. 8–noon (arrive at least 15 min. early).*

LINDOS
19 km (12 miles) southwest of Epta Piges, 48 km (30 miles) southwest of Rhodes Town.

Lindos, cradled between two harbors, had a particular importance in antiquity. It had a revered sanctuary, consecrated to Athena, whose cult probably succeeded that of a pre-Hellenic divinity named Lindia, and the sanctuary was dedicated to Athena Lindia. Lindos prospered during the Middle Ages, and under the Knights of St. John. Only at the beginning of the 19th century did the age-old shipping activity cease. The population decreased radically, reviving only with the 20th-century influx of foreigners.

Lindos is enchanting and remarkably well preserved. Many 15th-century houses are still in use. Everywhere are examples of Crusader architecture: substantial houses of finely cut Lindos limestone, with windows crowned by elaborate arches. Intermixed with these Crusader buildings are whitewashed, geometric, Cycladic-style houses. Many floors are paved with black-and-white pebble mosaics. The narrow alleyways can get crowded in summer.

Fodor's Choice **Acropolis of Lindos.** For about €5, you can hire a donkey for the 15-
★ minute climb from the modern town up to the Acropolis of Lindos. The
🅒 winding path leads past a gauntlet of Lindian women who spread out their lace and embroidery like fresh laundry over the rocks. The final approach ascends a steep flight of stairs, past a marvelous 2nd-century BC **relief of the prow of a Lindian ship,** carved into the rock.

The entrance to the Acropolis takes you through the **Medieval Castle** built by the Knights of St. John, then to the Byzantine **Chapel of St. John** on the next level. The Romans, too, left their mark on the acropolis, with a temple dedicated to Diocletian. On the **upper terraces,** begun by classical Greeks around 300 BC, are the remains of elaborate **porticoes** and **stoas,** commanding an immense sweep of sea and making a powerful statement on behalf of Athena and the Lydians (who dedicated the monuments on the Acropolis to her); the lofty white columns of the temple and stoa on the summit must have presented a magnificent picture. The main portico of the stoa had 42 Doric columns, at the center of which an opening led to the staircase up to the **Propylaia** (or sanctuary). The **Temple of Athena Lindia** at the very top is surprisingly modest, given the drama of the approach. As was common in the 4th century BC, both the front and the rear are flanked by four Doric columns. Numerous inscribed statue bases were found all over the summit, attesting in many cases to the work of Lindian sculptors, who were clearly second to none. ⊠ *Above New Town* ☎ *22440/31258* ⊕ *www.culture.gr* 🖼 *€6* ☉ *May–Oct., Tues.–Sun. 8–5:40, Mon. 8–2:40; Nov.–Apr., Tues.–Sun. 8–2:40.*

Church of the Panayia. A graceful building with a beautiful bell tower, the Church of the Panayia probably antedates the Knights, though the bell tower bears the arms of Grand Master d'Aubusson with the dates 1484–90. Frescoes in the elaborate interior were painted in 1779 by Gregory of Symi, and the black-and-white pebble floor is a popular Byzantine design. ⊠ *Off main square* ☻ *May–Oct., daily 9–2 and 5–9; Nov.–Apr., call number posted on church to have door unlocked.*

SHOPPING

3

Lovers of handicrafts will really enjoy shopping in Rhodes. There's an abundance of ceramics, both traditional and modern, wooden bowls, reproductions of ancient statuary, woven rugs, jewelry, lace, and edibles such as delicious honey, olive oil, and of course, olives themselves. Cotton clothing is perfect for the summer temperatures. Strong handcrafted sandals and leather goods are also excellent choices.

Souvenir shopping in Rhodes Town is concentrated on Sokratous Street and the labyrinth of narrow alleyways in the old Turkish Quarter. You'll find the same merchandise in the alleyways of Lindos, where every inch of wall space is used for display—sometimes to the detriment of pedestrian traffic flow. Rhodes Town has a number of high-class jewelers and camera shops, whereas Lindos has more art galleries. The winding path that leads up to the citadel of Lindos is traditionally where Lindian women spread out their lace and embroidery over the rocks like fresh laundry.

Astero Antiques. Mahalis Hatziz, owner of Astero Antiques, travels throughout Greece each winter to fill his shop with some of the most enticing goods on offer on the island. ⊠ *Ayiou Fanouriou 4, off Sokratous, Rhodes Town* ☎ *22410/34753.*

BEACHES

Rhodes is a popular island with European vacationers, and the beaches all around the island have well-developed facilities.

Lachania. Stretching uninterrupted for several miles, Lachania beach begins a mile north of Gennadi; drive alongside until you come to a secluded spot.

WHERE TO EAT

$$$
SEAFOOD
★

✕ **Dinoris.** The great hall that holds Dinoris was built in AD 310 as a hospital and then converted into a stable for the Knights in 1530. The fish specialties and the spacious, classy setting lure appreciative and demanding clients, from visiting celebs to Middle Eastern sheikhs. For appetizers, try the variety platter, which includes *psarokeftedakia* (fish balls made from a secret recipe) as well as mussels, shrimp, and lobster. Other special dishes are sea urchin salad and grilled calamari stuffed with cheese. In warm months, cool sea air drifts through the outdoor garden area enclosed by part of the city's walls. ⑤ *Average main: €25* ⊠ *Mouseou Sq. 14a, Rhodes Town* ☎ *22410/25824* ⌲ *Reservations essential* ☻ *Closed Jan.*

$$ ✕ **Mavrikos.** The secret of this longtime favorite, one of the finest
GREEK   restaurants on Rhodes, is an elegant, perfect simplicity. Seemingly
Fodor's Choice   straightforward dishes, such as sea-urchin salad, fried *manouri* cheese
★   with basil and pine nuts, swordfish in caper sauce, and lobster risotto,
become transcendent with the magic touch of third-generation chef
Dimitris Mavrikos, who now owns this 75-year-old family-run institu-
tion with his brother, Michalis. He combines the freshest ingredients
with classical training and an abiding love for the best of Greek vil-
lage cuisine. The meat dishes, including oven-baked lamb, are also
sublime. $ *Average main: €20* ⊠ *Main square, Lindos* ☎ *22440/31232*
⊘ *Closed Nov.–Mar.*

SANTORINI, GREECE

Updated by
Adrian Vrettos
and Alexia
Amvrazi

Undoubtedly the most extraordinary island in the Aegean, crescent-
shape Santorini remains a mandatory stop on the Cycladic tourist
route—even if it's necessary to enjoy the sensational sunsets from Ia,
the fascinating excavations, and the dazzling white towns with a mil-
lion other travelers. Arriving by boat, you are met by one of the world's
truly breathtaking sights, the caldera: a crescent of cliffs, striated in
black, pink, brown, white, and pale green, rising 1,100 feet, with the
white clusters of the towns of Fira and Ia perched along the top. The
encircling cliffs are the ancient rim of a still-active volcano, and you
are sailing east across its flooded caldera. Victims of their own success,
the main towns of Santorini can at peak times seem overburdened by
an unrelenting mass of backpackers and tour groups. Even so, if you
look beneath the layers of gimcrack tourism, you'll find that Santorini
is still a beautiful place.

ESSENTIALS
CURRENCY
The euro.

HOURS
Museums are generally open from 9 to 5, but many are closed on
Monday. Shops are open daily in the summer, from 9 to noon or 1,
reopening from 4 or 5 until 9 on Monday through Saturday; and from
9 to 6 on Sunday. Many shops and restaurants are closed between
October and April.

TELEPHONES
Tri-band GSM phones work in Greece. You can buy prepaid phone
cards at telecom shops, news vendors, and tobacconists in all towns
and cities. Phone cards can be used for local or international calls.
Vodafone is the leading mobile telecom company. OTE is the national
domestic provider. Calls can be made at OTE offices and paid for
after completion.

COMING ASHORE
Cruise ships anchor in the spectacular caldera, and in almost all cases
passengers are tendered to the small port of Skala Fira, a sheer 1,000
feet below the capital, Fira. You can either take the funicular to the
top or take a donkey ride up the steep winding path that claws its way

Santorini

0 —— 2 miles
0 —— 3 km

Baxedes

Ia ○ Perivolos

○ Thirassia
Thirassia Sprinisi

Skaros ○ **Imerovigli**

○ **Firostefani**

○ **Fira**

Karterados ○

Monolithos ○

*As
pronissi* *Palea
Kameni* **Nea
Kameni**

Messaria ○

Athinios ○

Pyrgos ○ ○ Agia
Paraskevi

Megalochori ○

Red Beach Akrotiri ○ ○ Kamari

Emborio ○

Perissa ○

Sea of Crete

Fira

cable car

**Archaeological
Museum** ♦

Agiou Mina *Ypapantis* *Erythrou Stavrou* *25 Martiou* *Kovaeou*

Marinatou

Agiou Athanassiou

Christi Odos

*Plateia
Theotokopoulou
Square*

Danezi

Decigala

**Panayia
Ypapantis** ♦

Museum of Prehistoric Thera ♦

0 —— 1/16 mi
0 —— 1/16 km

to the top; regardless of your mode of travel, the cost is the same (€5). The donkey drivers are very persistent, but be aware that donkey droppings make the path slippery and smelly (especially relevant if you decide to go up on foot, which is also possible).

Regular bus services (approximately every 30 minutes in summer, dropping to every 1½ hours in winter with shoulder seasons) travel from Thira to Ia and Akrotiri. Schedules are posted in the station. Ticket prices range from €1.40 to €3. The main taxi stand sits next to the bus station in the main town square. Fares are reasonable, with a trip from Fira to Ia costing approximately €15.

If you rented a car for the day, you could probably see most of what Santorini has to offer. The island is compact, and it's difficult to get lost. Prices are €50 per day for a subcompact manual vehicle, but you can get an ATV for around €25 or a motorbike or scooter with prices starting at about €10 a day, including third-party liability coverage. If you rent a quad, bike, or scooter don't wear shorts or sandals, insist on the helmet (which the law requires), and get a phone number, in case of breakdown. Don't rent a scooter if you aren't an experienced rider.

> ### SANTORINI BEST BETS
>
> **The view of Santorini from the ship.** The panoramic vista of the immense volcano with whitewashed settlements tumbling over the caldera edge is unique and quite unforgettable.
>
> **The remains of ancient Akrotiri.** A city frozen in time by volcanic ash, ancient Akrotiri tells a fascinating story of a rich Aegean civilization that seems to have escaped before disaster struck.
>
> **Strolling the streets of Ia.** Santorini's most beautiful village has foliage-draped Cycladic houses, boutiques, and eateries. The views are best at sunset.

EXPLORING SANTORINI

FIRA

Tourism, the island's major industry, adds more than 1 million visitors per year to a population of 7,000. As a result, Fira, the capital, midway along the west coast of the east rim, is no longer only a picturesque village but a major tourist center, overflowing with discos, shops, and restaurants. It soon becomes clear what brings the tourist here: with its white, cubical white houses clinging to the cliff hundreds of feet above the caldera, Fira is a beautiful place. The blocked-off Ypapantis Street (west of Panayia Ypapantis cathedral) leads to Kato Fira (Lower Fira), built into the cliff-side overlooking the caldera, where prices are higher and the vista wonderful. For centuries, the people of the island have been digging themselves rooms with a view right in the cliff face. Along Eikostis Pemptis Martiou (25th March Street), you'll find inexpensive restaurants and accommodations—many bars and hotel rooms now occupy the caves. The farther away from the caldera you get, the cheaper the restaurants.

Archaeological Museum. This fascinating squint into the island's millenia of history offers displays of pottery, statues, and grave artifacts

found at excavations mostly from ancient Thira and Akrotiri, from the Minoan through the Byzantine periods. ⊠ *Stavrou and Nomikos, Mitropoleos, behind big church* ☎ *22860/22217* 🖃 *€3, including Museum of Prehistoric Thera* ⊙ *Apr.–Oct., Tues.–Sun. 9–4; Nov.–Mar., Tues.–Sun. 8:30–3.*

★ **Museum of Prehistoric Thera.** This is the treasure house that displays pots and frescoes from the famed excavations at Akrotiri. Note the fresco fragments with the painted swallows (who flocked here

---

ANCIENT AKROTIRI

The best archaeological site on Santorini is near the tip of the southern horn of the island. Unfortunately, at this writing the site is closed (and has been for some time) for structural repairs. There was some hope that it might reopen, but such hopes have become commonplace for the past few years, so check ahead before you plan a visit.

---

because they loved the cliffs) and the women in Minoan dresses. The swallows, which still come in spring, remain the island's favorite design motif. The fossilized olive leaves from 60,000 BC prove the olive to be indigenous. ⊠ *Mitropoleos, behind big church* ☎ *22860/23217* ⊕ *www.culture.gr* 🖃 *€3, including Archaeological Museum* ⊙ *Summer, Tues.–Sun. 8–7:30; winter, 8:30–3.*

Panayia Ypapantis. The modern Greek Orthodox cathedral of Panayia Ypapantis is a major landmark; you'll quickly note how the local priests, with somber faces, long beards, and black robes, look strangely out of place in summertime, tourist-jammed Fira. ⊠ *Southern part of town.*

FIROSTEFANI

Firostefani used to be a separate village, but now it is an elegant suburb north of Fira. The 10-minute walk between it and Fira, along the caldera, is one of Santorini's highlights. From Firostefani's single white cliff-side street, walkways descend to traditional vaulted cave houses, which are fast becoming pensions. Though close to the action, Firostefani feels calm and quiet.

IMEROVIGLI

Imerovigli, on the highest point of the caldera's rim, is what Firostefani was like a decade and a half ago. It is now being developed, and for good reasons: it is quiet, traditional, and less expensive. The 25-minute walk from Fira, with incredible views, should be on everyone's itinerary. The lodgments, some of them traditional cave houses, are mostly down stairways from the cliff-side walkway. The big rock backing the village was once crowned by Skaros castle, where Venetial the conqueror raised his flag in 1207; it housed the island's administrative offices. It collapsed in an earthquake, leaving only the rock.

IA

Fodor's Choice

★ At the tip of the northern horn of the island sits Ia (or Oia), Santorini's second-largest town and the Aegean's most-photographed village. Ia is more tasteful than Fira (for one thing, no establishment here is allowed to play music that can be heard on the street), and the town's cubical white houses (some vaulted against earthquakes) stand out against the green-, brown-, and rust-color layers of rock, earth, and

solid volcanic ash that rise from the sea. Every summer evening, travelers from all over the world congregate at the caldera's rim—sitting on whitewashed fences, staircases, beneath the town's windmill, on the old **Kastro**—each looking out to sea in anticipation of the performance: the Ia sunset. The three-hour rim-edge walk from Ia to Fira at this hour is unforgettable.

Ia is set up like the other three towns—Fira, Firostefani, and Imerovigli—that adorn the caldera's sinuous rim. There is a car road, which is new, and a cliff-side walkway (Nikolaos Nomikou), which is old. Shops and restaurants are all on the walkway, and hotel entrances mostly descend from it—something to check carefully if you cannot negotiate stairs easily. In Ia there is a lower cliff-side walkway writhing with stone steps, and a long stairway to the tiny blue bay with its dock below. Short streets leading from the car road to the walkway have cheaper eateries and shops. There is a parking lot at either end, and the northern one marks the end of the road and the rim. Nothing is very far from anything else.

The main walkway of Ia can be thought of as a straight river, with a delta at the northern end, where the better shops and restaurants are. The most-luxurious cave-house hotels are at the southern end, and a stroll by them is part of the extended evening promenade. Although it is not as crowded as Fira, where the tour boats deposit their thousands of hasty shoppers, relentless publicity about Ia's beauty and tastefulness, accurate enough, are making it impassable in August. The sunset in Ia may not really be much more spectacular than in Fira, and certainly not better than in higher Imerovigli, but there is something tribally satisfying at the sight of so many people gathering in one spot to celebrate pure beauty. Happily, the night scene isn't as frantic as Fira's—most shop owners are content to sit out front and don't cotton to the few revelers' bars in operation. In winter Ia feels pretty uninhabited.

Fodor's Choice **Naval Museum of Thera.** Set in an old neoclassic mansion, once destroyed
★ in the big earthquake, the Naval Museum of Thera has now risen like a phoenix from the ashes. The collection displays ships' figureheads, seamen's chests, maritime equipment, and models—all revealing the extensive nautical history of the island, Santorini's main trade until tourism took over. ⊠ *Near telephone office* ☎ *22860/71156* 🖃 *€3* ☉ *Apr.–Oct., Wed.–Mon. 10–2 and 5–8.*

NEA KAMENI

Nea Kameni. To peer into a live, sometimes smoldering volcano, join one of the popular excursions to Nea Kameni, the larger of the two Burnt Isles. After disembarking, you hike 430 feet to the top and walk around the edge of the crater, wondering if the volcano is ready for its fifth eruption during the last hundred years—after all, the last was in 1956. Some tours continue on to Therassia, where there is a village. Tours (about €20) are scheduled regularly.

SHOPPING

The dramatic landscapes and light of Santorini are an inspiration to the creative—the archipelago is home to artists working in many genres. There are many galleries selling exquisite one-of-a-kind jewelry and hundreds of others selling artistic accessories for the home.

The locals say that in Santorini there is more wine than water, and it may be true: Santorini produces more wine than any two other Cyclades. Thirty-six varieties of grape thrive here. Farmers twist the vines into a basketlike shape, in which the grapes grow, protected from the wind.

Fodor's Choice
★
Bead Shop. Marina Tsiagkouri's shop has expanded, but beads are still the main reason to go. Who can resist her unique beads made from Santorini's volcanic rock? ⊠ *Opposite entrance to Museum of Prehistoric Thera, Fira* ☎ *22860/25176.*

Costas Dimitrokalis. With purchases that can be mailed anywhere, Costas Dimitrokalis and Matthew Dimitrokalis sell locally made embroideries of Greek linen and Egyptian cotton, rugs, pillowcases in hand-crocheted wool with local designs, and more. ⊠ *1 block from cable car, Fira* ☎☎ *22860/22957.*

Kostas Antoniou Jewelry. Many of Kostas's pieces were inspired by ancient Thera. Master jeweler Gerry Kafieris sells his Triton jewelry collection here, including delicate minautre mosaics. ⊠ *In Spiliotica shopping area, near Archaeological Museum, Fira* ☎ *22860/22633.*

★
Phenomenon. Christoforos Asimis studied painting at Athens University, and has had many exhibitions there and abroad. The nearby cathedral's murals are his. His paintings specialize in the light and landscape of his home island. His wife, Eleni, who also studied in Athens, creates some of Santorini's most elegant jewelry. ⊠ *Ypapantis walkway, Palia Fabrika, Fira* ☎ *22860/23041* ⊕ *www.santorini.info/paliafabrika/index.html.*

BEACHES

Santorini's volcanic rocks have produced unusual beaches of black and red sand that make for dramatic vistas. One thing to note is that this sand absorbs the suns rays and gets much hotter than golden sand. The black-sand beaches of **Kamari** (and of Perissa) are popular and consequently overdeveloped. Deck chairs and umbrellas can be rented, and tavernas and refreshment stands abound.

Red Beach. This comes up a winner on several fronts: it is quiet, has a taverna, and is covered with red-hued sands (have your Nikon handy). ⊠ *On southwest shore below Akrotiri, Akrotiri.*

WHERE TO EAT

$$
GREEK
★
✕ **Kastro.** Spyros Dimitroulis's restaurant is primarily patronized for its view of the famous Ia sunset, and at the magical hour it is always filled. Happily, the food makes a fitting accompaniment. A good starter is olives stuffed with cream cheese, dipped in beer dough, and fried,

served on arugula with a balsamic sauce. For a main dish try mussels with oil-pepper sauce. Lunch is popular. $ *Average main: €20* ⊠ *Near Venetian castle, Ia* ☎ *22860/71045.*

$ ✕ **Lithos.** Dimitris Anastopoulos's restaurant deftly proves you can eat GREEK well, inexpensively, and have a caldera view. Start with steamed mussels with ouzo and masticha liqueur or pastry flutes with Edam, sun-dried tomatoes, capers, and yogurt. For a main dish, try chicken with artichokes and capers in lemon cream sauce, or Lithos pork tenderloin, with mushrooms and kefalotiri cheese in red-wine sauce. Desserts are a specialty, and cheesecake with wild blackberries tastes as good as it looks. The oil and wine are from Dimitris's farm in the Peloponnese, and the fish is local. From the high caldera street, walk down to the lower until you see the sign. This neighborhood jumps at night. $ *Average main: €13* ⊠ *Caldera, Fira* ☎ *22860/24421* ⊕ *www.lithossantorini. com* ☉ *Closed Nov.–Mar.*

$ ✕ **Skaros Fish Taverna.** This rustic open-air taverna, one of the few res-GREEK taurants in Imerovigli, has spectacular caldera views. It serves fresh fish and Santorini specialties, such as octopus in onion sauce, and mussels with rice and raisins. $ *Average main: €14* ⊠ *On cliff-side walkway, Imerovigli* ☎ *22860/23616* ☉ *Closed Nov.–Mar.*

SPLIT, CROATIA

Updated by   The heart of Split lies within the walls of Roman emperor Diocletian's
Jane Foster   retirement palace, which was built in the 3rd century AD. Born in the nearby Roman settlement of Salona in AD 245, Diocletian achieved a brilliant career as a soldier and became emperor at the age of 40. In 295 he ordered this vast palace to be built in his native Dalmatia, and when it was completed he stepped down from the throne and retired to his beloved homeland. In 615, when Salona was sacked by barbarian tribes, refugees took shelter within the stout palace walls and divided up the vast imperial apartments into more modest living quarters. Thus, the palace developed into an urban center. Under the rule of Venice (1420–1797), Split became one of the Adriatic's main trading ports. When the Habsburgs took control during the 19th century, an overland connection to Central Europe was established by the construction of the Split–Zagreb–Vienna railway line. The Tito years saw a period of rapid urban expansion: industrialization accelerated.

ESSENTIALS

CURRENCY
The Croatian kuna.

HOURS
Offices are open weekdays from 8:30 to 4. Shops often close for lunch around 1 and may close for as long as three hours; banks also sometimes close for lunch. Post offices are open on Saturday during the main summer season, from June through September.

TELEPHONES
Most tri- and quad-band GSM phones will work in Croatia. Public phones use calling cards, which can be purchased at the post office, newsstands, and hotels. Major mobile phone companies include TMobile and VIPNet.

COMING ASHORE

Cruise ships dock in the city port, which is a 10-minute walk from Split's charming Old Town, which itself lies within the walls of Diocletian's Palace overlooking the sea. In the Old Town, you will find a useful tourist information office. Immediately opposite the port lie the train station and bus station, and there's also a taxi stand at the port.

Since the Old Town is compact and pedestrian-friendly, we recommend that you not rent a car in Split. However, if you do choose to rent, to explore further afield, expect to pay about €55 for a manual compact vehicle, though you can rent a semiautomatic Smart car at some outlets for about €50.

SPLIT BEST BETS

Diocletian's Palace. Explore this vast ancient palace, which now hosts the heart of Split's magnificent Old Town, a UNESCO World Heritage site.

Meštroviæ Gallery. See the works of Croatia's finest 20th-century sculptor—pieces in wood, marble, and bronze, displayed in his former summer villa.

Green retreat. Stroll across Marjan Peninsula, planted with pine trees and fragrant Mediterranean herbs, for superb views down onto the Old Town and out to sea.

EXPLORING SPLIT

The Old Town (often referred to as the Grad), where most of the architectural monuments are found, lies within the walls of Diocletian's Palace, which fronts on the seafront promenade, known to locals as the Riva. West of the center, Varoš is a conglomeration of stone fishermen's cottages built into a hillside, behind which rises Marjan, a 3½-km-long (2-mile-long) peninsula covered with pinewoods.

★ **Dioklecijanova Palača** (*Diocletian's Palace*). The original palace was a combination of a luxurious villa and a Roman garrison, based on the ground plan of an irregular rectangle. Each of the four walls bore a main gate, the largest and most important being the northern *Zlatna Vrata* (Golden Gate), opening onto the road to the Roman settlement of Salona. The entrance from the western wall was the *Željezna Vrata* (Iron Gate), and the entrance through the east wall was the *Srebrena Vrata* (Silver Gate). The *Mjedna Vrata* (Bronze Gate) in the south wall faced directly onto the sea, and during Roman times boats would have docked here. The city celebrated the palace's 1,700th birthday in 2005. ⊠ *Obala Hrvatskog Narodnog Preporoda, Grad.*

★ **Galerija Meštrović** (*Meštrović Gallery*). A modern villa surrounded by extensive gardens, this building designed by Ivan Meštrović was his summer residence during the 1920s and '30s. Some 200 of his sculptural works in wood, marble, stone, and bronze are on display, both indoors and out. There is a small open-air cafe in the garden with a lovely sea view. ⊠ *Šetalište Ivana Meštrovića 46, Meje* ☎ *021/340–800* ⊕ *www.mdc.hr* 💶 *30 Kn* ☉ *May–Sept., Tues.–Sun. 9–7; Oct.–Apr., Tues.–Sat. 9–4, Sun. 10–3.*

Kaštelet. Entrance to the Galerija Meštrović is also valid for the nearby Kaštelet, housing a chapel containing a cycle of New Testament

bas-relief wood carvings that many consider Meštrović's finest work. ✉ Šetalište Ivana Meštrovicá 39, Meje.

Galerija Vidović (*Vidović Gallery*). Emanuel Vidović (1870–1953) is acknowledged as Split's greatest painter. Here you can see 74 of his works, donated to the city by his family. Large, bold canvasses depict local landmarks cast in hazy light, while the sketches done outdoors before returning to his studio to paint are more playful and colorful. ✉ *Poljana Kraljice Jelene bb, Grad* ☏ *021/360–155* ⊕ *www.galerija-vidovic.com* 🎫 *10 Kn* 🕐 *June–Sept., Tues.–Fri. 9–9, weekends 9–4; Oct.–May, Tues.–Fri. 10–5, Sat. 9–1, Sun. 10–1.*

Gradski Muzej (*City Museum*). Split's city museum is worth a quick look both to marvel at the collection of medieval weaponry and to see the interior of this splendid 15th-century town house. The dining room, on the first floor, is furnished just as it would have been when the Papalić family owned the house, giving some idea of how the aristocracy of that time lived. ✉ *Papaličeva 1, Grad* ☏ *021/360–171* ⊕ *www.mgst. net* 🎫 *10 Kn* 🕐 *May.–Sep, Tues.–Fri. 9–9, Sat.–Mon. 10–4; Oct.–Apr., Tues.–Fri. 10–5, Sat.–Mon. 9–1.*

Jupiterov Hram (*Jupiter's Temple*). This Roman temple was converted into a baptistery during the Middle Ages. The entrance is guarded by the mate (unfortunately damaged) of the black-granite sphinx that

stands in front of the cathedral. Inside, beneath the coffered barrel vault and ornamented cornice, the 11th-century baptismal font is adorned with a stone relief showing a medieval Croatian king on his throne. Directly behind it, the bronze statue of St. John the Baptist is the work of Meštrović. ✉ *Kraj Sv Ivana, Grad* 🖾 *5 Kn* 🕒 *May–Oct., daily 8–7.*

Katedrala Sveti Dujam (*Cathedral of St. Dominius*). The main body of the cathedral is the 3rd-century octagonal mausoleum designed as a shrine to Emperor Diocletian. During the 7th century, refugees from Salona converted it into an early Christian church, ironically dedicating it to Sv Duje (St. Domnius), after Bishop Domnius of Salona, one of the many Christians martyred during the late emperor's persecution campaign. The cathedral's monumental main door is ornamented with magnificent carved wooden reliefs, the work of Andrija Buvina of Split. Inside, the hexagonal Romanesque stone pulpit, with richly carved decoration, is from the 13th century. The high altar, surmounted by a late-Gothic canopy, was executed by Bonino of Milan in 1427. ✉ *Peristil, Grad* 🖾 *Cathedral free, bell tower 10 Kn* 🕒 *Nov.–Apr, daily 8–6; May–Oct., daily 8–7.*

Marjan (*Marjan Hill*). Situated on a hilly peninsula, this much-loved park is planted with pine trees and Mediterranean shrubs and has been a protected nature reserve since 1964. A network of paths crisscrosses the grounds, offering stunning views over the sea and islands. ✉ *Marjan.*

Muzej Hrvatskih Arheološki Spomenika (*Museum of Croatian Archaeological Monuments*). This modern building displays early Croatian religious art from the 7th through the 12th centuries. The most interesting exhibits are fine stone carvings decorated with plaitwork designs, surprisingly similar to the geometric patterns typical of Celtic art. In the garden you can see several stećci, monolithic stone tombs dating back to the cult of the Bogomils (an anti-imperial sect that developed in the Balkans during the 10th century). ✉ *Šetalište Ivana Meštrovića 18, Meje* ☎ *021/323–901* ⊕ *www.mhas-split.hr* 🖾 *10 Kn* 🕒 *Mon.–Fri. 9–1 and 5–8, Sat. 9–2.*

Narodni trg (*People's Square*). A pedestrianized expanse paved with gleaming white marble, and rimmed by open-air cafés, this is contemporary Split's main square. Although religious activity has to this day centered on Peristil, Narodni trg became the focus of civic life during the 14th century. In the 15th century the Venetians constructed several important public buildings here: the Town Hall (housing a contemporary art gallery, with erratic opening hours), plus the Rector's Palace and a theater, the latter two sadly demolished by the Habsburgs in the 19th century. The Austrians, for their part, added a Secessionist building at the west end of the square. ✉ *Grad.*

Peristil (*Peristyle*). From Roman times up to the present day, the main public meeting place within the palace walls, this spacious central courtyard is flanked by marble columns topped with Corinthian capitals and richly ornamented cornices linked by arches. There are six columns on both the east and west sides, and four more at the south end, which mark the monumental entrance to the Vestibul. During summer, occasional live concerts are held here. ✉ *Grad.*

Vestibul. The cupola of this domed space would once have been decorated with marble and mosaics. Today there's only a round hole in the top of the dome, but it produces a stunning effect: the dark interior, the blue sky above, and the tip of the cathedral's bell tower framed in the opening. ⊠ *Peristil, Grad.*

Zlatna Vrata (*Golden Gate*). Formerly the main entrance into the palace, Zlatna Vrata, on the north side of the palace, is the most monumental of the four gates. Just outside the Zlatna Vrata stands Meštrović's gigantic bronze **statue of Grgur Ninski** (Bishop Gregory of Nin). During the 9th century, the bishop campaigned for the use of the Slav language in the Croatian Church, as opposed to Latin, thus infuriating Rome. This statue was created in 1929 and placed on Peristil to mark the 1,000th anniversary of the Split Synod, then moved here in 1957. Note the big toe on the left foot, which is considered by locals to be a good luck charm and has been worn gold through constant touching. ⊠ *Dioklecijanova, Grad.*

SHOPPING

Dalmatian women—and those from Split in particular—are renowned for their elegant sense of style. Despite a poor local economy, you'll find countless exclusive little boutiques selling women's clothes, some representing the new generation of young Croatian designers, and shoes imported from Italy. However, the city's most memorable shopping venue remains the *pazar,* the colorful open-air market held each morning just outside the palace walls. When looking for gifts, bear in mind that Dalmatia produces some excellent wines, which you can buy either in Split or while visiting the islands.

Croata. Overlooking Trg Brace Radića, close to the seafront, Croata specializes in "original Croatian ties" in presentation boxes. ⊠ *Mihovilova Širina 7, Grad* ☎ *021/346–336.*

Vinoteka Terra. Vinoteka Terra is a stone cellar close to Bačvice Bay, where you can taste Croatian regional wines, accompanied by savory appetizers, before purchasing bottles. It also stocks truffle products and olive oils. ⊠ *Prilaz Braće Kaliterna 6, Bačvice* ☎ *021/314–800* ⊕ *vinoteka.hr.*

BEACHES

Uvala Bačvica (*Bačvice Bay*). This is the area's best beach and it's a 10-minute walk east of the Old Town. It does get very busy in summer, but if you don't mind the crowds, you can rent beach chairs and umbrellas, and there's a string of cafés and bars along this stretch of coast. **Amenities:** food and drink; showers. **Best for:** partiers; swimming. ⊠ *Šetalište Petra Preradovića, Bačvica.*

WHERE TO EAT

$$$$ ✕**Kod Jose.** This typical Dalmatian *konoba* is relaxed and romantic,
EASTERN with exposed stone walls and heavy wooden furniture set off by candle-
EUROPEAN light. The waiters are wonderfully discreet, and the *rižot frutta di mare*
(seafood risotto) delicious. You'll find it just outside the palace walls,
a five-minute walk from Zlatna Vrata (Golden Gate)—it's slightly hidden away, so many tourists miss it. There are also tabels outside on a
small open-air terrace if you come here in summer. $ *Average main:*
€*90* ✉ *Sredmanuška 4, Manuš* ☎ *021/347–397.*

$$ ✕**Pizzeria Galija.** The best pizzas in town, as well as delicious pasta
PIZZA dishes and a range of colorful salads, good draft beer and wine sold
by the glass, are to be found in this centrally located pizzeria, which
is close to the fish market. A favorite with locals, its dining room is
bustling and informal, with heavy wooden tables and benches. There's
also a terrace for open-air dining out front. The owner, Željko Jerkov,
is a retired Olympic gold medal–winning basketball player. $ *Average
main:* €*60* ✉ *Tončićeva 12, Grad* ☎ *021/347–932* ▭ *No credit cards.*

The North Sea

PORTS IN BELGIUM, GREAT BRITAIN, IRELAND, AND THE NETHERLANDS

Bruges, Belgium

WORD OF MOUTH

"Amsterdam is so walkable and safe, you can easily just 'follow your nose' without needing a walking plan. We loved wandering around that lovely city, at all hours of the day and night."

—MaureenB

"In Edinburgh we walked the Royal Mile (more than once), visited Holyrood Palace, the Britannia, Mary King's Close."

—d1carter

Ports in the United Kingdom have long been the starting points for many transatlantic crossings, but these days your ship is more likely to begin its journey in Harwich than Southampton, and may cruise around the North Sea and British Isles or continue to the Baltic or even around the Mediterranean.

Some ships by U.S.-based cruise lines are even based year-round or part of the year in England to facilitate easier cruising in Europe. These increasingly busy ports sometimes include more exotic destinations such as the Canary Islands on their itineraries.

ABOUT THE RESTAURANTS

All the restaurants we recommend serve lunch; they may also serve dinner if your cruise ship stays late in port and you choose to dine off the ship. Europeans tend to eat a leisurely meal at lunch, but in most ports there are quicker and simpler alternatives for those who just want to grab a quick bite before returning to the ship. You'll be able to pay in euros only in Belgium, Ireland, and the Netherlands; prices in England and Scotland are in British pounds. All restaurant prices are based on the average cost of a main course at dinner. Price categories in the United Kingdom are based on the euro-equivalent costs of eating in restaurants.

AMSTERDAM, NETHERLANDS

Updated by Liz Humphreys

Amsterdam has as many facets as a 40-carat diamond polished by one of the city's gem cutters: the capital, and spiritual "downtown," of a nation ingrained with the principles of tolerance; a veritable Babylon of old-world charm; a font for homegrown geniuses such as Rembrandt and Van Gogh; a cornucopia bursting with parrot tulips and other greener—more potent—blooms; and a unified social zone that takes in cozy bars, archetypal "brown" cafés, and outdoor markets. Although impressive gabled houses bear witness to the Golden Age of the 17th century, their upside-down images reflected in the waters of the city's canals symbolize and magnify the contradictions within the broader Dutch society. With a mere 768,000 friendly souls and with almost everything a scant 10-minute bike ride away, Amsterdam is actually like a village that happens to pack the cultural wallop of a megalopolis.

ESSENTIALS

CURRENCY

The euro. ATMs are common and credit cards are widely accepted in all but restaurants, where only European cards with PIN are accepted widely.

HOURS

Shops open Tuesday, Wednesday, Friday, and Saturday from 9 or 10 until 6; they are open later on Thursday. Most stores are closed on Sunday and some on Monday. Museums open from 9 until 6, with one late-opening night during the week.

PRIVATE TOURS

If you want a private chauffeured tour around Amsterdam or other parts of Holland (including such options as the flower market at Aalsmeer, Delft, the fishing villages of Vollendam and Marken, and more), Amsterdam City Tours offers private cars or minibuses starting at €225 and provides tours lasting from three to eight hours. They also offer Amsterdam group city tours by bus (1 hour, 45 min., €13) or bus and boat (3 hours, €29).

Contacts **Amsterdam City Tours.** ☎ *31/299411111*
⊕ *www.amsterdamcitytours.*

TELEPHONES

Most tri- and quad-band GSM mobile phones should work in the Netherlands, which operates a 3G mobile system with dual-band handsets. Most public phones take phone cards (available at numerous shops) and some take credit cards, and will connect international calls. Major telecom companies are Vodafone and Orange.

COMING ASHORE

Ships dock at the cruise terminal on the IJ River, a 15-minute walk (one tram stop) from the main train station, the transport hub of the city. The terminal, constructed of glass in the shape of a wave, is attached to the Mövenpick Hotel and the Muziekgebouw concert hall. It has tourist information, shopping facilities, a Subway restaurant, an ATM (available from 7–7 daily), luggage lockers, and free Internet access on dedicated consoles. Passengers can walk directly from the terminal into the town or rent a bike (or a Segway, also available at the terminal) and take to the cycle tracks that crisscross the city. For trips to other locations around the Netherlands, take Tram 26 to reach the main train station (Centraal Station) or Tram 25 to the bus station on the southeast side of Centraal Station.

The so-called Canal Bus (which is actually a boat) picks up passengers from the cruise terminal and makes nine stops around Amsterdam, including some of Amsterdam's major museums, traveling around on the water. A day-ticket for the Canal Bus is €22; save 10% if you buy your ticket in advance online. The bus makes a stop just outside the central train station. Public bus and tram services are also useful for visiting the attractions; single tickets cost €2.60 for a maximum one-hour journey, while a day ticket is €7.50. In Amsterdam, most transit tickets have been replaced with reusable plastic chipcards, which you can purchase at Centraal Station; you can also buy one-hour and one-day disposable chipcards on board the bus or tram.

EXPLORING AMSTERDAM

Fodor's Choice   **Amsterdam Museum** (*Amsterdam Historical Museum*). Any city that
★   began in the 13th century as a boggy swamp to become the trading
☺   powerhouse of the world in the 17th century has a fascinating story
to tell, and this museum does it superbly. It's housed in a rambling
amalgamation of buildings, once a convent, which was used as Amsterdam's Civic Orphanage. Before visiting the actual museum, walk past
the entrance and check out the glassed Schuttersgalerij (Civil Guards
Gallery) lined with huge portraits of city militias—though not in the
same league as *The Night Watch*, you can see them for free. Recently,
21st-century renditions of civil guard paintings have been added to the
collection, notably one featuring the "Maid of Amsterdam," with a
joint in one hand and Rembrandt's face tattooed on her chest. ⊠ *Kalverstraat 92 and Sint Luciënsteeg 27, Centrum* ☎ *020/523–1822* ⊕ *www.
amsterdammuseum.nl* ⌨ *€10* ☾ *Daily 10–5.*

Fodor's Choice   **Anne Frankhuis** (*Anne Frank House*). Anne Frank, one of the most
★   famous authors of the 20th century, wrote the inspiring diary of a
Jewish girl who was forced to hide with her family here in a hidden
apartment from the Nazis. In the pages of *The Diary of Anne Frank*
(published posthumously in 1947 as *The Annex* by her father—the title
she chose) the young Anne recorded two increasingly fraught years living in secret in a warren of rooms at the back of this 1635 canal house
with her family, the Van Pels family, and the dentist Fritz Pfeffer, a total
of five adults and three children. The entrance to the flat was hidden
behind a hinged bookcase. Here, like many *onderduikers* ("people in
hiding") throughout Amsterdam, Anne dreamed her dreams, wrote her
diary, and pinned up movie-star pictures to her wall (still on view). It's
hard to imagine how the group lived and tried to avoid capture and
attention. All but Otto Frank were ultimately killed during the war.
Miep Gies, one of the friends who helped with the hiding, found Anne's
diary after the raid and kept it through the war. ■TIP➔ The line to get
into the Anne Frank House is extremely long, especially in the summer. It
moves (sort of) quickly, but it's best to arrive early or book tickets online to
avoid the worst crowds. ⊠ *Prinsengracht 263-267, Centrum* ☎ *020/556-
7105* ⊕ *www.annefrank.nl* ⌨ *€9* ☾ *Mar.–Sept., daily 9–9 (Sat. until 10);
July–Aug., daily 9–10; Sept.–Mar., daily 9–7 (Sat. until 9).*

Fodor's Choice   **Brouwersgracht** (*Brewers' Canal*). Regularly voted Amsterdam's most
★   beautiful street, this wonderful canal at the northern border of the
Jordaan is lined by residences and former warehouses for brewers, fish
processors, and tanneries that traded here in the 17th century when
Amsterdam was the "warehouse of the world." Without sacrificing
the ancient vibe, most of the buildings have been converted into luxury
apartments. Of particular note are Nos. 204–212 and their trapezium
gables. At No. 162, there are two dried fish above the door. This decoration on a metal screen was the forerunner of the gable stone denoting
occupation. The canal provides long views down the grand canals that
are perfect for photo ops. The Brouwersgracht runs westward from the
end of the Singel (a short walk along Prins Hendrikkade from Centraal
Station) and forms a cap to the western end of the Grachtengordel.

On top of the old canal mansions dotting the Brouwersgracht are symbols referring to the breweries that used this waterway to transport their goods to thirsty drinkers hundreds of years ago. ⊠ *Jordaan.*

Dam (*Dam Square*). Home to the Koninklijk Paleis (Royal Palace) and the Nieuwe Kerk, Dam Square (or just Dam), is Amsterdam's main square. It traces its roots to the 12th century and the dam built over the Amstel (hence the city's name). The waters of the Damrak (the continuation of the Amstel) once reached right up to the Dam, with ships and barges sailing to the weigh house. Folks came here to trade, talk, protest, and be executed. In the 17th century it was hemmed in by houses and packed with markets. Behind the Nieuwe Kerk there's an atmospheric warren of alleys with *proeflokaal* (liquor tasting house) *De Drie Fleschjes* (the Three Small Bottles) on Gravenstraat dating from 1650. In the 19th century the Damrak was filled in to form the street leading to Centraal Station, and King Louis, Napoléon's brother, demolished the weigh house in 1808 because it spoiled the view from his bedroom window in the Royal Palace. Today the Dam is a bustling meeting point with street performers and fairs on high days and holidays. ⊠ *Amsterdam.*

> ## AMSTERDAM BEST BETS
>
> **Canal-boat trip.** It may seem kitschy, but this is the best way to get a feel for the canal ring historic area and to take in the wonderful architecture of the Old City.
>
> **Vincent van Gogh.** The world's richest repository of the tragic artist's work has been transferred from the Van Gogh Museum to the grand Hermitage Amsterdam museum while the Van Gogh undergoes renovations; it's expected to reopen in April 2013.
>
> **Rijksmuseum.** This grand gallery reopened in April 2013; it's a must-see.

Fodor's Choice ★ **Magere Brug** (*Skinny Bridge*). Of Amsterdam's 60-plus drawbridges, the Magere Brug is the most famous and provides gorgeous views of the Amstel and surrounding area. It was purportedly first built in 1672 by two sisters living on opposite sides of the Amstel who wanted an efficient way of sharing that grandest of Dutch traditions: the *gezellige* (socially cozy) midmorning coffee break. Walk by at night when it's spectacularly lit. Many replacements to the original bridge have come and gone, and this, dating from 1969, is just the latest. ⊠ *Between Kerkstraat and Nieuwe Kerkstraat, Centrum.*

Fodor's Choice ★ **Museum het Rembrandthuis** (*Rembrandt House Museum*). This is the house that Rembrandt bought, flush with success, for 13,000 guilders (a princely sum) in 1639, and where he lived and worked until 1656 when declared bankrupt. The inside is a remarkable reconstruction job, as the contents have been assembled based on inventories made when Rembrandt was forced to sell everything, including an extravagant collection of art and antiquities (a contributing factor in his money troubles). He originally chose this house on what was then the main street of the Jewish Quarter, to experience firsthand the faces he would use in his Old Testament religious paintings. The house interior has been restored with contemporaneous elegant furnishings and artwork in the

reception rooms, a collection of rarities that match as closely as possible the descriptions in the inventory, and the main studio, occasionally used by guest artists, which is kept fully stocked with paints and canvases. But it doesn't convey much of the humanity of Rembrandt himself. The little etching studio is perhaps the most atmospheric. Littered with tools of the trade, a printing press, and a line hung with drying prints (there are demonstrations), it's easy to imagine Rembrandt finding respite here, experimenting with form and technique, away from uncomfortable schmoozing for commissions (and loans) in the grander salon. The museum owns a huge collection of etchings with 260 of the 290 he made represented, and a changing selection is on permanent display. ⊠ *Joden-breestraat 4–6, Centrum* ☎ *020/520–0400* ⊕ *www.rembrandthuis.nl* ⊠ *€10* ♡ *Daily, 10–5.*

Fodor's Choice   **Ons' Lieve Heer op Solder** (*Our Lord in the Attic Museum*). With its
★   elegant gray-and-white facade and spout gable, this appears to be just another lovely 17th-century canal house, and on the lower floors it is. But tucked away in the attic is a clandestine place of Catholic worship, a *schuilkerk* (hidden church), one of the very few to survive more or less in its original state. Catholic Masses were officially forbidden from 1578, but the Protestant authorities in Amsterdam turned a blind eye provided the churches were not recognizable as such from the outside. The Oude Kerk was de-Catholicized and stripped of its patron, St. Nicholas, so this little church, consecrated in 1663, was dedicated to him until the St. Nicolaaskerk opened in 1887. The chapel itself is a triumph of Dutch classicist taste, with magnificent marble columns, gilded capitals, a colored-marble altar, and the *Baptism of Christ in the Jordan* (1716) painting by Jacob de Wit presiding over all.

The grandeur continues through the house, which was renovated by merchant Jan Hartan between 1661 and 1663. Even the kitchen and chaplain bedroom remain furnished in the style of the age, and the drawing room, or *sael*, looks as if it were plucked from a Vermeer painting. Besides boasting canvases by Thomas de Keyser, Jan Wynants, and Abraham de Vries, the house also displays impressive collections of church silver and sculptures. The new part of the museum, on the other side of the alley, hosts temporary exhibitions. ⊠ *Oudezijds Voorburg-wal 40, Centrum* ☎ *020/624–6604* ⊕ *www.opsolder.nl* ⊠ *€8* ♡ *Mon.–Sat. 10–5, Sun. 1–5.*

★   **Oude Kerk** (*Old Church*). Amsterdam's oldest church has evolved over three centuries to look as it does today. What began as a wooden chapel in 1306 was built up to a hall church and then a cross basilica between 1366 and 1566 (and fully restored between 1955 and 1979). It was violently looted during the Reformation and stripped of its altars and images of saints—though the looters did leave the 14th-century paintings still visible on its wooden roof, as well as the Virgin Mary stained-glass windows that had been set in place in 1550. The famed Vater-Müller organ was installed in 1726. Don't miss the carved choir stalls that illustrate proverbs relating to cardinal sins, among other things. Within this open, atmospheric space, there's a gravestone for Rembrandt's wife Saskia van Uylenburgh and also for Kiliaen van Rensselaer, one of the Dutch founders of what is now New York, and by the

door, a bronzed hand cupping a naked breast. This is one of a series of sculptures placed throughout Amsterdam in 1982 by an anonymous artist. The Oude Kerk is as much exhibition space as a place of worship, hosting the annual World Press Photography competition and top-notch modern-art shows. Its carillon is played every Tuesday at 2 and every Saturday at 4—the best place to listen is the bridge in front of the church. ⊠ *Oudekerksplein 23, Centrum* ☎ *020/625–8284* ⊕ *www. oudekerk.nl* ≦ *€5* ☉ *Mon.–Sat. 11–5, Sun. 1–5:30.*

Fodor's Choice
★

Rijksmuseum (*State Museum*). Rembrandt's *The Night Watch*, Vermeer's *The Love Letter*, Frans Hals's *Portrait of a Young Couple* . . . you get the picture. The Netherlands' greatest museum, the famed Rijksmuseum is home to a near infinite selection of masterpieces by these top masters along with Steen, Ruisdael, Hobbema, Cuyp, and the rest of their Golden Age ilk. As of Spring 2013 the revamped museum will finally open its doors after a massive renovation both indoors and out.

While the collection encompasses both the West and Asia, and ranges from the 9th through the 19th centuries, the bulk is of 15th- to 17th-century paintings, mostly Dutch. But if your time is limited, head directly for Rembrandt's *The Night Watch,* with its central figure, the "stupidest man in Amsterdam," Frans Banningh Cocq. Other unmissable masterpieces include Vermeer's *The Little Street*—a magical sliver of 17th-century Delft life—and his incomparable *The Love Letter*, in which a well-appointed interior reveals a mistress and her maid caught in the emotional eddies of a recently opened and read billet-doux. Ostensibly, a more sedate missive is being read in Vermeer's *Woman in Blue Reading a Letter*, on view nearby.

For an institution dedicated to antiquity and art history, the Rijksmuseum has shown a remarkable technical savvy in making its vast collection more accessible via its incredible website. On the sub-site Rijksstudio you can see, download, share, and do basically anything else you like with images of 125,000 works from the museum's collection. ■ TIP→ **Don't leave the country without visiting the mini-museum at Schiphol Airport** (⊠ *Holland Boulevard between piers E and F behind passport control* ☎ *020/653–5036* ☉ *Daily 6 am–8 pm*). ⊠ *Stadhouderskade 42, Museum District* ☎ *020/674–7000* ⊕ *www.rijksmuseum. nl* ≦ *€14 (subject to change after the reopening)* ☉ *Daily 9–6. Library, Print Room, and Reading Room (ID required): Tues.–Sat. 10–5.*

Fodor's Choice
★

Stedelijk Museum of Modern Art. Amsterdam's celebrated treasure house of modern art, the Stedelijk finally reopened (in September 2012) following a massive refurbishment of this wedding-cake Neo-Renaissance structure built in 1895. In true Amsterdam fashion, the locals were quick to nickname the futuristic addition by globally acclaimed local architects Benthem/Crouwel the *Badkuip* (Bathtub); it incorporates a glass-walled restaurant (which you can visit, along with the museum shop, without a museum ticket). The new Stedelijk boasts twice the exhibition space compared to the old, thanks, in part, to the new Bathub, which will now host temporary shows (watch out for Suprematist Malevich in 2013 and the noted South-African-Dutch painter Marlene Dumas in 2014).

As for the Stedelijk's old building, it is now home to the museum's own fabled collection of modern and contemporary art. While this collection harbors many works by such ancients of modernism as Chagall, Cézanne, Picasso, Monet, Mondriaan, and Malevich, there is a definite emphasis on the post-World War II period: with such local CoBrA boys as Appel and Corneille; American pop artists as Warhol, Johns, Oldenburg, and Liechtenstein; abstract expressionists as de Kooning and Pollock; and contemporary German expressionists as Polke, Richter, and Baselitz; and displays of Dutch essentials like De Stijl school, including the game-changing *Red Blue Chair* that Gerrit Rietveld designed in 1918 and Mondriaan's 1920 trail-blazing *Composition in Red, Black, Yellow, Blue, and Grey.* ⊠ *Paulus Potterstraat 13, Museum District* 🕾 *020/573–2911* ⊕ *www.stedelijk.nl* 🎟 *€15* ⊙ *Tues. and Wed. 11–5; Thurs. 11–10; Sat. and Sun. 10–6; closed Mon.*

Fodor'sChoice
★
Willet-Holthuysen Museum. Here's a rare chance to experience what it was like to live in a gracious mansion on the Herengracht in the 18th century. In 1895, widow Sandrina Louisa Willet-Holthuysen bequeathed this house to the city, along with all of its contents. It was actually built in 1687 but has been renovated several times and is now under the management of the Amsterdam Museum. Take an hour or so to discover its interiors and artwork, including a sumptuous ballroom and a rarities cabinet. Complete the Dutch luxury experience by lounging in the French-style garden in the back. ⊠ *Herengracht 605, Centrum* 🕾 *020/523–1822* ⊕ *www.willetholthuysen.nl* 🎟 *€8* ⊙ *Weekdays 10–5, weekends 11–5.*

SHOPPING

Souvenir shops are filled with wooden clogs and ceramics bearing windmill or tulip motifs, but Amsterdam offers more than just cheap and cheerful items. There's a major market in diamonds and also in antiques. At the lower end of the price scale, there's a market in collectibles and one-of-a-kind items, plus cutting-edge design for the home.

Kalverstraat, the city's main pedestrians-only shopping street, is where much of Amsterdam does its day-to-day shopping. Running parallel to Kalverstraat is the **Rokin,** a main tram route lined with shops offering high-priced trendy fashion, jewelry, accessories, antiques, and even an old master painting or two. Shoppers will love to explore the **Negen Straatjes** (Nine Streets), nine charming, tiny streets that radiate from behind the Royal Palace. Here, in a sector bordered by Raadhuisstraat and Leidsestraat, specialty and fashion shops are delightfully one-of-a-kind. Heading even farther to the west, you enter the chic and funky sector of the **Jordaan,** where generation after generation of experimental designers have set up shop to show their imaginative creations. Though adventurous collectors are increasingly looking to the Jordaan district for unique finds, the more expensive **Spiegelkwartier** is the city's mainstay for high-end antiques. The **De Baarsjes** neighborhood in the western part of the city is progressively attracting small galleries that showcase exciting works of art.

★ Whether hunting for treasures or trash, you could get lucky at one of Amsterdam's flea markets. The best is **Waterlooplein** flea market (Monday–Saturday 9–5), which surrounds the perimeter of the Stopera (Muziektheater/Town Hall complex) building. The **Bloemenmarkt** (along the Singel canal, between Koningsplein and Muntplein), is another of Amsterdam's must-see markets, where flowers and plants are sold from permanently moored barges (Monday–Saturday 9–5).

WHERE TO EAT

$ ✕**Bakkerswinkel.** This genteel yet unpretentious bakery and tearoom
EUROPEAN evokes an English country kitchen, one that lovingly prepares and serves
Fodor'sChoice breakfasts, high tea, hearty-breaded sandwiches, soups, and divine slabs
★ of quiche. The closely clustered wooden tables don't make for much privacy, but this place is a true oasis if you want to indulge in a healthful breakfast or lunch. The convenient location on busy Zeedijk will only be open until 2014, when the original Bakkerswinkel reopens at Warmoesstraat 69 after renovations. There are several other locations: such as one complete with a garden patio in the Museum District and another at Westergasfabriek, plus a takeout-only counter at Warmoesstraat 133. $ *Average main: €8* ⊠ *Zeedijk 37, Red Light District* ☎ *020/489–8000* ⊕ *www.debakkerswinkel.com* ⊘ *No dinner.*

$ ✕**Pancake Bakery.** It's hard to go wrong when going out for Dutch pan-
DUTCH cakes in Amsterdam. But the quaint Pancake Bakery rises above the
★ pack of similar eateries with its medieval vibe, canal-side patio near the
☾ Anne Frank House, and a mammoth menu with more than 75 choices of sweet and savory toppings. There are also omelets, and a convincing take on the folk dish of *erwtensoep* (a superthick, smoked sausage–imbued pea soup—only available from Oct. to April). But don't rise too early for your pancakes—the bakery doesn't open till noon—and be prepared to wait: reservations are only taken for groups of six or more. $ *Average main: €11* ⊠ *Prinsengracht 191, Western Canal Ring* ☎ *020/625–1333* ⊕ *www.pancake.nl* ⚠ *Reservations not accepted.*

WHERE TO STAY

$$$$ ⌂**Conservatorium Hotel.** An impressive early 20th-century bank turned
HOTEL music school is a visual feast, with a glass-roofed, tree-filled courtyard
Fodor'sChoice lobby and dramatically modern guest rooms, many of them duplexes,
★ with huge windows, muted tones, and splashes of color. **Pros:** stunning contemporary surroundings; spacious and beautiful accommodations; spa with lap pool; near museums. **Cons:** quite expensive; a bit removed from city center. $ *Rooms from: €325* ⊠ *Van Baerlestraat 27, Museum District and Environs* ☎ *020/570–0000* ⊕ *www.conservatoriumhotel. com* ⇥ *129 rooms, 42 suites* ⫶⃝*No meals.*

$$$$ ⌂**Dylan Amsterdam.** Lacquered trunks, mahogany screens, modernist
HOTEL hardwood tables, and luxurious upholstery all lend design flair to these lovely quarters on the site of the historic Municipal Theater, which burned down in the 17th century (an arched entryway remains). **Pros:** a taste of old Amsterdam; good for celebrity spotting; updated business facilities. **Cons:** some parts of the hotel feel overdesigned; few

rooms have canal views. ⑤ *Rooms from: €275* ✉ *Keizersgracht 384, Western Canal Ring* ☎ *020/530–2010* ⊕ *www.dylanamsterdam.com* ⤳ *40 rooms, 8 suites* ⑩ *No meals.*

$$$
HOTEL
Fodor's Choice
★
☾

🏨 **Mövenpick.** Most of the business-like rooms in this striking glass sky-scraper built on an island within the blossoming docks area offer stun-ning views of the Amsterdam sky-line and beyond. **Pros:** upper-floor suites offer the best views in town; the terrace is a great waterfront spot for refreshments; atmosphere is casual and welcoming. **Cons:** lacks Dutch character; a bit off the beaten path. ⑤ *Rooms from: €229* ✉ *Piet Heinkade 11, Eastern Dock-lands, Station and Docklands* ☎ *020/519–1200* ⊕ *www.moevenpick-amsterdam.com* ⤳ *408 rooms, 31 suites* ⑩ *No meals.*

> ## TAX-FREE SHOPPING
>
> Since 2007, the minimum amount spent by non-EU cruise passen-gers to become eligible for a tax refund dropped from €136 to €50. Participating shops display the Duty-Free Shopping sticker.

ANTWERP, BELGIUM

Updated by
Liz Humphreys

In its heyday, Antwerp (*Antwerpen* in Flemish, *Anvers* in French) played second fiddle only to Paris. It became Europe's most important com-mercial center in the 16th century, and this wealth funded many archi-tectural and artistic projects. Masters such as Rubens and Van Dyck established the city as one of Europe's leading art centers, and its inno-vative printing presses produced missals for the farthest reaches of the continent. It also became, and has remained, the diamond capital of the world. Antwerp is today Europe's second-largest port, and has much of the zest often associated with a harbor town. The historic Oude Stad, the heart of the city, distills the essence of Antwerp. The narrow, wind-ing streets, many of them restricted to pedestrian traffic, are wonder-ful for strolling, the squares are full of charm, and the museums and churches are the pride of the city.

ESSENTIALS

CURRENCY
The euro. ATMs are common.

HOURS
Museums and attractions are usually open from 9:30 to 5; many are closed on Monday. Most shops are open Monday–Saturday 9–6.

PRIVATE TOURS
You can arrange for a personal English-speaking guide through the *Toerisme Antwerpen* (the city tourist office). However, this requires two days' to three weeks' notice, depending on the season. You can ask your guide to show you any part of the city that interests you, either by neighborhood or by theme (fashion, history, architecture, etc.). The tourism bureau also sells booklets that sketch out walks through the city focusing on fashion and architecture.

Contacts Toerisme Antwerpen. ⊕ *www.visitantwerpen.be.*

Antwerp

TO PORT OF ANTWERP

Waasland Tunnel

Scheldt

TO ANTWERPEN MINIATUUR-STAAD

Museum aan de Stroom

A. Brouwerstr.
Godefridus kaai
Brouwersvliet
Oude Leeuwenrui
Waasland Tunnel

Entrepotkaai
Italiëlei
Langedijkstr.
Van Aerdtstr.
Cassiersstr.
Van den Wervestr.
Oude Steenweg
Dambruggestr.

Falcon plein
Falconrui
Stijfselrui
Ankerrui

Sint-Pauluskerk
Paardenmarkt
Paardenmarkt
Vondel-str.
Rotterdam-str.
Hollandstr.
Van Maerlant-str.

Noorderterras
Orteliuskaai
St. Paulusstr.
Vee Markt
Nosestr.
Zw. zu. str.
Zirkstr.
Klap
Mutsaertstr.
Venusstr.
Vekestr.
Kauwenberg
Lange Winkelstr.
V. Hoboken
Prinsesstr.
Prinsstr.
Blindestr.
Rodestr.
Osystr.
Van Stratenstr.

Jordaenskaai
Repenstr.
Oude Beurs
Gridk str.
Grote Markt
Wolstr.
Keizerstr.
Rockoxhuis
Kipdorp
St. Jacobsmkt.
Ossen Markt
Italiëlei
Molenberg
Franklin Roosevelt plaats
Gemeentestr.

Suikerrui
Reynders-str.
Onze-Lieve-Vrouwekathedraal
Eiermarkt
Lange Nieuw str.
Sint-Jacobskerk
K. larensstr.
Jezusstr.
Leysstr.
Kon. Astrid Pl.

Zuiderterras
E. van Dijckkaai
Oever
Hoogstr.
H.G. str.
H.G. perlenstr.
Schoenmarkt
Meir
Meir
Wapper
De Keyserlei

Plantinkaai
Muntstr.
Plantin-Moretus Museum/Prentenkabinet
Vrijdagmarkt
Lombardenvest
Gasthuisstr.
Huide-vettersstr.
K.
Rubenshuis
Hopland
Kipdorp Vest
Frankrijklei
Ouellinstr.
Appelmanstr.
Pelikaanstr.
Simonsstr.
Mechalostr.
Diamondland

Mode Museum (MoMu)
Kammenstr.
Everdijstr.
Oudaan
Jodenstr.
Kolvenierssstr.
Diamantwijk

Kloosterstr.
Lange Ridders
St. Adries
Beukelaer
Franken
Nationalestraat
Sleutel str.
St. Antoniusstr.
Schoytestr.
Lange Gasthuisstr.
Museum Mayer Van den Bergh
Komediepl.
Leopoldstr.
Oude Vaartpl.
Tabak Vest
Lange Herentalsestr.
Van Leriusstr.
Matsijslei
Plantin en Moretuslei

Aaimoezenier str.
Begijnenstr.
Vleminckveld
Frankrijklei
Rubenslei
Quinten
Van Eycklei

Museum van Hedendaagse Kunst (M HKA)
St. Rochusstr.
Stads Park

Kronenburg-str.
Kasteelpleinstr.
Begijnenvest
Britselei

Marnix-plaats
Tol straat
Justitiestr.
Mechelsesteen weg
TO BERCHEM (AIRPORT)

Volkstr.
Koninklijk Museum voor Schone Kunsten
Amerikalei
Anselmostr.

Scheldestr.

TO MIDDELHEIM

0 — 1/4 mi
0 — 1/4 km

TELEPHONES

Tri-band GSM phones work in Belgium. You can buy prepaid phone cards at telecom shops, news vendors, and tobacconists in all towns and cities. Phone cards can be used for local or international calls. Proximus, Mobistar, and BASE are the leading telecom companies.

COMING ASHORE

The cruise port couldn't be better placed for passengers, as vessels dock directly at the heart of the city. All the major attractions and museums of the historic center are within walking distance of the dock. The commercial port has no facilities for disembarking passengers, but a wealth of shopping options and restaurants lies just outside the gates.

Antwerp's tram and metro public transit system is extensive and reliable. A €1.20 ticket is good for one hour on all forms of public transport, including buses. You'll pay €2 if you buy your ticket on the bus, so prepay at a ticket machine at a bus stop, at the station, at the tourist office, or at news vendors in the city; a day pass buys unlimited travel for one full day. Passes are €5 if you prepay, €6 if you buy on the bus or tram. Car-rental offices are in Antwerp (and are quite expensive at around €100 per day for a compact manual vehicle). Travel by taxi has a per-km charge of around €1.90 on top of an initial pick-up price of €2.95, which makes it expensive for day tours but acceptable for short trips. Rates are higher at night.

ANTWERP BEST BETS
Museum Aan de Stroom. Don't miss this comprehensive new museum that strives to showcase Antwerp's history and relations with the world through often-fascinating and highly detailed exhibits.
Sint-Pauluskerk. This late-Gothic church features outstanding religious art by a range of Flemish masters including Rubens and Van Dyck.
Onze-Lieve-Vrouwekathedraal. A triumph of the Gothic architectural style, decorated by some of Peter Paul Rubens' finest religious works.

EXPLORING ANTWERP

Diamondland. A spectacular showroom, Diamondland was created to enable visitors to get a sense of the activity that goes on behind closed doors in the security-conscious Diamantwijk. All explanations are in English and you can watch several diamond cutters at work. Many of the hundreds of jewelry pieces on display (and for sale) are specially designed by an in-house jeweler. ⊠ *Appelmansstraat 33A, Diamantwijk* ☎ *03/229–2990* ⊕ *www.diamondland.be* ☉ *Mon.–Sat. 9:30–5:30, by appointment only* Ⓜ *Trams 2, 6, 9, or 15.*

Diamantwijk. The diamond trade has its own quarter in Antwerp, where the skills of cutting and polishing the gems have been handed down for generations by a tightly knit community. Multimillion-dollar deals are agreed upon with a handshake, and the Antwerp Diamond High Council was established in 1975 to further the industry. Some 85% of the world's uncut diamonds pass through Antwerp. Twenty-five million carats are cut and traded here every year, more than anywhere else in

the world. The district occupies a few nondescript city blocks west of Centraal Station. A large part of the community is Jewish, so you'll see shop signs in Hebrew and Hasidic men with traditional dark clothing and side curls. Below the elevated railway tracks, a long row of stalls and shops gleams with jewelry and gems.

Diamond cutting began in Brugge but moved to Antwerp in the late 15th century when a new technique for polishing and cutting gems evolved here. When a flood of rough diamonds from South Africa hit the markets in the 19th century, Antwerp rose to the top of the field. Today the industry employs some 8,000 workers, including expert polishers and cutters, serving 1,800 dealers. Jewish establishments close on Saturday for the Sabbath, but there are still enough shops open in the neighborhood to have a good browse. ⊠ *Bounded by De Keyserlei, Pelikaanstraat, Lange Herentalsestraat, and Lange Kievitstraat, Diamantwijk* Ⓜ *Tram 2 or 15.*

Grote Markt. The heart of the Oude Stad, the Grote Markt is dominated by a huge fountain splashing water onto the paving stones. Atop the fountain stands the figure of the legendary Silvius Brabo, who has been poised to fling the hand of the giant Druon Antigon into the river Scheldt since the 19th century. Another famous monster slayer, St. George, is perched on top of a 16th-century guild house at Grote Markt 5, while the dragon appears to be falling off the pediment. ⊠ *Grote Markt, Oude Stad.*

Stadhuis. The triangular square is lined on two sides by guild houses and on the third by the Renaissance Stadhuis. Antwerp's town hall was built in the 1560s during the city's Golden Age, when Paris and Antwerp were the only European cities with more than 100,000 inhabitants. In its facade, the fanciful fretwork of the late-Gothic style has given way to the discipline and order of the Renaissance. The public rooms are suitably impressive, though the heavy hand of 19th-century restoration work is much in evidence. You can see the interior with guided tour. Tours take place (in English) on Sundays at 2 pm (tickets are 8 euros and can be purchased from the tourist office). ⊠ *Grote Markt, Oude Stad* ☎ *03/232–0103* Ⓜ *Metro 2, 3, or 5.*

Mode Museum (MoMu). To get up to speed on the latest clothing designers, head to MoMu for a fashion crash course. Housed within ModeNatie, an early 19th-century building with a 20th-century makeover, you'll find comprehensive exhibits, some highlighting the avant-garde work of contemporary Flemish designers such as the renowned Antwerp Six. Rotating exhibits also make the most of the museum's collections of clothing, accessories, and textiles dating back to the 18th century; you can ponder the workmanship of delicate antique lace alongside deconstructed blouses from the late 1990s. Also in the museum's complex are the Flanders Fashion Institute, the fashion academy of the Royal Academy of Fine Arts (the designer wellspring), a brasserie, library, reading room, and a boutique. You can pick up a brochure with information in English. ⊠ *Nationalestraat 28, Sint-Andrieskwartier* ☎ *03/470–2770* ⊕ *www.momu.be* ⊠ *€8* ☉ *Tues.–Sun. 10–6; every first Thurs. of the month 10–9* Ⓜ *Tram 4, 8, or 15.*

Fodor's Choice **Museum aan de Stroom** (*MAS*). This ambitious museum in a striking red
★ sandstone and glass building next to Antwerp's old dock area aims to
place Antwerp's history into a world context. Five floors of exhibits
explore themes such as trade and shipping, men and gods, here and
elsewhere, and prestige and symbols, showcasing everything from pre-
Columbian artifacts to gas masks from World War II. It's all capped
off with a panoramic rooftop view and a Michelin 2-star restaurant, 't
Zilte. Note that most of the museum's documentation is not in English;
for a translation, use your Smartphone to read the QR codes placed
next to many exhibits, or borrow a MAS Smartphone from the information desk. ⊠ *Hanzestedenplaats 1, Oude Stad* ☎ *03/338–4434* ⊕ *www.
mas.be* 🖾 *€10* ⊙ *Tues.–Fri. 10–5, Sat.–Sun. 10–6; last tickets sold one
hour before closing.*

Fodor's Choice **Museum Mayer Van den Bergh.** Pieter Bruegel the Elder's arguably greatest
★ and most enigmatic painting, *Dulle Griet,* is the showpiece here (room
9). Often referred to in English as "Mad Meg," it portrays an irate
woman wearing helmet and breastplate—a sword in one hand, and
food and cooking utensils in the other—striding across a field strewn
with the ravages and insanity of war. There is no consensus on how to
read this painting. Some consider it one of the most powerful antiwar
statements ever made. Others claim that it denounces the Inquisition.
Either way, nothing could be further from the Bruegelian villages than
this nightmare world. In 1894, Mayer Van den Bergh bought *Dulle
Griet* for 480 Belgian francs. Today it is priceless. The museum also
has a set of Bruegel's witty, miniature illustrations of *Twelve Proverbs,*
based on popular Flemish sayings.

Mayer Van den Bergh was a passionate art connoisseur who amassed
a private collection of almost 4,000 works in the 19th century. The
collection includes treasures such as a life-size polychrome statue from
about 1300 of St. John resting his head on Christ's chest (room 6). It is,
however, the Bruegels that make this small museum a must. There's an
English-language pamphlet included with admission that reviews part
of the collection. ⊠ *Lange Gasthuisstraat 19, Kruidtuin* ☎ *03/338–8188*
⊕ *www.mayervandenbergh.be* 🖾 *€8 (€10 in combination with Rubenshuis)* ⊙ *Tues.–Sun. 10–5; free last Wed. of the month.* Ⓜ *Tram 7 or 8.*

Museum van Hedendaagse Kunst (M HKA). One of Belgium's most important contemporary art venues; here you'll find paintings, installations,
video art, and experimental architecture from international artists,
including works by the mysterious Flemish theater director/choreogra-
pher/artist Jan Fabre, whose sculptures and installations, often based
on or involving insects, have established him as a leading figure in the
Belgian art world. The museum, which also contains an art house cin-
ema and library, is housed in a renovated grain silo. There's also a roof
terrace café. ⊠ *Leuvenstraat 32, Het Zuid* ☎ *03/260–9999* ⊕ *www.
muhka.be* 🖾 *€8* ⊙ *Tues.–Wed. and Fri.–Sun. 11–6; Thurs. 11–9* Ⓜ *Bus
6 or 23, or Tram 8.*

Fodor's Choice **Onze-Lieve-Vrouwekathedraal.** A miracle of soaring Gothic lightness, the
★ Cathedral of Our Lady contains some of Rubens' greatest paintings and
is topped by its 404-foot-high north spire—now restored to its original

gleaming white and serving as a beacon that can be seen from far away. Work began in 1352 and continued in fits and starts until 1521. Despite this, it is a homogeneous monument, thanks to a succession of remarkable architects, including Peter Appelmans, Herman and Domien de Waghemakere, and Rombout Keldermans the Younger. The tower holds a 49-bell carillon played at various times throughout the year.

The cathedral's art treasures were twice vandalized, first by Calvinists in 1566 and again by the French revolutionary army at the end of the 18th century. The French even broke up the floor so that their horses would not slip on it. The masterpieces were either sold at auction or carried off to Paris. Some, but by no means all, have subsequently been returned. Other works, either donated or purchased, make up an outstanding collection of 17th-century religious art, including four Rubens altarpieces, glowing with his marvelous red, allegedly fortified by pigeon's blood. The panels of *De Kruisafneming* (*The Descent from the Cross*) triptych—Mary's visit to Elizabeth (with the painter's wife as Mary) and the presentation of Jesus in the temple—are among the most delicate and tender biblical scenes ever painted. *De Hemelvaart van de Maagd Maria* (*The Assumption of the Virgin Mary*), painted for the high altar, shows the Virgin being carried upward by massed ranks of cherubs toward the angel waiting to crown her Queen of the Angels. *De Hemelvaart* (*The Assumption*) is skillfully displayed so that the rays of the sun illuminate it exactly at noon. ✉ *Handschoenmarkt, Oude Stad* ☎ *03/213–9951* ⊕ *www.dekathedraal.be* ⊠ *€5* ۞ *Weekdays 10–5, Sat. 10–3, Sun. 1–4* Ⓜ *Tram 2, 3, 4, 5, 8, 9, 10, 11, or 15.*

★ **Plantin-Moretus Museum/Prentenkabinet.** This was the home and printing plant of an extraordinary publishing dynasty. For three centuries, beginning in 1576, the family printed innumerable Bibles, breviaries, and missals; Christophe Plantin's greatest technical achievement was the *Biblia Regia* (in room 16): eight large volumes containing the Bible in Latin, Greek, Hebrew, Syriac, and Aramaic, complete with notes, glossaries, and grammars.

The first three rooms were the family quarters, furnished in 16th-century luxury and containing several portraits by Rubens. Others remain as they were when occupied by accountants, editors, and proofreaders, while many contain Bibles and religious manuscripts dating back to the 9th century, including one owned by King Wenceslas of Bohemia. The workshops are filled with Plantin's 16 printing presses. Two typefaces designed here, Plantin and Garamond, are still in use. The presses are in working order—you can even purchase a copy of Plantin's sonnet, *Le Bonheur de ce monde* ("An Ode to Contentment"), in any of seven European languages, printed on an original press. There's a free information brochure available in English. ✉ *Vrijdagmarkt 22–23, Sint-Andrieskwartier* ☎ *03/221–1450* ⊕ *www.museumplantinmoretus. be* ⊠ *€8; free last Wed. of the month* ۞ *Tues.–Sun. 10–5; last ticket sold at 4:30* Ⓜ *Tram 3, 9, or 15; bus 22, 25, or 26.*

Rockoxhuis. This was the splendid Renaissance home of Rubens' friend and patron Nicolaas Rockox (1560-1640), seven times mayor of Antwerp. A humanist and art collector, Rockox moved here in 1603. The

art on display includes two of Rubens' works. One is *Madonna en Kind* (*Madonna and Child*), a delicate portrait of Rubens' first wife, Isabella, and their son, Nicolaas; the other is a sketch for the *Kruisiging* (*Crucifixion*). The collection also includes works by Van Dyck, Frans Snijders, Joachim Patinier, Jordaens, and David Teniers the Younger. The setting makes visiting this collection an exceptional experience. Rather than being displayed on museum walls, the paintings are shown in the context of an upper-class baroque home, furnished in the style of the period. A documentary slide show in English describes Antwerp at that time. ⊠ *Keizerstraat 10–12, Stadswaag* ☎ *03/201–9250* ⊕ *www. rockoxhuis.be* ⊠ *€2.50* ☉ *Tues.–Sun. 10–5; free on the last Wednesday of the month* Ⓜ *Tram 2, 3, 10, 11, or 15.*

★ **Rubenshuis.** A fabulous picture of Rubens as painter and patrician is presented here at his own house. Only the elaborate portico and temple, designed by Rubens in Italian baroque style, were still standing three centuries after the house was built. Most of what's here is a reconstruction (completed in 1946) from the master's own design. It represents Rubens at the pinnacle of his fame, a period during which he was appointed court painter to Archduke Albrecht and, with his wife, was sent on a diplomatic mission to Madrid, where he also painted some 40 portraits. He conducted delicate peace negotiations in London on behalf of Philip IV of Spain, and while in London he painted the ceiling of the Whitehall Banqueting Hall and was knighted by Charles I of Great Britain. The most evocative room in Rubens House is the huge studio, where drawings by Rubens and his pupils, as well as old prints, help to re-create the original atmosphere. In Rubens' day, visitors could view completed paintings and watch from the mezzanine while Rubens and his students worked. Rubens completed about 2,500 paintings, nearly all characterized by the energy and exuberance that were his hallmark. A few Rubens works hang in the house, including a touching sketch in the studio of the Annunciation and a self-portrait in the dining room. Unfortunately, his young widow promptly sold off some 300 pieces after his death in 1640. ⊠ *Wapper 9, Meir* ☎ *03/201–1555* ⊕ *www. rubenshuis.be* ⊠ *€8 (€10 in combination with Museum Mayer Van den Bergh); free last Wed. of the month* ☉ *Tues.–Sun. 10–5; last ticket at 4:30* Ⓜ *Tram 2, 3, 5, or 15; bus 22, 25, or 26.*

Sint-Jacobskerk. Peter Paul Rubens is buried in the white sandstone St. Jacob's Church. A painting depicting him as St. George posed between his two wives, Isabella Brant and Helena Fourment, hangs above his tomb. The three-aisle church blends late-Gothic and baroque styles; the tombs are a who's who of prominent 17th-century Antwerp families. A notable visitor (W. A. Mozart) allegedly played the organ here during his 1727 stay in the city. ⊠ *Lange Nieuwstraat 73–75, Meir* ☎ *03/225–0414* ⊕ *www.mkaweb.be* ⊠ *€2* ☉ *Apr.–Oct., Mon.–Fri. 2–5* Ⓜ *Tram 10 or 11.*

Sint-Pauluskerk. The late-Gothic St. Paul's Church, built 1530–71, is a repository of more than 50 outstanding paintings, including a series known as the 15 mysteries of the Rosary by Antwerp's finest painters of the time. There are three by Rubens, including a visceral depiction of Jesus's flagellation, as well as early works by Jordaens and Van

Dyck. The church is further enriched by more than 200 17th- and 18th-century sculptures, including the ten baroque confessionals attributed to Peeter Verbruggen the Elder. A baroque altar completed in 1639 towers over the more somber Gothic nave. Sint-Pauluskerk was restored in 1968 after damage from a major fire. ✉ *Veemarkt 14, Oude Stad* ☎ *03/231–3321* ⊕ *www.mkaweb.be* 🎫 *Free* ☽ *Apr. 1–Oct. 14, daily 2–5* Ⓜ *Tram 4 or 7; Bus 6 or 34.*

SHOPPING

Antwerp has a reputation for edgy chic, due in large part to its clothing designers; followers of fashion consider the city in a league with Milan and Paris. Credit for this development goes to the so-called Antwerp Six (students of Linda Loppa from the class of 1981 at Antwerp's Fashion Academy) and in equal measure to the new wave of talent that has more recently stormed the catwalks. Ready-to-wear by stalwarts Ann Demeulemeester, Dirk Bikkembergs, Dries Van Noten, Martin Margiela, and relative newcomers Raf Simons, Véronique Branquinho, and Wim Neels command high prices. However, in the shopping area south of Groenplaats, prices are less astronomical. And, of course, the Diamantwijk is prime territory for glittering precious stones.

The elegant **Meir**, together with its extension to the east, **De Keyserlei**, and at the opposite end, **Huidevettersstraat**, is where you will find high-street standbys and long-established names. Shopping galleries branch off all three streets. The area in and around the glamorous **Horta Complex,** on Hopland, is also a popular shopping hub. For avant-garde tastes, the best-known area is **De Wilde Zee,** which straddles the Meir and Oude Stad. The nearby Schuttershofstraat, Kammenstraat, and Nationalestraat are also fizzing with new spots. Another pedestrian area for general shopping is **Hoogstraat.**

Ann Demeulemeester. Ann Demeulemeester sells her clothes in an elegant corner store not far from the M HKA (Museum van Hedendaagse Kunst). ✉ *Leopold de Waelplaats, Het Zuid* ☎ *03/216–0133* ⊕ *www. anndemeulemeester.be.*

Diamondland. The largest diamond showroom is Diamondland, where tours of polishers, goldsmiths, and setters at work can be arranged before you settle down to business. Loose diamonds can be set while you wait. The store is open by appointment only, Mon.–Sat., 9:30–5:30. ✉ *Appelmansstraat 33a, Diamantwijk* ☎ *03/229–2990* ⊕ *www. diamondland.be.*

Het Modepaleis. Dries Van Noten collections for men and women can be found in the splendid Modepaleis, a five-story Belle Époque building that he bought in 1989. ✉ *Nationalestraat 16, Sint-Andrieskwartier* ☎ *03/470–2510* ⊕ *www.driesvannoten.be.*

WHERE TO EAT

$$$ ✗ **Zuiderterras.** A stark, glass-and-black-metal construction, this riverside café and restaurant was designed by avant-garde architect bOb (his spelling) Van Reeth; it resembles a docked cruise ship. You're

BELGIAN

virtually assured a good view, since large windows stretch on all sides. You'll have the river traffic on one side and, on the other, a view of the cathedral and the Oude Stad. The food is as modern as the surroundings, with dishes such as ravioli with fennel, parmesan, and pistachio crumble. $ *Average main: €25* ⊠ *Ernest Van Dijckkaai 37, Oude Stad* ☎ *03/234–1275* ⊕ *www.zuiderterras.be.*

$$ ✕ **'t Hofke.** It's worth visiting here for the location alone, in the Vlaeykens-
BELGIAN   gang alley, where time seems to have stood still. The cozy dining room has the look and feel of a private home. The lunch menu includes a large selection of salads and omelets, as well as more substantial fare in the evening. Try for a table in the courtyard. $ *Average main: €17* ⊠ *Vlaeykensgang, Oude Koornmarkt 16, Oude Stad* ☎ *03/233–8606* ⊕ *www.thofke.com* Ⓜ *Tram 2, 3, 4, 5, 8, or 15.*

COBH, IRELAND (FOR CORK)

The major metropolis of the South, Cork is Ireland's second-largest city—but it runs a distant second, with a population of 119,400, roughly a tenth the size of Dublin. Cork is a spirited place, with a formidable pub culture, a lively traditional music scene, a respected and progressive university, attractive art galleries, and offbeat cafés. The city received a major boost in 2005 when it was named a Capital of Culture by the EU—the smallest city ever to receive the designation. The result was a burst in development; one of the lasting legacies is a striking but controversial redesign of the city center (Patrick Street and Grand Parade) by Barcelona-based architect Beth Gali. Outside the city, the rolling countryside gives way to rugged coastline hosting tiny villages, each with their own piece of history. Many set sail for the New World from here; some were destined not to arrive.

ESSENTIALS

CURRENCY
The euro. ATMs are common.

HOURS
Shops and businesses are generally open Monday through Saturday from 9:30 to 5:30 or 6; some open later and some open on Sunday. Most museums are open Monday–Saturday 9–5 and may have shorter hours on Sunday.

PRIVATE TOURS
Adams & Butler conducts special-interest tours; topics include gardens, architecture, ghosts, and golf.

Contacts Adams & Butler ⊠ *58 Foster Ave., the Carriage House, Mount Merrion, Co. Dublin* ☎ *01/288–9355* ⊕ *www.adamsandbutler.com.*

TELEPHONES
Most tri- and quad-band GSM phones will work in Ireland, and the country's mobile system is 3G compatible with excellent coverage. Public phones accept prepaid call cards (available in shops and telecom offices) and credit cards. Eircom, BT Ireland, and Vodafone are the major telecom suppliers.

COMING ASHORE

Large ships dock at Cobh's dedicated cruise terminal adjacent to the Cobh Heritage Centre. There are basic facilities for passengers, including restrooms, taxis, and tourist information, but no cafés, restaurants, or shops.

There is a rail link between Cobh and Cork. It runs once or twice an hour throughout the day, so it would be possible to explore Cork and Cobh in the same day by public transport. Smaller vessels dock at the City Quays in the heart of Cork City; from here you can tour the town on foot.

Renting a car would be an advantage for touring the Kerry countryside around the town and the associated attractions. The cost for a compact manual vehicle is approx €50. Taxis can be engaged to run tour itineraries, although charges are complicated, and the costs are fairly expensive, best shared among four people. Drivers can choose to charge by the minute rather than per kilometer.

> ### CORK BEST BETS
>
> **Strolling along Patrick Street.** The historic storefronts along this famous thoroughfare have graced a thousand tourist brochures—it's an atmospheric place to browse for a souvenir or two.
>
> **Kissing the Blarney Stone.** The "magic" stone at Blarney Castle is said to give you the gift of gab to get what you want.
>
> **Visiting the Queenstown Story at Cobh Heritage Centre.** This site tells the story of the millions of emigrants who set sail to the United States, and of the tragic last voyage of the *Lusitania*.

EXPLORING COUNTY CORK

COBH

24 km (15 miles) southeast of Cork City.

Many of the people who left Ireland on immigrant ships for the New World departed from Cobh, a pretty fishing port and seaside resort 24 km (15 miles) southeast of Cork City on R624.

Fodor'sChoice
★
Cobh Heritage Centre. Many of the people who left Ireland on immigrant ships for the New World departed from Cobh, which was formerly known as Queenstown. The center's Queenstown Story exhibit, in the old Cobh railway station, re-creates the experience of the 2.5 million emigrants who left from here between 1848 and 1950. It also tells the stories of great transatlantic liners, including the *Titanic,* whose last port of call was Cobh, and the *Lusitania,* which was sunk by a German submarine off this coast on May 7, 1915. Many of the *Lusitania*'s 1,198 victims are buried in Cobh, which has a memorial to them on the local quay. ✉ *Old Railway Building, Lower Rd.* ☎ *021/481–3591* ⊕ *www.cobhheritage.com* 🎫 €7.50 ۞ *Nov.–Mar., Mon.–Sat. 9:30–5, Sun. 11–5; Apr.–Sept., daily 9:30–6.*

St. Colman's Cathedral. The best view of Cobh, well worth the uphill stroll, is from St. Colman's Cathedral, an exuberant neo-Gothic granite church designed by the eminent British architect E. W. Pugin in 1869, and completed in 1919. Inside, granite niches portray scenes of the

Roman Catholic Church's history in Ireland, beginning with the arrival of St. Patrick. ☎ *021/481–3222* ⊕ *www.cobhcathedralparish.ie.*

CORK CITY

Bishop Lucey Park. This tiny green park in the heart of the city opened in 1985 in celebration of the 800th anniversary of Cork's Norman charter. During its excavation, workers unearthed portions of the city's original fortified walls, now preserved just inside the arched entrance. Sculptures by contemporary Cork artists are found throughout the park. ⊠ *Grand Parade, Washington Village.*

Cork City Gaol. This castle-like building contains an austere, 19th-century prison. Life-size wax figures occupy the cells, and sound effects illustrate the appalling conditions that prevailed into the 20th century. Also here, in the Governor's House, the **Radio Museum Experience** exhibits genuine artifacts from the 1923 radio station, 6CK, and tells the story of radio broadcasting in Cork. ⊠ *Sunday's Well Rd., Sunday's Well* ☎ *021/430–5022* ⊕ *www.corkcitygaol.com* ⚑ *€8* ⊙ *Nov.–Feb., daily 10–4; Mar.–Oct., daily 9:30–5.*

Court House. A landmark in the very center of Cork, this magnificent classical building has an imposing Corinthian portico and is still used as the district's main courthouse. The exterior has been cleaned and fully restored and looks every bit as good as it did when it was built in 1835. ⊠ *Washington St., Washington Village* ☎ *021/427–2706* ⊙ *Weekdays 9–5.*

★ **Crawford Art Gallery.** The large redbrick building was built in 1724 as the customs house and is now home to Ireland's leading provincial art gallery. An imaginative expansion has added gallery space for visiting exhibitions and adventurous shows of modern Irish artists. The permanent collection includes landscape paintings depicting Cork in the 18th and 19th centuries. Take special note of works by Irish painters William Leech (1881–1968), Daniel Maclise (1806–70), James Barry (1741–1806), and Nathaniel Grogan (1740–1807). The café, run by the Allen family of Ballymaloe, is a good place for a light lunch or a homemade sweet. ⊠ *Emmet Pl., City Center South* ☎ *021/490–7855* ⊕ *www.crawfordartgallery.ie* ⚑ *Free* ⊙ *Mon.–Sat. 10–5; Thurs. 10–8 pm.*

★ **English Market.** Food lovers (and, who, pray, isn't?): be sure to make a beeline for one of the misleadingly small entrances to this large and famous mecca for foodies. Fetchingly housed in an elaborate, brick-and-cast-iron Victorian building, it bears the official name of the Princes Street Market, but it's also known locally as the Covered Market along with its general nickname. Among the 140 stalls, keep an eye out for the Alternative Bread Co., which produces more than 40 varieties of handmade bread every day. Iago, Sean Calder-Potts's deli, has fresh pasta, lots of cheeses, and charcuterie. The Olive Stall sells olive oil, olive-oil soap, and olives from Greece, Spain, France, and Italy. Kay O'Connell's Fish Stall, in the legendary fresh-fish alley, purveys local smoked salmon. O'Reilly's Tripe and Drisheen is the last existing retailer of a Cork specialty, tripe (cow's stomach), and *drisheen* (blood sausage). Upstairs is the Farmgate, an excellent café. ⊠ *Entrances on Grand Parade and Princes St., City Center South* ⊕ *www.corkenglishmarket.ie* ⊙ *Mon.– Sat. 9:30–5:30.*

☾ **Fitzgerald's Park.** This small, well-tended park is beside the River Lee's north channel in the west of the city. The park contains the **Cork Public Museum,** a Georgian mansion that houses a well-planned exhibit about Cork's history since ancient times, with a strong emphasis on the city's Republican history. ⊠ *Western Rd., Western Road* ☎ *021/427–0679* ⊕ *www.corkcity.ie/services/recreationamenityculture/museum* ⌨ *Free* ☉ *Mon.–Sat. 11–1 and 2:15–5, Sun. 3–5; closed Sun. Oct.–Mar.*

Patrick's Bridge. From here you can look along the curve of Patrick Street and north across the River Lee to St. Patrick's Hill, with its tall Georgian houses. The hill is so steep that steps are cut into the pavement. Tall ships that served the butter trade used to load up beside the bridge at Merchant's Quay before heading downstream to the sea. The design of the large, redbrick shopping center on the site evokes the warehouses of old. ⊠ *Patrick St., City Center South.*

Paul Street. A narrow stretch between the River Lee and Patrick Street and parallel to both, Paul Street is the backbone of the trendy shopping district that now occupies Cork's old French Quarter. The area was first settled by Huguenots fleeing religious persecution in France. Musicians and other street performers often entertain passersby in the Rory Gallagher Piazza, named for the late rock guitarist, whose family was from Cork. The shops here offer the best in modern Irish design—from local fashions to hand-blown glass. ⊠ *City Center South.*

St. Anne's Church. The church's pepper-pot Shandon steeple, which has a four-sided clock and is topped with a golden, salmon-shaped weather vane, is visible from throughout the city and is the chief reason why St. Anne's is so frequently visited. The Bells of Shandon were immortalized in an atrocious but popular 19th-century ballad of that name. Your reward for climbing the 120-foot-tall tower is the chance to ring the bells, with the assistance of sheet tune cards, out over Cork. Beside the church, Firkin Crane, Cork's 18th-century butter market, houses two small performing spaces. Adjacent is the **Shandon Craft Market.** ⊠ *Church St., Shandon* ☎ *021/450–5906* ⌨ *€6* ☉ *Easter–Oct., Mon.–Sat. 10–4; Nov.–Easter, Mon.–Sat. 11–3.*

St. Fin Barre's Cathedral. On the site that was the entrance to medieval Cork, this compact, three-spire Gothic cathedral, which was completed in 1879, belongs to the Church of Ireland and houses a 3,000-pipe organ. According to tradition, St. Fin Barre established a monastery on this site around AD 650 and is credited as being the founder of Cork. ⊠ *Bishop St., Washington Village* ☎ *021/496–3387* ⊕ *cathedral.cork. anglican.org* ☉ *Weekdays 9:30–5, Sat. 10–5.*

★ **University College Cork.** The Doric, porticoed gates of UCC stand about 2 km (1 mile) from the city center. The college, which has a student body of roughly 10,000, is a constituent of the National University of Ireland. The main quadrangle is a fine example of 19th-century university architecture in the Tudor-Gothic style, reminiscent of many Oxford and Cambridge colleges. Several ancient ogham stones are on display in the North Quadrangle (near the visitor center), and the renovated Crawford Observatory's 1860 telescope can be visited. The Honan Collegiate Chapel, east of the quadrangle, was built in 1916 and modeled on

the 12th-century, Hiberno-Romanesque style, best exemplified by the remains of Cormac's Chapel at Cashel. The UCC chapel's stained-glass windows, as well as its collection of art and crafts, altar furnishings, and textiles in the Celtic Revival style, are noteworthy. Three large, modern buildings have been successfully integrated with the old, including the Boole Library, named for mathematician George Boole (1815–64), who was a professor at the college. Both indoors and out the campus is enhanced by works of contemporary Irish art. The **Lewis Glucksman Gallery,** in a striking new building astride the college's entrance gates, displays works from the college's outstanding collection and hosts cutting-edge contemporary-art exhibitions. ⊠ *College Rd., Western Road* ☎ *021/490–1876* ⊕ *www.ucc.ie* ⊠ *Free* ☉ *Visitor center weekdays 9–5; call for hrs Easter wk, July, Aug., and mid-Dec.–mid-Jan.; guided tours by arrangement.*

4

BLARNEY

10 km (6 miles) northwest of Cork City.

★ **Blarney Castle.** In the center of Blarney is Blarney Castle, or what remains of it: the ruined central keep is all that's left of this mid-15th-century stronghold. The castle contains the famed **Blarney Stone**; kissing the stone, it's said, endows the kisser with the fabled "gift of gab." It's 127 steep steps to the battlements. To kiss the stone, you must lie down on the battlements, hold on to a guardrail, and lean your head way back. It's good fun and not at all dangerous. Expect a line from mid-June to early September; while you wait, you can admire the views of the wooded River Lee valley and chuckle over how the word "blarney" came to mean what it does. As the story goes, Queen Elizabeth I wanted Cormac MacCarthy, Lord of Blarney, to will his castle to the Crown, but he refused her requests with eloquent excuses and soothing compliments. Exhausted by his comments, the queen reportedly exclaimed, "This is all Blarney. What he says he rarely means."

You can take pleasant walks around the castle grounds; Rock Close contains oddly shaped limestone rocks landscaped in the 18th century, and a grove of ancient yew trees that is said to have been a site of Druid worship. In early March there's a wonderful display of naturalized daffodils. ☎ *021/438–5252* ⊕ *www.blarneycastle.ie* ⊠ *€10* ☉ *May and Sept., Mon.–Sat. 9–6:30, Sun. 9–5:30; June–Aug., Mon.–Sat. 9–7, Sun. 9–5:30; Oct.–Apr., Mon.–Sat. 9–sunset Sun. 9–5 or sunset.*

KINSALE

29 km (18 miles) southwest of Cork City on R600.

Foodies flock to Kinsale, a picturesque port that pioneered the Irish small-town tradition of fine dining in unbelievably small restaurants. In the town center, at the tip of the wide, fjord-like harbor that opens out from the River Bandon, upscale shops and eateries with brightly painted facades line small streets. Kinsale is also a center for sailing.

★ **Charles Fort.** The British built Charles Fort on the east side of the Bandon River estuary in the late 17th century, after their defeat of the Spanish and Irish forces. One of Europe's best-preserved "star forts" encloses some 12 cliff-top acres and is similar to Fort Ticonderoga in New York State. If the sun is shining, take the footpath signposted Scilly Walk; it

winds along the harbor's edge under tall trees and then through the village of Summer Cove. ✉ *3 km (2 miles) east of town* ☎ *021/477–2263* ⊕ *www.heritageireland.ie* 💷 *€4* 🕑 *Mid-Mar.–Oct., daily 10–6; Nov.–mid-Mar., daily 10–5.*

Desmond Castle and the International Museum of Wine. This museum occupies a 15th-century fortified town house—originally a custom house—that has a dark history. It was used as a prison for French and American seamen in the 1700s, and was subsequently a jail and then a workhouse. Now it contains displays that tell the story of the wine trade and its importance to the Irish diaspora in France, America, Australia, and New Zealand. ✉ *Cork St.* ☎ *021/477–4855* ⊕ *www.winegeese.ie* 💷 *€3* 🕑 *Mid-Apr.–mid-Oct., daily 10–6.*

SHOPPING

Ireland is *the* place to buy linen and wool products, but the Waterford crystal factory is no longer operating (the name lives on, but no crystal is currently produced in Ireland). The area is still good for ceramics and antiques. Celtic motifs are found on everything from jewelry to coffee cups. In Cork, Paul Street is the backbone of the trendy shopping scene, while Patrick Street has high-end names mixed with antique and souvenir shops. Blarney and Kinsale both have a range of shops selling arts and crafts from around the country.

Blarney Woollen Mills. With the largest stock and the highest turnover of Blarney's crafts shops, this noted emporium sells everything from Irish-made high fashion to Aran hand-knit items to leprechaun key rings. ☎ *021/451–6111* ⊕ *www.blarney.com.*

Quills. A good selection of Irish-made apparel for women and men is always available at Quills. ✉ *107 Patrick St., City Center South, Cork City* ☎ *021/427–1717.*

WHERE TO EAT

$ ✕**Farmgate Café.** One of the best—and busiest—informal lunch spots
IRISH in town is on a terraced gallery above the fountain at the Princes Street entrance to the atmospheric English Market. All ingredients used at the café are purchased in the market below. One side of the gallery opens onto the market and is self-service; the other side is glassed in and has table service (reservations advised). Tripe and *drisheen* (blood sausage) is one dish that is always on the menu; daily specials include less challenging but no less traditional dishes, such as corned beef with *colcannon* (potatoes and cabbage mashed with butter and seasonings) and loin of smoked bacon with *champ* (potatoes mashed with scallions or leeks). 💲 *Average main: €14* ✉ *English Market, City Center South, Cork City* ☎ *021/427–8134* ⊕ *www.corkenglishmarket.ie* 🕑 *Closed Sun. No dinner.*

$$$ ✕**Jim Edwards.** One of Ireland's original bar-restaurants, this is a famous
EUROPEAN Kinsale institution known for its generous portions of local steak, lamb,
★ and duck, and fresh seafood, all prepared under the careful eye of the owner and his wife, Paula. Choose from the inexpensive daily specials in the busy bar ($), or have a more leisurely meal among the

mahogany tables and dark-red decor of the somewhat baronial restaurant. With seafood this fresh, the preparation is kept simple: Kinsale oysters au naturel or crab claws tossed in garlic butter to start, followed by 10 ounces of prime fillet steak or medallions of monkfish (caught this morning) in a spring onion, ginger, and lime sauce. Fresh lobster from the tank is always available. The classic homemade desserts (profiteroles, crème brûlée) are substantial, and the Irish coffee is renowned. ⑤ *Average main: €26* ⊠ *Market Quay* ☎ *021/477–2541* ⊕ *www.jimedwardskinsale.com.*

DOVER, UNITED KINGDOM

Updated by
Ellin Stein

Although the southeast of England is the most densely populated part of Britain, once you escape London's sprawling suburbs, you will find hundreds of small farms set in a gentle landscape. Kent, the most southeasterly county, is known as the garden of England, famous for its apples, hops (used for brewing beer), and, increasingly, excellent vineyards. The Kent landscape is dotted with oast houses, small round towers with tilted pointed roofs originally used for drying hops, although most have now been converted into desirable homes. The area is rich in history, notably the cathedral in Canterbury, the center of the Anglican Church and the site of the murder of St. Thomas á Becket. On the coast you'll find both seaside resorts and Britain's busiest port, Dover, historically the gateway to continental Europe.

ESSENTIALS
CURRENCY
The British pound sterling. ATMs are common and credit cards are widely accepted.

HOURS
Museums are open daily during normal business hours and some evenings, while shops usually open from 9 until 5:30 or 6. Many are open on Sunday.

TELEPHONES
Dual-band GSM phones work in the United Kingdom. You can buy prepaid phone cards at telecom shops and news vendors in all towns and cities. Phone cards can be used for local or international calls. Vodafone, T-Mobile, Virgin, and Orange are the leading telecom companies.

COMING ASHORE
Ships dock at the Western Docks in Dover. There are two passenger terminals. Terminal 1 is in a converted Victorian railway station, while Terminal 2 is a purpose-built passenger facility opened in 2000. The terminals have currency-exchange facilities, car-rental kiosks, and cafés, plus a taxi stand.

There are direct trains to London Victoria and London Charing Cross (about two hours) from Dover Priory Station (take a taxi to the station). Ticket prices start at £21 round-trip but vary depending on the time of the train. There is also a faster but less frequent service to London St. Pancras. The train journey to Canterbury is around 30 minutes, with several trains per hour. Tickets are around £8 per single journey.

London Victoria Coach Station (⇨ *see Harwich, below*) can also be reached in 2½ hours by bus. There are also bus departures from the Eastern Docks (a taxi ride or a 15-minute walk along the seafront) and, occasionally, directly from the cruise terminal.

A car rental is recommended for exploring the Kent countryside but not for a visit to London, where traffic, congestion charges, and parking difficulties abound. Rental rates begin at £32 per day for an economy manual vehicle. But given the distance, this is a good opportunity to see the beauty of Kent rather than trek all the way into central London.

GETTING TO THE AIRPORT

If you choose not to purchase aiport transfers from your cruise line, the easiest way to get to the airport from the cruise port to Heathrow airport is to contract a private taxi or transfer company. Several companies offer the services with prices of a one-way transfer of around €185 for vehicles carrying a maximum of three people. For other transport options, including bus and train, it's necessary to connect through central London, which may be tiring depending on how much luggage you are carrying and may not be a money-saving option depending on how many travelers are in your party.

Contacts Prompt Airport Cars. ☎ 020/3384–4659 ⊕ www.promptexecutivehire. co.uk. **Road Express.** ☎ 0844/822–2616 ⊕ www.road-express.co.uk.

EXPLORING DOVER AND VICINITY

DOVER

122 km (76 miles) southeast of London.

The busy passenger port of Dover has for centuries been Britain's gateway to Europe. Its chalk **White Cliffs** are a famous and inspirational sight, though you may find the town itself a bit disappointing; the savage bombardments of World War II and the shortsightedness of postwar developers left the city center an unattractive place. However, there are still some historic legacies, notably the castle, as well the ruins of a Roman lighthouse and a late Saxon church on its grounds, and a well-preserved Roman residence.

★   **Dover Castle.** Spectacular and with plenty to explore, Dover Castle, towering high above the ramparts of the white cliffs, is a mighty medieval castle that has served as an important strategic center over the centuries, even in World War II. Most of the castle, including the keep, dates to Norman times. It was begun by Henry II in 1181 but incorporates additions from almost every succeeding century. There's a lot to see besides the castle rooms, and many of the exhibits will appeal to kids, including the Siege of 1216, the Princess of Wales Regimental Museum, and Castle Fit for a King. ■**TIP→** **Tour the secret wartime tunnels, a medieval and Napoleonic-era system that was used again during World War II.** ⊠ *Castle Rd.* ☎ *01304/211067* ⊕ *www.english-heritage.org.uk* 🎟 *£16.50* ☉ *Apr.–July and Sept., daily 10–6; Aug., daily 9:30–6; Oct.–early Nov., daily 10–5; mid-Nov.–Mar., weekends 10–4.*

Roman Painted House. Believed to have been a hotel, this structure includes some Roman wall paintings, along with the remnants of an ingenious heating system. ⊠ *New St.* ☎ *01304/203279* ⊕ *www.theromanpaintedhouse.co.uk* 🎟 *£3* ☉ *Early–mid-Apr., daily 10–5; late Apr.–May, Tues. and Sat. 10–5; Jun.–mid-Sept, Tues.–Sun. 10–5; last admission 30 min before closing.*

CANTERBURY

28 km (17 miles) northwest of Dover.

A bustling medieval cathedral town, charming Canterbury has good shopping, plenty of history, and just enough to see in a day. Thousands flocked to the city's magnificent cathedral, the Church of England's equivalent to the Vatican, in the 12th century, a pilgrimage immortalized in Geoffrey Chaucer's *Canterbury Tales*, and it remains well worth a visit. They flocked here to see the shrine of the murdered archbishop St. Thomas á Becket, and buildings that served as pilgrims' inns (and survived the World War II bombing of the city) still dominate the city center. Going back even further, there's evidence of a prosperous society in the Canterbury area as early as the Bronze Age (around 1000 BC), and it was an important Roman city, as well as a center of Anglo-Saxon culture in the Kingdom of Kent.

Fodor's Choice   **Canterbury Cathedral.** The focal point of the city was the first of ★   England's great Norman cathedrals. Nucleus of worldwide Anglicanism, the Cathedral Church of Christ Canterbury (its formal name) is a living textbook of medieval architecture. The building was begun

in 1070, demolished, begun anew in 1096, and then systematically expanded over the next three centuries. When the original choir section burned to the ground in 1174, another replaced it, designed in the new Gothic style, with tall, pointed arches. The cathedral is popular, so arrive early or late in the day to avoid the crowds. You can just walk around, or you can buy a guidebook with an overview of the building's history, use an audio guide for the most detail, or take a tour.

The cathedral was only a century old, and still relatively small, when Thomas à Becket, the archbishop of Canterbury, was murdered here in 1170. Becket, a defender of ecclesiastical interests, had angered his friend Henry II, who was supposedly heard to exclaim, "Will no one rid me of this troublesome priest?" Thinking they were carrying out the king's wishes, four knights burst in on Becket in one of the side chapels and killed him. Two years later Becket was canonized, and Henry II's subsequent penitence and submission to the authority of the Church helped establish the cathedral as the center of English Christianity.

Becket's tomb, destroyed by Henry VIII in 1538 as part of his campaign to reduce the power of the Church and confiscate its treasures, was one of the most extravagant shrines in Christendom. In **Trinity Chapel,** which held the shrine, you can still see a series of 13th-century stained-glass windows illustrating Becket's miracles. So hallowed was this spot that in 1376, Edward, the Black Prince, warrior son of Edward III and a national hero, was buried near it. The actual site of Becket's murder is down a flight of steps just to the left of the nave. In the corner, a second flight of steps leads down to the enormous Norman **undercroft,** or vaulted cellarage, built in the early 12th century. A row of squat pillars whose capitals dance with animals and monsters supports the roof.

If time permits, explore the **cloisters** and the small monastic buildings to the north of the cathedral. The 12th-century octagonal water tower is still part of the cathedral's water supply. The Norman staircase in the northwest corner of the Green Court dates from 1167 and is a unique example of the architecture of the times. ⊠ *Cathedral Precincts* ☎ *01227/762862* ⊕ *www.canterbury-cathedral.org* 🎫 *£9, free for services and ½ hr before closing; £5 for tour; £3.50 for audio guide* ☉ *Easter–Sept., Mon.–Sat. 9–5:30, Sun. 12:30–2:30; Oct.–Easter, Mon.–Sat. 9–5, Sun. 12:30–2:30. Last entry ½ hr before closing. Restricted access during services.*

DOVER BEST BETS

Canterbury Cathedral. One of Britain's greatest churches, this was an important place of pilgrimage and the scene of one of the country's darkest crimes.

The White Cliffs of Dover. Best seen from the water, these iconic cliffs are part of the national psyche and, on a sunny day, an exceptionally breathtaking vista.

Rye. Though there are no attractions as such here, the sheer quaintness and "Englishness" of Rye makes it a great place to relax, soak in the atmosphere, and shop for souvenirs.

Canterbury Roman Museum. Belowground, at the level of the remnants of Roman Canterbury, this museum features colorful mosaic Roman pavement and a hypocaust—the Roman version of central heating. Displays of excavated objects (some of which you can hold in the Touch the Past area) and computer-generated reconstructions of Roman buildings and the marketplace help re-create the past. ■ **TIP→ Up to four kids get in free with an adult.** ✉ *Butchery La.* ☎ *01227/785575* ⊕ *www.canterbury. co.uk* 🖾*£6; combined ticket with Canterbury Heritage Museum £10* ⊙ *Daily 10–5; last admission at 4. Closed last wk in Dec.*

🐾 **The Canterbury Tales.** It's a kitschy audiovisual (and occasionally olfactory) dramatization of 14th-century English life—touristy but popular. You'll "meet" Chaucer's pilgrims and view tableaus illustrating five tales. In summer, actors in period costume play out scenes from the town's history. ✉ *St. Margaret's St.* ☎ *01227/479227* ⊕ *www. canterburytales.org.uk* 🖾*£8.25* ⊙ *Nov.–Feb., daily 10–4:30; Mar.– June, Sept., and Oct., daily 10–5; July and Aug., daily 9:30–5.*

Medieval city walls. For an essential Canterbury experience, follow the circuit of the 13th- and 14th-century walls, built on the line of the Roman walls. Those to the east survive intact, towering some 20 feet high and offering a sweeping view of the town. You can access these from a number of places, including Castle Street and Broad Street.

FAVERSHAM
45 km (28 miles) northwest of Dover.

In Roman times, Faversham was a thriving seaport. Today the port is hidden from sight, and you could pass through this market town without knowing it was there. Still, Faversham is a worthwhile stop for those in search of Ye Quaint Olde Englande: The town center, with its Tudor houses grouped around the 1574 Guildhall and covered market, looks like a perfect stage set. There are no actual sights here, as such, but it's a lovely place to take a break and have a stroll.

BROADSTAIRS
36 km (22 miles) north of Dover.

Like other Victorian seaside towns on this stretch of coast, Broadstairs was once the playground of vacationing Londoners. Charles Dickens spent many summers here between 1837 and 1851 and wrote glowingly of its bracing freshness. Today grand 19th-century houses line the waterfront. In the off-season Broadstairs is a peaceful retreat, but day-trippers pack the town in July and August.

Dickens House Museum. This house was originally the home of Mary Pearson Strong, on whom Dickens based the character of Betsey Trotwood, David Copperfield's aunt. Dickens lived here from 1837 to 1839 while writing *The Pickwick Papers* and *Oliver Twist*. Some rooms have been decorated to look as they would have in Dickens's day, and there's a reconstruction of Miss Trotwood's room as described by Dickens. ✉ *2 Victoria Parade* ☎ *01843/861232* ⊕ *www.dickensfellowship.org* 🖾*£3.50* ⊙ *Apr.–Oct., daily 2–5.*

RYE

★ *64 km (40 miles) south of Dover.*

With cobbled streets and ancient timbered dwellings, Rye is an artist's dream. Once a port (the water retreated, and the harbor is now 2 miles away), the town starts where the sea once lapped at its ankles and then winds its way to the top of a low hill that overlooks the Romney Marshes. Virtually every building in the little town center is intriguingly old; some places were smugglers' retreats. This place can be easily walked without a map, but if you prefer guidance, the local tourist office has an interesting audio tour of the town, as well as maps.

SHOPPING

The little towns of Kent are great places to browse for collectibles, china, silver, and secondhand books. The streets of Canterbury have an excellent selection of souvenirs, some of them decidedly kitsch. Rye has great antiques shops, perfect for an afternoon of rummaging, with the biggest cluster at the foot of the hill near the tourist information center. The English can find bargains; it's harder for Americans, given the exchange rate. The town still has a number of potteries.

Black Sheep Antiques. This shop has a superior selection of antique crystal and silver. ✉ *72 The Mint* ☎ *01797/224508.*

Collectors Corner. A good mix of furniture, art, and silver is found at Collectors Corner. ✉ *2 Market Rd.* ☎ *01797/225796.*

David Sharp Pottery. Like the ceramic name plaques that are a feature of the town? They are on offer at this tidy shop. ✉ *55 The Mint* ☎ *01797/222620.*

WHERE TO EAT

$ ✕**City Fish Bar.** Long lines and lots of satisfied finger licking attest to the
BRITISH   deserved popularity of this excellent fish-and-chips outlet in the center of town. Everything is freshly fried, the batter crisp and the fish tasty; the fried mushrooms are also surprisingly good. There's no seating, so your fish is wrapped up in paper, and you eat it where you want, perhaps in the park. This place closes at 7. ⑤ *Average main: £6* ✉ *30 St. Margaret's St., Canterbury* ☎ *01227/760873* ▭ *No credit cards.*

$$ ✕**Webbes at the Fish Café.** One of Rye's most popular restaurants occu-
SEAFOOD   pies a brick building that dates to 1907, but the interior has been
Fodor's Choice   redone in a sleek, modern style. The ground-floor café has a relaxed
★   atmosphere, and upstairs is a more formal dining room. Most of the seafood here is caught nearby, so it's very fresh. Sample the shellfish platter with oysters, whelks, winkles, shrimp, and crab claws, or try the grilled squid with bok choy. Reservations are recommended for dinner. ⑤ *Average main: £15* ✉ *17 Tower St., Rye* ☎ *01797/222226* ⊕ *www. webbesrestaurants.co.uk* ⊗ *Closed Mon. Oct.–Apr. No dinner Sun.*

WHERE TO STAY

$$ 🛏 **Abode Canterbury.** This glossy boutique hotel inside the Old City
HOTEL   walls offers an up-to-date style in traditional Canterbury. **Pros:** central
location; luxurious handmade beds; great restaurants and bars. **Cons:**
one of the priciest hotels in town; bar gets quite crowded. $ *Rooms
from: £135* ✉ *30–33 High St., Canterbury* ☎ *01227/766266* ⊕ *www.
abodehotels.co.uk* 🛏 *73 rooms.*

DUBLIN, IRELAND

In his inimitable, irresistible way, James Joyce immortalized the city
of Dublin in works like *Ulysses* and *Dubliners*. He claimed to have
chosen Dublin as the setting for his work because it was a "center of
paralysis" where nothing much ever changed. What would he make
of Temple Bar—the city's erstwhile down-at-the-heels neighborhood,
now crammed with restaurants and hotels? Or of the city's newfound
status as a bustling hub of the European economy? Yet despite all
these advances, traditional Dublin is far from buried. The fundamen-
tals—the Georgian elegance of Merrion Square, the Norman drama of
Christ Church Cathedral, the foamy pint at an atmospheric pub—are
still on hand to gratify. Most of all, there are the locals themselves:
the nod and grin when you catch their eye on the street, the eager-
ness to share a tale or two, and their paradoxically dark but warm
sense of humor.

ESSENTIALS
CURRENCY
The euro. ATMs are common.

HOURS
Shops and businesses are generally open Monday through Saturday
from 9:30 to 5:30 or 6; some open later and some open on Sunday.
Most museums open daily Monday through Saturday from 9 until 5;
museums may have shorter hours on Sunday.

TELEPHONES
Most tri- and quad-band GSM phones will work in Ireland, and the
country's mobile system is 3G compatible with excellent coverage. Pub-
lic phones accept prepaid call cards (available in shops and telecom
offices) and credit crads. Eircom, BT Ireland, and Vodafone are the
major telecom suppliers.

COMING ASHORE
Small ships dock at the quayside of the River Liffey, close to the
downtown area. Larger ships berth at Alexandra Quay, 1.2 miles
from downtown. Alexandra Quay is part of the great Dublin Port,
with a range of visitor facilities including cafés, shops, information
desks, and restrooms. Buses 53 and 53A run from the port into the
city. Ticket prices are set according to the number of zones traveled,
beginning at €1.40.

Taxis can be hired to run tour itineraries, although charges are compli-
cated. Initial charges are a maximum of €4.10, then €1.03 per km (½

Belvidere Pl.

Portland Row

North Strand Rd.

West Rd.

Church Rd.

East Rd.

Sean McDermott St.

Killarney St.

Amiens St.

Church Rd.

Church Rd.

Railway St.

Foley St.

Seville Pl.

Connolly Station

Gardiner St.

Talbot St.

Lower Sheriff St.

Upper Sheriff St.

Inner Dock

Commons St.

New Wapping St.

Mayor St.

Castleforbes Rd.

Custom House

Georges Dock

Custom House Quay

North Wall Quay

Butt Br.

Talbot Mem. Br.

George's Quay

City Quay

River Liffey

East Link Toll Br.

Tara St. Station

Gloucester St.

Sir John Rogerson's Quay

nsend St.

Pearse St.

Cardiff's La.

Hanover Quay

Grand Canal Dock

Lombard St. E.

Mageanis Pl.

Westland Row

Pearse Station

Pearse St.

Macken St.

Grand Canal Quay

Ringsend Rd.

South Lotts Rd.

Leinster St.

Lincoln Place

Clare St.

Fenian St.

Hogan Pl.

Lower Grand Canal St.

rick St.

◆ National Gallery of Ireland

Merrion Sq. N.

Upper Grand Canal St.

Bath Av.

◆ National Museum of Archaeology

Merrion Sq. S.

◆ Merrion Square

Lower Mount St.

Northumberland Rd.

Shelbourne Rd.

Lansdowne Rugby Ground

Merrion Row

Fitzwilliam La.

Lower Fitzwilliam St.

Upper Mount St.

Herbert Rd.

Pembroke St. Lower

Baggot St.

Herbert Pl.

Percy Pl.

Haddington Rd.

Lansdowne Park

Lansdowne Rd.

Upper Fitzwilliam St.

Lad La.

Herbert St.

Lansdowne Rd.

Shelbourne Rd.

Lower Leeson St.

Wilton Terrace

Upper Baggot St.

Pembroke Rd.

Pembroke Rd.

Mespil Rd.

Pembroke Ln.

Beattys Av.

Herbert Rd.

uth

Burleigh Ct.

Wellington Rd.

Elgin Rd.

Raglan Ln.

Pembroke Rd.

rth

mouth

Sussex Rd.

Burlington Rd.

Waterloo Lane

Heysbury Lane

Raglan Rd.

Clyde Rd.

Shelbourne Rd.

South

Upper Leeson St.

Waterloo Rd.

Wellington Rd.

Clyde Ln.

Anglesea Rd.

Serpentine Av.

thbrook Rd.

Wellington Pl.

rthbrook

The Appian Way

HERBERT PARK

Merrion Rd.

0 ——— 1/4 mi

0 ——— 1/4 km

mile). Drivers can choose to charge by the minute rather than per km. Don't rent a car if you are planning to tour Dublin, but a rental car does offer freedom to explore the countryside and coast around the city. The cost per day for a compact manual vehicle begins at €60.

EXPLORING DUBLIN

City Hall. Facing the Liffey from Cork Hill at the top of Parliament Street, this grand Georgian municipal building (1769–79), once the Royal Exchange, marks the southwest corner of Temple Bar. Today it's the seat of the Dublin Corporation, the elected body that governs the city. Thomas Cooley designed the building with 12 columns that encircle the domed central rotunda, which has a fine mosaic floor and 12 frescoes depicting Dublin legends and ancient Irish historical scenes. The 20-foot-high sculpture to the right is of Daniel O'Connell, "The Liberator." He looks like he's about to begin the famous speech he gave here in 1800. The building houses a multimedia exhibition—with artifacts, kiosks, graphics, and audiovisual presentations—tracing the evolution of Ireland's 1,000-year-old capital. ⊠ *Dame St., Dublin West* ☎ *01/222–2204* ⊕ *www.dublincity.ie/RecreationandCulture* ☜ *€4* ⊙ *Mon.–Sat. 10–5:15.*

Custom House. Seen at its best when reflected in the waters of the Liffey during the short interval when the high tide is on the turn, the Custom House is the city's most spectacular Georgian building. Extending 375 feet on the north side of the river, this is the work of James Gandon, an English architect who arrived in Ireland in 1781, when the building's construction commenced (it continued for 10 years). Crafted from gleaming Portland stone, the central portico is linked by arcades to pavilions at either end. A statue of Commerce tops the copper dome, whose puny circumference, unfortunately, is out of proportion to the rest of the building. Statues on the main facade are based on allegorical themes. Note the exquisitely carved lions and unicorns supporting the arms of Ireland at the far ends of the facade. After Republicans set fire to the building in 1921, it was completely restored and reconstructed to house government offices. A visitor center traces the building's history and significance, and the life of Gandon. ⊠ *Custom House Quay, Northside* ☎ *01/888–2538* ⊕ *www.visitdublin.com* ☜ *Free* ⊙ *Mid-Mar.–Oct., weekdays 10–12:30, weekends 2–5; Nov.–mid-Mar., Wed.–Fri. 10–12:30, Sun. 2–5.*

★ **Dublin City Gallery, The Hugh Lane.** The Francis Bacon studio, reconstructed here exactly as the artist left it on his death (including his diary, books, walls, floors, ceiling, and even dust!), makes this already impressive gallery a must-see for art lovers and fans of the renowned British artist. Built as a town house for the Earl of Charlemont in 1762, this residence was so grand that the Parnell Square street on which it sits was nicknamed "Palace Row" in its honor. Sir William Chambers, who also built the Marino Casino for Charlemont, designed the structure in the best Palladian manner. Its delicate and rigidly correct facade, extended by two demilune (half-moon) arcades, was fashioned from the "new" white Ardmulcan stone (now seasoned to gray). Charlemont

was one of the cultural locomotives of 18th-century Dublin—his walls were hung with Titians and Hogarths, and he frequently dined with Oliver Goldsmith and Sir Joshua Reynolds—so he would undoubtedly be delighted that his home is now a gallery, named after Sir Hugh Lane, a nephew of Lady Gregory (W. B. Yeats's aristocratic patron). Lane collected both impressionist paintings and 19th-century Irish and Anglo-Irish works. A complicated agreement with the National Gallery in London (reached after heated diplomatic dispute) stipulates that a portion of the 39 French paintings amassed by Lane shuttle between London and here. Time it right and you'll be able to see Pissarro's *Printemps,* Manet's *Eva Gonzales,* Morisot's *Jour d'Été,* and, the jewel of the collection, Renoir's *Les Parapluies.*

> **DUBLIN BEST BETS**
>
> **Admire the Georgian architecture.** The magnificent neoclassical buildings form an impressive framework on which the life of the 21st-century city hangs.
>
> **Have a pint of Guinness.** The people of Dublin have a reputation for friendliness and a love of life that's infectious, so find a seat in a pub and enjoy.
>
> **Wander through St. Stephen's Green.** This park offers recreation as well as history—scattered throughout are memorials to the city's literary giants.

Irish artists represented include Roderic O'Conor, well known for his views of the west of Ireland; William Leech, including his *Girl with a Tinsel Scarf* and *The Cigarette*; and the most famous of the group, Jack B. Yeats (W. B.'s brother). The museum has a dozen of his paintings, including *Ball Alley* and *There is No Night.* The mystically serene Sean Scully Gallery displays seven giant canvasses by Ireland's renowned abstract modernist. ⊠ *Parnell Sq. N, Northside* ☎ *01/222–5550* ⊕ *www.hughlane.ie* 🖼 *Free* ☉ *Tues.–Thurs. 10–6, Fri. and Sat. 10–5, Sun. 11–5.*

Grafton Street. It's no more than 200 yards long and about 20 feet wide, but brick-lined Grafton Street, open only to pedestrians, can claim to be the most humming street in the city, if not in all of Ireland. It's one of Dublin's vital spines: the most direct route between the front door of Trinity College and St. Stephen's Green, and the city's premier shopping street, with Dublin's most distinguished department store, Brown Thomas, as well as tried and trusted Marks & Spencer. Grafton Street and the smaller alleyways that radiate off it offer dozens of independent stores, a dozen or so colorful flower sellers, and some of the Southside's most popular watering holes. In summer, buskers from all over the world line both sides of the street, pouring out the sounds of drum, whistle, pipe, and string.

Fodor's Choice
★ **Guinness Storehouse.** Ireland's all-dominating brewery—founded by Arthur Guinness in 1759 and at one time the largest stout-producing brewery in the world—spans a 60-acre spread west of Christ Church Cathedral. Not surprisingly, it's the most popular tourist destination in town—after all, the Irish national drink is Guinness stout, a dark brew made with roasted malt. The brewery itself is closed to the public, but the Guinness Storehouse is a spectacular attraction, designed to woo— some might say brainwash—you with the wonders of the "dark stuff."

In a 1904 cast-iron-and-brick warehouse, the museum display covers six floors built around a huge, central glass atrium, which is shaped like a giant pint glass. Beneath the glass floor of the lobby you can see Arthur Guinness's original lease on the site, for a whopping 9,000 years. The exhibition elucidates the brewing process and its history, with antique presses and vats, a look at bottle and can design through the ages, a history of the Guinness family, a fascinating archive of Guinness advertisements, and a chance to pull your own perfect pint. The star attraction is undoubtedly the top-floor **Gravity Bar,** with 360-degree floor-to-ceiling glass walls that offer a nonpareil view out over the city at sunset while you sip your free pint. One of the bar's first clients was one William Jefferson Clinton. You'll find the Guinness logo on everything from piggy banks to underpants in the Guinness Store on the ground floor. ⊠ *St. James' Gate, Dublin West* ☎ *01/408–4800* ⊕ *www.guinness-storehouse.com* ⊠ *€14.40* ⊙ *July and Aug., daily 9:30–7; Sept.–June, daily 9:30–5.*

James Joyce Centre. Few may have read him, but everyone in Ireland has at least heard of James Joyce (1882–1941)—especially since owning a copy of his censored and suppressed *Ulysses* was one of the top status symbols of the early 20th century. Joyce is of course now acknowledged as one of the greatest modern authors, and his *Dubliners, Finnegan's Wake,* and *A Portrait of the Artist as a Young Man* can even be read as quirky "travel guides" to Dublin. Open to the public, this restored 18th-century Georgian town house, once the dancing academy of Professor Denis J. Maginni (which many will recognize from a reading of *Ulysses*), is a center for Joycean studies and events related to the author. It has an extensive library and archives, exhibition rooms, a bookstore, and a café. The collection includes letters from Beckett, Joyce's guitar and cane, and a celebrated edition of *Ulysses* illustrated by Matisse. The interactive "James Joyce and Ulysses" exhibition allows you to delve into the mysteries and controversies of the novel. The center is the main organizer of "Bloomstime," which marks the week leading up to the Bloomsday celebrations. (Bloomsday, June 16, is the single day *Ulysses* chronicles, as Leopold Bloom winds his way around Dublin in 1904.) ⊠ *35 N. Great George's St., Northside* ☎ *01/878–8547* ⊕ *www.jamesjoyce.ie* ⊠ *€5, guided tour €10* ⊙ *Tues.–Sat. 10–5, Sun. noon–5.*

Fodor's Choice ★ **Merrion Square.** Created between 1762 and 1764, this tranquil square a few blocks east of St. Stephen's Green is lined on three sides by some of Dublin's best-preserved Georgian town houses, many of which have brightly painted front doors crowned by intricate fanlights. Leinster House, the National Museum of Natural History, and the National Gallery line the west side of the square. It's on the other sides, however, that the Georgian terrace streetscape comes into its own—the finest houses are on the north border. Even when the flower gardens here are not in bloom, the vibrant, mostly evergreen grounds, dotted with sculpture and threaded with meandering paths, are worth strolling through. Several distinguished Dubliners have lived on the square, including Oscar Wilde's parents, Sir William and "Speranza" Wilde (No. 1); Irish national leader Daniel O'Connell (No. 58); and authors W. B. Yeats (Nos. 52 and 82) and Sheridan LeFanu (No. 70). Until 50

years ago the square was a fashionable residential area, but today most of the houses serve as offices. At the south end of Merrion Square, on Upper Mount Street, stands the Church of Ireland St. Stephen's Church. Known locally as the "pepper canister" church because of its cupola, the structure was inspired in part by Wren's churches in London. An open-air art gallery featuring the works of local artists is held on the square on Sundays. ✉ *Southeast Dublin* ⊕ *www.merrionsquareart.com* ⊙ *Daily sunrise–sunset.*

Fodor'sChoice
★
National Gallery of Ireland. Caravaggio's *The Taking of Christ* (1602), Van Gogh's *Rooftops of Paris* (1886), Vermeer's *Lady Writing a Letter with Her Maid* (circa 1670) . . . you get the picture, or rather, you'll *find* the picture here. Established in 1864 and designed by Francis Fowke (who also designed London's Victoria & Albert Museum), the National Gallery of Ireland is one of Europe's finest smaller art museums, with "smaller" being a relative term: the collection holds more than 2,500 paintings and some 10,000 other works. But unlike Europe's largest art museums, the National Gallery can be thoroughly covered in a morning or afternoon without inducing exhaustion.

A highlight of the museum is the major collection of paintings by Irish artists from the 17th through 20th centuries, including works by Roderic O'Conor (1860–1940), Sir William Orpen (1878–1931), and William Leech (1881–1968). The Yeats Museum section contains works by members of the Yeats family, including Jack B. Yeats (1871–1957), the brother of writer W. B. Yeats, and by far the best-known Irish painter of the 20th century.

The collection also claims exceptional paintings from the 17th-century French, Dutch, Italian, and Spanish schools, and works by French impressionists Monet, Sisley, and Renoir. The amply stocked gift shop is a good place to pick up books on Irish artists. Free, guided tours are available on Saturday at 2 and on Sunday at 1 and 2. ✉ *Merrion Sq. W, Southeast Dublin* ☎ *01/661–5133* ⊕ *www.nationalgallery.ie* ✍ *Free; special exhibits €10* ⊙ *Mon.–Wed., Fri., and Sat. 9:30–5:30, Thurs. 9:30–8:30, Sun. noon–5:30.*

★
National Museum of Archaeology. Just south of Leinster House is Ireland's National Museum of Archaeology, one of four branches of the National Museum of Ireland, and home to a fabled collection of Irish artifacts dating from 7000 BC to the present. Organized around a grand rotunda, the museum is elaborately decorated, with mosaic floors, marble columns, balustrades, and fancy ironwork. It has the largest collection of Celtic antiquities in the world, including gold jewelry, carved stones, bronze tools, and weapons.

The Treasury collection, including some of the museum's most renowned pieces, is open on a permanent basis. Among the priceless relics on display are the 8th-century Ardagh Chalice, a two-handled silver cup with gold filigree ornamentation; the bronze-coated iron St. Patrick's Bell, the oldest surviving example (5th–8th century) of Irish metalwork; the 8th-century Tara Brooch, an intricately decorated piece made of white bronze, amber, and glass; and the 12th-century bejeweled oak Cross of Cong, covered with silver and bronze panels.

The *Or: Ireland's Gold* exhibition gathers together the most impressive pieces of surprisingly delicate and intricate prehistoric gold work—including sun disks and the late Bronze Age gold collar known as the Gleninsheen Gorget—that range in dates from 2200 to 500 BC. Upstairs, Viking Ireland is a permanent exhibit on the Norsemen, featuring a full-size Viking skeleton, swords, leatherworks recovered in Dublin and surrounding areas, and a replica of a small Viking boat. The newest attraction is an exhibition entitled *Kinship and Sacrifice*, centering on a number of Iron Age "bog bodies" found along with other objects in Ireland's peat bogs.

The 18th-century Collins Barracks, near Phoenix Park (⇨ *see Phoenix Park*), houses the National Museum of Decorative Arts and History, a collection of glass, silver, furniture, and other decorative arts. ⊠ *Kildare St. Annex, 7–9 Merrion Row, Southeast Dublin* ☎ *01/677-7444* ⊕ *www.museum.ie* ⊠ *Free* ☉ *Tues.–Sat. 10–5, Sun. 2–5.*

Newman House. One of the finest examples of Georgian Dublin, Newman House is actually two imposing town houses joined together. The earlier of the two, No. 85 St. Stephen's Green (1738), has two landmarks of Irish Georgian style: the Apollo Room, decorated with stuccowork depicting the sun god and his muses; and the magnificent Saloon, crowned with an exuberant ceiling aswirl with cupids and gods, created by the Brothers Lafranchini–the finest *stuccadores* (plaster workers) of 18th-century Dublin. Next door at No. 86 (1765), the staircase, set against pastel walls, is one of the city's most beautiful rococo examples—with floral swags and musical instruments picked out in cake-frosting white. To explore the rich history and architecture of the houses you must join a guided tour. At the back of Newman House hides Dublin's "secret garden" (⇨ *see Iveagh Gardens).* ⊠ *85–86 St. Stephen's Green, Southside* ☎ *01/475-7255* ⊕ *www.ucd.ie/campusdevelopment/developmentprojects* ⊠ *House and garden €5* ☉ *Tours June–Aug., Tues.–Fri. at 2, 3, and 4.*

O'Connell Street. Dublin's most famous thoroughfare, which is 150 feet wide, was previously known as Sackville Street, but its name was changed in 1924, two years after the founding of the Irish Free State. After the devastation of the 1916 Easter Uprising, the Northside street had to be almost entirely reconstructed, a task that took until the end of the 1920s. At one time the main attraction of the street was Nelson's Pillar, a Doric column towering over the city center and a marvelous vantage point, but it was blown up in 1966, on the 50th anniversary of the Easter Uprising. A major cleanup and repaving have returned the street to some of its old glory. The large monument at the south end of the street is dedicated to Daniel O'Connell (1775–1847), "The Liberator," and was erected in 1854 as a tribute to the orator's achievement in securing Catholic Emancipation in 1829. Look closely and you'll notice that O'Connell is wearing a glove on one hand, as he did for much of his adult life, a self-imposed penance for shooting a man in a duel. But even the great man himself is dwarfed by the newest addition to O'Connell Street: the 395-foot-high spire was built in Nelson's Pillar's place in 2003, and today this gigantic, stainless-steel monument dominates the street.

★ **Royal Hospital Kilmainham.** This replica of Les Invalides in Paris is regarded as the most important 17th-century building in Ireland. Commissioned as a hospice for disabled and veteran soldiers by James Butler—the Duke of Ormonde and viceroy to King Charles II—it was completed in 1684, making it the first building erected in Dublin's golden age. It survived into the 1920s as a hospital, but after the founding of the Irish Free State in 1922, the building fell into disrepair. The entire edifice has since been restored. The architectural highlight is the hospital's baroque chapel, distinguished by its extraordinary plasterwork ceiling and fine wood carvings. ⊕ *www.rhk.ie.*

Irish Museum of Modern Art. The Royal Hospital also houses the Irish Museum of Modern Art, which concentrates on the work of contemporary Irish artists such as Richard Deacon, Richard Gorman, Dorothy Cross, Sean Scully, Matt Mullican, Louis Le Brocquy, and James Coleman. The museum also displays works by some non-Irish 20th-century greats, including Picasso and Miró, plus recent hotshots like Damien Hirst, and regularly hosts touring shows from major European museums. The Grass Roots Café serves light fare such as soups and sandwiches. The hospital is a short ride by taxi or bus from the city center. ⊠ *Kilmainham La., Dublin West* ☎ *01/612–9900* ⊕ *www.imma. ie* ⊡ *Free* ⊙ *Royal Hospital: Mon, Tues., and Thurs.–Sat. 10–5:30, Wed. 10:30–5:30, Sun. noon–5:30. Museum: Tues. and Thurs.–Sat. 10–5:30, Wed. 10:30–5:30, Sun. noon–5:30; tours Wed. and Fri. at 2:30, Sat. at 11:30*

Fodor's Choice **St. Stephen's Green.** Dubliners call it simply Stephen's Green, and green
★ it is (year-round)—a verdant, 27-acre Southside square that was used for the public punishment of criminals until 1664. After a long period of decline, it became a private park in 1814—the first time in its history that it was closed to the public. Its fortunes changed again in 1880, when Sir Arthur Guinness paid for it to be laid out anew. Flower gardens, formal lawns, a Victorian bandstand, and an ornamental lake with lots of waterfowl are all within the park's borders, connected by paths guaranteeing that strolling here or just passing through will offer up unexpected delights (such as palm trees). Among the park's many statues are a memorial to W. B. Yeats and another to Joyce by Henry Moore. In the 18th century, the walk on the north side of the green was referred to as the Beaux Walk because most of Dublin's gentlemen's clubs were in town houses here. Today it's dominated by the legendary Shelbourne hotel. On the south side is the alluring Georgian Newman House. ⊠ *Southside* ⊡ *Free* ⊙ *Daily sunrise–sunset.*

Fodor's Choice **Trinity College Dublin.** Founded in 1592 by Queen Elizabeth I to "civi-
★ lize" (Her Majesty's word) Dublin, Trinity is Ireland's oldest and most famous college. The memorably atmospheric campus is a must; here you can track the shadows of some of the noted alumni, such as Jonathan Swift (1667–1745), Oscar Wilde (1854–1900), Bram Stoker (1847–1912), and Samuel Beckett (1906–89). Trinity College, Dublin (familiarly known as TCD), was founded on the site of the confiscated Priory of All Hallows. For centuries Trinity was the preserve of the Protestant Church; a free education was offered to Catholics—provided that they accepted the Protestant faith. As a legacy of this condition, until 1966

Catholics who wished to study at Trinity had to obtain a dispensation from their bishop or face excommunication.

Trinity's grounds cover 40 acres. Most of its buildings were constructed in the 18th and early 19th centuries. The extensive **West Front,** with a classical pedimented portico in the Corinthian style, faces College Green and is directly across from the Bank of Ireland; it was built between 1755 and 1759, and is possibly the work of Theodore Jacobsen, architect of London's Foundling Hospital. The design is repeated on the interior, so the view is the same from outside the gates and from the quadrangle inside. On the lawn in front of the inner facade stand statues of two alumni, orator Edmund Burke (1729–97) and dramatist Oliver Goldsmith (1730–74). On the right side of the cobblestone quadrangle of **Parliament Square** (commonly known as Front Square) is Sir William Chambers's theater, or Examination Hall, dating from the mid-1780s, which contains the college's most splendid Adamesque interior, designed by Michael Stapleton. The hall houses an impressive organ retrieved from an 18th-century Spanish ship and a gilded oak chandelier from the old House of Commons; concerts are sometimes held here. The chapel, left of the quadrangle, has stucco ceilings and fine woodwork. The looming campanile, or bell tower, is the symbolic heart of the college; erected in 1853, it dominates the center of the square. ☎ 01/896–1000 ⊕ www.tcd.ie.

SHOPPING

There's a tremendous variety of stores in Dublin, many of which are quite sophisticated. Department stores stock internationally known fashion designer goods and housewares, and small boutiques sell Irish crafts and other merchandise. If you're at all interested in modern and contemporary literature, be sure to leave yourself time to browse through the bookstores. Don't forget a bottle of Irish whiskey or a bottle or two of Guinness.

Francis Street is the hub of Dublin's antiques trade. **Grafton Street** has mainly chain stores. The smaller streets off Grafton Street have worthwhile crafts, clothing, and designer houseware shops. **Nassau Street,** Dublin's main tourist-oriented thoroughfare, has some of the best-known stores selling Irish goods. **Temple Bar** is dotted with small boutiques—mainly intimate, quirky shops that traffic in a selection of trendy goods, from vintage clothes to some of the most avant-garde Irish garb anywhere in the city. Note that many museums have excellent gift shops selling crafts, books, and prints, among other items.

Fodor'sChoice   **Cathach Books.** Head here for a fine array of first editions of Irish litera-
★   ture and many other books of Irish interest, plus old maps of Dublin and Ireland. ⊠ 10 Duke St., Southside ☎ 01/671–8676 ⊕ www.rarebooks.ie.

WHERE TO EAT

$ ✕ **Busyfeet & Coco Café.** This bustling, quirky bohemian café emphasizes
CAFÉ   good, wholesome food. Organic ingredients play a prominent role on a menu that's laden with delicious salads and sandwiches. Try the grilled

goat-cheese salad served with walnut-and-raisin toast and sun-dried-tomato tapenade on a bed of arugula. The delicious Mediterranean quesadilla wrap—with roasted vegetables, napolitana sauce, and mature cheddar—is a must. It's also one of the city center's best-situated spots for a bit of people-watching, as Dublin's young and hip stroll by all day long. Live music every Saturday night. ⑤ *Average main: €8* ⌂ *41–42 S. William St., Southside* ☎ *01/671–9514* ⌂ *Reservations not accepted.*

GREENOCK, SCOTLAND (FOR GLASGOW)

Updated
by Mike
Gonzalez

In the days when Britain still ruled over an empire, Glasgow pronounced itself the Second City of the Empire. The term "Clyde-built" (from Glasgow's River Clyde) became synonymous with good workmanship and lasting quality. Glasgow had fallen into a severely depressed state by the mid-20th century, but during the century's last two decades the city cleaned up and started looking forward. Modern Glasgow has undergone an urban renaissance: A booming cultural life, stylish restaurants, and an air of confidence make it Scotland's most exciting city. Glasgow is particularly remarkable for its architecture, from the unique Victorian cityscapes of Alexander "Greek" Thomson (1817–75) to the cutting-edge art nouveau vision of Charles Rennie Mackintosh (1868–1928). The city also has some of the most exciting museum collections outside London.

ESSENTIALS
CURRENCY
The British pound sterling. ATMs are common and credit cards are widely accepted.

HOURS
Museums are open from 9 until 5, while shops usually open from 9 until 5:30 or 6. Shops are open on Sunday.

PRIVATE TOURS
Private tours can be arranged through Glasgow Taxis or Little's Chauffeur Drive.

Contacts Glasgow Taxis. ☎ *0141/429–7070* ⊕ *glasgowtaxisltd.co.uk.*
Little's Chauffeur Drive. ☎ *0141/883–2111* ⊕ *www.littles.co.uk.*

TELEPHONES
Dual-band GSM phones work in the United Kingdom. You can buy prepaid phone cards at telecom shops and news vendors in all towns and cities. Phone cards can be used for local or international calls. Vodafone, T-Mobile, Virgin and Orange are the leading telecom companies.

COMING ASHORE
Vessels dock at Greenock's Ocean Terminal in the main port. Passengers walk the few yards to the terminal building, which has tourist information, refreshments, currency exchange, car-rental kiosks, and a taxi stand. A new waterfront walkway leads into the town of Greenock, where there are shops, restaurants, and some fine Victorian architecture dating from the time when the town was an important transatlantic port. However, there's little to hold visitors here.

Glasgow

↑ TO BBC
SCOTLAND

Kelvin Bridge

Queen's
Cross Church

Maryhill Rd.

North Woodsi

Belmont St.

Hunterian
Art Gallery

Great Western Road

St. George's Rd.

University Ave.

Bank St.

Park Rd.

U

Kelvin Way

River Kelvin

Woodlands Road

Garnet St.

Buccl

Riverside
Museum:
Scotland's
Museum of
Transport and Travel

Argyle St.

Kelvingrove
Art Gallery
and Museum

Kelvingrove
Park

Renfrew St.

Argyle St.

Sauchiehall St.

Elderslie St.

North St.

Newton St.

Elmbank St.

Holland St.

Pitt St.

W. Reg

Berkeley St.

Argyle St.

St. Vincent St.

Mitchell St.

Douglas

Clydeside   Expressway

Argyle St.

Bellahouston
Park

Dumbreck Rd.

Finnieston St.

Lancefield   Quay

M8

Argyle St.

Mosspark Blvd.

M77

River Clyde

Dumbreck Rd.

Mavisbank Quay

Pollok
Country
Park

Burrell
Collection ♦

Paisley Rd.

Wallace St.

Guidmans Rd.

Burrell
Collection
(see inset)
↓

TO SCOTLAND
STREET SCHOOL

Cook St.

Pollok Ave.

KEY

Pedestrian Zone
Rail Lines
U Metro Stop
i Tourist information

0   1/4 mi
0   1/4 km

Possil Rd.
Keppochhill Rd.
Garscube Rd.
Saracen St.
Craighall Rd.
Garscube Rd.

Dobbie's Loan
Dobbie's Loan
M8

Cowcaddens Rd.
Buchanan St.
Bus Station
Glasgow
School of Art
Dalhouse St.
Cambridge St.
W. Campbell St.
Sauchiehall St.
Bath St.
Nelson
Mandela
Pl.
Queen St.
Station
U
North Hanover St.
Cathedral St.
N. Frederick St.
St. James Rd.
Castle St.
Glasgow
Cathedral
St. Mungo
Museum of
Religious
Life and Art
Strathclyde
University
Taylor St.
eorge St.
St. Vincent St.
Hope St.
Renfield St.
W. George St.
George Square
St. Vincent Pl.
i
S. Frederick St.
John St.
Rotten Row
Rotten Row E.
Blythswood
Bothwell St.
Gordon St.
Buchanan St.
Hanover St.
Queen St.
George St.
Ingram St.
MERCHANT
CITY
Duke St.
Waterloo St.
nderston
oss Bus
ation
Royal
Exchange
Square
Central
Station
Union St.
W. Nile St.
Princes Sq.
Miller St.
Virginia St.
Glassford St.
Hutcheson St.
Wilson
Candleriggs
Albion St.
Bell St.
High St.
U
St. Enoch
Shopping
Centre
Argyll
Arcade
Jamaica St.
Oswald St.
Glassford St.
Trongate
Osborne St.
Bridgegate
London Rd.
Gallowgate
Millroad St.
Clyde St.
R. Clyde
Saltmarket
Greendyke St.
Lanark St.
Charlotte St.
London Rd.
Monteith Row
Green St.
The Green
Nelson St.
Norfolk St.
Gorbals St.
Glasgow Green

A black taxi to downtown Glasgow is a fixed-price of £45 one-way. Private hire firms operate to and from Greenock but must be booked in advance. They are significantly cheaper. In Glasgow, Network Cars (which will also pick up from Greenock if booked) and Inverclyde Taxis in Greenock) are the best choices. From the station in Greenock (Greenock West), regular train services run into Glasgow city. From the port to the railway station it's a £4 taxi trip. The journey to Glasgow takes 30 to 40 minutes; trains run three or more times per hour, and tickets start at £6.80 round trip (off-peak is the cheapest ticket, after 9:30 am and not between 4:30 and 6:30 pm). You can also take Buses 901, 906, and 907 into Glasgow from the Greenock bus station. A Daytripper ticket, which covers transport to and from Glasgow and within the city for a day, costs £19 for 2 adults and up to 4 children or £10.70 for 1 adult and 2 children.

GLASGOW BEST BETS

Kelvingrove Art Gallery and Museum. A fantastic collection of European art, featuring such luminaries as Rembrandt and Monet, set in a stunning neo-Renaissance edifice.

Glasgow School of Art. Designed by Charles Rennie Mackintosh, this building is a tour de force of British art nouveau and one of the finest architectural statements in a city full of fine civic buildings. Tickets for the Mackintosh Trail are £16 and entry to all Mackintosh sites in the city and transport between them. Purchase at the tourist office in Glasgow.

Hunterian Art Gallery. This gallery features works by Tintoretto, Sir Joshua Reynolds, and Auguste Rodin—all donated by a private collector.

Once in Glasgow, Subway (tickets £1.40 a single trip or £3.80 for a whole day Discovery ticket, use after 9.30 a.m.) and bus services (tickets £1.85) can get you around easily. There are also numerous metered taxis. If you want to explore the majestic landscapes of southwestern Scotland independently, it pays to rent a vehicle (approximately £50–£70 per day for a manual economy vehicle) or take a custom guided tour.

Contacts Network Cars. ☎ 01415/571110. **Inverclyde Taxis.** ☎ 01475/734563.

EXPLORING GLASGOW

The Greater Glasgow and Clyde Valley Tourist Board, at 11 George Square, provides information on all services available in and around the city, as well as details of tours within and around the city. Most tours begin from here, too, and can be booked in advance. It also has a well-stocked shop.

Fodor's Choice ★ **Burrell Collection.** An elegant, ultramodern building of pink sandstone and stainless steel houses thousands of items of all descriptions, from ancient Egyptian, Greek, and Roman artifacts to Chinese ceramics, bronzes, and jade. You can also find medieval tapestries, stained-glass windows, Rodin sculptures, and exquisite French-impressionist paintings—Degas's *The Rehearsal* and Sir Henry Raeburn's *Miss Macartney,* to name two. Eccentric millionaire Sir William Burrell (1861–1958)

donated this collection of some 8,000 pieces to the city in 1944. The 1983 building was designed with large glass walls so that the items on display could relate to their surroundings in Pollok Country Park: art and nature, supposedly in perfect harmony. You can get here via Buses 45, 48, and 57 from Union Street, or it's a leisurely 15-minute walk from the Pollokshaws West rail station. ☒ *2060 Pollokshaws Rd., South Side* ☏ *0141/287–2550* ⊕ *www.glasgowmuseums.com* ☒ *Free* ☉ *Mon.–Thurs. and Sat. 10–5, Fri. and Sun. 11–5.*

George Square. The focal point of Glasgow is lined with an impressive collection of statues of worthies: Queen Victoria; Scotland's national poet, Robert Burns (1759–96); the inventor and developer of the steam engine, James Watt (1736–1819); Prime Minister William Gladstone (1809–98); and towering above them all, Scotland's great historical novelist, Sir Walter Scott (1771–1832). The column was intended for George III (1738–1820), after whom the square is named, but when he was found to be insane toward the end of his reign, his statue was never erected. On the square's east side stands the magnificent Italian Renaissance–style **City Chambers**; the handsome **Merchants' House** fills the corner of West George Street, crowned by a globe and a sailing ship. ☒ *Between St. Vincent and Argyle Sts., City Center* Ⓜ *Buchanan St.*

Fodor's Choice
★
Glasgow Cathedral. The most complete of Scotland's cathedrals (it would have been more complete had 19th-century vandals not pulled down its two rugged towers), this is an unusual double church, one above the other, dedicated to Glasgow's patron saint, St. Mungo. Consecrated in 1136 and completed about 300 years later, it was spared the ravages of the Reformation—which destroyed so many of Scotland's medieval churches—mainly because Glasgow's trade guilds defended it. A late-medieval open-timber roof in the nave and lovely 20th-century stained glass are notable features. In the lower church is the splendid crypt of St. Mungo, who was originally known as St. Kentigern (*kentigern* means "chief word"), but who was nicknamed St. Mungo (meaning "dear one") by his early followers in Glasgow. The site of the tomb has been revered since the 6th century, when St. Mungo founded a church here. Mungo features prominently in local legends; one such legend is about a pet bird that he nursed back to life, and another tells of a bush or tree, the branches of which he used to miraculously relight a fire. The bird, the tree, and the salmon with a ring in its mouth (from another story about him) are all to be found on the city of Glasgow's coat of arms, together with a bell that Mungo brought from Rome. ☒ *Cathedral St., City Center* ☏ *0141/552–8198* ⊕ *www.glasgow-cathedral.com* ☒ *Free* ☉ *Apr.–Sept., Mon.–Sat. 9:30–5:30, Sun. 1–5; Oct.–Mar., Mon.–Sat. 9:30–4:30, Sun. 1–4:30* Ⓜ *Buchanan St.*

★ **Glasgow School of Art.** The exterior and interior, structure, furnishings, and decoration of this art nouveau building, built between 1897 and 1909, form a unified whole, reflecting the inventive genius of Charles Rennie Mackintosh, who was only 28 years old when he won the competition for its design. Architects and designers from all over the world come to admire it. Book ahead for daily guided tours, which cost £8.75 and begin at 11 and 3 (sometimes more frequently in the summer). Otherwise, you can visit four galleries that host frequently changing exhibitions. A

visitor center has a small Mackintosh exhibition and sells a good selection of prints, postcards, and books. ⊠ *11 Dalhousie St., City Center* ☎ *0141/353–4526* ⊕ *www.gsa.ac.uk/tours* ✉ *£8.75* ⊘ *Building: daily 10:30–5. Exhibitions: Mon.–Sat. 10:30–4:30, Sat. 10–2.* Ⓜ *Cowcaddens.*

★ **Hunterian Art Gallery.** Opposite Glasgow University's main gate, this gallery houses William Hunter's (1718–83) collection of paintings (his antiquarian collection is housed in the nearby Hunterian Museum). You'll also find prints, drawings, and sculptures by Tintoretto, Rembrandt, and Auguste Rodin, as well as a major collection of paintings by James McNeill Whistler, who had a great affection for the city that bought one of his earliest paintings. Also in the gallery is a replica of **Charles Rennie Mackintosh's town house,** which once stood nearby. The rooms contain Mackintosh's distinctive art nouveau chairs, tables, beds, and cupboards, and the walls are decorated in the equally distinctive style devised by him and his artist wife, Margaret. The gallery is free, but the Mackintosh House and occasional special exhibitions are £5. ⊠ *Hillhead St., West End* ☎ *0141/330–5431* ⊕ *www.hunterian.gla.ac.uk* ✉ *Free, Mackintosh house £5* ⊘ *Tues.–Sat. 10–5, Sun. 11–4* Ⓜ *Hillhead.*

Fodor's Choice **Kelvingrove Art Gallery and Museum.** Worthy of its world-class reputation,
★ the Kelvingrive Art Gallery and Museum attracts local families as well
☸ as international visitors. This combination of cathedral and castle was designed in the Renaissance style and built between 1891 and 1901. The stunning red-sandstone edifice is an appropriate home for works by Botticelli, Rembrandt, Monet, and others; the museum has been hailed as "one of the greatest civic collections in Europe." The Glasgow Room houses extraordinary works by local artists. There's a Mackintosh and the Glasgow Style room, a picture promenade, and a natural-history exhibit on creatures of the past. Whether the subject is Scottish culture, design, or storytelling, every wall and room begs you to look deeper; labels are thought provoking and sometimes witty. You could spend a weekend here, but in a pinch three hours would do one level justice—there are three. Leave time to visit the gift shop and the attractive basement restaurant. ⊠ *Argyle St., West End* ☎ *0141/276–9599* ⊕ *www. glasgowmuseums.com* ✉ *Free* ⊘ *Mon.–Thurs. and Sat. 10–5, Fri. and Sun. 11–5* Ⓜ *Kelvinhall.*

Queen's Cross Church. Head for the Charles Rennie Mackintosh Society Headquarters, housed in the only church Mackintosh designed, to learn more about the famous Glasgow-born architect and designer. Although one of the leading lights in the art nouveau movement, Mackintosh died in relative obscurity in 1928. Today he's widely accepted as a brilliant innovator. The church has beautiful stained-glass windows and a light-enhancing, carved-wood interior. The center's library and shop provide further insight into Glasgow's other Mackintosh-designed buildings, which include Scotland Street School, the Martyrs Public School, and the Glasgow School of Art. The church sits on the corner of Springbank Street at the junction of Garscube Road with Maryhill Road; a cab ride can get you here, or take a bus toward Queen's Cross from stops along Hope Street. ⊠ *870 Garscube Rd., West End* ☎ *0141/946–6600* ⊕ *www.crmsociety.com* ✉ *£4* ⊘ *Apr.–Oct., Mon., Wed., and Fri. 10–5; Nov.–Mar., Mon., Wed., and Fri. 10–4.*

Fodor's Choice **Riverside Museum: Scotland's Museum of Transport and Travel.** An extraor-
★ dinary new riverside museum designed by Zaha Hadid celebrates the
☺ area's industrial heritage with flair. Its huge metal structure with curving
walls echoes the covered yards where ships were built on the Clyde.
Glasgow's history of shipbuilding is celebrated in the world-famous
collection of Clyde-built ship models. Some of the locomotives built
at the nearby St. Rollox yards are also on display. There are cars from
every age and many countries suspended on a kind of flying roadway
above the main museum. You can wander down Main Street, circa
1930, without leaving the building: the pawnbroker and the Italian
café, the subway train and the funeral parlor are frozen in time. Relax
with a coffee in the café, wander out onto the expansive riverside walk,
or board the tall ship that is moored permanently behind the museum.
Bus 100 from George Square brings you here, or you can walk from
the Partick subway station in 10 minutes. ⊠ *100 Poundhouse Pl., West
End* ☎ *0141/287–2720* ⊕ *www.glasgowlife.org.uk/museums* 🖃 *Free*
☉ *Mon.–Thurs. and Sat. 10–5, Fri. and Sun. 11–5* Ⓜ *Partick.*

St. Mungo Museum of Religious Life and Art. An outstanding collection of
artifacts, including Celtic crosses and statuettes of Hindu gods, reflects
the many religious groups that have settled throughout the centuries
in Glasgow and the west of Scotland. This rich history is depicted in
the stunning Sharing of Faiths Banner, which celebrates the city's many
different faiths. A Zen garden creates a peaceful setting for rest and con-
templation, and elsewhere stained-glass windows include a depiction
of St. Mungo himself. ⊠ *2 Castle St., City Center* ☎ *0141/276–1625*
⊕ *www.glasgowmuseums.com* 🖃 *Free* ☉ *Tues.–Thurs. and Sat. 10–5,
Fri. and Sun. 11–5* Ⓜ *Buchanan St.*

SHOPPING

Glasgow is a shopper's dream, with its large department stores, designer
outlets, quirky boutiques, and unique markets. Choice items include
such traditional Scottish crafts as tartans, kilts, knitwear, and of course,
whisky. Join the throngs of style-conscious and unseasonably tan locals
along Argyle, Buchanan, and Sauchiehall streets. Should the weather
turn *dreich,* you can avoid getting *drookit* by sheltering in one of the
many covered arcades in the city center. For more unusual items, head
to the West End's Byres Road and Great Western Road.

Many of Glasgow's young and upwardly mobile make their home in
Merchant City, on the edge of the city center. Shopping here is expensive,
but the area is worth visiting if you're seeking the youthful Glasgow
style. If you're an antiques connoisseur and art lover, a walk along **West
Regent Street,** particularly its **Victorian Village,** is highly recommended,
as there are various galleries and shops, some specializing in Scottish
antiques and paintings.

Glasgow School of Art. The Glasgow School of Art sells books, cards, jewelry, and ceramics. Students often display their work during the degree
shows in June. ⊠ *167 Renfrew St., City Center* ☎ *0141/353–4526.*

Hector Russell Kiltmakers. Hector Russell Kiltmakers specializes in High-land outfits, wool and cashmere clothing, and women's fashions. ⌧ *110 Buchanan St., City Center* ☎ *0141/221–0217.*

Princes Square. By far the best shopping center is the art nouveau Princes Square, with high-quality shops alongside pleasant cafés and restaurants. Look for the Scottish Craft Centre, which carries an outstanding collection of work created by some of the nation's best craftspeople. ⌧ *48 Buchanan St., City Center* ☎ *0141/221–0324.*

ACTIVITIES

Royal Troon. Founded in 1878, Royal Troon has two 18-hole courses: the Old, or Championship, Course and the Portland Course. The views are magnificent, but the courses can get windy. Access for non-members is limited between May and mid-October to Monday, Tuesday, and Thursday only; day tickets cost £220 and include two rounds, morning coffee, and a buffet lunch, but there are cheaper options. ⌧ *Craigend Rd., Troon* ☎ *01292/311555* ⊕ *www.royaltroon.co.uk* ⅃ *Old Course: 18 holes, 7,150 yds, SSS 74. Portland Course: 18 holes, 6,289 yds, SSS 70.*

WHERE TO EAT

$ ✕ **Café Gandolfi.** Occupying what was once the tea market, this trendy
BRITISH café draws the style-conscious crowd. Wooden tables and chairs crafted by Scottish artist Tim Stead are so fluidly shaped it's hard to believe they're inanimate. The café opens early for breakfast, serving croissants, eggs *en cocotte* (casserole-style), and strong espresso. Don't miss the smoked venison or the finnan haddie (smoked haddock). The bar on the second floor is more intimate and much less busy—and lets you order from the same menu. Ⓢ *Average main: £13* ⌧ *64 Albion St., Merchant City* ☎ *0141/552–6813* ⊕ *www.cafegandolfi.com.*

$ ✕ **Willow Tearoom.** This Sauchiehall Street eatery takes up part of a
BRITISH department store originally designed by Charles Rennie Mackintosh. The original tearoom is now reduced to a gallery at the back of a Mackintosh-themed jewelry and gift shop, but it retains his trademark furnishings, including high-back chairs with elegant lines and subtle curves. The St. Andrew's Platter is an exquisite selection of trout, salmon, and prawns. Scottish and Continental breakfasts are available throughout the day, and the scrambled eggs with salmon is traditional Scots food at its finest. The in-house baker guarantees fresh scones, cakes, and pastries. Ⓢ *Average main: £8* ⌧ *217 Sauchie-hall St., City Center* ☎ *0141/332–0521* ⊕ *www.willowtearooms.co.uk* ☉ *No dinner.*

HARWICH, UNITED KINGDOM (FOR LONDON)

Updated by
Ellin Stein

An urban center since Roman times, London combines streets redolent with history with the vibrant modernity of a world city. If London offered only famous landmarks like the Tower, Big Ben, and St. Paul's Cathedral, it would nevertheless be a top international destination. But it is so much more: the green oases of the parks and squares; a dining scene that encompasses both superstar chefs and affordable restaurants serving cuisines from around the world; and shops and galleries that reflect the city's status as a hotbed of trailblazing style and art. At the same time, London's traditional character remains. Double-decker red buses still trundle around, soldiers in tall bearskin hats still guard Buckingham Palace, the theaters still offer some of the world's best productions, and there is still an abundance of museums containing incomparable collections. Far from being a monument to the past, London is constantly growing and changing. Harwich is now commonly used as the point of embarkation for many ships that use "London" as a base.

ESSENTIALS

CURRENCY

The British pound sterling. ATMs are common and credit cards are widely accepted.

HOURS

Museums are open daily during normal business hours and some evenings, while shops usually open from 9 until 5:30 or 6. Many are open on Sunday.

TELEPHONES

Dual-band GSM phones work in the United Kingdom. You can buy prepaid phone cards at telecom shops and news vendors in all towns and cities. Phone cards can be used for local or international calls. Vodafone, T-Mobile, Virgin, and Orange are the leading telecom companies.

COMING ASHORE

Vessels dock in the commercial port at Harwich, which is small but busy with commercial and ferry traffic. Port amenities include a main-line train station for transfers into London, a café, bar, ATMs, and an exchange bureau.

When larger cruise ships dock, the port schedules extra trains between Harwich International station (*not* Harwich Town) and Liverpool Street station in London. The journey time for these and normal weekday trains is 80 minutes. On weekends, one change is required, and the journey is one hour 45 minutes. Ticket prices are around £19 round-trip. Taxi (private hire or minicab) transfer to London is prohibitively expensive at around £160 or more.

GETTING TO THE AIRPORT

If you do not purchase airport transfers from your cruise line there are several ways to reach the Heathrow airport from the cruise port. The easiest but costliest way would be to book a private direct tranfer by taxi or private hire company. Costs are around £170, but this covers from one to three people traveling in the same vehicle. Depending on traffic conditions, the transfer should be around one hour.

There are several public transport options, but each of these involves a transfer between rail and Underground stations within London, which may not be practical if you have bulky luggage. Once at Liverpool Street station, it's generally best to transfer to your chosen mode of transport to take you from central London to Heathrow airport unless you take a transfer offered by your cruise line direct to the airport.

The least expensive option is the London Underground, but carriages can be busy with little luggage space. From Liverpool Street take the Hammersmith and City line to King's Cross. From King's Cross the Piccadily line takes you directly to Heathrow. The time for the journey is around 1:20 hours and costs £5.30.

Aimed more at travelers than commuters, Heathrow Express offers a much quicker journey, 15 minutes from Paddington Station to Heathrow. To reach Paddington, take the Hammersmith and City line from Liverpool Street. Heathrow Express tickets cost £18 one-way.

The Heathrow Connect train links Paddington with Heathrow airport, stopping at selected minor stations along the 30-minute route. Prices are £8.50 one-way.

Contacts **Cruise Transfer.com.** ☎ *0800/043–2752, 888/556–8616 from U.S.* ⊕ *www.cruisetransfer.com.* **Prompt Airport Cars.** ☎ *020/3384–4659* ⊕ *www.promptexecutivehire.co.uk.* **Airport Express.** ☎ *0800/783–7899, 07702/787–600 from U.S.* ⊕ *www.aidg.co.uk.*

> ## LONDON BEST BETS
>
> **Buckingham Palace.** A prime chance to catch sight of British royalty.
>
> **The British Museum.** One of the world's richest historical and archaeological collections, and it's completely free.
>
> **The Tower of London.** Experience the city's rich history, from dirty deeds to the dazzling Crown Jewels.

EXPLORING LONDON

Fodor'sChoice
★

British Museum. With a facade like a great temple, this celebrated treasure house, filled with plunder of incalculable value and beauty from around the globe, occupies an immense Greco-Victorian building that makes a suitably grand impression. Inside are some of the greatest relics of humankind: the Parthenon Sculptures (Elgin Marbles), the Rosetta Stone, the Sutton Hoo Treasure—almost everything, it seems, but the Ark of the Covenant. The three rooms that comprise the **Sainsbury African** Galleries are a must-see in the Lower Gallery—together they present 200,000 objects, highlighting such ancient kingdoms as the Benin and Asante. The museum's focal point is the **Great Court**, a brilliant modern design with a vast glass roof that reveals the museum's covered courtyard. The revered **Reading Room** has a blue-and-gold dome and hosts temporary exhibitions. If you want to navigate the highlights of the almost 100 galleries, join the free **eyeOpener** 30- to 40-minute tours by museum guides (details at the information desk).

The collection's greatest hits include the **Rosetta Stone,** found by French soldiers in 1799, and carved in 196 BC by decree of Ptolemy V in Egyptian hieroglyphics, demotic (a cursive script developed in Egypt), and Greek. Maybe the **Parthenon Sculptures** should be back in Greece, but while the debate rages on, you can steal your own moment with the Elgin Marbles. Also in the West Wing is one of the Seven Wonders of the Ancient World—in fragment form: the **Mausoleum of Halikarnassos.** Upstairs are some of the most popular galleries, especially beloved by children, are the **Egyptian mummies.** Nearby are the glittering 4th-century **Mildenhall Treasure** and the equally splendid 8th-century Anglo-Saxon **Sutton Hoo Treasure** (with magnificent helmets and jewelry). ⊠ *Great Russell St., Bloomsbury* ☎ *020/7323–8000* ⊕ *www.britishmuseum.org* ✉ *Free; donations encouraged* ☉ *Galleries Sat.–Thurs. 10–5:30, Fri. 10–8:30. Great Court Sat.–Thurs. 9–6, Fri. 9 – 8.30* Ⓜ *Russell Square, Holborn, Tottemham Court Rd.*

Fodor's Choice
★
Buckingham Palace. It's rare to get a chance to see how the other half— well, other minute fraction—lives and works. But when the Queen heads off to Scotland on her annual summer holiday (you can tell because the Union Jack flies above the palace instead of the Royal Standard), the palace's 19 State Rooms open up to visitors (although the north wing's private apartments remain behind closed doors). With fabulous gilt moldings and walls adorned with masterpieces by Rembrandt, Rubens, and other old masters, the State Rooms are the grandest of the palace's 775 rooms. The **Changing the Guard,** also known as **Guard Mounting,** remains one of London's best free shows and culminates in front of the palace. ⊠ *Buckingham Palace Rd., St. James* ☎ *020/7766–7300* ⊕ *www.royalcollection.org.uk* ✉ *£18* ☉ *Aug.–late Sept., daily 9:45–6 (last admission 3:45); times subject to change; book ahead for disabled access; check website before visiting* Ⓜ *Victoria, St. James's Park, Green Park.*

Houses of Parliament. If you want to understand some of the centuries-old traditions and arcane idiosyncrasies that make up constitution-less British parliamentary democracy, the Palace of Westminster, as the complex is still properly called, is the place to come. The architecture in this 1,100-room labyrinth impresses, but the real excitement lies in stalking the corridors of power. A palace was first established on this site by Edward the Confessor in the 11th century. William II started building a new palace in 1087, and this gradually became the seat of English administrative power. However, fire destroyed most of the palace in 1834, and the current complex dates largely from the middle of the 19th century.

Visitors aren't allowed to snoop too much, but the **Visitors' Galleries** of the House of Commons do afford a view of democracy in process when the banks of green-leather benches are filled by opposing MPs (members of Parliament). When they speak, it's not directly to each other but through the Speaker, who also decides who will get time on the floor. After the 1834 fire, the **Clock Tower** was completed in 1858, and contains the 13-ton bell known as **Big Ben.** At the southwest end of the main Parliament building is the 323-foot-high Victoria Tower. ⊠ *St. Stephen's Entrance, St. Margaret St., Westminster*

☎ *020/7219–4272, 0844/847–1672* ⊕ *www.parliament.uk/visiting* ✉ *Free; £15 tours (must book ahead)* ⊙ *Call to confirm hrs for Visitors Galleries. Tours: Aug., Mon., Tues., Fri., Sat. 9.15–4.30, Wed. and Thurs. 1.15–4.30; Sept., Mon., Fri., Sat. 9.15–4.30, Tues., Wed., Thurs. 1.15–4.30* Ⓜ *Westminster.*

★ **London Eye.** To mark the start of the new millennium, architects David
🕐 Marks and Julia Barfield conceived a beautiful and celebratory structure that would allow people to see this great city from a completely new perspective. They came up with a giant Ferris wheel, which, as well as representing the turn of the century, would also be a symbol of regeneration. The London Eye is the largest cantilevered observation wheel ever built and among the tallest structures in London. The 25-minute slow-motion ride inside one of the enclosed passenger capsules is so smooth you'd hardly know you were suspended over the Thames. On a clear day you can see for up to 25 miles, with a bird's-eye view over London's most famous landmarks as you circle through 360 degrees. If you're looking for a special place to celebrate, champagne and canapés can be arranged ahead of time. ■ **TIP→ Buy your ticket online to avoid the long lines and get a 10% discount. For an extra £10, you can save even more time with a Fast Track flight for which you check in 15 minutes before your "departure."** You can buy a combination ticket for the Eye and other London attractions—check online for details—or board the London Eye River Cruise here for a 40-minute sightseeing voyage on the Thames. ⊠ *Riverside Building, County Hall, Westminster Bridge Rd., South Bank* ☎ *0870/990–8883* ⊕ *www.londoneye.com* ✉ *£18.60; cruise £12* ⊙ *June and Sept., daily 10–9; July and Aug., daily 10–9:30; Oct.–Mar., daily 10–8:30* Ⓜ *Waterloo.*

Fodor'sChoice **National Gallery.** Standing proudly on the north side of Trafalgar Square
★ is one of the world's supreme art collections, with more than 2,300
🕐 masterpieces on show. Picasso, van Gogh, Michelangelo, Leonardo, Monet, Turner, and more—all for free. Watch our special temporary exhibitions as well.

This brief selection is your jumping-off point, but there are hundreds of other paintings to see, enough to fill a full day. In chronological order: (1) **Van Eyck** (circa 1395–1441), *The Arnolfini Portrait*—a solemn couple holds hands, the fish-eye mirror behind them mysteriously illuminating what can't be seen from the front view. (2) **Holbein** (1497–1543), *The Ambassadors*—two wealthy visitors from France stand surrounded by what were considered luxury goods at the time. Note the elongated skull at the bottom of the painting, which takes shape when viewed from an angle. (3) **Leonardo da Vinci** (1452–1519), *The Virgin and Child*—this exquisite black-chalk "Burlington Cartoon" depicts the master's most haunting Mary. (4) **Velazquez** (1599–1660), *Christ in the House of Martha and Mary*—in this enigmatic masterpiece the Spaniard plays with perspective and the role of the viewer. (5) **Turner** (1775–1851), *Rain, Steam and Speed: The Great Western Railway*, the whirl of rain, mist, steam, and locomotion is nothing short of astonishing (spot the hare). (6) **Caravaggio** (1573–1610), *The Supper at Emmaus* —a cinematically lightened, freshly resurrected Christ blesses bread in an astonishingly domestic

vision from the master of chiaroscuro. (7) **Van Gogh** (1853–1890), *Sunflowers* — painted during his sojourn with Gauguin in Arles, this is quintessential Van Gogh. (8) **Seurat** (1859–91), *Bathers at Asnières*— this static summer day's idyll is one of the pointillist extraordinaire's best-known works. ⊠ *Trafalgar Square, Westminster* ☎ 020/7747–2885 ⊕ *www.nationalgallery.org.uk* ⊠ *Free; charge for special exhibitions; audio guide £3.50* ☯ *Sun.–Thurs. 10–6, Fri. 10–9* Ⓜ *Charing Cross, Embankment, Leicester Square.*

Fodor'sChoice
★ **St. Paul's Cathedral.** St. Paul's is simply breathtaking. The structure is Sir Christopher Wren's masterpiece, completed in 1710 after 35 years of building, and, much later, miraculously spared (mostly) by World War II bombs. Wren's first plan, known as the New Model, did not make it past the drawing board. The second, known as the Great Model, got as far as the 20-foot oak rendering before it also was rejected. You can see it displayed in the Trophy Room. The third plan was accepted, with the fortunate proviso that the architect be allowed to make changes as he saw fit. Without that, there would be no dome, because the approved design had a steeple—and St. Paul's simply would not be St. Paul's as we know it without the dome, the third largest in the world and easily recognizable on the skyline from many an angle around London. Up 163 spiral steps is the **Whispering Gallery,** an acoustic phenomenon; you whisper something to the wall on one side, and a second later it transmits clearly to the other side, 107 feet away. Behind the high altar is the **American Memorial Chapel,** dedicated to the 28,000 GIs stationed in the United Kingdom who lost their lives in World War II. Among the famous figures whose remains lie in the **Crypt** are the Duke of Wellington and Admiral Lord Nelson. The Crypt also has a gift shop and a café. ⊠ *St. Paul's Churchyard, The City* ☎ 020/7236–4128 ⊕ *www. stpauls.co.uk* ⊠ *£15 (includes multimedia guides and guided tours)* ☯ *Cathedral Mon.–Sat. 8:30–4; Shop Mon.–Sat. 9–5, Sun. 10–5; Crypt Café Mon.–Sat. 9–5, Sun. noon–4* Ⓜ *St. Paul's.*

Fodor'sChoice
★
☙ **Tate Britain.** The stately neoclassical institution may not be as ambitious as its sibling Tate Modern on the South Bank, but Tate Britain's bright galleries lure only a fraction of the Modern's crowds and are a great place to explore British art from 1500 to the present. First opened in 1897, funded by the sugar magnate Sir Henry Tate, the museum includes the Linbury Galleries on the lower floors, which stage temporary (and often popular) exhibitions, whereas the upper floors show the permanent collection. Pictures are regularly re-hung and whatever is on view, you can find classic works by John Constable, Thomas Gainsborough, George Stubbs, David Wilkie, Francis Bacon, Duncan Grant, Barbara Hepworth, and Ben Nicholson and an outstanding display from J.M.W. Turner in the Clore Gallery, including many later vaporous and light-infused works such as *Sunrise with Sea Monsters*. Sumptuous Pre-Raphaelite pieces are a major drawcard while the Contemporary British Art galleries bring you face to face with Damien Hirst's *Away from the Flock* and other recent conceptions. The Tate Britain also hosts the annual Turner Prize exhibition, with its accompanying furor over the state of contemporary art, from about October to January each year. ⊠ *Millbank, Westminster* ☎ 020/7887–8888 ⊕ *www.tate.org.uk/britain*

⌧ *Free, special exhibitions £9–£15; Tate-to-Tate shuttle £5 each way; River Roamer ticket £12.60* ☉ *Sat.–Thurs. 10–6 (last entry at 5.15), Fri. 10–10 (last entry at 9:15)* Ⓜ *Pimlico (signposted 5-min walk).*

Fodor's Choice
★
☻
Tate Modern. This spectacular renovation of a mid-20th-century power station is the most-visited museum of modern art in the world. Its great permanent collection, which starts in 1900 and ranges from modern masters like Matisse to the most cutting-edge contemporary artists, is arranged thematically—Landscape, Still Life, and the Nude. Its blockbuster temporary exhibitions showcase the work of individual artists like Gaugin, Warhol, and Gerhard Richter. The vast **Turbine Hall** is a dramatic entrance point used to showcase big, audacious installations that tend to generate a lot of publicity. Past highlights include Olafur Eliasson's massive glowing sun and Carsten Holler's huge metal slides. ⌧ *Bankside, South Bank* ☎ *020/7887–8888* ⊕ *www.tate.org.uk/modern* ⌧ *Free, charge for special exhibitions* ☉ *Sun.–Thurs. 10–6, Fri. and Sat. 10–10 (last admission to exhibitions 45 min before close)* Ⓜ *Southwark, Mansion House, St. Paul's.*

Fodor's Choice
★
Tower of London. Nowhere else does London's history come to life so vividly as it does in this minicity of 20 towers filled with heraldry and treasure, the intimate details of lords and dukes and princes and sovereigns etched in the walls (literally, in some places), and quite a few pints of royal blood spilled on the stones. This is one of Britain's most popular sights—the Crown Jewels are here—and you can avoid lines by buying a ticket in advance on the website, by phone, at any tube station, or from the automatic kiosks on arrival. The visitor center provides an introduction to the Tower. Allow at least three hours for exploring, and take time to stroll along the battlements for a wonderful overview. The Crown Jewels are worth the wait, the White Tower is essential, and the Medieval Palace and Bloody Tower should at least be breezed through. ⌧ *H. M. Tower of London, Tower Hill, The City* ☎ *0844/482-7777, 0844/482-7799* ⊕ *www.hrp.org.uk* ⌧ *£19* ☉ *Mar.–Oct., Tues.–Sat. 9–5:30, Sun. and Mon. 10–5:30; last admission at 5. Nov.–Feb., Tues.–Sat. 9–4:30, Sun. and Mon. 10–4:30; last admission at 4* Ⓜ *Tower Hill.*

Trafalgar Square. This is literally the center of London: a plaque on the corner of the Strand and Charing Cross Road marks the spot from which distances on U.K. signposts are measured. **Nelson's Column** stands at the heart of the square (which is named after the great admiral's most important victory), guarded by haughty lions designed by Sir Edwin Landseer and flanked by statues of two generals who helped establish the British Empire in India, **Charles Napier** and **Henry Havelock.** The fourth plinth is given over to rotating works by contemporary sculptors. Great events, such as New Year's Eve celebrations, political protests, and sporting triumphs always see the crowds gathering in the city's most famous square. Although Trafalgar Square is known to Chinese tourists as Pigeon Square, feeding the birds is now banned and the gray flocks have flown. ⌧ *Trafalgar Sq., Westminster* Ⓜ *Charing Cross.*

Fodor's Choice
★
Westminster Abbey. A monument to the nation's rich—and often bloody and scandalous—history, the abbey rises on the Thames skyline as one of London's most iconic sites. The mysterious gloom of the lofty medieval interior is home to more than 600 statues, tombs, and commemorative tablets. About 3,300 people, from kings to composers to wordsmiths, are buried in the abbey. It has been the scene of 16 royal weddings and no fewer than 38 coronations—the first in 1066, when William the Conqueror was made king here.

There's only one way around the abbey, and as there will almost certainly be a long stream of shuffling tourists at your heels, you'll need to be alert to catch the highlights. Enter by the north door then turn around and look up to see the **painted-glass rose window**, the largest of its kind. Step into the small Chapel of St. Michael, where a tomb effigy of Joseph Gascoigne Nightingale fights off a sheet-draped figure of death. Next enter the adjacent Tomb of St. John the Baptist past a lovely statue of the Virgin Mary and child.

As you walk east toward the apse you'll see the **Coronation Chair**, at the foot of the Henry VII Chapel, which has been briefly graced by nearly every regal posterior since Edward I ordered it in 1301. Continue through the South Ambulatory to the **Chapel of St. Edward the Confessor,** which contains the shrine to the pre-Norman king. Because of its great age, you must join one of the vergers' tours to be admitted to the chapel (details available at the admission desk; there is a small charge), or attend Holy Communion within the shrine on Tuesdays at 8 am). To the left, you'll find **Poets' Corner**. Geoffrey Chaucer was the first poet to be buried here in 1400, and other statues and memorials include those to William Shakespeare, D.H. Lawrence, T.S. Eliot, and Dylan Thomas as well as non-poets, Laurence Olivier and George Frederick Handel among them; look out for the 700-year old frescoes. ⊠ *Broad Sanctuary, Westminster* ☎ *020/7222–5152* ⊕ *www.westminster-abbey.org* ⊠ *Abbey and museum, £15 adults; children under 11 free if accompanied by adult; free audio tour* ⊙ *Abbey, weekdays 9:30–3:30; closes 1 hr after last admission. Museum, daily 10:30–4; Cloisters, daily 8–6; College Garde, Apr.–Sept., Tues.–Thurs. 10–6; Oct.–Mar., Tues.–Thurs. 10–4. Chapter House, daily 10–4; services may cause changes to hrs, so call ahead* Ⓜ *Westminster.*

SHOPPING

Napoléon was being scornful when he called Britain a nation of shopkeepers, but Londoners have had the last laugh, as the city has become a leading international shopping destination. You can shop like royalty at the Duchess of Cambridge's favorite boutique, discover unusual silver spoons in an antiques shop, or find an early edition of Wuthering Heights on Charing Cross Road. If your time is limited, head for one of the city's grand department stores, such as Selfridges or Liberty, where you can find enough booty for your entire gift list.

The main shopping drags are Regent Street (upscale) and Oxford Street (mass-market). Knightsbridge and Bond Street are for top international designers, Hoxton and Shoreditch for young edgy ones. Chelsea has

fashionable boutiques plus home furnishings stores, Covent Garden quirky shoe stores.

Fodor's Choice ★ **Fortnum & Mason.** Although popularly known as the Queen's grocer, and the impeccably mannered staff wear traditional tailcoats, F&M's food hall stocks gifts for all budgets, such as loads of irresistibly packaged luxury foods stamped with the gold "By Appointment" crest for less than £5. Try the teas, preserves (unusual products include rose-petal jelly), condiments, chocolate, tins of pâté, or Gentleman's Relish (anchovy paste). The store's famous hampers are always a welcome gift. The gleaming food hall spans two floors and includes a sleek wine bar designed by David Collins, with the rest of the store devoted to upscale homewares, men and women's gifts, toiletries, and accessories, women's jewelry and cosmetics, and clothing and toys for children. If you start to flag, break for afternoon tea at one of the four other restaurants (one's an indulgent ice-cream parlor)—or a treatment in the Beauty Rooms. ⊠ *181 Piccadilly, St. James's* ☎ *020/7734–8040* ⊕ *www.fortnumandmason.com* Ⓜ *Green Park.*

★ **Harrods.** With an encyclopedic assortment of luxury brands, this Knightsbridge institution has more than 300 departments and 20 restaurants, all spread over 1 million square feet on a 5-acre site. If you approach Harrods as a tourist attraction rather than as a fashion hunting ground, you won't be disappointed. Focus on the spectacular food halls, the huge ground-floor perfumery, the marble-lined accessory rooms, the excellent Urban Retreat spa, and the Vegas-like Egyptian Room. At the bottom of the nearby Egyptian escalator, there's a bronze statue depicting the late Princess Diana and Dodi Fayed, son of the former owner, dancing beneath the wings of an albatross. Nevertheless, standards of taste are enforced with a customer dress code (no shorts, ripped jeans, or flip-flops). ■ TIP→ Be prepared to brave the crowds (avoid visiting on a Saturday if you can), and be prepared to pay if you want to use the bathroom on some floors(!). ⊠ *87–135 Brompton Rd., Knightsbridge* ☎ *020/7730–1234* ⊕ *www.harrods.com* Ⓜ *Knightsbridge.*

WHERE TO EAT

$$$ MODERN EUROPEAN ✕ **Medlar.** What's there *not* to like about Medlar? Sensationally assured Modern European cuisine, effortless service and elegant oak-wood floors, mirrored walls, and a luxe gray/lime-green stenciled color scheme make for a complete neighborhood package at the quieter World's End stretch of the King's Road. Set lunch is a steal at £25, where you'll find such winners as crab ravioli with fondant leeks and samphire, rabbit with red onion marmalade, or fillet steak with snails and triple-cooked chips. Desserts—like pear and frangipane tart and clotted cream—couldn't be more delicious. Ⓢ *Average main: £22* ⊠ *438 King's Rd., Chelsea* ☎ *020/7349–1900* ⊕ *www.medlarrestaurant.co.uk* ⌂ *Reservations essential* Ⓜ *Fulham Broadway, Sloane Sq.*

$$ BURGER ✕ **The Riding House Café.** Stuffed squirrel lamp holders peer down on trendy diners at this groovy New York–style small-plates-and-deluxe-burgers all-dayer just north of Oxford Circus. Everything's reclaimed, salvaged, or bespoke, so you'll find stuffed birds and taxidermy dotted

around, reclaimed blue theater seats at the counter bar, bright orange leather banquettes, or old snooker table legs holding up your dining table. Opt for a £5 small plate of sea bass ceviche with lime and chili, and head straight for the poached-egg chorizo hash browns or a mighty decadent foie gras hamburger, with gherkin and chips—a bargain at £13.90. ⑤ *Average main: £14* ✉ *43 Great Titchfield St., Noho* ☎ *020/7927* ⊕ *www.ridinghousecafe.co.uk* ⌖ *Reservations essential* Ⓜ *Oxford Circus.*

WHERE TO STAY

$$ ⌖ **B&B Belgravia.** At this modern guesthouse near Victoria Station, a
B&B/INN clean, chic white color scheme, simple modern furniture, and a lounge where a fire crackles away in the winter are all geared to stylish comfort. **Pros:** nice extras like free use of a laptop in the hotel lounge; coffee and tea always available. **Cons:** bathrooms and rooms are small; unimaginative breakfasts; can be noisy, especially on lower floors. ⑤ *Rooms from: £135* ✉ *64–66 Ebury St., Victoria* ☎ *020/7259–8570* ⊕ *www. bb-belgravia.com* ⇥ *17 rooms* ⦿ *Breakfast* Ⓜ *Knightsbridge.*

$$$ ⌖ **Charlotte Street Hotel.** Modern flair and the traditional are fused with
HOTEL real style in public spaces and bedrooms beautifully decorated with unique printed fabrics from designer Kit Kemp; bathrooms are truly impressive, lined with gleaming granite and oak—with walk-in showers and flat-screen TVs, so you can catch up on the news while you soak in the deep baths. **Pros:** elegant, luxurious; great attention to detail. **Cons:** the popular bar can be noisy; reservations are necessary for the restaurant. ⑤ *Rooms from: £288* ✉ *15 Charlotte St., Bloomsbury* ☎ *020/7806–2000, 800/553–6674 in U.S.* ⊕ *www.charlottestreethotel. com* ⇥ *46 rooms, 6 suites* Ⓜ *Goodge St.*

$$$ ⌖ **Millennium Gloucester.** Although the sleek lobby, with polished wood
HOTEL columns, a warming fireplace, and glittering chandeliers, is quite opulent, guest rooms have a traditionally masculine look, done in neutral creams and earth tones and furnished with blond-wood desks and leather chairs. **Pros:** good deals available if you book in advance. **Cons:** lighting in some bedrooms is a bit too subtle; bathrooms are relatively small but have all you need; public areas and restaurant can get crowded. ⑤ *Rooms from: £145* ✉ *4–18 Harrington Gardens, Kensington* ☎ *020/7373–6030* ⊕ *www.millenniumhotels.co.uk/ millenniumgloucester* ⇥ *143 rooms* ⦿ *Breakfast* Ⓜ *Gloucester Rd.*

INVERGORDON, SCOTLAND

Updated
by Mike
Gonzalez
The port of Invergordon is your gateway to the Great Glen, an area of Scotland that includes Loch Ness and the city of Inverness. Inverness, the capital of the Highlands, has the flavor of a Lowland town, its winds blowing in a sea-salt air from the Moray Firth. The Great Glen is also home to one of the world's most famous monster myths: in 1933, during a quiet news week, the editor of a local paper decided to run a story about a strange sighting of something splashing about in Loch Ness. But there's more to look for here besides Nessie, including

inland lochs, craggy and steep-sided mountains, rugged promontories, deep inlets, brilliant purple and emerald moorland, and forests filled with astonishingly varied wildlife, including mountain hares, red deer, golden eagles, and ospreys.

ESSENTIALS

CURRENCY

The British pound sterling. ATMs are common and credit cards are widely accepted.

HOURS

Museums are open from 9 until 5, while shops usually open from 9 until 5:30 or 6. Shops are open on Sunday.

PRIVATE TOURS

Around Lochness (⊕ *www.aroundlochness.com* ☎ *01456/486675*) and Montains to Sea (⊕ *www.mountains2sea.co.uk* ☎ *07826/688871*) arrange tours of the area from Invergordon. From Inverness, tours run regularly to and around Loch Ness. They are run by the Jacobite Experience (⊕ *www.jacobite.co.uk* ☎ *01463/233999*). They have their own bus services to collect you from Inverness. Prices vary according to the length of tour. It is advisable to book these tours ahead. Jacobite also runs a combined tour of Inverness and Loch Ness.

There are hop on/hop off bus tours of Inverness (tickets £10) and a bus tour combining the city tour with Loch Ness (tickets £21). You can get information from the visitor center.

Contacts Around Lochness. ☎ *01456/486675* ⊕ *www.aroundlochness.com.* **Montains To Sea.** ☎ *07826/688871* ⊕ *www.mountains2sea.co.uk.* **The Jacobite Experience.** ☎ *01463/233999* ⊕ *www.jacobite.co.uk.*

TELEPHONES

Dual-band GSM phones work in the United Kingdom. You can buy prepaid phone cards at telecom shops and news vendors in all towns and cities. Phone cards can be used for local or international calls. Vodafone, T-Mobile, Virgin, and Orange are the leading telecom companies.

GREAT GLEN BEST BETS

Monster hunting at Loch Ness. Even though numerous scientific studies have failed to prove the existence of Scotland's most famous monster, you're sure to be on the lookout, just in case he makes an appearance.

Urquhart Castle. A sublime setting on the banks of Loch Ness makes Urquhart one of the world's most romantic and wistful fortresses.

Aviemore. The rugged landscapes of the Cairngorm Mountains contrast sharply with the verdant lowland glens; a mountain train takes the strain, so you don't need to work up a sweat.

4

COMING ASHORE

There is no dedicated cruise terminal at Invergordon. Ships dock at one of the town quays—usually Admiralty Quay, the closest to the town. At the pier there is a tourist information kiosk manned only when ships are in dock.

Passengers can walk into the center of Invergordon for public transportation to surrounding sights. The X99 bus goes directly to Inverness. Scotrail trains connect with Inverness to the south and Dornoch to the north. The Invergordon railway station is 1 km (½ mile) from the port.

A car is a great asset for exploring the Great Glen, especially since the best of the area is away from the main roads. You can use the main A82 from Inverness to Fort William, or use the smaller B862/B852 roads (former military roads) to explore the much quieter east side of Loch Ness.

Taxis do not meet the ships as a matter of course.

EXPLORING INVERGORDON AND THE GREAT GLEN

INVERNESS

Inverness seems designed for the tourist, with its banks, souvenirs, high-quality woolens, and well-equipped visitor center. Compared with other Scottish towns, however, Inverness has less to offer visitors who have a keen interest in Scottish history. Throughout its past, Inverness was burned and ravaged by the restive Highland clans competing for dominance in the region. Thus, a decorative wall panel here and a fragment of tower there are all that remain amid the modern shopping

facilities and 19th-century downtown developments. The town does make a good base, however, for exploring the northern end of the Great Glen.

Inverness Castle. One of Inverness's few historic landmarks is reddish sandstone Inverness Castle (now the local Sheriff Court), nestled above the river off Castle Road on Castle Hill. The current structure is Victorian, built after a former fort was blown up by the Jacobites in the 1745 campaign.

☺ **Inverness Museum and Art Gallery.** The excellent, although small, Inverness Museum and Art Gallery covers archaeology, art, local history, and the natural environment in its lively displays. ⊠ *Castle Wynd* ☎ *01463/237114* ⊕ *www.invernessmuseum.com* ⊠ *Free* ☉ *Tues.–Sat. 10–5.*

CULLODEN MOOR

★ **Culloden Moor.** Culloden was the scene of the last major battle fought on British soil—to this day considered one of the most infamous and tragic of all. Here, on a cold April day in 1746, the outnumbered, fatigued Jacobite forces of Bonnie Prince Charlie were destroyed by the superior firepower of George II's army. The victorious commander, the duke of Cumberland (George II's son), earned the name of the "Butcher" of Cumberland for the bloody reprisals carried out by his men on Highland families, Jacobite or not, caught in the vicinity. In the battle itself, the duke's army—greatly outnumbering the Scots—killed more than 1,000 soldiers. The National Trust for Scotland has re-created a slightly eerie version of the battlefield as it looked in 1746 that you can explore with a guided audio tour. An innovative visitor center enables you to get closer to the sights and sounds of the battle and to interact with the characters involved. Academic research and technology have helped re-create the Gaelic dialect, song, and music of the time. The excellent on-site café serves homemade soups, sandwiches, and cakes. ⊠ *B9006, Culloden* ☎ *0844/4932159* ⊕ *www.nts. org.uk/Culloden* ⊠ *£10* ☉ *Nov–Mar, daily 10–4; Apr.–Oct., daily 9–6; last entry half hr before closing.*

FORT GEORGE

★ **Fort George.** As a direct result of the battle at Culloden, the nervous government in London ordered the construction of a large fort on a promontory reaching into the Moray Firth: Fort George was started in 1748 and completed some 20 years later. It's perhaps the best-preserved 18th-century military fortification in Europe. A visitor center and tableaux at the fort portray the 18th-century Scottish soldier's way of life. The fort is 14 miles northeast of Iverness. ⊠ *Off B9006, Ardersier* ☎ *01667/460232* ⊕ *www.historic-scotland.gov.uk* ⊠ *£6.90* ☉ *Apr.–Sept., daily 9:30–5; Oct.–Mar., daily 10–4; last admission 45 mins before closing.*

CAWDOR CASTLE

Fodor's Choice **Cawdor Castle.** Shakespeare's (1564–1616) Macbeth was Thane of Caw-
★ dor, but the sense of history that exists within the turreted walls of
☺ Cawdor Castle is more than fictional. Cawdor is a lived-in castle, not an abandoned, decaying structure. The earliest part of the castle is the 14th-century central tower; the rooms contain family portraits,

tapestries, fine furniture, and paraphernalia reflecting 600 years of history. Outside the castle walls are sheltered gardens and woodland walks. Children will have a ball exploring the lush and mysterious Big Wood, with its wildflowers and varied wildlife. There are lots of creepy stories and fantastic tales amid the dank dungeons and drawbridges. If you like it here, the estate has cottages to rent. ✉ *B9090, 5 miles southwest of Nairn, Cawdor* 🕿 *01667/404401* ⊕ *www.cawdorcastle.com* 🎫 *Grounds £5.50; castle £9.50* ⊘ *May–mid-Oct., daily 10–5.*

LOCH NESS EXHIBITION CENTRE

🎏 **Loch Ness Centre & Exhibition.** If you're in search of the infamous beast Nessie, head to the Loch Ness Centre & Exhibition, which explores the facts and the fakes, the photographs, the unexplained sonar contacts, and the sincere testimony of eyewitnesses. You'll have to make up your own mind on Nessie. All that's really known is that Loch Ness's huge volume of water has a warming effect on the local weather, making the loch conducive to mirages in still, warm conditions. Whether or not the *bestia aquatilis* lurks in the depths is more than ever in doubt since 1994, when the man who took one of the most convincing photos of Nessie confessed on his deathbed that it was a fake. You can take a cruise of the loch from the center, too. ✉ *A82, Drumnadrochit* 🕿 *01456/450573* ⊕ *www.lochness.com* 🎫 *£6.50* ⊘ *Easter–May, Sept., and Oct., daily 9:30–5; June, 9–5:30; July and Aug., daily 9–6; Nov.– Easter, daily 10–3:30; last admission ½ hr before closing.*

URQUHART CASTLE

Urquhart Castle. About 2 miles southeast of Drumnadrochit, this castle is a favorite Loch Ness monster–watching spot. This romantically broken-down fortress stands on a promontory overlooking the loch, as it has since the Middle Ages. Because of its central and strategic position in the Great Glen line of communication, the castle has a complex history involving military offense and defense, as well as its own destruction and renovation. The castle was begun in the 13th century and was destroyed before the end of the 17th century to prevent its use by the Jacobites. The ruins of what was one of the largest castles in Scotland were then plundered for building material. A visitor center relates these events and gives an idea of what life was like here in medieval times. ✉ *A82, Drumnadrochit* 🕿 *01456/450551* ⊕ *www.historic-scotland. gov.uk/places* 🎫 *£7.20* ⊘ *Apr.–Sept., daily 9:30–6; Oct., 9:30–5; Nov.– Mar., daily 9:30–4:30; last admission 45 mins before closing.*

LOCH NESS

Loch Ness. From the A82 you get many views of the formidable and famous Loch Ness, which has a greater volume of water than any other Scottish loch, a maximum depth of more than 800 feet, and its own monster—at least according to popular myth. Early travelers who passed this way included English lexicographer Dr. Samuel Johnson (1709–84) and his guide and biographer, James Boswell (1740–95), who were on their way to the Hebrides in 1783. They remarked at the time about the poor condition of the population and the squalor of their homes. Another early travel writer and naturalist, Thomas Pennant (1726–98), noted that the loch kept the locality frost-free in

winter. Even General Wade came here, his troops blasting and digging a road up much of the eastern shore. None of these observant early travelers ever made mention of a monster. Clearly, they had not read the local guidebooks.

AVIEMORE

Once a quiet junction on the Highland Railway, Aviemore now has all the brashness and concrete boxiness of a year-round holiday resort. The Aviemore area is a versatile walking base, but you must be dressed properly and carry emergency safety gear for high-level excursions onto the near-arctic plateau.

★ **Cairngorms National Park.** A rugged wilderness of mountains, moorlands, glens, and lochs, Cairngorms National Park is the country's second-oldest national park. Past Loch Morlich at the high parking lot on the exposed shoulders of the Cairngorm Mountains are dozens of trails for hiking and cycling. The park is especially popular with birding enthusiasts, as it's the best place to see the Scottish crossbill, the only bird unique to Britain. Weather conditions in the park change abruptly, so be sure to have the proper gear or seek out many of the guided options. This is a massive park, but a good place to start exploring is the visitor center in Aviemore. ☎ *01479/873535* ⊕ *www.cairngorms.co.uk.*

CairnGorm Mountain Railway. A funicular railway to the top of Cairn Gorm (the mountain that gives its name to the region), the CairnGorm Mountain Railway operates both during and after the ski season and affords extensive views across the Cairngorms and the broad valley of the Spey. At the top is a visitor center and restaurant. Prebooking is recommended. ✉ *B970* ☎ *01479/861261* ⊕ *www.cairngormmountain. co.uk* 🎫 *£9.95* ⊙ *Daily 10–4:30.*

SHOPPING

All things "Highland" make the best souvenirs. Tartans and kilts, tweed clothing, and woolen and cashmere knits are made here in the glens. Modern breathable outdoor clothing is also in great abundance. The beauty of the landscape inspires artists and craftspeople, and you'll find their paintings, ceramics, and wooden carved items in markets and specialty shops. Foodies will love the natural smoked salmon.

INVERNESS

★ **Riverside Gallery.** The Riverside Gallery sells paintings, etchings, and prints of Highland landscapes, as well as abstract and representational contemporary work by Highland artists. ✉ *11 Bank St., Inverness* ☎ *01463/224781* ⊕ *www.riverside-gallery.co.uk.*

Victorian Market. Don't miss the atmospheric indoor Victorian Market, built in 1870. It houses more than 40 privately owned specialty shops. ✉ *Academy St., Inverness.*

WHERE TO EAT

$$ ✕ **Riva.** Facing Inverness Castle, Riva has views over the River Ness from
ITALIAN   its window seats. The dining room has subtly lighted deep-red walls lined
with black-and-white photographs of Italian cityscapes. Tasty Italian
dishes include pasta carbonara (with eggs, cream, and bacon), as well as
more unusual concoctions like ravioli *alla granchio* (crab-and–tiger prawn
ravioli on arugula). The service can be inconsistent. ⑤ *Average main: £16*
✉ *4–6 Ness Walk, Inverness* ☎ *01463/237377* ⊘ *No lunch Sun.*

$$ ✕ **Rocpool Restaurant.** Highly recommended by locals, the Rocpool has
BRASSERIE   a calming mix of dark and light woods and cream and pale mint fur-
nishings. The frequently changing menu may include such favorites
as sweet-pea-and-spinach risotto for lunch and loin of venison with
creamed parsnips and wild mushrooms for dinner. ⑤ *Average main: £18*
✉ *1 Ness Walk, Inverness* ☎ *01463/717274* ⊘ *Closed Sun.*

4

LEITH, SCOTLAND (FOR EDINBURGH)

Updated
by Mike
Gonzalez

One of the world's stateliest cities and proudest capitals, Edinburgh is
built—like Rome—on seven hills, making it a striking backdrop for the
ancient pageant of history. In a skyline of sheer drama, Edinburgh Castle
watches over the capital city, frowning down on Princes Street as if disap-
proving of its modern razzmatazz. Nearly everywhere in Edinburgh (the
"-burgh" is always pronounced *burra* in Scotland) there are spectacular
buildings, whose Doric, Ionic, and Corinthian pillars add touches of neoclassical grandeur to the largely Presbyterian backdrop. The city is justly
proud of its gardens, green lungs that bring a sense of release to frenetic
modern life. Conspicuous from Princes Street is Arthur's Seat, a child-size
mountain with steep slopes and little crags, like a miniature Highlands
set down in the middle of the busy city. Appropriately, these theatrical
elements match Edinburgh's character—after all, the city has been a stage
that has seen its fair share of romance, violence, tragedy, and triumph.

ESSENTIALS

CURRENCY
The British pound sterling. ATMs are common and credit cards are
widely accepted.

HOURS
Museums are open from 9 until 5, while shops usually open from 9
until 5:30 or 6. Shops are open on Sunday.

PRIVATE TOURS
Private tours may be difficult to arrange, but there are a number of
city sightseeing tours departing from the street outside Waverley station. There is no need to book these in advance. Tickets are £12. Uncle
Bob's Audio Walking Tours provide downloadableAudio tours for those
wanting to walk the city on their own. Rabbie's Trail Burners run tours
to the area around the city, including a day trip to the Rosslyn Chapel
made famous by Dan Brown.

Contacts Rabbie's Trail Burners. ☎ *0131/2263133* ⊕ *www.robbies.com.*
Uncle Bob's Audio Walking Tours. ⊕ *www.edinburghtour.com.*

Edinburgh

TO LEITH AND
BRITANNIA
ROYAL YACHT

*Calton
Hill*

◆ **Calton Hill**

St. James
Centre

Leith St.

Regent Rd.

*Calton New
Burial
Ground*

Abbey Hill

Waterloo Pl.

*Calton
Burial
Ground*

Calton Rd.

Abbey
Strand

**Palace of
Holyroodhouse**

North Bridge

**Edinburgh
Waverley
Station**

Tolbooth Wynd

E. Market St.

Jeffrey St.

Canongate

Bull's Close

CANONGATE

St.

Royal Mile

St. Mary's St.

Holyrood Rd.

*Holyrood
Park*

Blackfriars St.

Cowgate

Old
Fishmarket
Close

South Bridge

Chambers St.

Drummond St.

Salisbury Crags

**National Museum
of Scotland**

Pleasance

Queen's Drive

Buccleuch St.

Nicolson St.

**TO ARTHUR'S SEAT →
AND DUDDINGSTON**

*George
Square*

0   1/8 mi

0   1/8 km

TELEPHONES

Dual-band GSM phones work in the United Kingdom. You can buy pre-paid phone cards at telecom shops and news vendors in all towns and cities. Phone cards can be used for local or international calls. Vodafone, T-Mobile, Virgin, and Orange are the leading telecom companies.

COMING ASHORE

Currently ships larger than 220 meters (720 feet) must anchor offshore at Leith and passengers must be tendered ashore. Smaller ships can dock at the quayside in Leith Town. The whole waterfront area, named Ocean Terminal, has received a multimillion-pound redevelopment since the late 1990s, and significantly more is due to be

> ### EDINBURGH BEST BETS
>
> **Edinburgh Castle.** The twists and turns of Scottish history have unfolded in this true bastion atop a volcanic peak. Stay for the firing of the one o'clock gun, but remember to cover your ears!
>
> **The Palace of Holyroodhouse.** Home to Scottish and English monarchs throughout the ages, Holyroodhouse has many stories to tell—including one of the most vile deeds in Edinburgh's history.
>
> **Calton Hill.** The architectural panorama of Edinburgh plays out before your eyes from this height.

invested in the years up to 2019; a tram system to link the Leith waterfront to central Edinburgh should be open sometime in 2013. There are few facilities at the passenger terminal itself, but a huge complex of shopping, eating, and entertainment venues sits right outside the door.

From Leith, Buses 11, 22, 34, 35 and 36 make the 15-minute trip to the Princes Street stop in central Edinburgh; one-way fare is £1.20, and a day ticket £3. Taxis are plentiful and wait at the Ocean Terminal taxi line. Costs include an initial charge of £2.50, then £0.25 for every 225 meters (758 feet) until 2 km (1½ miles), after which charges climb to £0.25 per 210 meters (688 feet). Don't rent a car if you plan to spend your port day in Edinburgh, but a car will open up much of the surrounding countryside to exploration if you want to venture further. Rental rates for a compact manual vehicle are approximately £55 per day.

EXPLORING EDINBURGH

Calton Hill. Robert Louis Stevenson's favorite view of his beloved city was from the top of this hill. The architectural styles represented by the extraordinary collection of monuments here include mock Gothic—the Old Observatory, for example—and neoclassical. Under the latter category falls the monument by William Playfair (1789–1857) designed to honor his talented uncle, the geologist and mathematician John Playfair (1748–1819), as well as his cruciform **New Observatory.** The piece that commands the most attention, however, is the so-called **National Monument,** often referred to as "Scotland's Disgrace." Intended to mimic Athens's Parthenon, this monument to the dead of the Napoleonic Wars was started in 1822 to the specifications of a design by Playfair. But in 1830, only 12 columns later, money ran out, and the facade became a monument to high aspirations and poor fund-raising. The tallest monument on Calton Hill is the 100-foot-high

Nelson Monument, completed in 1815 in honor of Britain's naval hero Horatio Nelson (1758–1805); you can climb its 143 steps for sweeping city views. The **Burns Monument** is the circular Corinthian temple below Regent Road. Devotees of Robert Burns may want to visit one other grave—that of Mrs. Agnes McLehose, or "Clarinda," in the Canongate Graveyard. ✉ *Bounded by Leith St. to the west and Regent Rd. to the south, New Town* ☎ *0131/556–2716* ∰ *www.cac.org.uk* 🎟 *Nelson Monument £3* ⊙ *Nelson Monument Oct.–Mar., Mon.–Sat. 10–3; Apr.–Sept., daily 10–6.*

Charlotte Square. At the west end of George Street is the New Town's centerpiece—an 18th-century square with one of the proudest achievements of Robert Adam, Scotland's noted neoclassical architect. On the north side, Adam designed a palatial facade to unite three separate town houses of such sublime simplicity and perfect proportions that architects come from all over the world to study it. Happily, the Age of Enlightenment grace notes continue within, as the center town house is now occupied by the **Georgian House** museum, and to the west stands **West Register House.** ✉ *West end of George St., New Town.*

Fodor's Choice
★
🜨

Edinburgh Castle. The crowning glory of the Scottish capital, Edinburgh Castle is popular not only because it's the symbolic heart of Scotland but also because of the views from its battlements: on a clear day the vistas—stretching to the "kingdom" of Fife—are breathtaking. ■ TIP→ There's so much to see that you need at least three hours to do the site justice, especially if you're interested in military sites.

You enter across the **Esplanade,** the huge forecourt built in the 18th century as a parade ground. The area comes alive with color and music each August when it's used for the Military Tattoo, a festival of magnificently outfitted marching bands and regiments. Heading over the drawbridge and through the gatehouse, past the guards, you can find the rough stone walls of the **Half-Moon Battery,** where the one-o'clock gun is fired every day in an impressively anachronistic ceremony; these curving ramparts give Edinburgh Castle its distinctive appearance from miles away. Climb up through a second gateway and you come to the oldest surviving building in the complex, the tiny 11th-century **St. Margaret's Chapel,** named in honor of Saxon queen Margaret (1046–93), who had persuaded her husband, King Malcolm III (circa 1031–93), to move his court from Dunfermline to Edinburgh. Edinburgh's environs—the Lothians—were occupied by Anglian settlers with whom the queen felt more at home, or so the story goes (Dunfermline was surrounded by Celts). The **Crown Room,** a must-see, contains the "Honours of Scotland"—the crown, scepter, and sword that once graced the Scottish monarch. Upon the **Stone of Scone,** also in the Crown Room, Scottish monarchs once sat to be crowned. In the section now called **Queen Mary's Apartments,** Mary, Queen of Scots, gave birth to James VI of Scotland. The **Great Hall** displays arms and armor under an impressive vaulted, beamed ceiling. Scottish parliament meetings were conducted here until 1840.

Military features of interest include the **Scottish National War Memorial,** the **Scottish United Services Museum,** and the famous 15th-century Belgian-made cannon *Mons Meg.* This enormous piece of artillery has

been silent since 1682, when it exploded while firing a salute for the duke of York; it now stands in an ancient hall behind the Half-Moon Battery. Contrary to what you may hear from locals, it's not *Mons Meg* but the battery's gun that goes off with a bang every weekday at 1 pm, frightening visitors and reminding Edinburghers to check their watches. ⊠ *Castle Esplanade and Castlehill, Old Town* ☎ *0131/225–9846 Edinburgh Castle, 0131/226–7393 War Memorial* ⊕ *www.edinburghcastle. gov.uk* ☞ *£14* ☉ *Apr.–Sept., daily 9:30–6; Oct.–Mar., daily 9:30–5; last entry 45 mins before closing.*

High Kirk of St. Giles. Sometimes called St. Giles's Cathedral, this is one of the city's principal churches. However, anyone expecting a rival to Paris's Notre Dame or London's Westminster Abbey will be disappointed: St. Giles is more like a large parish church than a great European cathedral. There has been a church here since AD 854, although most of the present structure dates from either 1120 or 1829, when the church was restored. The tower, with its stone crown towering 161 feet above the ground, was completed between 1495 and 1500. The most elaborate feature is the **Chapel of the Order of the Thistle,** built onto the southeast corner of the church in 1911 for the exclusive use of Scotland's only chivalric order, the Most Ancient and Noble Order of the Thistle. It bears the belligerent national motto "nemo me impune lacessit" ("No one provokes me with impunity"). Inside the church stands a life-size statue of the Scot whose spirit still dominates the place—the great religious reformer and preacher John Knox, before whose zeal all of Scotland once trembled. The church lies about one-third of the way along the Royal Mile from Edinburgh Castle. ⊠ *High St., Old Town* ☎ *0131/225–9442* ⊕ *www.stgilescathedral.org.uk* ☞ *£3 suggested donation* ☉ *May–Sept., weekdays 9–7, Sat. 9–5, Sun. 1–5; Oct.–Apr., Mon.–Sat. 9–5, Sun. 1–5.*

Fodor's Choice
★

National Gallery of Scotland. Opened to the public in 1859, the National Gallery presents a wide selection of paintings from the Renaissance to the postimpressionist period within a grand neoclassical building designed by William Playfair. Most famous are the old master paintings bequeathed by the Duke of Sutherland, including Titian's *Three Ages of Man.* Many masters are here; works by Velázquez, El Greco, Rembrandt, Goya, Poussin, Turner, Degas, Monet, and Van Gogh, among others, complement a fine collection of Scottish art, including Sir Henry Raeburn's *Reverend Robert Walker Skating on Duddingston Loch* and other works by Ramsay, Raeburn, and Wilkie. The Weston Link connects the National Gallery of Scotland to the Royal Scottish Academy and provides expanded gallery space as well as a restaurant, bar, café, shop, and information center. ⊠ *The Mound, New Town* ☎ *0131/624–6336* ⊕ *www.nationalgalleries. org* ☞ *Free* ☉ *Fri.–Wed. 10–5, Thurs. 10–7.*

Fodor's Choice
★
♲

National Museum of Scotland. This museum traces the country's fascinating story from the oldest fossils to the most recent popular culture, making it a must-see for first-time visitors to Scotland or anyone interested in history. One of the most famous treasures is the Lewis Chessmen, 11 intricately carved ivory chess pieces found in the 19th century on one of Scotland's Western Isles: other pieces are in London's British Museum. An extensive renovation in 2011 freed up space in the

basement, creating a dramatic, crypt-like entrance. Visitors now rise to the light-filled, birdcage wonders of the Victorian grand hall and the upper galleries in glass elevators. Highlights include the hanging hippo and sea creatures of the Wildlife Panorama, a life-size skeleton cast of a *Tyrannosaurus rex*, Viking brooches, Pictish stones, Jacobite relics, the Stevenson family's inventions, including lighthouse optics, and Queen Mary's *clarsach* (harp). All this is free, but donations are welcomed to help renovate 11 other galleries. ⊠ *Chambers St., Old Town* ☎ *0131/225–7534* ⊕ *www.nms.ac.uk* 🖾 *Free* ⊙ *Daily 10–5.*

★ **Palace of Holyroodhouse.** Once the haunt of Mary, Queen of Scots, and the setting for high drama—including at least one notorious murder, several major fires, and centuries of the colorful lifestyles of larger-than-life, power-hungry personalities—this is now Queen Elizabeth's official residence in Scotland. A doughty and impressive palace standing at the foot of the Royal Mile in a hilly public park, it's built around a graceful, lawned central court at the end of Canongate. When the queen or royal family is not in residence, you can take a tour. The free audio guide is excellent. ■ TIP→ There's plenty to see here, so make sure you have at least two hours to tour the palace, gardens (in summer), and the ruins of the 12th-century abbey. The **King James Tower** is the oldest surviving section, containing the rooms of Mary, Queen of Scots, on the second floor, and Lord Darnley's rooms below. Though much has been altered, there are fine fireplaces, paneling, plasterwork, tapestries, and 18th- and 19th-century furnishings throughout. **The Queen's Gallery,** in a former church and school at the entrance to the palace, holds rotating exhibits from the Royal Collection. There is a separate admission charge.

Behind the palace lie the open grounds and looming crags of Holyrood Park, the hunting ground of early Scottish kings. From the top of Edinburgh's mini mountain, **Arthur's Seat** (822 feet), views are breathtaking. ⊠ *Abbey Strand, Old Town* ☎ *0131/556–5100* ⊕ *www.royalcollection. org.uk* 🖾 *£10.75, £6 Queen's Gallery, £15.10 joint ticket* ⊙ *Apr.–Oct., daily 9:30–6; Nov.–Mar., daily 9:30–4:30; last admission 1 hr before closing. Closed during royal visits.*

Royal Scottish Academy. The William Playfair–designed academy hosts temporary art exhibitions (Monet paintings, for example), but is also worth visiting for a look at the imposing, neoclassic architecture. The underground Weston Link connects the museum to the National Gallery of Scotland. ⊠ *The Mound, New Town* ☎ *0131/225–6671* ⊕ *www. royalscottishacademy.org* 🖾 *Free* ⊙ *Mon.–Sat. 10–5, Sun. noon–5.*

Scottish National Portrait Gallery. A magnificent red-sandstone Gothic building dating from 1889 houses this must-see institution. Conceived as a gift to the people of Scotland, the recently revamped gallery is organized under five broad themes: Reformation, Enlightenment, Empire, Modernity, and Contemporary. The refurbished complex features a photography gallery, a gallery for contemporary art, and a fancy glass elevator. New spaces hold exhibits on various aspects of Scots history and life, including *The Visual Culture of the Jacobite Cause* and *Playing for Scotland: The Making of Modern Sport.* ⊠ *1 Queen St., New Town* ☎ *0131/624–6200* ⊕ *www. nationalgalleries.org* 🖾 *Free* ⊙ *Fri.–Wed. 10–5, Thurs. 10–7.*

SHOPPING

Despite its renown as a shopping street, **Princes Street** in the New Town disappoints some visitors with its dull, anonymous modern architecture, average chain stores, and fast-food outlets. It is, however, one of the best spots to shop for tartans, tweeds, and knitwear, especially if your time is limited. One block north of Princes Street, **Rose Street** has many smaller specialty shops; part of the street is a pedestrian zone, so it's a pleasant place to browse.

The streets crossing George Street—Hanover, Frederick, and Castle—are also worth exploring. **Dundas Street,** the northern extension of Hanover Street, beyond Queen Street Gardens, has several antiques shops. **Thistle Street,** originally George Street's "back lane," or service area, has several boutiques and more antiques shops. **Stafford and William streets** form a small, upscale shopping area in a Georgian setting.

As may be expected, many shops along the **Royal Mile** sell what may be politely or euphemistically described as tourist ware—whiskies, tartans, and tweeds. Careful exploration, however, will uncover some worthwhile establishments. Shops here also cater to highly specialized interests and hobbies. Close to the castle end of the Royal Mile, just off George IV Bridge, is **Victoria Street,** with specialty shops grouped in a small area. Follow the tiny West Bow to **Grassmarket** for more specialty stores.

Ocean Terminal. The Ocean Terminal houses a large collection of shops, as well as bars and eateries. Here you can also visit the former royal yacht *Britannia.* ⊠ *Ocean Dr., Leith.*

WHERE TO EAT

$

BRITISH

✕ **The King's Wark.** Along the shoreline at Leith is a gastropub with a pleasant atmosphere and quality food that continues to win plaudits. At lunchtime, the dark-wood bar does a roaring trade in simple fare such as gourmet burgers and fish cakes, but in the evening the kitchen ups the ante with such dishes as sea trout stuffed with smoked mackerel risotto. Old stone walls attest to the building's 15th-century origins. Book early to sample the legendary breakfast. ⑤ *Average main: £14* ⊠ *36 The Shore, Leith* ☎ *0131/554–9260.*

$$

ITALIAN

✕ **Valvona & Crolla VinCaffe.** Every Scot with a passion for food knows Valvona & Crolla, the country's first Italian delicatessen and wine merchant. This eatery of the same name may lack the old-world feel of the original on Elm Row, but the menu created by food writer and cook Mary Contini is as wonderful as you would expect. The fare is relatively simple, but the quality of the ingredients ensure that treats such as the white pizza with cured bacon, fried calamari, and linguine with crab meat do nothing to tarnish the brand's reputation. Watch for tastings and cultural events staged here. ⑤ *Average main: £15* ⊠ *11 Multrees Walk, New Town* ☎ *0131/557–0088* ⊕ *www.vincaffe.com.*

ROTTERDAM, NETHERLANDS

Rotterdam is the industrial center of Holland and the world's largest port. When Rotterdam's city center and harbor were completely destroyed in World War II, the authorities decided to start afresh rather than try to reconstruct its former maze of canals. The imposing, futuristic skyline along the banks of the Maas River has been developing since then, thanks in large part to the efforts of major figures such as Rem Koolhaas, Eric van Egeraat, and UN Studio. Elsewhere in the region you can step back in time: wander through the ancient cobbled streets in Leiden and buy china in Delft that once colored the world with its unique blue. Many other colors are on view in Holland's fabled tulip fields. Every spring, green thumbs everywhere make a pilgrimage to Lisse to view the noted tulip gardens at Keukenhof and to drive the Bollenstreek Route, which takes them through miles of countryside glowing with gorgeous hues and blooms.

ESSENTIALS

CURRENCY

The euro. ATMs are common and credit cards are widely accepted in all but restaurants, where only European cards with PIN are accepted widely.

HOURS

Shops open Tuesday, Wednesday, Friday, and Saturday from 9 or 10 until 6; they are open later on Thursday. Most stores are closed on Sunday and some on Monday. Museums open from 9 until 6 with one late opening night during the week.

PRIVATE GUIDES

Private tour guides are available from Gilde-Rotterdam for walking, bus, or bicycle tours within the city. Tours start at €4 and run on weekdays. Spido offers a 75-minute guided Rotterdam Harbour boat tour several times daily at a cost of €10.50.

Contacts Gilde-Rotterdam. ☎ *31/104362844* ⊕ *www.gilderotterdam.nl.*
Spido. ☎ *31/102759988* ⊕ *spido.nl/en/rotterdam-harbour-tour.*

TELEPHONES

Most tri- and quad-band GSM mobile phones should work in the Netherlands, which operates a 3G mobile system with dual-band handsets. Most public phones take phone cards (available at numerous shops) and some take credit cards, and will connect international calls. Major telecom companies are Vodafone and Orange.

COMING ASHORE

Ships dock at the historic terminal building in the city dock, once the headquarters of the Holland America Line. The terminal offers handicraft displays, shopping facilities, and an information desk. A hotel including restaurants, a café, a theater, and a shopping center is currently being built next to the terminal and is expected to open in 2013. A shuttle service operates between the terminal and the town. Each bus has an English-speaking host who can answer any questions that you have. A water-taxi service also operates from the port across the River Maas into the heart of the Old Town. A 15-minute round-trip costs approximately €30.

The terminal has a taxi service desk where you can arrange for trips at fixed prices. It is also possible to book journeys and trips ahead of time. All drivers speak English. Public transport is efficient and modern. Tram routes Erasmus, 20, 23, and 25 link the port with Rotterdam Central Station (this station area is currently undergoing a comprehensive renovation program). All public transport is now paid for with an electronic chip card which deducts the amount of the journey from the amount registered on the card. The easiest option for cruise passengers is to purchase a disposable chip card that can be loaded with a single one-hour travel pass good for the tram, bus, and metro (equivalent to a single ticket); a two-journey travel pass; or a one-, two-, or three-day travel card. If you intend to use public transport throughout the day, the one-day travel card would be simplest; it costs €7. While the one-hour travel card can be purchased from personnel aboard trams and buses, the other passes must be purchased from machines at stations. Rotterdam is bicycle-friendly. Bikes can be rented at the central train station at a cost of €6.50 per day.

The train journey from Rotterdam to Delft takes 15 minutes, and there are several services per hour; ticket prices are €10.20 round-trip for first-class and €6 round-trip for second-class. The train journey from Rotterdam to Leiden takes 34 minutes, with several services every hour;

ticket prices are €22.80 round-trip for first-class and €13.40 round-trip for second-class. The journey to Amsterdam takes one hour, or 40 minutes on the faster Fyra train, with several services every hour; round-trip tickets are €46.20 in first-class and €27.20 in second-class.

EXPLORING ROTTERDAM AND VICINITY

ROTTERDAM

Cobbled streets, gabled houses, narrow canals overhung with lime trees, and antiques shops give the historic center a tangible feeling of history, and Leiden's university's academic buildings, the historic Waag (Weigh House) and the Burcht fortress, the stately mansions lining the Rapenburg—the most elegant canal in the town—and no fewer than 35 hofjes (groups of houses surrounding little courtyards) make it a rewarding place for a stroll. As you walk about, keep a watch for verses painted on lofty gables, a project started some 10 years ago. The proverbs, sayings, and poems now number more than 70, and are in a multitude of languages.

Delfshaven. The last remaining nook of old Rotterdam is the old port area, reconstructed to appear just as it was when originally built—an open-air museum with rows of gabled houses lining the historic waterfront, trendy galleries, cafés, and restaurants. Walk along the Voorhaven, Achterhaven, and neighboring Piet Heynplein and marvel at the many historic buildings. For historic sights in the environs, check out the working mill of **Korenmolen de Distilleerketel** (open Wednesday and Saturday only), the fascinating **Museum de Dubbelde Palmboom** on Rotterdam city history, and the **Oudekerk/Pilgrimvaders Kerk.** Tram No. 4 connects Delfshaven with the rest of the city, as does the nearby Delfshaven metro station. ⊠ *Achterhaven and Voorhaven, Delfshaven.*

Euromast. For a bird's-eye view of the contrast between Delfshaven and the majority of the city, as well as a spectacular panorama of city and harbor, visit the 600-foot-high Euromast. Designed by Rotterdam architect Huig Maaskant in 1960, this was the Netherland's tallest building for many years; when a new medical facility for the Erasmus University usurped the honor in 1970, an additional 25 feet were added to the tower in six days, restoring Euromast to its premier position. On a clear day, you can just about see the coast. The main observation deck is at 315 feet, but the **Euroscoop** is a rotating panoramic elevator that will carry you another 300 feet from there to the top of the mast. For the thrill seekers among us, on weekends from May to September you can skip the elevator and rappel down from the observation deck, or shoot down the rope slide in about 10 seconds on Europe's fastest "zip wire" (make reservations via the Web at ⊕ *www.abseilen.nl*). There's also a restaurant at the top. You can even stay up the tower overnight in one of two special suites, but be warned the prices are as high as the experience. Down below, the park at the base of the Euromast is where many Rotterdammers spend time when the weather is good. ⊠ *Parkhaven 20, Delfshaven* ☎ *010/436–4811* ⊕ *www.euromast.nl* ☜ *€9.25; rappel or rope slide €49.50* ☉ *Apr.–Sept., daily 9:30 am–11 pm; Oct.–Mar., daily 10 am–11 pm.*

Kunsthal. This "art house" sits at one end of the visitor-friendly museum quarter and hosts major temporary exhibitions. There is no permanent collection, other than the massive, multistory boxlike center itself, designed by architect-prophet Rem Koolhaas. Opinions about the building are sharply divided: some say the design bridging the gap between the Museumpark and the dike is a clever spatial creation; others consider it an ugly mix of facades (part glass, part brick, and part corrugated iron) that has led to rusted iron, stained concrete, and cracks in the central walkway. The biggest complaint is the lack of elevator, compounded by the hazards of the central ramp, whose steep angle makes this a potential ski slope for wheelchair users. Fortunately, the eclectic exhibitions, usually three or four at any one time, are always fascinating, regardless of the setting. ⊠ *Westzeedijk 341, Museumpark* ☎ *010/440–0301* ⊕ *www.kunsthal.nl* ☑ *€11* ☉ *Tues.– Sat. 10–5, Sun. 11–5.*

> ### ROTTERDAM BEST BETS
>
> **Modernist architecture.** Rotterdam eschewed rebuilding the city after the destruction of WWII and instead strode resolutely into modernism.
>
> **The Kinderdijk Windmills.** This archetypal Dutch landscape isn't a theme park—the windmills were grouped to pump water out of the polders. Today the vista is picture-perfect.
>
> **Old Delft.** This tangle of canals and medieval streets, with its array of ornate decoration and flower-bedecked windows, offers some of the prettiest views in Holland.

Fodor's Choice
★
☺
Maritiem Museum Rotterdam. A sea lover's delight, the Maritime Museum is Rotterdam's noted nautical collection. Appropriately perched at the head of the Leuvehaven harbor, it was founded by Prince Hendrik in 1874. Set against the background of modern and historical maritime objects, the seafaring ways of old Rotterdammers make more sense. Star attraction of the ground floor is a large model of the Europoort, which shows how the Rotterdam area has developed over the centuries into the major seaport of today. The upper floors are mainly given over to rotating exhibitions on seafaring themes. Children have half a floor dedicated to them, called "Professor Plons" (Professor Plunge), where museum staff are on hand to help with looking through a real periscope, donning a hard hat and taking to the driving seat of a scaled-down crane, and engaging in many other activities dealing with the themes of water and ships. Kids will also love the museum's prize exhibit, the warship *De Buffel,* moored in the harbor outside, dating back to 1868. The ship has been perfectly restored and is fitted out sumptuously, as can be seen in the mahogany-deck captain's cabin. ⊠ *Leuvehaven 1, Witte de With* ☎ *010/413–2680* ⊕ *www. maritiemmuseum.nl* ☑ *€7.50* ☉ *July and Aug., Mon.–Sat. 10–5, Sun. 11–5; Sept.–June, Tues.–Sat. 10–5, Sun. 11–5.*

Fodor's Choice
★
Museum Boijmans van Beuningen. Rotterdam's finest shrine to art, with treasures ranging from Pieter Bruegel the Elder's 16th-century *Tower of Babel* to Mondriaan's extraordinary *Composition in Yellow and Blue,* ranks among the greatest art galleries in Europe. The top attraction

here is the collection of old masters, which covers West European art from the 14th to the 19th century. In particular 15th- to 17th-century Dutch and Flemish art are well represented, including painters such as Van Eyck, Rubens, Hieronymous Bosch, and Rembrandt. The modern art section runs the gamut from Monet to Warhol and beyond, picking up Kandinsky, Magritte, and Dalí in between. In the Decorative Art and Design collection, both precious ornamental objects and everyday utensils dating from medieval times are displayed. In the museum café, note the fantastic collection of chairs, each by a different designer. More artworks embellish the museum gardens. ⊠ *Museumpark 18–20, Museumpark* ☎ *010/441–9400* ⊕ *www.boijmans. nl* ⊠ *€12.50* ☉ *Tues.–Sun. 11–5.*

Museum de Dubbelde Palmboom (*Double Palm Tree Museum*). Devoted to the history of Rotterdam and its role as an international nexus, this museum traces the city's history from prehistoric times to the current day. The focus is on how exotic wares imported by the East India Company affected the city. The building itself is redolent of history: not only do its heavy beams and brick floors waft you back to yesteryear, but there even seems to be a faint smell of grains, recalling the many years the building spent as a warehouse. Ask for the informative guide in English, as all labeling is in Dutch. The first floor has some fascinating archaeological finds: one of the spouted ancient jugs has been traced to a town near Cologne, providing proof that traveling merchants were apparently very active in trading ceramics. ⊠ *Voorhaven 12, Delfshaven* ☎ *010/476–1533* ⊕ *www.museumrotterdam.nl* ⊠ *€6, ticket also valid for a same-day visit to the Schielandshuis* ☉ *Tues.–Sun. 11–5.*

Toren op Zuid. An office complex by celebrated modern architect Renzo Piano, this structure houses the head offices of KPN Telecom. Its eye-catching billboard facade glitters with 1,000-odd green lamps flashing on and off, creating images provided by the city of Rotterdam, in addition to images provided by KPN and an art academy. The facade fronting the Erasmus Bridge leans forward by 6 degrees, which is the same as the angle of the bridge's pylon. It is also said that Piano could have been making a humorous reference to his homeland, as the Tower of Pisa leans at the same angle. ⊠ *Wilhelminakade 123, Kop van Zuid.*

DELFT

15 km (9 miles) northwest of Rotterdam.

Fodor's Choice
★

With time-burnished canals and streets, Delft radiates a peaceful calm that recalls the quieter pace of the Golden Age of the 17th century. Back then the town counted among its citizens the artist Johannes Vermeer, who decided one spring day to paint the city gates and landscape across the Kolk harbor from a house's window on the Schieweg (now the Hooikade). The result was the 1660 *View of Delft* (now the star of the Mauritshuis Museum in The Hague), famously called by Marcel Proust "the most beautiful painting in the world." Spending a few hours in certain parts of Delft, in fact, puts you in the company of Vermeer. Imagine a tiny Amsterdam, canals reduced to dollhouse proportions, narrower bridges, merchants' houses less grand, and you have the essence of Old

Delft. But even though the city has one foot firmly planted in the past, another is planted in the present: Delft teems with hip cafés, jazz festivals, and revelers spilling out of bars.

Fodor'sChoice ★ **Museum Het Prinsenhof.** A former dignitary-hosting convent of St. Agatha, the Prinsenhof Museum is celebrated as the residence of Prince William the Silent, beloved as *Vader des Vaderlands* (Father of the Nation) for his role in the Spanish Revolt and a hero whose tragic end here gave this structure the sobriquet "cradle of Dutch liberty." The complex of buildings was taken over by the government of the new Dutch Republic in 1572 and given to William of Orange for his use as a residence. On July 10, 1584, fevered by monies offered by Philip II of Spain, Bathasar Gerard, a Catholic fanatic, gained admittance to the mansion and succeeded in shooting the prince on the staircase hall, since known as Moordhal (Murder Hall). The fatal bullet holes—the *teykenen der koogelen*—are still visible in the stairwell. Today, the imposing structure is a museum, with a 15th-century chapel, a quaint courtyard, and a bevy of elegantly furnished 17th-century rooms filled with antique pottery, silver, tapestries, and House of Orange portraits, along with exhibits on Dutch history. ⊠ *Sint Agathaplein 1* ☎ *015/260–2358* ⊕ *www. prinsenhof-delft.nl* ☒ *€7.50; combined ticket to Het Prinsenhof and Nusantara museums €10* ☉ *Tues.–Sun. 11–5.*

Fodor'sChoice ★ **Vermeer Centrum** (*Vermeer Center*). Housed in the former St. Lucas Guild, where Delft's favorite son was dean for many years, the Center takes visitors on a multimedia journey through the life and work of Johannes Vermeer. Touch screens, projections, and other interactive features are interspersed with giant reproductions of the master's work, weaving a tale of 17th-century Delft and drawing you into the mind of the painter. ☎ *015/213–8588* ⊕ *www.vermeerdelft.nl* ☒ *€7* ☉ *Daily 10–5.*

KINDERDIJK

Fodor'sChoice ★ **Kinderdijk.** The sight of the 19 windmills at Kinderdijk under sail is magnificently and romantically impressive. Not surprisingly, this landmark sight (so valued it is found on the UNESCO World Heritage list) is one of the most visited places in the Netherlands. These are water-pumping mills whose job was to drain water from the Alblasserwaard polder enclosed by the rivers Noord and Lek—a function now performed by the 1950 pumping station with its humongously sized water screws, which you pass on the way to the site. The somewhat chocolate-boxy name (which means "child's dyke") comes from a legend involving a baby who washed up here in a cradle after the great floods of 1421, with a cat sitting on its tummy to keep them both from tumbling out.

Rarer than ever, these windmills date all the way back to 1740. Just 150 years ago 10,000 windmills were in operation across the country, but today only 1,000 remain. These have been saved from the wrecking ball thanks to the help of heritage organizations. The windmills are open in rotation, so there is always one interior to visit. A walk through a working windmill gives fascinating insight into how the millers and their families lived. The mills can be seen in full action (wind permitting) from 1 pm to 5 pm on Saturdays in July and August, as well as on National

Windmill Day (second Saturday of May) and National Monument Day (second weekend of September). Throughout the first week following the first Monday of September the mills are illuminated at night, really pulling out the tourist stops. You can walk around the mills area whenever you like, so it's a great way to spend a leisurely afternoon. There are a couple of cafés for snacks, but if the weather is good bring a picnic. ⊠ *Molenkade, Kinderdijk* ☎ *078/691–2830* ⊕ *www.molenskinderdijk. nl* ⊠ *Interior of mill: €6.00 (incl. film at visitor's center)* ☉ *Interior of mill: Apr.–Oct., daily 9:30–5:30.*

SHOPPING

Rotterdam is the number-one shopping city in the south of Holland, and it offers some excellent interior design galleries. Its famous **Lijn-baan** and **Beurstraverse** shopping centers, as well as the surrounding areas, offer a dazzling variety of shops. The archways and fountains of the Beurstraverse—at the bottom of the Coolsingel, near the Stadhuis—make this newer, pedestrianized area more pleasing to walk around. **Van Oldenbarneveldtstraat** and **Nieuwe Binnenweg** are the places to be if you want something different; there is a huge variety of alternative fashion to be found here. Exclusive shops and boutiques can be found in the Entrepotgebied, Delfshaven, Witte de Withstraat, Nieuwe and Oude Binnenweg, and Van Oldenbarneveldtstraat. **West Kruiskade** and its vicinity offers a wide assortment of multicultural products in the many Chinese, Suriname, Mediterranean, and Arabic shops. You should also walk through the **Entrepot Harbor design district,** alongside the city marina at Kop van Zuid, where there are several interior-design stores.

De Bijenkorf. De Bijenkorf is a favorite department store, the best in Rotterdam, designed by Marcel Breuer (the great Bauhaus architect) with an exterior that looks like its name, a beehive. There's a good range of clothing and shoes from both designers and the store's own label, plus a selection of cosmetics and perfume on the ground floor, with a Chill Out department on the same floor geared toward street- and club-wear; here, on some Saturdays a DJ keeps it mellow, and you can even get a haircut at in-store Kinki Kappers. De Bijenkorf is well known for its excellent household-goods line, ranging from lights and furniture to sumptuous fabrics and rugs. Check out the second-floor restaurant with its view out over the Coolsingel and Naum Gabo's sculpture *Constructie.* ⊠ *Coolsingel 105, Centrum* ☎ *0800/0918* ⊕ *www.debijenkorf.nl.*

De Porceleyne Fles. It's corny, even sometimes a little tacky (miniature clogs, anyone?), but no visit to Delft would be complete without stopping at a Delft porcelain factory to see plates and tulip vases being painted by hand and perhaps picking up a souvenir or two. De Porceleyne Fles is the original and most famous home to the popular blue-and-white pottery. Regular demonstrations of molding and painting pottery are given by the artisans. On the bottom of each object is a triple signature: a plump vase topped by a straight line, the stylized letter "F" below it, and the word "Delft." Blue is no longer the only

official color. In 1948, a rich red cracked glaze was premiered depicting profuse flowers, graceful birds, and leaping gazelles. There is New Delft, a range of green, gold, and black hues, whose exquisite minuscule figures are drawn to resemble an old Persian tapestry; the Pynacker Delft, borrowing Japanese motifs in rich oranges and golds; and the brighter Polychrome Delft, which can strike a brilliant sunflower-yellow effect. ⊠ *Royal Delftware Factory, Rotterdamseweg 196* ☎ *015/251–2030* ⊕ *www.royaldelft.com* ✉ *museum €12* ⊙ *mid-Mar.–Oct., daily 9–5; Nov.–mid-Mar., Mon.–Sat. 9–5.*

WHERE TO EAT

$ ✕ **Café Dudok.** Lofty ceilings, a cavernous former-warehouse interior,
CAFÉ   long reading tables stacked with international magazines and papers— little wonder this place attracts an artsy crowd. At its most mellow, the spot is perfect for a lazy afternoon treat of delicious homemade pastries, but you can come here for breakfast, lunch, high tea, dinner, or even a snack after midnight. They offer a small selection for vegetarians. The brasserie, on a mezzanine above the open kitchen at the back, looks out over the Rotte River. Since it's terribly crowded at times, you should get here unfashionably early to avoid disappointment—there's nowhere else like it in Rotterdam. $ *Average main: €10* ⊠ *Meent 88, Centrum* ☎ *010/433–3102* ⊕ *www.dudok.nl.*

$ ✕ **Café Floor.** Adjacent to the Stadsschouwburg (Municipal Theater),
CONTEMPORARY   this popular spot doesn't look too inviting from the outside, but the interior is modern, light, and airy; the staff are friendly; and the kitchen produces excellent food. Try the lamb brochette, so tender the meat practically dissolves on your tongue. There's also a good selection of tapas available and a delicious passion-fruit cheesecake. The beautiful garden at the back, and accompanying birdsong from the local fauna, make this a restful stop. This place is a favorite with local and international regulars, so be prepared to be patient if you go late-ish on a Saturday. $ *Average main: €12* ⊠ *Schouwburgplein 28, Centrum* ☎ *010/404–5288* ⊕ *www.cafefloor.nl.*

SOUTHAMPTON, UNITED KINGDOM

Updated by   Southampton, in the county of Hampshire, may not be in every tourist
Ellin Stein   brochure, but this city and its environs hold all kinds of attractions— and not a few quiet pleasures. Close to London, the green fields of Hampshire divide the cliffs and coves of the West Country from the hustle and bustle of the big city. Two important cathedrals, Winchester and Salisbury (pronounced *sawls*-bree), are nearby, as are stately homes, intriguing market towns and hundreds of haunting prehistoric remains; Stonehenge, the most famous of these, should not be missed. These, however, are just the highlights. Anyone spending time in the region should rent a car and set out to discover the quiet back-road villages that were home to numerous literary greats lived—such as Chawton, where Jane Austen lived—or the semiwilderness of the New Forest.

Hampshire

ESSENTIALS

CURRENCY
The British pound sterling. ATMs are common and credit cards are widely accepted.

HOURS
Museums are open from 9 until 5, while shops usually open from 9 until 5:30 or 6. Some shops are open on Sunday.

TELEPHONES
Dual-band GSM phones work in the United Kingdom. You can buy prepaid phone cards at telecom shops and news vendors in all towns and cities. Phone cards can be used for local or international calls. Vodafone, T-Mobile, Virgin, and Orange are the leading telecom companies.

COMING ASHORE
Southampton is a busy cruise port, and has four separate cruise terminals, each with its own dock, refreshment facilities, and dedicated taxi rank. City Cruise Terminal and Mayflower Terminal are situated in the Western Docks closest to the city (5 minutes by car), while Ocean Terminal and Queen Elizabeth II Terminal are in the Eastern Docks, a couple of minutes farther away from the downtown. Taxi fares to downtown/railway station are around £6. The Eastern Docks have a public bus link (routes U1 and U6) that runs to downtown.

There are four or five train services every hour, and fares start at £39.40 round-trip. By bus, the journey takes around 2½ hours; prices start at £14 round-trip. The rail journey from Southampton to Salisbury takes 40 minutes and starts at £16.80 round-trip; there are trains every half hour. Bus services take around 40 minutes with return ticket prices around £6.40. The rail journey from Southampton to Winchester takes around 20 minutes; fares start at £11.60 round-trip. Bus services take around 30 minutes, with return ticket prices around £4.80.

Renting a car for the day would allow you to explore towns and attractions in the surrounding area more easily. Rental prices are approximately £35 for an economy manual vehicle.

> ## HAMPSHIRE BEST BETS
>
> **Stonehenge.** This world-famous megalithic monument has captured the popular imagination. Although we're sure of its age, its origins and exact purpose remain a mystery.
>
> **Winchester.** Once the capital of England, this diminutive city has many architectural treasures on show, including one of the finest cathedrals in Britain.
>
> **Chawton.** Jane Austen lived here for many years; devotees can be inspired by the atmosphere in the very room where she wrote her greatest works.

GETTING TO THE AIRPORT

If you do not purchase airport transfers from your cruise line, the simplest way to reach Heathrow Airport is by private transfer company or hire cab. The journey time is around two hours from terminal to terminal, but prices for a vehicle for one to three people are expensive, at around £116.

Aside from bespoke transfer, the easiest other option is by bus. National Express runs direct services between Southampton Bus Station and Heathrow departing once every 1 hour, 45 minutes or so. Journey time is just over 2 hours. Single journey price is £12.50.

Trains from Southampton terminate at Waterloo Station in London. The journey time is about 90 minutes. There are four or five train services every hour, and fares start at £39.40 round-trip. To reach Heathrow, the least expensive option is the London Underground, but carriages can be busy with little luggage space. From Waterloo Station take the Bakerloo Line to Piccadilly Circus, from where the Piccadilly line will take you directly to Heathrow. The time for the journey is around 1:20 hours and costs £5.30.

Aimed more at travelers than commuters, the Heathrow Express offers a much quicker, direct journey, 15 minutes from Paddington Station to Heathrow. To reach Paddington, take the Bakerloo Underground line from Waterloo Station. Heathrow Express tickets cost £18 one-way.

The Heathrow Connect train runs every half-hour from Paddington to Heathrow, stopping at local stations along the 30-minute route. Prices are £8.50 one-way.

From the cruise terminal to downtown Southampton (bus or train station) the taxi fare should be around £7 to £10. If you are traveling from airport to cruise terminal, be sure to note the name of the terminal your ship is docked at, because the four terminals are a couple of miles apart.

EXPLORING HAMPSHIRE

SOUTHAMPTON

Central Southampton is about 2 km (1 mile) from the cruise-ship docks.

Seafaring Saxons and Romans used Southampton's outer harbor as a commercial trading port for centuries, allowing the city to become one of England's wealthiest. Though still home to England's second-largest container terminal, it is now primarily used for passenger traffic. As the home port of many great ocean liners of the 20th century, including the *Queen Mary* and the ill-fated *Titanic,* as well as being the departure point for Henry V's fleet bound for Agincourt and the *Mayflower,* Southampton has one of the richest maritime traditions in England. Much of the city center is unremarkable, having been hastily rebuilt after World War II bombing, but bits of the city's history peek out from between modern buildings. The Old Town retains its medieval air, and considerable parts of Southampton's castellated town walls remain. Other attractions include an art gallery, extensive parks, and a couple of good museums. The Southampton International Boat Show, a 10-day event in mid-September, draws huge

Mayflower Park and the Pilgrim Fathers' Memorial. This memorial was built to commemorate the departure of 102 passengers on the North America–bound *Mayflower* from Southampton on August 15, 1620. A plaque also honors the 2 million U.S. troops who embarked from Southampton during World War II. ⊠ *Western Esplanade.*

SeaCity Museum. This new £15 million museum is devoted to Southampton's storied maritime history. The Gateway to the World gallery brings together artifacts from Roman, Saxon, and medieval times with models, mementos, and pieces of furniture from the age of the great clippers and cruise ships. The *Titanic* gallery displays a wealth of memorabilia relating to one of the most famous of the cruise ships that sailed from the city—footage, photos, crew lists, and so on. Boat buffs will relish plenty of vital statistics dealing with the history of commercial shipping. ⊠ *Havelock Rd.* ☎ *023/8083–3007* ⊕ *www.seacitymuseum.co.uk* ⌨ *£8.50* ⊙ *Daily 10–5.*

WINCHESTER

25 km (16 miles) northeast of Southampton.

One of the region's most compelling and historically rich destinations, and still a thriving market town, Winchester is among the most historic of English cities. For more than four centuries it served first as the capital of the ancient kingdom of Wessex and then of England. Alfred the Great, whose court was here, laid out the street plan. Its imposing cathedral, the final resting place of notables ranging from Saxon kings to Jane Austen, still dominates the skyline.

Great Hall. A short walk west of the cathedral, this hall is all that remains of the city's Norman castle, and it's still used today for events and ceremonies. Here the English Parliament met for the first time in 1246; Sir Walter Raleigh was tried for conspiracy against King James I in 1603; and Dame Alice Lisle was sentenced to death by the brutal Judge Jeffreys for sheltering fugitives, after Monmouth's Rebellion in 1685. The

hall's greatest relic hangs on its west wall: King Arthur's Round Table has places for 24 knights and a portrait of Arthur bearing a remarkable resemblance to King Henry VIII. In fact, the animal skin–covered table dates back only to the 13th century and was repainted by order of Henry on the occasion of a visit by the Holy Roman Emperor Charles V; the real Arthur was probably a Celtic chieftain who held off the invading Saxons after the fall of the Roman Empire in the 5th or 6th century. The Tudor monarchs revived the Arthurian legend for political purposes. Take time to wander through the garden named for the two Queen Eleanors—a re-creation of a medieval shady retreat. ⊠ *Castle Hill* ☏ *01962/846476* ⊕ *www.hants.gov.uk/greathall* ▱ *Free* ⊙ *Daily 10–5.*

★ **Winchester Cathedral.** The city's greatest monument, begun in 1079 and consecrated in 1093, presents a sturdy, chunky appearance in keeping with its Norman construction, so that the Gothic lightness within is even more breathtaking. Its tower, transepts, and crypt, and the inside core of the great Perpendicular nave, reveal some of the world's best surviving examples of Norman architecture. Other features, such as the arcades, the presbytery (behind the quire, holding the high altar), and the windows, are Gothic alterations carried out between the 12th and 14th century. Little of the original stained glass has survived, however, thanks to Cromwell's Puritan troops, who ransacked the cathedral in the 17th century during the English Civil War, but you can still see the sumptuously illuminated 12th-century Winchester Bible in the Library and Triforium Gallery.

Among the many well-known people buried in the cathedral are William the Conqueror's son, William II ("Rufus"), mysteriously murdered in the New Forest in 1100; Izaak Walton (1593–1683), author of *The Compleat Angler*, whose memorial window in Silkestede's Chapel was paid for by "the fishermen of England and America"; and Jane Austen, whose grave lies in the north aisle of the nave. The tombstone makes no mention of Austen's literary status, though a brass plaque in the wall, dating from 80 years after her death, celebrates her achievements, and modern panels provide an overview of her life and work. Firmly in the 20th century, Antony Gormley's evocative statue *Sound II* (1986) looms in the crypt, as often as not standing in water (as it was designed to do), because of seasonal flooding. You can also explore the bell tower—with far-reaching views in fair weather—and other recesses of the building on a tour. Special services or ceremonies may mean the cathedral is closed to visits, so call ahead. Outside the cathedral, explore the Close, the area that nearly envelopes the cathedral and contains neat lawns and the Deanery, Dome Alley, and Cheyney Court. ⊠ *The Close, Cathedral Precincts* ☏ *01962/857200* ⊕ *www.winchester-cathedral.org.uk* ▱ *Cathedral £4.80; bell tower £6; cathedral and bell tower £9.50* ⊙ *Cathedral Mon.–Sat. 10–4 (last admission 3), Sun. 12:30–2:30. Library and Triforium Gallery Apr.–Oct., Mon. 2–4, Tues.–Sat. and national holidays 10:30–4; Nov.–Mar., Sat. 10:30–3:30. Free tours on the hr Mon.–Sat. 10–3, bell tower tours June–Aug., Mon., Wed., and Fri. 2:15; Sat. 11:30 and 2:15; Sept.–late May, Wed. 2:15, Sat. 11:30 and 2:15.*

CHAWTON

49 km (30 miles) northeast of Southampton.

In this tiny Hampshire village you'll find the elegant but understated house where Jane Austen (1775–1817) lived the last eight years of her life and wrote three of her novels. Now a museum, it effectively evokes her life there.

★ **Jane Austen's House.** Here, in an unassuming redbrick house, Jane Austen wrote *Emma, Persuasion,* and *Mansfield Park,* and revised *Sense and Sensibility, Northanger Abbey,* and *Pride and Prejudice.* Now a museum, the house retains the modest but genteel atmosphere suitable to the unmarried daughter of a clergyman. In the left-hand parlor, there's a piano similar to the one Jane would play every morning before repairing to a small writing table in the family dining parlor—leaving her sister, Cassandra, to do the household chores ("I find composition impossible with my head full of joints of mutton and doses of rhubarb," Jane wrote). In the early 19th century the road near the house was a bustling thoroughfare, and one traveler reported that a window view proved that the Misses Austen were "looking very comfortable at breakfast." Jane was famous for working through interruptions, but one protection against the outside world was the famous door that creaked. She asked that its hinges remain unattended to because they gave her warning that someone was coming. The museum often schedules readings and other special events, so call ahead. ⊠ *Signed off A31/A32 roundabout* ☎ *01420/83262* ⊕ *www.jane-austens-house-museum.org. uk* ✉ *£7.50* ⊙ *Jan.–mid-Feb., weekends 10:30–4:30; mid-Feb.–May and Sept.–Dec., daily 10:30–4:30; June–Aug., daily 10–5; last admission 30 mins before closing.*

SALISBURY CATHEDRAL

Fodor's Choice **Salisbury Cathedral.** Salisbury is dominated by the towering cathedral,
★ a soaring hymn in stone. It is unique among cathedrals in that it was conceived and built as a whole in the amazingly short span of 38 years (1220–58). The spire, added in 1320, is the tallest in England and a miraculous feat of medieval engineering—even though the point, 404 feet above the ground, is 2½ feet off vertical. For a fictional, keenly imaginative reconstruction of the drama underlying such an achievement, read William Golding's novel *The Spire.* The excellent model of the cathedral in the north transept, the "arm" of the church to your left as you look toward the altar, shows the building about 20 years into construction, and makes clear the ambition of Salisbury's medieval builders. For all their sophistication, the height and immense weight of the great spire have always posed structural problems. In the late 17th century Sir Christopher Wren was summoned from London to strengthen the spire, and in the mid-19th century Sir George Gilbert Scott, a leading Victorian Gothicist, undertook a major program of restoration. He also initiated a clearing out of the interior and removed some less-than-sympathetic 18th-century alterations, returning a more authentically Gothic feel. Despite this, the interior seems spartan and a little gloomy, but check out the remarkable lancet windows and sculpted tombs of crusaders and other medieval notables. The clock in

the north aisle—probably the oldest working mechanism in Europe, if not the world—was made in 1386.

The **cloisters** are the largest in England, and the octagonal **Chapter House** contains a marvelous 13th-century frieze showing scenes from the Old Testament. Here you can also see one of the four original copies of the **Magna Carta,** the charter of rights the English barons forced King John to accept in 1215; it was sent here for safekeeping in the 13th century. ■ TIP→ Join a free 45-minute tour of the church, leaving two or more times a day. There are also daily tours of the roof and spire (except on Sunday from October through April). For a peaceful break, the café in the cloister offers freshly baked cakes and pastries. ✉ *Cathedral Close, Salisbury* ☎ *01722/555120* ⊕ *www.salisburycathedral.org.uk* ☎ *Cathedral and Chapter House free; suggested donation £6.50; tower tour £10* ☉ *Cathedral Mon.–Sat. 10–5, Sun. 12–4. Chapter House Mon.–Sat. 9:30–4:30, Sun. 12:45–3:45.*

STONEHENGE

Fodor's Choice   **Stonehenge.** Mysterious and ancient, Stonehenge has baffled archaeolo-
★   gists for centuries. One of England's most visited monuments, the cir-
cle of giant stones standing starkly against the wide sweep of Salisbury Plain still has the capacity to fascinate and move those who view it. This World Heritage site is now enclosed by barriers due to incidents of vandalism and growing fears that its popularity could threaten its existence, and visitors are kept on a paved path a short distance away from the stones. But if you visit in the early morning before the crowds have arrived, or in the evening, when the sky is heavy with scudding clouds, you can experience Stonehenge as it once was: a mystical, awe-inspiring place. Stonehenge was begun about 3000 BC and continued being changed and in use until around 1600 BC. It was made up of an outer circle of 30 sarsen stones, huge sandstone blocks weighing up to 25 tons, which are believed to have originated from the Marlborough Downs, and an earlier inner circle of bluestones that was constructed around 2500 BC. Within these circles was a horseshoe-shape group of sarsen trilithons (two large vertical stones supporting a third stone laid horizontally across it) and within that another horseshoe-shape grouping of bluestones. The sarsens used in the trilithons averaged 45 tons. Many of the huge stones were brought here from great distances before the invention of the wheel, and it's not certain what ancient form of transportation was used to move them. The bluestones, for example, are thought to have come from the Preseli Hills on the Atlantic coast of Wales, and may have been moved by raft over sea and river, and then dragged on rollers across country despite weighing as much as 4 tons each—a total journey of 149 miles as the crow flies. However, every time a reconstruction of the journey has been attempted, it has failed. The labor involved in quarrying, transporting, and carving these stones is astonishing, all the more so when you realize that it was accomplished about the same time as the construction of Egypt's major pyramids. Stonehenge (the name derives from the Saxon term for "hanging stones") has been excavated several times over the centuries, although some of the site's mysteries have been solved, the primary reason for its erection

remains unknown. It's fairly certain that it was a religious site, and that worship here involved the cycles of the sun; the alignment of the stones on the axis of the midsummer sunrise and midwinter sunset makes this clear. The Druids certainly had nothing to do with the construction: the monument had already been in existence for nearly 2,000 years by the time they appeared. Some historians have maintained that Stonehenge was a kind of Neolithic computer, with a sophisticated astronomical purpose—an observatory of sorts—though evidence from excavations in the early 20th century shows that it had once been used as a burial ground. Excavations at Durrington Walls, another archaeological site a couple of miles northeast (off A345), have unearthed a seasonally occupied settlement dating from around 2500 BC, which may have been built and occupied by those who constructed Stonehenge. Another possibility is that this Neolithic village was home to those who performed the religious rites at Stonehenge, where people gathered from far and wide to feast and worship. The finds show Stonehenge not to be an isolated monument, but part of a much larger complex of ceremonial structures. Since it's no longer possible to closely examine the prehistoric carvings, some of which show axes and daggers, bring a pair of binoculars to help make out the details on the monoliths. To fully engage your imagination, or to get that magical photo, it's worth exploring all aspects of the site, both near and far. It has a particularly romantic aspect at dawn and dusk, or by a full moon. Your ticket entitles you to an informative audio tour, but in general, visitor amenities at Stonehenge are limited, especially for such a major tourist attraction. A new visitor center was under construction at the time of this writing, and this may cause some travel disruption. ■TIP→ English Heritage arranges access to the stone circle outside of normal hours. These tours require a payment of £15.30 well in advance. ⊠ *Junction of A303 and A344/A360, Amesbury* ☎ *0870/333–1181, 01722/343830 for private tours* ⊕ *www.english-heritage.org.uk* 🎫 *£7.80* ⊙ *Mid-Mar.–May and Sept.–mid-Oct., daily 9:30–6; June–Aug., daily 9–7; mid-Oct.–mid-Mar., daily 9:30–4. Last admission 30 mins before closing.*

SHOPPING

Almost every town in this part of England has a tempting array of shops selling antiques, collectibles, and one-of-a-kind items. English china makes a fitting souvenir, as do copies of the various Austen novels set in the region. For a post-tour pick-me-up, try English blended teas in presentation sets.

King's Walk, off Friarsgate in Winchester, has a number of stalls selling antiques, crafts, gift items, and bric-a-brac.

WHERE TO EAT

$$ ✕ **Chesil Rectory.** The timbered and gabled building may be Old English–
MODERN BRITISH   it dates back to the mid-15th century–but the cuisine is modern British, using locally sourced ingredients. Dishes might include venison carpaccio for a starter, followed by slow-cooked pork rib eye or oven-roasted

halibut. Good-value fixed-price lunches and early-evening dinners are available. Service and the heritage charm of the surroundings enhance the quality of the food. ⑤ *Average main: £17* ⊠ *1 Chesil St., Winchester* ☎ *01962/851555* ⊕ *www.chesilrectory.co.uk.*

$$ ✕ **The Pig.** Funkier sister of glamorous Lime Wood hotel, this New
MODERN BRITISH Forest "restaurant with rooms" puts the emphasis on localism and seasonality and is a local favorite. Lunch and dinner are served in a large conservatory overlooking lawns, and 95% of the ingredients are sourced within 15 miles. The frequently changing menu may include dishes like Lymington pollock with Dorset clams or Lyme Bay scallops with bacon. As the name suggests, porcine dishes feature prominently. You can overnight in one of the 26 comfortable rooms in the main building (an 18th-century former royal hunting lodge) or the converted stable block. All combine a slightly retro, shabby-chic style with modern bathrooms. Guests may accompany the "staff forager" on expeditions to find edible fauna such as wild garlic. ⑤ *Average main: £16* ⊠ *Beaulieu Rd., Brockenhurst* ☎ *01590/622354* ⊕ *www.thepighotel.com.*

ZEEBRUGGE, BELGIUM (FOR BRUGES)

Updated by
Liz Humphreys

Long thought of as a Sleeping Beauty reawakened, Bruges is an ancient town where the rhythm of medieval life resonates from every street corner. The city thrived during the 13th century as a member of the Hanseatic League, and an era of unprecedented wealth began under such Burgundian rulers as Philip the Good and Charles the Bold in the 15th century. At this time, Hans Memling and Jan van Eyck took art in a new direction with the famed Flemish Primitive style of painting, while fine civil and domestic buildings advertised the wealth generated by trade. When the city fell into poverty as its rivers silted in the 16th century, this architecture was preserved as if in aspic. Today Bruges is a compact and atmospheric maze of tangled streets, narrow canals, handsome squares, and gabled buildings. The town has not only awakened from its slumbers, but is also bright-eyed with spruced-up shops, restaurants, and cafés.

ESSENTIALS
CURRENCY
The euro. ATMs are common and credit cards are widely accepted.

HOURS
Shops open Tuesday, Wednesday, Friday, and Saturday from 9 or 10 until 6; they are open later on Thursday. Most stores are closed on Sunday and some on Monday. Museums open from 9 until 6 with one late opening night during the week.

PRIVATE TOURS
Though there are no guided tours that leave from Zeebrugge itself, you can take a variety of tours once you get to Bruges. And if you book in advance with Toerisme Brugge, you can hire a guide for a two-hour private tour for €60 (€30 for each additional hour).

Contacts Toerisme Brugge. ☎ *32/50444646* ⊕ *www.brugge.be.*

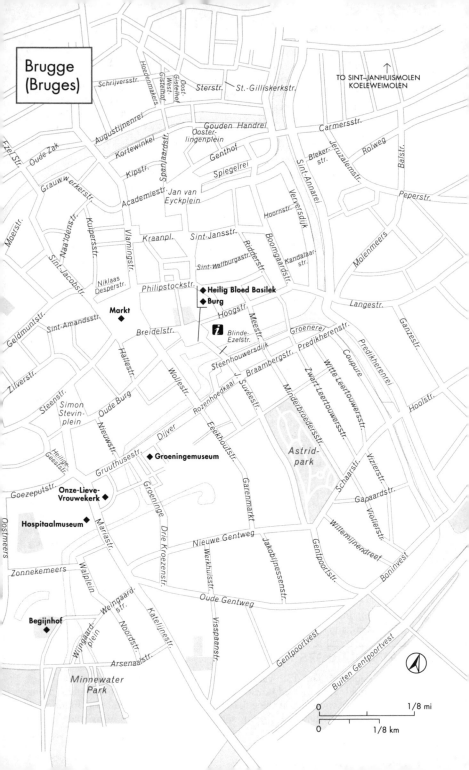

Brugge (Bruges)

Schrijversstr.

Sterstr.

St.-Gilliskerkstr.

TO SINT-JANHUISMOLEN
KOELEWEIMOLEN

Hoedenmakers

Oost-
Gistelhof
West-
Gistelhof

Carmersstr.

Augustijnenrei

Gouden Handrei

Oosterlingenplein

Kortewinkel

Kipstr.

Spanjaardstr.

Genthof

Bleker-
str.

Jeruzalemstr.

Rolweg

Balstr.

Ezel Str.

Oude Zak

Grauwwerkersstr.

Academiestr.

Jan van Eyckplein

Spiegelrei

Sint-Annarei

Peperstr.

Moerstr.

Sint-Jan-denstr.

Kuipersstr.

Vlamingstr.

Kraanpl.

Sint-Jansstr.

Hoornstr.

Verversdijk

Molenmeers

Sint-Jacobstr.

Niklaas
Desperstr.

Philipstockstr.

Sint-Walburgastr.

Ridderstr.

Boomgaardstr.

Kandelaar-
str.

Langestr.

Ganzestr.

◆ **Heilig Bloed Basilek**
◆ **Burg**

Geldmuntstr.

Sint-Amandsstr.

◆ **Markt**

Hallestr.

Breidelstr.

Hoogstr.

Meestr.

*Blinde-
Ezelstr.*

Groenerei

Predikherenstr.

Coupure

Predikherenrei

Zilverstr.

Steenstr.

Simon
Stevin-
plein

Oude Burg

Nieuwstr.

Wollestr.

Steenhouwersdijk

Braambergstr.

Rozenhoedkaai

Suveestr.

Zwart Leertouwersstr.

Witte Leertouwersstr.

Mindelbroedersstr.

Hoolstr.

Heilige
Geeststr.

Gruuthusestr.

Dijver

◆ **Groeningemuseum**

Eeekhoutstr.

Garenmarkt

*Astrid-
park*

Schaarstr.

Vizierstr.

Goezeputstr.

◆ **Onze-Lieve-
Vrouwekerk**

Groeninge

Vlotietstr.

Gapaardstr.

◆ **Hospitaalmuseum**

Mariastr.

Drie Kroezenstr.

Nieuwe Gentweg

Werkhuisstr.

Jakobijnessenstr.

Gentpoortstr.

Willemijnendreef

Boninvest

Oostmeers

Zonnekemeers

Walplein

Weingaard-
str.

Oude Gentweg

Visspaanstr.

◆ **Begijnhof**

Wijngaard-
plein

Noordstr.

Katelijnestr.

Arsenaalstr.

Gentpoortvest

Buten Gentpoortvest

*Minnewater
Park*

0   1/8 mi

0   1/8 km

TELEPHONES

Tri-band GSM phones work in Belgium. You can buy prepaid phone cards at telecom shops, news vendors, and tobacconists in all towns and cities. Phone cards can be used for local or international calls. Proximus, Mobistar, and BASE are the leading telecom companies.

COMING ASHORE

Cruise ships dock at Zeebrugge—14 km (9 miles) from the city of Bruges—at the King Leopold II dam or at Zweedse Kaai (Swedish Quay). From Zweedse Kaai, the Zeebrugge port authority provides a free shuttle to the exit of the cruise terminal. These locations are 2 km (1½ miles) from Zeebrugge train station. There are no passenger facilities within the port itself. The reliable and modern rail system ensures swift and efficient transfer from the station to a range of Belgian cities, including Ghent, Antwerp, and Brussels. The dock is within walking distance of the seafront of Zeebrugge Town, with its seafront promenade, Russian submarine exhibit, and historic fishing district.

> **BRUGES BEST BETS**
>
> **Boat trip on the canals.** The lifeblood of medieval Bruges, the canals now offer some of the finest views of the city's delightful architecture and distinctive streets and alleyways.
>
> **Belfort.** Climb the medieval tower for exceptional views across the tiled rooftops and ornate gables of this tiny enclave.
>
> **Groeningemusem.** The art of the Flemish Primitives and their successors form the core of this gallery, one of the finest of its kind in the world.

Taxis wait at the dockside to transfer passengers not booked on organized trips into Zeebrugge, or you can walk to the train stations, though the roads are rather industrial. There are two stations, Zeebrugge Dorp, nearest to the Swedish Quay and open on weekdays from September to June, and Zeebrugge Strand, nearest to King Leopold II and open on weekends from September to June and daily in July and August. By rail from the center of Zeebrugge it is a 20-minute journey to Bruges at a current cost of €4.40 one-way for first-class and €2.90 one-way for second-class; the rail journey to Antwerp takes about two hours, at a cost of €24.60 one-way for first-class and €16 one-way for second-class. It is 15 minutes by road from the Zeebrugge docks to Bruges. You can also take a taxi into Bruges for a fixed rate of €50. Travel by taxi has a per-km (per-½ mile) charge of around €2.50, which makes it expensive for day tours but acceptable for short trips.

Vehicle-rental offices are located in Bruges (around €100 per day for a compact manual shift vehicle), but rail transport is most practical for independent travelers unless you really want to see more of the Belgian countryside.

EXPLORING BRUGES

Begijnhof. This 13th-century béguinage is a pretty and serene cluster of small whitewashed houses, a pigeon tower, and a church surrounding a pleasant green at the edge of a canal. The Begijnhof was founded in 1245 by Margaret, Countess of Constantinople, to bring together the

Beguines—girls and widows from all social backgrounds who devoted themselves to charitable work but who were not bound by religious vows. The last of the Beguines died about 50 years ago; today the site is occupied by the Benedictine nuns, who still wear the Beguine habit. Although most of the present-day houses are from the 16th and 17th centuries, they have maintained the architectural style of the houses that preceded them. One house (No.1) has been set aside as a small museum. Visitors are asked to respect the order's vow of silence. The horse-and-carriage rides around the town have a 10-minute stop outside the béguinage—long enough for a quick look round. ⊠ *Oude Begijnhof, off Wijngaardstraat* ☎ *050/33-00-11* 🖾 *Free, No. 1 house visit €2* ⊗ *Begijnhof daily 6:30–6:30; house Mon.–Sat. 10–5, Sun. 2:30–5* Ⓜ *Bus 12.*

THE NAME GAME
You'll find two spellings of the town name. That's because Belgium has two languages, Flemish and French. In French the spelling is Bruges; in Flemish it's Brugge. Since the city sits in the mainly Flemish-speaking region of Flanders, Brugge is more technically correct—though you won't have a problem if you call the city Bruges, as most tourists do.

Fodor's Choice
★ **Burg.** A popular daytime meeting place and an enchanting, floodlighted scene after dark, the Burg is flanked by striking, centuries-old civic buildings. Named for the fortress built by Baldwin of the Iron Arm, the Burg was also the former site of the 10th-century Carolingian Cathedral of St. Donaas, which was destroyed by French Republicans in 1799. You can wander through the handsome, 18th-century law court, the Oude Gerechtshof, the Voormalige Civiele Griffie with its 15th-century front gable, the Stadhuis, and the Heilig Bloed Basiliek. The Burg is not all historic splendor, though—in sharp contrast to these buildings stands a modern construction by Japanese artist Toyo Ito, added in 2002. Public opinion is sharply divided over Ito's pavilion; you'll either love it or hate it. ⊠ *Hoogstraat and Breidelstraat* Ⓜ *Bus 1 or 12.*

Fodor's Choice
★ **Groeningemuseum.** The tremendous holdings of this gallery give you the makings for a crash course in the Flemish Primitives and their successors. Petrus Christus, Hugo Van der Goes, Hieronymus Bosch, Rogier van der Weyden, Gerard David, Pieter Bruegel (both Elder and Younger), Pieter Pourbus—all the greats are represented here. Here you can see Jan van Eyck's wonderfully realistic *Madonna with Canon Van der Paele,* in which van Eyck achieved texture and depth through multiple layers of oil and varnish. There's also one of Hans Memling's greatest works, the *Moreel Triptych.* As if this weren't enough, the museum also encompasses a strong display of 15th- to 21st-century Dutch and Belgian works, sweeping through to Surrealist and contemporary art. The Groeninge is set back from the street in a pocket-size park behind a medieval gate. ⊠ *Dijver 12* ☎ *050/44-87-11* 🖾 *€8* ⊗ *Tues.–Sun. 9:30–5* Ⓜ *Bus 1 or 12.*

Heilig Bloed Basiliek. The Basilica of the Holy Blood manages to include both the austere and the ornate under one roof—not to mention one of Europe's most precious relics. The 12th-century Lower Chapel retains a stern, Romanesque character. From this sober space, an elaborate,

external Gothic stairway leads to the stunningly lavish Upper Chapel, which was twice destroyed—by Protestant iconoclasts in the 16th century and by French Republicans in the 18th—but both times rebuilt. (Note that the Upper Chapel is closed to visitors during Eucharistic Mass on Sunday 11 to noon.) The original stained-glass windows were replaced in 1845, and then again after an explosion in 1967, when they were restored by the Brugge painter De Loddere. The basilica's name-sake treasure is a vial thought to contain a few drops of the blood of Christ, brought from Jerusalem to Brugge in 1149 by Derick of Alsace when he returned from the Second Crusade. It is exposed here every Friday in the Lower Chapel 8:30 to 10 and in the Upper Chapel 10 to 11 and 3 to 4, and on other apparently random occasions for veneration: queue up to place your right hand on the vial and take a moment for quiet reflection. The small museum next to the basilica is the usual home of the basilica's name-sake reliquary. ✉ *Burg 13* ⊕ *www.holyblood.com* ▨ *Museum, €2* ☉ *Apr.–Sept., daily 9:30–noon and 2–5; Oct.–Mar., daily 10–noon and 2–4* Ⓜ *Bus 1 or 12.*

Fodor's Choice   **Hospitaalmuseum.** Home to the greatest collection of Hans Memling
★   paintings in the world, the **Oud Sint-Janshospitaal** is one of the oldest surviving medieval hospitals in Europe. It was founded in the 12th century and remained in use until the early 20th century. Furniture, paintings, and hospital-related items are attractively displayed; the 13th-century middle ward, the oldest of three, was built in Romanesque style. Other fascinating 18th-century paintings show patients arriving by sedan chair and being fed and ministered to by sisters and clerics. Some of the actual sedan chairs that were used are also on display. But the highlights of the collection are the six major works (and plenty of minor ones) by Hans Memling (1440–94) that are of breathtaking quality and rank among the greatest—and certainly the most spiritual—of the Flemish Primitive school. Memling was born in Germany, but spent the greater part of his life in Brugge. ✉ *Mariastraat 38* ☎ *050/44–87–11* ▨ *€8* ☉ *Tues.–Sun. 9:30–5* Ⓜ *Bus 1 or 12.*

Fodor's Choice   **Markt.** Used as a marketplace since 958, this square is still one of the
★   liveliest places in Brugge. In the center stands a memorial to the city's medieval heroes, Jan Breydel and Pieter De Coninck, who led the commoners of Flanders to their short-lived victory over the aristocrats of France. On the east side of the Markt stand the provincial government house and the post office, an excellent pastiche of Burgundian Gothic. Old guild houses line the west and north sides of the square, their step-gabled facades overlooking the cafés spilling out onto the sidewalk. These buildings aren't always as old as they seem, though—often they're 19th-century reconstructions. The medieval **Belfort** (Belfry) on the south side of the Markt, however, is the genuine article. The tower dates to the 13th century, its crowning octagonal lantern to the 15th century. The valuables of Brugge were once kept in the second-floor treasury; now the Belfort's riches are in its remarkable 47-bell carillon, which rings even truer thanks to the new bells it was given in 2010. (Impressing Belgians with a carillon is no mean feat, as Belgium has some of the best in the world.) If you haven't walked enough, you can climb 366 winding steps to the clock mechanism, and from the

carillon enjoy a gorgeous panoramic view. Back in the square, you may be tempted by the **horse-drawn carriages** that congregate here; a half-hour ride for up to five people, with a short stop at the Begijnhof, costs €39 plus "something for the horse." ✉ *Intersection of Steenstraat, St-Amandstraat, Vlamingstraat, Philipstockstraat, Breidelstraat, and Wollestraat* ☎ *050/44–87–11* ✆ *Belfort €8* ⊙ *Belfort daily 9:30–5.*

Onze-Lieve-Vrouwekerk. The towering spire of the plain Gothic Church of Our Lady, begun about 1220, rivals the Belfry as Brugge's symbol. It is 381 feet high, the tallest brick construction in the world. While brick can be built high, it cannot be sculpted like stone; hence the tower's somewhat severe look. The art history highlight here is the *Madonna and Child* statue carved by Michelangelo, an early work. The great sculptor sold it to a merchant from Brugge when the original client failed to pay. It was stolen by Napoléon, and during World War II by Nazi leader Hermann Göring; now the white-marble figure sits in a black-marble niche behind an altar at the end of the south aisle. The choir museum contains many 13th- and 14th-century polychrome tombs, as well as two mausoleums: that of Mary of Burgundy, who died in 1482 at the age of 25 after a fall from her horse; and that of her father, Charles the Bold, killed in 1477 while laying siege to Nancy in France. Note that while you can enter the church for free, you'll need a ticket to see most of the major artworks, including the Michelangelo statue. ✉ *Dijver and Mariastraat* ✆ *Church free; choir museum €4* ⊙ *Tues.–Fri. 9:30–5, Sat. 9:30–4:45, Sun. 1:30–5* Ⓜ *Bus 1 or 12.*

SHOPPING

Bruges has many trendy boutiques and shops, especially along Nordzandstraat, as well as Steenstraat and Vlamingstraat, both of which branch off from the Markt. Ter Steeghere mall, which links the Burg with Wollestraat, deftly integrates a modern development into the historic center. The largest and most pleasant mall is the Zilverpand off Zilverstraat, where 30-odd shops cluster in Flemish gable houses. Souvenir shops crowd around the Markt, Wollestraat, Breidelstraat, and Minnewater. Bruges has been a center for lace-making since the 15th century. Handmade lace in intricate patterns, however, takes a long time to produce, and this is reflected in the price. For work of this type, you should be prepared to part with €250 or more. Art and antiques abound, with furniture and decorative objects from the surrounding Flanders region. You also can't go far in the city center without seeing a tempting window display of handmade chocolates, truffles, and pralines. These are delicious to enjoy while you stroll.

ACTIVITIES

CYCLING

The city is easy to explore on two wheels, and many Bruges city dwellers use bicycles daily. Cyclists can go in both directions along more than 50 one-way streets, marked on the tarmac with an image of a bicycle circled in blue. The Bruges tourist office sells a cycling brochure outlining five different routes around the city. The Green Bike Tour provides bike

rental and a guided tour (leaving 10 am daily from the Concertgebouw at 't Zand 34 from April to October) for €15. Tours return in the early afternoon. You can rent bicycles in several places.

Contacts The Green Bike Tour. ⊠ *St. Kwintensstraat 12, Bruges* ☎ *32/50612667.*

WHERE TO EAT

$$$

FRENCH

✕ **Chez Olivier.** Set above a quiet canal, with white swans gliding below, this French charmer is purely romantic. Chef Olivier Foucad uses impeccably fresh ingredients for "light food," such as scallops in ginger and herbs, duck in rosemary honey, and lightly marbled Charolais beef. Lunches are a bargain and the staff is flexible—if you want one main course or two starters instead of the full prix fixe menu, just ask. For the best views, request a window seat next to the water. $ *Average main:* €28 ⊠ *Meestraat 9* ☎ *050/33–36–59* ⊕ *www.chezolivier.be* ⊗ *Closed Thurs. and Sun. and 2 wks in July. No lunch Sat.* Ⓜ *Bus 1.*

$

BELGIAN

✕ **De Torre.** For traditional Belgian food at honest prices, this is the place. From noon until 10 pm, Flemish stew, tomato with shrimp, mussels, or fillet of sole are served as they are in many Flemish homes. The 18th-century house is decorated in art deco style, and the sunny terrace has a lovely view of the Reien. $ *Average main: €15* ⊠ *Langestraat 8* ☎ *050/34–29–46* ⊕ *www.de-torre.com* ⊗ *Apr.–Sept, closed Tues.; Oct.– Mar., closed Tues., Wed.* Ⓜ *Bus 6 or 16.*

The Baltic

PORTS IN DENMARK, ESTONIA, FINLAND, GERMANY, LATVIA, POLAND, RUSSIA, AND SWEDEN

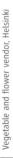

Vegetable and flower vendor, Helsinki

WORD OF MOUTH

"We did the Baltic in June, and St. Petersburg was the highlight of the trip. . . . The sights are amazing . . . . For us, we disembarked in every port except St. Petersburg on our own, so we did not have to wait in lines for a tour to assemble and begin."

—jacketwatch

Northern European itineraries are increasingly popular. You may depart from Stockholm or Copenhagen and visit several of the Baltic's top ports. A special treat for Baltic cruisers is often a stop in St. Petersburg, Russia, and this is why many people take these cruises.

Some Baltic itineraries begin in a U.K. port or even in Amsterdam (⇨ *"The North Sea" for more information about these ports*). Some may include stops in Norway (⇨ *"Norway" for Norwegian ports*). These cruises may be longer than the typical Mediterranean cruise and may cost more, which is one reason why they aren't as popular with first-timers to European cruising. But the number of ships doing Baltic itineraries continues to expand, and there are now some one-week cruises in these northern waters during the summer.

ABOUT THE RESTAURANTS

All the restaurants we recommend serve lunch; they may also serve dinner if your cruise ship stays late in port and you choose to dine off the ship. Cuisine in Europe is varied, but Europeans tend to eat a leisurely meal at lunch; in most ports there are quicker and simpler alternatives for those who just want to grab a quick bite before returning to the ship. Note that several Baltic countries do not use the euro, including Denmark, Estonia, Finland, Latvia, Poland, Russia, and Sweden. Price categories in those countries are based on the euro-equivalent costs of eating in restaurants.

COPENHAGEN, DENMARK

Updated by
Gelu Sulugiuc

Copenhagen—"København" in Danish—has no glittering skylines, few killer views, and only a handful of meager skyscrapers. Bicycles glide alongside manageable traffic at a pace that's utterly human. The early-morning air in the pedestrian streets of the city's core, Strøget, is redolent of freshly baked bread and soap-scrubbed storefronts. If there's such a thing as a cozy city, this is it. Filled with museums, restaurants, cafés, and lively nightlife, the city has its greatest resource in its spirited inhabitants. The imaginative, unconventional, and affable Copenhageners exude an egalitarian philosophy that embraces nearly all lifestyles and leanings. Despite a tumultuous history, Copenhagen survives as the liveliest Scandinavian capital, with some excellent galleries and museums. With its backdrop of copper towers and crooked rooftops, the venerable city is amused by playful street musicians and performers, soothed by one of the highest standards of living in the world, and spangled by the thousand lights and gardens of Tivoli.

ESSENTIALS

CURRENCY

The monetary unit in Denmark is the krone (DKr), divided into 100 øre. Even though Denmark hasn't adopted the euro, the Danish krone is firmly bound to it at about DKr 7.5 to 1€, with only minimal fluctuations in exchange rates.

HOURS

Museum hours vary, though the major collections are open Tuesday through Sunday from 10 to 5. Stores are open weekdays from 9:30 to 5:30 (or sometimes 7).

TELEPHONES

Tri-band GSM phones work in Denmark. You can buy prepaid phone cards at telecom shops, news vendors, and tobacconists in all towns and cities. Phone cards can be used for local or international calls.

COMING ASHORE

The city's main cruise port at Langelinie Pier is one of the best in Europe. Although it's a 10-minute drive or 30-minute walk from the downtown core, the port is within walking distance of the Little Mermaid and the attractions of the seafront. Taxis wait outside the cruise terminal. The on-site Copenhagen Cruise Information Center is run by the city tourist office, and there is a selection of shops housed in the renovated old wharf warehouses selling typical souvenirs.

Some ships dock at the Freeport Terminal, which is a further 30 minutes on foot from the downtown core (i.e., a full hour's walk from the center). Taxis wait outside the terminal, and the cost is around DKr 125 for the trip into town. A small number of ships (primarily smaller vessels) dock at the quayside at Nordre Toldbod, which sits beside the Little Mermaid and is a 10-minute walk from the city center; however, there are no passenger facilities here.

City Bikes is a citywide project offering free bike rental. There's a City Bike rack at Langelinie Pier, so you can pick up a bike here and cycle along the waterfront to the center or take a bike from a rack in the center to cycle back to the ship at the end of your day.

A water-taxi service to the city center leaves from the end of Langelinie Pier hourly. The boat stops at various parts of the city, and you can hop on and hop off as you wish. A one-day ticket costs DKr 40. A taxi direct to downtown (10 to 15 minutes) costs around DKr 70–DKr 90 from Langelinie.

There is a dedicated cruise lounge at the Illum department store on Strøget in the city center, where you can wait for transfers, leave purchases for later collection, have a free coffee, or rest during your day ashore.

Car rentals cost around DKr 1,185 per day for an economy manual vehicle; however, public transport is much more convenient for a short city visit. The metro and bus services are clean and efficient, with tickets costing DKr 24 for a single-ride two-zone ticket for one hour of unlimited travel; stamp your ticket as you board the bus or before boarding the train.

Copenhagen

NØRREBRO

ØSTERBRO

TO ASSISTENS KIERKEGÅRD

Øster Anlæg

Statens Museum for Kunst

Botanisk Have

Kongens Have

Ørsteds Parken

DOWNTOWN

Vor Frue Kirken

Gammel- torv

Østergade

Strøget

Rådhus Pl.

Rådhus

Nationalmuseet

Christiansborg Slot

Tivoli

Central Railway Station (Hovedbanegården)

Ny Carlsberg Glyptotek

VESTERBRO

Carlsberg Bryggeri

TO ARKEN

KEY

7 Tourist
Information

Rail Lines

TO
CRUISE TERMINAL

**Den Lille
Havfrue**

Dag Hammarskjölds Al.

Østbaneg.

Folke Bernadottes Al.

Forbindelsesv.

Langelinie

Østerport
Station

Oslo
Plads

Churchill-
parken

Yderhavn

NYBODER

Skt. Kongensg.

Grøningen

Esplanaden

Rigensg.

Kronprincessestr.

Fredericiag.

Bredg.

Amalieg.

SANKT ANNÆ
KVARTER

Store Kongensg.

Toldbodg.

Dronningens Tværg.

Bredg.

Amalienborg

Adelg.

Borgerg.

Amalieg.

Sankt Annæ Plads

**Trapholt Museum
for Moderne Kunst**

5

Inderhavn

HOLMEN

Ny Østerg.

Kr. Bernikg.

Nyhavn Canal

Nyhavn

Kongens
Nytorv

Bremerholm

Heibergsg.

Holmenskanal

Holbergsg.

Holmenskanal

Havneg.

Christiansborg
Slotsplads

Børsg.

Chr.
IV's
Bro

CHRISTIANSHAVN

Stadsgraven

Christians Brygge

Knippelsbro

Strandg.

Wildersg.

Torveg.

Christianshavn

Bådsmandsstr.

Skt Annæg.

0   1/4 mi

0   1/4 km

Dronningensg.

Princessg.

Langerbrog.

GETTING TO THE AIRPORT

If you do not purchase airport transfers from your cruise line, there are easy and inexpensive options for travel between the cruise terminals and the airport.

For Langelinie Pier, take the metro (DKr 28.50) upstairs in the airport train station at Terminal 3. Trains depart every 4 minutes during the day and every 15 minutes during night hours. There are two possible routes to and from the airport to Langelinie Pier: Either get off at Copenhagen Central Station and then take a taxi to the cruise terminal, or get off at Østerport Station (three more minutes of travel) and take Bus 26 (DKr 25), which stops at the cruise terminal. The 20-minute taxi ride between airport and pier costs around DKr 250.

For Freeport Terminal, take the metro to Copenhagen Central Station (DKr 28.50); a taxi from the station to the terminal will cost around DKr 75. A taxi direct from the airport to Freeport Terminal will cost around DKr 300.

> **COPENHAGEN BEST BETS**
>
> **Tivoli Gardens.** One of Europe's finest and most famous planned green spaces, Tivoli is part formal garden, part woodland, part theme park.
>
> **Amalianborg Palace.** These rococo palaces, built by the Royal Family at the height of Danish influence, are architectural delights filled with artistic treasures gathered from around Europe.
>
> **The Little Mermaid.** This diminutive statue is the city's most famous landmark, and though she's a little disappointing in real life, you haven't been to Copenhagen if you don't say hello to her.

EXPLORING COPENHAGEN

★ **Amalienborg.** The four identical rococo buildings occupying this square have housed royals since 1784. It's still the queen's winter residence. The Christian VIII palace across from the royal's wing houses the Amalienborg Museum, which displays the second part of the Royal Collection (the first is at Rosenborg Slot) and chronicles royal lifestyles between 1863 and 1947. Here you can view the study of King Christian IX (1818–1906) and the drawing room of his wife, Queen Louise. Rooms are packed with royal heirlooms and treasures.

In the square's center is a magnificent equestrian statue of King Frederik V by the French sculptor Jacques François Joseph Saly. It reputedly cost as much as all the buildings combined. Every day at noon, the Royal Guard and band march from Rosenborg Slot through the city for the changing of the guard. At noon on Queen Margrethe's birthday, April 16, crowds of Danes gather to cheer their monarch, who stands and waves from her balcony. On Amalienborg's harbor side is the garden of Amaliehaven, at the foot of which the queen's ship often docks. ⊠ *Christian VIII's Palace, Amalienborg Pl., Frederiksstaden* ☎ *33/12–21–86* ⊕ *dkks.dk/amalienborgmuseet* ⊠ *Museum: DKr 65* ☉ *Museum: May–Oct. daily 10–4, Nov.–Dec. Tues.–Sun. 11–4.*

Carlsberg Bryggeri (*Carlsberg Brewery*). A large, ornate chimney makes this mid-19th-century brewery visible from a distance. J. C. Jacobson, one of Denmark's most important historical figures, named the brewery after his son Carl; "berg," or mountain, signifies the brewery's location on Valby Hill. The four giant granite elephants that guard the main entrance illustrate that Jacobsen was a well-traveled man who adored art. The elephants are in fact inspired by Bernini's famous obelisk in Rome. In the visitor center, new interactive displays, also in English, take you step by step through the brewing process. At the end of your visit, you're rewarded with a complimentary beer sampling. The Carlsberg Museum, also on the grounds, tells the story of the Jacobsen family, their beer empire, and Carlsberg's extensive philanthropy, which still greatly benefits Danish culture. Large-scale beer production has now moved outside of the city and the old brewery complex is being transformed into a combined neighborhood for arts, culture, and living. ⊠ *Gamle Carlsberg Vej 11, Vesterbro* ☎ *33/27–12–82* ⊕ *www.visitcarlsberg.com* ⊠ *DKr 70 (includes 2 beers or soft drinks)* ⊙ *Tues.–Sun. 10–5.*

Fodor's Choice
★

Christiansborg Slot. Surrounded by canals on three sides, the massive granite Christiansborg Castle is where the queen officially receives guests. From 1441 until the fire of 1795, it was used as the royal residence. Even though the first two castles on the site were burned, Christiansborg remains an impressive neobaroque and neoclassical compound. It now houses parliament and the prime minister's office. ⊠ *Slotsholmen, (area around Christiansborg; bordered by Boørsgade, Vindebrogade, and Frederiksholms Kanal), Centrum.*

Kongelige Repræsantationslokaler (*Royal Reception Chambers*). At the Kongelige Repræsantationslokaler, you're asked to don slippers to protect the floors in this impossibly grand space. ⊠ *Christiansborg Slot, Slotsholmen* ☎ *33/92–64–92* ⊠ *DKr 70* ⊙ *Tours: May–Sept., daily at 3, Oct.–Apr., Tues–Sun., 3.*

Ruins of Bishop Absalon's castle. While Christiansborg was being rebuilt around 1900, the national museum excavated the ruins of Bishop Absalon's castle beneath it. The resulting dark, subterranean maze contains fascinating models and architectural relics. ⊠ *Christiansborg Slot, Slotsholmen* ☎ *33/92–64–92* ⊠ *DKr 40* ⊙ *May–Sept., daily 10–5; Oct.–Apr., Tues.–Sun., 10–5.*

Christianshavn. Cobbled avenues, antique street lamps, and Left Bank charm make up one of the oldest neighborhoods in the city. Today the area harbors restaurants, cafés, and shops, and its ramparts are edged with green areas and walking paths, making it the perfect neighborhood for an afternoon amble.

Den Lille Havfrue (*The Little Mermaid*). Somewhat overhyped, this 1913 statue commemorates Hans Christian Andersen's lovelorn Little Mermaid. (You may want to read the original Hans Christian Andersen tale in advance; it's a heart-wrenching story that's a far cry from the Disney animated movie.) Donated to the city by Carl Jacobsen, the son of the founder of Carlsberg Breweries, the innocent waif has also been the subject of some cruel practical jokes, including decapitation

5

and the loss of an arm, but she's currently in one piece. The Langelinie promenade is thronged with Danes and visitors making their pilgrimage to the statue, especially on sunny Sundays. Although the statue itself is modest, the views of the surrounding harbor are not. ⊠ *Langelinie promenade, Østerbro.*

Fodor'sChoice   **Nationalmuseet** (*National Museum*). One of the best museums of its kind
★   in Europe, the Nationalmuseet is inside an 18th-century royal residence
☻   that's peaked by massive overhead windows. Extensive permanent exhibits chronicle Danish cultural history from prehistoric to modern times. The museum has one of the largest collections of Stone Age tools in the world, as well as Egyptian, Greek, and Roman antiquities. The exhibit on Danish prehistory features a great section on Viking times. The children's museum, with replicas of period clothing and a scalable copy of a real Viking ship, makes history fun for those under 12. Displays have English labels, and the do-it-yourself walking tour, History of Denmark in 60 Minutes, offers a good introduction to Denmark; the guide is free at the information desk. ⊠ *Frederiksholms Kanal 12, Centrum* ☎ *33/13–44–11* ⊕ *www.natmus.dk* ⊠ *Free* ☉ *Tues.–Sun. 10–5.*

★   **Ny Carlsberg Glyptotek.** The exquisite antiquities and a world-class collection of impressionist masterpieces make this one of Copenhagen's most important museums. The neoclassical building was donated in 1888 by Carl Jacobsen, son of the founder of the Carlsberg Brewery. Surrounding its lush indoor garden, a series of rooms house works by Pissarro, Degas, Monet, Sisley, Rodin, and Gauguin. The museum is also renowned for its extensive assemblage of Egyptian and Greek pieces, not to mention Europe's finest collection of Roman portraits and the best collection of Etruscan art outside Italy. A modern wing, designed by the acclaimed Danish architect Henning Larsen, provides a luminous entry to the French painting section. From June to September, guided English-language tours start at 2. The café overlooking the winter garden is well known among Copenhageners for its Sunday brunch. ⊠ *Dantes Pl. 7, Centrum* ☎ *33/41–81–41* ⊕ *www.glyptoteket. dk* ⊠ *DKr 50; free Sun.* ☉ *Tues.–Sun. 11–5.*

★   **Statens Museum for Kunst.** Old-master paintings—including works by
☻   Rubens, Rembrandt, Titian, El Greco, and Fragonard—as well as a comprehensive array of antique and 20th-century Danish art make up the National Art Gallery collection. Also notable is the modern art, which includes pieces by Henri Matisse, Edvard Munch, Henri Laurens, Emil Nolde, and Georges Braque. The space also contains a children's museum, which puts on shows for different age groups at kids' eye-level. Wall texts are in English. The bookstore and café are also worth a visit. ⊠ *Sølvgade 48–50, Østerbro* ☎ *33/74–84–94* ⊕ *www.smk.dk* ⊠ *Museum: Free. Special exhibitions: DKr 95* ☉ *Tues. and Thurs.–Sun. 10–5, Wed. 10–8.*

★   **Strøget.** Though it is referred to by one name, the city's pedestrian spine, pronounced *Stroy*-et, is actually a series of five streets: Frederiksberggade, Nygade, Vimmelskaftet, Amagertorv, and Østergade. By midmorning, particularly on Saturday, it is congested with people, baby strollers, and street performers. Past the swank and trendy—and sometimes flashy and trashy—boutiques of **Frederiksberggade** is the double

square of **Gammeltorv** (Old Square) and **Nytorv** (New Square). In addition to shopping, you can enjoy Strøget for strolling, as hundreds do. In summer the sidewalks have a festive street-fair atmosphere.

Fodor's Choice ★ ☺ **Tivoli.** Copenhagen's best-known attraction, conveniently next to its main train station, attracts an astounding 4 million people from mid-April to mid-September. Tivoli is more than just an amusement park: among its attractions are a pantomime theater, an open-air stage, 38 restaurants (some of them very elegant), and frequent concerts, which cover the spectrum from classical to rock to jazz. Fantastic flower exhibits color the lush gardens and float on the swan-filled ponds.

The park was established in the 1840s, when Danish architect George Carstensen persuaded a worried King Christian VIII to let him build an amusement park on the edge of the city's fortifications, rationalizing that "when people amuse themselves, they forget politics." The Tivoli Guard, a youth version of the Queen's Royal Guard, performs every day. Try to see Tivoli at least once by night, when 100,000 colored lanterns illuminate the Chinese pagoda and the main fountain. Some evenings there are also fireworks displays. Call to check the season's opening and closing dates as well as family discounts. Tivoli is also open select hours around Halloween and from mid-November until late December. ⊠ *Vesterbrog. 3 (on border of Vesterbro district), Centrum* ☎ *33/15–10–01* ⊕ *www.tivoli.dk* ☞ *Grounds: DKr 95. Unlimited ride pass: DKr 199* ☉ *Apr.–Sept., Sun.–Thurs. 11 am to 10 or 11 pm, Fri. 11 am–12:30 am, Sat. 11–midnight.*

Fodor's Choice ★ **Trapholt Museum for Moderne Kunst** (*Trapholt Museum of Modern Art*). Just east of town is the Trapholt Museum for Moderne Kunst, one of Denmark's largest—and most highly acclaimed—modern-art museums. Rising over the banks of the Kolding Fjord, this sprawling white complex has been artfully incorporated into its surroundings, affording lovely water and parkland views from its floor-to-ceiling windows. A collection of 20th-century Danish paintings is displayed in the light-filled galleries; it includes works by Anna Ancher, Ejler Bille, Egill Jakobsen, J.A. Jerichau, Jais Nielsen, Richard Mortensen, Aksel Jørgensen, and Franciska Clausen. A true highlight is the Danish Furniture Museum, housed in a specially designed annex that is accessed via a circular ramp topped by a skylight. The superbly displayed collection includes the world's largest assemblage of Danish-designed chairs, offering a unique historical overview of the birth and popularization of the nation's furniture design. The museum keeps its furniture storage room open to the public, so you can peruse the entire collection even when it's not officially on display.

The Danish ceramics collection, one of the largest in Denmark, is also well worth a look, featuring works by Thorvald Bindesbøll and one-of-a-kind ceramics by Axel Salto, whose pieces often resemble living organisms. Famous designer Arne Jacobsen's summer cottage was moved to Trapholt and opened on its grounds. Café Trapholt serves coffee, beverages, and light meals. The gift shop sells local and international art and design-related gifts. ⊠ *Æblehaven 23, Kolding* ☎ *76/30–05–30* ⊕ *www. trapholt.dk* ☞ *DKr 65* ☉ *Tues.–Sun. 10–5, Wed. 10–8.*

5

SHOPPING

A showcase for world-famous Danish design and craftsmanship, Copenhagen seems to have been set up with shoppers in mind. In fact, its very name (København in Danish), means the "merchant's harbor," because it was once a major center of trade. The spirit of those days remains, with countless specialty shops in almost every corner of the city. The best buys are such luxury items as amber, crystal, porcelain, silver, and furs. Danish clothing design is now coming into fashion and is considered one of the nation's most important exports.

Look for offers and sales (*tilbud* or *udsalg* in Danish) and check antiques and secondhand shops for classics at cut-rate prices. Although prices are inflated by a hefty 25% Value-Added Tax (Danes call it *moms*), non–European Union citizens can receive about an 18% refund if they are willing to do the paperwork. For more details and a list of all tax-free shops, ask at the tourist office for a copy of the *Tax-Free Shopping Guide, or visit the website Global Blue* (⊕ *www.global-blue.com*).

Georg Jensen. This elegant, austere shop is aglitter with sterling, which is what you'd expect from one of the most recognized names in international silver. Jensen has its own museum next door. ⊠ *Amagertorv 4, Centrum* ☎ *33/11–40–80* ⊕ *www.georgjensen.com*.

Illums Bolighus. Part gallery and part department store, Illums Bolighus will surround you with cutting-edge Danish and international design—art glass, porcelain, silverware, carpets, and loads of grown-up toys. Staff will help you file your value-added tax refund on site—don't forget to get some documents stamped at customs upon leaving Denmark and mail them back. ⊠ *Amagertorv 10, Downtown* ☎ *33/14–19–41* ⊕ *www.illumsbolighus.dk*.

Information Center for Danish Crafts and Design. The Information Center for Danish Crafts and Design provides helpful information on galleries, shops, and workshops specializing in Danish crafts and design, including jewelry, ceramics, wooden toys, and furniture. Its website has listings and reviews of the city's best crafts shops. ⊠ *Kongens Nytorv 1E, 1., Centrum* ☎ *33/12–61–62* ⊕ *www.danishcrafts.dk*.

Royal Copenhagen Factory Outlet. The Royal Copenhagen Factory Outlet has a good deal of stock, often at reduced prices. You can also buy Holmegaard Glass at the Royal Copenhagen store in Centrum and this factory outlet. ⊠ *Søndre Fasanvej 9, Frederiksberg* ☎ *38/34–10–04* ⊕ *www.royalcopenhagen.com* ☉ *Weekdays 10–6, Sat. 10–2.*

WHERE TO EAT

$

SCANDINAVIAN

★

✕ **Ida Davidsen.** This five-generations-old, world-renowned lunch spot is synonymous with smørrebrød, the Danish open-face sandwich. The often-packed dining area is dimly lighted, with worn wooden tables and news clippings of famous visitors on the walls. Creative sandwiches include the H. C. Andersen, with liver pâté, bacon, and tomatoes. The terrific duck is smoked by Ida's husband, Adam, and served alongside a horseradish-spiked cabbage salad. ⑤ *Average main: Dkr 200* ⊠ *Store Kongensgade 70, Centrum* ☎ *33/91–36–55* ⊕ *www.idadavidsen.dk* ⌁ *Reservations essential* ☉ *No dinner. Closed weekends and July.*

$$ ✕**Søren K.** Occupying a bright corner of the Royal Library's mod-
EUROPEAN ern Black Diamond extension, this cool-toned restaurant, with clean
lines, blond-wood furnishings, and recessed lighting, serves French-
Scandinavian concoctions. For waterfront views, choose a table inside
up against the glass walls or outside. Signature dishes include dried
Danish ham with thyme and *beurre noir* or scallops, corn purée, and
watercress. The menu always has vegetarian dishes and a fish of the day.
It's the perfect lunchtime spot, with a two-course menu for about DKr
200. ⑤ *Average main: Dkr 205* ⊠ *Søren Kierkegaards Pl. 1, Centrum*
☎ *33/47–49–49* ⊕ *www.soerenk.dk* ⊘ *Closed Sun.*

WHERE TO STAY

$$ 🏨**Copenhagen Marriott Hotel.** This large Marriott on the waterfront is a
HOTEL well-oiled machine. **Pros:** all rooms have both tub and shower combo
and either city or canal-side views. **Cons:** no restaurants nearby; small
windows in the rooms; slightly generic. ⑤ *Rooms from: Dkr 1899*
⊠ *Kalvebod Brygge 5, Centrum* ☎ *88/33–99–00* ⊕ *www.marriott.com/
cphdk* ⇌ *401 rooms, 10 suites* ⦿| *No meals.*

$$$$ 🏨**Copenhagen Strand.** You can't stay closer to the harbor than here.
HOTEL **Pros:** close to city attractions, most bathrooms have both a tub and
shower. **Cons:** restaurant only serves breakfast; tight quarters; morning
street noise; very expensive. ⑤ *Rooms from: Dkr 4000* ⊠ *Havneg. 37,
Centrum* ☎ *33/48–99–00* ⊕ *www.copenhagenstrand.dk* ⇌ *174 rooms,
2 suites* ⦿| *Breakfast.*

$$ 🏨**Radisson Blu Scandinavia Hotel.** South across the Stadsgraven from
HOTEL Christianshavn stands one of Denmark's largest hotels, as well as
Copenhagen's only casino. **Pros:** good-size rooms with great city views;
several on-site restaurants. **Cons:** it's about a mile to Centrum; feels
like the business hotel it is, which isn't to everyone's taste. ⑤ *Rooms
from: Dkr 1605* ⊠ *Amager Blvd. 70, Amager* ☎ *33/96–50–00* ⊕ *www.
radissonblu.dk/scandinaviahotel-koebenhavn* ⇌ *542 rooms, 42 suites*
⦿| *No meals.*

GDAŃSK, POLAND

Updated by   Gdańsk is special to Poles—and to Scandinavians and Germans, who
Dorota Wąsik   visit the region in great numbers. From 1308 to 1945 Gdańsk was an
independent city-state called Danzig. In 1997 Gdańsk celebrated its
1,000th year as a Baltic city. It remains well known as the cradle of
the anti-Communist workers' movement that came to be known as
Solidarność (Solidarity)—after the collapse of the Soviet bloc in 1989,
Solidarity leader Lech Wałesa became president of Poland in the nation's
first free elections since World War II. Although Gdańsk was almost
entirely destroyed during World War II, the streets of its Główne Miasto
(Main Town) have been lovingly restored and still retain their historical
and cultural richness. The Stare Miasto (Old Town) contains several
churches and the beautifully reconstructed Ratusz Główny (Old Town
Hall). At the north end of the Old Town sit the shipyards that captivated
world attention during the 1970s and '80s but have since undergone

a difficult restructuring process. It might be tempting to see its lot as a metaphor to the last few decades of Polish history. Gdańsk is part of the so-called Tri-city—the other two of the triplets being Sopot, a fashionable 19th-century resort, and Gdynia, a 1920s, modernist-style port town, where most cruise ships arrive. The three components of the Tri-city are not very far apart, and they are conveniently linked by a suburban rail system (SKM).

ESSENTIALS

CURRENCY
The Złoty. U.S. currency is not accepted, and credit cards are not universally accepted, especially in smaller shops and eateries. ATMs are widespread.

HOURS
Shopping hours are generally weekdays from 7 am until 6 or 7 pm, with shorter hours on the weekend. Museums are typically open Tuesday through Sunday from 10 am until 4 pm.

TELEPHONES
Most international mobile phones (3G included) work in Poland, but do check your roaming charges in advance. Major local telecom companies are Era, Plus, and Orange. It is easy to get a prepaid phone and recharge it as you need it (you can get the cards at mobile operators' shops, newsagents, gas stations, even supermarkets). Due to the fast growth of the mobile network, there are fewer public phones now, but you will still find them. They operate with phone cards, which can be bought at newsstands. Public phones support international calls.

COMING ASHORE
Most cruise ships arrive at Gdynia, either at the Francuskie (French) or Pomorskie (Pomeranian) Quay. The port is within a 20-minute walk (about 1 km) of the SKM (suburban rail) stop, which is right next to the main railway station in Gdynia. This train is the easiest and most economical means of transportation within the Tri-city, and the ride into Gdańsk city center takes about 30 minutes. Taxis are readily available, but a ride between Gdańsk to Gdynia will cost you about zł 100 .

A few ships arrive in Gdańsk itself. These will dock at two sites in the outer harbor of the city: Oliwskie Quay on the east bank and Westerplatte Quay on the west bank. Both lie 6 km (3.7 miles) from the downtown center. Facilities at Oliwskie Quay, the bigger of the two, include shops and taxi kiosks. It is 1 km (½ mile) to the Oliwa train station for the journey into downtown Gdańsk, or 300 meters to a tram stop (Routes 2, 5, 10, 14, and 15 head into the city). Westerplatte Quay has almost no facilities, with only restrooms and a taxi kiosk. Bus route 106 travels into the city. The downtown core can be easily explored on foot.

Car rentals are not useful for exploring the city, but would allow you to visit the surrounding Pomeranian region. An economy manual vehicle is approximately €63 per day. Companies will pick you up at the port but may add an extra charge. Taxis or limousines can be hired for touring. Taxi rates are zł 5–zł 7 at pickup then zł 3 per km.

EXPLORING GDAŃSK

★ **Brama Wyżynna** (*High Gate*). The historic entrance to the Old Town of Gdańsk is marked by this magnificent Renaissance gate, which marks the beginning of the so-called Royal Route, along which the king passed through the city on his annual visit. The gate is adorned with the flags of Poland, Gdańsk, and the Prussian kingdom. Its builder, Hans Kramer of Dresden, erected it as a link in the chain of modern fortifications put up to frame the western city borders between 1574 and 1576. The brick gate was renovated and decorated in 1588 by Flemish sculptor Willem van den Blocke, whose decorations you can still see today. ⊠ *Off Wały Jagiellońskie, at ul. Długa, Stare Miasto.*

Brama Zielona (*Green Gate*). The eastern entrance to the medieval city of Gdańsk is at the water's edge. Construction, supervised by Regnier of Amsterdam and Hans Kramer of Dresden, lasted from 1568 to 1571. This 16th-century gate also doubled as a royal residence. Unfortunately, the name no longer fits: the gate is now painted brown. ⊠ *At eastern end of Długi Targ, Stare Miasto.*

Brama Złota (*Golden Gate*). Brama Złota Just behind the Brama Wyżynna, the Golden Gate was the second through which the king passed on the Royal Route. This structure dates from 1614, and combines characteristics of both the Italian and Dutch Renaissance. It was built to the design of Abraham van den Blocke. The stone figures (by Pieter Ringering) along the parapet (on the Wały Jagiellońskie facade) represent allegories of the city's citizen's virtues: Prudence, Justice, Piety, and Concord. On the Długa street facade there are allegories of Peace, Freedom, Fortune, and Fame—the pursuits of Gdańsk city over the centuries. Next to the Golden Gate squats the house of the **St George's Brotherhood**, erected by Glotau between 1487 and 1494 in the late-Gothic style. ⊠ *Off Wały Jagiellońskie, at western end of ul. Długa, Stare Miasto.*

★ **Dwór Artusa** (*Artus Mansion*). Behind the Fontanna Neptuna on Długi Targ, one of the more significant of the grand houses was constructed over a period from the 15th through the 17th centuries and is now a museum. The mansion was named for mythical English King Arthur, who otherwise has no affiliation with the place. This and the other stately mansions on the Długi Targ are reminders of the traders and aristocrats who once resided in this posh district. The court's elegant interior houses a huge, 40-foot-high Renaissance tiled stove, possibly the world's largest, a mid-16th-century masterpiece by George Stelzener. The mansion's collection also includes Renaissance furnishings, paintings, and holy figures. The building was the meeting place of the Gdańsk city nobles. ⊠ *Długi Targ 43, Stare Miasto* ☎ *058/346–33–58* 💳 *zł 10* 🕐 *Mon. 11–3, Tues.–Sat. 10–6, Sun. 11–6.*

Fodor's Choice **Fontanna Neptuna** (*Neptune Fountain*). One of the city's most distinctive
★ landmarks is the elaborately gilded, 17th-century fountain at the western
☾ end of Długi Targ. The fountain itself is perhaps the best-known symbol of Gdańsk, emphasizing its bond with the sea. It was sculpted by Peter Husen and Johann Rogge. The general conceptual design was developed by Abraham van den Blocke. The magnificent surrounding fencing was

added in 1634. Between 1757 and 1761 Johann Karl Stender remade the fountain chalice and plinth in the rococo style and added a whole array of sea creatures. ✉ *ul. Długa, east of Wały Jagiellońskie, Stare Miasto.*

Fodor's Choice ★ **Katedra w Oliwie** (*Oliwa Cathedral*). The district of Oliwa, northwest of the Old Town, is worth visiting if only for its magnificent cathedral complex. Originally part of a Cistercian monastery, the church was erected during the 13th century. Like most other structures in Poland, it has been rebuilt many times, resulting in a hodgepodge of styles from Gothic to Renaissance to rococo. The cathedral houses a **museum** as well as one of the most impressive rococo organs you're ever likely to hear—and see. It has more than 6,000 pipes, and when a special mechanism is activated, wooden angels ring bells and a wooden star climbs up a wooden sky. Demonstrations of the organ and a brief narrated church history are given almost hourly on weekdays in summer (May through September), less frequently on weekends and the rest of the year. ✉ *ul. Cystersów 10, Oliwa* ⊕ *www.archikatedraoliwa.pl* ☉ *Church daily; museum June–mid-Sept., weekdays 10–5, Sat. 10–3.*

> ## GDAŃSK BEST BETS
>
> **Stocznia Gdańska.** This shipyard was the seat of the social movement that began the downfall of Communism in Eastern Europe, so the site resonates with living history.
>
> **Stroll the lanes and alleyways of the Old Town.** This district is a triumph of Renaissance architecture and a riot of ornate gables, cornices and lintels.
>
> **Kościół Najświetszej Marii Panny.** This is the largest brick-built church in the world and the largest church of any kind in Poland.

Fodor's Choice ★ **Kościół Najświetszej Marii Panny** (*St. Mary's Church*). The largest brick church in the world—and the largest church of any kind in Poland—St. Mary's is on the north side of ulica Piwna. The sanctuary can accommodate 25,000 people. This enormous 14th-century church underwent major restoration after World War II. Although it originally held 22 altars, 15 of them have been relocated to museums in Gdańsk and Warsaw. The highlight of a visit is the climb up the hundreds of steps to the top of the church tower. The church also contains a 500-year-old, 25-foot-high astronomical clock that has only recently been restored to working order after years of neglect. It keeps track of solar and lunar progressions, and it displays the signs of the zodiac, something of an anomaly in a Catholic church. ✉ *Podkramarska 5, at ul. Piwna, Stare Miasto* ⊕ *www.bazylikamariacka.pl* 🎫 *zł 4 (church); zł 5 (tower)* ☉ *Church Mon.–Sat. 9–5, Sun. 1–5; tower Apr.–Oct. only.*

Kościół świetej Brygidy (*St. Brigitte's Church*). This church, a few blocks north of the shipyards, is a prime example of the fundamental link in the Polish consciousness between Catholicism and political dissent. After the Communist government declared martial law in 1981 in an attempt to force Solidarity to disband, the union's members began meeting here secretly during celebrations of mass. A statue of Pope John Paul II can be seen in front of the church. ✉ *ul. Profesorska 17, near Ratusz Główny (Old Town Hall), Stare Miasto* ⊕ *www.brygida.gdansk.pl.*

5

Kościół świetej Katarzyny (*St. Catherine's Church*). The former parish church in Gdańsk's Old Town is supposedly the oldest church in the city: its construction was begun in the 1220s; the tower was constructed in the 1480s; the carillon of 37 bells was added in 1634. The 17th-century astronomer Jan Hevelius is buried in the presbytery of the church, below which lies what's left of the town's oldest Christian cemetery (which dates from the 10th century). At this writing, the church is undergoing renovation but can still be visited. ⊠ *Wielki Młyn, Stare Miasto* ☎ *058/301–15–95* ⊕ *www.gdansk.karmelici.pl.*

Muzeum Archeologiczne Gdańska (*Gdańsk Archaeological Museum*). Gdańsk's small archaeological museum displays Slavic tribal artifacts, including jewelry, pottery, boats, and bones. ⊠ *ul. Mariacka 25–26, Stare Miasto* ☎ *058/322–21–00* ⊕ *www.archeologia.pl* 💰 *Zł 6* ⊙ *Tues.–Sun. 10–4.*

★ **Muzeum Narodowe w Gdańsku** (*National Museum in Gdańsk*). The former Franciscan monastery, just south of the old walls of the Main Town, exhibits 14th- to 20th-century art and ethnographic collections. Hans Memling's triptych *Last Judgment* is the jewel of the collection. ⊠ *ul. Toruńska 1, off ul. Okopowa, Stare Miasto* ☎ *058/301–70–61* ⊕ *www.muzeum.narodowe.gda.pl* 💰 *zł 10 (free Sun.)* ⊙ *Oct.–April, Tue.–Fri. 9–4, Sat. and Sun. 10–5; May–Sept. Tues.–Sun. 10–5; June–Aug., Thurs. 12–7.*

Muzeum Sztuki Współczesnej (*Modern Art Museum*). Two museums can be found in a beautiful park surrounding the cathedral in Oliwa in the former Abbots' Palace. The Modern Art Museum has a large collection of works by Polish artists from the inter-war period onward. The Ethnographic Museum has the same hours and contact information but a separate admission fee. ⊠ *Pałac Opatów, Cystersów 18, Oliwa* ☎ *058/552–12–71* ⊕ *www.muzeum.narodowe.gda.pl* 💰 *Zł 10* ⊙ *Tues.–Sun. 9–4.*

Muzeum Etnograficzne (*Ethnographic Museum*). Connected to the Modern Art Museum, administratively and physically, is the Muzeum Etnograficzne, in the former Abbots' Granary. The museum display has fine examples of local crafts from the 19th century and also has an interesting display of amber folk jewelry. It has a separate entrance from the Modern Art Museum and a separate admission fee, but the hours and other contact information are the same for both museums. ⊠ *ul. Cystersów 19, Oliwa* ☎ *058/552–12–71* ⊕ *www.muzeum.narodowe.gda.pl* 💰 *zł 8* ⊙ *Tues.–Sun. 9–4.*

★ **Ratusz Główny** (*Old Town Hall*). Although Gdańsk's original town hall was completely destroyed during World War II, a careful reconstruction of the exterior and interior now recreates the glory of Gdańsk's medieval past. During the summer season the tower is accessible to visitors and well worth climbing for the view. Inside, the **Muzeum Historii Miasta Gdańska** (Gdańsk Historical Museum) covers more than five centuries of Gdańsk's history in exhibits that include paintings, sculptures, and weapons. ⊠ *ul. Długa 47, Stare Miasto* ☎ *058/301–48–72* 💰 *Museum zł 10 (free Tues.)* ⊙ *Tues. 10–3, Wed.–Sat. 10–4, Sun. 11–4.*

Fodor'sChoice
★ **Stocznia Gdańska** (*Gdańsk Shipyard*). Stocznia Gdańska Three huge and somber crosses perpetually draped with flowers stand outside the

gates of the former Lenin Shipyards, which gave birth to the Solidarity movement. The crosses outside the entrance to the shipyards are the **Pomnik Poległych Stoczniowców** (Monument to Fallen Shipyard Workers) There are also plaques that commemorate the struggle, and a quotation by Pope John Paul II inspired by his visit to the monument in 1987: "The Grace of God could not have created anything better; in this place, silence is a scream." Formerly inside the shipyard gates (and now a bit further away), the **Roads to Freedom** exhibition once consisted of a number of symbolic gates, which until recently led to a multimedia exhibition in the historic BPH room on Plac Solidarności, where the Gdańsk Agreements were signed. The BPH room, which has been renovated, reopened in 2007 in a new location at Wały Piastowskie Street (a short walk from the shipyard itself, halfway between the shipyards and the Main Railway Station). The exhibition traces the beginning and development of the Solidarity movement, taking you on a virtual tour through 1980s Poland. ⊠ *Wały Piastowskie 24, Stare Miasto* ☎ *058/308–44–28* ⊕ *www.ecs.gda.pl* ▢ *Zł 6* ⊙ *Oct.–Apr., Tues.–Sun. 10–5; May–Sept., Tues.–Sun. 10–6.*

Żuraw Gdański (*Harbor Crane*). Żuraw Gdański, built in 1444, Gdańsk's crane was medieval Europe's largest—and today it's also Europe's oldest. It used to play the double role of a port crane and city gate. The structure was given its present shape between 1442 and 1444. Today it houses the **Muzeum Morskie** (Maritime Museum), with a collection of models of the ships constructed in the Gdańsk Shipyards since 1945. At the museum ticket office, inquire about tickets for tours of the *Sołdek,* a World War II battleship moored nearby on the canal. ⊠ *Szeroka 67, Stare Miasto* ☎ *058/301–69–38* ⊕ *www.cmm.pl* ▢ *Zł 8* ⊙ *Oct.–June, Tues.–Sun. 10–3; July–Sept., Tues.–Sun. 10–4.*

SHOPPING

The Tri-city is not a shopping destination. Nevertheless, Gdańsk and Sopot are good places to look for amber jewelry. You'll find souvenir shops and stores specializing in amber everywhere in town. In fact, they can't be missed they are so ubiquitous.

WHERE TO EAT

$$
POLISH

✕ **Czerwone Drzwi.** "Behind the red door" (that's what *Czerwone Drzwi* means in Polish) is an elegant café-cum-restaurant, a favorite with Gdańsk's fashionable people (with well-stocked wallets). The menu changes with the seasons. ⑤ *Average main: zł 50* ⊠ *ul. Piwna 52/53, Stare Miasto* ☎ *058/301–57–64* ⊕ *www.reddoor.gd.pl.*

$$$
SEAFOOD
Fodor's Choice
★

✕ **Pod Łososiem.** "The Salmon" is certainly the most famous restaurant in Gdańsk, with a long-standing reputation. It is memorable for its elegant baroque-era dining rooms, well-oiled maître d', attentive service, and excellent seafood (the menu also extends to game and fowl dishes). Try the salmon or smoked eel to start, followed by flounder or grilled trout. You may want to try the famous Goldwasser vodka—after all, this is its original source. ⑤ *Average main: zł 75* ⊠ *ul. Szeroka 52/53* ☎ *058/301–76–52* ⊕ *www.podlososiem.com.pl.*

HAMBURG, GERMANY

Updated by
Giulia Pines

Water—in the form of the Alster Lakes and the Elbe River—is Hamburg's defining feature and the key to the city's success. A harbor city with an international past, Hamburg is the most tolerant and open-minded of German cities. The media have made Hamburg their capital. Add to that the slick world of advertising and you have a populace of worldly and fashionable professionals. Not surprisingly, the city of movers and shakers is also the city with most of Germany's millionaires. Hamburg has been a major port for more than 1,000 years, but it reached the crest of its power during the 19th century. What you see today is the "new" Hamburg. World War II bombing raids destroyed more than half of the city. In spite of the 1940–44 raids, Hamburg now stands as a remarkably faithful replica of that glittering prewar city—a place of enormous style, verve, and elegance, with considerable architectural diversity, including turn-of-the-20th-century art nouveau buildings.

ESSENTIALS

CURRENCY
The euro. ATMs are common if you need cash.

HOURS
Stores are open Monday through Saturday from 8 am until 8 pm. Museum hours vary, but core hours are 10 am until 5 pm, with shorter opening on Sundays. Some state museums are closed on Monday.

TELEPHONES
Tri- and quad-band GSM phones should work in Germany, where the mobile system supports 3G technology. Phone cards for public phones are available at newsagents and will allow international calls. Major companies include Vodafone, T2, and T-Mobile.

COMING ASHORE
Hamburg has constructed a state-of-the-art cruise port and terminal as part of the regeneration of the Überseequartier district and surrounding HafenCity (a totally new city district). The main terminal, called HafnCity 2012, will have a hotel, restaurants, and direct metro access to downtown. The port is already accepting cruise ships, but not all facilities are open at this writing.

The older Hafn City Terminal is currently the main welcome terminal for cruise passenegers. It has a Welcome Center and a café. Public bus access is a short stroll through the terminal exit gate. Altona Terminal is a modern structure that provides facilities including shops and an information desk, but at present there are no cafés or restaurants. There is a bus stop for public transport into downtown Hamburg. Although city attractions are not far from the terminals, it would be sensible to take transportation to the attractions rather than walking, due to the heavy construction going on in the area.

Passengers exploring the city will find no benefit in renting a car; in fact, many major attractions are within walking distance of each other. But if you want to explore the area by car, a car rental costs €51 for a compact manual vehicle. Taxi meters start at €2.90, and the fare is €2

per km (½ miles) for the first 5 km, €1.90 for between 5 and 10 km and €1.40 for each km thereafter. Waiting time is €25 per hour. You can hail taxis on the street or at stands, or order one by phone.

The HVV, Hamburg's public transportation system, includes the U-bahn (subway), the S-bahn (suburban train), and buses. At this writing, a one-way fare starts at €2.85 for a one-zone ticket covers *one* unlimited ride in the Hamburg inner-city area. Tickets are available on all buses and at automatic machines in all stations and at most bus stops. A *Single-Tageskarte* (all-day ticket) for the inner-city districts, valid until 6 am the next day, costs €6.95. If you're traveling with family or friends, a *Partner Day Ticket* (group or family ticket) is a good value—a group of up to five adults (children count as half an adult) can travel for the entire day for €9.90–€19.30 (depending on the number of fare zones the ticket covers).

EXPLORING HAMBURG

Fodor's Choice
★ **Alster** (*Alster lakes*). These twin lakes provide downtown Hamburg with one of its most memorable vistas. The two lakes meet at the Lombardsbrücke and Kennedybrücke (Lombard and Kennedy bridges). The boat landing at the Jungfernstieg, below the Alsterpavillon, is the starting point for lake and canal cruises. Small sailboats and rowboats, hired from yards on the shores of the Alster, are very much a part of the summer scene. Every Hamburger dreams of living within sight of the Alster, but only the wealthiest can afford it. Some lucky millionaires own the magnificent garden properties around the Alster's perimeter, known as the Millionaire's Coast. But you don't have to be a guest on one of these estates to enjoy the waterfront—the Alster shoreline has 6 km (4 miles) of tree-lined public pathways. The Aussenalster 50-minute lake tour costs €12; the Fleet-Fahrt costs €19. The Dämmertour costs €19 and includes one drink. ■TIP➔ Popular among joggers, these trails are a lovely place for a stroll. Ⓜ *Jungfernstieg (U-bahn).*

★ **Deichstrasse.** The oldest residential area in the Old Town of Hamburg, which dates from the 14th century, now consists of lavishly restored houses from the 17th through the 19th century. Many of the original houses on Deichstrasse were destroyed in the Great Fire of 1842, which broke out in No. 38 and left approximately 20,000 people homeless; only a few of the early dwellings escaped its ravages. Today Deichstrasse and nearby Peterstrasse, which is steps away from the site of the former city wall, are of great historical interest. At No. 35–39 Peterstrasse, for example, is the replica of the baroque facade of the Beylingstift complex, built in 1751. Today, the Johannes Brahms Museum sits in No. 39, the composer's former home. All the buildings in the area have been painstakingly designed to look like the original buildings, thanks largely to nonprofit foundations. ⊠ *Altstadt* Ⓜ *Rödingsmarkt (U-bahn).*

★ **Tierpark Hagenbeck** (*Hagenbeck Zoo*). One of the country's oldest and most popular zoos is family-owned. Founded in 1907, it was the world's first zoo to let wild animals such as lions, elephants, chimpanzees, and others roam freely in vast, open-air corrals. In summer, you can ride a

pony. The Tropen-Aquarium sits on the same property as the zoo and a tour through it is like a trip around the world. Sea life, insects, curious reptiles, marvelous birds, and exotic mammals live in replicas of their natural habitat. Detailed recreations of deserts, oceans, rain forests, and jungles are home to birds, fish, mammals, insects, and reptiles from almost every continent, including a "Madagascar" village with black-tailed lemurs. ⊠ *2 Lokstedter Grenzstr. at Hamburg-Stellingen, Stellingen* ☎ *040/530–0330* ⊕ *www.hagenbeck.de* ⊡ *€20 for zoo, €14 for aquarium, €30 for zoo and aquarium* ☉ *Zoo: Mar.–June, Sept., and Oct., daily 9–6; July and Aug., daily 9–7; Nov.–Feb., daily 9–4:30. Aquarium: daily 9–6* Ⓜ *Hagenbecks Tierpark (U-bahn).*

> ### HAMBURG BEST BETS
>
> **Enjoy the art in the Kunsthalle.** With works ranging from the Renaissance to the modern era, the gallery offers a visual timeline of European art.
>
> **Tour the Rathaus.** The sumptuous decor of the Town Hall epitomizes the power and confidence of the 19th-century city.
>
> **Tour the Alster Lakes.** Wonderful vistas of the city pass by at a genteel pace when you take a boat cruise here.

★ **Jungfernstieg.** This wide promenade looking out over the Alster lakes is the beginning of the city's premier shopping district. Laid out in 1665, it used to be part of a muddy millrace that channeled water into the Elbe. Hidden from view behind the sedate facade of Jungfernstieg is a network of several small shopping centers that together account for almost a mile of shops selling everything from souvenirs to haute couture. Many of these passages have sprung up in the past two decades, but some have been here since the 19th century; the first glass-covered arcade, called Sillem's Bazaar, was built in 1845. ⊠ *Neustadt* Ⓜ *Jungfernstieg (U-bahn).*

★ **Hamburger Kunsthalle** (*Art Gallery*). One of the most important art museums in Germany, the Kunsthalle has 3,500 paintings, 650 sculptures, and a coin and medal collection that dates from the ancient Roman era. In the postmodern, cube-shaped building designed by Berlin architect O. M. Ungers, the **Galerie der Gegenwart** has housed a collection of international modern art since 1960, including works by Andy Warhol, Joseph Beuys, Georg Baselitz, and David Hockney. With 1,200 drawings and other visuals, graphic art is well represented, including works by Pablo Picasso and Horst Janssen, a Hamburg artist famous for his satirical worldview. In the other areas of the museum, you can view works by local artists dating from the 16th century. The outstanding collection of German Romantic paintings includes pieces by Caspar David Friedrich. Paintings by Holbein, Rembrandt, Van Dyck, Tiepolo, and Canaletto are also on view, while late-19th-century impressionism is represented by works by Leibl, Liebermann, Manet, Monet, and Renoir. ⊠ *Glockengiesserwall, Altstadt* ☎ *040/4281–31200* ⊕ *www.hamburger-kunsthalle.de* ⊡ *Permanent exhibition €8.50* ☉ *Tues., Wed., and Fri.–Sun. 10–6, Thurs. 10–9* Ⓜ *Hauptbahnhof (U-bahn and S-bahn).*

Fodor's Choice **Rathaus** (*Town Hall*). To most Hamburgers this large building is the
★ symbolic heart of the city. As a city-state—an independent city and
simultaneously one of the 16 federal states of Germany—Hamburg
maintains city and state governments, both of which have their
administrative headquarters in the Rathaus. An ostentatious neo-
Renaissance affair, the building dictates political decorum in the city.
To this day, the mayor of Hamburg never welcomes VIPs at the foot
of its staircase, but always awaits them at the very top—whether it's
a president or the queen of England. The immense neo-Renaissance
building, with its 647 rooms and imposing central clock tower, is not
the most graceful structure in the city, but the sheer opulence of its
interior is astonishing. A 40-minute tour begins in the ground-floor
Rathausdiele, a vast pillared hall. Although you can only view the
state rooms, their tapestries, huge staircases, glittering chandeliers,
coffered ceilings, and grand portraits give you a sense of the city's
great wealth in the 19th century and its understandable civic pride.
⊠ *Rathausmarkt, Altstadt* ☎ *040/42831–2470* ⊕ *www.hamburgische-
buergerschaft.de* ✒ *Tours €3* ☉ *Tours weekdays, half-hourly 10:15–
3:15; Sat., half-hourly 10:15–5:15; Sun., half-hourly 10:15–6:15;
English tours weekdays 11:15, 1:15, and 3:15; Sat. 11:15, 1:15,
3:15, and 5:15; Sun. 11:15, 1:15, 3:15, and, if there is demand, 4:15*
Ⓜ *Rathaus (U-bahn), Jungfernstieg (U-bahn/S-bahn).*

★ **St. Jacobi Kirche** (*St. James's Church*). This 15th-century church was
almost completely destroyed during World War II. Only the interiors
survived, and reconstruction was completed in 1963. The interior is not
to be missed—it houses such treasures as a massive baroque organ and
three Gothic altars from the 15th and 16th centuries. ⊠ *Jacobikirchhof
22, at Steinstr., Altstadt* ☎ *040/303–7370* ✉ *info@jacobus.de* ⊕ *www.
jacobus.de* ☉ *Apr.–Sept., Mon.–Sat. 10–5, Sun. after 11 am; Oct.–
Mar., Mon.–Sat. 11–5, Sun. after 11 am. English guided tours available on request at info@jacobus.de* Ⓜ *Rathaus (U-bahn), Jungfernstieg
(U-bahn/S-bahn).*

Fodor's Choice **St. Michaelis Kirche** (*St. Michael's Church*). The Michel, as it's called
★ locally, is Hamburg's principal church and northern Germany's finest
baroque-style ecclesiastical building. Constructed between 1649 and
1661 (the tower followed in 1669), it was razed after lightning struck
almost a century later. It was rebuilt between 1750 and 1786 in the
decorative Nordic baroque style, but was gutted by a terrible fire in
1906. The replica, completed in 1912, was demolished during World
War II. The present church is a reconstruction.

The distinctive 436-foot brick-and-iron tower bears the largest tower
clock in Germany, 26 feet in diameter. Just above the clock is a viewing platform (accessible by elevator or stairs) that affords a magnificent
panorama of the city, the Elbe River, and the Alster lakes. ■TIP➔ **Twice
a day, at 10 am and 9 pm (Sunday at noon), a watchman plays a trumpet
solo from the tower platform.** In the crypt a 30-minute movie about the
1,000-year history of Hamburg and its churches is shown.

For a great view of Hamburg's skyline, head to the clock tower at
night. In the evenings you can sip a complimentary soft drink while

listening to classical music in a room just below the tower, usually held from 5:30 pm to 11:00 pm. Check ⊕ *www.nachtmichel.de* or call ☎ *040/2851–5791* to confirm times. ✉ *Englische Planke 1, Neustadt* ☎ *040/376–780* ⊕ *www.st-michaelis.de* ☜ *Tower €4; show, tower, and crypt €6* ⊙ *May–Oct., daily 9–8; Nov.–Apr., daily 10–5:30* Ⓜ *Rödingsmarkt (U-bahn), Stadthausbrücke (S-bahn).*

Fodor's Choice ★ ☾ **Speicherstadt** (*Warehouse District*). This imposing cluster of massive brick buildings sits along canals near the Elbe and reveals yet another aspect of Hamburg's extraordinary architectural diversity. Once home to tons of cargo imported by Hamburg, today the area is a mix of offices, restaurants, amusements, and warehouses. These warehouses are still used to store and process every conceivable commodity, from coffee and spices to raw silks and hand-woven Oriental carpets. An entire residential area was torn down (including many Renaissance and baroque buildings) to store the wares. Today, the area is home to Hamburg Dungeon, a haunted-house attraction; the Miniatur Wunderland, the site of the largest model railway in the world; and a few museums celebrating the area's shipping past.

Speicherstadtmuseum. Although you won't be able to tour the storage spaces, the nonstop comings and goings will give you a good sense of a port at work. If you want to learn about the history and architecture of the old warehouses, detour to the Speicherstadtmuseum. ✉ *Am Sandtorkai 30, Speicherstadt* ☎ *040/321–191* ⊕ *www.speicherstadtmuseum. de* ☜ *€3.50* ⊙ *Apr.–Oct., weekdays 10–5, weekends 10–6; Nov.–Mar., Tues.–Sun. 10–5* Ⓜ *Baumwall (U-bahn)* ✉ *Speicherstadt is bounded by Am Sandtorkai and Brooktorkai and the Elbe River., Speicherstadt* ☎ *040/3690–1799* ⊕ *www.hafencity.com* ☜ *Free* ⊙ *Visitor center: May–Sept., Tues., Wed., and Fri.–Sun. 10–6, Thurs. 10–8* Ⓜ *Messberg (U-bahn).*

SHOPPING

Hamburg's shopping districts are among the most elegant on the continent, and the city has Europe's largest expanse of covered shopping arcades, most of them packed with small, exclusive boutiques. The streets **Grosse Bleichen** and **Neuer Wall**, which lead off Jungfernstieg, are a high-price-tag zone. The Grosse Bleichen leads to six of the city's most important covered (or indoor) malls, many of which are connected. The marble-clad **Galleria** is modeled after London's Burlington Arcade. Daylight streams through the immense glass ceilings of the **Hanse-Viertel**, an otherwise ordinary reddish-brown brick building. The **Kaufmannshaus**, also known as the Commercie, and the upscale (and former first-class hotel) **Hamburger Hof** are two of the oldest and most fashionable indoor malls. There are also the **Alte Post** and the **Bleichenhof**, while over-the-top, stunningly designed **Europa Passage** is the city's latest arrival on the luxury shopping mall scene.

Some of the country's premier designers, such as Karl Lagerfeld, Jil Sander, and Wolfgang Joop, are native Hamburgers, or at least worked here for quite some time, so high-class fashion is well in evidence. For souvenirs, the most famous must-buys are *Buddelschiffe* (ships in bottles) and other maritime memorabilia.

Alsterhaus. Alsterhaus is Hamburg's famous and high-end department store. A favorite with locals, it's a large and elegant landmark. For a treat, check out the gourmet food hall and the champagne bar. ✉ *Jung-fernstieg 16–20, Neustadt* ☎ *040/3590–1218.*

Antik-Center Hamburg. The Antik-Center Hamburg has a treasure trove of "antiques" from the '50s, '60s, and '70s. The staff ships purchases anywhere in the world. ✉ *Gertigstrasse 67, Altstadt* ☎ *0172/400–4011* ⊕ *www.wirtschaftswunder-welt.de.*

WHERE TO EAT

$$ ✕**Rive.** This harborside oyster bar is known for both its German nou-
GERMAN velle cuisine and its classic local dishes. Choose between such dishes as hearty *Matjes mit dreierlei Saucen* (herring with three sauces) or *Dorade in der Salzkruste* (dorado cooked in salt crust). Media types come to this shiplike building for the fresh oysters, clams, and spectacular view. ✉ *Van-der-Smissen Str. 1, Kreuzfahrt-Center, Altona* ☎ *040/380–5919* ⊕ *www.rive.de* ⌕ *Reservations essential* Ⓜ *Königstrasse (S-bahn).*

$ ✕**River-Kasematten.** There is no other restaurant in town that better
ECLECTIC embodies Hamburg's international spirit and its lust for style, enter-
★ tainment, and good seafood. Once a legendary jazz club with perfor-mances by Ella Fitzgerald and the like, it now hosts a fascinating mix of hip guests. Sushi, spiced-up regional fish dishes, and exotic soups are the order of the day. The lunch buffet (weekdays noon–3) for just €9.90 is a steal; it's even better on the outside terrace. The ambience— black oak floors, leather seats, and redbrick walls—is elegant yet casual. ✉ *St. Pauli Fischmarkt 28–32, St. Pauli* ☎ *040/300–60190* ⊕ *www. river-kasematten.de* ⌕ *Reservations essential* Ⓜ *Fischmarkt (Bus 112), Reeperbahn (S-bahn).*

HELSINKI, FINLAND

Updated by
David Dunne

A city of the sea, Helsinki was built along a series of oddly shaped pen-insulas and islands jutting into the Gulf of Finland. Nature dictates life in this Nordic land, where winter brings perpetual darkness, and sum-mer perpetual light. A disastrous fire in the early 1800s destroyed many of Helsinki's traditional wooden structures, and as a result, Helsinki has some of the purest neoclassical architecture in the world. Add to this foundation the influence of Stockholm and St. Petersburg sprinkled with the local inspiration of 20th-century Finnish design, and the result is a European capital city that is as architecturally eye-catching as it is distinct. Today Helsinki is still a meeting point of eastern and western Europe, a fact reflected in its cosmopolitan image, its influx of Russians and Estonians, and its generally multilingual population. Outdoor sum-mer bars (*terrassit,* as the locals call them) and cafés in the city center are perfect for people-watching on a summer afternoon.

ESSENTIALS

CURRENCY

The euro. Local banks and Forex offices usually give the best rates and charge a minimal commission. ATMs are common and credit cards are widely accepted.

HOURS

Smaller stores are generally open weekdays from 9 am to 6 pm and Saturday from 9 am to 1 pm; larger department stores are open until 9 pm weekdays and until 6 pm on Saturday. Stores are often open on Sunday from June through August and during December. The majority of museums are closed on Monday.

TELEPHONES

Most tri-band and quad-band GSM phones work in Finland, but the Finnish mobile system is not 3G-compatible. You can buy prepaid phone cards at telecom shops, news vendors and tobacconists in all towns and cities. Phone cards can be used for local or international calls. Major companies include Elisa and Finnish 2G.

COMING ASHORE

Helsinki is a busy cruise destination and sees many ships throughout the season. Ships dock at one of three distinct areas.

Katajanokka Quay has a terminal with souvenir shop, toilets, and taxi station. From Katajanokka Terminal, local Bus 13 or Tram T4 will take you to Helsinki city center, but this is also reachable on foot. If you want to ride, Trams 4 and 4T stop here.

South Harbour has a terminal at Olympia Quay with shopping, information, a taxi rank, currency exchange, and Internet access and a second quay called Makasiini Quay. It's a 15-minute walk into downtown from the South Harbour port entrance. Trams 1A, 3B, and 3T run from the port into town.

Hernasaari Harbour has two quays with access to the dedicated cruise terminal with shops, information desk, taxi rank, and Internet access. It's a longer walk into Helsinki from here, but the terminal is served by Bus routes 14B and 16.

Taxis wait at all terminals to take visitors downtown, and this may be the most convenient way to travel if you don't want to take the cruise shuttle service. Journey times are short from all the terminals, the longest being around 15 minutes. Taxis are plentiful (albeit expensive) and make a convenient way to link attractions. Taxis take credit cards. A 5-km (3-mile) trip is currently €10.30, while a 10-km (6-mile) trip is €16.10. A car rental is not a sensible option if you intend to explore the city, as parking is difficult. Expect to pay €76 per day for a compact manual vehicle.

Tickets for the Helsinki public transport system cost €2.50 from the driver, or €2 from a ticket machine. Day tickets are €6.80—these are valid on trams, buses, the metro and the ferry to Soumenlinna. Ticket machines sell one-day tickets. Tram services 3B and 3T link many of the most important city attractions so in conjunction with a day ticket could be used as hop-on hop-off services.

EXPLORING HELSINKI

★ **Ateneumin Taidemuseo** (*Ateneum Art Museum of the Finnish National Gallery*). The best traditional Finnish art is housed in this splendid neo-classical complex, one of three museums organized under the Finnish National Gallery umbrella. The gallery holds major European works, but the outstanding attraction is the Finnish art, particularly the works of Akseli Gallen-Kallela, inspired by the national epic *Kalevala*. The rustic portraits by Albert Edelfelt are enchanting, and many contemporary Finnish artists are well represented. The two other museums that make up the National Gallery are **Kiasma** and **Synebrychoff**. ⊠ *Kaivok. 2, Keskusta* ☎ *09/6122–5510 information* ⊕ *www.fng.fi; www.ateneum. fi* ✉ *€8, extra charge for special exhibits* ☉ *Tues. and Fri. 10–6, Wed. and Thurs. 10–8, weekends 11–5.*

Cygnaeuksen Galleria (*Cygnaeus Gallery*). This diminutive gallery, in a cottage with a tower overlooking the harbor, is the perfect setting for works by various Finnish painters, sculptors, and folk artists. This was once the summer home of Fredrik Cygnaeus (1807–1881), a poet and historian who generously left his cottage and all the art inside to the Finnish public. ⊠ *Kalliolinnantie 8, Kaivopuisto* ☎ *09/4050–9628* ⊕ *www.nba.fi/en/gygnaeusgallery* ✉ *€6.50* ☉ *May–Sept., daily 11–5* Ⓜ *Trams 3B and 3T, Kaivopuisto.*

Fodor's Choice **Designmuseo** (*Design Museum*). The best of Finnish design can be seen
★ here in displays of furnishings, jewelry, ceramics, and more. ⊠ *Korkeavuorenk. 23, Keskusta* ☎ *09/622–0540* ⊕ *www.designmuseum.fi* ✉ *€8* ☉ *Sept.–May, Tues. 11–8, Wed.–Sun. 11–6; June–Aug., daily 11–6* Ⓜ *Bus 16, Tram 10.*

Finlandiatalo (*Finlandia Hall*). This white, winged concert hall was one of Alvar Aalto's last creations. It's especially impressive on foggy days or at night. If you can't make it to a concert here, try to take a guided tour. ⊠ *Mannerheimintie 13e, Keskusta* ☎ *09/402–41* ⊕ *www.finlandiatalo.fi* ✉ *€11.50 for guided tours on Wed. 2pm* ☉ *Symphony concerts usually held Wed. and Thurs. nights* Ⓜ *Trams 4, 7 and 10 stop at Mannerheimintie next to Finlandia Hall (National Museum's stop).*

Gulf of Finland Archipelago. In winter, Finns walk across the frozen sea with dogs and even baby buggies to the nearby islands. On the land side, the facades of the Eira and Kaivopuisto districts' grandest buildings form a parade of architectural splendor. One tradition that remains, even in this upscale neighborhood, is rug washing in the sea—an incredibly arduous task. You may be surprised to see people leave their rugs to dry in the sea air without fear of theft. ⊠ *South of Merisatamaranta, Merisatama.*

Havis Amanda. This fountain's brass centerpiece, a young woman perched on rocks surrounded by dolphins, was commissioned by the city fathers to embody Helsinki. Sculptor Ville Vallgren completed her in 1908 using a Parisian girl as his model. Partying university students annually crown the Havis Amanda with their white caps on the eve of Vappu, the May 1 holiday. ⊠ *Eteläespl. and Eteläranta, Keskusta/Kauppatori.*

Sibeliusken Puisto

Taivallahti

Taivalsaari

Suomen Kansallisooppera

Töölön-lahti

Sibeliuksenk.
Topeliuksenk.
Sibeliuksenk.
Töölönk.
Valskärink.
Mechelinink.
Mannerheimintie
Runebergink.
Töölönk.

Pohjoinen Hesperiank.
Eteläinen Hesperiank.

Apollonk.

Finlandiatalo

Cygnaeuksenk.

Suomen Kansallismuseo

Museok.

Tunturik.

Helsingin Taidehalli

Mannerheimintie

Hietakannaksent.
Mechelinink.
Väinämöisenk.
Caloniuk.k.
Rune bergi nk.
Temppelik.
Nervanderink.
Aurorank.

Hietaniemi Cemetery

Samonk.
Itmarink.
Dagm.k.

Hietaniemenkatu

Temppeliaukio Kirkko

Arkadiank.

Musiikkitalo

Nykytaiteenmuseo (Kiasma)

Kai vo

Lapinlahti

Hietaniemenk.

Etel. Rautatiek.
Pohj Rautatiek.

Salomonk.

Urho Kekkosenk.

Simonk.

Mannerheimintie

Mechelininkatu

Runeberginkatu

Malmink.

Fredrikink.

Lapinlahdenk.
Lapinrinne

Lapinlahdentie

Lastenkodink.

Eerikink.

Kalevank.

Bulevardi
Annank.

Länsiväylä

Ruoholahdenk.
Abrahamink.
Lonnrotink.
Albertink.

Uudenmaank.

Porkkalank.

Hietalahdenk.
Köydenpunojank.

Bulevardi

Itämerenk.

Ruoholahden

Hietalah denranta

Iso Roobertink.
Punavuorenk.
Merimiehenk.
Pursimiehenk.

Ruoholahti

Mallask.

Telekkak.

Sepänk.

Tehtaan-puisto

Tehtaankatu

Munkkisaarenk.

Rehbinderinti

Hietalahti

Hernesaarenk.

KEY

🚢 Ferry

┼┼┼┼ Rail Lines

Helsinki

TO PORVOO →

Eläintarhantie

Siltasaarenk.

Porthanink.

Hämeentie

Sörnäistenrantatie

Eläintarhan-
lahti

Sörnäisten satama

Kaisaniemenlahti

Siltavuoren-
salmi

Unionink.

Siltavuorenranta

0 _____ 1/4 mi

0 _____ 1/4 km

Kluuvi
Gloet

Liisank.

Maurink.

Maneesik

Pohjoissatama
(North Harbor)

Vuorik.

Kaisaniemenk.

Unionink.

Snellmanink.

Virونk.

Meritullink.

Pohjoisranta

Rautatientori

Rautatieasema

Fabianinkatu

Rauhank.

Kirkkok

Tuomiokirkko ◆

Kluuvikatu

Kirkkok

Yliopistonk.

Mariank.

Ateneumin
Taidemuseo ◆

Mikonk.

Senaatintori ◆

Keskusk.

Aleksanterink.

Uspenski
Katedraali ◆

Laivastok

Raha-
pajank

Luotsik

Pohjoisesplanadi

Obeliski
Keisarinnan Kivi

KATAJANOKKA

Eteläesplanadi

Havis
Amanda ◆

Kanavakatu

Kruunuvuorenk.

Kauppiaank

Yrjönk.

◆ Kauppatori

Eteläranta

Katajanokkalaituri

Linnankatu

Katajano-
kanranta

Pohj Makasiinik

◆ Vanha
Kauppahalli

Etel Makasiinik

Pieni
Roobertink.

Laivasillank.

Bernhardink.

Eteläsatama
(South Harbor)

◆ Designmuseo

Korkeavuorenk.

Kasarmik.

Tähtitorninvuori

Valkosaari

Suomenlinna ◆

Jääkärink.

Tähtitornink.

Vuorimiehenk.

Uttank.

Iso Puistotie

Cygnaeuksen
Galleria ◆

Ehrenströmintie

Luoto

Ryssänsaari

Kalliolinnantie

Pietarink.

Neitsytp.

Puistok.

Kaivohuoneen-
rinne

Itäinen Puistotie

Pikkuluoto

Kaivopuisto

5

Helsingin Taidehalli (*Helsinki Art Gallery*). Here you'll see the best of contemporary Finnish art, including painting, sculpture, architecture, and industrial art and design. ⊠ *Nervanderink. 3, Keskusta* ☎ *09/454–2060 office, 40/450–7211 tickets* ⊕ *www.taidehalli.fi* 🖃 *€8, can vary for special exhibitions* ☉ *Tues., Thurs., and Fri. 11–6; Wed. 11–8; weekends 11–6* Ⓜ *Kamppi stop.*

★ **Kauppatori** (*Market Square*). At this Helsinki institution, open year-round, wooden stands with orange and gold awnings bustle in the mornings when everyone—tourists and locals alike—comes to shop, browse, or sit and enjoy coffee and conversation. You can buy a freshly caught perch for the evening's dinner, a bouquet of bright flowers for a friend, or a fur pelt. In summer, the fruit and vegetable stalls are supplemented by an evening arts-and-crafts market. The crepes, made-to-order by one of the tented vendors, are excellent. ⊠ *Eteläranta and Pohjoisespl., Keskusta/Kauppatori* ☉ *Weekdays 6:30–6, Sat. 6:30–4, and in the summer Sun. 10–5.*

> ### HELSINKI BEST BETS
>
> **Temppeliaukio Kirkko.** This church, seemingly rising out of living rock, pushes the boundaries of architecture.
>
> **Senaatintori.** The symmetry of this neoclassical city square is a joy to the eye.
>
> **Kauppatori.** Enjoy a steaming cup of coffee while browsing in the market or immersing yourself in daily life.

Musiikkitalo (*Helsinki Music Center*). Since it opened in 2011, the Helsinki Music Center has been praised for its acoustics and daring design. It's home to the Sibelius Academy and two symphony orchestras. Guided tours are available, but most are in Finnish—check the website for details. The one-hour guided walking tour introduces participants to what happens here, as well as to the architecture, main audience, and the concert hall. ⊠ *Mannerheimintie 13 a, Töölö* ☎ *0600/900–900 tour tickets, 020/707–0421 service desk* ⊕ *www.musiikkitalo.fi.*

★ **Nykytaiteenmuseo (Kiasma)** (*Museum of Contemporary Art*). Praised for the boldness of its curved steel shell but condemned for its encroachment on the territory of the Mannerheim statue, this striking museum displays a wealth of Finnish and foreign art from the 1960s to the present. Look for the "butterfly" windows, and don't miss the view of Töölönlahti from the north side of the fifth-floor gallery. ⊠ *Mannerheiminaukio 2, Keskusta/Pääposti* ☎ *09/1733–6501 information and theater tickets* ⊕ *www.kiasma.fi* 🖃 *€8* ☉ *Tues. 10–5; Wed. and Thurs. 10–8.30; Fri: 10–10; weekends 10–5.*

Obeliski Keisarinnan Kivi (*Czarina's Stone*). This obelisk with a double-headed golden eagle, used by Imperial Russia, was erected in 1835, toppled during the Russian Revolution in 1917, and fully restored in 1972. ⊠ *Kauppatori along Pohjoisespl., Keskusta/Kauppatori.*

Rautatieasema (*Central Train Station*). This outdoor square and the adjoining train station are the city's bustling commuter hub. The station's huge granite figures are by Emil Wikström; the solid building they adorn was designed by Eliel Saarinen, one of the founders of the early-20th-century National Romantic style. ⊠ *Kaivok. 1, Rautatientori, Keskusta*

☎ *0600/41–902 information in English (€1 for answered call plus local network charge)* ⊕ *www.vr.fi/en* ⊙ *Information, daily 7–10 pm.*

★ **Senaatintori** (*Senate Square*). The harmony of the three buildings flanking Senaatintori exemplifies one of the purest styles of European architecture, as envisioned and designed by German architect Carl Ludvig Engel. This is the heart of neoclassical Helsinki. On the square's west side is one of the main buildings of Helsingin Yliopisto (Helsinki University), and up the hill is the university library. On the east side is the pale yellow Valtionneuvosto (Council of State), completed in 1822 and once the seat of the Autonomous Grand Duchy of Finland's Imperial Senate. At the lower end of the square, stores, and restaurants now occupy former merchants' homes. ⊠ *Bounded by Aleksanterink. to south and Yliopistonk. to north, Senaatintori* ⊙ *Cathedral on Senate Square: daily 9–6.*

Suomen Kansallismuseo (*National Museum of Finland*). Architect Eliel Saarinen and his partners combined the language of Finnish medieval church architecture with elements of art nouveau to create this vintage example of the National Romantic style. The museum's collection of archaeological, cultural, and ethnological artifacts gives you insight into Finland's past. ⊠ *Mannerheimintie 34, Keskusta* ☎ *09/40–501, 09/4050–9544 ticket office, 09/4050–9552 guided tours* ⊕ *www.nba. fi/en/nationalmuseum* 🎟€8 ⊙ *Tue. 11–8; Wed.–Sun. 11–6* Ⓜ *Trams 7A, 7B, 4, 4T and 10 stop at Kansallismuse/Nationalmuseum (National Museum of Finland).*

Fodor's Choice **Suomen Kansallisooppera** (*Finnish National Opera*). Grand gilded operas,
★ classical ballets, and booming concerts all take place in Helsinki's splendid opera house, a striking example of modern Scandinavian architecture. All events at the opera house draw crowds, so buy your tickets early. ⊠ *Helsinginkatu 58, Keskusta* ☎ *09/4030–2210 house tours, 09/4030–2211 box office* ⊕ *www.opera.fi/en* ⊙ *Box office Tues.–Fri. 10–5; house tours, in English, in summer Tues. and Thurs. at 3, or by appointment* Ⓜ *Trams 3T, 4, 7A/7B, 8 and 10.*

Fodor's Choice **Suomenlinna** (*Finland's Castle*). A former island fortress, Suomenlinna is
★ a perennially popular collection of museums, parks, and gardens, and has been designated a UNESCO World Heritage site. In 1748 the Finnish army helped build the impregnable fortress, long referred to as the Gibraltar of the North; since then it has expanded into a series of interlinked islands. Although Suomenlinna has never been taken by assault, its occupants surrendered once to the Russians in 1808 and came under fire from British ships in 1855 during the Crimean War. Today Suomenlinna makes a lovely excursion from Helsinki, particularly in early summer when the island is engulfed in a mauve-and-purple mist of lilacs, introduced from Versailles by the Finnish architect Ehrensvärd.

Suomenlinna is easily reached by public ferry (€2.50 one-way, €3.60 round-trip) or private boat (€3.50 one-way, €5.50 round-trip), both of which leave from Helsinki's Kauppatori. The ferry ride from South Harbor to Suomenlinna takes about 15 minutes. Plan to spend an afternoon on the islands; you'll need about four hours to explore the fortress and museums. Note that the days open and the hours of sites are limited off-season.

Although its fortification occupied six islands, its main attractions are now concentrated on three: Iso Mustasaari, Susisaari, and Kustaanmiekka. There are no street names on the island, so get a map for about €2 from the Helsinki City Tourist Office before you go, or buy one at the visitor center on the island. ☎ *029/53–38410* ⊕ *www.suomenlinna.fi/en.*

Suomenlinna Visitor Centre. From June through August, guided English-language tours leave daily at 11 am and 2 pm from the Suomenlinna Visitor Centre; call to arrange tours at other times. The center, which is in the same building as the Suomenlinna Museum, is on the shore of Tykistölahti Bay, about 400 yards south of the main ferry terminal ⊠ *Suomenlinna C 74, Suomenlinna* ☎ *029/53–38410, 029/53–38410 tours* ⊕ *www. suomenlinna.fi* ☉ *Oct.–Apr., daily 10:30–4:30; May–Sept., daily 10–6.*

Suomenlinna Museo (*Suomenlinna Museum*). The Suomenlinna Museo is housed in the same building as the visitor center. Exhibits cover the building of the fortress and the fleet and early life on islands; the ticket price includes the *Suomenlinna Experience* multimedia show. ⊠ *Suomenlinna museum, Suomenlinna C 74, Suomenlinna* ☎ *09/684–1850* ⊕ *www.nba.fi/fi/suomenlinna_museo* 🎟 *€6.50* ☉ *May-Sept., daily 10–6; Oct.–Apr., daily 10:30–4:30.*

★ **Temppeliaukio Kirkko** (*Temple Square Church*). Topped with a copper dome, the church looks like a half-buried spaceship from the outside. It's really a modern Lutheran church carved into the rock outcrops below. The sun shines in from above, illuminating a stunning interior with birch pews, modern pipe organ, and cavernous walls. Ecumenical and Lutheran services in various languages are held throughout the week. ⊠ *Lutherinkatu 3, Töölö* ☎ *09/2340–5940* ⊕ *www. helsinginseurakunnat.fi* ☉ *Mon.–Thurs. 10–8; Fri. and Sat. 10–5:45; Sun. 11:45–5:45; closed during weddings, concerts, and services.*

Fodor'sChoice
★ **Tuomiokirkko** (*Lutheran Cathedral of Finland*). The steep steps and green domes of the church dominate Senaatintori. Completed in 1852, it is the work of famous architect Carl Ludvig Engel, who also designed parts of Tallinn and St. Petersburg. Wander through the tasteful blue-gray interior, with its white moldings and the statues of German reformers Martin Luther and Philipp Melanchthon, as well as the famous Finnish bishop Mikael Agricola. Concerts are frequently held inside the church. The crypt at the rear is the site of frequent historic and architectural exhibitions and bazaars. ⊠ *Unioninkatu 29, Senaatintori* ☎ *09/2340–6120* ⊕ *www.helsinginseurakunnat.fi* ☉ *Sept.–May, daily 9–6; June–Aug., 9–midnight.*

★ **Uspenski Katedraali** (*Uspenski Orthodox Cathedral*). Perched atop a small rocky cliff over the North Harbor in Katajanokka is the main cathedral of the Orthodox Church in Finland. Its brilliant gold onion domes are its hallmark, but its imposing redbrick edifice, decorated by 19th-century Russian artists, is no less distinctive. The cathedral was built and dedicated in 1868 in the Byzantine-Slavonic style and remains the biggest Orthodox church in Scandinavia. ⊠ *Kanavak. 1, Katajanokka* ☎ *0207/220–683* ⊕ *www.ort.fi* ☉ *Oct.–Apr., Tue.–Fri. 9:30–4, Sat. 9.30–2, Sun. noon–3; May–Sept., weekdays 9:30–4, Sat. 9:30–2, Sun. noon–3; closed for weddings and other special events.*

★ **Vanha Kauppahalli** (*Old Market Hall*). Piles of colorful fish roe, marinated Greek olives, and much more—the old brick market hall on the waterfront is a treasury of delicacies. The vendors set up permanent stalls with decorative carved woodwork. ⊠ *Eteläranta, along South Harbor, Kauppatori* ⊙ *Weekdays 8–6, Sat. 8–4.*

SHOPPING

From large, well-organized malls to closet-size boutiques, Helsinki has shopping for every taste. Most sales staff in the main shopping areas speak English and are helpful. Smaller stores are generally open weekdays 9–6 and Saturday 9–1. Small grocery stores are often open on Sunday year-round; other stores are often open on Sunday from June through August and December. The Forum and Kamppi complexes and Stockmann's department store are open weekdays 9–9, Saturday 9–6, and (in summer and Christmastime) Sunday noon–6. An ever-expanding network of pedestrian tunnels connects the Forum, Stockmann's, and the train-station tunnel.

The area south and west of Mannerheimintie has been branded Design District Helsinki. It includes roughly 170 venues, most of them smaller boutiques and designer-run shops selling handmade everything from jewelry to clothing to housewares. The majority are located on Fredrikinkatu and Annankatu; look for a black Design District Helsinki sticker in the window. You can pick up a map detailing the shops in the district at most participating stores. Kiosks remain open late and on weekends; they sell such basics as milk, juice, camera film, and tissues. Stores in Asematunneli, the train-station tunnel, are open weekdays 10–10 and on weekends noon–10.

Design Forum Finland. This shop sells items from many of the nearby stores as well as items by designers without places of their own. It also puts on exhibitions featuring particular artists and it has a café. ⊠ *Erottajank. 7, Punavouri* ☏ *09/6220–8130* ⊕ *www.designforum.fi.*

Hietalahden Tori. At the outdoor flea market (open weekdays 8–7, Saturday 8–4) that's held here, you can get an ever-changing assortment of used items; the indoor market brims with food, flowers, fish, and more. ⊠ *Bulevardi and Hietalahdenkatu* ☏ *09/3107–1396* ⊙ *Weekdays 6:30–6, Sat. 6:30–4 (with extended summer hours).*

Marimekko. Since the 1950s Marimekko has been selling bright, unusual clothes for men, women, and children in quality fabrics. Though the products are expensive, they're worth a look even if you don't plan to buy. There are four locations in central Helsinki. ⊠ *Pohjoisespl. 2, Esplanadi* ☏ *09/686–0240* ⊕ *www.marimekko.com* ⊠ *Pohjoisespl. 33, Kämp Galleria, Esplanadi* ☏ *09/686–0240* ⊕ *www.marimekko. com* ⊠ *Kamppi shopping center, Urho Kekkosen Katu 1, Keskusta* ☏ *010/344–3300.*

ACTIVITIES

Taking a sauna is the big Finnish pastime. It's a place to get cleansed and do some socializing.

WHERE TO EAT

$$$
SCANDINAVIAN
Fodor's Choice
★

✕ **Kosmos.** Just a short walk from Stockmann's department store, this cozy restaurant has become a lunchtime favorite among businesspeople working nearby. Come evening, it's given over to artists and journalists. Its high ceilings and understated interior give it a Scandinavian air of simplicity and efficiency. Menu highlights include reindeer fillet in a sauce of spruce shoots and rosemary that's served with roasted potatoes, and *vorschmack*, a ground meat and anchovy dish, which is served here with *Duchesse* potatoes (a rich version of mashed), pickles, and beets. $ *Average main: €25* ✉ *Kalevank. 3, Keskusta* ☎ *09/647–255* ⊕ *www. kosmos.fi* ☉ *Closed Sun. and in July. No lunch Sat.* Ⓜ *Trams 3B, 6, 9, 10: Student House stop.*

$$
SCANDINAVIAN

✕ **Salutorget Scandinavian Bistro.** Right beside City Hall, this building retains Doric columns and deep wood panels that harken back to the days when it was a bank rather than an elegant restaurant. Toast skagen, a Nordic classic, is a good bet for a starter—it's shrimp, mayo, and chives on toasted bread, topped with a generous dollop of whitefish roe. Moose Wallenbergare, served with potato purée, game sauce, and cranberry jam, is definitely worth trying as a main course. Salutorget has adopted with gusto the very British concept of afternoon tea. Two Sunday brunch sittings are available, at noon and 3. $ *Average main: €21* ✉ *Pohjoisesplanadi 15, Esplanadi, Helsinki* ☎ *09/6128–5950* ⊕ *www. salutorget.fi/en.*

RĪGA, LATVIA

Updated by
Dorota Wąsik

Rīga has an upscale, big-city feel unmatched in the region. The capital (almost as large as Tallinn and Vilnius combined) is the business center of the area while original, high-quality restaurants and hotels have earned Rīga some bragging rights among its Western European counterparts. The city also doesn't lack for beauty—Rīga's Old Town (now a UNESCO World Heritage site) is one of Europe's most striking examples of the art nouveau architectural style. Long avenues of complex and sometimes whimsical Jugendstil facades hint at Rīga's grand past. Many were designed by Mikhail Eisenstein, the father of Soviet director Sergei. This style dominates the city center; you can see the finest examples at Alberta 2, 2a, 4, 6, 8, and 13; Elizabetes 10b; and Strēlnieku 4a.

ESSENTIALS
CURRENCY
The monetary unit in Latvia is the lat. In addition to banks, which change cash and traveler's checks, there are numerous currency-exchange booths and ATMs. Credit cards are accepted in major hotels, restaurants, and shops (mostly Visa and MasterCard, with American Express accepted occasionally).

HOURS

Banks are open weekdays 9–4, but some open as early as 8 and close as late as 7. Most are closed on Saturday, but some stay open 9–3. Museums are generally open Wednesday–Sunday 11–5. Some stay open until 6. Shops open between 10 and 11 and close between 5 and 7, with shorter hours on Saturday. Most shops are closed on Sunday; however, convenience stores are open 7 days a week.

TELEPHONES

The Latvian mobile phone system is 3G-compatible, Tele2, and Latvijas Mobilias Telefons being the main providers. Public phones support international calls. Some kiosks accept credit cards. Phone cards are available at tobacconists/newspaper shops.

COMING ASHORE

In addition to larger cruise ships, ferries connect Rīga with Kiel and Lübeck (in Germany) and Stockholm (in Sweden). The cruise port is in the main port, close to the historic downtown core. The walk from port to the downtown core is 15 minutes along the waterfront. The passenger welcome center has good facilities, including restaurants, restrooms, currency-exchange facilities, and ATMs.

To reach the Old Town you can take an inexpensive shuttle transfer or taxi. Taxis are more expensive from the port than within the city

center. Drivers must display an operating license and a meter. Stick to the state cabs with orange and black markings. Insist that the meter be turned on; if there is no meter, choose another taxi or decide on a price beforehand. Public transportation can be paid for by the ride, or you can get a 24-hour pass. Services run from 5:30 am to midnight. Some routes have 24-hour service. Trams 6 and 11 connect the Old Town with the Esplanāde area and run regularly throughout the day. Buy tickets at numerous outlets and validate them in the machine on board.

EXPLORING RĪGA

In many ways, the wonder of Rīga resides less in its individual attractions and more in the fabric of the town itself. In the medieval **Old Town,** an ornate gable or architrave catches the eye at every turn. The somber and the flamboyant are both represented in this quarter's 1,000 years of architectural history. Don't hesitate to just follow where your desire leads—the Old Town is compact and bounded by canals, so it's difficult to get totally lost.

When the Old Town eventually became too crowded, the city burst out into the newer inner suburbs. The rich could afford to leave and build themselves fine fashionable mansions in the style of the day; consequently, city planners created a whole new Rīga. Across the narrow canal, you'll find the **Esplanāde,** a vast expanse of parkland with formal gardens and period mansions where the well-heeled stroll and play. Surrounding this is the **art nouveau district.** Encompassing avenues of splendid family homes (now spruced up in the postcommunist era), the collection has been praised by UNESCO as Europe's finest in the art nouveau style. The best examples are at Alberta 2, 2a, 4, 6, 8, and 13; Elizabetes 10b; and Strēlnieku 4a.

If the weather permits, eschew public transport and stroll between the two districts, taking in the varied skylines and multifaceted facades, and perhaps stopping at a café or two as you go. The city has churches in five Christian denominations and more than 50 museums, many of which cater to eclectic or specialist tastes.

☾ **Brīvdabas muzejs.** The Open-Air Ethnographic Museum is well worth the 9-km (5-mile) trek from downtown. At this countryside living museum, farmsteads and villages have been crafted to look like those in 18th- and 19th-century Latvia, and costumed workers engage in traditional activities (beekeeping, smithing, and so on). ✉ *Brīvības 440* ☎ *6799–4515* ⊕ *www.brivdabasmuzejs.lv* 🎟 *Ls 2.50* ☉ *Daily 10–5.*

★ **Brīvības piemineklis.** The central Freedom Monument, a 1935 statue whose upheld stars represent Latvia's united peoples (the Kurzeme, Vidzeme, and Latgale), was the rallying point for many nationalist protests during the late 1980s and early 1990s. Watch the changing of the guard every hour on the hour between 9 and 6. ✉ *Brīvības and Raina.*

Doma baznīca (*Dome Cathedral*). In Doma laukums (Dome Square), the nerve center of the Old Town, the stately 1210 cathedral dominates.

Reconstructed over the years with Romanesque, Gothic, and baroque elements, this place of worship is astounding as much for its architecture as for its size. The massive 6,768-pipe organ is among the largest in Europe, and it is played nearly every evening at 7 pm. Check at the cathedral for schedules and tickets. ⊠ *Doma laukums* ☎ *6/722-7573* ⊕ *www.doms.lv* ⊙ *Tues.–Fri. 1–5, Sat. 10–2.*

Melngalvju Nams. The fiercely Gothic Blackheads House was built in 1344 as a hotel for wayfaring merchants (who wore black hats). Partially destroyed during World War II and leveled by the Soviets in 1948, the extravagant, ornate building was renovated and reopened in 2000 for Rīga's 800th anniversary. The facade is a treasured example of Dutch Renaissance work. ⊠ *Ratslaukums 7* ☎ *6/7043678* ⊕ *www.melngalvjunams.lv* ⊙ *Tues.–Sun. 10–5.*

Nacionālā Opera. Latvia's restored 18th-century National Opera House, where Richard Wagner once conducted, is worthy of a night out. ⊠ *Aspazijas 3* ☎ *6/707-3777* ⊕ *www.opera.lv* ⊙ *Mon.–Sat. 10–7, Sun. 11–7.*

★ **Okupācijas muzejs.** The Latvian Occupation Museum details the devastation of Latvia at the hands of the Nazis and Soviets during World War II, as well as the Latvians' struggle for independence in September 1991. In front of the museum is a monument to the Latvian sharpshooters who protected Lenin during the 1917 revolution. ⊠ *Strēlnieku laukums 1* ☎ *6/721-2715* ⊕ *www.okupacijasmuzejs.lv/en* 🎫 *Donations accepted* ⊙ *May–Sept., daily 11–6; Oct.–Apr., Tues.–Sun. 11–5.*

Pētera baznīca. Towering St. Peter's Church, originally built in 1209, had a long history of annihilation and conflagration before being destroyed most recently in 1941. Rebuilt by the Soviets, it lacks authenticity but has a good observation deck on the 200-foot spire. ⊠ *Skārnu 19* ☎ *6/722-9426* ⊕ *www.peterbaznica.lv* ⊙ *Tues.–Sun. 10–7.*

Rīgas motormuzejs. At the Motor Museum, the Western cars on display can impress, but the Soviet models—including Stalin's iron-plated limo and a Rolls-Royce totaled by Brezhnev himself—are the most fun. ⊠ *Eizensteina 6* ☎ *6/7025888* ⊕ *www.motormuzejs.lv* 🎫 *Ls 2* ⊙ *Daily 10–6.*

Trīs Brāli. The Three Brothers—a trio of houses on Mazā Pils—show what the city looked like before the 20th century. The three oldest stone houses in the capital (No. 17 is the oldest, dating from the 15th century) span several styles, from the medieval to the baroque. The building at No. 19 is the city's **architecture museum.** ⊠ *Mazā Pils 17, 19, 21* ☎ *6/722-0779* ⊕ *www.archmuseum.lv* ⊙ *Mon. 9–6, Tues.–Thurs. 9–5, Fri. 9–4.*

RĪGA BEST BETS

Elizabetes Street. The heart of art nouveau Rīga has some exceptional period architecture and is a testament to the wealth generated here by shipping and trade in the early 20th century.

Old Town. The fabric of this medieval core remains remarkably intact, with Gothic spires sheltering church naves and winding cobbled streets revealing sturdy gables.

The Esplanāde. The green lung of the city, this huge park has fine formal gardens and planned woodlands. Enjoy a picnic here in warm weather.

5

Valsts mākslas muzejs. The National Art Museum has a gorgeous interior, with imposing marble staircases linking several large halls of 19th- and 20th-century Latvian paintings. ⊠ *K. Valdemāra 10a* ☎ *6732–4461* ⊕ *www.lnmm.lv* ⊠ *Ls 3* ⊘ *Mon., Wed., Thurs, and weekends 11–5, Fri. 11–8.* ⊘ *Closed Tues.*

SHOPPING

You'll find many souvenir and gift shops in the streets of the Old Town, many of which specifically cater to visitors. Latvia is famed for its linen, which is fashioned into clothes and household items such as tea towels and table runners. Woolen sweaters, mittens, and socks with traditional patterns have been worn by generations of locals during the winter. Amber items are everywhere, although their quality can vary, so shop around. Also popular are jewelry, carved ornaments, and Rīga Black Balsam, a liqueur made from an ancient recipe incorporating herbs and medicinal roots.

WHERE TO EAT

$ ✕ **Cydonia.** One of Rīga's premier dining establishments, Cydonia gastropub serves outstanding Mediterranean cuisine, with an emphasis on seafood, as well as light soups and salads. The dining room is furnished in a fashionable Scandinavian style—simple yet cozy, with an abundance of natural materials like wood and stone. There's also a lovely kids' corner with toys and crayons. ⑤ *Average main: Ls7* ⊠ *Berga Bazārs, Dzirnavu 84/1* ☎ *6/7282055* ⊕ *www.cydonia.lv.*

MEDITERRANEAN

$ ✕ **Staburags.** Found in the the the art nouveau Hotel Viktorija in downtown Rīga, this may be the capital's best place to sample Latvian national cuisine, with such offerings as roast leg of pork, sauerkraut, an assortment of potato dishes, and smoked chicken. ⑤ *Average main: Ls5* ⊠ *Caka 55* ☎ *6729–9787* ⊕ *www.hotelviktorija.lv.*

EASTERN
EUROPEAN

ST. PETERSBURG, RUSSIAN FEDERATION

Commissioned by Peter the Great as "a window looking into Europe," St. Petersburg is a planned city built on more than 100 islands in the Neva Delta linked by canals and arched bridges. It was first called the "Venice of the North" by Goethe. Little wonder it's the darling of today's fashion photographers. With its strict geometric lines and perfectly planned architecture, so unlike the Russian cities that came before it, St. Petersburg is almost too European to be Russian. And yet it's too Russian to be European. Memories of revolutionary zeal and one of the worst ordeals of World War II, when the city—then known as Leningrad—withstood a 900-day siege and blockade by Nazi forces, are still fresh in the minds of citizens. Nevertheless, St. Petersburg is filled with pleasures and tantalizing treasures, from golden spires and gilded domes to pastel palaces and candlelit cathedrals.

ESSENTIALS

CURRENCY

The ruble. There are ATMs in the city, but exchange bureaus are more plentiful. Credit cards are increasingly accepted, but ask first to be sure.

HOURS

Stores have recently extended their opening hours considerably—many stay open until 8 or 9 pm, or on Sunday.

PRIVATE TOURS

Cruise passengers who do not wish to take expensive and crowded tours offered by their ships but who still do not wish to deal with the bureaucracy and cost of getting a Russian visa can still visit St. Petersburg on a private tour with an accredited company. These tours must be arranged in advance, but they offer the opportunity to get fast entry to major museums without having to stand in long lines and include the services of a knowledgeable guide. While privately arranged tours are often cheaper than the ones offered by ships, this is not the case in St. Petersburg, where a private tour might even be more expensive if you are just, say, a couple. However, you get superior service and more personal attention on these tours and do not have to travel in a large bus with dozens of other passengers. For many people, this is worth the cost.

Contacts Alla Tours. ☎ *(7)812/312–5355* ⊕ *www.alla-tour.com.* **SPb Tours.** ☎ *(7)812/331–5383* ⊕ *www.spb-tours.com.*

TELEPHONES

Some tri- and quad-band mobile phones may work in St. Petersburg, but mobile service on the whole is patchy. The network does not yet support 3G services, and handsets are single-band. Public phones take phone cards, which can be bought at newsstands. Note that public phones in Metro stations work on a different system and require a different card.

COMING ASHORE

Independent travel is not as easy in St. Petersburg as in other destinations, as you need to obtain a tourist visa prior to the cruise departure to explore without a certified guide; for the vast majority of travelers, it is simply not a practical matter to get a separate visa for a typical two-night cruise visit. It is also worth considering that independent travelers need to line up for tickets at museums and attractions, while guided groups do not. This can cut down your sightseeing time considerably. Whether you travel independently or with an accredited small tour company, it is approximately 20 minutes on foot to the port entrance, from where you will be able to take a taxi.

EXPLORING ST. PETERSBURG

★ **Dvortsovaya Ploshchad** (*Palace Square*). One of the world's most mag-
☾ nificent plazas, the square is a stunning ensemble of buildings and open space, a combination of several seemingly incongruous architectural styles in perfect harmony. It's where the city's imperial past has been preserved in all its glorious splendor, but it also resonates with the

St. Petersburg

PETROGRAD SIDE

Maly pr.

Bolshoy pr.

Krasnogo kursanta ul.

Dobrolubova

Kamennostrovsky pr.

Skorochodova ul.

Mira ul.

Kronverksky pr.

Pirogovskaya nab.

Bolshaya Nevka

Petrogradskaya nab.

Petrovskaya nab.

Svobody most

Kuybysheva ul.

Troitskaya Pl.

Kronverk Canal

Peter and Paul Fortress

Troitsky most

Malaya Neva

Makarova

VASILIEVSKY ISLAND

4-5 Liniya

Syezdovskaya l.

Bolshoy pr.

Mend. l.

Stock Exchange

Birzhevoy most

Dvortsovy most

Dvortsovaya nab.

Marble Palace

Sadovaya ul.

Engineer's Castle

Mokhovaya ul.

State Hermitage Museum

Winter Palace

Universitetskaya nab.

Neva

Admiralteistvo

Dvortsovaya Ploshchad

Admiralteysky pr.

Gorokhovaya ul.

Nevsky pr.

Ethnography Museum

State Museum of Russian Art

most Leytenanta Shmidta nab.

Anglijskaya nab.

Truda ul.

St. Isaac's Cathedral

Konnogvardeysky bulvar

Kazanskaya ul.

Kazan Cathedral

Pl. Iskusstv

Lomonosova

Z. Rossi ul.

Moika

reka

Pisareva ul.

Maklina

Dekabristov ul.

Voznesensky pr.

Griboyedov Canal

Sadovaya ul.

Lomonosov Pl.

Zagorodny pr.

Zvenigorodskaya ul.

Rimskogo-Korsakova

St. Nicholas Cathedral

reka Fontanka

Vitebsky Station

Turgenyeva ploshchad

Moskovsky pr.

Ruzovskaya ul.

Klinsky

0   1/2 mi

0   1/2 km

history of the revolution that followed. Here, the fate of the last Russian tsar was effectively sealed, on Bloody Sunday in 1905, when palace troops opened fire on peaceful demonstrators, killing scores of women and children. It was across Palace Square in October 1917 that Bolshevik revolutionaries stormed the Winter Palace and overthrew Kerensky's Provisional Government, an event that led to the birth of the Soviet Union. Almost 75 years later, during tense days, huge crowds rallied on Palace Square in support of perestroika and democracy. Today, the beautiful square is a bustling hubbub of tourist and marketing activity, lively yet seemingly imperturbable as ever. Horseback and carriage rides are available for hire here. A carriage ride around the square costs about 200R per person. A 20-minute tour of the city in the direction of your choosing costs about 2,000R, for up to six people. ⊠ *City Center* Ⓜ *Nevsky Prospekt.*

> ## ST. PETERSBURG BEST BETS
>
> **The State Hermitage Museum.** This immense and ornate royal palace is one of the finest art repositories in the world.
>
> **Dvortsovaya Ploshchad.** The seeds of the revolution were sown in this historic and architecturally stunning square.
>
> **The downtown core.** Known by the epithet "Venice of the North," St. Petersburg offers marvelous vistas at every turn.

Kazan Cathedral (*Kazansky Sobor*). After a visit to Rome, Tsar Paul I (1754–1801) commissioned this magnificent cathedral, wishing to copy—and perhaps present the Orthodox rival to—that city's St. Peter's. It was erected between 1801 and 1811 from a design by Andrei Voronikhin. Inside and out, the church abounds with sculpture and decoration. On the prospect side the frontage holds statues of St. John the Baptist and the apostle Andrew as well as such sanctified Russian heroes as Grand Prince Vladimir (who advanced the Christianization of Russia) and Alexander Nevsky. Note the enormous bronze front doors—exact copies of Ghiberti's Gates of Heaven at Florence's Baptistery. ⊠ *2 Kazanskaya Pl., City Center* ☎ *812/314–4663* ⊙ *Open daily 8:30–8; services weekdays at 10 am and 6 pm, weekends at 7 and 10 am and 6 pm* Ⓜ *Nevsky Prospekt.*

Fodor's Choice
★

Peter and Paul Fortress (*Petropavlovskaya Krepost*). The first building in Sankt-Piter-Burkh, as the city was then called, the fortress was erected in just one year, between 1703 and 1704. The date on which construction began on the fortress is celebrated as the birth of St. Petersburg.

The fortifications display several gates, along with arsenal buildings and the **Engineer's House** (*Inzhenerny Dom*), which is now a branch of the Museum of the History of St. Petersburg (as are all exhibits in the fortress) and presents displays about the city's pre-revolutionary history.

The main attraction of the fortress, however, is the **Cathedral of Sts. Peter and Paul** (*Petropavlovsky Sobor*). Constructed between 1712 and 1733 on the site of an earlier wooden church, it's highly unusual for a Russian Orthodox church. Instead of the characteristic bulbous domes, it's adorned by a single, slender, gilded spire whose height (400 feet)

made the church the city's tallest building for more than two centuries. Starting with Peter the Great, the cathedral served as the burial place of the tsars.

Several of the fortress's bastions were put to use over the years mainly as political prisons. One of them, **Trubetskoi Bastion,** is open to the public as a museum. Famous prisoners include some of the People's Will terrorists, who killed Alexander II in 1881; plus revolutionaries Leon Trotsky and Maxim Gorky. ✉ *3 Petropavlovskaya Krepost, Petrograd Side ☎ 812/230–6431; 812/232–9454 excursions ✇ Cathedral 140R, cathedral and other sights and exhibitions 250R, audio guide in English, French, German, Spanish, or Italian 250R (purchase guide at the Fortress's Information Center, at Ioanovsky Ravelin; the deposit of 2,000R or a document, such as a passport or driver's license, is required) ◷ Thurs.–Tues. 11–6, kassa open until 5 Thurs.–Mon., until 4 on Tues. Cathedral of Sts. Peter and Paul closed Wed., fortress closed last Tues. of month Ⓜ Gorkovskaya.*

Fodor'sChoice
★ **St. Isaac's Cathedral** (*Isaakievsky Sobor*). St. Isaac's is the world's third-largest domed cathedral, and the first monument you see of the city if you arrive by ship. Tsar Alexander I commissioned the construction of the cathedral in 1818 to celebrate his victory over Napoléon.

The interior of the cathedral is lavishly decorated with malachite, lazulite, marble, and other precious stones and minerals. Gilding the dome required 220 pounds of gold. When the city was blockaded during World War II, the gilded dome was painted black to avoid its being targeted by enemy fire. Despite efforts to protect it, the cathedral nevertheless suffered heavy damage, as bullet holes on the columns on the south side attest. ✉ *1 Isaakievskaya Pl., Admiralteisky ☎ 812/315–9732 ✇ Cathedral 200R, colonnade 100R ◷ Cathedral May–Sept., Thurs.–Tues. 10 am–7 pm and 8 pm–10:30 pm; Oct.–Apr., Thurs.–Tues. 11–6 and 7 pm–9:30 pm Ⓜ Sennaya Ploshchad.*

Fodor'sChoice
★ **State Hermitage Museum** (*Gosudarstvenny Ermitazh Muzey*). Leonardo's *Benois Madonna* . . . Rembrandt's *Danaë* . . . Matisse's *The Dance* . . . you get the picture. As the former private art collection of the tsars, this is one of the world's most famous museums, virtually wallpapered with celebrated paintings. In addition, the walls are works of art themselves, for this collection is housed in the lavish Winter Palace, one of the most outstanding examples of Russian baroque magnificence. The museum takes its name from Catherine the Great (1729–96), who used it for her private apartments. Between 1764 and 1775 the empress undertook to acquire some of the world's finest works of art.

A wealth of Russian and European art is on show: Florentine, Venetian, and other Italian art through the 18th century, including Leonardos and Michelangelos, two Raphaels, eight Titians, and works by Tintoretto, Lippi, Caravaggio, and Canaletto. The Hermitage also houses a superb collection of Spanish art, of which works by El Greco, Velázquez, Murillo, and Goya are on display. Its spectacular presentation of Flemish and Dutch art contains roomfuls of Van Dycks. Also here are more than 40 canvases by Rubens and an equally impressive number of Rembrandts. There is a smattering of excellent British

paintings including works by Joshua Reynolds, Thomas Gainsborough, and George Morland.

Reflecting the Francophilia of the empresses Elizabeth and Catherine, the museum is second only to the Louvre in its assortment of French art. Along with earlier masterpieces by Lorrain, Watteau, and Poussin, the collection runs the whole gamut of 19th-century genius, with Delacroix, Ingres, Corot, and Courbet. There is also a stunning collection of impressionists and postimpressionists, including works by Monet, Degas, Sisley, Pissarro, and Renoir. Sculptures by Auguste Rodin and a host of pictures by Cézanne, Gauguin, and van Gogh are followed by Picasso and a lovely room of Matisse.

Possibly the most-prized section of the Hermitage is the first-floor's **Treasure Gallery,** also referred to as the *Zolotaya Kladovaya* (Golden Room). This spectacular collection of gold, silver, and royal jewels includes ancient Scythian gold and silver treasures, plus precious stones, jewelry, and jewel-encrusted items from the 16th through the 20th centuries. ⊠ *2 Dvortsovaya Pl., City Center* ☎ *812/710–9625 recorded information in Russian; 812/710–9079 information desk; 812/571– 8446 tours* ⊕ *www.hermitagemuseum.org* ✉ *State Hermitage Museum 400R (free 1st Thurs. of month), two-day combined-entrance ticket 780R (this can only be purchased through the website), personal excursion guide 7,000R for groups up to seven people, Treasure Gallery 300R in addition to the entrance ticket price (check the schedule for the tours to the gallery a day before your visit by calling the tour service phone)* ⊗ *Tues.–Sat. 10:30–6, Sun. 10:30–5; kassa (ticket window) open Tues.–Sat. until 5, Sun. until 4* Ⓜ *Nevsky Prospekt.*

Fodor'sChoice
★ **State Museum of Russian Art** (*Gosudarstvenny Russky Muzey*). In 1898 Nicholas II turned the stupendously majestic neoclassical Mikhailovsky Palace (Mikhailovsky Dvorets) into a museum that has become one of the country's most important art galleries. The collection at the museum, which is sometimes just referred to as the Russian Museum, has scores of masterpieces on display, from outstanding icons to mainstream art of all eras. For many years much of this work was unknown in the West, and it's fascinating to see the stylistic parallels and the incorporation of outside influences into a Russian framework. Painters of the World of Art movement—Bakst, Benois, and Somov—are also here. There are several examples of 20th-century art, with works by Kandinsky and Kazimir Malevich. ⊠ *4/2 Inzhenernaya ul., City Center* ☎ *812/595–4248* ⊕ *www.rusmuseum.ru* ✉ *350R* ⊗ *Mon. 10–5, Wed.– Sun. 10–6, kassa open until 1 hr before closing* Ⓜ *Nevsky Prospekt.*

Fodor'sChoice
★ **Winter Palace** (*Zimny Dvorets*). With its 1,001 rooms swathed in malachite, jasper, agate, and gilded mirrors, this famous palace—the residence of Russia's rulers from Catherine the Great (1762) to Nicholas II (1917)—is the focal point of Palace Square. The palace, now the site of the State Hermitage Museum, is the grandest monument of that strange hybrid: the Russian rococo, in itself an eye-popping mix of the old-fashioned 17th-century baroque and the newfangled 18th-century neoclassical style. Now "Russianized," the palace's neoclassic ornament lost its early gracefulness and Greek sense of proportion and evolved

toward the heavier, more monumental, imperial style. Still, the exterior is particularly successful and pleasing.

The palace, which was created by the Italian architect Bartolomeo Francesco Rastrelli, stretches from Palace Square to the Neva River embankment. It was the fourth royal residence on this site, commissioned in 1754 by Peter the Great's daughter Elizabeth. By the time it was completed, in 1762, Elizabeth had died and the craze for the Russian rococo style had waned. Catherine the Great left the exterior unaltered but had the interiors redesigned in the neoclassical style of her day. In 1837, after the palace was gutted by fire, the interiors were revamped once again. Three of the palace's most celebrated rooms are the **Gallery of the 1812 War,** where portraits of Russian commanders who served against Napoléon are on display; the **Great Throne Room,** richly decorated in marble and bronze; and the **Malachite Room,** designed by the architect Alexander Bryullov. ⊠ *34 Dvortsovaya Pl., City Center* ☎ *812/710–9625 recorded information in Russian or 812/710–9079 directory service in Russian and English* ⊕ *www.hermitagemuseum.org* 🎫 *400R; 2-day combined-entrance ticket 780R (this can only be purchased through the website* ⊙ *Tues.–Sat. 10:30–6, Sun. 10:30–5 kassa open Tues.–Sat. until 5, on Sun. until 4* Ⓜ *Nevsky Prospekt.*

SHOPPING

Pick up a copy of Russian *Vogue* and you may be surprised to see that it nearly outdoes its Parisian and American counterparts for sheer glitz and trendy garb. And all those nifty threads that the models are wearing are fully stocked in the international boutiques around the city.

A two-tiered system of stores exists in St. Petersburg. Western-style shops taking credit-card payment have replaced the old *Beriozkas* (Birch Trees) emporiums, which were stocked only for foreigners. State-run shops are also better stocked now than before. Only rubles (as opposed to credit cards) are accepted in the state-run shops, however, and you'll have a tough time maneuvering through the cashiers if you don't speak some Russian.

The central shopping district is Nevsky prospekt and the streets running off it. Don't expect too many bargains beyond the bootlegged CDs and videos (which could be confiscated at customs in the United States), however, because prices for items such as clothes and electronic goods are just as high as in the West, and in the chic stores in hotels they are even higher.

For true souvenirs of the city, think quality crafts just like the tsars did. Ceramic painted eggs, á la Fabergé, and almost anything ornate and gilded are typical of the "imperial" style. Look also for good quality linens. Furs may not be to everybody's taste, but wealthy locals still prefer them during the freezing winters. For kitsch, what better than a set of Russian dolls? These vary in quality and in price.

WHERE TO EAT

$ ✕ **Teremok.** Don't be intimidated by the café's spartan setting. Teremok's
CAFÉ   owners penny-pinch only on furnishings and presentation. Cooked
in front of your eyes, their famous blini—priced at 40R–300R—are
deservedly rated the best in town. Stuffed with mushrooms, ham, pork,
grilled chicken, cream, honey, and a dozen other fillings, the blini, rich
in flavor and never over- or underdone, taste as if a Russian mom
cooked them. A single blini is so rich and hefty, it may leave you stuffed.
Be conservative when you order unless you are absolutely starving. In
addition to this café, Teremok also runs a chain of 15 street stands. ✉ *60
Nevsky pr., City Center* ☎ *No phone* Ⓜ *Nevsky Prospekt.*

$$ ✕ **Tinkoff.** The crowded, loftlike Tinkoff was St. Petersburg's first micro-
AMERICAN   brewery. Trendy people come to enjoy beer and tasty comfort food in
a relaxed, club-like dining room. Frequent Western jazz, lounge, and
cool pop acts appear at Tinkoff, but when they're here the cover price
gets very high, usually around 1,500R. There's a sushi bar, with combos
starting from 250R, but you're better off sticking with the beer and
burgers. ✉ *7 Kazanskaya ul., City Center* ☎ *812/718–5566* ⊕ *www.
tinkof.ru* Ⓜ *Nevsky Prospekt.*

STOCKHOLM, SWEDEN

Updated
by Lola
Akinmade-
Åkerström

Stockholm is a city in the flush of its second youth. In the last 10 years
Sweden's capital has emerged from its cold, Nordic shadow to take the
stage as a truly international city. The streets are flowing with a young
and confident population keen to drink in everything the city has to
offer. The glittering feeling of optimism, success, and living in the "here
and now" is rampant in Stockholm. Of course, not everyone is looking
to live so much in the present; luckily, Stockholm also has plenty of his-
tory. Stockholm boasts a glorious medieval Old Town, grand palaces,
ancient churches, sturdy edifices, public parks, and 19th-century muse-
ums—its history is soaked into the very fabric of its airy boulevards,
built as a public display of the city's trading glory.

ESSENTIALS
CURRENCY
The unit of currency is the krona (plural kronor). Sweden is not in the
euro zone.

HOURS
Banks are open weekdays 9:30–3; larger branches until 5 and 6 on
Thursday. The bank at Arlanda International Airport is open every day
with extended hours, and the Forex and X-Change currency-exchange
offices also have extended hours. Take a queue-number ticket from
near the door and wait your turn. It's not uncommon to come across
cashless bank branches in some smaller towns so it's worth checking
before traveling.

TELEPHONES
Most tri- or quad-band GSM phones work in Sweden, though handsets
are single-band, where the system is 3G-compatible. Public phones in
Sweden take phone cards or credit cards. Phone cards can be bought

Tegnérgatan
Tegnér-
lunden
Kammakargatan

◆ Stockholms
Stadsbiblioteket

Humlegården

Sturegatan

Brunnsgatan

Sture
Plan

Humlegårdsgatan

Barnhusgatan

Drottninggatan

Olof Palmes Gata

Hötorget

Kungsgatan

Malmskillnadsgatan

Mäster Samuelsgatan

Biblioteksgatan

Birger Jarlsgatan

Nybrogatan

Vasagatan

Kungsgatan

Sjöldgatan

Sveavägen

Smålandsgatan

Norr
Malmstorg

Nybro-
plan

Bryggargatan

Drottninggatan

Hamngatan 🛈

NORRMALM

Klarabergsgatan

Regeringsgatan

Kungsträdgårdsgatan

Arsenalsgatan

Nybrokajen

Klaberstrands-
leden

Klarabergsviadukten

Kulturhuset

Kungsträdgården ◆

Karl XII:s
Torg

Södra

Blasieholmsh.

🛈

◆ Train
Station

Vattugatan

Herkulesgatan

Operan ◆

Gustav
Adolfs
Torg

Strömbron

Kungsholms
Strand

Jakobsgatan

Fredsgatan

Riksbron

Norrbro

Hantverkargatan

Tegel
Backen

Stadshus-
bron

Vasabron

HELGEANDS
HOLMEN

Skeppsbron

Kungliga
Slottet ◆

Norr Mälar-
strand

Stadshuset ◆

Klara
Mälarstrand

Gångbron

Centralbron

Myntgatan

Slottsbacken

← Mälaren

Storkyrkobrinken

GAMLA
STAN

RIDDAR
HOLMEN

Riddarhus
Torget

Nobelmuseet ◆

Köpmang. Brunnsgr.

Stortorget ◆

Västerlånggatan

Österlånggatan

🛈

Riddarfjärden

Stora Nygatan

Lilla Nygatan

Kornhamns-
torg

Skeppsbron

Söder Mälarstrand

Centralbron

Söderm.
torg

Stadsgården

SÖDERMALM

Bastugatan

Tavastgatan

Brännkyrkagatan

Bleektornsgränd

Bellmansgatan

Södergatan

Katarinavägen

Hornsgatan

KEY
🚢 Ferry
⊢┼⊣ Rail Lines
🛈 Tourist information

at telecom shops, newsstands, and tobacconists. Public phones support international calls. Main providers include Telia, Tele2, Comviq, Vodafone, and T-Mobile.

COMING ASHORE

Most vessels dock at various quays in the heart of the Gamla Stan (Old Town). How far you have to walk to the attractions depends on which quay you are moored at. This is one port where you'll want to be out on deck as the ship arrives and the city comes within camera distance. If all berths are full (eight of them), there is a mooring buoy in the harbor, and passengers will be tendered ashore. You can reach everything in the city (museums, shops, restaurants, and cafés) from the quays on foot.

Alternatively, some vessels dock at Nynasham outside the city. It is a 15-minute walk from the port at Nynasham to the railway station for the one-hour journey into central Stockholm. A one-day travel card covers this journey and all other public transport trips within the city. SL (Stockholm Transport) runs a modern and reliable public transit system. Tickets are valid for one hour from validation and cost SKr 30 per journey within Zone 1 (central Stockholm). A one-day card is SKr 100.

Taxis are plentiful but expensive, and most drivers speak some English. Current rates are SKr 45 for pick-up, then around SKr 9 per km depending on the company. So expect to pay SKr100 (over US$14) for about a five-minute taxi ride.

EXPLORING STOCKHOLM

Fodor's Choice ★ **Fotografiska.** Opened in 2010, this contemporary photography museum housed in a 1906 redbrick art nouveau building along Stockholm's waterfront spotlights edgy fine art photography and past exhibitions have included celebrity photographer Annie Leibovitz and director Anton Corbijn. ⊠ *Stadsgårdsleden 22, Södermalm* ☎ *08/50900500* ⊕ *www.fotografiska.eu* ☕ *Skr 110* ☉ *Daily 10–9.*

♻ **Gröna Lund Tivoli.** Smaller than Copenhagen's Tivoli or Göteborg's Liseberg, this amusement park has managed to retain much of its historical charm, while making room for some modern, hair-raising rides among the pleasure gardens, amusement arcades, and restaurants. If you're feeling especially daring, try the Power Tower. At 350 feet, it's one of Europe's tallest free-fall amusement-park rides and one of the best ways to see Stockholm, albeit for about three seconds, before you plummet. There isn't an adult who grew up in Stockholm who can't remember the annual excitement of Gröna Lund's April opening. Go and you will see why. ⊠ *Allmänna Gränd 9, Djurgården* ☎ *08/58750100* ⊕ *www. gronalund.com* ☕ *SKr 95, not including tickets or passes for rides* ☉ *Late Apr.–mid-Sept., daily. Hrs vary but are generally noon-11pm. Call ahead for specific information.*

♻ **Kulturhuset** (*Culture House*). Since it opened in 1974, architect Peter Celsing's cultural center, a glass-and-stone monolith on the south side of Sergels Torg, has become a symbol of modernism in Sweden. Stockholmers are divided on the aesthetics of this building—most either love it or hate it. Here there are exhibitions for children and adults, a library,

a theater, a youth center, an exhibition center, and a restaurant. Head to Café Panorama, on the top floor, to savor traditional Swedish cuisine and a great view of Sergels Torg down below. ✉ *Sergels torg 3, City* ☎ *08/50831508* ⊕ *www.kulturhuset.stockholm.se* ☉ *Weekdays 9–7, weekends 11–5.*

Fodor's Choice **Kungliga Slottet** (*Royal Palace*). Designed by Nicodemus Tessin, the ★ Royal Palace was completed in 1760 and replaced the previous palace that had burned down at the location in 1697. The four facades of the palace each have a distinct style: the west is the king's, the east the queen's, the south belongs to the nation, and the north represents royalty in general. Watch the changing of the guard in the curved terrace entrance, and view the palace's fine furnishings and Gobelin tapestries on a tour of the Representationsvän (State Apartments). To survey the crown jewels, which are no longer used in this self-consciously egalitarian country, head to the Skattkammaren (Treasury). The Livrustkammaren (Royal Armory) has an outstanding collection of weaponry, coaches, and royal regalia. Entrances to the Treasury and Armory are on the Slottsbacken side of the palace. ✉ *Slottsbacken 1, Gamla Stan* ☎ *08/4026130* ⊕ *www.royalcourt.se* 💳 *SKr 150* ☉ *Mid-May–mid-Sept., daily 10–5; mid-Sept.–mid-May, daily noon-4.*

Kungsträdgården. Once the royal kitchen garden, this is now Stockholm's smallest but most central park. It is often used to host festivals and events, but is best seen in its everyday guise: as a pleasant sanctuary from the pulse of downtown. Several neat little glass-cube cafés sell light lunches, coffee, and snacks. ✉ *Kungsträdgården* ☎ *08/55510090* ⊕ *www.kungstradgarden.se.*

Moderna Museet (*Museum of Modern Art*). The museum's excellent collection includes works by Picasso, Kandinsky, Dalí, Brancusi, and other international artists. You can also view examples of significant Swedish painters and sculptors and an extensive section on photography. The building itself is striking. Designed by the well-regarded Spanish architect Rafael Moneo, it has seemingly endless hallways of blond wood and walls of glass. ✉ *Skeppsholmen, Exercisplan, City* ☎ *08/51955200* ⊕ *www.modernamuseet.se* 💳 *SKr 120* ☉ *Tues. 10–8, Wed.–Sun. 10–6.*

Fodor's Choice **Nationalmuseum.** Allow at least an hour if you want to see most of the ★ paintings and sculptures on display at this impressive museum. The emphasis is on Swedish and Nordic art, but other areas are well represented. Look especially for some fine works by Rembrandt. The print and drawing department is also impressive, with a nearly complete collection of Edouard Manet prints. ■**TIP→ From summer 2013, the Nationalmuseum will be undergoing major renovations. Many of its works will be temporararily relocated to the Royal Swedish Academy of Fine Arts at Fredsgatan 12, with different hours likely.** ✉ *Södra Blasieholmshamnen, City* ☎ *08/51954410* ⊕ *www.nationalmuseum.se* 💳 *SKr 100* ☉ *Jan.–Aug., Tues. 11–8, Wed.–Sun. 11–5; Sept.–Dec., Tues. and Thurs. 11–8, Wed., Fri., and weekends 11–5.*

Nobelmuseet. The Swedish Academy meets at Börshuset (the Stock Exchange) every year to decide the winner of the Nobel Prize for literature. The building is also the home of the Nobel Museum. Along with

exhibits on creativity's many forms, the museum displays scientific models, shows films, and has a full explanation of the process of choosing prizewinners. The museum does a good job covering the controversial selections made over the years. It's a must for Nobel Prize hopefuls and others. ⊠ *Börshuset, Stortorget 2, Gamla Stan* ☎ *08/53481800* ⊕ *www.nobelmuseum.se* ✉ *SKr 70* ⊗ *Mid-May–mid-Sept., Wed., Thurs., and Sat.–Mon., 10–6, Tues. and Fri. 10–8; mid-Sept.–mid-May, Tues. 11–8, Wed.–Sun. 11–5.*

Operan (*Opera House*). Stockholm's baroque Opera House is almost more famous for its restaurants and bars than for its opera

and ballet productions, but that doesn't mean an evening performance should be missed. There's not a bad seat in the house. For between just SKr 50 to 100 you can even get a listening-only seat (with no view). Still, its food and drink status can't be denied. It has been one of Stockholm's artistic and literary watering holes since the first Operakällaren restaurant opened on the site in 1787. ⊠ *Gustav Adolfs Torg, City* ☎ *08/7914400* ⊕ *www.operan.se.*

Östermalmstorg. The market square and its neighboring streets represent old, established Stockholm. **Saluhall** looks more like a collection of boutiques than the indoor food market it is; the fish displays can be especially intriguing. At the other end of the square, **Hedvig Eleonora Kyrka,** a church with characteristically Swedish faux-marble painting throughout its wooden interior, is the site of frequent lunchtime concerts in spring and summer. ⊠ *Nybrog. at Humlegårdsg., Östermalm* ⊕ *www.ostermalmshallen.se.*

Fodor's Choice **Rosendals Trädgården** (*Rosendal's Garden*). This gorgeous slice of greenery is a perfect place to spend a few hours on a late summer afternoon. When the weather's nice, people flock to the garden café, which is in one of the greenhouses, to enjoy tasty pastries and salads made from the locally grown vegetables. Pick your own flowers from the vast flower beds (paying by weight), stroll through the creative garden displays, or take away produce from the farm shop. ⊠ *Rosendalsterrassen 12, Djurgården* ☎ *08/54581270* ⊕ *www.rosendalstradgard.se* ✉ *Free* ⊗ *May–Sept., weekdays 11–5, weekends 11–6; Oct.–Apr. call ahead for specific information.*

★ **Skansen.** The world's first open-air museum, Skansen was founded in 1891 by philologist and ethnographer Artur Hazelius, who is buried here. Drawing from all parts of the country, he preserved examples of traditional Swedish architecture, including farmhouses, windmills, barns, a working glassblower's hut, and churches. Not only is Skansen

a delightful trip out of time in the center of a modern city, but it also provides insight into the life and culture of Sweden's various regions. In addition, the park has a zoo, carnival area, aquarium, theater, and cafés. ✉ *Djurgårdsslätten 49–51, Djurgården* ☎ *08/4428000* ⊕ *www. skansen.se* 🖃 *Park and zoo: Jan.–Apr. SKr 70, May and Sept. SKr 90, June–Aug. SKr 110. Aquarium: SKr 100.* ⊙ *Nov.–Feb., weekdays 10–3, weekends 10-4; Mar., Apr., and Oct., daily 10–4; May–June 19, daily 10–8; June 20–Aug. 10–8; Sept., daily 10–8.*

Fodor's Choice **Stadshuset** (*City Hall*). The architect Ragnar Östberg, one of the found-
★ ers of the National Romantic movement, completed Stockholm's city hall in 1923. The headquarters of the city council, the building is functional but ornate: its immense **Blå Hallen** (Blue Hall) is the venue for the annual Nobel Prize dinner, Stockholm's main social event. You must take a tour to visit City Hall. You can also take a trip to the top of the 348-foot tower, most of which can be achieved by elevator, to enjoy a breathtaking panorama of the city and Riddarfjärden. ✉ *Hantverkarg. 1, Kungsholmen* ☎ *08/50829058* ⊕ *www.stockholm.se* 🖃 *SKr 90, tower Skr 40* ⊙ *Tours of City Hall in English, Sept.–May, daily on the hour 10–3; June–Aug., daily every 30 min. 9:30–4. Tower open May–Sept., daily 9:15–4:30.*

Stockholms Stadsbiblioteket (*Stockholm City Library*). The Stockholm City Library is among the most captivating buildings in town. Designed by the famous Swedish architect E. G. Asplund and completed in 1928, the building's cylindrical, galleried main hall gives it the appearance of a large birthday cake. Inside is an excellent "information technology" center with free Internet access—and lots of books, too. ✉ *Sveav. 73, Vasastan* ☎ *08/50830900* ⊕ *www.biblioteket.se* ⊙ *Mon.–Thurs. 9–9, Fri. 9–7, weekends noon–4.*

Stortorget (*Great Square*). Here in 1520 the Danish king Christian II ordered a massacre of Swedish noblemen. The slaughter paved the way for a national revolt against foreign rule and the founding of Sweden as a sovereign state under King Gustav Vasa, who ruled from 1523 to 1560. One legend holds that if it rains heavily enough on the anniversary of the massacre, the old stones still run red. ✉ *Near Kungliga Slottet, Gamla Stan.*

Vasamuseet (*Vasa Museum*). The warship *Vasa* sank 10 minutes into its maiden voyage in 1628, consigned to a watery grave until it was raised from the seabed in 1961. Its hull was preserved by the Baltic mud, free of the shipworms (really clams) that can eat through timbers. Now largely restored to her former glory (however short-lived it may have been), the man-of-war resides in a handsome museum. The sheer size of this cannon-laden hulk inspires awe and fear in equal measure. The political history of the world may have been different had she made it out of harbor. Daily tours are available year-round. ✉ *Galärvarvsv. 14, Djurgården* ☎ *08/51954800* ⊕ *www.vasamuseet.se* 🖃 *SKr 110* ⊙ *June–Aug., daily 8.30–6; Sept.–May, Thurs.–Tues. 10–5, Wed. 10–8.*

SHOPPING

If you like to shop till you drop, then charge on down to MOOD, PUB, NK, and Gallerian, the four main department stores and malls in the central city area. All of them carry top-name brands for both men and women. For souvenirs and crafts peruse the boutiques and galleries in Västerlånggatan, the main street of Gamla Stan. For jewelry, crafts, and fine art, hit the shops that line the raised sidewalk at the start of Hornsgatan on Södermalm. Drottninggatan, Birger Jarlsgatan, Biblioteksgatan, Götgatan, and Hamngatan also offer some of the city's best shopping.

Gallerian. Just down the road from Sergels Torg, this large indoor mall has designer chic to spare, selling toys to fashion in beautiful surroundings. ⊠ *Hamng. 37, City* ☎ *08/53337300* ⊕ *www.gallerian.se.*

Fodor'sChoice
★
Hötorgshallen. For a good indoor market hit Hötorgshallen, directly under the Filmstaden movie theater. The market is filled with butcher shops, coffee and tea shops, and fresh-fish markets. It's closed on Sunday. ⊠ *Hötorget, City* ☎ *08/230001* ⊕ *www.hotorgshallen.se.*

MOOD. Stockholm's newest destination for high-end shopping spans an entire city block. ⊠ *Jakobsbergsg. 15, Norrmalm* ⊕ *www. moodstockholm.com.*

Fodor'sChoice
★
NK. Sweden's leading department store is the unmissable NK; the initials, pronounced enn-*koh,* stand for Nordiska Kompaniet. You pay for the high quality here. ⊠ *Hamng. 18–20, across street from Kungsträdgården, City* ☎ *08/7628000* ⊕ *www.nk.se.*

PUB. Before becoming a famous actress, Greta Garbo used to work at PUB, which has 42 independent boutiques. Garbo fans will appreciate the small exhibit on level H2—a collection of photographs begins with her employee ID card. ⊠ *Drottningg. 63 and Hötorget, City* ☎ *08/7891930* ⊕ *www.pub.se.*

WHERE TO EAT

Most Stockholm restaurants specialize in the preparation of perennially popular, Swedish-style fish and shellfish. Innovative and traditional herring assortments and locally sourced roe are especially popular as starters. These starters are often large enough for a light, affordable lunch. Note that many restaurants are closed on Sunday.

$$
VEGETARIAN
Fodor'sChoice
★
✕ **Hermans.** Hermans is a haven for vegetarians out to get the most bang for their kronor. The glassed-in back deck and open garden both provide breathtaking vistas across the water of Stockholm harbor, Gamla Stan, and the island of Djurgården. The food, served buffet style, includes various vegetable and pasta salads, warm casseroles, and such entrées as Indonesian stew with peanut sauce and vegetarian lasagna. The fruit pies, chocolate cakes, and cookies are delicious. $ *Average main: SKr 155* ⊠ *Fjällg. 23B* ☎ *08/6439480* ⊕ *www.hermans.se.*

$$$$
SCANDINAVIAN
Fodor'sChoice
★
✕ **Mathias Dahlgren.** From the elegant modern dining room to what's on the plate—simple, artistically rendered local food that its eponymous chef has dubbed "natural cuisine"—this place doesn't disappoint. And for his trouble Dahlgren has picked up two Michelin stars since opening in late 2007. Don't miss this place—and keep in mind that prices in

the bar, where lunch is served on weekdays, are much lower than in the dining room. $ *Average main: SKr 1,650* ⊠ *Grand Hotel, S Blasieholmshamen 6* ☎ *08/6793584* ⊕ *www.mathiasdahlgren.com* ⌂ *Reservations essential* ⊘ *No lunch weekends. Closed Sun.*

$$ ✕ **Pelikan.** Beer, beer, and more beer is the order of the day at this traditional drinking hall, a relic of the days when Södermalm was the dwelling place of the city's blue-collar brigade. Today's more bohemian residents find it just as enticing, with the unvarnished wood-paneled walls, faded murals, and glass globe lights fulfilling all their down-at-the-heel pretensions. The food here is some of the best traditional Swedish fare in the city. The herring, meatballs, and salted bacon with onion sauce are all great choices. $ *Average main: SKr 216* ⊠ *Blekingeg. 40* ☎ *08/55609090* ⊕ *www.pelikan.se* ⊘ *No lunch Fri.–Sun.*

SCANDINAVIAN

Fodor's Choice

★

$$$ ✕ **Prinsen.** Still in the same location as when it opened in 1897, the Prince serves both traditional and modern Swedish cuisine, but it's the traditional that brings most people here. The interior is rich with mellow, warm lighting; dark-wood paneling; and leather chairs and booths. The restaurant is rightly known for its scampi salad and *Wallenbergare,* a classic dish of veal, cream, and peas. Downstairs you'll find a bar and a space for larger parties. $ *Average main: SKr 295* ⊠ *Mäster Samuelsg. 4, Norrmalm* ☎ *08/6111331* ⊕ *www.restaurangprinsen.eu* ⌂ *Reservations essential.*

SCANDINAVIAN

★

5

WHERE TO STAY

Stockholm can be a relatively stagnant town when it comes to hotel development, with few new openings each year. But while the hotel choices here are often not trendily brand-new, they're still plentiful and include everything from grand five-star properties down to basic, affordable hostel accommodation.

$$$$ ⌂ **Grand Hotel.** At first glance the Grand seems like any other world-class international hotel, and in many ways it is. **Pros:** unadulterated luxury; world-class service; great bar. **Cons:** some rooms are small; faded in parts; very expensive. $ *Rooms from: SKr 3,000* ⊠ *Södra Blasieholmshamnen 8, City* ☎ *08/6793500* ⊕ *www.grandhotel.se* ⇄ *269 rooms, 31 suites* ⫿⊘⫿ *Breakfast.*

HOTEL

Fodor's Choice

★

$$ ⌂ **Radisson Blue Strand Hotel.** An art nouveau monolith, built in 1912 for the Stockholm Olympics, this hotel has been completely and tastefully modernized. **Pros:** central location; elegant rooms; energized public areas. **Cons:** has a slight chain-hotel feel; beds too soft for some. $ *Rooms from: SKr 1,895* ⊠ *Nybrokajen 9, City* ☎ *08/50664000* ⊕ *www.radissonblu.com* ⇄ *149 rooms, 3 suites* ⫿⊘⫿ *Breakfast.*

HOTEL

$$ ⌂ **Scandic Grand Central.** The eco-friendly Scandic Grand Central is in an impressive 130-year-old building, just steps away from the city's main train station, right in the heart of Stockholm's business district. **Pros:** central to everything; everything's new (hotel opened in late 2011). **Cons:** noisy location. $ *Rooms from: SKr 1650* ⊠ *Kungsg. 70, City* ☎ *08/51252000* ⊕ *www.scandichotels.com* ⇄ *391 rooms* ⫿⊘⫿ *Breakfast.*

HOTEL

Fodor's Choice

★

$$ ⌂ **Sheraton Hotel.** Popular with businesspeople, the Sheraton is also an ideal hotel for the tourist on a generous budget looking for comfort

HOTEL

and luxury. **Pros:** great location; big rooms; extremely comfortable beds. **Cons:** lower-floor rooms can be noisy; terrible view from courtyard rooms. $ *Rooms from: SKr 1,995* ⊠ *Tegelbacken 6, City* ☎ *08/4123400* ⊕ *www.sheratonstockholm.com* ⤴ *436 rooms, 29 suites* ⦿| *Breakfast.*

TALLINN, ESTONIA

Updated by
Dorota Wąsik

Tallinn's tiny gem of an Old Town, the most impressive in the region, is an ideal cruise destination. It has romantic towers, ankle-wrenching cobblestone streets, cozy nooks, city-wall cafés, and a dozen other attractions–all within 1 square km. In many ways still the same town as during the medieval era, it is compact enough to reveal itself on a short visit. In this eminently walkable city it is possible to see the main sights and venture into intimate corners during your trip and feel that you've found your own personal Tallinn. The city has blossomed in the post-Communist era and revels in its resurgent popularity, but it hasn't forgotten its roots. It's still charming and distinctive, despite having strode headlong into the 21st century.

ESSENTIALS
CURRENCY
Since 2011, Estonia has used the euro. National banks, with branches in all major and most minor cities, change cash and traveler's checks at fair commissions. There is a good network of ATMs, and credit cards are widely accepted in Estonia, although Visa and MasterCard are more common than American Express.

HOURS
Banks are open weekdays 9–4, but some open as early as 8 and close as late as 7. Most are closed on Saturday, but some stay open 9–3. Museums are generally open Wednesday–Sunday 11–5. Some stay open until 6. Shops open between 10 and 11 and close between 5 and 7, with shorter hours on Saturday. Most shops are closed on Sunday, except for shopping centers and malls, which stay open 7 days a week, until late.

TELEPHONES
Most tri- and quad-band mobile phones should work in Estonia. The mobile service is dual-band and supports text and data services. Pay phones take phone cards. Buy cards at any kiosk. You can use these to make international calls.

COMING ASHORE
The Old City Harbor Port sits in the very heart of modern Tallinn and is half a mile from the city center. Terminal facilities are comprehensive, and include a restaurant, bank–exchange facilities, tourist information shops, and restrooms. Taxis wait outside the terminal building for journeys into the Old Town; otherwise, it's only a short walk from the port.

Taxi drivers are bound by law to display an operating license and a meter. There is no need to rent a car while in Tallinn, as all the major attractions are in the Old Town, which is very close to the cruise pier.

EXPLORING TALLINN

Tallinn's tiny Old Town, the most impressive in the region, has romantic towers, ankle-wrenching cobblestone streets, cozy nooks, city-wall
cafés, and a dozen other attractions—all within 1 square km (½ square
mile). In the 1990s, Vanalinn (the lower Old Town)—historically the
domain of traders, artisans, and ordinary citizens—sprouted glitzy
neon signs in otherwise charming alleys and sights. The stately, sedate
Toompea (Upper Town), a hillock that was the site of the original Estonian settlement, is on the burial mound of Kalev, the epic hero of Estonia. Toompea Castle, crowning the hill, is now the seat of the country's
parliament and is not open to visitors. Summer visitors can experience
the unforgettable white nights, when the sun never completely sets.

Aleksandr Nevski Khram. The 19th-century Russian Orthodox Alexander
Nevsky Cathedral, with the country's largest bell, is a symbol of the
centuries of Russification endured by Estonia. ⊠ *Lossi pl. 10, Toompea*
☎ *644–3484* ☾ *Daily 8–7.*

Dominiiklaste Kloostri Muuseum. Wander through the ages in the ancient
stone galleries and narrow hallways of the Dominican Monastery
Museum, founded in 1246 and now displaying 15th- and 16th-century
stone carvings. At 5 pm enjoy a half-hour baroque music concert.
⊠ *Vene 16, Vanalinn* ☎ *644–4606* ⊕ *kloostri.ee* ☾ *Daily 10–6.*

Kadriorg Palace Foreign Art Museum. The baroque palace, built for Catherine I by her husband Peter the Great in 1721, merits a visit not just for its impressive and thorough exhibition of 16th- to 20th-century art, but also for the palace's architectural beauty and manicured gardens. Kadriorg Palace offers a glimpse into history, from Russian imperial splendor to Soviet Socialist Realist art, with Estonian and European masterpieces along the way. ⊠ *Weizenbergi 37* ☎ *606–6400* ⊕ *www.kadriorumuuseum.ee/en* ⌐ *€4.80* ☿ *May–Sept., Tues.–Sun. 10–5; Oct.–Apr., Wed.–Sun. 10–5.*

★ **Kiek-in-de-Kök.** At the southern end of the Old Town looms this magnificent, six-story tower church (the name is Low German for "peep in the kitchen"), so called because during the 15th century one could peer into the kitchens of lower town houses from here. The tower has a museum of contemporary art and ancient maps and weapons. ⊠ *Komandandi 2, Vanalinn* ☎ *644–6686* ⊕ *www.linnamuuseum.ee/kok* ⌐ *€4.50* ☿ *Mar.–Oct., Tues.–Sun. 10:30–6; Nov.–Feb., Tues.–Sun. 10:30–5.*

Niguliste Kirik. The 15th-century Church of St. Nicholas, part of the Estonian Art Museum, is famed for its fragment of a treasured frieze, Bernt Notke's (1440–1509) *Danse Macabre,* a haunting depiction of death. ⊠ *Niguliste 3, Vanalinn* ☎ *631–4330* ⊕ *www.nigulistemuuseum.ee/en* ⌐ *€3.50* ☿ *Wed.–Sun. 10–5.*

Paks Margareeta. The stocky guardian of the northernmost point of the Old Town, Fat Margaret, is a 16th-century fortification named for a particularly hefty cannon it contained. Now it houses the Maritime Museum and a roof with a view of Old Town. ⊠ *Pikk 70, Vanalinn* ☎ *641–1408* ⊕ *www.meremuuseum.ee* ⌐ *€4* ☿ *Wed.–Sun. 10–6.*

Fodor's Choice ★ **Raekoja Plats.** Tallinn's Town Hall Square has a long history of intrigue, executions, and salt (Tallinn's main export in the Middle Ages). You can tour the only surviving Gothic **town hall** in northern Europe. Old Thomas, its weather vane, has been atop the town hall since 1530. Near the center of the square, an L-shaped stone marks the site of a 17th-century execution, where a priest was beheaded for killing a waitress who had offered him a rock-hard omelet. Across the square stands the town **apothecary,** which dates from 1422. ⊠ *Raekoja plats 11* ☎ *645–7900 for town hall, 631–4860 for apothecary* ⌐ *Town Hall: €4* ☿ *Town Hall: Mon.–Sat. 10–4.*

☻ **Rocca al Mare.** A 15-minute taxi ride from the center, the 207-acre Open-Air Ethnographic Museum provides a breath of fresh air and

---

TALINN BEST BETS

Shopping in Vanalinn. These alleyways have been a bustling commercial center for more than 500 years. History practically oozes from every stone and the galleries are a shopper's delight.

Raekoja Plats. One of the finest city squares in the Baltic, Raekoja Plats is the social center of the city, hosting markets, concerts, and parades.

Aleksandr Nevski Khram. This Orthodox church is a wonderfully ornate example of its type, with onion domes and an interior full of votives and icons.

an informative look into Estonia's past, from farm architecture to World War II–era deportations. ✉ *Vabaõhumuuseumi 12* ☎ *654–9101* ⊕ *www.evm.ee/keel/eng* 🎫 *€3* ⊘ *Late Apr.–late Sept., daily 10–8; late Sept.–late Apr., daily 10–5.*

Toomkirik. The Lutheran Dome Church (Cathedral of Saint Mary the Virgin) is the oldest church in the country, founded by the occupying Danes in the 13th century and rebuilt in 1686. ✉ *Toom-kooli 6, Toompea* ☎ *644–4140* ⊕ *www.eelk.ee/tallinna.toom* ⊘ *Tues.–Sun. 9–5.*

SHOPPING

Tallinn has a wide range of crafts on sale. Fragrant juniper wood is carved into bowls and dolomite stone is fashioned into candlesticks and coasters. A whole range of handblown glass, ceramics, delicate wrought iron, and art is sold in tiny galleries. Hand-knitted sweaters, gloves, and socks keep the locals snug in winter and are signature souvenirs here. Warming quilts are also available, as well as a good range of leather goods. Sweet tooths will love the chocolates made by Kalev and the hand-painted marzipan that's sold in presentation boxes. The Old Town is the place to browse, with some excellent shops around Katerina kälk (Catherine Passage).

WHERE TO EAT

$$$
ECLECTIC
✕ **Gloria.** The art nouveau interior compliments the French-influenced menu of highbrow European food like beef Stroganoff or tournedos Rossini. To maintain its tradition of decadence, Gloria offers a *tabacalera* (tobacco shop) complete with Cuban cigars and an extensive wine cellar. 💲 *Average main: €25* ✉ *Müürivahe 2* ☎ *640–6800* ⊕ *www. gloria.ee* ⌚ *Reservations essential Jacket and tie* ⊘ *Closed Sun. No lunch Sat.*

$
EASTERN
EUROPEAN
Fodor's Choice
★
✕ **Olde Hansa.** In a 15th-century building in the Old Town, this restaurant recreates medieval times with waiters in period costume, candlelit tables, and historic Eastern European recipes for such dishes as nobleman's smoked filet mignon in mushroom sauce and wild boar with game sauce and forest berries. The honey beer is out of this world, and the old-fashioned food is always fresh and tasty. 💲 *Average main: €15* ✉ *Vanaturg 1* ☎ *627–9020* ⊕ *www.oldehansa.ee.*

VISBY, SWEDEN

Updated
by Lola
Akinmade-
Åkerström

Gotland is Sweden's main holiday island, a place of ancient history, a relaxed summer-party vibe, wide sandy beaches, and wild cliff formations called *raukar* (the remnants of reefs formed more than 400 million years ago). Measuring 125 km (78 miles) long and 52 km (32 miles) at its widest point, Gotland is where Swedish sheep farming has its home. In its charming glades, 35 varieties of wild orchids thrive, attracting botanists from all over the world. Gotland's capital, Visby, reflects this full and fascinating history, and the architecture of its downtown core is classified as a World Heritage site.

ESSENTIALS

CURRENCY
The unit of currency is the krona (plural kronor). Sweden is not in the euro zone.

HOURS
Banks are open weekdays 9:30–3; larger branches until 5 and 6 on Thursday. The bank at Arlanda International Airport is open every day with extended hours, and the Forex and X-Change currency-exchange offices also have extended hours. Take a queue-number ticket from near the door and wait your turn. It's not uncommon to come across cashless bank branches in some smaller towns so it's worth checking before traveling.

TELEPHONES
Most tri- or quad-band GSM phones work in Sweden, though handsets are single-band, where the system is 3G-compatible. Public phones in Sweden take phone cards or credit cards. Phone cards can be bought at telecom shops, newsstands, and tobacconists. Public phones support international calls. Main providers include Telia, Tele2, Comviq, Vodafone, and T-Mobile.

COMING ASHORE
Vessels dock in the town port; from here it is a 5- to 10-minute walk into the center of town. The port has only the most basic facilities, but shops and restaurants are on hand in town.

You don't need public transport to explore Visby. However, if you want to discover all that Gotland has to offer independently, you'll need transportation. Renting a car would free you up to explore at your own pace. An economy manual vehicle starts at SKr 800 per day.

EXPLORING GOTLAND

VISBY
Gotland's capital, Visby, is a delightful hilly town of about 22,000 people. Medieval houses, ruined fortifications, churches, and cottage-lined cobbled lanes make Visby look like it's from a fairy tale. Thanks to a very gentle climate, the roses that grow along many of the town's facades bloom even in November. In its heyday Visby was protected by a wall, of which 3 km (2 miles) survive today, along with 44 towers and numerous gateways. It is considered the best-preserved medieval city wall in Europe after that of Carcassonne, in southern France. Take a stroll to the north gate for an unsurpassed view of the wall.

Fodor's Choice
★
☺
Fårö. It takes a five-minute ferry crossing to reach tiny, secluded Fårö from Gotland, to the south. A popular summer retreat for Scandinavians, the island has just 600 year-round residents. Legendary Swedish filmmaker Ingmar Bergman once called this island home; every June, film fanatics head over to celebrate Bergman Week. And in September, the island celebrates Fårönatta—a night when its shops, restaurants, and attractions stay open all night and the church holds a midnight mass. Head to the Digerhuvud area to find some impressive natural "sea stacks," weather rock formations that are known as *raukar*. They often take on human

Gotland

Farö	**Farö**
Kappelshamn	Farösund
◆ Lummelundagrottan	
Visby see detail map	Slite
Hejdeby	
	Gothem
Kneippbyn	Romakloster
Vastergarn	Östergarnsholm
◆ Klintehamn	Östergarn
◆ Vikingabyn	
◆ Stora and Lilla Karlsö	Stänga	Ljugarn
Hemse	
Haydhem	
Burgsvik	
Sundre	
Hoburgen	

0   6 mi
0   9 km

Baltic Sea

STRAND-GÄRDET

Nordergravar

Silverhättan

Backg.

Bergsg.

Norderväg

Norderport

Strandpromenaden

Studentallén

Botaniska Trädgården

Tranhusg.

Skt. Nikolaig.

Norra Kyrkog.

Österavar

◆ **St. Maria Kyrka**

Dalmansporten

Fiskarporten

Speckarum

Strandg.

Kung Magnus väg

Strandväg.

Almedalen

Mellang.

Skt. Hansg.

Storatorget

Norra Murg.

Nyg.

Donnersg.

Gotland Museum

Klinttorget

Polhemsg.

Jägarg.

Hamnplan

Donners plats

Skt. Hans plan

Wallers plats

Hästg.

Osterport

Östervag

Scheeleg.

Holmen

Korsg.

Skt. Hansg.

Kinbergs plats

Berggrand

Adelsg.

Skolportssg.

Na Hanseg.

Inrehamnen

Fårleden

Södra Murg.

Avag.

Palisaderna

Söder-torg

Söderport

SOLBORGA

Skansporten

Kneippbyn

0   1,00 yards
0   1,00 m

Visby

profiles, fueling local myths and legends. Note that basic services, including police, medical services, and banks, are virtually nonexistent on Fårö itself. If you really want to retreat from the world, Fårö is it. ⊕ *www.gotland.info.*

Gotland Museum. The Länsmuseet på Gotland, Gotland's county museum, contains examples of medieval artwork, prehistoric gravestones and skeletons, and silver hoards from Viking times. Be sure to also check out the ornate "picture stones" from AD 400–600, which depict ships, people, houses, and animals. ⊠ *Strandg. 14* ☎ *0498/292700* ⊕ *www.gotlandsmuseum.se* 🖻 *SKr 100* ⏱ *Daily 11–6.*

VISBY BEST BETS

Follow your whim along the streets of Visby. The wealth of architectural splendor funded by Hanseatic trade means there's a wonderful vista on almost every corner.

Explore the dramatic and windswept countryside beyond the city walls. Wild orchids, rocky coastal precipices, and grassy meadows abound.

Church-hopping. Gotland has about 100 old churches that are still in use (Visby itself has 13); exploring them is a major pastime.

☺ **Kneippbyn.** This resort with a water park and amusement park brings droves of families in summer; there are over 600 rooms, cabins, apartments, and camping sites. Locations from the Pippi Longstocking TV show, including her house, Villa Villekulla, are here. ⊠ *3 km south of Visby, Gotland* ⊕ *www. kneippbyn.se* 🖻 *Skr 135–245* ⏱ *Parks open May–Aug.*

St. Maria Kyrka. Visby's cathedral is the only one of the town's 13 medieval churches that is still intact and in use. Built between 1190 and 1225 as a place of worship for the town's German parishioners, the church has few of its original fittings because of the extensive and sometimes clumsy restoration work done over the years. That said, the sandstone font and the unusually ugly angels decorating the pulpit are both original features worth a look. ⊠ *Västra kyrkog., Visby* ☎ *0498/206800* ⊕ *www.svenskakyrkan.se* ⏱ *Daily 10–5.*

GOTLAND

There's a lot to see out on the island, so if you want to spend the day exploring, you can see a fair amount in your day in port. Definitely get out of Visby itself if you want to see some of the island's churches.

Lummelundagrottan. The 4 km (2½ miles) of stalactite caves at Lummelunda, about 18 km (11 miles) north of Visby on the coastal road, are unique in this part of the world and well worth a visit. ⊠ *Lummelunds Bruk* ☎ *0498/273050* ⊕ *www.lummelundagrottan.se* 🖻 *SKr 130* ⏱ *May–Sept., daily 10–5.*

Stora and Lilla Karlsö. These two bird sanctuaries are off the coast south of Visby. The bird population consists mainly of guillemots, which look like penguins. Visits to these sanctuaries are permitted only in the company of a recognized guide. Contact each sanctuary for its tour times. ☎ *0498/240450 for Stora, 0498/241139 for Lilla* ⊕ *www. storakarlso.se; www.lillakarlso.org* 🖻 *SKr 325 for Stora, SKr 300 for Lilla* ⏱ *May–Aug., daily.*

CLOSE UP

Gotland's Churches

The island has about 100 old churches dating from Gotland's great commercial era that are still in use today. **Barlingbo,** from the 13th century, has vault paintings, stained-glass windows, and a remarkable 12th-century font. The exquisite **Dalhem** was constructed around 1200. **Gothem,** built during the 13th century, has a notable series of paintings of that period. **Grötlingbo** is a 14th-century church with stone sculptures and stained glass (note the 12th-century reliefs on the facade). **Öja,** a medieval church decorated with paintings, houses a famous holy rood from the late-13th century. The massive ruins of a Cistercian monastery founded in 1164 are now called the **Roma Kloster Kyrka** (Roma Cloister Church). **Tingstäde** is a mix of six buildings dating from 1169 to 1300.

5

Ⓒ **Vikingabyn** (*Viking Village*). Be a Viking for a day at this 10th-century village re-creation. Kids and adults can try their hands at baking Viking bread, axe throwing, archery, and other activities. There are also performances along with guided tours and lectures. ⊠ *Tofta Strand, Gotland* ☎ *0498/297100* ⊕ *www.vikingabyn.se* ⊠ *Skr 120* ☉ *June–Aug., Mon.–Sat. 10–5.*

SHOPPING

Gotlanders are self-sufficient and resourceful people and have developed many handicrafts, so there is a range of handcrafted souvenirs to choose from, including blown glass, metal objects, sculptures, woven items, and ceramics. Sheepskin and wool items are a particular specialty.

ACTIVITIES

The unspoiled countryside and onshore waters are a perfect playground if you want to get active. Many visitors simply rent a bike and take to the safe open roads, or try kayaking or windsurfing on the water.

Fodor'sChoice **Gotland Active Store.** Adventure tours and packages that cover Gotland
★ and nearby islands are available from this company. ⊠ *Hamng. 4, Visby* ☎ *0772/070400* ⊕ *www.gotlandactive.se.*

Gotlands Cykeluthyrning. Bicycles, tents, and camping equipment can be rented from Gotlands Cykeluthyrning. ⊠ *Skeppsbron 2, Visby* ☎ *0498/214133* ⊕ *www.gotlandscykeluthyrning.com.*

Gotlands Upplevelser. For an aquatic adventure, Gotlands Upplevelser will rent you a canoe and a life jacket or windsurfing equipment. They also offer rock-climbing courses. ⊠ *Getsvältans väg 8, Högklint* ☎ *0730/751678* ⊕ *www.gotlandsupplevelser.se.*

WHERE TO EAT

$$ X **Bakfickan.** It may have one of the best locations in town—right in
SWEDISH   Stora Torget next to medieval ruins of St. Karin—but this restaurant
is decorated in what could be called Fisherman's Shack Rustic, with
wood benches, shellfish and seafood displays, details from fishing boats,
small metal buckets resting on shelves, and menus scribbled on chalk-
boards. Expect a tight squeeze—there isn't much space to maneuver
inside. Try the fried Baltic herring with mashed potatoes, or on a brisk
day, warm up with its hearty fish stew with a dollop of aioli. $ *Aver-
age main: SKr 185* ⊠ *Stora Torget 1, Visby* ☎ *0498/271807* ⊕ *www.
bakfickan-visby.nu.*

$$$ X **Donners Brunn.** Bo Nilsson, the chef proprietor of this atmospheric
SCANDINAVIAN   restaurant, was once chef at the renowned Operakällaren in Stockholm.
Fodor's Choice   Now, in a beautiful orange-brick house on a small square in Visby, he
★   cooks for a mix of locals and visitors, who dine in cellar-like halls surrounded by white stone walls. The menu uses excellent local ingredients
to make French-influenced dishes that are reasonably priced, given their
quality. Its house specialty of Gotland lamb shanks with sweetbread
and turnips is absolutely delicious; you may want to finish with a rich
and sticky-sweet crème brûlée topped with a mixed-berry compote.
$ *Average main: SKr 285* ⊠ *Donners Plats 3* ☎ *0498/271090* ⊕ *www.
donnersbrunn.se* ⌂ *Reservations essential* ☉ *No lunch. Closed Sun.*

WARNEMÜNDE, GERMANY (FOR BERLIN)

Updated by
Giulia Pines

Since the fall of the Iron Curtain, no city in Europe has seen more
development and change. Two Berlins that had been separated for 40
years struggled to meld into one, and in the scar of barren borderland
between them sprang government and commercial centers that have
become the glossy spreads of travel guides and architecture journals.
But even as the capital moves forward, history is always tugging at
its sleeve. Between the wealth of neoclassical and 21st-century buildings, there are constant reminders, both subtle and stark, of the events
of the 20th century. For every relocated corporate headquarters, a
church stands half ruined, a synagogue is under 24-hour guard, and an
empty lot remains where a building either crumbled in World War II
or went up in dynamite as East Germany cleared a path for its wall.
There are few other cities where the past and the present collide with
such energy.

ESSENTIALS
CURRENCY
The euro. ATMs are common and credit cards are widely accepted.

HOURS
Stores are open Monday through Saturday from 8 am to 8 pm. Museum
hours vary, but core hours are from 10 am to 5 pm, with shorter hours
on Sunday. Some state museums are closed on Monday.

TELEPHONES

Most tri- and quad-band GSM phones will work in Germany, where the mobile system supports 3G technology. Phone cards for public phones are available at newsagents and will allow international calls. Major companies include Vodafone, T2, and T-Mobile.

COMING ASHORE

A state-of-the-art Warnemünde cruise terminal opened in 2005, but it has limited passenger facilities. The best thing about the terminal is that it is within 300 yards of a railway station for easy onward connections through the town of Rostock. Travel time into Rostock is 20 minutes, with train journeys to Berlin taking 2 hours 45 minutes. Prices to Berlin are €39 round-trip. Trains from Rostock to Berlin run approximately three times per hour depending on time of day.

Once in Berlin, you'll find an integrated network of subway (U-bahn) and suburban (S-bahn) train lines, buses, and trams (in eastern Berlin only). Most visitor destinations are in the broad reach of the fare zones A and B. At this writing, both the €2.40 ticket (fare zones A and B) and the €3.10 ticket (fare zones A, B, and C) allow you to make a one-way trip with an unlimited number of changes between trains, buses, and trams.

Buy a Kurzstreckentarif ticket (€1.40) for short rides of up to six bus or tram stops or three U-bahn or S-bahn stops. The best deal if you plan to travel around the city extensively is the Tageskarte (day card for zones A and B), for €6.50, good on all transportation (€7 for A, B, C zones).

There is a Hertz rental office at the port. Alternatively, you can easily travel by train into nearby Rostock and pick up a vehicle there. If you want to visit Berlin, public transport is more practical than a car rental. However, renting a vehicle would allow you to explore the other towns along the Baltic coastline and enjoy the countryside and beaches. The cost for a compact manual vehicle is approximately €80 per day.

EXPLORING BERLIN

Berliner Fernsehturm (*Berlin TV Tower*). Finding Alexanderplatz is no problem: just head toward the 1,207-foot-high tower piercing the sky. Built in 1969 as a signal to the West (clearly visible over the wall, no less) that the East German economy was thriving, it is deliberately higher than both western Berlin's broadcasting tower and the Eiffel Tower in Paris. You can get the best view of Berlin from within the tower's disco ball–like observation level; on a clear day you can see for 40 km (25 miles). One floor above, the city's highest restaurant rotates for your panoramic pleasure. ■TIP➜ **During the summer season, order VIP tickets online to avoid a long wait.** ✉ *Panoramastr. 1a, Mitte* ☎ *030/247–5750* ⊕ *www.tr-turm.de* 🎫*€12* ☉ *Nov.–Feb., daily 10 am–midnight; Mar.–Oct., daily 9 am–midnight; last admission ½ hr before closing* Ⓜ *Alexanderplatz (U-bahn and S-bahn).*

Voltastr.

Wollinerstr.

Schwedtstr.

FORMER LOCATION OF BERLIN WALL

Danziger Str.

Fennstr.

Müllerstr.

Sellerstr.

Neue Hoch- Str.

Liesenstr.

Bernauer str.

U BERNAUER STR.

Schönhauser Allee

Kastanienallee

Boyen- str.

Chausseestr.

Gedenkstätte Berliner Mauer ◆

Brunnenstr.

Berg str.

Scharnhorststr.

FORMER LOCATION OF BERLIN WALL

NORDBAHNHOF S

Gartenstr.

Weinbergsw.

Choriner str.

Kollwitzstr.

Heide-str.

Invalidenstr.

Torstr.

Linienstr.

Auguststr.

Rosenthaler str.

Mollstr.

Prenzlauer Allee

S HAUPT-BAHNHOF

Luisenstr.

Oranien-burger

ORANIENBURGER STR.

Memhard str.

Moltke str.

Reichstag

Friedrichstr.

S HACKESCHER MARKT

◆ Berliner Fernsehturm

S U

S U FRIEDRICHSTR.

◆ Museumsinsel

Deutsches ◆ Historisches Museum

ALEXANDERPL.

Dulles Allee

Brandenburger Tor ◆

Unter den Linden

◆ Unter den Linden

Schloss-pl.

Rathaus str.

KLOSTERSTR. U

Stralauerstr.

S UNTER DEN LINDEN

Entlastungsstr.

Wilhelm str.

Denkmal für die Ermordeten Juden Europas ◆

U FRANZÖSISCHE STR.

Gendarmen-markt

HAUSVOGTEIPL. U

MÄRKISCHES MUSEUM U

STADTM. U

Leipziger Str.

Wallstr.

POTSDAMER PL. S U

◆ Kulturforum

FORMER LOCATION OF BERLIN WALL

FORMER LOCATION OF BERLIN WALL

KOCHSTR. U

◆ Mauermuseum-Museum Haus am Checkpoint Charlie

Oranienstr.

H.-Heine-Str.

ANHALTER BHF.

S

Schöneberger str.

Stresemann-str.

Wilhelm str.

Friedrichstr.

Linden str.

Ritterstr.

Prinzenstr.

MORITZPL. U

◆ Jüdisches Museum Berlin

HALLESCHES TOR U

Gitschinerstr.

Obentrautstr.

Urbanstr.

Yorckstr.

Gneisenaustr.

KEY	
S	*S-Bahn*
U	*U-Bahn*
i	*Tourist information*

Fodor's Choice
★

Brandenburger Tor (*Brandenburg Gate*). Once the pride of Prussian Berlin and the city's premier landmark, the Brandenburger Tor was left in a desolate no-man's-land when the wall was built. Since the wall's dismantling, the sandstone gateway has become the scene of the city's Unification Day and New Year's Eve parties. This is the sole remaining gate of 14 built by Carl Langhans in 1788–91, designed as a triumphal arch for King Frederick Wilhelm II. Its virile classical style pays tribute to Athens's Acropolis. The quadriga, a chariot drawn by four horses and driven by the Goddess of Victory, was added in 1794. Troops paraded through the gate after successful campaigns— the last time in 1945, when victorious Red Army troops took Berlin. The upper part of the gate, together with its chariot and Goddess of Victory, was destroyed in the war. In 1957 the original molds were discovered in West Berlin, and a new quadriga was cast in copper and presented as a gift to the people of East Berlin. A tourist-information center is in the south part of the gate. ⊠ *Pariser Pl., Mitte* Ⓜ *Unter den Linden (S-bahn).*

Denkmal für die Ermordeten Juden Europas (*Memorial to the Murdered Jews of Europe*). An expansive and unusual memorial dedicated to the 6 million Jews who were killed in the Holocaust, the monument was designed by American architect Peter Eisenman. The stunning place of remembrance consists of a grid of more than 2,700 concrete stelae, planted into undulating ground. The abstract memorial can be entered from all sides and offers no prescribed path. ∎ TIP→ An information center that goes into specifics about the Holocaust lies underground at the southeast corner. ⊠ *Cora-Berliner-Str. 1, Mitte* ☎ *030/2639–4336* ⊕ *www.stiftung-denkmal.de* ⌨ *Free* ☉ *Daily 24 hrs; information center: Oct.–Mar., Tues.–Sun. 10–7; Apr.–Sept., Tues.–Sun. 10–8* Ⓜ *Unter den Linden (S-bahn).*

Deutsches Historisches Museum (*German History Museum*). The museum is composed of two buildings. The magnificent pink, baroque Prussian arsenal (Zeughaus) was constructed between 1695 and 1730, and is the oldest building on Unter den Linden. It also houses a theater, the Zeughaus Kino, which regularly presents a variety of films, both German and international, historic and modern. The new permanent exhibits, reopened after much debate in mid-2006, offer a modern and fascinating view of German history since the early Middle Ages. Behind the arsenal, the granite-and-glass Pei-Bau building by I. M. Pei holds often stunning and politically controversial changing exhibits, such as 2010's unprecedented blockbuster, *Hitler und die Deutschen* (*Hitler and the Germans*), which explored the methods of propaganda used by Hitler and the Nazis to gain power. ⊠ *Unter den Linden 2, Mitte* ☎ *030/203–040* ⊕ *www.dhm.de* ⌨ *€8* ☉ *Daily 10–6.*

Gedenkstätte Berliner Mauer (*Berlin Wall Memorial Site*). This site combines memorials and a museum and research center on the Berlin Wall. The division of Berlin was particularly heart wrenching on Bernauer Strasse, where neighbors and families on opposite sides of the street were separated overnight. The Reconciliation Chapel, completed in 2000, replaced the community church dynamited by the Communists in 1985. The church had been walled into the "death strip," and was

seen as a hindrance to patrolling it. A portion of the wall remains on Bernauer Strasse, and an installation meant to serve as a memorial unfortunately only confuses those wondering what the border once looked like. For a wealth of images and information, head into the museum, where German-speakers can even hear radio broadcasts from the time the wall was erected. ⊠ *Bernauer Str. 111, Wedding* ☎ *030/464–1030* ⊕ *www.berliner-mauer-gedenkstaette.de* 🖾 *Free, tours €3* ☉ *Apr.–Oct., Tues.–Sun. 9:30–7; Nov.–Mar., Tues.–Sun. 9:30–6* Ⓜ *Bernauer Strasse (U-bahn), Nordbahnhof (S-bahn).*

BERLIN BEST BETS

Brandenburger Tor. The gate is the symbolic heart of the city, and one of the few survivors of the WWII era.

Museumsinsel. Berlin's most famous museums are all here, including the Neuesmuseum and its Egyptian collection, as well as the grand altar of Pergamon.

Reichstag. The historic seat of Germany's federal parliament, the Reichstag is also remarkable for its synthesis of architectural styles.

Jüdisches Museum Berlin (*Jewish Museum*). The history of Germany's Jews from the Middle Ages through today is chronicled here, from prominent historical figures to the evolution of laws regarding Jews' participation in civil society. A few of the exhibits document the Holocaust itself, but this museum celebrates Jewish life and history far more than it focuses on the atrocities committed during WWII. An attraction in itself is the highly conceptual building, designed by Daniel Libeskind, who will also direct the construction of a new adjacent building holding a library and temporary exhibitions. Various physical "voids" in the oddly constructed and intensely personal modern wing of the building represent the idea that some things can and should never be exhibited when it comes to the Holocaust. ▪**TIP→ Reserve at least three hours for the museum and devote more time to the second floor if you're already familiar with basic aspects of Judaica, which are the focus of the third floor.** ⊠ *Lindenstr. 9–14, Kreuzberg* ☎ *030/2599–3300* ⊕ *www.jmberlin.de* 🖾 *€5* ☉ *Mon. 10–10, Tues.–Sun. 10–8* Ⓜ *Hallesches Tor (U-bahn).*

Kaiser-Wilhelm-Gedächtnis-Kirche (*Kaiser Wilhelm Memorial Church*). A dramatic reminder of World War II's destruction, the ruined bell tower is all that remains of this once massive church, which was completed in 1895 and dedicated to the emperor, Kaiser Wilhelm I. The Hohenzollern dynasty is depicted inside in a gilded mosaic, whose damage, like that of the building, will not be repaired. The exhibition revisits World War II's devastation throughout Europe. On the hour, the tower chimes out a melody composed by the last emperor's great-grandson, the late Prince Louis Ferdinand von Hohenzollern. ⊠ *Breitscheidpl., Western Downtown* ☎ *030/218–5023* ⊕ *www.gedaechtniskirche-berlin.de* 🖾 *Free* ☉ *Memorial Church daily 9–7; old tower Mon.–Fri. 10–6, Sat. 10–5:30, Sun. 12–5:30.* Ⓜ *Zoologischer Garten (U-bahn and S-bahn).*

5

★ **Kulturforum** (*Cultural Forum*). This unique ensemble of museums, galleries, and the Philharmonic Hall was long in the making. The first designs were submitted in the 1960s and the last building completed in 1998. Now it forms a welcome modern counterpoint to the thoroughly restored Prussian splendor of Museum Island.

Gemäldegalerie (*Paintings Gallery*). The Gemäldegalerie reunites formerly separated collections from East and West Berlin. It's one of Germany's finest art galleries, and has an extensive selection of European paintings from the 13th to 18th century. Seven rooms are reserved for paintings by German masters, among them Dürer, Cranach the Elder, and Holbein. A special collection has works of the Italian masters—Botticelli, Titian, Giotto, Lippi, and Raphael—as well as paintings by Dutch and Flemish masters of the 15th and 16th centuries: Van Eyck, Bosch, Brueghel the Elder, and van der Weyden. The museum also holds the world's second-largest Rembrandt collection. ⊠ *Matthäikirchpl. 4, Tiergarten* ☎ *030/266–424242* ⊕ *www.smb.museum* ✆ *€8* ⊙ *Tues., Wed., and Fri.–Sun. 10–6; Thurs. 10–10* Ⓜ *Potsdamer Platz (U-bahn and S-bahn).*

Mauermuseum-Museum Haus am Checkpoint Charlie. Just steps from the famous crossing point between the two Berlins, the Wall Museum–House at Checkpoint Charlie presents visitors with the story of the wall and, even more riveting, the stories of those who escaped through, under, and over it. The homespun museum reviews the events leading up to the wall's construction and, with original tools and devices, plus recordings and photographs, shows how East Germans escaped to the West (one ingenious contraption was a miniature submarine). Exhibits about human rights and paintings interpreting the wall round out the experience. ■**TIP**➔ **Come early or late in the day to avoid the multitudes dropped off by tour buses.** (Monday can be particularly crowded.) ⊠ *Friedrichstr. 43–45, Kreuzberg* ☎ *030/253–7250* ⊕ *www.mauermuseum.com* ✆ *€12.50* ⊙ *Daily 9 am–10 pm* Ⓜ *Kochstrasse (U-bahn).*

Fodor'sChoice
★ **Museumsinsel** (*Museum Island*). On the site of one of Berlin's two original settlements, this unique complex of five state museums, a UNESCO World Heritage site, is an absolute must.

The **Alte Nationalgalerie** (Old National Gallery, entrance on Bodestrasse) houses an outstanding collection of 18th-, 19th-, and early-20th-century paintings and sculptures. Works by Cézanne, Rodin, Degas, and one of Germany's most famous portrait artists, Max Liebermann, are part of the permanent exhibition. Its Galerie der Romantik (Gallery of Romanticism) collection has masterpieces from such 19th-century German painters as Karl Friedrich Schinkel and Caspar David Friedrich, the leading members of the German Romantic school. The **Altes Museum** (Old Museum), a red-marble, neoclassical building abutting the green Lustgarten, was Prussia's first building purpose-built to serve as a museum. Designed by Karl Friedrich Schinkel, it was completed in 1830. The permanent collection of the Altes Museum consists of everyday utensils from ancient Greece as well as vases and sculptures from the 6th to 4th century BC. Etruscan art is its highlight, and there are

a few examples of Roman art. Antique sculptures, clay figurines, and bronze art of the Antikensammlung (Antiquities Collection) are also housed here; the other part of the collection is in the Pergamonmuseum. At the northern tip of Museum Island is the **Bode-Museum,** a somber-looking gray edifice graced with elegant columns. The museum presents the state museums' stunning collection of German and Italian sculptures since the Middle Ages, the Museum of Byzantine Art, and a huge coin collection. Museum Island's new shining star, however, is the **Neues Museum** (New Museum), which reopened in 2009. Originally designed by Friedrich August Stüler in 1843–55, the building was badly damaged in World War II and only now has been elaborately redeveloped by British star architect David Chipperfield, who has been overseeing the complete restoration of Museum Island. Instead of completely restoring the Neues Museum, the architect decided to integrate modern elements into the historic landmark, while leaving many of its heavily bombed and dilapidated areas untouched. The result is a stunning experience. Home to the Egyptian Museum, including the famous bust of Nefertiti (who, after some 70 years, has returned to her first museum location in Berlin), it also features the Papyrus Collection and the Museum of Prehistory and Early History. Even if you think you aren't interested in the ancient world, make an exception for the **Pergamonmuseum** (entrance on Am Kupfergraben). The museum's name is derived from its principal display, the Pergamon Altar, a monumental Greek temple discovered in what is now Turkey and dating from 180 BC. The altar was shipped to Berlin in the late 19th century. Equally impressive are the gateway to the Roman town of Miletus and the Babylonian processional way. If you get tired of antiques and paintings, drop by any of the museums' cafés. ⊠ *Entrance to Museumsinsel: Am Kupfergraben, Mitte* ☎ *030/2664–24242* ⊕ *www.smb.museum* 🖃 *All Museum Island museums: €14; individual museum admissions €8–€10* ⊘ *Pergamonmuseum: Fri.–Wed. 10–6, Thurs. 10–10. Alte Nationalgalerie: Tues., Wed., and Fri.–Sun. 10–6; Thurs. 10–10. Altes Museum: Fri.–Wed. 10–6, Thurs. 10–10. Neues Museum: Sun.–Wed. 10–6, Thurs.–Sat. 10–8. Bode-Museum: Tues., Wed., and Fri.–Sun. 10–6; Thurs. 10–10* Ⓜ *Hackescher Markt (S-bahn).*

★ **Reichstag** (*Parliament Building*). After last meeting here in 1933, the Bundestag, Germany's federal parliament, returned to its traditional seat in the spring of 1999. British architect Sir Norman Foster lightened up the gray monolith with a glass dome, which quickly became a main attraction: you can circle up a gently rising ramp while taking in the rooftops of Berlin and the parliamentary chamber below. At the base of the dome is an exhibit on the Reichstag's history, in German and English. ■ **TIP→ After terrorism warnings at the end of 2010, the Reichstag tightened its door policy, asking all visitors to register their names and birthdates in advance either for regular admission or to reserve a place on a guided tour.** A riverwalk with great views of the government buildings begins behind the Reichstag. ⊠ *Pl. der Republik 1, Tiergarten* ⊠ *Bundeskanzleramt, Besucherdienst* ☎ *030/2273–2152, 030/2273–5908 Reichstag* 🖷 *030/2273–0027 Reichstag, 030/4000–1881 Bundes-*

kanzleramt ⊕ www.bundestag.de ✉ Free ☉ Daily at 10:30, 1:30, 3:30, 6:30 Ⓜ Brandenburger Tor (S-bahn), Bundestag (U-bahn).

Tiergarten (*Animal Garden*). The quiet greenery of the 630-acre Tiergarten is a beloved oasis, with some 23 km (14 miles) of footpaths, meadows, and two beer gardens. The inner park's 6½ acres of lakes and ponds were landscaped by garden architect Joseph Peter Lenné in the mid-1800s.

Unter den Linden. The name of this historic Berlin thoroughfare, between the Brandenburg Gate and Schlossplatz, means "under the linden trees," and it was indeed lined with fragrant and beloved lindens until the 1930's. Imagine Berliners' shock when Hitler decided to fell the trees in order to make the street more parade-friendly. The grand boulevard began as a riding path that the royals used to get from their palace to their hunting grounds (now the central Berlin park called Tiergarten). It is once again lined with linden trees planted after World War II.

★ **Zoologischer Garten** (*Zoological Gardens*). Even though Knut, the polar
♺ bear cub who captured the heart of the city, is sadly no longer with us, there are 14,000 other animals to see here, many of whom may be happy to have their time in the spotlight once again. There are 1,500 different species (more than any other zoo in Europe), including those rare and endangered, which the zoo has been successful at breeding. New arrivals in the past years include a baby rhinoceros. ■ TIP→ Check the feeding times posted to watch creatures such as seals, apes, hippos, crocodiles, and pelicans during their favorite time of day. The animals' enclosures are designed to resemble their natural habitats, though some structures are ornate, such as the 1910 Arabian-style Zebra House. Pythons, frogs, turtles, invertebrates, Komodo dragons, and an amazing array of strange and colorful fish are part of the three-floor aquarium. ✉ *Hardenbergpl. 8 and Budapester Str. 32, Western Downtown ☎ 030/254–010 ⊕ www.zoo-berlin.de ✉ Zoo or aquarium €13, combined ticket €20 ☉ Zoo: Oct.–mid-Mar., daily 9–5; mid-Mar.–Oct., daily 9–7. Aquarium: daily 9–6 Ⓜ Zoologischer Garten (U-bahn and S-bahn).*

SHOPPING

Although Ku'damm is still touted as the shopping mile of Berlin, many shops are ho-hum retailers. The best stretch for exclusive fashions are the three blocks between Leibnizstrasse and Bleibtreustrasse. For gift items and unusual clothing boutiques, follow this route off Ku'damm: Leibnizstrasse to Mommsenstrasse to Bleibtreustrasse, then on to the ring around Savignyplatz. Fasanenstrasse, Knesebeckstrasse, Schlüterstrasse, and Uhlandstrasse are also fun places to browse.

The finest shops in Mitte (historic Berlin) are along Friedrichstrasse. Nearby, Unter den Linden has just a few souvenir shops and a Meissen ceramic showroom. Smaller clothing and specialty stores populate the Scheunenviertel. The area between Hackescher Markt, Weinmeister Strasse, and Rosa-Luxemburg-Platz alternates pricey independent designers with groovy secondhand shops. Neue Schönhauser Strasse

curves into Alte Schönhauser Strasse, and both streets are full of stylish casual wear. Galleries along Gipsstrasse and Sophienstrasse round out the mix.

Kaufhaus des Westens (*KaDeWe*). The largest department store in continental Europe, classy Kaufhaus des Westens (KaDeWe) has a grand selection of goods on seven floors, as well as food and deli counters, champagne bars, beer bars, and a winter garden on its top floor. Its wealth of services includes fixing umbrellas and repairing leather and furs. ⊠ *Tauentzienstr. 21–24, Western Downtown* ☎ *030/21210* ⊕ *www.kadewe.de* ☉ *Mon.–Thurs. 10–8, Sat. 10–9, Sun. 9:30–8.*

WHERE TO EAT

$$ ✕ **Café Einstein Stammhaus.** The Einstein is a Berlin landmark and a leading coffeehouse in town. Set in the historic grand villa of silent movie star Henny Porten, it charmingly recalls the elegant days of the Austrian-Hungarian empire, complete with slightly snobbish waiters gliding across squeaking parquet floors. The Einstein's very own roasting facility produces some of Germany's best coffee, and the cakes are fabulous, particularly the fresh strawberry cake best enjoyed in the shady garden behind the villa in summer. The café also excels in preparing solid Austrian fare such as schnitzel or goulash for an artsy, highbrow clientele. ⊠ *Kurfürstenstr. 58, Schoeneberg* ☎ *030/2639–1918* ⊕ *www. cafeeinstein.com* Ⓜ *Kurfürstenstrasse (U-bahn).*

AUSTRIAN

Fodor'sChoice

★

$$$ ✕ **Lutter & Wegner.** One of the city's oldest vintners (*Sekt,* German champagne, was first conceived here in 1811 by actor Ludwig Devrient), Lutter & Wegner has returned to its historic location across from Gendarmenmarkt. The dark-wood-panel walls, parquet floor, and multitude of rooms take you back to 19th-century Vienna. The cuisine is mostly Austrian, with superb game dishes in winter and, of course, a Wiener schnitzel with lukewarm potato salad. The sauerbraten (marinated pot roast) with red cabbage has been a national prizewinner. ■ **TIP**➜ **In the Weinstube, meat and cheese plates are served until 3 am.** ⊠ *Charlottenstr. 56, Mitte* ☎ *030/2029–5417* ⊕ *www.l-w-berlin.de* Ⓜ *Französische Strasse and Stadtmitte (U-bahn).*

GERMAN

5

Norway

ÅLESUND, BERGEN, FLÅM, GEIRANGER,
HAMMERFEST, HONNINGSVAG, KRISTÌANSAND,
OSLO, TROMSØ, TRONDHEIM

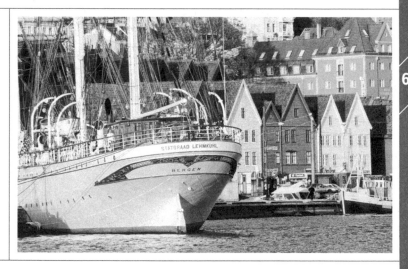

Bergen harbour, Norway

WORD OF MOUTH

"We sailed from Bergen to Kirkenes in late July. It never did get dark, just a very long twilight. By October, say, the days would be quite short. Some ports—Aalesund, for example—were visited for several hours. Others, only minutes. It's a wonderful, scenic voyage, so free of hassles."

—USNR

Updated by
Anne-Sophie
Redisch

Norway's most renowned cruise itinerary is the *Hurtigruten,* which literally means "Rapid Route." Ships that follow this route, which were historically known as coastal steamers, depart from Bergen and stop at 34 ports along the coast in a week, ending in Kirkenes, near the Russian border, before turning back.

Ships may stop in one port for just a few minutes to load and unload passengers who use the scenic route for transportation, so these steamers are more than just pleasure cruises for the people who choose to live in the isolated coastal villages in Norway's northern reaches. But many passengers on these routes are Americans, here to enjoy the dramatically beautiful Norwegian scenery.

Many of these ships, which are operated primarily by Hurtigruten (the Norwegian cruise line, which was once known in the United States as Norwegian Coastal Voyage), are more than just ferries. They do have some cruise ship–style amenities, though not "big-ship" amenities. So you can expect to find a sauna on board some of the ships but not a full-fledged spa, a restaurant but not a choice of restaurants. And while food is included in your cruise fare (unless you book a transportation-only passage, as some backpackers and short-haul travelers do), you pay extra (and dearly) for alcohol; luckily, the ships allow you to carry your own alcohol on board.

Norway is also a popular destination among major cruise lines—both luxury and mainstream—and many northern European cruises in the summer include some stops in Norway, though they may also include Århus or Copenhagen in Denmark or stops in Sweden, *which are covered in "The Baltic."*

ABOUT THE RESTAURANTS

Most of the restaurants we recommend serve lunch; they also serve dinner if your cruise ship stays late in port and you choose to dine off the ship. Cuisine in Europe is varied, though you should expect restaurants in Norway to focus primarily on Norwegian specialties; you'll have more choices in larger cities like Oslo and Bergen. Europeans tend to eat a leisurely meal at lunch, but in most ports there are quicker and simpler alternatives for those who just want to grab a quick bite before returning to the ship.

ÅLESUND, NORWAY

On three islands and between two bright blue fjords is Ålesund, home to 45,000 inhabitants and one of Norway's largest harbors for exporting dried and fresh fish. About two-thirds of its 1,040 wooden houses were destroyed by a fire in 1904. In the rush to shelter the 10,000 homeless victims, Germany's Kaiser Wilhelm II, who often vacationed here, led a swift rebuilding that married German art nouveau (*Jugendstil*) with Viking flourishes. Winding streets are crammed with buildings topped

with turrets, spires, gables, dragons' heads, and curlicues. Today Ålesund is considered one of the few art nouveau cities in the world. Inquire at the tourism office for one of the insightful guided walking tours.

ESSENTIALS

CURRENCY

Norway is a non-EU country and has opted to keep its currency, the Norwegian krone. ATMs are readily available.

HOURS

Banks are generally open weekdays 9 to 3. Many offices and embassies close at 3 from June to August. Stores are generally open weekdays 9 to 5 or 6 and Saturday 9 to 1 or 2. Some grocery stores are open until 11 pm on weekdays and Saturdays. All stores are closed Sunday.

TELEPHONES

The country code for Norway is 47. There are no area codes—you must dial all eight digits of any phone number wherever you are. Most tri- and quad-band GSM phones work in Norway, so if your service provider offers service in Europe, you will likely be able to use your mobile phone along the Norwegian coast, even while hugging the shoreline on ship. Public telephones are relatively rare.

COMING ASHORE

Ålesund is at the entrance to the world-famous Geirangerfjord. Turrets, spires, and medieval ornaments rise above the skyline of the colorful town and its charming architecture. Cruise ships dock in the center of town.

EXPLORING ÅLESUND

Aalesunds Museum. This gem of a museum highlights the city's past, including the great fire of 1904 and the escape route that the Norwegian Resistance established in World War II—its goal was the Shetland Islands. Handicrafts on display are done in the folk-art style of the area. You can also see the art nouveau room and learn more about the town's unique architecture. ⊠ *Rasmus Rønnebergsgt. 16* ☎ *70–12–31–70* ⊕ *www.aalesunds.museum.no* ⬛ *NKr 50* ⊙ *Mid-Sept.–Apr., weekdays 9–3; May–mid-Aug., weekdays 9–4, weekends noon–4; mid-Aug.–mid-Sept., weekdays 9–3, Sun. noon–4.*

☼ **Atlanterhavsparken** (*Atlantic Sea Park*). Teeming with aquatic life, this is one of Scandinavia's largest aquariums. Right on the ocean, 3 km (2 miles) west of town, the park emphasizes aquatic animals of the North Atlantic, including anglers, octopus, and lobster. See the daily diving show at which the fish are fed. The divers actually enter a feeding frenzy of huge, and sometimes aggressive, halibut and wolffish. The Humbodt penguins are also popular with children. After your visit, have a picnic, hike, or take a refreshing swim at the adjoining Tueneset Park. The bus that leaves from St. Olavs Plass makes the 15-minute journey to the park once every hour during the day, Monday through Saturday. There's also a shuttle bus from the cruise terminal (NKr 200 round-trip). ⊠ *Tueneset* ☎ *70–10–70–60* ⊕ *www.atlanterhavsparken. no* ⬛ *NKr 140* ⊙ *June–Aug., Sun.–Fri. 10–7, Sat. 10–4; Sept.–May, Mon.–Sat. 11–4, Sun. 11–6.*

Kniven. You can drive or take a bus up the nearby mountain Aksla to this vantage point, "the knife," for a splendid view of the city, which absolutely glitters at night.

Runde. Norway's southernmost major "bird rock"—one of the largest in Europe—is the breeding ground for some 200 species, including puffins, gannets, and cormorants. The region's wildlife managers maintain many observation posts here. In summer, straying into the bird's nesting areas is strictly forbidden. Contact the local tourist office for more information. ☎ 70–15–76–00 ⊕ www.visitalesund-geiranger.com/en/The-bird-island-Runde.

SHOPPING

The first Saturday of each month is known as "Town Saturday," when shops in the city center are open later than usual.

WHERE TO EAT

$ | ✕ **Fjellstua.** This mountaintop restaurant has tremendous views over
NORWEGIAN | the surrounding peaks, islands, and fjords. There is also a terrace that's open when the weather allows. On the menu might be Norwegian salt cod, baked salmon, or homemade rissoles (similar to croquettes). ⑤ Average main: NKr 175 ✉ Top of Aksla Mountain ☎ 70–10–74–00 ⊕ www.fjellstua.no ☉ Closed Dec. and Jan.

BERGEN, NORWAY

Many visitors fall in love with Bergen, Norway's second-largest city, at first sight. Seven rounded lush mountains, pastel wood houses, the historic wharf, winding cobblestone streets, and Hanseatic relics all make it a place of enchantment. Surrounded by forested mountains and fjords, it's only natural that most Bergensers feel at home either on the mountains (skiing, hiking, walking, or at their cabins) or at sea (fishing and boating). As for the rainy weather, most visitors quickly learn the necessity of rain jackets and umbrellas. The surviving Hanseatic wooden buildings on Bryggen (the quay, or wharf) are topped with triangular cookie-cutter roofs and painted in red, blue, yellow, and green. Monuments in themselves (they are on the UNESCO World Heritage List), the buildings tempt travelers and locals to the shops, restaurants, and museums inside.

COMING ASHORE

Cruise ships dock at Skoltegrunnskaien and Jekteviken/Dokkeskjærskaien. Both are within a 15-minute walk of the city center. Free shuttle buses are available from Jekteviken/Dokkeskjærskaien. From Skoltegrunnskaien, buses stop near the docks. The trip to the city center costs NKr 27 on the public bus. Once in the city center, nearly all of the attractions are within walking distance.

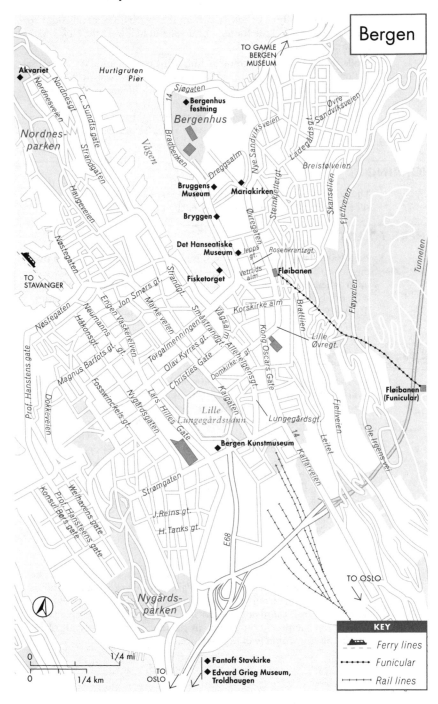

Bergen

Akvariet
Hurtigruten Pier
TO GAME BERGEN MUSEUM
Sjøgaten
Bergenhus festning
Bergenhus
Nordnes-parken
Bradbenken
Dreggsalm
Nye Sandviksveien
Øvre Sandviksveien
Lådegårdsgt.
Breistølveien
Skanselien
Fjellveien
Bruggens Museum
Mariakirken
Steinkjellergt.
Øvregaten
Bryggen
Det Hanseatiske Museum
Jepps gt.
Rosenkrantzgt.
Tunnelen
Fisketorget
Vetrlids alm.
Fløibanen
TO STAVANGER
Brattlien
Fløyveien
Korskirke alm.
Vågsalm.
Lille Øvregt.
Strandgt.
Jon Smørs gt.
Marke veien
Smästrandgt.
Allehelgensgt.
Kong Oscars Gate
Engen Vaskerelven
Neumanns
Torgalmenningen
Olav Kyrres gt.
Domkirke gt.
Magnus Barfots gt. gt.
Håkonsgt.
Christies Gate
Kaigaten
Fjellveien
Fløibanen (Funicular)
Fosswinckels gt.
Lars Hilles Gate
Nygårdsgaten
Lille Lungegårdsunn
Lungegårdsgt.
Prof. Hanstens gate
Dokkeveien
Bergen Kunstmuseum
Leitet
Ole Irgensvei
Strømgaten
J. Reins gt.
H. Tanks gt.
E68
Kalfarveien
14
TO OSLO
Welhavens gate
Prof. Hansteens gate
Konsul Børs gate
Nygårds-parken
0   1/4 mi
0   1/4 km
TO OSLO
Fantoft Stavkirke
Edvard Grieg Museum, Troldhaugen

KEY

⛴	*Ferry lines*
••••	*Funicular*
┼┼┼	*Rail lines*

EXPLORING BERGEN

☺ **Akvariet.** The Bergen Aquarium is one of the largest collections of North Sea fish and invertebrates in Europe. It has 60 tanks and two outdoor pools with seals and penguins. Tanks inside are filled with schools of colorful tropical fish as well as Norwegian salmon and common eels, which tend to wrap around each other. There is also a section with alligators from different parts of the world on display. *The Aquarium: Bergen and the Local Coastline*—a 360-degree video directed by one of Norway's most beloved animators, the late Ivo Caprino—is shown every hour, as is the 3D-film *SOS Planet*. The aquarium is on Nordnes Peninsula, a 20-minute walk from the fish market. You can also take Bus 11 or the ferry from the fish market. ⊠ *Nordnesbakken 4, Nordnes* ☎ *55–55–71–71* ⊕ *akvariet.no* ⊠ *NKr 200, NKr 150 in winter* ☺ *May–Aug., daily 9–7; Sept.–Apr., daily 10–6.*

Bergenhus festning (*Bergenhus Fortress*). The major buildings at the medieval Bergenhus are Håkonshallen (Haakon's Hall) and Rosenkrantztårnet (Rosenkrantz Tower). Both are open to visitors. **Håkonshallen** is a royal ceremonial hall erected during the reign of Håkon Håkonsson in the mid-1200s. It was badly damaged by the explosion of a German ammunition ship in 1944, but was restored by 1961. Erected in the 1560s by the governor of Bergenhus, Erik Rosenkrantz, **Rosenkrantztårnet** served as a combined residence and fortified tower. ⊠ *Bryggen* ☎ *81–57–04–00 Bergenhus festning, 55–31–60–67 Håkonshallen* ⊕ *www.bymuseet.no* ☺ *Grounds open daily 6:30 am–11 pm. Late Sept.–mid-May: Håkonshallen, Thurs. 3–6, Fri.–Wed. noon–3; Rosenkrantztårnet, Sun noon–3. Mid-May–late Sept.: both open daily 10–4.*

Fodor's Choice ★ **Bergen Kunstmuseum** (*Bergen Art Museum*). An important Bergen institution and one of the largest museums in Norway, the Bergen Art Museum is housed in several buildings along Lake Lille Lungeårdsvann. Works by Max Ernst, Paul Klee, Vassily Kandinsky, Pablo Picasso, Joan Miró, and the Dutch Renaissance masters are all on display. Norwegian artists include Edvard Munch, J.C. Dahl, Adolph Tidemand, Hans Gude, Harriet Backer, and Per Krogh. ⊠ *Rasmus Meyers allé 3, Downtown* ☎ *55–56–80–00* ⊕ *www.kunstmuseene.no/Default. asp?enhet=kunstmuseum&sp=2* ⊠ *NKr 100* ☺ *Mid-May–mid-Sept., daily 11–5; mid-Sept.–mid-May, Tues.–Sun. 11–5.*

Fodor's Choice ★ **Bryggen** (*The Wharf*). A trip to this merchant city is incomplete without a trip to the historic Hanseatic harborside, Bryggen. A row of mostly reconstructed 14th-century wooden buildings that face the harbor makes this one of the most charming walkways in Europe, especially on a sunny day. Several fires, the latest in 1955, destroyed some of the original structures. Today the old houses hold boutiques and restaurants. Bryggen has been a UNESCO World Heritage site since 1979. ⊠ *Bryggen.*

★ **Det Hanseatiske Museum.** One of the best-preserved buildings in Bergen, the Hanseatic Museum was the 16th-century office and home of an affluent German merchant. The apprentices lived upstairs, in boxed-in beds with windows cut into the wall. Although claustrophobic, the snug rooms had the benefit of being relatively warm—a blessing in the unheated building. In summer, there are daily guided tours in Norwegian,

German, French, and English. ✉ *Finnegården 1A, Bryggen* ☎ *55–54–46–90* ⊕ *www.museumvest. no/?action=static&id=8* 🖃 *NKr 60* ⏱ *Mid-May–mid-Sept., daily 9–5; mid-Sept.–mid-May, Tues.–Sat. 11–2, Sun. 11–4.*

Edvard Grieg Museum, Troldhaugen. Built in 1885, Troldhaugen was the home of Norway's most famous composer, Edvard Grieg. He composed many of his best-known works in a garden cottage by the lakeshore. In 1867 he married his cousin Nina, a Danish soprano. They lived in the white clapboard house with green gingerbread trim for 22 years. A salon and gathering place for many Scandinavian artists then, it now houses mementos—a piano, paintings, prints—of the composer's life. The interior has been kept as it was during Grieg's time here. Concerts are held both at Troldhaugen and at Troldsalen next door. ✉ *Troldhaugsveien 65, Paradis* ☎ *55–92–29–92* ⊕ *www. kunstmuseene.no/troldhaugen* 🖃 *NKr 80* ⏱ *Oct.–Apr., daily 10-4; May-Sept., daily 9–6.*

Fodor's Choice ★ Fantoft Stavkirke (*Fantoft Stave Church*). During the Middle Ages, when European cathedrals were built in stone, Norway used wood to create unique stave churches. These cultural symbols stand out for their dragons' heads, carved doorways, and walls of staves (vertical planks). Though as many as 750 stave churches may have once existed, only 30 remain standing. The original stave church here, built in Fortun in Sogn in 1150 and moved to Fantoft in 1883, burned down in 1992. Since then, the church has been reconstructed to resemble the original structure. From the main bus station next to the railway station, take any bus leaving from Platform 19, 20, or 21. ✉ *Fantoftvn. 38* ☎ *55–28–07–10* ⊕ *fantoftstavkirke.com* 🖃 *NKr 44* ⏱ *Mid-May–mid-Sept., daily 10:30–6.*

Fisketorget (*Bergen Fish Market*). The busy fish market is one of Bergen's most popular attractions. Turn-of-the-20th-century photographs of this pungent square show fishermen in Wellington boots and raincoats and women in long aprons. Now the fishmongers wear bright-orange rubber overalls as they look over the day's catch. In 2012, some of the market moved indoors, to a brand-new food hall. Fruits, vegetables, and flowers are on offer, as are handicrafts and souvenirs. Try a classic Bergen lunch of shrimp or salmon on a baguette with mayonnaise and cucumber. ✉ *Bryggen* ☎ *55–55-20-00* ⊕ *www.torgetibergen.no/english. asp* ⏱ *June–Aug., daily 7–7; Sept.–May, Mon.–Sat. 7–4.*

BERGEN BEST BETS

Bryggen. Bergen's historic seafront promenade, which dates from the 11th century, is the city's most atmospheric street.

Mariakirken. This Romanesque church is the oldest structure in Bergen still used for its original purpose.

Rasmus Meyer Collection. The prescient collector purchased most of the works here while the artists were still unknown. His collection is now on display at the Bergen Art Museum. The collection of Munch paintings is the best in Norway outside of Oslo.

NIGHTLIFE

Bergen is a university town, and the thousands of students who live and study here year-round contribute to making the city's nightlife livelier than you might expect in a small town. Most nightspots center on Ole Bulls Plass, the plaza at one end of Torgallmenningen. Within a stone's throw of the plaza you can find dozens of relaxing bars, bustling pubs, dancing, live music, and trendy cafés.

Altona vinbar. For a quiet glass of wine in intimate and historic surroundings, try Altona, a hotel bar in a 400-year-old wine cellar. The food is good, too. ⊠ *Augustin Hotel, Strandgaten 81, Nordnes* ☎ *55–30–40–00.*

Café Opera. A classic—both sumptuous and stylish. It's often crowded on Friday and Saturday nights, when there are DJs. There's also a quiz night on Monday, readings, and more. ⊠ *Engen 18, Downtown* ☎ *55–23–03–15* ⊕ *www.cafeopera.org.*

Kafe Kippers. Head to this large outdoor café at sunset for cozy wool blankets and a spectacular view of the water. ⊠ *Georgernes Verft 12, Nordnes* ☎ *55–30–40–80.*

Logen Teater. If you prefer conversation over dancing, try Logen Teater, a popular meeting place with live acoustic music every Sunday. Edvard Grieg has performed here, and so have Sergei Rachmaninoff and Rickie Lee Jones. ⊠ *Øvre Ole Bulls pl. 6, Downtown* ☎ *55–23–20–15* ⊕ *www. logen-teater.no.*

6

SHOPPING

Bergen has several cobblestoned pedestrian shopping streets, including Gamle Strandgaten, (Gågaten), Torgallmenningen, Hollendergaten, and Marken. Stores selling Norwegian handicrafts are concentrated along the Bryggen boardwalk. Near the cathedral, the tiny Skostredet has become popular with young shoppers. The small, independent specialty stores here sell everything from army surplus gear to tailored suits and designer trinkets. Most Bergen shops are open Monday–Wednesday and Friday from 9 to 5; Thursday from 9 to 7; and Saturday from 10 to 3. Bergen's shopping centers—Galleriet, Kløverhuset, and Bergen Storsenter—are open weekdays from 9 to 9 and Saturday from 9 to 6.

Galleriet. This is the best of the downtown shopping malls, with over 70 shops, including GlasMagasinet and more exclusive small shops along with all the chains. ⊠ *Torgallmenningen 8, Downtown* ☎ *55–30–05–00* ⊕ *www.galleriet.com.*

Hjertholm. At this gift shop, most everything is of Scandinavian design. The pottery and glassware are of the highest quality—much of it is made by local artisans. ⊠ *Galleriet Shopping Center, Torgallmenningen 8, 5th fl., Downtown* ☎ *55–31–70–27* ⊕ *www.hjertholm.no.*

Norsk Flid. Established in 1895, the Bergen branch of this famous handicraft store sells national costumes and other Norwegian crafts, clothes, blankets and gift items. ⊠ *Vågsallmenningen 3, Downtown* ☎ *55–54–47–40* ⊕ *www.norskflid.no/bergen.*

ACTIVITIES

Bergen is literally wedged between the mountains and the sea, and there are plenty of opportunities to enjoy the outdoors. Bergensers are quick to do so on sunny days. In summer, don't be surprised to see many Bergensers leaving work early to enjoy sports and other outdoor activities, or to just relax in the parks.

HIKING

Like most Norwegians, Bergensers love to go hiking, especially on one of the seven mountains that surround the city.

Bergen Turlag (DNT). The Bergen Trekking Association arranges hikes and maintains cabins for hikers. You can pick up maps of many self-guided walking tours from the office, as well as from local bookstores. ⊠ *Tverrgt. 4–6, Downtown* ☎ *55–33–58–10* ⊕ *www.bergen-turlag.no.*

Mt. Fløyen. Take the funicular up Mt. Fløyen, and minutes later you'll be in the midst of a forest. From the nearby shop and restaurant, well-marked paths fan out over the mountains. Follow Fløysvingene Road down for an easy stroll, with great views of the city and harbor. ⊠ *Vetrlidsallmenningen 21, Bryggen* ☎ *55–33–68–00* ⊕ *www.floibanen.no.*

Mt. Ulriken. Mt. Ulriken is popular with walkers and hikers of all levels. The easiest way to reach the summit is via the cable car from Haukeland University Hospital. (To get there, take the double-decker bus that leaves from Torget.) Once you get off the cable car, you'll find trails leading across the mountain plateau, Vidden, which is above the tree line. The plateau connects the Fløyen and Ulriken mountains, and you can hike between them in four to six hours. Views from the alpine trail are spectacular. Be advised that foggy and rainy weather, even in the summer months, can make hiking here dangerous. Consult the tourist information center or Bergen Turlag for maps and general advice. ☎ *53–64–36–43* ⊕ *www.ulriken643.no.*

WHERE TO EAT

$$$
NORWEGIAN
★

✕ **Bølgen & Moi.** In late 2012, this branch of the trendy Bølgen & Moi chain moved to grand and majestic quarters, with marble walls, tall columns, chandeliers, fabulous ceiling details, and a new champagne and seafood bar. What hasn't changed is its very good-value lunch menu, which includes their famous fish soup and a crayfish sandwich. Dinner might include turbot with asparagus and a citrus hollandaise, a modern take on a Norwegian classic. $ *Average main: NKr 290* ⊠ *Vågsalmenningen 16* ☎ *55–59–77–00* ⊕ *www.bolgenogmoi.no.*

$$$
NORWEGIAN

✕ **Wesselstuen.** Housed in an 18th-century wine cellar, this distinctive restaurant is known for its convivial atmosphere and unpretentious, authentic Norwegian fare. This is a good place to try reindeer steak or salt cod. Light meals and more international options are also available. Note that the restaurant doesn't open until 2 pm on Sunday. $ *Average main: NKr 270* ⊠ *Øvre Ole Bulls pl. 6, Downtown* ☎ *55–55–49–49* ⊕ *www.wesselstuen.no.*

FLÅM

Flåm is on an arm of the world's longest (at 204 km [127 miles]) and deepest (at 1,308 meters [4,291 feet]) fjord. The village of only 500 inhabitants is set against a backdrop of steep mountains, thundering waterfalls, narrow valleys, and deep canyons. Cruise ships—bringing primarily British and German passengers—began transiting the majestic Sognefjord to Flåm in the late 19th century. Today, it's Norway's fourth most popular port of call, a fact that can be attributed not only to the beauty of the fjord but also to the popularity of the Flåm Railway, considered to be one of Europe's most dramatic rail excursions.

COMING ASHORE

Ships dock directly in the harbor of Flåm. Sights are easily accessible from the dock. The train station is a five-minute walk from the pier.

EXPLORING FLÅM

Flåmsbana (*Flåm Railway*). This trip is only 20 km (12 miles) long, but it takes 40 to 55 minutes (one-way) to travel the 2,850 feet up the steep mountain gorge. The line includes 20 tunnels and a bridge. A masterpiece of Norwegian engineering, it took 20 years to complete, and is today one of Norway's prime tourist attractions, with more than 600,000 visiting each year. ⊠ *Flåm train station* ☎ *57–63–21–00* ⊕ *www.visitflam.no/flaamsbana.*

Flåmsbana Museet. If you have time to kill before the train departs, make sure you visit the Flåm Railway Museum. Building the Flåm Railway was a remarkable feat in engineering, and this museum illustrates the challenges the builders faced in detail. You'll find it in the old station building, 300 feet from the present one. ⊠ *Flåm train station* ☎ *57–63–23–10* ⊕ *www.visitflam.no/flaamsbana-museet* 🎫 *Free* ☉ *May–Sept., daily 9–5; Oct.–Apr., daily 1:30–3.*

Fretheim Hotell. One of western Norway's most beautiful hotels, the Fretheim has a classic, timeless look and is worth your time if you want to drop in to see the lobby. ⊠ *Flåm Harbor* ☎ *57–63–63–00* ⊕ *www.fretheim-hotel.no.*

GEIRANGER, NORWAY

85 km (52½ miles) southwest of Åndalsnes.

★ The Geirangerfjord, which made the UNESCO World Heritage List in 2005, is Norway's most spectacular and perhaps best-known fjord. The 16-km-long (10-mile-long), 960-foot-deep Geirangerfjord's most stunning attractions are its roaring waterfalls—the Seven Sisters, the Bridal Veil, and the Suitor. Perched on mountain ledges along the fjord, deserted farms at Skageflå and Knivsflå are being restored and maintained by local enthusiasts.

EXPLORING GEIRANGER

The village of Geiranger, at the end of the fjord, is home to only 250 year-round residents, but in spring and summer its population swells to 5,000 due to visitors traveling from Hellesylt to the east. In winter, snow on the mountain roads means that the village is often isolated.

★ **Trollstigen.** The most scenic route to Geiranger from Åndalsnes is the two-hour drive along Route 63 over Trollstigen (the Troll's Ladder). After that, the Ørneveien (Eagles' Road) to Geiranger, which has 11 hairpin turns and was completed in 1952, leads to the fjord.

SHOPPING

The handful of shops in Geiranger emphasize traditional Norwegian cottage crafts such as wood carvings and woven and knitted goods, like Norwegian sweaters. All the shops are along the main street.

ACTIVITIES

HIKING

Trekking through fjord country can occupy a few hours or several days. Trails and paths are marked by signs or cairns with a red "T" on them. Area tourist offices and bookshops have maps, and you can always ask residents for directions or destinations.

GUDVANGEN, NORWAY

On an arm of Sognefjord, Gudvangen is at the foot of steep cliffs soaring 5,500 feet above the water's surface and plunging deep to form one of the region's deepest fjord basins. Snow-capped mountains, green cliffs, and veils of tumbling waterfalls characterize the vertical landscape on the approach to Gudvangen. The fjord is so narrow in places that during winter the sun can't reach the valley floor. Mystical Gudvangen is the site of white caves and medieval stave churches. Standing sentinel over the ornate entrances to the venerable wooden sanctuaries are visages of fierce trolls and dragons, carved by long-dead Viking craftsman from the region.

COMING ASHORE

Cruise passengers are brought ashore by tender at one of two small piers, which are both in the center of town.

EXPLORING GUDVANGEN

Stalheim Hotel. In the spectacular Nærøyfjorden, a UNESCO World Heritage site of steep mountains and waterfalls that form a beautiful valley, drivers must navigate 13 hairpin turns on Stalheimskleiva, a section of road not quite a mile in length, to reach this hotel. An inspiration to painters and other artists, Stalheim Hotel is furnished with a spectacular collection of Scandinavian furniture and antiques, and it also has a large collection of buildings dating back from the 16th and 17th centuries. ✉ *Stalheimsvegen 131, Stalheim* ⊕ *stalheim.dnn.gasta.no.*

Tvindefossen. From Stalheim it's not a long drive to Tvinde, a name derived from the Norwegian word for two. En route, you'll pass the villages of Oppheim and Vinje, as well as Oppheim Lake. But the best waterfall of this area is Tvindefossen, which has a 152-meter (500-ft) drop down steep stone cliffs. Nearby is the town of Voss, the bottling source of one of the world's most expensive waters.

Undredal stavkirke (*Stave Church*). The village of Undredal, home to 80 humans and 500 goats, also has Norway's smallest stave church, which was probably built in 1147. ⊠ *Undredal* ⊕ *naroyfjorden.no/ verdsarvbygdene/undredal?lang=en.*

White Caves (*De hvite grottene i Gudvangen*). These impressive caves are composed of anorthosite, a type of marble that contains both gold and aluminum. A stone bar-and-restaurant serves refreshments. The caves are just off the E16 to Voss, about 6 km from Gudvangen. Only pre-booked groups can visit. ⊠ *Gudvangen* ☎ *48–07–55–55* ⊕ *gudvangen. com/magical-white-caves.*

SHOPPING

Gudvangen Fjordtell, which is right at the port, has two souvenir shops that are open daily during the cruising season. Look for Viking souvenirs, Dale sweaters, and accessories made of seal, fox, reindeer, and moose.

6

ACTIVITIES

FISHING
The Nærøy River is one of 20 salmon rivers that receive special protection from the Norwegian government.

HIKING AND WALKING
Heritage Adventures. This outfitter offers multiday hikes, and leisurely day-hikes (5 or 10 km) in pristine forests and pastures along the shores of the breathtaking Nærøyfjord, a UNESCO World Heritage site. A picnic lunch and a short scenic fjord cruise are also included. All hikes must be booked in advance. ☎ *56–52–95–90* ⊕ *www. heritageadventures.no.*

RAFTING
Because of the different grades of the rivers, ranging from two to five, rafting in Gudvangen is suitable for beginners as well as experienced rafters. Strandaelva and Raundalselva (the Stranda and Raundal rivers) have been rated between three and five for experienced rafters. The Vosso is a grade two, recommended for families with children.

WATERFALL ABSEILING
This waterborne experience allows you to rappel down Skjervefossen, a waterfall that plunges 100 meters (330 feet).

Sørøysundet

The Royal and Ancient
Polar Bear Society

Storelv-
bakken

Bratt-
bakken

Ballast-
bakken

Mørenveien

Idrettsveien

Strandgata

Nybakken

Hammegata

Batteriet

Pargata

Storgata

Sjøgata

Rådhus-
plassen

Mellomgata

Sørøygata

Corn. Moes gate

Sjøgata

Kirkegata

Salsgata

◆ Museum of Post-War
Reconstruction

Nedre Haven

Øvre Haven

Turistveien

| 0 | | | 1/8 mi |
| 0 | | | 1/8 km |

HAMMERFEST, NORWAY

More than 600 miles north of the Arctic Circle, the world's northern-most town is also one of the most widely visited and oldest places in Northern Norway. *Hammerfest* means "mooring place" and refers to the natural harbor (remarkably free of ice year-round thanks to the Gulf Stream) that is formed by the crags in the mountain. Hammerfest is the gateway to the Barents Sea and the Arctic Ocean, a jumping-off point for Arctic expeditions. Once a hunting town, Hammerfest's town emblem features the polar bear. In 1891 the residents of Hammerfest, tired of the months of darkness that winter always brought, decided to brighten their nights: they purchased a generator from Thomas Edison, and Hammerfest thus became the first city in Europe to have electric street lamps.

COMING ASHORE

Ships dock either at quay number 1 or 2 in the city center, or at quay number 9 at Fuglenes, about a mile away. If you'd rather not walk, there are buses and taxis to take you the short distance to the city center. Ships sometimes anchor and tender passengers ashore to the dock in the town center. There is no terminal in the port area and only limited facilities, but the town center is only a few steps away, and it has everything you might need.

EXPLORING HAMMERFEST

In addition to two museums, there are several shops within Hammerfest's small city center. There is also a market selling souvenirs and other goods outside the town hall.

Museum of Post-War Reconstruction (*Gjenreisningsmusee*). Although it covers the county of Finnmark's history since the Stone Age, this museum primarily focuses on World War II, when the German army forced Finnmark's population to evacuate, and the county was burned to the ground as part of a scorched-earth policy. Through photographs, videos, and sound effects, the museum recounts the residents' struggle to rebuild their lives. The exhibition includes authentic rooms that were built in caves after the evacuation, as well as huts and postwar houses. ✉ *Kirkegt. 21* ☎ *78–40–29–30* ⊕ *www.gjenreisningsmuseet.no* ✉ *Nkr 50* ⊙ *June–mid-Aug., daily 10–4; mid-Aug.–May, daily 11–2.*

The Royal and Ancient Polar Bear Society. Isbjørnklubben was founded by two businessmen whose goal was to share the town's history as a center of hunting and commerce. Exhibits depict aspects of Arctic hunts, including preserved and stuffed polar bears, seals, lynx, puffins, and wolves. You can only become a member by visiting in person, so it's a very exclusive club open only to those who have actually visited the world's northernmost city. Members get a membership card and diploma, and a sought-after silver-and-enamel polar bear pin. Part of the fee is donated to the World Wildlife Foundation. ✉ *Havnegata 3* ☎ *78–41–31–00* ⊕ *www.isbjornklubben.no* ✉ *Membership NKr 180* ⊙ *June and July, weekdays 6–6, weekends 6–4; Aug.–May, weekdays 9–4, weekends 10–2.*

ACTIVITIES

Hammerfest Turist (*Tourist information*). Stop at the tourist office to learn about activities in the region, including golf, walking tours, birdwatching trips, and boating. A popular activity is coast sightseeing, in which a catamaran takes you to small fishing villages on Sørøya Island. Also popular are city tours; highlights include a ride up Salen Mountain for spectacular views of the city, and a visit to the Meridian Column, erected in 1854 to mark the first international measurement of the earth's circumference and shape. ✉ *Havnegata 3* ☎ *78–41–21–85* ⊕ *www.hammerfest-turist.no.*

HIKING AND WALKING

Hammerfest is a paradise for those who enjoy long ambles. The tourist office organizes a four-hour scenic walking excursion to reach Kjøttvikvarden, a landmark built in 1850 to help fishermen become oriented on long journeys. They also provide suggested walking routes such as the Gammelveien trail, a 30-minute walk that starts from the town church and heads up an old road. ✉ *Havnegt. 3* ☎ *78–41–31–00* ⊕ *www.hammerfest-turist.no.*

HONNINGSVÅG, NORWAY

Searching in 1553 for a northeast passage to India, British navigator Richard Chancellor came upon a crag 307 yards above the Barents Sea. He named the jut of rock North Cape, or *Nordkapp*. Today Europe's northernmost point is a rite-of-passage journey for nearly all Scandinavians and many others. Most cruise passengers visit Nordkapp from Honningsvåg, a fishing village on Magerøya Island. The journey from Honningsvåg to Nordkapp covers about 35 km (22 miles) across a landscape characterized by rocky tundra and grazing reindeer, which are rounded up each spring by Sami herdsmen in boats. The herdsmen herd the reindeer across a mile-wide channel from their winter home on the mainland. Honningvåg's northerly location makes for long, dark winter nights and perpetually sun-filled summer days. The village serves as the gateway to Arctic exploration and the beautiful Nordkapp Plateau, a destination that calls to all visitors of this region.

Most of those who journey to Nordkapp, the northernmost tip of Europe, are in it for a taste of this unique, otherworldly, rugged yet delicate landscape. You'll see an incredible treeless tundra, with crumbling mountains and sparse dwarf plants. The subarctic environment is very vulnerable; so don't disturb the plants. Walk only on marked trails and don't remove stones, leave car marks, or make campfires. Because the roads are closed in winter, the only access is from the tiny fishing village of Skarsvåg via Sno-Cat, a thump-and-bump ride that's as unforgettable as the desolate view.

COMING ASHORE

One of Northern Norway's largest ports welcomes about 100 cruise ships annually during the summer season. The port itself has no services, but within 100 yards are shops, museums, tourist information, post office, banks, restaurants, and an ice bar.

EXPLORING HONNINGSVÅG AND NORDKAPP

HONNINGSVÅG

Nordkappmuseet (*North Cape Museum*). On the third floor of Nordkapphuset (North Cape House), this museum documents the history of the Arctic fishing industry and the history of tourism at North Cape. You can learn how the trail of humanity stretches back 10,000 years, and about the development of society and culture in this region. ☒ *Fiskerivn. 4, Honningsvåg* ☎ *78–47–72–00* ⊕ *www.nordkappmuseet.no* ☒ *Nkr 50* ☉ *June–mid-Aug., Mon.–Sat. 10–7, Sun. noon–7; mid-Aug.–May, weekdays noon–4.*

NORDKAPP

34 km (21 miles) north of Honningsvåg.

On your journey to Nordkapp you'll see an incredible expanse of treeless tundra, with crumbling mountains and sparse, dwarf plants. The subarctic environment is very vulnerable; so don't disturb the plants. Walk only on marked trails and don't remove stones, leave car marks, or make campfires. The roads are open for buses through most of winter.

Nordkapphallen (*North Cape Hall*). The contrast between the near-barren territory outside and this tourist center is striking. Blasted into the interior of the plateau, the building is housed in a cave and includes an ecumenical chapel, a souvenir shop, and a post office. Exhibits trace the history of the cape, from Richard Chancellor, an Englishman who drifted around it and named it in 1533, to Oscar II, king of Norway and Sweden, who climbed to the top of the plateau in 1873. Celebrate your pilgrimage to 71° North at one of the cafés. The hefty admission covers the exhibits, parking, other facilities, and entrance to the plateau itself. ☎ 78–47–68–60 ⊕ *www.rica-hotels.com/special-offers/tilbud/nordkapphallen* ✑ *NKr 235. Ticket is valid for 48 hrs* ◷ *Mid-May–mid-Aug., daily 11 am–1 am; mid- to late Aug., daily 11 am–10 pm; Sept.–mid-May, daily 11–3.*

SHOPPING

Honningsvåg has several shops selling Norwegian souvenirs and handicrafts.

Arctic Suvenirs. This shop, in the same building as the tourist center, stays open until late at night, when cruise ships call. The shop features a range of Norwegian souvenirs, T-shirts, books, knitting products, and pewter—all tax-free. ⊠ *Nordkapphallen, Fiskeriveien 4, Honningsvåg* ☎ 78–47–37–12.

WHERE TO EAT

$

SCANDINAVIAN

✕ **Corner.** The daily catch often dictates the menu here, though pasta is always available—and so is crispy cod tongue. ⑤ *Average main: NKr 190* ✉ *Fiskeriveien 2A, Honningsvåg* ☎ *78-47-63-41* ⊕ *www.corner.no.*

KRISTIANSAND, NORWAY

326 km (202 miles) southwest of Oslo and 232 km (144 miles) southeast of Stavanger.

Nicknamed "Sommerbyen" ("Summer City"), Norway's fifth-largest city has 78,000 inhabitants. Norwegians come here for its sun-soaked beaches and beautiful harbor.

According to legend, in 1641 King Christian IV marked the four corners of Kristiansand with his walking stick, and within that framework the grid of wide streets was laid down. The center of town, called Kvadraturen, still retains the grid, even after numerous fires. In the northeast corner is Posebyen, one of northern Europe's largest collections of low, connected wooden house settlements. There's a market here every Saturday in summer. *Fisketorvet* (the fish market) is near the south corner of the town's grid, right on the sea.

COMING ASHORE

Cruise ships dock directly at Kristiansand's cruise-ship terminal. The town's main sights are a 1/3-mile or 10-minute walk from the terminal.

EXPLORING KRISTIANSAND

Agder naturmuseum og botaniske hage (*Agder Natural History Museum and Botanical Garden*). The area's natural history from the Ice Age to the present is on display here, starting with the coast and moving on to the high mountains. There's a rainbow of minerals on display, as well as a rose garden with varieties from 1850. There's even the country's largest collection of cacti. ✉ *Gimle gård, Gimlevn. 23* ☎ *38-05-86-20* ⊕ *www.naturmuseum.no* ◻ *NKr 50* ⊙ *Mid-June–mid-Aug., daily 11–5; mid-Aug.–mid-June, Tues.–Fri. 10–3, Sun. noon–4; closed Mon. and Sat.*

Christiansholm Festning (*Christiansholm Fortress*). This circular fortress with 16-foot-thick walls, on a promontory opposite Festningsgata, was completed in 1674. Its role has been much more decorative than defensive; it was used once, in 1807 during the Napoleonic Wars, to defend the city against British invasion. Now it contains art exhibits. However, the best part is walking around the grounds—the gates open early in the morning. ✉ *Østre Strandgt 52B* ☎ *38-07-51-50 number is for Kristiansand municipality* ⊕ *www.kristiansand.kommune.no/Anlegg-lokaler-og-utstyr-til-leie/Leie-av-arealer-til-utendors-arrangement1/Christiansholm-festning* ⊙ *Mid-May–Sept., daily 9–9.*

★ **Dyreparken Kristiansand** (*Kristiansand Zoo and Amusement Park*). One ↻ of Norway's most popular attractions, Dyreparken Kristiansand is actually five separate parks, including a water park (bring bathing suits and

towels); a forested park; an entertainment park; a theme park; and a zoo, which contains an enclosure for Scandinavian animals such as wolves, snow foxes, lynxes, and elks. The theme park, Kardemomme By (Cardamom Town), is named for a book by the Norwegian illustrator and writer Thorbjørn Egner. In the zoo, the *My Africa* exhibition allows you to move along a bridge observing native savanna animals such as giraffes and zebras. The park is 11 km (6 miles) east of town. ✉ *Kardemomme By* ☎ *97–05–97–00* ⊕ *www.dyreparken.no* 🔲 *NKr 399, includes admission to all parks and rides; discounts offered off-season, reduced fee for kids* ⊙ *June–Aug., daily 10–7; Sept.–May, weekdays 10–3, weekends 10–5.*

🄲 **Kristiansand Kanonmuseum** (*Cannon Museum*). At the Kristiansand Kanonmuseum you can see the cannon that the occupying Germans rigged up during World War II. With a caliber of 15 inches, the cannon was said to be capable of shooting a projectile halfway to Denmark. In the bunkers, related military materials are on display. This little museum is a gem. Kids love running around the grounds, but keep an eye on them, since there aren't railings everywhere. ✉ *Kroodden* ☎ *38–08–50–90* ⊕ *www.kanonmuseet.no* 🔲 *NKr 65* ⊙ *Mid-May–mid-June and mid-Aug.–late Sept., Mon.–Wed. 11–3, Thurs.–Sun. 11–5; mid-June–mid-Aug., daily 11–6; late Sept.–late Nov. and Feb.–mid-May, Sun. noon–4.*

Oddernes kirke (*Oddernes Church*). The striking rune stone in the cemetery of Oddernes kirke says that Øyvind, godson of Saint Olav, built this church in 1040 on property he inherited from his father. One of the oldest churches in Norway, it has a baroque pulpit from 1704 and is dedicated to Saint Olav. ✉ *Jegersbergvn. 2* ☎ *38–19–68–60* ⊕ *www.visitkrs.no/en/TellusView/?&TLl=en&TLp=431420* 🔲 *Free* ⊙ *July–mid-Aug., weekdays 11–2.*

Fodor's Choice ★ **Ravnedalen** (*Raven Valley*). A favorite with hikers and strolling nannies, Ravnedalen is a lush park that's filled with flowers in springtime. Wear comfortable shoes to hike the narrow, winding paths up the hills and climb the 200 steps up to a 304-foot lookout. There is a café on-site, and open-air concerts in summer. ⊕ *ravnedalen.no.*

🄲 **Vest-Agder-museet Kristiansand** (*County Museum*). The region's largest cultural museum has more than 40 old buildings on display. The structures, transported from other locations in the area, include two *tun*—farm buildings traditionally set in clusters around a common area—which suited extended families. If you have children with you, check out the old-fashioned toys, which can still be played with. The museum is 4 km (2½ miles) east of Kristiansand on Route E18. ✉ *Vigevn. 22B, Kongsgård* ☎ *38–10–26–80* ⊕ *www.vestagdermuseet.no* 🔲 *NKr 50* ⊙ *Mid-June–Aug., weekdays 10–5, weekends noon–5; Sept.–mid-June, weekdays 9–3, Sun. noon–5.*

6

ACTIVITIES

Samsen Kulturhus. Whether you're an experienced pro or just a gung-ho beginner, you can rent climbing equipment or learn more about the sport from Samsen Kulturhus. ✉ *Vestervn. 2, Kristiansand* ☎ *38–00–64–00* ⊕ *www.samsen.com.*

Troll Mountain. Troll Mountain, about one hour's drive from Kristiansand, organizes many activities. Be it mountain climbing, sailing, biking, rafting, paintball, or even beaver or deer safaris, this is the place for outdoorsy types. ✉ *Setesdal Rafting og Aktivitetssenter, Rte. 9, Evje* ☎ *37–93–11–77* ⊕ *www.troll-mountain.no.*

FISHING

Lillesand Tourist Office. You can get a permit at any sports store or at the Lillesand Tourist Office. ☎ *37–40–19–10, 93–01–17–81* ⊕ *www.lillesand.com.*

HIKING

Baneheia Skog (*Baneheia Forest*). In addition to the gardens and steep hills of Ravnedalen, the Baneheia Skog is full of evergreens, small lakes, and paths that are ideal for a lazy walk or a challenging run. It's just a 15-minute walk north from the city center.

HORSEBACK RIDING

Islandshestsenteret (*The Icelandic Horse Center*). If you're at home in the saddle, then head to Islandshestsenteret. Specializing in the Icelandic horse breed, this center offers courses, trips, and camping for children and adults. ✉ *Søgne, Kristiansand* ☎ *38–16–98–82* ⊕ *www.islandshestsenteret.no.*

SHOPPING

There are many shops next to Dyreparken in Kristiansand.

Kvadraturen. You'll find 300 stores and eating spots in this part of the Old Town, which was commissioned by King Christian IV in the mid-1600s. ⊕ *www.kvadraturen.no.*

Sørlandssenteret. One of the region's larger shopping centers, Sørlandssenteret contains 130 stores, a pharmacy, and a post office. ✉ *Barstølveien 31–35* ☎ *38–04–91–00* ⊕ *www.sorlandssenteret.no.*

OSLO, NORWAY

What sets Oslo apart from other European cities is not so much its cultural traditions or its internationally renowned museums as its simply stunning natural beauty. How many world capitals have subway service to the forest, or lakes and hiking trails within the city limits? But Norwegians will be quick to remind you that Oslo is a cosmopolitan metropolis with prosperous businesses and a thriving nightlife. During the mid-19th century, Norway and Sweden were ruled as one kingdom, under King Karl Johan. It was then that the grand main street that is his namesake was built, and Karl Johans Gate has been at the center of city life ever since. In 1905 the country separated from

Sweden, and in 1925 an act of Parliament finally changed the city's name back to Oslo from Kristiania, its Swedish name. Today Oslo is Norway's political, economic, industrial, and cultural capital. The Norwegian royal family lives in Oslo, and it is also where the Nobel Peace Prize is awarded.

COMING ASHORE

Cruise ships navigate beautiful Oslofjord en route to Oslo and dock in the compact city center. Many of Oslo's attractions can be explored on foot from the docks, but Oslo has a good subway system, as well as plentiful buses and taxis.

Taxis are radio dispatched from a central office, and it can take up to 30 minutes to get one during peak hours. Taxi stands are all over town. It is possible to hail a cab on the street, but cabs are not allowed to pick up passengers within 100 yards of a stand. Never take pirate taxis; all registered taxis should have their roof lights on when they're available. Rates start at around NKr 109 for hailed or rank cabs, and NKr 91 for ordered taxis, depending on the time of day and the company.

EXPLORING OSLO

6

Fodor'sChoice
★
Aker Brygge. This area was the site of a disused shipbuilding yard until redevelopment saw the addition of residential town houses and a commercial sector. Postmodern steel and glass buildings dominate the skyline now. The area has more than 60 shops and 35 restaurants, including upmarket fashion boutiques, pubs, cinemas, a theater, a comedy club, and a shopping mall. There is an open boulevard for strolling. Service facilities include banks, drugstores, and a parking garage for 1,600. ⊠ *Aker Brygge* ☎ *22–83–26–80* ⊕ *www.akerbrygge.no* ☒ *Free* ⊙ *Shopping hrs weekdays 10–8, Sat. 10–6; grocery store and restaurants are open later.*

Akershus Festning og Slott (*Akershus Fortress and Castle*). Dating to 1299, this stone medieval castle and royal residence was developed into a fortress armed with cannons by 1592. After that time, it withstood a number of sieges and then fell into decay. It was finally restored in 1899. Summer tours take you through its magnificent halls, the castle church, the royal mausoleum, reception rooms, and banqueting halls. Explore Akershus Fortress on your own with the Fortress Trail Map, which you can pick up at the visitor center. Note that the castle is closed during official visits, which happen a couple weekends a year. ⊠ *Akershus festning, Sentrum* ☎ *23–09–35–53* ⊕ *www.forsvarsbygg.no/festningene/ Festningene/Akershus-festning* ☒ *Fortress grounds and concerts: free. Castle: NKr 70, including audio guide* ⊙ *Sept.–Apr., weekends noon–5; May–Aug., Mon.–Sat. 10–4, Sun. noon–4.*

★
ℭ
Fram-Museet. This was the ship used by the legendary Polar explorer Roald Amundsen when be became the first man to reach the South Pole, in December 1911. Once known as the strongest vessel in the world, this enormous Norwegian polar ship has advanced farther north and south than any other surface vessel. Built in 1892, it made three voyages to the Arctic (they were conducted by Fridtjof Nansen and Otto Sverdrup, in addition to Amundsen). Climb on board and peer

Oslo

Vigelandsparken

Holmenkollbakken
og Skimuseet

TO HOLMENKOLLEN

Vigelands-
parken

Kirkeveien

Halvdan Svartes gt.

Nordraaks gt.

Gyldenløves gt.

Tidemands gt.

Prof. Dahls gt.

Bogstadveien

Industrig!.

Eilert Sundts gt.

Uranienborg veien

Eckerbergs gt.

Arno
Bergs
Plass

Holte gt.

C. Colletts veien

Parkveien

Nobels gt.

Frognerveien

Løvenskiolds

Oscars gt.

Thomas Heftyes gt.

Gimleveien

Ridderrvolds gt.

Bygdøy allé

Elisenberg veien

Balders gt.

Lille Frogner Allé

Krusesgt.

Gyldenløves gt.

Skovveien

Slottet

Drammens veien

Thomas Heftyes

Fred. Stangs gt.

Gabels gt.

Bygdøy allé

Parkveien

Lapsetorget

Drammensveien

U.S.
Embassy

Frognerstranda

Niels Juels gate

Drammensveien

Parkveien

Cort Adelers

Munkedamsveien

Munkedamsveien

Frognerkilen

E18

E18

Dokkveien

Filipstadveien

Aker
Brygge

Pipervika

Norsk Folkemuseum

Vikingskiphuset

Filipstadkaia

Langvikbukta

Oslofjorden

TO AIRPORT
Kon-Tiki Museum

Fram-Museet

KEY
🛈 Tourist information

0   1/2 mi

0   1/2 km

inside the captain's quarters, which has explorers' sealskin jackets and other relics on display. Surrounding the ship are many artifacts from expeditions. ⊠ *Bygdøynesvn. 36, Bygdøy* ☎ *23–28–29–50* ⊕ *www.frammuseum.no* 🎫 *NKr 80* ☉ *June–Aug., daily 9–6; Sept. and May, daily 10–5; Oct. and Mar.–Apr., daily 10–4; Nov.–Feb., weekdays 10–3, weekends 10–4.*

Fodor's Choice
★
Holmenkollbakken og skimuseet (*Holmenkollen Ski Jump and Ski Museum*). A feat of world-class engineering, this beloved ski jump was first constructed in 1892 and has been rebuilt numerous times, remaining a distinctive part of Oslo's skyline. The cool, futuristic-looking jump you see today was finished in 2010. It offers spectacular views and some repose from Oslo's

> ## OSLO BEST BETS
>
> **Aker Brygge.** Once a dilapidated shipyard, this is now an upscale residential and commercial district.
>
> **Munch Museet.** Munch is Norway's most famous artist. You can see a version of *The Scream* here; there's another version in the Nasjonalgalleriet if you want a broader introduction to Norwegian art.
>
> **Vigelandsparken.** The 212 bronze, granite, and wrought-iron sculptures by Gustav Vigeland skillfully and artistically detail his life, thoughts, and interpretations of his childhood.

urbanity, and it still hosts international competitions. The ski-jump simulator puts you in the skis of real jumpers, and the world's oldest ski museum presents 4,000 years of ski history. Check on hours before visiting; they're subject to change, particularly in the fall through spring months. Guided tours of the museum and jump tower are both available. ⊠ *Kongevn. 5, Holmenkollen* ☎ *22–92–32–00* ⊕ *holmenkollen.com* 🎫 *Jump tower and museum (joint ticket): NKr 110* ☉ *Oct.–Apr., daily 10–4; May and Sept., daily 10–5; June–Aug, daily 9–8.*

★
☾
Kon-Tiki Museum. The museum celebrates Norway's most famous 20th-century explorer. Thor Heyerdahl made a voyage in 1947 from Peru to Polynesia on the *Kon-Tiki,* a balsa raft, to lend weight to his theory that the first Polynesians came from the Americas. His second craft, the *Ra II,* was used to test his theory that this sort of boat could have reached the West Indies before Columbus. The museum also has a film room and artifacts from Peru, Polynesia, and the Easter Islands. ⊠ *Bygdøynesvn. 36, Bygdøy* ☎ *23–08–67–67 press 4 for English* ⊕ *www.kon-tiki.no* 🎫 *NKr 80* ☉ *Mar.–May, Sept., and Oct. daily 10–5; June–Aug, daily 9:30–6; Nov.–Feb. daily 10–4.*

Fodor's Choice
★
Munchmuseet (*Munch Museum*). Edvard Munch, Norway's most famous artist, bequeathed his enormous collection of works (about 1,100 paintings, 3,000 drawings, and 18,000 graphic works) to the city when he died in 1944. The museum is a monument to his artistic genius, housing the largest collection of his works and also mounting changing exhibitions. Munch actually painted four different versions of *The Scream,* the image for which he's best known, and one of them is on display here. While most of the Munch legend focuses on the artist as a troubled, angst-ridden man, he moved away from that pessimistic and dark approach to more optimistic themes later in his career. ⊠ *Tøyengt. 53,*

Tøyen ☎ *23–49–35–00* ⊕ *www.munch.museum.no* ▣ *NKr 95* ☉ *Sept.–May, Tues.–Sat. 10–4, Sun. 10–5; June–Aug., daily 10–5.*

★ **Nasjonalgalleriet** (*National Gallery*). The gallery, part of the National Museum of Art, Architecture and Design, houses Norway's largest collection of art created before 1945. The deep-red Edvard Munch room holds such major paintings as *The Dance of Life,* one of two existing oil versions of *The Scream,* and several self-portraits. Classic landscapes by Hans Gude and Adolph Tidemand—including *Bridal Voyage on the Hardangerfjord*—share space in galleries with other works by major Norwegian artists. The museum also has works by Monet, Renoir, Van Gogh, and Gauguin, as well as contemporary works by 20th-century Nordic artists. ✉ *Universitetsgt. 13, Sentrum* ☎ *21–98–20–00* ⊕ *www. nasjonalmuseet.no* ▣ *NKr 50; free on Sun.* ☉ *Tues., Wed., and Fri. 10–6, Thurs. 10–7, weekends 11–5.*

Fodor'sChoice ★ ☾ **Norsk Folkemuseum** (*The Norwegian Museum of Cultural History*). One of the largest open-air museums in Europe, this is a perfect way to see Norway in a day. From the stoic stave church (built in AD 1200) to farmers' houses made of sod, the old buildings here span Norway's regions and most of its recorded history. Indoors, there's a fascinating display of folk costumes. The displays of richly embroidered, colorful *bunader* (national costumes) from every region include one set at a Telemark country wedding. The museum also has stunning dragon-style wood carvings from 1550 and some beautiful *rosemaling,* or decorative painted floral patterns. The traditional costumes of the Sami (Lapp) people of Northern Norway are exhibited around one of their tents. If you're visiting in summer, ask about Norwegian Evening, a summer program of folk dancing, guided tours, and food tastings. On Sundays in December, the museum holds Oslo's largest Christmas market. ✉ *Museumsvn. 10, Bygdøy* ☎ *22–12–37–00* ⊕ *www.norskfolkemuseum.no* ▣ *NKr 110* ☉ *Mid–Sept.–mid-May, weekdays 11–3, weekends 11–4; mid-May–mid-Sept., daily 10–6.*

Fodor'sChoice ★ **Operahuset.** Oslo's opera house opened in 2008 with a fanfare that included the presence of the Norwegian king and a host of celebrities. The white marble and glass building, designed by renowned Norwegian architect firm Snøhetta, is a stunning addition to the Oslo waterfront, and the pride of Norwegians. It doesn't just look good; acoustics inside the dark oak auditorium are excellent, too. The program includes ballet, orchestra concerts, rock, and opera. Locals and tourists alike enjoy visiting at off hours, eating in the venue's restaurants, and walking on the building's roof. ✉ *Kirsten Flagstads pl. 1* ☎ *21–42–21–00* ⊕ *www.operaen.no* ▣ *Free entrance; guided tours NKr 100* ☉ *Tours in English in summer.*

Rådhuset (*City Hall*). This redbrick building is best known today for the awarding of the Nobel Peace Prize, which takes place here every December. Inside, many museum-quality masterpieces are on the walls. After viewing the frescoes in the main hall, walk upstairs to the banquet hall to see the royal portraits. Free drop-in guided tours are available. Meet in the main hall for the 45-minute tour at the noted times. To visit the City Hall Gallery, enter harborside. Special exhibits

6

are hung throughout the year. On festive occasions, the central hall is illuminated from outside by 60 large spotlights that simulate daylight. ✉ *Fridtjof Nansens Plass, Sentrum* ☎ *02180* ⊕ *www.radhusetsforvaltningstjeneste.oslo.kommune.no/english* 💷 *Free* ☉ *Drop-in guided tours of City Hall: Sept.–May, Wed. at 10, noon, and 2; June–Aug., daily at 10, noon, and 2.*

Slottet (*The Royal Palace*). At one end of Karl Johans Gate, the vanilla-and-cream-color neoclassical palace was completed in 1848. The equestrian statue out in front is of Karl Johan, King of Sweden and Norway from 1818 to 1844. The palace is only open to the public in summer, when there are guided tours (in English). ■**TIP→** **Kids of all ages will love the Royal Palace's changing of the guard ceremony, accompanied by the Norwegian Military Band, that takes place daily, rain or shine, at 1:30.** ✉ *Slottsplassen* ☎ *81–53–31–33 Billettservice, for tickets* ⊕ *www. kongehuset.no* 💷 *Tours: NKr 95* ☉ *Tours: Mid-June–mid-Aug., Mon.– Thurs. and Sat. at noon, 2, and 2:20; Fri. and Sun. 2, 2:20, and 4.*

Fodor's Choice **Vigelandsparken** (*Vigeland Sculpture Park*). A vast green lung and a
★ favorite hangout for locals, Vigelandsparken has 212 bronze, granite,
☾ and wrought-iron sculptures by Gustav Vigeland (1869–1943) as well as ample park space. The 56-foot-high granite *Monolith* is a column of 121 upward-striving nudes surrounded by 36 groups on circular stairs. The *Angry Boy*, a bronze of an enraged cherubic child stamping his foot, draws legions of visitors and has been filmed, parodied, painted red, and even stolen. Kids love to climb on the statues. There's also a museum on-site for those wishing to delve deeper into the artist's work. ✉ *Frognerparken, Frogner* ☎ *23–49–37–00* ⊕ *www.vigeland.museum. no* 💷 *Park: free. Museum: NKr 50* ☉ *Park: year-round, dawn–dusk. Museum: May–Aug.: Tues.–Sun. 10–5, Sept.–Apr.: Tues.–Sun. noon–4.*

Fodor's Choice **Vikingskipshuset** (*Viking Ship Museum*). The Viking legacy in all its glory
★ lives on at this classic Oslo museum. Chances are you'll come away fas-
☾ cinated by the *Gokstad, Oseberg,* and *Tune,* three blackened wooden Viking ships that date to AD 800. Discovered in Viking tombs around the Oslo fjords between 1860 and 1904, the boats are the best-preserved Viking ships ever found; they have been on display since the museum's 1957 opening. In Viking times, it was customary to bury the dead with food, drink, useful and decorative objects, and even their horses and dogs. Many of the well-preserved tapestries, household utensils, dragon-style wood carvings, and sledges were found aboard ships. The museum's rounded white walls give the feeling of a burial mound. Avoid summertime crowds by visiting at lunchtime. ✉ *Huk Aveny 35, Bygdøy* ☎ *22–13–52–80* ⊕ *www.ukm.uio.no/vikingskipshuset* 💷 *NKr 60* ☉ *May–Sept., daily 9–6; Oct.–Apr., daily 10–4.*

SHOPPING

Oslo is the best place in the country for buying anything Norwegian. Popular souvenirs include knitwear, wood and ceramic trolls, cheese slicers, boxes with rosemaling, gold and silver jewelry, items made from pewter, smoked salmon, caviar, akvavit, chocolate, and geitost,

the sweet brown goat cheese that can be found in just about every Norwegian kitchen.

Established Norwegian brands include Porsgrund porcelain, Hadeland and Magnor glass, David Andersen jewelry, and Husfliden handicrafts (most of which are sold in branches of the Norsk flid crafts chain). You may also want to look for popular, classical, or folk music CDs; English translations of Norwegian books; or clothing by Norwegian designers, such as Moods of Norway.

Prices in Norway, as in all of Scandinavia, are generally much higher than in other European countries. Prices of handmade articles, such as knitwear, are controlled, making comparison shopping pointless. Otherwise, shops have both sales and specials—look for the words *salg* and *tilbud*. In addition, if you are a resident of a country other than Norway, Sweden, Finland, or Denmark, you can have the Norwegian value-added tax (MVA) refunded at the airport when you leave the country. When you make a purchase, you must clearly state your country of residence in order to have the necessary export document filled in by store staff.

Basarhallene, the arcade behind Oslo *domkirke* (cathedral), is worth a browse for glass and crystal and handicrafts made in Norway. Walk 15 minutes west of the city center and you can wander up the tree-lined Bygdøy Allé and browse the fashionable **Frogner** and **Bygdøy** areas, which are brimming with modern- and antique-furniture stores, interior design shops, food shops, art galleries, haute couture, and Oslo's beautiful people. The streets downtown around **Karl Johans Gate** draw many of Oslo's shoppers. The concentration of department stores is especially high in this part of town. **Majorstuen** starts at the *T-bane* (subway) station with the same name and proceeds down Bogstadveien to the Royal Palace. Oslo is not famed for its markets, but there's a small flower market on Stortorget in front of the cathedral, and a few stalls selling souvenirs and secondhand records on Youngstorget. Every Saturday, a flea market is open at **Vestkanttorget**, at Amaldus Nilsens Plass near Frognerparken. **Grünerløkka,** a 15-minute walk north of the center, is blooming with trendy new and bohemian fashion boutiques, vintage stores, and many other quirky little shops.

Aker Brygge. More than a shopping center, essentially a waterside pedestrian paradise, this renovated shipyard is where Oslo hangs out. Open late, it has 60 shops and 35 restaurants. ☎ 22–83–26–80 ⊕ *www.akerbrygge.no.*

GlasMagasinet. More an amalgam of shops under one roof than a true department store, GlasMagasinet has stores selling handcrafted items made with glass, silver, and pewter. It's opposite the cathedral. ⊠ *Stortorvet 9, Sentrum* ☎ *22–82–23–00* ⊕ *www.glasmagasinet.no.*

Paleet. The elegant Paleet opens up into a grand, marbled atrium and has many high-end clothing, accessories, and food stores—and there's a food court in the basement. ⊠ *Karl Johans gt. 37–43, Sentrum* ☎ *23–08–08–11* ⊕ *www.paleet.no.*

6

ACTIVITIES

Oslo's natural surroundings and climate make it ideally suited to out-door pursuits. The Oslofjord and its islands, the forested woodlands called the *marka,* and as many as 18 hours of daylight in summer all make the Norwegian capital an irresistible place for outdoor activities.

NIGHTLIFE

Oslo's cafés, restaurant-bars, and jazz clubs are laid-back and mellow. But if you're ready to party, there are many pulsating, live-rock and dance clubs to choose from. Day or night, people are usually out on Karl Johans Gate, and many clubs and restaurants in the central area stay open until the early hours. Aker Brygge, the wharf area, has many bars and some nightclubs, attracting mostly tourists, couples on first dates, and other people willing to spend extra for the waterfront location. Grünerløkka and Grønland have even more bars, pubs, and cafés catering to a younger crowd. An older crowd ventures out to the less-busy west side of Oslo, to Frogner and Bygdøy.

Drinking out is very expensive, starting at around NKr 70 for a beer or a mixed drink. Many Norwegians save money by having a *vorspiel*—a "pre-party" at friends' houses before heading out on the town. Some bars in town remain quiet until 11 pm or midnight when the first groups of vorspiel partiers arrive.

Bibliotekbaren og Vinterhaven. If you're more partial to lounging than drinking, the Bibliotekbaren og Vinterhaven (Library Bar and Winter Garden) is a stylish hangout with old-fashioned leather armchairs, huge marble columns, and live piano music. Politicians, actors, musicians, journalists, and locals have come here for nearly 100 years for informal meetings, quiet chats, or just to enjoy the tempting sandwich and cake buffet. ⊠ *Hotel Bristol, Kristian IVs gt. 7, Sentrum* ☎ *22–82–60–00.*

Blå. This is one of the most important Nordic clubs for jazz, electronica, hip-hop, and related sounds. The patio, along the Akerselva River, is popular in summer. ⊠ *Brennerivn. 9C, Grünerløkka* ☎ *98–25–63–86* ⊕ *www.blaaoslo.no.*

Herr Nilsen. At Herr Nilsen, some of Norway's most celebrated jazz artists perform in a stylish space. There's live music several nights a week and jazz on Saturday at 4 pm. ⊠ *C.J. Hambros pl. 5, Sentrum* ☎ *22–33–54–05* ⊕ *www.herrnilsen.no.*

WHERE TO EAT

$ ✕ **Asylet.** This popular pub right by Grønland Torg serves homemade NORWEGIAN traditional Norwegian food in an atmospheric setting. The building, ⊙   which dates from the 1730s, was once an orphanage. The big lunch menu features a good selection of *smørbrød* (open-faced sandwiches) as well as smoked-salmon salad and the traditional *karbonade* (a sort of open-faced hamburger, served with fried onions). There is a fireplace inside, and a beer garden for enjoying the sun in summer. ⑤ *Average main: NKr 180* ⊠ *Grønland 28* ☎ *22–17–09–39* ⊕ *www.asylet.no.*

$ ✕ **Beach Club.** This diner, its American origins "adjusted to a Norwegian
AMERICAN way of life," has been drawing the crowds since it opened in 1989.
The classics burgers are all there, but for something a bit different try
the "Favourite," with cheese, bacon and chili con carne; or the Zorba
(chicken burger with tzatziki); and then a Beach Lime Pie for dessert.
Full American-style breakfasts are also available, and there's also a
small kids' menu. The original Keith Haring on the walls and the big terrace for sunny days are two more pluses here. $ *Average main: NKr 150*
✉ *Bryggetorget 14, Aker Brygge* ☎ *22–83–83–82* ⊕ *www.beachclub.no.*

$$$ ✕ **Det Gamle Rådhus.** If you're in Oslo for just one night and want an
NORWEGIAN authentic dining experience, head to the city's oldest restaurant—
Fodor's Choice housed in Oslo's first town hall, a building that dates from 1641. It's
★ known for its traditional fish and game dishes such as the moose entre-
cote or the Røros reindeer. An absolute must, if you're lucky enough
to be visiting at the right time, is the house specialty, the pre-Christmas
lutefisk platter. The backyard has a charming outdoor area for dining
in summer. $ *Average main: NKr 270* ✉ *Nedre Slottsgt. 1, Sentrum*
☎ *22–42–01–07* ⊕ *www.gamleraadhus.no* ☯ *Closed Sun.*

$ ✕ **Fru Hagen.** The classic chandeliers and velvet sofas here make it look
BISTRO like a vintage neighborhood hangout. Locals gather here for fresh, well-
executed comfort food—burgers, pasta, sandwiches, and salads—or the
spicy chicken salad, a house specialty. At night, Fru Hagen lets its hair
down further, becoming a disco/bar that's open until 3 am. $ *Average
main: NKr 150* ✉ *Thorvald Meyers gt. 40, Grünerløkka* ☎ *45–49–19–
04* ⊕ *www.fruhagen.no.*

WHERE TO STAY

$$ ⌂ **Grand Hotel.** This very central hotel is the choice of visiting heads
HOTEL of state, rock musicians, and Nobel Peace Prize winners. **Pros:** period
Fodor's Choice features have been preserved throughout; Ladies Floor, with 13 unique
★ rooms designed for women travelers; beautiful pool and spa. **Cons:** gets
busy during festivals and in December, during Nobel Peace Prize week.
$ *Rooms from: NKr 1440* ✉ *Karl Johans gt. 31, Sentrum* ☎ *23–21–
20–00* ⊕ *www.grand.no* ⇗ *292 rooms, incl. 54 suites* ⦿ *Breakfast.*

$$$$ ⌂ **Hotel Continental.** History meets modernity at this landmark—it's a
HOTEL sophisticated stay with stylish guest rooms and posh common areas.
Fodor's Choice **Pros:** exemplary service; beautiful, well-appointed rooms; great gym.
★ **Cons:** restaurant and bars are very busy with locals as well as guests;
very expensive. $ *Rooms from: NKr 3300* ✉ *Stortingsgt. 24–26, Sen-
trum* ☎ *22–82–40–00* ⊕ *www.hotelcontinental.no* ⇗ *155 rooms, 23
suites* ⦿ *No meals.*

$$ ⌂ **Radisson Blu Plaza Hotel.** The understated elegance helps keep the
HOTEL rooms filled at this business hotel. **Pros:** great top floor bar; very good
★ breakfast buffet; luxuriously grand bathtubs; excellent location. **Cons:**
this is northern Europe's tallest hotel, so it's not very intimate; the
breakfast room can get crowded. $ *Rooms from: NKr 1495* ✉ *Sonja
Henies pl. 3* ☎ *22–05–80–00* ⊕ *www.radissonblu.com/plazahotel-oslo*
⇗ *676 rooms, 20 suites* ⦿ *Breakfast.*

6

TROMSØ, NORWAY

Tromsø surprised visitors in the 1800s: they thought it very sophisticated and cultured for being so close to the North Pole—hence
its nickname, the Paris of the North. It looks the way a polar town
should—with ice-capped mountain ridges and jagged architecture that
is an echo of the peaks. The midnight sun shines from May 21 to July
21, and it is said that the northern lights decorate the night skies over
Tromsø more than over any other city in Norway. Tromsø is home to
only 69,000 people, but it's very spread out—the city's total area, 2,558
square km (987 square miles), is the most expansive in Norway. The
downtown area is on a small, hilly island connected to the mainland
by a slender bridge. The 13,000 students at the world's northernmost
university are one reason the nightlife here is uncommonly busy.

COMING ASHORE

Cruise ships dock either in the city center at Prostneset or 4 km (2½
miles) north of the city center at Breivika. Step off the ship in Prostneset, and you're in the city center. A shuttle is offered between Breivika
and the city center.

EXPLORING TROMSØ

Fjellheisen. To get a sense of Tromsø's immensity and solitude, take this
cable car from the mainland, just across the bridge and behind the
cathedral, up to the island's mountains. *Storsteinen* (Big Rock), 1,386
feet above sea level, has a great city view. In summer a restaurant is
open at the top of the lift. ✉ *Sollivn. 12, Tromsdalen* ☎ *77–63–87–37*
⊕ *www.fjellheisen.no* 🎫 *NKr 120* ◷ *Mid-May–July, daily 10 am–1 am;
Aug., daily 10–10; Sept., daily 10–5; Oct.–Dec., daily 11–4; Feb.–Mar.,
10–4; Apr.–mid-May, daily 10–5.*

Ishavskatedralen (*Arctic Cathedral*). Tromsø's signature structure was
designed by Jan Inge Hovig to evoke the shape of a Sami tent as well as
the iciness of a glacier. Opened in 1964, it represents northern Norwegian
nature, culture, and faith. The immense stained-glass window depicts the
Second Coming. There are midnight sun concerts in summer, starting at
11:30 pm. ✉ *Hans Nilsens v. 41, Tromsdalen* ☎ *47–68–06–68* ⊕ *www.
ishavskatedralen.no* 🎫 *NKr 35; midnight sun concerts NKr 130* ◷ *June–
mid-Aug., Mon.–Sat. 9–7, Sun. 1–7; mid-Aug.–mid-Sept., daily 3–6; mid-
Sept.–mid-May, daily 4–6; mid-May through end of May, daily 3-6.*

Polaria. Housed in a striking modern building by the harbor, the adventure center Polaria examines life in and around the polar and Barents regions. Explore the exhibits on polar travel and arctic research,
then check out two panoramic films, *Svalbard—Arctic Wilderness* and
Northern Lights in Arctic Norway. The aquarium has sea mammals,
including bearded seals. ✉ *Hjalmar Johansens gt. 12* ☎ *77–75–01–00*
⊕ *www.polaria.no* 🎫 *NKr 105* ◷ *Mid-May–mid-Aug., daily 10–7; mid-
Aug.–mid-May, daily 11–5.*

Polarmuseet (*Polar Museum*). Inside a customs warehouse from 1830,
Polarmuseet documents the history of the polar regions. There are
exhibitions on wintering in the Arctic, trapping, Arctic seal hunting,

and on famous Norwegian polar explorers like Fridtjof Nansen and Roald Amundsen. Part of the University of Tromsø, the museum opened in 1978, on the 50th anniversary of Amundsen leaving Tromsø for the last time, in search of his explorer colleague Umberto Nobile. ✉ *Søndre Tollbodgt. 11B* ☎ *77–62–33–60* ⊕ *www.polarmuseum.no* 🎫 *NKr 50* ⊗ *Mid-Aug.–mid-June daily 11–5; mid-June–mid-Aug. daily 10–7.*

♧ **Tromsø Museum** (*Tromsø University Museum*). Dating from 1872, Northern Norway's oldest scientific institution is dedicated to the nature and culture of the region. Learn about the northern lights, wildlife, fossils and dinosaurs, minerals and rocks, and church art from 1300 to 1800. Outdoors you can visit a Sami *gamme* (turf hut), and a replica of a Viking longhouse. The pretty Arctic-Alpine Botanical Garden is the most northern in the world, at roughly the same latitude as Alaska's north coast. ✉ *Lars Thørings v. 10* ☎ *77–64–50–00* ⊕ *uit.no/tmu* 🎫 *NKr 50* ⊗ *June–Aug., daily 9–6; Sept.–May, weekdays 10–4:30, Sat. noon–3, Sun. 11–4.*

ACTIVITIES

HIKING AND WALKING

With wilderness at its doorstep, Tromsø has more than 100 km (62 miles) of walking and hiking trails in the mountains above the city. They're reachable by funicular.

OUTDOOR ACTIVITY OUTFITTERS

Tromsø has more than 100 km (62 miles) of walking and hiking trails in the mountains above the city. They're reachable by funicular.

Lyngsfjord Adventure. This tour company offers dog sledding, reindeer sledding, snowmobile safaris, snowshoeing, northern lights viewing, and the chance to sleep in Sami tents. ☎ 77–71–55-88 ⊕ *www. lyngsfjord.com.*

Tromsø Villmarkssenter. This outfitter, located a half hour outside the city, organizes winter dogsledding trips, northern lights safaris, glacier walking, kayaking, summit tours, and Sami-style dinners, which take place around a campfire inside a *lavvu* (a Sami tent). ⊠ *Straumsvegen 603, Kvaløya* ☎ *77–69–60–02* ⊕ *www.villmarkssenter.no.*

SHOPPING

One of Norway's leading regions for handmade arts and crafts, Tromsø is a treasure trove of shops, particularly along the main pedestrian street Storgata, where a market sells regional and international products. Pick up art from the city's many galleries or craft shops (such as glass-blowing and candle-making studios), or score such Arctic delicacies as reindeer sausages.

WHERE TO EAT

$$ ✕ **Vertshuset Skarven.** The several restaurants and bars here mostly
SEAFOOD emphasize seafood, but there's also a steak house. The menu in this Arctic pantry might include soup of Kamchatka crab, delicious halibut and coalfish, Arctic reindeer, or whale carpaccio. The fish lunch at Skarven is a good value. The pleasant terrace is usually packed in summer. ⑤ *Average main: NKr 255* ⊠ *Strandtorget 1* ☎ *77–60–07–20* ⊕ *www.skarven.no.*

TRONDHEIM, NORWAY

One of Scandinavia's oldest cities, Trondheim was the first capital of Norway, from AD 997 to 1380. Founded in 997 by Viking king Olav Tryggvason, it was first named Nidaros (still the name of the cathedral), a composite word referring to the city's location at the mouth of the Nidelva River. Today, it's Central Norway's largest (and Norway's third-largest) city, with a population of 150,000. The wide streets of the historic city center remain lined with brightly painted wood houses and striking warehouses. But it's no historic relic: it's also the home to NTNU (Norwegian University of Science and Technology) and is Norway's technological capital.

Trondheim

Trondheimfjord

Ytre Bassin

TO →
RINGVE
MUSEUM

Central
Station

Dyre Halses

Østre | Kanalhavn

Fjordgata

Vestre Kanalhavn

Olav Tryggvasons gt.

Thomas Agnells gt.

Bakke bru

Dronningens gata

Nedre gt.

Søndre gt.

Krambugt.

Liepmannsgata

Munkegata

Sandgata

Tordenskiolds gt.

Stiftsgården

Kongens gate

Kongensgata

Erling Skakkes gt.

Elvegata

Kalvskinnsgt.

Prinsens gata

Munkegata

Nordenfjeldske
Kunstindustrimuseum

Gamle
Bybru

Nedre Bakklandet

Kristiansten
festning

Gangbrua

Sverres gata

Bispegata

Brubakken

Trondheim Kunstmuseum

Klostergata

Nidelva

Elgeseter bru

Nidarosdomen

Erkebispegården

Øvre Bakklandet

Lillegardsbakken

Sverresborg Trøndelag
Folkemuseum

0 ___ 1/4 mi
0 ___ 1/4 km

6

COMING ASHORE

Cruise ships dock at one of two piers. Both of these are within easy
walking distance of the city center. There are no facilities at the piers,
but you'll find everything you need—from banks to tourist offices—in
the city.

EXPLORING TRONDHEIM

Trondheim is home to some wonderful historical buildings and sites.
Take in the cathedral where Norway's kings are blessed (they're no
longer crowned), visit some of the oldest buildings in the country, and
marvel at the country's largest entirely wooden palace. If that's not your
thing, stop in at a museum, or just enjoy the relatively mild climate as
you walk along Nidelva River, admiring the view.

Erkebispegården (*Archbishop's Palace*). Erkebispegården is the oldest
secular building in Scandinavia, dating from around 1160. It was the
residence of the archbishop until the Reformation in 1537. The Archbishop's Palace Museum has original sculptures from Nidaros Cathedral
and archaeological pieces from throughout its history. Within Erkebispegården's inner palace is the Rustkammeret/Resistance Museum,
which traces military development from Viking times to the present
through displays of uniforms, swords, and daggers. The dramatic events

of World War II get a special emphasis. ■**TIP→** Opening times for the various museums and wings in the Erkebispegården and for the cathedral vary greatly by season. ✉ *Kongsgårdsgt. 1* ☎ *73-89-08-00* ⊕ *www. nidarosdomen.no* 🔲 *NKr 120 (includes entry to Nidaros Cathedral)* ⊙ *Hrs. vary greatly.*

Kristiansten festning. Built by J. C. Cicignon after the great fire of 1681, the Kristiansten Fort saved the city from conquest by Sweden in 1718. During World War II, the German occupying forces executed members of the Norwegian Resistance here; there's a plaque in their honor. The fort has spectacular views of the city, the fjord, and the mountains. ☎ *81-57-04-00* ⊕ *www.forsvarsbygg.no/festningene/Festningene/ Kristiansten-festning* 🔲 *Free* ⊙ *Grounds open daily 8 am-1 am.*

Nidarosdomen (*Nidaros Cathedral*). Trondheim's cathedral was built on the grave of King Olav, who formulated a Christian religious code for Norway in 1024. The town quickly became a pilgrimage site for Christians from all over Northern Europe, and Olav was canonized in 1164. Construction of Nidarosdomen began in 1070, but the oldest existing parts of the cathedral date from around 1150. It has been ravaged on several occasions by fire and rebuilt each time, generally in a Gothic style. Since the Middle Ages, Norway's kings have been crowned and blessed in the cathedral. The crown jewels are on display here. Forty-five-minute guided tours are offered in English from mid-June to mid-August. ✉ *Kongsgårdsgt. 2* ☎ *73-89-08-00* ⊕ *www. nidarosdomen.no* 🔲 *NKr 120 with Erkebispegården, otherwise NKr 60* ⊙ *Hrs. vary greatly with seasons.*

★ **Nordenfjeldske Kunstindustrimuseum.** The Tiffany windows are magnificent at this museum of decorative arts, which houses an impressive collection of furniture, silver, and textiles. The Scandinavian Design section features a room interior designed by the Danish architect Finn Juhl in 1952. The 1690 bridal crown by Adrian Bogarth is also memorable. *Three Women–Three Artists* features tapestries by Hannah Ryggen and Synnøve Anker Aurdal, and glass creations by Benny Motzfeldt. ✉ *Munkegt. 5* ☎ *73-80-89-50* ⊕ *www.nkim.no* 🔲 *NKr 80* ⊙ *June–late Aug., Mon.–Sat. 10–5, Sun. noon–5; late Aug.–May, Tues.–Sat. 10–3, Sun. noon–4.*

Fodor's Choice ★ **Stiftsgården.** Built in the 1770s, Stiftsgården is now the official royal residence in Trondheim; Princess Märtha Louise held her wedding reception here in 2002. The architecture and interior are late baroque and highly representative of 18th-century high society's taste. Tours offer insight into the festivities marking the coronations and blessings of the kings in the cathedral. ✉ *Munkegt. 23* ☎ *73-84-28-80 guided tour information* ⊕ *www.nkim.no/stiftsgarden* 🔲 *NKr 80* ⊙ *June–mid-Aug., Mon.–Sat. 10–4, Sun. noon–4. Tours on the hr.*

↻ **Sverresborg, Trøndelag Folkemuseum.** Near the ruins of King Sverre's medieval castle is this open-air historical museum that depicts everyday life in Trøndelag during the 18th and 19th centuries. The stave church here, built in the 1170s, is the northernmost preserved church of its type in Norway. In the Old Town you can visit a 1900s dentist's office and an old-fashioned grocery store that sells sweets. In the summer

there are farm animals on-site, and a range of activities for children. ✉ *Sverresborg allé 13* ☎ *73–89–01–10* ⊕ *www.sverresborg.no* ✍ *NKr 100 in summer; NKr 55 the rest of the year* ☉ *June–Aug., daily 11–6; Sept.–May, weekdays 11–3, weekends noon–4.*

Trondheim Kunstmuseum (*Trondheim Art Museum*). The town's art museum houses some 4,000 works of art, including many by regional artists. ✉ *Bispegt. 7B* ☎ *73–53–81–80* ⊕ *www.tkm.museum.no* ✍ *NKr 60* ☉ *Tues and Thurs.–Sun. 11–3, Wed. 11–9.*

SHOPPING

Arne Ronning. Sweaters by Dale of Norway and other designers are available here. ✉ *Nordregt. 10* ☎ *73–53–13–30* ⊕ *www.arneronning.no.*

Gullsmed Møller. Founded in 1770, this is Northern Europe's oldest goldsmith. It sells versions of the Trondheim Rose, the city symbol since the 1700s. ✉ *Munkegt. 3* ☎ *73–52–04–39* ⊕ *www.gullsmedmoller.no.*

Jens Hoff Garn & Ide. For knitted clothes and blankets, try this shop. ✉ *Sirkus Shopping, Solsiden* ☎ *90–26–31–40* ⊕ *www.jenshoff.no.*

Norsk Flid. Trondheim's branch of the popular handicraft store. ✉ *Olav Tryggvasongt. 18* ☎ *73–83–32–30* ⊕ *www.norskflid.no/trondheim.*

ACTIVITIES

CYCLING

Trondheim Bysykkel. Some 125 city bikes can be borrowed in the city center. Parked in easy-to-see stands at central locations, the distinctive red-and-white bikes come with shopping baskets. To rent a bicycle, you need to buy a subscription—ask at the tourist office for more information. ⊕ *www.bysykler.no/trondheim_bysykkel.asp.*

HIKING AND WALKING

Bymarka. This wooded area on Trondheim's outskirts has a varied and well-developed network of trails—60 km (37 miles) of gravel paths, 80 km (50 miles) of ordinary paths, 250 km (155 miles) of ski tracks.

Ladestien (*Lade Trail*). This 8-km trail along the edge of Lade Peninsula has great views of Trondheimsfjord. It's a nice hike whatever your fitness level. ⊕ *www.trondheim.kommune.no/content/1094810105/Ladestien.*

Nidelvstien Trail. This trail runs along the river from Tempe to the Leirfossene waterfalls. ⊕ *www.trondheim.kommune.no/content.ap?thisId=1094810136.*

WHERE TO EAT

Trondheim is known for the traditional dish *surlaks* (marinated salmon served with sour cream). A sweet specialty is *tekake* (tea cake), which looks like a thick-crust pizza topped with a lattice pattern of cinnamon and sugar.

$$$ ✕ **Havfruen.** The long-running "Mermaid" is Trondheim's foremost and
SEAFOOD   most stylish fish restaurant. Taking its cues from France, the restaurant
★   excels at bouillabaisse as well as many other fish dishes, which change
seasonally. The warm decor uses orange, greens, and reds accented by
wood. The wine list includes a wide range of whites, highlighting dry
French varieties. ⑤ *Average main: NKr 299* ⊠ *Kjøpmannsgt. 7* ☎ *73–
87–40–70* ⊕ *www.havfruen.no* ⊘ *Closed Sun. No lunch.*

$$ ✕ **Vertshuset Tavern.** Housed in what was once a 1739 tavern in down-
NORWEGIAN   town Trondheim, this restaurant is now part of the Sverresborg folk
museum. The traditional menu includes homemade fish cakes and
meatballs; *rømmegrøt* (sour-cream porridge); creamed fish soup and
spekemat (cured meat). On weekends, the restaurant opens at 2 pm.
⑤ *Average main: NKr 200* ⊠ *Sverresborg allé 11* ☎ *73–87–80–70*
⊕ *www.tavern.no* ⊘ *No lunch weekdays.*

Atlantic Islands

PORTS IN THE CANARY ISLANDS, ICELAND, AND MADEIRA

WORD OF MOUTH

"As I started reading more about all the various islands (especially in the Canaries), it struck my mind that cruises might be more efficient at [letting you see] everything. I checked online, and sure enough, there are a ton of them."

—mistadobalina

Though not in the Mediterranean proper, a few islands in the Atlantic are commonly included on many so-called Mediterranean-cruise itineraries. The Canary Islands and Iceland are sometimes included on transatlantic crossings, but the Canary Islands or Madeira may also be included on longer western Mediterranean cruises, while Iceland is included in some summer Scandinavia cruises. All of these islands offer dramatically beautiful scenery, and although their respective influences are vastly different, they each offer something unique. All are popular summer vacation destinations for Europeans.

FUNCHAL, MADEIRA

Updated by
Joanna Styles

Wine connoisseurs through the ages have savored Madeira's eponymous export, but a sip of this heady elixir provides only a taste of the island's many delights. The natural beauty of this island is like no other, from the cliffs that plummet seaward to mountain summits cloaked in silent fog. The magic has captivated travelers for centuries. Multiple microclimates, exotic topography and vegetation, and designated nature reserves create an amazing ecodestination. The Laurissilva Forest that occupies a lofty coastal strip above the sea has been classified as part of the Madeira Nature Reserve and a UNESCO World Natural Heritage site. The island is the only region in the world where ancient forest dating back before the Ice Age can be found. Flora and fauna in the four nature reserves are still being discovered to this day. With this awesome heritage, Madeira has the power to keep its core a sanctuary for centuries to come.

ESSENTIALS

CURRENCY

The euro. ATMs are common and credit cards are widely accepted.

HOURS

Most shops are open weekdays from 9 to 1 and 3 to 7, Saturday from 9 to 1; malls and supermarkets often remain open until at least 10, and some stores are also open on Sunday. Most museums are closed Monday, and churches generally close for a couple of hours in the middle of the day.

TOUR OPERATOR

Madeira Explorers run guided walks and tours around the island's most spectacular sights. Half- and full-day trips are available.

Contacts **Madeira Explorers.** ☎ *291/763701* ⊕ *www.madeira-levada-walks.com.*

TELEPHONES

Most tri- and quad-band GSM phones will work in Madeira, and Portugal has a well-organized 3G-compatible mobile network, which extends to Madeira. You can buy prepaid phone cards at telecom shops, news vendors, and tobacconists in all towns and cities. Phone cards can be used for local or international calls. Major companies include Vodafone and Optimus.

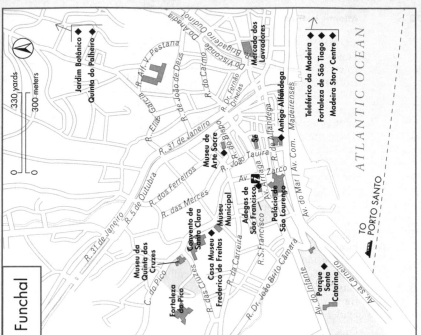

Funchal

Jardim Botânico ◆
Quinta do Palheiro ◆

Teleférico da Madeira ◆
Fortaleza de São Tiago ◆
Madeiro Story Centre ◆

Mercado dos Lavadores

Antiga Alfândega ◆

Museu de Arte Sacre ◆

Sé

Convento de Santa Clara ◆
Museu Municipal ◆
Museu da Quinta das Cruzes ◆
Casa Museu Frederico de Freitas ◆

Adegas de São Francisco ◆
Palácio de São Lourenço ◆

Fortaleza do Pico ◆

Parque Santa Catarina ◆

R. Alf.-V. Pestana
R. do Visconde do Anadia
R. do Bispo Brigadeiro Oudinot
R. do Carmo
R. D. Fernão Ornelas
R. de João de Deus
R. da Alfândega
R. Jão de Taulra
R. do Aljube
Av. Arriaga
Av. Zarco
R. da Carreira
R.S. Francisco
R. Dr. João Brito Câmara
Av. do Infante
Av. Sá Carneiro
Av. do Mar | Av. Com. Madeirenses
R. Elias Garcia
R. 31 de Janeiro
R. 5 de Outubro
R. dos Ferreiros
R. das Merces
R. das Cruzes
C. do Pico

TO PORTO SANTO

ATLANTIC OCEAN

330 yards
300 meters

Madeira

ATLANTIC OCEAN

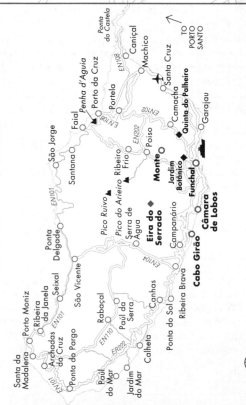

Santa da Madalena
Porto Moniz
Ribeira da Janela
Seixal
São Vicente
Ponta Delgada
Santana
São Jorge
Faial
Penha d'Aguia
Porto da Cruz
Ponta do Castela
Caniçal
Machico
Santa Cruz
TO PORTO SANTO

Archadas da Cruz
Paúl da Serra
Rabaçal
Ribeiro Frio
Portela
Poiso
Monte
Camacha
Quinta do Palheiro
Garajau

EN101
EN110
ER222
EN104
EN202
EN102
EN108

Ponta do Pargo
Paúl do Mar
Jardim do Mar
Calheta
Ponta do Sol
Ribeira Brava
Canhas
Campanário
Serra de Água
Pico do Arieiro
Pico Ruivo
Eira do Serrado
Jardim Botânico
Funchal
Câmara de Lobos
Cabo Girão

6 miles
9 km

COMING ASHORE

Funchal's cruise port is close to the town center, but ships dock away from the entrance. There may be a shuttle into Funchal; otherwise, there are cabs at the port entrance, or it is a pleasant half-mile walk. There are few tourist facilities at the port itself, though a few souvenir kiosks open when the boats are in dock.

Taxis are numerous, and the prices are government-controlled. There's a base of €2 (€2.60 on weekends), then €0.63 per km. Fares for public buses begin at €1.90 for your initial journey including the price of a rechargeable electronic Giro card, and €1.25 thereafter provided you have sufficient funds on the card. A full-day Giro card is €4.40, and this may be the most practical and easy solution if you intend to use public transport to get around. You'll need to pass this card over an electronic reader as you enter and leave the bus to register your fare.

Funchal is the center of a good network of bus routes to the major sights of the island, but check on the frequency and times of return to Funchal before you set out.

If you plan to spend your day ashore in Funchal, you should not rent a car; however, a vehicle would enable you to explore other areas of the island during your day. A manual economy vehicle is approximately €45 per day.

> ## MADEIRA BEST BETS
>
> **Take a trip down the toboggan run at Serra do Monte.** This unique and exhilarating experience is a must, but hold onto your hat!
>
> **View the *poios* (terraces).** An ancient method of growing crops in mountainous areas, terraces are rare in Europe, yet there are thousands here on Madeira.

EXPLORING MADEIRA

FUNCHAL

When colonists arrived in Madeira in July 1419, the valley they settled was a mass of bright yellow fennel (*funchal* in Portuguese). Today the bucolic fields are gone, and the community that replaced them is the self-governing island's bustling business and political center.

Adegas de São Francisco. The St. Francis Wine Lodge takes its original name from the convent that once stood on this site. Today the operation is owned by the island's famous winemaking Blandy family and is also known as the Old Blandy Wine Lodge. Here you can see how the wine and wine barrels are made, visit cellars where the wine is stored, and hear tales about Madeira wine. One legend has it that when the Duke of Clarence was sentenced to death in 1478 for plotting against his brother, King Edward IV, he was given his choice of execution methods. He decided to be drowned in a "vat of Malmsey," a barrel of the drink. There's plenty of time for tasting at the end of the visit and a shop for purchasing the wine. ⊠ *Av. Arriaga 28* ☎ *291/740110* ⊕ *www.madeirawinecompany.com* ⬛ *€5* ⊙ *Tours weekdays at 10:30, 2:30, 3:30, and 4:30, Sat. at 11. Wine shop weekdays 10–6:30, Sat. 10–1.*

Antiga Alfândega. The stately Old Customs House is home to Madeira's parliament (closed to the public). From here deputies govern the island, which is part of Portugal but enjoys greater autonomy than the mainland provinces. The building's original 16th-century Manueline style was given baroque touches during renovations that followed the devastating 18th-century earthquake that almost leveled faraway Lisbon. ⊠ *Av. do Mar and Av. das Comunidades Madeirenses* ☎ *291/210500.*

Casa Museu Frederico de Freitas. This delightful museum has been renovated in the style of a 19th-century quinta, inside the attractive 18th-century Casa Calçada. Inside you can find antique furniture, oriental carpets, and paintings collected by the 20th-century lawyer and veteran traveler, Dr. Frederico de Freitas. Don't miss the adjacent Casa dos Azulejos, a museum dedicated to decorative tiles from Spain, Persia, Turkey, Holland, and Syria that date from medieval times to the nineteenth century as well as Portuguese tiles rescued from demolished buildings on the island. ⊠ *Calçada de Santa Clara 7* ☎ *291/202570* ⊠ *€2.50* ☽ *Tues.–Sat. 10–5:30.*

Convento de Santa Clara. Inside the working 17th-century Santa Clara Convent (ring for entry), the painted wood walls and the ceiling are lined with ceramic tiles, giving the sanctuary an Arabic look. There are two beautiful internal cloisters; one is filled with orange trees. The adjacent church contains the tomb of Zarco, the discoverer of Madeira. ⊠ *Calçada de Santa Clara 15* ☎ *291/742602* ☽ *Mon.–Sat. 10–noon and 3–5.*

Fortaleza do Pico. The Fort of the Peak was built in 1611 to protect the settlement against pirate attacks. It's a steep walk to get here, but worth the effort for the dazzling views of the city. The fortress has been in the possession of the navy since 1933, but you can view parts of the ramparts, and there's a small room that has prints of the building over the years on display. ⊠ *Calçada do Pico* ☎ *No phone* ⊠ *Free* ☽ *Daily 9–6.*

Fortaleza de São Tiago. This robust construction was started by 1614, if not earlier, when French corsairs began to threaten Funchal's coveted deepwater harbor. Thanks to continuous use—by British troops when their nation was allied with Portugal against Napoléon, and during the visit of the Portuguese king Dom Carlos in 1901—much of the military stronghold has been preserved. You can wander around the ramparts, which offer interesting views over the Old Town and sea below. A former governor's house inside it is now the **Museu de Arte Contemporânea,** which has changing exhibitions of works from the 1960s and later, most by local artists. ⊠ *Rua do Portão de São Tiago* ☎ *291/213340* ⊠ *€2.50 for exhibitions, free at other times* ☽ *Mon.–Sat. 10–12:30 and 2:30–5:30.*

Fodor's Choice ★ **Jardim Botânico.** The Botanical Garden is on the grounds of an old plantation 3 km (2 miles) northeast of Funchal. Its well-labeled plants—including anthuriums, bird-of-paradise flowers, and a large cactus collection—come from four continents. Savor wonderful views of Funchal, and check out the petrified trunk of a 10-million-year-old heather tree. There's also a natural-history museum, and a small

exotic-birds garden. You can get here on Bus 29, 30, or 31, which stop across the street from the market in front of Madeira's Electric Company. You can also take another cable car from the top of the gardens to Monte (⊘ *Daily 9:30–6* ⊠*€8.25 single, €12.75 return*). ⊠ *Caminho do Meio* ☎ *291/211200* ⊕ *www.madeirabotanicalgarden. com* ⊠ *€3* ⊘ *Gardens daily 9–6.*

↻ **Madeira Story Centre.** Fun for children, this museum is a great introduction to Madeira for first-time visitors. It's not high-tech, but a series of models, paintings, archive TV footage and multimedia displays explain the history and culture of the island, from the days of pirates to the flying boats that brought the first plane passengers to Funchal. There's a roof terrace with fine views over town, a souvenir shop, and daily activities for kids. ⊠ *Rua Dom Carlos I 27–29* ☎ *291/100770* ⊕ *www. storycentre.com* ⊠ *€10* ⊘ *Daily 10–6, shop until 7.*

Fodor's Choice   **Mercado dos Lavradores** *(Farmers' Market).* In the center patio of the
★   Farmers' Market, women—sometimes in Madeira's native costume of a full, homespun skirt with yellow, red, and black vertical stripes and an embroidered white blouse—sell orchids, bird-of-paradise flowers (the emblem of Madeira), anthuriums, and other blooms. The lower-level seafood market displays the day's catch. Note the rows of fierce-looking espada. Their huge, bulging eyes are caused by the fatal change in pressure between their deepwater habitat and sea level. ⊠ *Largo dos Lavradores* ⊘ *Weekdays 7 am–8 pm, Sat. 7 am–2 pm.*

Museu de Arte Sacra. Funchal's Museum of Sacred Art has Flemish paintings, polychrome wood statues, and other treasures displayed in a former bishop's palace. Most of the priceless paintings were commissioned by the first merchants of Madeira, who traded sugar for Flemish art so they could decorate their private chapels. The *Adoration of the Magi* was painted in 1518 for a wealthy trader from Machico and was paid for not in gold, but in sugar. You can tell how important this commodity was to the island by examining Funchal's coat of arms: it depicts five loaves of sugar in the shape of a cross. ⊠ *Rua do Bispo 21* ☎ *291/228900* ⊕ *www.museuartesacrafunchal.org* ⊠ *€3* ⊘ *Tues.–Sun. 10–12:30 and 2:30–6, Sun. 10–1.*

↻ **Museu Municipal.** Animals found on Madeira and in its seas—including a ferocious-looking collection of stuffed sharks—are on display in the city museum. Attached is a small aquarium, where you can watch the graceful movements of an octopus and view a family of sea turtles. ⊠ *Rua Mouraria 31* ☎ *291/229761* ⊠ *€3.60* ⊘ *Tues.–Fri. 10–6, weekends noon–6.*

Museu da Quinta das Cruzes *(Crosses Manor Museum).* Once the home of a Genoese wine-shipping family, the 17th-century building and grounds of this museum are as impressive as its collection of antique furniture. Of special interest are the palanquins—lounge chairs once used to carry the grand ladies of colonial Madeira around town. Don't miss the small garden filled with ancient stone columns, window frames, arches, and tombstone fragments rescued from buildings that have been demolished around the island. It also has an alluring café. ⊠ *Calçada do Pico 1* ☎ *291/740670* ⊠ *€2.50* ⊘ *Tues.–Sun. 10–12:30 and 2–5:30.*

Palácio de São Lourenço. Built in the 17th century as Madeira's first fortress, the St. Lawrence Palace is still used as a military headquarters. At certain times its grand rooms are open to visitors and you can see the grand Ballroom and other state rooms filled with sumptuous works of art and antique furniture. ⊠ *Entrance on Av. Zarco* ☎ *291/202530* ✉ *Free* ⊙ *Wed. 10 am, Fri. 3 pm, Sat. 11 am.*

Parque Santa Catarina. Abloom with flowers all year-round, St. Catarina Park covers an area of around 43,000 square yards with fantastic views over Funchal and its bay up to the Ponta do Garajau. In the center of the park rests the tiny **Capela de Santa Catarina** (St. Catherine's Chapel), built by Madeira's discoverer João Gonçalves Zarco in 1425. It's one of the island's oldest buildings. Just above the park is a pink mansion called **Quinta Vigia,** the residence of the president of Madeira—it's closed to the public but you can visit its eighteenth-century chapel, lined with beautiful tiles. ⊠ *Between Av. do Infante and Av. Sá Carneiro, overlooking the harbor.*

Quinta do Palheiro. Also known as the Blandy Gardens, this 30-acre estate 5 km (3 miles) northeast of Funchal is owned by the Blandy wine family. The formal gardens have flowering perennials. You can stroll the gardens and the grounds, where camellia trees bloom between December and April, but you can't tour the family's house. To get here, head out of town on N101, the road to the airport. At the fork make a left onto N102 and follow the signs toward Camacha. Also, bus 36A departs weekday mornings at 9:45 from in front of the Palácio de São Lourenço, on Avenida das Comunidades Madeirenses (next to the marina). It returns at 12:35. ⊠ *Caminho Quinta do Palheiro 32* ☎ *291/793 044* ⊕ *www.palheiroestate.com* ✉ *€10.50* ⊙ *Weekdays 9:30–4:30 pm.*

Sé. Renowned for its ceiling with intricate geometric designs of inlaid ivory, Funchal's cathedral dates from 1514 and reveals an Arabic influence throughout. Don't miss the carved, gilded choir stalls in the side entrance and in the chancel (they depict the prophets and the apostles), or the intricate tile work at the side entrance and in the belfry. ⊠ *Largo da Sé* ☎ *No phone* ⊙ *Daily 8–6.*

Fodor's Choice
★

Teleférico da Madeira. The sleek, Austrian-engineered cable-car service has more than 40 cars that travel from Funchal's Old Town waterfront up to Monte at 1,804 feet above sea level. The trip takes 15 minutes one way, and there are great views to enjoy as you float silently up and over the city. ⊠ *Caminho das Barbosas 8* ☎ *291/780280* ⊕ *www.madeiracablecar.com* ✉ *€10 one-way, €15 round-trip* ⊙ *Daily 9:30–6 (last round-trip 5:30, last uphill trip 5:45).*

MONTE

6 km (4 miles) northeast of Funchal.

Madeira Cable Car. The most enjoyable approach to Monte is on the cable car that departs from Funchal's Old Town. A second cable car departs from Monte down to the Jardim Botânico ⊠ *Caminho das Barbosas 8* ☎ *291/780280* ⊕ *www.madeiracablecar.com* ✉ *€10 one-way, €15 round-trip* ⊙ *Daily 9:30–6 (last round-trip 5:30, last uphill trip 5:45).*

★ **Tábuas de Madeira.** The village of Monte is home to one of Madeira's oddest attractions: *tábuas de Madeira* or *carrinhos do Monte* (the snowless sled ride). The sleds were first created to carry supplies from Monte to Funchal; later, passenger sleighs hauled as many as 10 people at a time and required six drivers. Nowadays the rides are just for fun, and no one in Madeira should miss this experience that will take 10 years off your life and stay with you forever. Dressed in white and wearing goatskin boots with soles made of rubber tires, drivers line up on the street below the Nossa Senhora do Monte church. The sleds, which have cushioned seats, look like big wicker baskets; their wooden runners are greased with lard. Two drivers run alongside the sled, controlling it with ropes as it races downhill on a 10-minute trip nearly back to Funchal (you will have to walk about 1 km (½ mile) to reach Funchal or take one of the many taxis that line up at the end of the ride). If the sled starts going too fast, the drivers jump on the back to slow it down. ⊠ *Serra do Monte* 🖼 *€20 for 1 person, €25 for 2, €37.50 for 3 people* ⊙ *Mon.–Sat. 9–6, Sun. 9–1.*

CÂMARA DE LOBOS
20 km (12 miles) west of Funchal.

On coastal route N101 you'll pass many banana plantations on the way to Câmara de Lobos—a fishing village made famous by Winston Churchill, who came here (in a borrowed Rolls-Royce equipped with a bar) to paint pictures of the multicolored boats and the fishermen's tiny homes. A plaque marks the spot where he set up his easel. The promenade that protrudes from the main plaza offers magnificent views west to Cabo Girão.

CABO GIRÃO
16 km (10 miles) west of Câmara de Lobos.

At 1,900 feet, Cabo Girão is on one of the highest sea cliffs in the world. Totally uninhabited, it offers unimpeded views of ribbons of terraces carved out of even the steepest slopes and farmers daringly cultivating grapes or garden vegetables. Through centuries, thousands upon thousands of *poios* (terraces) have been built in Madeira.

EIRA DO SERRADO
16 km (10 miles) northwest of Funchal.

The *miradouro* (viewpoint) at Eira do Serrado overlooks the Grande Curral—the crater of a long-extinct volcano in the center of the island, sometimes referred to as Madeira's belly button. From here Pico Ruivo and the craggy central summits look like a granite city.

SHOPPING

Madeira has many thriving forms of handicraft, including lots of basketwork and rattan furniture. Embroidery was introduced to the island at the start of the 20th century. Tropical flowers are perfectly packaged for onward transportation. (It's legal to bring flowers into the United States from Madeira as long as they're inspected at the U.S. airport upon arrival.)

Fortified Madeira wine served as an aperitif or with dessert, depending on its sweetness, is the island's most famous product. The four varieties, from driest to sweetest, are Sercial, Verdelho, Boal, and Malmsey. Unlike other wines, Madeira is heated to produce its distinctive mellow flavor—a process that supposedly developed after thirsty sailors sampled the Madeira that had been shipped through equatorial heat and discovered its improved taste.

Bordal. This store specializes in traditional Madeiran embroidery and produces beautifully handcrafted linen, pillowcases, table cloths, towels, and baby clothes. ⊠ *Rua Doutor Fernão Ornelas 77* ☎ *291/222965* ⊕ *www.bordal.pt* ☉ *Weekdays 9–1 and 2–7, Sat. 9:30–1.*

Casa do Turista. This store sells museum-quality Madeiran crafts of all types. Prices are reasonable, if not the cheapest in town. ⊠ *José S. Ribeiro 2, on corner with seafront* ☎ *291/224907.*

Madeira Wine Company. This company sells an exhaustive selection of the local tipple, covering virtually every vintage produced on the island for the past 35-odd years. ⊠ *Av. Arriaga 28* ☎ *291/740100* ⊕ *www. madeirawinecompany.com.*

WHERE TO EAT

$ ✕ **Gavião Novo.** It's best to make reservations or to arrive early to bag a
PORTUGUESE table at this cozy, traditional restaurant in the heart of the Old Town. The family-run restaurant offers simple local food such as grilled limpets, tuna with fried cornmeal, fish stews, and delicious kebabs. ⊠ *Rua de Santa Maria 131* ☎ *291/229238.*

$ ✕ **Golden Gate Grand Café.** Just across from the tourist office in the heart
CAFÉ of Funchal, this restaurant-café has been open for business off and on since 1814. Sit in the airy interior, capture one of the tables that flank the sidewalk, or—even better—bag a seat on the balcony. You can pop in for coffee, light local dishes, or British-style afternoon tea, or you can settle in for a feast of creative Portuguese and international dishes. Don't miss the delicious desserts such as *sorvete de banana e maracujá* (banana and passion-fruit sorbet). ⊠ *Av. Arriaga 29* ☎ *291/234383.*

GRAN CANARIA, CANARY ISLANDS (LAS PALMAS)

Updated by
Joanna Styles

The circular island of Gran Canaria has three distinct identities. Its capital, Las Palmas, population 382,000, is a thriving business center and shipping port; the white-sand beaches of the south coast are tourist magnets; the interior is rural. Las Palmas, the largest city in the Canary Islands, is for the most part a dirty port city, overrun by sailors, tourists, traffic jams, diesel-spewing buses, and hordes of shoppers. One side of the city is lined with docks for huge container ships, while the other oddly harbors Europe's famous 7-km (4½-mile) Canteras beach. A quaint historic quarter redeems the city's mismatched commercial buildings. The south coast, a boxy 1960s development along wide avenues, is a family resort. At the southern tip of the island, the popular Playa del Inglés

gives way to the empty dunes of Maspalomas, the most spectacular sight of the island. The isle's more pristine interior is a steep highland that reaches 6,435 feet at Pozo de las Nieves. Although it's green in winter, Gran Canaria does not have the luxurious tropical foliage of the archipelago's western islands.

ESSENTIALS

CURRENCY

The euro. ATMs are common and credit cards are widely accepted.

HOURS

Shops are generally open Monday to Saturday from 9 to 1 and again from 4 to 8 or 9. Most places close for siesta, but some resort shops may stay open throughout the day and may also be open on Sunday. Museums are usually open from 10 until noon, but have varied afternoon opening hours.

TELEPHONES

Most tri- and quad-band GSM phones will work in the Canary Islands, where mobile services are 3G-compatible. Public kiosks accept phone cards that support international calls (cards sold in press shops, bars, and telecom shops).

COMING ASHORE

Ships dock at the busy Santa Catalina terminal in the Las Palmas port. There are toilets, ATMs, bus stops, and a taxi stand at the terminal itself, while the huge El Muelle shopping center beckons directly across from the port gates. The terminal is a 10-minute walk from the north end of the city center. The southern end, where most sights are located, is a mile on foot (about 5 minutes by taxi).

Because Gran Canaria is quite large—1,560 sq km (602 sq miles)—renting a car will not get you to all of the island's far corners during your short stay; however, a car will surely aid in island exploration. (We recommend that you go no farther than Maspalomas.) An economy manual vehicle costs approximately €30 to €40 per day. There are numerous car-rental offices in Las Palmas, but the easiest option is to prebook a car online using Cicar (⊕ www.cicar.com), though Gran Canaria has several other rental agencies. Taxis also wait outside the terminal building, and they can be contracted for tourist itineraries, at €0.51 per km (½ mile), with waiting rate of €12.75 per hour. They can also be negotiated off the meter for around €25 per hour.

GRAN CANARIA BEST BETS

■ **Casa de Colón.** Gran Canaria was supposedly the last landfall for Christopher Columbus before his arrival in the New World; the museum contains various artifacts of early transatlantic voyages.

■ **Dunas de Maspalomas.** Trek down south to witness the grand reminder that the Canaries share their latitude with the Sahara.

■ **La Vegueta and Triana.** Stroll the historic quarters of Las Palmas.

EXPLORING GRAN CANARIA

LAS PALMAS

Las Palmas is a long, sprawling city, strung out for 10 km (6 miles) along two waterfronts of a peninsula. Though most of the action centers on the peninsula's northern end along the lovely Las Canteras beach, the sights are clustered around the city's southern edge. Begin in the old quarter, La Vegueta, at the **Plaza Santa Ana** (don't miss the bronze dog statues), for a tour of interesting colonial architecture. Then make your way into the neighboring quarter of Triana, a treasure trove of small shops and cafés and restaurants. It's quite a walk from one end of town to the other, so at any point you may want to hop one of the many canary-yellow buses. Buses 1, 2 and 3 run the length of the city.

Casa Museo Colón (*Columbus Museum*). The Casa Museo Colón is in a palace where Christopher Columbus may have stayed when he stopped to repair the *Pinta*'s rudder. Nautical instruments, copies of early navigational maps, and models of Columbus's three ships are on display in the palace, which retains many original features. Two rooms hold pre-Columbian artifacts, and one floor is dedicated to paintings from the 16th to the 19th century. There's a focus on self-portraits. ⊠ *Colón 1, Vegueta* ☎ *928/311255* ☒ *Free* �l *Weekdays 9–7, Sat. 9–6, Sun. 9–3.*

Catedral Santa Ana. St. Anne's Cathedral took four centuries to complete, so the neoclassical Roman columns of the 19th-century exterior contrast sharply with the Gothic ceiling vaulting of the interior. Baroque statues are displayed in the cathedral's **Museo de Arte Sacro** (Museum of Religious Art), arranged around a peaceful cloister. Ask the curator to open the *sala capitular* (chapter house) to see the 16th-century Valencian tile floor. Be sure to check out the black stone dog sculptures outside the cathedral's main entrance—these are four examples of the Gran Canaria hounds that gave the island its name. ⊠ *Espíritu Santo 20, facing Plaza Santa Ana, Vegueta* ☎ *928/314989* ☒ *€3* �l *Weekdays 10–4:30, Sat. 10–1:30.*

Centro Atlántico de Arte Moderno (*Atlantic Center for Modern Art*). The Centro Atlántico de Arte Moderno has earned a name for curating some of the best avant-garde shows in Spain, with a year-round calendar of exhibitions. The excellent permanent collection includes Canarian art from the 1930s and 1940s and works by the well-known Lanzarote artist César Manrique. The center also has a fine collection of contemporary African art. ⊠ *Los Balcones 11, Vegueta* ☎ *928/311800* ⊕ *www. caam.net* ☒ *Free* �l *Tues.–Sat. 10–9, Sun. 10–2.*

Ermita de San Telmo. Destroyed by Dutch attackers in 1599, this chapel was rebuilt in the 17th century. Inside is a fine baroque altarpiece with rich gold leaf and wooden details. ⊠ *Plaza de San Telmo, Triana.*

Parque Santa Catalina. Ride a *guagua* (bus) to Parque Santa Catalina, or get off at the neighboring Parque Doramas (stops are listed on big yellow signs; the 2, 3, and 30 generally cover the entire city), to peek at the elegant Santa Catalina Hotel. Next to the Parque Doramas is the **Pueblo Canario,** a model village with typical Canarian architecture. ⊠ *Las Palmas.*

Las Palmas

Ermita de San Telmo

Parque Santa Catalina

Playa de las Canteras

STA. CATALINA

Av. Franc Roca

Av. José Mesa y López

ALCARAVANERAS

Av. Juan XXIII

C. Guanarteme

Playa de las Alcaravaneras

Puerto de Luz

Av. del Alcalde J. R. Bethencourt

Parque Doramas

Av. León y Castillo

Paseo de Chil

León y Castillo Monument

ESCALERITAS

Prolongación A. de Escaleritas

Autovía Santa Catalina - Lomo Blanco

Autovía Las Palmas-Galdar

ARENALES

SCHAMANN

ATALAYA

TRIANA

Ctra. de Matas

Av. de Canarias

Plaza Santa Ana

Ctra. del Centro

Casa Museo Colón

Catedral Santa Ana

Centro Atlántico de Arte Moderno

1 mi
1 km

Gran Canaria

Morro de la Vieja

Las Palmas

Pta. del Camello

Arucas

Jardín Canario Viera y Clavijo

Tafira Alta

Tamaraceite

Pta. de la Cueva

Pta. de Gando

Pta. de la Sal

Pta. de Guanarteme

Firgas

Tafira Baja

Moya

Teror

Santa Brígida

San Mateo

Telde

Valsequillo

Carrizal

Ingenio

Agüimes

Arinaga

Pta. Tenefe

Pta. Sardina

Gáldar

Sardina del Nort

Santa María de Guía

Agaete

Puerto de las Nieves

Cruz de Tejeda

Tejeda

Artenara

Tamadaba

Pico de las Nieves

Roque Nubio

Vecindario

Fataga

San Agustín

ATLANTIC OCEAN

Parque Natural de Tamadaba

La Aldea de San Nicolás

Mt. de la Sandara

Palmitos Park

Aqualand

Holiday World

Dunas de Maspalomas

Maspalomas

Playa del Inglés

Pta. de la Aldea

Pta. de la Soga

Pta. de las Telas

Mogán

Puerto Rico

Puerto de Mogán

Pta. del Parchel

4 mi
4 km

MASPALOMAS AND THE SOUTHERN COAST

60 km (36 miles) southwest of Las Palmas.

One of the first places in Spain to welcome international tourists (starting in 1962), Maspalomas remains a beach resort with all the trappings. It's somewhat incongruously backed by empty sand dunes that resemble the Sahara—despite beachfront overdevelopment in the town, it retains appealing stretches of isolated beach on the outskirts, as well as a bird sanctuary. Much of the area around the dunes is a protected nature reserve.

Aqualand Maspalomas. The largest water park in the Canary Islands has wave pools, slides, and just about everything else splash-related. ⊠ *Ctra. Palmitos Park, Km 3* ☎ *928/140525* ⊕ *www.aqualand.es* ⊑ *€25* ☼ *July–Aug., daily 10–6; Sept.–June, daily 10–5.*

Holiday World. This amusement park has bumper cars and other carnival rides, including a Ferris wheel visible from miles away. ⊠ *Av. Touroperator Tui 18* ☎ *928/730498* ⊕ *www.holidayworld-maspalomas.com* ⊑ *Admission free; rides vary; unlimited rides €30* ☼ *Apr.–Sept., daily 6 pm–midnight; Oct.–March, Sun.–Thurs. 5 pm–11 pm, Fri.–Sat. 5 pm–midnight.*

Palmitos Park. One of the main attractions in this part of the island, this part–botanical garden and part-zoo has 1,500 tropical birds, a butterfly sanctuary, an orchid house, 160 species of tropical fish, many crocodiles, and parrot shows. ⊠ *Ctra. Palmitos, 6 km, inland from Maspalomas* ☎ *928/797070* ⊕ *www.palmitospark.es* ⊑ *€28.50* ☼ *Daily 10–6.*

TEJEDA

About 34 km (21 miles) southwest of Las Palmas, on the rustic 811 local road.

At the village of Tejeda, the road begins to ascend through a pine forest dotted with picnic spots to the **Parador Cruz de Tejeda.** From the parador, continue uphill about 21 km (13 miles) to the **Mirador Pico de las Nieves,** the highest lookout on Gran Canaria. Here, too, is the **Pozo de la Nieve,** a well built by clergymen in 1699 to store snow.

SAN MATEO

17 km (11 miles) southwest of Las Palmas, en route to Tejeda.

From Tejeda, the road winds down to San Mateo, whose local cheese is famous throughout the island. You can find it at the weekend market. Pass **Santa Brígida** and turn right toward the golf club on the rim of the Bandama crater. Continue to the village of Atalaya, where there are cave houses and pottery workshops.

TAFIRA ALTA

7 km (4½ miles) southwest of Las Palmas.

Along the main road leading into Las Palmas from San Mateo is Tafira Alta, an exclusive suburb where many of the city's wealthiest families live.

Jardín Canario Viero y Clavijo. In Tafira Alta (just north of Las Palmas) is one of Spain's largest botanical gardens, with plants from all the islands grouped in their natural habitats. ⊠ *Ctra. de Centro, Km 7* ☎ *928/219580* ⊕ *www.jardincanario.org* ☼ *Daily 8–6:30.*

BEACHES

The beaches along Gran Canaria's eastern and southern coasts are the island's major attractions.

LAS PALMAS

Las Canteras. One of the best urban beaches in Spain is found at the northwest end of the city. Its perfect yellow sands are flanked by a pleasant promenade, which goes for just over 3 km (nearly 2 miles), from the Alfredo Kraus Auditorium, in the south, where surfers congregate, to the Playa del Confital, in the north. The beach is protected by a natural volcanic reef, La Barra, which runs parallel to most of the beach and makes for safe swimming. Lounge chairs and sunshades can be rented year-round. This is a very popular beach that can be extremely crowded in summer. **Amenities:** food and drink; lifeguards; showers; toilets; water sports. **Best for:** sunset; surfing (at southern end); swimming; walking. ⊠ *Las Canteras.*

MASPALOMAS AND THE SOUTHERN COAST

All of these beaches abut one another, and you can walk them in sequence (hindered only by a pair of rocky dividers) along the shore. A boardwalk links Playa de Tarajalillo to the rest of the beaches until the dunes separate the boardwalk from the Maspalomas beach and Playa de la Mujer.

Fodor's Choice **Maspalomas.** The island's most emblematic beach and one of the most
★ beautiful, Maspaloma has golden sand that stretches for 2.7 km (1.7 miles) along the southern tip of Gran Canaria. Behind this beach are the famous Maspalomas dunes as well as palm groves and a saltwater lagoon, which lend an air of isolation and refuge to the beach. Bathing is safe everywhere except at La Punta de Maspalomas, where currents converge. Topless bathing is acceptable and there's a nudist area at La Cañada de la Penca. This beach is busy year-round. **Amenities:** food and drink; lifeguards; showers; toilets. **Best for:** nudists; sunrise; sunset; swimming; walking. ⊠ *Maspalomas.*

Playa de Tarajalillo. To the east of San Agustín, this black-sand and gravel beach is quieter than many of the others in the area. It's a popular spot with fishermen and windsurfers. The almost permanent strong breeze and waves mean bathers should be careful. **Amenities:** none. **Best for:** solitude; sunrise; windsurfing. ⊠ *San Agustín.*

Playa de San Agustín. To the east of Maspalomas, this smaller beach consists of golden sands and some rocks. The promenade has lush vegetation nearby, making it one of the most picturesque on the island. This is a quieter beach than Maspalomas and Playa del Inglés. Bathing is safe in calm conditions, but watch out for strong currents when the waves get up. Lounge chairs and sunshades line the beach. **Amenities:** food and drink; lifeguards; showers; toilets; water sports. **Best for:** sunrise; walking. ⊠ *San Agustín.*

Playa de las Burras. Sandwiched between Playa del Inglés and Playa de San Agustín, this little sandy beach is protected by a breakwall, making it a favorite with families. Small fishing boats are moored in the bay and the seafront promenade connects the neighboring resorts. Swimming's

safe. There are plenty of lounge chairs and sunshades. **Amenities:** food and drink; lifeguards; showers; toilets. **Best for:** sunrise; swimming. ⊠ *San Agustín.*

★ **Playa del Inglés.** Rivaling Maspalomas for popularity, Playa del Inglés has a lot going, including partying at the beach bars, sports, competitions, and concerts. There's nearly 3 km (1.9 miles) of golden sands, flanked by a pleasant seafront promenade that's great for early morning and evening strolls. Swimming is generally safe, although windy conditions can create waves—it's a favorite spot with surfers. Lounge chairs and sunshades are available along the beach, and there's also a nudist area, which is signposted. **Amenities:** food and drink; lifeguards; showers; toilets; water sports. **Best for:** partiers, nudists, sunrise; swimming; walking; windsurfing. ⊠ *Playa del Inglés.*

Playa de las Mujeres. "The Women's Beach" is around the corner from the Maspalomas lighthouse in Meloneras. Consisting of gray shingles and small rocks, this quiet beach currently has no amenities, although the expansion of Meloneras, along with the construction of several high-end hotels, may change that in the future. Swimming is generally safe. **Amenities:** none. **Best for:** solitude; sunset. ⊠ *Urb Meloneras, Maspalomas.*

BOATING AND SAILING

Escuela de Vela de Puerto Rico sailing school. Some of Spain's best sailors have trained and taught here. It's about 13 km (8 miles) west of Maspalomas. ⊠ *Playa de Puerto Rico, Puerto Rico* ☎ *928/291567.*

Multiacuatic. Two-hour whale- and dolphin-watching trips leave from Puerto Rico, about 13 km (8 miles) west of Maspalomas. ⊠ *Muelle Puerto Base, Puerto Rico* ☎ *928/153747* ⊕ *www.dolphinwhales.es* 🎫 *€25* 🕙 *Departures Mon.–Sat. at 10:30 and 1.*

GOLF

Lopesan Meloneras Golf. Half of the 18 holes at this par-71 course face the mountains, and the other half face the sea. Several are practically on the beach. ⊠ *Autopista GC 500, s/n, Meloneras* ☎ *928/145309* ⊕ *www. lopesan.com.*

Maspalomas Golf. Surrounded by the famous Maspalomas dunes, this 18-hole, par-73 course has ocean views from many of its long, wide greens. The course was designed by Mackenzie Ross. ⊠ *Av. T.O. Neckerman s/n, Maspalomas* ☎ *928/762581* ⊕ *www.maspalomasgolf.net.*

Oasis Golf. Just ten minutes outside Las Palmas, this 18-hole, par-54 course, designed by Blake Stirling, is one of the best places to play on the island; some golfers think it's one of the best courses in the world. It's the only course on the island that allows night play. ⊠ *Autopista del Sur, km 6.4, Telde* ☎ *928/684890.*

WINDSURFING

Club Mistral. Rent windsurfing gear, kayaks, and boogie boards from Club Mistral. Classes are also available. ⊠ *Playa del Tarajalillo, Ctra. del Sur, Km 44, Maspalomas* ☎ *928/157158* ⊕ *www.club-mistral.com.*

SHOPPING

Las Palmas has easily the best shopping on the islands. The main commercial areas are located around Calle Mesa y López (south of the port) and Triana in the old quarter. Here you'll find all the major international and Spanish fashion stores, duty-free stores, and shops selling local crafts, hats and clothes, Russian caviar, tackle for fishing and catching crabs, and lots more.

Centro Comercial El Muelle. This modern shopping mall opposite the Santa Catalina Park has stores selling all the major Spanish fashion brands, several sports shops, and a movie theater. ⊠ *Muelle de Santa Catalina s/n, Las Canteras, Las Palmas* ☎ *928/327527* ⊕ *www.ccelmuelle.es* ⊙ *Mon.–Sat. 10 am–10 pm.*

El Corte Inglés. If you want to one-stop-shop for souvenirs, try the department store El Corte Inglés, in Las Canteras. ⊠ *Mesa y Lopez 18, Las Canteras, Las Palmas* ☎ *928/263600* ⊕ *www.elcorteingles.es* ⊙ *Mon.– Sat., 9:30–9:30.*

FEDAC. As the official artisan shop, FEDAC carries a selection of genuine Gran Canaria crafts and handiwork. ⊠ *Domingo J. Navarro, Triana, Las Palmas* ☎ *928/369661* ⊙ *Weekdays 9:30–1:30 and 4:30–8.*

La Despensa del Sur. Canary cheese, wine, and mojo are all available at this store; the adjoining restaurant serves traditional fare and snacks. ⊠ *Cano 33, Triana, Las Palmas* ☎ *928/360195* ⊕ *www. ladespensadelsur.com* ⊙ *Weekdays 9–9, Sat. 10–4.*

WHERE TO EAT

$$ ✕ **Casa Montesdeoca.** The hallways of this 14th-century mansion in the
SPANISH historic quarter are stone labyrinths. During the Inquisition, the Jew-
★ ish Montesdeoca family escaped from their pursuers through hidden doors and secret tunnels. Today the mansion only conceals a romantic restaurant with an outdoor patio draped with bougainvillea. Fresh fish—including *cherne* (sea bass) and *rape* (monkfish)—is prepared on an outdoor grill steps from your table. The wine list has the best bottles from each island. ⑤ *Average main: €16* ⊠ *Montesdeoca 10, Vegueta, Las Palmas* ☎☎ *928/333466* ⊙ *Closed Sun. and Aug.*

$ ✕ **Te lo dije Pérez.** Just below the cathedral square is one of the island's
INTERNATIONAL best bars for having a beer—there's a huge selection—along with some tapas. The bar feels a bit like a French café, with high ceilings and black and red furnishings. Some unusual tapas plates include nachos with eggplant and ginger sauce and a genuine German sausage as well as spinach and walnut croquettes. There are inside and outside tables, but you may have to stand at this very busy venue. ⑤ *Average main: €8* ⊠ *Obispo Codina 6, Vegueta, Las Palmas* ☎☎ *928/249087* ⊕ *www. telodijeperez.com* ⊙ *Closed Sun.*

LANZAROTE, CANARY ISLANDS

The most easterly Canary, Lanzarote, is right out of a science-fiction film, with solidified lava and dark, disconcerting dunes in its interior. The entire island has been declared a UNESCO Biosphere Reserve with its unique moonlike landscapes. It was named for the Italian explorer Lancelotto Alocello. The founder of modern-day Lanzarote, however, was artist and architect César Manrique, the unofficial artistic guru of the Canary Islands. He designed most of the esoteric tourist attractions and gave the island its distinctive low-rise whitewashed buildings. Overall, Lanzarote has avoided the high-rise destruction that mars its western counterparts, though an abundance of budget resorts on the east side of the island are less than attractive. Outside of the port and touristy beaches, Lanzarote's austere and barren landscape is strangely breathtaking, with the greatest scenery within Parque Nacional Timafaya.

ESSENTIALS

CURRENCY
The euro. ATMs are common and credit cards are widely accepted.

HOURS
Shops are generally open Monday through Saturday from 9 to 1 and again from 4 until 8 or 9. Most places close for siesta, but some resort shops may stay open throughout the day and also stay open on Sunday. Museums are usually open from 10 until noon, but have varied afternoon opening hours.

TELEPHONES
Most tri- and quad-band GSM phones will work in the Canary Islands, where mobile services are 3G-compatible. Public kiosks accept phone cards that support international calls (cards sold in press shops, bars, and telecom shops).

COMING ASHORE
Cruise ships dock at Puerto Mármoles, about 3 km (2 miles) west of the capital. A walkway goes along the shoreline from the port to the center of town. Although it takes you away from the busy main road, it's a long and not very attractive walk, so it's best to take either a shuttle bus or a taxi from just outside the cruise terminal into Arrecife proper.

Lanzarote Vision Tour Bus. Take in the whole island via these distinctive tours on yellow hop-on, hop-off buses. The Green Route visits the north of the island, including Costa Teguise, Arrecife, the Fundación César Manrique, and the Cueva de los Verdes; the Red Route heads south, to Playa Blanca, Puerto del Carmen, two bodegas, and the Parque Nacional de Timanfaya. Tickets, which are valid for a single day, can be bought online, at official Lanzarote Vision sales points throughout the island, and through hotels and travel agencies. ⊠ *Av. de las Playas, Puerto del Carmen* ☎ *928/511089* ⊕ *www.lanzarotevision. es* 🖼 *€19.50.*

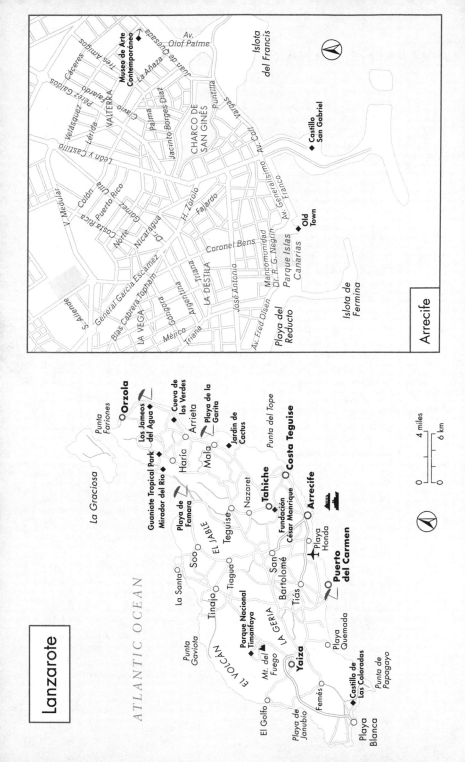

Lanzarote

ATLANTIC OCEAN

La Graciosa

Punta Fariones

Orzola

Guaniate Tropical Park
Mirador del Río
Los Jameos del Agua

Cueva de los Verdes

Playa de la Garita

Arrieta

Punta Gaviota

La Santa

Soo

El JABLE

Haría

Mala

Jardín de Cactus

Tiagua

Teguise

Nazaret

Costa Teguise

Punta del Tope

Tinajo

San Bartolomé

Tahiche

Fundación César Manrique

Arrecife

Parque Nacional Timanfaya

Mt. del Fuego

EL VOLCÁN

LA GERIA

Tías

Playa Honda

Puerto del Carmen

El Golfo

Yaiza

Playa Quemada

Femés

Castillo de Las Coloradas

Punta de Papagayo

Playa Blanca

Playa de Janubio

0   4 miles
0   6 km

Arrecife

Av. Olof Palme

Tres Amigos

Cáceres

Velázquez

Pérez Galdós

Fajardo

VALTERRA

Ciavijo

Museo de Arte Contemporáneo

La Añaza

tren de La Añaza

Palma

Jacinto Borges Díaz

Islota del Francis

V. Medular

S. Allende

Colón

Costa Rica

Puerto Rico

Gómez

Norte

Nicaragua

León y Castillo

Uría

CHARCO DE SAN GINÉS

Puntilla

Vegas

Av. Coll

Castillo San Gabriel

General García Escámez

Blas Cabrera Topham

LA VEGA

Argentina

Triana

LA DESTILA

Méjico

Triana

Góngora

H. Zerolo

José Antonio

Coronel Bens

Mancomunidad Dr. R. G. Negrín

Av. Generalísimo Franco

Parque Islas Canarias

Old Town

Islota de Fermina

Av. Fred Olsen

Playa del Reducto

EXPLORING LANZAROTE

ARRECIFE

Although Arrecife has fully 50,000 of the 130,000 people that live on Lanzarote, this small city remains a place where life moves at a more sedate pace than it does in bustling Santa Cruz or Las Palmas. The coastline here is strung with line after line of rocky reefs (in fact, "reef" is what *arrecife* means in Spanish). A stroll around the back streets near the lagoon gives you an idea of the old Arrecife. The local Playa del Reducto is a good place to get in some beach time if you're spending the day here.

Castillo San Gabriel. The Castillo San Gabriel is a double-wall fortress once used to keep pirates at bay. A museum, due to open in 2013, will cover important events in the city's past. ⊠ *Arrecife.*

Museo de Arte Contemporáneo (*Museum of Contemporary Art*). The old, waterfront fortress **Castillo San José** was turned into this stunning museum by the architect César Manrique. One of his paintings is on display, along with other modern Spanish works. ⊠ *Av. de Naos s/n* ☎ *928/812321* 🎟 *Free* ⊙ *Daily 11–9.*

Old Town. Arrecife isn't the most attractive part of Lanzarote, but the Old Town is interesting, particularly the area around the Charco de San Ginés (lagoon). The **tourist office**, housed in the original bandstand in the municipal park, has detailed maps and information about local points of interest. ⊠ *Parque Municipal* ☎ *928/816174* ⊙ *Office open Weekdays 10–7; Sat., 10–1.*

COSTA TEGUISE

7 km (4½ miles) northeast of Arrecife.

Costa Teguise is a green-and-white complex of apartments and several large hotels. It's a typical '80s resort and past its heyday, although it still draws thousands of visitors every year. King Juan Carlos owns a villa here, near the Meliá Salinas hotel.

☺ **Guinate Tropical Park.** In the northern part of the island, Guinate Tropical Park has 1,300 species of exotic birds and animals, and amazing views of La Graciosa Island and the ocean. ⊠ *Costa Teguise* ☎ *928/835500* ⊕ *www.guinatepark.com* 🎟 *€14* ⊙ *Daily 10–5.*

Jardín de Cactus (*Cactus Garden*). The Jardín de Cactus, north of Costa Teguise between Guatiza and Mala, was César Manrique's last creation for Lanzarote. The giant metal cactus that marks the entrance comes close to tacky, but the gardens artfully display nearly 10,000 cacti of more than 1,500 varieties from all over the world. ⊠ *Costa Teguise* ☎ *928/529397* 🎟 *€5* ⊙ *Daily 10–5:45.*

★ **Los Jameos del Agua.** These water caverns, 15 km (9 miles) north of the Costa Teguise, were created when molten lava streamed through an underground tunnel and hissed into the sea. Look for the tiny albino crabs on the rocks in the underground lake—this species, which is blind, is found nowhere else in the world. There are bars and restaurants around the lake, and the **Casa de los Volcanes** is a good museum of volcanic science. Night visits are possible on Tuesdays and Saturdays. ⊠ *Costa Teguise* ☎ *928/848020* 🎟 *Days €8, nights €78* ⊙ *Daily 10–6:30; night visits Tues. and Sat. 7 pm–midnight.*

Cueva de los Verdes (*Green Caves*). If the Jameos del Agua caverns weren't enough for you, then head to this cave, just across the highway. Guided walks take you through a 1-km (½-mile) section of underground volcanic passageway. It's one of the best tours on the island. ✉ *Costa Teguise* ☎ *928/848484* 🎫 *€8* ⊙ *June–Sept., daily 10–7; Oct.–May, daily 10–6.*

Mirador del Río. Designed by César Manrique, this lookout in the most northern point of the island lets you see the islet of **La Graciosa** from at altitude of 474 meters (1,550 feet). From the lookout you can also see smaller protected isles—Montaña Clara, Alegranza (the Canary closest to Europe), and Roque del Este. ✉ *Costa Teguise* 🎫 *€4.50* ⊙ *Daily 10–5:45.*

Orzola. The little fishing village of Orzola is 9 km (5½ miles) north of Jameo del Agua. Small boat excursions leave here each day for the neighboring islet of La Graciosa, where there are fewer than 500 residents and plenty of quiet beaches. ✉ *Costa Teguise.*

PUERTO DEL CARMEN
11 km (7 miles) southwest of Arrecife.

Most beach-bound travelers to Lanzarote head to the sandy strands of the Puerto del Carmen area, the island's busiest resort. The small fishing port and marina are surrounded by numerous cafés and restaurants, with the main commercial center behind them. Puerto Carlero, nearby, is a newer addition to the resort; this attractive marina makes a quieter base for a holiday.

TAHÍCHE
6 km (3½ miles) north of Arrecife.

★ **Fundación César Manrique.** The former home of this accomplished artist and architect is now a museum and foundation displaying a collection of his paintings and sculptures, as well as works by other 20th-century artists. The real attraction is the house itself, designed by Manrique to blend with the volcanic landscape. Built into a series of lower-level caves, with palm trees ascending into the upper floor, are a series of unusual, whitewashed living rooms. The maze of spaces invites you to walk from room to room through indoor tunnels and outdoor courtyards. ✉ *Ctra. Tahíche–San Bartolomé, 2 km (1 mile) west of Tahíche* ☎ *928/843138* ⊕ *www.fcmanrique.org* 🎫 *€8* ⊙ *July–Oct., daily 10–7; Nov.–June, Mon.–Sat. 10–6, Sun. 10–3.*

LAZNAROTE BEST BETS

Parque Nacional Timanfaya. The vast volcanic, otherworldly landscape will ambush your senses. The volcano-grilled barbecue lunch at Restaurante del Diablo is unforgettable.

Cesar Manrique's Landmarks. Lanzarote's architectural hero made his mark across the island, most notably at the Cactus Garden and Fundaion Cesar Manrique.

Teguise. Wander the street of Lanzarote's charming former capital, circa 1852.

YAIZA

18 km (11 miles) west of Arrecife.

Yaiza is a quiet, whitewashed village with good restaurants. Largely destroyed by a river of lava in the 1700s, it's best known as the gateway to the volcanic national park.

Fodor's Choice ★ **Parque Nacional Timanfaya** (*Timanfaya National Park*). The Parque Nacional Timanfaya, popularly known as "the Fire Mountains," takes up much of southern Lanzarote. As you enter the park from Yaiza, the first thing you'll see is the staging area for the Canaries' best-known **camel rides**. A bumpy camel trek lasts about 20 minutes. The volcanic landscape inside Timanfaya is a violent jumble of exploded craters, cinder cones, lava formations, and heat fissures. The park is protected, and you can visit only on a bus tour or a camel ride. A taped English commentary explains how the parish priest of Yaiza took notes during the 1730 eruption that buried two villages. He had plenty of time—the eruption lasted six years, making it the longest known eruption in volcanic history. By the time it was over, more than 75% of Lanzarote was covered in lava. Throughout the park, on signs and road markers, you'll see a little devil with a pitchfork; this *diablito* was designed by Manrique.

The **Ruta de los Volcanes** bus tour takes you around the central volcanic area on a 14-km (9-mile) circuit that was designed to have minimal impact on this natural park. Tickets can be bought at the stand at the entrance to the National Park. ■TIP→ **During summer, visit in late afternoon to avoid the crowds.** ✉ *Centro de Visitantes Mancha Blancha, Ctra. de Yaiza a Tinajo, Km 11.5, Tinajo* ☎ *928/118042* ☜ *Ruta de los Volcanes €8* ☉ *Visitor center weekdays 9–3. Ruta de los Volcanes July–Sept., daily 9–7; Oct.–June, daily 9–5:45.*

SHOPPING

The Canary Islands are known for lacy, hand-embroidered tablecloths and placemats, plus locally made ceramics and *timples* (typical musical instrument). Vegetation is scarce on Lanzarote, but the grapes grown by farmers in volcanic ash produce a distinctive Canarian wine. Locals also take great pride in the island's tiny potatoes, which you will on most menus as *papas canarias*, accompanied by fresh mojo sauces. The Canary Islands are free ports—no value-added tax is charged on luxury goods—but while the streets are packed with shops selling jewelry, cameras, and electronics, prices are still fairly high, so don't expect any phenomenal bargains.

Shopping is low-key in Arrecife. The main shops are on and around the pedestrian-only Calle León y Castilla. For island crafts and produce, go to the open market in the village of **Teguise** on Sunday between 9 and 2. Some vendors set up stalls in the plaza; others just lay out a blanket in the street and sell embroidered tablecloths, leather goods, costume jewelry, African masks, and other items.

ACTIVITIES

Due to its climate and popularity with European vacationers, Lanzarote is well equipped for a range of sports and activities throughout the year, from water sports and diving to golf. Staff speak good English.

BIKING

Lanzarote Freeride. Biking is a popular and practical way to tour the island, as Lanzarote is not particularly hilly. Lanzarote Freeride's bike rentals start at €22 a day. ☎ *696/972982* ⊕ *www.lanzarotefreeride.eu.*

DIVING

One of the island's official diving centers is near Las Cucharas beach.

Calipso Diving Lanzarote. A well-established dive school with PADI Resort Center status. ✉ *CC Calipso, local 3, Av. Islas Canarias, Costa Teguise* ☎ *928/590879* ⊕ *www.calipso-diving.com.*

GOLF

Costa Teguise Golf. These 18 holes, which are outside the Costa Teguise development, have unusual sand traps filled with black-lava cinders. The course is par 72. ✉ *Av. del Golf s/n, Costa Teguise* ☎ *928/590512* ⊕ *www.lanzarote-golf.com.*

BEACHES

Playa de Famara. Directly opposite Costa Teguise on the north coast of Lanzarote is one of the island's most attractive beaches. Set in a natural cove, its 6 km (3.7 miles) of sand are flanked by spectacular cliffs. The riptide here makes for excellent surfing and windsurfing, and Playa de Famara is regularly used for world championships for those sports. That said, the strong currents mean swimming can be dangerous. **Amenities:** food and drink; lifeguards; showers; toilets; water sports. **Best for:** sunset; surfing; walking; windsurfing. ✉ *Teguise.*

☾ **Playa de la Garita.** Not far from the Jardín de Cactus, Playa de la Garita is a wide bay of crystalline water favored by surfers in winter and snorkelers in summer. The 850 meters (½ mile) of golden sands are safe for swimming, making this a popular spot for families. The beach does get busy in the summer, but is reasonably quiet the rest of the year. Lounge chairs and umbrellas are available for rent. **Amenities:** food and drink; lifeguards; showers; toilets; water sports. **Best for:** snorkeling; surfing; swimming. ✉ *Haria.*

Playa de las Cucharas. This is the best of Costa Teguise's several small beaches. The sands are protected from high wind and waves by the natural bay formed in the coastline. A pleasant seafront promenade takes you around the beach and into the southern stretches of the resort. Getting a spot for your towel in the summer can be a challenge, especially at weekends. **Amenities:** food and drink; lifeguards; showers; toilets; water sports. **Best for:** sunrise; swimming. ✉ *Costa Teguise.*

Playa del Reducto. It may not be in the same league as some of the beaches in the south, but Playa del Reducto is still an attractive urban beach, ideal for relaxing after you've looked around Arrecife. It's well maintained and protected by natural reefs, so swimming is usually like

swimming in a warm lake (though do watch out for rocky outcrops at low tide). The beach is backed by a pleasant promenade that goes all the way to Puerto del Carmen. **Amenities:** food and drink; showers; toilets. **Best for:** sunrise; walking. ⊠ *Arrecife.*

Playa de los Pocillos. Slightly north of Puerto del Carmen, this beach is near most of the area's development; hotels and apartments are restricted, however, to the other side of the highway, leaving the 2-km (1-mile) yellow-sand beach surprisingly pristine. Finding a spot to place your towel can be difficult in summer. Lounge chairs and umbrellas are available. **Amenities:** food and drink; lifeguards; showers; toilets; water sports. **Best for:** sunrise; swimming; walking. ⊠ *Tías.*

Playa Grande. Puerto del Carmen's main beach is a busy strip of yellow sand that's as close as you can get to an urban beach on Lanzarote outside Arrecife. Lounge chairs and umbrellas are available for rent. Backing the beach is a seafront promenade with plenty of souvenir shops and restaurants. You can take the promenade all the way to Arrecife. **Amenities:** food and drink; lifeguards; showers; toilets; water sports. **Best for:** swimming. ⊠ *Puerto del Carmen.*

Playa Matagorda. On this northern extension of Playa de los Pocillos, there are alternating sections of gravel and gray sand. A perpetually windy spot, this busy beach has gentle waves that are perfect for those learning to surf. Lounge chairs and beach umbrellas are available. **Amenities:** food and drink; lifeguards; showers; toilets; water sports. **Best for:** surfing; swimming; walking. ⊠ *Tías.*

Playa Mujeres. Facing west across to Fuerteventura and the Isla de Lobos, this is a very popular beach. The sandy bay provides safe swimming conditions, and the beach is cleaned regularly. Amenities are limited to a few small bars. On the way to the beach, look out for the ruins of some bunkers from World War II. **Amenities:** food and drink. **Best for:** snorkeling; sunset; swimming. ⊠ *Playa Blanca.*

Playa Papagayo. The rugged coastline to the east of Playa Blanca has several stunning beaches, but most people think that Playa Papagayo is the island's most beautiful. This small bay with fine white sand is perfect for sunbathing, as it's protected from the wind by cliffs at both ends. You have to walk along a dirt path to get here, so take suitable footwear as well as plenty of drinking water. Despite its remoteness, this is a busy beach, particularly in summer. **Amenities:** none. **Best for:** snorkeling; sunrise; swimming. ⊠ *Playa Blanca.*

WHERE TO EAT

$$ ✕ **Lilium.** Creative cooking with Canarian roots is the philosophy behind the dishes at this modern restaurant that's just around the corner from the beach. Although there are a few tables outdoors, the dining mainly takes place inside, where copper and chocolate tones accompany floral touches. Standout dishes here include plantain croquettes and a slow-cooked suckling pig, served with a fruit reduction. Reservations are a good idea on weekends. ⑤ *Average main: €16* ⊠ *Primo de Rivera 103, Arrecife* ☎ *928/524978* ⊕ *restaurantelilium.com* ☾ *Closed Sun.*

SPANISH

★

$$
SPANISH
★

✕ **El Diablo.** This must be one of the world's most unusual restaurants. Here, in the middle of Timanfaya National Park, chicken, steaks, and spicy sausages are cooked over a volcanic crater using the earth's natural heat. You have to be on the Ruta de los Volcanes bus tour to get here. ⑤ *Average main: €15* ✉ *Timanfaya National Park, Yaiza* ☎ *928/840057.*

REYKJAVÍK, ICELAND

Iceland is an epic land. It tempts with epithets like "The Land of Fire and Ice," but these just hint at the delights this island has in store. It is a land of dazzling white glaciers and black sands, blue hot springs, rugged lava fields, and green, green valleys. This North Atlantic island offers insight into the ferocious powers of nature, ranging from the still-warm lava volcanic eruptions to the chilling splendor of the Vatnajökull Glacier. Ice caps cover 11% of the country, more than 50% is barren, 6% consists of lakes and rivers, and less than 2% of the land is cultivated. There's hardly a tree to be seen, making the wildflowers and delicate vegetation all the more lovely. Sprawling Reykjavík, the nation's nerve center and government seat, is home to half the island's population. On a bay overlooked by proud Mt. Esja (pronounced *eh-shyuh*), with its ever-changing hues, Reykjavík presents a colorful sight, its concrete houses painted in light colors and topped by vibrant red, blue, and green roofs. In contrast to the almost treeless countryside, Reykjavík has many tall, native birches, rowans, and willows, as well as imported aspens, pines, and spruces.

ESSENTIALS

CURRENCY

The Icelandic krona has experienced a dramatic drop in value relative to foreign currencies; although prices have been adjusted upward in some cases (particularly for exported goods), prices still favor Americans and Europeans at this writing.

HOURS

Most businesses close early on weekdays and are closed on Sunday. Some museums are open only in summer. Shops are typically open weekdays from 9 to 6, but a growing number of stores—especially food stores—are open on weekends with shorter hours. Souvenir shops (along with bakeries and kiosks) are open daily.

TELEPHONES

Iceland has no area codes; within the country, simply dial the seven-digit number. Non-800 numbers starting with 8 often indicate cellular phones. Most tri- and quad-band GSM phones work in Iceland. You can also buy prepaid phone cards at telecom shops and newsstands.

COMING ASHORE

Ships dock at Skarfabakki Quay in Reykjavik, which sits 4 km (2½ miles) from the city center. The Cruise Visitor Welcome Centre has a range of facilities, including currency exchange, V.A.T. refunds, car rental, a shop, Internet access (including Wi-Fi), and toilets. Free shuttle buses transfer passengers downtown, but taxis also generally wait to meet the ship. If

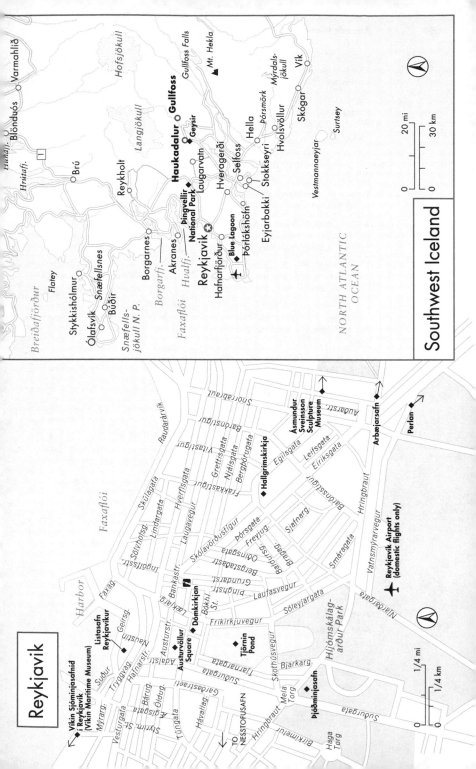

Reykjavik

Faxaflói

Harbor

Vikin Sjóminjasafnið
í Reykjavík
(Vikin Maritime Museum)

Listasafn
Reykjavíkur

Austurvöllur
Square

Dómkirkjan

Tjörnin
Pond

Hallgrímskirkja

Ásmundur
Sveinsson
Sculpture
Museum

Árbæjarsafn

Perlan

Reykjavik Airport
(domestic flights only)

Þjóðminjasafn

TO
NESSTOFUSAFN

Hljómskála-
garður Park

Skúlagata
Lindargata
Sölvhólsg.
Ingólfsstr.
Raudarárvík
Vitastígur
Barónsstígur
Snorrabraut
Hverfisgata
Frakkastígur
Njálsgata
Bergþórugata
Grettisgata
Laugavegur
Bankastr.
Lækjarg.
Skólavörðustígur
Þórsgata
Óðinsgata
Freyjug.
Baldursg.
Bragi
Sjafnarg.
Egilsgata
Leifsgata
Eiríksgata
Bergstaðastr.
Grundarstr.
Þingholtsstr.
Bókhl.
St.
Laufásvegur
Sóleyjargata
Frikirkjuvegur
Skothúsvegur
Smáragata
Barónsstígur
Hringbraut
Vatnsmýrarvegur
Njarðargata
Garðastræti
Suðurgata
Tjarnargata
Bjarkarg.
Mela
Torg
Austurstr.
Aðalstr.
Hafnarstr.
Tryggvag.
Geirsg.
Faxag.
Naustin
Suður.
Mýrarg.
Bárug.
Öldug.
Egilsgata
Túngata
Vesturgata
Sturlag.
Hávallag.
Birkimelur
Haga
Torg
Hringbraut
Suðurgata

0   1/4 mi
0   1/4 km

Southwest Iceland

Varmahlíð
Blönduós
Hofsjökull
Gullfoss Falls
Mt. Hekla
Hrútafj.
Brú
Langjökull
Gullfoss
Haukadalur
Geysir
Mýrdals-
jökull
Vík
Reykholt
Laugarvatn
Hveragerði
Þórsmörk
Þingvellir
National Park
Selfoss
Hella
Hvolsvöllur
Skógar
Borgarnes
Akranes
Reykjavík
Blue Lagoon
Hafnarfjörður
Þorlákshöfn
Eyjarbakki
Stokkseyri
Surtsey
Vestmannaeyjar
Flatey
Stykkishólmur
Ólafsvík
Búðir
Snæfells-
jökull N. P.
Snæfellsnes
Borgarfj.
Hvalfj.
Faxaflói
Breiðafjörður

NORTH ATLANTIC
OCEAN

0   20 mi
0   30 km

you want to walk, it is an easy stroll into town, but you can never be sure of the weather.

A car rental is expensive in summertime per day for a compact manual vehicle. All the international companies have offices in the city. Many roads outside the capital are hard surface but not asphalt, so a car is necessary if you want to explore on your own. Driving can be difficult in snow and ice.

There are many companies in Reykjavík offering group or individual tours, but the costs for these activities can be high. Tourist information centers in Reykjavík have many brochures for day tours. Taxis can also perform tour services. Prices may be fixed or, for shorter journeys, metered, and taxis accept credit cards.

> **ICELAND BEST BETS**
>
> **The "Golden Triangle."** Iceland in miniature, Strukkur, Gullfoss, and Þingvellir epitomize the raw and vital beauty of Iceland's landscapes.
>
> **The National Museum.** A fascinating treasure trove of Viking artifacts is beautifully displayed in this museum that charts the history of Iceland from the first settlers to today.
>
> **Blue Lagoon.** Luxuriate in the earth's gift of volcanically heated water gushing to the surface. The luxury pool and spa let you simply surrender to the bliss.

EXPLORING SOUTHWESTERN ICELAND

REYKJAVÍK

Árbæjarsafn. At the Open-Air Municipal Museum, 19th- and 20th-century houses furnished in old-fashioned style display authentic household utensils and tools for cottage industries and farming. During the summer you can see demonstrations of farm activities and taste piping-hot *lummur* (chewy pancakes) cooked over an old farmhouse stove. To get to the museum, take Bus 12 or 19. ⊠ *Ártúnsblettur, Kistuhyl 4* ☎ *411–6300* ⊕ *www.minjasafnreykjavikur.is* ✉ *ISK 1,100* ☉ *June–Aug., daily 10–5; Sept.–May, guided tours daily 1 pm.*

Ásmundur Sveinsson Sculpture Museum. Some of Ásmundur Sveinsson's original sculptures, depicting ordinary working people, myths, and folktale episodes, are exhibited in the museum's gallery and studio and in the surrounding garden. It's on the southwest edge of Laugardalur Park, opposite the traffic circle at its entrance. Take Bus 15 or 17 from Hlemmur station (a 5-minute ride). ⊠ *Sigtún 105* ☎ *553–2155* ⊕ *www.artmuseum.is* ✉ *ISK 1,100* ☉ *Daily May–Sept., 10–5; Oct.–Apr., 1–5.*

Austurvöllur Square. East Field is a peculiar name for a west-central square. The reason: it's just east of the presumed spot where first settler Ingólfur Arnarson built his farm, today near the corner of Aðalstræti.

★ **Dómkirkjan** (*Lutheran Cathedral*). A place of worship has existed on this site since AD 1200. The small, charming church, built 1788–96, represents the state religion, Lutheranism. It was here that sovereignty and independence were first blessed and endorsed by the church. It's

also where Iceland's national anthem, actually a hymn, was first sung in 1874. Since 1845, members and cabinet ministers of every Alþing parliament have gathered here for a service before the annual session. Among the treasured items inside is a baptismal font carved and donated by the famous 19th-century master sculptor Bertel Thorvaldsen, who was half Icelandic. ⊠ *Austurvöllur* ☎ *520–9700* ⊕ *www.domkirkjan.is/ enska.html* ⊙ *Mon.–Fri. 10–4:30, unless in use for services.*

★ **Hallgrímskirkja** (*Hallgrímur's Church*). Completed in 1986 after more than 40 years of construction, the church is named for the 17th-century hymn writer Hallgrímur Pétursson. It has a stylized concrete facade recalling both organ pipes and the distinctive columnar basalt formations you can see around Iceland. You may luck into hearing a performance or practice on the church's huge pipe organ. In front of Hallgrímskirkja is a statue of Leifur Eiríksson, the Icelander who discovered America 500 years before Columbus. (Leif's father was Eric the Red, who discovered Greenland.) The statue, by American sculptor Alexander Calder, was presented to Iceland by the United States in 1930 to mark the millennium of the Alþing parliament. ⊠ *At the top of Skólavörðustígur* ☎ *510–1000* ⊕ *www.hallgrimskirkja.is* 🎫 *Tower ISK 600* ⊙ *Daily 9–5.*

Listasafn Reykjavíkur (*Reykjavík Art Museum*). Also known as Hafnarhús, this former warehouse of the Port of Reykjavík now houses the city's art museum. The six galleries occupy two floors, and there's a courtyard and multipurpose space. The museum's permanent collection includes a large number of works donated by the contemporary Icelandic artist, Erró. There are also regular temporary exhibitions. ⊠ *Tryggvagata 17* ☎ *590–1200* ⊕ *www.artmuseum.is* 🎫 *ISK 1,100* ⊙ *Fri.–Wed. 10–5, Thurs. 10–8.*

Perlan. On top of Öskjuhlíð, the hill overlooking Reykjavík Airport, Perlan (the Pearl) was opened in 1991 as a monument to Iceland's invaluable geothermal water supplies. Among the indoor and outdoor spectacles are art exhibits, musical performances, markets, a permanent Viking history exhibit, and fountains that spurt water like geysers. Above the six vast tanks, which once held 24 million liters of hot water, the panoramic viewing platform offers telescopes and a cafeteria complete with ice cream parlor. The crowning glory is a revolving restaurant under the glass dome; it's pricey, but the view is second to none ⊠ *Öskjuhlíð Hill* ☎ *562–0200* ⊕ *www.perlan.is* ⊙ *Daily 10–9.*

Þjóðminjasafn (*National Museum*). Viking treasures and artifacts, silver work, wood carvings, and some unusual whalebone carvings are on display here, as well as maritime objects, historical textiles, jewelry, and crafts. There is also a coffee shop. ⊠ *Suðurgata 41* ☎ *530–2200* ⊕ *www.natmus.is* 🎫 *ISK 1,200* ⊙ *May 1–Sept. 15, daily 10–5; Sept. 16–Apr. 30, Tues.–Sun. 11–5.*

☺ **Tjörnin Pond.** This natural pond by the city hall attracts birds—and bird lovers—year-round and is also popular among ice-skaters in winter. Children love feeding bread to the many varieties of swans and ducks in the pond. ⊠ *Next to the Raðhús* 🎫 *Free.*

Víkin Sjóminjasafnið í Reykjavík (Víkin Maritime Museum). Housed in an old fish factory with great views of the harbor, the maritime museum features an exhibition on Icelandic fisheries, trading vessels, and displays a whole Costal Guard vessel that can be explored. ⊠ *Grandargarði 8* ☎ *517–9400* ⊕ *www.maritimemuseum.is* ⌧ *ISK 1,200* ۩ *June 1–Sept. 15, daily 10–5; Sept. 16–May 31, Tues–Sun. 11–5.*

BLUE LAGOON

15 km (9 miles) from Keflavík Airport and 50 km (31 miles) from Reykjavík (turn off toward the village of Grindavík).

Fodor's Choice **Blue Lagoon.** This world-renowned therapeutic wonder is now in a shel-
★ tered site where man-made structures blend with geologic formations. A reception area includes food concessions and boutiques where you can buy health products made from the lagoon's mineral-rich ingredients. Bathing suits are available to rent, and futuristic bracelets keep track of your locker code, any other purchases, and the length of your visit (all of which no doubt make useful marketing statistics). Buses run from the BSÍ bus terminal in Reykjavík to the Blue Lagoon twice daily and three times a day in July and August, or you can get to the airport on your own by taking a special FlyBus. ⊠ *Bláalónið, Grindavík* ☎ *420–8800* ⊕ *www.bluelagoon. com* ⌧ *ISK 4,800* ۩ *Sept.1–May 31, 10–8; June 1–Aug. 31, 9–9pm.*

ÞINGVELLIR

About 50 km (31 miles) northeast of Reykjavík. Take Ring Rd. about 9 km (5½ miles) just past the town of Mosfellsbær; turn right on Rte. 36.

This has been the nation's most hallowed place since AD 930, when the settler Grímur Geitskór chose it as the first site for what is often called the world's oldest parliament, the Icelandic Alþingi (General Assembly). In July of each year delegates from all over the country camped at Þingvellir, meeting to pass laws and render judicial sentences. Iceland remained a nation-state, ruled solely by the people without a central government, until 1262, when it came under the Norwegian crown; even then, the Alþingi continued to meet at Þingvellir until 1798, but it had long lost its lawmaking powers.

Þingvellir National Park. Þingvellir National Park, at the northern end of Þingvallavatn—Iceland's largest lake—is a potent symbol of Icelandic heritage. Many national celebrations are held here, and it was named a UNESCO World Heritage Site in 2004. Besides its historic interest, Þingvellir holds a special appeal for naturalists: it is the geologic meeting point of two continents. At Almannagjá, on the west side of the plain, is the easternmost edge of the North American tectonic plate, otherwise submerged in the Atlantic Ocean. Over on the plain's east side, at the Heiðargjá Gorge, you are at the westernmost edge of the Eurasian plate.

A path down into Almannagjá from the top of the gorge overlooking Þingvellir leads straight to the high rock wall of **Lögberg** (Law Rock), where the person chosen as guardian of the laws would recite them from memory. At the far end of the gorge is the **Öxarárfoss** (Öxará Waterfall). Beautiful, peaceful picnic spots are a bit beyond it. Just behind Lögberg, the river cascades down and forms the forbidding **Drekkingarhylur** pool, where women were drowned during the late middle ages. ⊠ *Þingvellir* ⊕ *www.thingvellir.is.*

Þingvallabær. Across the plain from Lögberg stand the church and the gabled manor house of Þingvallabær, where the government of Iceland often hosts visiting heads of state. Free, one-hour tours are offered on weekdays in the summer leaving at 10 am from the church. ⊠ *Þingvellir* ☏ *482–2660* ⊕ *www.thingvellir.is* ⊙ *Church May–Sept., daily 9–5:30; Information center summer daily 9–5, winter Sat.–Sun. 9–5.*

Nikulásargjá Gorge. The Nikulásargjá Gorge, reached by a footbridge, is better known these days as Peningagjá (Money Gorge) because it's customary to fling a coin into the gorge's icy-cold water and make a wish. Don't even dream about climbing down to wade here—it might look shallow, but it's more than 30 feet deep. ⚠ **The water is ice cold.** ⊠ *Þingvellir* ⊕ *www.thingvellir.is.*

HAUKADALUR
About 35 km (22 miles) northeast of Laugarvatn via Rte. 37 and then Rte. 35.

Fodor's Choice ★ The geothermal field in Haukadalur, home of the Geysir and Strokkur geysers, is one of Iceland's classic tourist spots.

The famous **Geysir** hot spring (the literal origin of the term, geyser) only erupts a few times a year, but the more reliable **Strokkur** spouts up boiling water as high as 100 feet at five-minute intervals. In the same area there are small natural vents from which steam rises, as well as beautiful, exotic-colored pools. Don't crowd Strokkur, and always be careful when approaching hot springs or mud pots—the ground may be treacherous, suddenly giving way beneath you. Stay on formal paths or established tracks.

To get here from Laugarvatn, take Route 37 (from Lake Laugarvatn you can take the short spur, Route 364, southwest to Route 37) northeast for 25 km (16 miles) to the junction with Route 35. Take Route 35 about 10 km (6 miles) northeast to Hótel Geysir, which is next to the springs.

GULLFOSS
About 6 km (4 miles) east of Geysir along Rte. 35.

Gullfoss. Measuring 105 feet high, thundering Gullfoss (Golden Falls) is a double cascade in the Hvítá River, turning at right angles in mid-drop. Gullfoss enters a dramatic chasm, which nonetheless has its gentle sides. The modest visitor center is named in memory of Sigríður Tómasdóttir, who fought against flooding the falls for a hydroelectric reservoir scheme in the early 20th century. She is said to have threatened to throw herself into the falls; a trailside plaque further honors her.

SHOPPING

Reykjavík is a happening and fun shopping town. The main shopping downtown is on and around Austurstræti, Aðalstræti, Hafnarstræti, Hverfisgata, Bankastræti, Laugavegur, and Skólavörðustígur. There are also two large American-style shopping malls. Both Kringlan and Smáralind make great places to shop when the weather turns inclement.

Sheepskin rugs and Viking-inspired jewelry are popular souvenirs. An amble along **Skólavörðustígur** from Laugavegur to Hallgrímskirkja church takes you past many tempting woolen, jewelry, and crafts shops, as well as art galleries. Laugavegur and Skólavörðustígur streets are both filled with jewelry stores that craft unique pieces, often incorporating gold or silver with materials found in Iceland, like lava rock, creating a very eye-catching effect.

ICELAND VAT REFUNDS

A 25.5% *virðisaukaskattur* (value-added tax, or V.A.T.), commonly called VSK, applies to most goods and services. V.A.T. is almost always included in a price; if not, that fact must be stated explicitly. Foreign visitors who purchase ISK 4,000 or more on one receipt can claim a partial refund on the V.A.T.

Anna María design. Founded in 1986, this workshop and store sells a variety of jewelry for both men and women, made from a variety of materials that encompass silver, gold, and Icelandic stones. ⊠ *Skólavörðustígur 3* ☎ *551–0036* ⊕ *www.annamariadesign.is.*

Handprjónasambandið. The Handknitting Association of Iceland, Handprjónasambandið, has its own outlet, selling, of course, only hand-knit items of various kinds. ⊠ *Skólavörðurstígur 19* ☎ *552–1890* ⊕ *www. handknit.is* ☉ *Mon.–Sat. 9–6; Sun. 11–5.*

ACTIVITIES

If you are looking for a more active adventure, there are numerous opportunities for adventure sports, including ATV Tours, quad biking, Jeep safaris, and glacier tours. You can also explore the countryside on horseback, and whale-watching is a growth activity.

Iceland Tour Guide Association ⊠ *Mörkin 6* ☎ *588–8670* ⊕ *www. touristguide.is.* **Reykjavík Excursions** ⊠ *BSÍ Bus Terminal, Vatnsmýrarvegi 10* ☎ *580–5040* ⊕ *www.re.is* ☉ *Daily 4 am–11 pm.*

WHERE TO EAT

$
FAST FOOD
★

✕ **Bæjarins beztu.** Facing the harbor in a parking lot, this tiny but well-known fast-food hut is famous for serving the original Icelandic hot dog; one person serves about a thousand hot dogs a day from the window. Ask for *AYN-ah-med-UTL-lou,* which will get you "one with everything": mustard, tomato sauce, *rémoulade* (mayonnaise with finely chopped pickles), and chopped raw and fried onions. ⑤ *Average main: IKr 320* ⊠ *Tryggvagata and Pósthússtræti* ☎ *894–4515* ⊕ *www.bbp.is/* ☉ *Sun.–Thurs., 10 am–12:30 am; Fri.–Sat., 10 am–4:30 am.*

$$$$
EUROPEAN
Fodor's Choice
★

✕ **Grillmarket.** A collaborative project by well-known culinary innovators Hrefna Rós Sætran (founder/owner of the Fish Market) and Guðlaugur P. Frímannsson, Grillmarkaðurinn emphasizes seasonal, organic, locally grown ingredients in a beautifully designed interior that's heavy on natural materials such as wood and stone. The menu is equally "earthy" featuring lots of smoked, grilled, and barbecued meat dishes. For something classic, try the grilled chicken wings or grilled

pork ribs; for something more unique, order the Minke whale steak. ⑤ *Average main: IKr 4,495* ✉ *Lækjargata 2a, Reykjavík* ☎ *571–7777* ⊕ *www.grillmarkadurinn.is.*

TENERIFE, CANARY ISLANDS (SANTA CRUZ DE TENERIFE)

Updated by
Joanna Styles

Tenerife is the largest of the Canary Islands but actually 112 km (70 miles) off the coast of southern Morocco. It is towered over by the volcanic peak of Mt. Teide, which at 12,198 feet is Spain's highest mountain. The slopes leading up to Teide are covered with pines in the north and with barren lava fields in the south. Popular with vacationing Europeans, the resort towns of Tenerife win no prizes for beauty, but the natural attractions and kind islanders more than compensate for the late-20th-century high-rise hotels and apartment blocks.

ESSENTIALS

CURRENCY

The euro. ATMs are common and credit cards are widely accepted.

HOURS

Shops are generally open Monday to Saturday between 9 and 1 and again from 4 until 8 or 9. Most places close for siesta, but some resort shops may stay open throughout the day and also open on Sunday. Museums are usually open from 10 until noon, but have varied afternoon opening hours.

TELEPHONES

Most tri- and quad-band GSM phones will work in the Canary Islands, where mobile services are 3G-compatible. Public kiosks accept phone cards that support international calls (cards sold in press shops, bars, and telecom shops).

COMING ASHORE

Vessels dock at the port of Santa Cruz, on the island's northeast side. If your ship docks at the berth farthest from the terminal, it is a 15-minute walk to the port exit. Once you reach the gates, the city of Santa Cruz is accessible on foot. There are few passenger facilities in the port, but the shopping district is close and taxis are readily available.

Renting a car would allow you to explore much of the island during your stopover. An economy manual vehicle begins at €40 per day. There are car-rental offices in Santa Cruz de Tenerife, but the easiest option is to prebook a car online for pick-up at Muelle Ribera (Ribera dock) using Cicar (⊕ *www.cicar.com*). Taxis also wait outside the terminal building, and they can be contracted for tourist itineraries, but on the meter these trips can be expensive; try to negotiate an hourly rate. Having private transport (rental car or taxi) would be more practical with only a day in port.

7

EXPLORING TENERIFE

SANTA CRUZ DE TENERIFE

Auditorio de Tenerife. A magnificent white shell of an auditorium dominates the west end of the city. Built by the architect Santiago Calatrava in 2003, the auditorium has a year-round program of concerts and opera. If you want a guided tour, it's best to book one ahead of time. ⊠ *Av. de la Constitución 1, Santa Cruz* ☎ *922/568625* ⊕ *www. auditoriodetenerife.com* ✉ *Tours €5* ⊙ *Tours in English: Oct.–June, Mon.–Sat. 12:30; July–Sept., weekdays 12:30 and 5:30, Sat. 12:30.*

Castillo San Cristóbal (*Saint Christopher's Castle*). The walls of the city castle were uncovered when the car park under the Plaza de España was built. The site is now a museum that includes an 18th-century cannon, a shot from which reputedly cost Britain's Admiral Nelson his right arm in an attack he led in 1794. Entrance to the museum is via a stairway opposite the lake. ⊠ *Pl. de España, Santa Cruz* ✉ *Free* ⊙ *Mon.–Sat. 10–6.*

Iglesia de Nuestra Señora de la Concepción (*Church of Our Lady of the Conception*). The Iglesia de Nuestra Señora de la Concepción has a six-story Moorish bell tower. The church was renovated as part of an urban-renewal project that razed blocks of slums in this area. Church opening times vary, but you can generally visit before and after Mass. ⊠ *Pl. de la Iglesia, Santa Cruz* ☎ *922/242387* ✉ *Free.*

Mercado de Nuestra Señora de Africa (*Market of Our Lady of Africa*). This colorful city market is part bazaar and part food emporium. Stalls outside sell household goods; inside, stands displaying everything from flowers to canaries are arranged around a patio. Downstairs, a stroll through the seafood section will acquaint you with the local fish. A flea market with antiques and secondhand goods is held here on Sunday. ⊠ *Av. de San Sebastián, Santa Cruz* ⊙ *Daily 6:30–3.*

Museo de Bellas Artes (*Museum of Fine Arts*). Old masters and modern works are in the two-story Museo de Bellas Artes, including canvases by Breughel and Ribera. Many works depict local events. The museum is on the Plaza Príncipe de Asturias. ⊠ *José Murphy 12, Santa Cruz* ☎ *922/274786* ✉ *Free* ⊙ *Tues.–Fri. 10–8, weekends 10–3.*

Museo de la Naturaleza y el Hombre (*Museum of Nature and Man*). Primitive ceramics and mummies are on display at the Museo de la Naturaleza y el Hombre. The ancient Guanches mummified their dead by rubbing the bodies with pine resin and salt and leaving them in the sun to dry for two weeks. ⊠ *Fuentes Morales s/n, Santa Cruz* ☎ *922/535816* ⊕ *www.museosdetenerife.org* ✉ *€3, free Sun.* ⊙ *Tues.–Sun. 9–7.*

Parque Marítimo César Manrique. Just west of the auditorium, this maritime park with its three saltwater pools and tropical gardens is a favorite with locals. Designed by the Lanzarote architect César Manrique, the park combines volcanic rock with palms and local flora. ⊠ *Av. de la Constitución 5, Santa Cruz* ☎ *922/229368* ⊕ *www.parquemaritimo. com* ✉ *€2.50* ⊙ *Daily 10–6.*

Plaza de España. The heart of Santa Cruz de Tenerife is the Plaza de España. The cross in the plaza is a monument to those who died in the

Tenerife

Punta del Hidalgo
Bajamar
Playa de las Teresitas
San Andrés
Los Rodeos Airport
Tacoronte
La Laguna
La Matanza de Acentejo
Santa Ursula
Bosque de la Esperanza
Santa Cruz de Tenerife
TO GRAN CANARIA, LANZAROTE, FUERTEVENTURA
Puerto de la Cruz
Garachico
Buenavista del Norte
Los Silos
Los Realejos
Valle de la Orotava
Las Caletillas
Candelaria
Arafo
Icod de los Vinos
Punta de Teno
Santiago del Teide
Mt. Teide
El Portillo
Güimar
Los Gigantes
Cable Car
Fasnia
Playa de la Arena
Guía de Isora
Vilaflor
Granadilla de Abona
Punta de Abona
Adeje
Playa de Cayado Hondo
Arona
Playa las Puntillas
San Miguel
Playa de las Américas
Los Cristianos
Reina Sofía Airport
El Médano
TO GOMERA
Costa del Silencio
Playa del Médano

0   10 miles
0   15 km

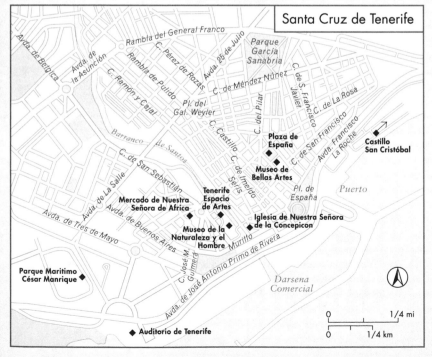

Santa Cruz de Tenerife

Avda. de Bélgica
Avda. de la Asunción
Rambla del General Franco
C. Pérez de Rozas
Rambla de Pulido
Avda. 25 de Julio
Parque García Sanabria
C. de Méndez Núñez
C. de S. Javier
C. de La Rosa
C. Ramón y Cajal
Pl. del Gal. Weyler
C. del Pilar
C. de San Francisco
Avda. Francisco La Roche
Barranco   de Santos
C. Castillo
C. de Imeldo Serís
Plaza de España
Castillo San Cristóbal
C. de San Sebastián
Museo de Bellas Artes
Pl. de España
Puerto
Avda. de La Salle
Tenerife Espacio de Artes
Avda. de Buenos Aires
Mercado de Nuestra Señora de Africa
Iglesia de Nuestra Señora de la Concepción
Avda. de Tres de Mayo
Museo de la Naturaleza y el Hombre
C. José M. Guimerá
Murillo
Avda. de José Antonio Primo de Rivera
Parque Marítimo César Manrique
Darsena Comercial

0   1/4 mi
0   1/4 km

Auditorio de Tenerife

Spanish civil war, which was actually launched from Tenerife by General Franco during his exile here. For two weeks before Lent each year, during Carnaval, Santa Cruz throbs to a Latin beat emanating from this plaza. Castillo San Cristóbal and the tourist office are both here. ⊠ *Pl. de España, Santa Cruz.*

Tenerife Espacio de Artes. Soon after it opened in 2008, this art museum quickly became the main landmark for contemporary art on the islands due to its sleek low-rise design as well as its avant-garde exhibitions. Designed by the Swiss architects Herzog & Meuron, it's next to the Museo de la Naturaleza. The emphasis is on the 20th and 21st centuries, and art incorporating or commenting on modern technology.

> **TENERIFE BEST BETS**
>
> **Venture to the summit of Mt. Teide.** Snow-capped for much of the year, this ancient volcano is the tallest in the Canaries and the highlight of any trip to Tenerife.
>
> **Explore the village of La Orotava.** Home to nobility in the 17th and 18th centuries, this village teems with elegant squares, streets, and churches renowned for their facades. But everything is closed on weekends.
>
> **Stroll the ramblas and cobbled streets of Santa Cruz.** Here the atmosphere of medieval Spain couldn't be more palpable.

A major permanent exhibition is dedicated to the Tenerife surrealist artist, Oscar Domínguez. ⊠ *Av. San Sebastián 8, Santa Cruz* ☎ *922/849057* ⊕ *www.teatenerife.es* ⊠ *€5* ⊗ *Tues.–Sun. 10–8.*

PUERTO DE LA CRUZ
36 km (22 miles) west of Santa Cruz.

Puerto de la Cruz is the oldest resort in the Canaries. Despite mass tourism, it has retained some of its Spanish charm and island character. The old sections of town have colonial plazas and *paseos* (promenades) for evening strolls.

Casa de Vino La Baranda. Wine and food lovers will want to head to this winery, which is about halfway between Puerto de la Cruz and Los Rodeos Airport, at the El Sauzal exit on the main highway. Opened by the Canary Islands' government to promote local vintners, it includes a wine museum, shop, and tasting room, where for a small fee you can sample some of Tenerife's best wines. The complex also has a tapas bar and a restaurant with nouvelle Canarian fare. Also here is a **honey museum,** with exhibits as well as tasting sessions. ⊠ *Simón 49, Autopista General del Norte, Km 21, El Sauzal* ☎ *922/572535* ⊕ *www.tenerife. es/casa-vino* ⊗ *Oct.–June, Tues. 10:30–6:30, Wed.–Sat. 9–9, Sun. 11–6; July–Sept., Tues. 10:30–6:30, Wed.–Sat., 10–7:30, Sun. 11–6.*

Jardín Botánico (*Botanical Garden*). Filled with over 4,000 varieties of tropical trees and plants, and sonorous birds, the Jardín Botánico was founded in 1788, on the orders of King Carlos III, to propagate warm-climate species brought back to Spain from the Americas. The gardens are closed during stormy weather or when the wind speed exceeds 40 kph (25 mph). ⊠ *Retama 2* ☎ *922/383572* ⊠ *€3* ⊗ *Oct.–Mar., daily 9–6; Apr.–Sept., daily 9–7.*

☺ **Lago Martiánez.** Because Puerto de la Cruz has uninviting black-sand beaches, the town commissioned Lanzarote artist César Manrique in 1965 to build Lago Martiánez, a forerunner of today's water parks. It's an immense, and immensely fun, public pool on the waterfront, with landscaped islands, bridges, and a volcano-like fountain that sprays sky-high. The complex also includes several smaller pools and a restaurant-nightclub. ✉ *Av. de Colón s/n* ☎ *922/385955* ⧉ *€4.50* ⊗ *Sept. 16–May, daily 10–6; June–Sept. 15, daily 10–7.*

☺ **Loro Parque.** This huge subtropical garden and zoo holds 1,300 parrots, many of which are trained to ride bicycles and perform other tricks. The garden also has the world's largest penguin zoo. The dapper Antarctic birds receive round-the-clock care from marine biologists and other veterinary specialists in a climate-controlled environment. Also here is one of Europe's largest aquariums, with an underwater tunnel, a dolphin-and killer-whale show, and some gorillas. Free trains leave for the park from the Plaza Reyes Católicos. ✉ *Av. Loro Parque s/n* ☎ *922/373841* ⊕ *www.loroparque.com* ⧉ *€33 (combined ticket with Siam Park €56)* ⊗ *Daily 8:30–6:45.*

Plaza del Charco. It's a two-minute walk from the Plaza de la Iglesia to this plaza, one of the prettiest and liveliest in town. ✉ *Pl. del Charco, Puerto de la Cruz.*

Puerto de la Cruz. The tourist office's building, a royal customhouse from the 17th century, is one of the best examples of a typical Canary house on the island. It's outfitted with balconies, an interior patio, and intricate wood carvings. ✉ *Casa de la Aduana, Las Lonjas s/n* ☎ *922/386000* ⊕ *turismo.puertodelacruz.es* ⊗ *Weekdays 9–8, weekends 9–5*

ICOD DE LOS VINOS
26 km (16 miles) west of Puerto de la Cruz.

Attractive plazas rimmed by unspoiled colonial architecture and pine balconies form the heart of Tenerife's most historic wine district. A 3,000-year-old **dragon tree** towers 57 feet above the coastal highway, C820. The Guanches worshiped these trees as symbols of fertility and knowledge; the sap, which turns red upon contact with air, was used in healing rituals.

GARACHICO
5 km (3 miles) west of Icod de los Vinos.

Garachico is one of the most idyllic and best-preserved towns on the islands, and it's well worth a quick visit. It was the main port of Tenerife until May 5, 1706, when Mt. Teide blew its top, sending twin rivers of lava downhill. One filled Garachico's harbor, and the other destroyed most of the town. Legend has it that the eruption was unleashed by an evil monk. One of the buildings that withstood the eruption was the **Castillo San Miguel,** a tiny 16th-century fortress on the waterfront. Island crafts, such as embroidery and basket making, are demonstrated inside. From the roof you can see the two rivers of lava, now solidified on the mountainside. You can also visit the **Convento de San Francisco,** which was unscathed, and the 18th-century parish church of **Santa Ana.**

MT. TEIDE

60 km (36 miles) southwest of Puerto de la Cruz, 63 km (39 miles) north of Playa de las Américas.

Parque Nacional del Teide (*Teide National Park*). This park includes the volcano itself and the **Cañadas del Teide**, a violent jumble of volcanic leftovers from El Teide and the neighboring Pico Viejo. Within this area you can find blue hills (the result of a process called hydrothermal alteration); spiky, knobby rock protrusions; and lava in varied colors and textures. The bizarre, photogenic rock formations known as the **Roques de García** are especially memorable; a two-hour trail around these rocks—one of 21 well-marked hikes inside the park—is recommended.

You enter the Parque Nacional del Teide at El Portillo. Exhibits at the visitor center explain the region's natural history; a garden outside labels the flora found within the park. The center also offers trail maps, video presentations, guided hikes, and bus tours. A second park information center, near Los Roques de García and next to the Parador Nacional Cañadas del Teide, has details and trail maps. ⊠ *Parque Nacional del Teide, Orotava* ☏ *922/922371* ۞ *Daily 9–4.*

Cable Car. On its way to the top of Mt. Teide, the cable car passes sulfur steam vents. You can get a good view of southern Tenerife and Gran Canaria from the top, although you'll be confined to the tiny terrace of a bar. The station also has a restaurant. ☏ *922/010440* ⊕ *www. telefericoteide.com* ☞ *€20* ۞ *Ascent: daily 9–4; descent: daily 9–5.*

Climbing the Teide Crater. If you're planning on hiking in the park, plan ahead. Take warm clothing even in summer, suitable footwear, sun protection, and plenty of drinking water. The trail to the top (No. 10) of the volcano is closed when it's snowy, usually about four months of the year. The difficult final 656 feet to the volcano crater itself takes about 40 minutes to climb, and you need a special free pass to do so—bring a photocopy of your passport's information page to the visitor center, or book online. If you stay at the refuge and access the crater before 8 am, you don't need a pass. ⊕ *www.reservasparquesnacionales.es.*

LOS CRISTIANOS AND PLAYA DE LAS AMÉRICAS

74 km (44 miles) southwest of Santa Cruz, 10 km (6 miles) west of Reina Sofía Airport.

The sunniest (and probably tackiest) tourist area on Tenerife is the southwestern shore, where high-rise hotels are built chockablock above the beaches. Sun, beaches, and nightlife constitute the attractions here for millions of northern Europeans desperate for a dose of warm sunshine. These loud and brash resorts aren't to everyone's taste. If you're looking for peace and quiet, you'll probably want to give this area a wide berth.

Siam Park. This giant water park covers just about all the aquatic bases, from sleepy, restful pools to the heart-stopping Tower of Power, which drops you 28 meters (90 feet) into a "shark-infested" aquarium. ⊠ *Autopista del Sur, take exit 28 or 29, San Eugenio bajo* ☏ *922/373841* ⊕ *www.siampark.net* ☞ *€33 (combined ticket with Loro Parque €56)* ۞ *May–Oct., daily 10–6; Nov.–Apr., 10–5.*

SHOPPING

The Canary Islands are free ports—no value-added tax is charged on luxury goods. The streets are packed with shops, but not all offer much in the way of savings. Choose a reputable store to buy electronic goods: make sure the boxed item is the one you want to purchase, and check your bill and credit card receipt carefully. The islands are also known for lacy, hand-embroidered tablecloths and place mats. If you're looking for the real thing, be prepared to pay for it, and watch out for cheap Asian imitations. Cuban-style cigars are also renowned, and many connoisseurs claim that Canary cigars are of better quality and cheaper than their Caribbean equivalents.

By Canary Island standards, Santa Cruz de Tenerife is a major shopping center, although it doesn't have the variety and number of stores found in Las Palmas. Calle Castillo, the main pedestrian street through the center of town, is lined with souvenir shops, trendy boutiques, and electronics stores. Calle del Pilar has higher-end fashions and the department stores Marks & Spencer and El Corte Inglés (another branch is next to the bus terminal).

Artenerife. Artenerife sells traditional crafts made by local artisans and guaranteed by the island's government as *productos artesanos*. The selection includes Tenerifan *calado*—exquisitely embroidered linen tablecloths and place mats—and clay pottery made using the same methods as those used by the island's aboriginal settlers. (The aborigines didn't use potter's wheels; rather, they rolled the clay into *churros*, or cylindrical strips, and hand-kneaded these into bowls. Pebbles, branches, and shells were used to buff the results.) ⊠ *Pl. de España, near tourist office, Santa Cruz* ☏ *922/291523* ⊕ *www.artenerife.com* ⊙ *Weekdays 10–5, Sat. 11–2.*

La Casa de Los Balcones. Near Plaza España, this shop stocks colorful Canarian blankets, embroideries, jars of mojo sauce, and hefty bags of gofio. ⊠ *Castillo 30, Santa Cruz* ☏ *922/245734* ⊕ *www.casa-balcones. com* ⊙ *Mon.–Sat. 9:30–8:30.*

La Cava La Cubana. Local and foreign cigars are available at this tobacco shop. ⊠ *Edif. Olimpo, Candelaria 28, Santa Cruz* ⊙ *Weekdays 10–2 and 4–6, Sat. 11–2.*

BEACHES

Tenerife's beaches are sandy but not extensive, and crowded with vacationers at all times of year. The newest and sunniest tourist area on Tenerife is the southwestern shore, where high-rise hotels are built chockablock above the beaches.

El Médano. More than 2 km (1 mile) long, this is the longest beach on the island and also one of the most distinctive—the conical top of Montaña Roja (Red Mountain) lies at its southern tip. The golden sands and exemplary facilities earn it the country's "Blue Flag" rating, and the gentle waves make for safe swimming. It's a good beach for those who want to try their hand at windsurfing. **Amenities:** food and drink; lifeguards; showers; toilets; water sports. **Best for:** sunset; swimming; walking; windsurfing. ⊠ *Arona.*

7

Las Vistas. Part of the eight beaches making up the sands in Playa de las Américas and Los Cristianos, Las Vistas has clean yellow sand and perfect bathing conditions thanks to a series of breakwalls that protect the beaches from high waves. Lounge chairs and parasols are available for rent. After sunbathing on this Blue Flag beach, take a stroll along the seafront promenade, one of the longest pedestrian stretches in Europe. **Amenities:** food and drink; lifeguards; showers; toilets; water sports. **Best for:** sunset; swimming; walking. ⊠ *Los Cristianos*.

Playa de las Teresitas. Santa Cruz's beach, Las Teresitas, is about 7 km (4½ miles) northeast of the city, near the town of San Andrés. The 1½ km (1 mile) of beach was created using white sand imported from the Sahara and planted with palms. A man-made barrier runs parallel to the sands and ensures safe bathing. Busy in the summer and on weekends, this beach is especially popular with local families. The 910 TITSA bus route connects the beach with Santa Cruz. There's a good choice of bars and restaurants, and plenty of lounge chairs for rent. **Amenities:** food and drink; lifeguards; showers; toilets. **Good for:** sunset; swimming; walking. ⊠ *San Andrés, Santa Cruz*.

ACTIVITIES

Due to its climate and popularity with European vacationers, Tenerife is well equipped for a range of sports and activities. There are 21 marked hiking trails around Mt. Teide. Maps are kept at the park visitor's center. Tenerife has six golf courses, and the climate means that you'll be able to get a round in most days of the year.

GOLF
Tenerife's noteworthy golf courses are all in the south of the island.

Amarilla Golf Club. In San Miguel, not far from Campo Golf, is this 18-hole course, where the greens front the ocean. ⊠ *Urb. Amarilla Golf, San Miguel, Los Cristianos* ☎ 922/730319 ⊕ *www.amarillagolf.es*.

Golf Abama. This course boasts over 22 lakes and more than 90,000 palms along its 18 holes. ⊠ *Ctra. Gral TF-47, km 9, Playa de San Juan, Guía de Isora, Los Cristianos* ☎ 922/126000 ⊕ *www. abamahotelresort.com*.

Golf Las Américas. Adjacent to Playa de las Américas, Golf Las Américas has an 18-hole course with views of the ocean and La Gomera Island. ⊠ *Playa de las Américas, Arona, Los Cristianos* ☎ 922/752005 ⊕ *www. golf-tenerife.com*.

Golf Costa Adeje. There's a 27-hole course and views of the sea at this club. ⊠ *Fince de los Olivos, Adeje, Los Cristianos* ☎ 922/710000 ⊕ *www.golfcostaadeje.com*.

WHERE TO EAT

$$
SPANISH
✕ **El Lateral 27.** This restaurant's key position in the main shopping street makes it a handy place to stop for a meal after sightseeing, especially since the kitchen is open from 11 am to midnight. If there are free tables, sit outside on the pleasant terrace in the leafy pedestrian street—inside is

less pretty. Specialties include a wide range of salads such as *ensalada de bacalao confitado con pimientos asados* (slow-cooked cod with baked peppers) and fresh fish. ⑤ *Average main: €13* ✉ *Bethencourt Alfonso 27, Santa Cruz* ☎ *922/287774* ⊘ *Closed Sun.*

$
SPANISH
✗ **Tasca Tagoror.** Opposite the Mencey Hotel, this tiny bar serves Canary cooking in abundant portions at reasonable prices. Tasca Tagoror (it means "meeting place" in Guanche) has a low, beamed ceiling with white walls dashed with gray rock. Seating is on wooden benches or stools around barrels, which doesn't exactly encourage lingering. Food is simple and unpretentious—daily specials might include fried fresh sardines with black potatoes or chicken breast with garlic and mushrooms. The wine list is surprisingly comprehensive. ⑤ *Average main: €8* ✉ *Doctor José Naveiras 9, Santa Cruz* ☎ *922/274163* ⊘ *Closed Sun. June–Oct.*

7

INDEX

A

A Coruña, Spain, 40–43
Abadia do Porto ✕, 122
Abbaye St-Victor, 153
Abbazia di San Fruttuoso, 205
Abu al-Abbas al-Mursi Mosque, 249
Achilleion, 268
Acquario di Genova, 95–96
Acropolis, 339
Acropolis of Lindos, 356
Acropolis Select ⊡, 345
Adega O Bebedeiro ✕, 42–43
Adegas de São Francisco, 578
Adio Mare ✕, 308
Aegean. ⇨ Eastern Mediterranean and Aegean
Agder naturmuseum og botaniske hage, 556
Ajaccio, Corsica, 43–52
Ajuntaments, 146, 158, 160
Aker Brygge, 559, 562
Akerhus Festning og Slott, 559
Akvariet, 545
Akvarij, 272
Al-Aqsa Mosque, 260–262
Albergo Santa Chiara ⊡, 89–90
Alberobello, 64–65
Alberobello-Martina Franca road, 65
Alcazaba, 140, 143
Alcázar, 72, 73
Aleksandr Nevski Khram, 521, 522
Ålesund, Norway, 540–543
Ålesunds Museum, 542
Alexandria, Egypt, 248–254
Alexandria National Museum, 251
Alghero, Sardinia, 197, 198–199
Alhambra, 140, 143
Alster, 485, 488
Amalienborg, 472
American Cemetery and Memorial, 109
Amsterdam, Netherlands, 372–382
Amsterdam Museum, 376
Anacapri, 180–181
Ancient Agora, 340
Ancient Akrotiri, 360, 361
Ancient Olympia, 295, 297–298
Andratx, Spain, 149
Anne Frankhuis, 376
Ano Mera, Mykonos, 332
Antibes, France, 76–80
Antiga Alfândega, 579
Antwerp, Belgium, 382–390
Apes' Den, 100
Apollo Hylates, 322
Aqualand Maspalomas, 587

Aqui Há Peixe ✕, 129
Árbæjarsafn, 600
Arc de Triomphe, 109, 112
Archaeological Museum (Delos), 330–331, 333
Archaeological Museum (Fira), 360–361
Archaeological Museum (Rhodes), 354
Archaeological Museum at Olympia, 298–299
Architecture museum, 503
Arkeoloji Müzeleri, 287, 290
Arrecife, 593
Art Escudellers (shop), 59–60
Art nouveau district, 502
Ashdod, Israel, 254–263
Ásmundur Sveinsson Sculpture Museum, 600
Atelier Exekias (shop), 299
Ateneumin Taidemuseo, 493
Athens, Greece, 335–345
Atlanterhavsparken, 542
Atlantic Islands, 576–613
castles and palaces, 593, 606
children, attractions for, 580, 587, 593, 596, 601, 609
churches, 579, 581, 585, 600–601, 606
currency, 576, 584, 591, 598, 605
docking, 578, 584, 591, 598, 600, 605
museums, 579, 580, 585, 593, 593, 594, 600, 601, 602, 606
private tours, 576, 595, 604
restaurants, 583, 590, 597–598, 604–605, 612–613
shopping, 582–583, 590, 595, 603–604, 611
sports and outdoor activities, 578, 582, 589, 596, 604, 612
wineries, 578, 608
Auditorio de Tenneriffe, 606
Austurvöllur Square, 600
Avenida dos Aliados, 117
Aviemore, 433, 436
Aya Sofya, 290
Ayios Lazarus, 323
Ayios Neophytos Monastery, 326
Ayuntamiento, 70
Azamara Club Cruises, 20–21

B

Baha'i Shrine and Gardens, 278, 279
Bakkerswinkel ✕, 381
Balcón de Europa, 142
Baltic, 468–537
castles and palaces, 472, 473, 480, 497–498, 509–510, 515

children, attractions for, 474, 480–481, 485, 488, 490, 502, 505, 507, 514–515, 516–517, 522–523, 524, 526, 527, 529
churches and mosques, 481–482, 489–490, 496, 498, 502–503, 507–508, 521, 522, 523, 527, 533
currency, 469, 478, 484, 492, 500, 505, 511, 520, 524, 526, 528
docking, 469, 478, 484–485, 492, 501–502, 505, 514, 520, 524, 529
lodging, 477, 519–520
museums, 474, 482, 483, 488, 490, 493, 496, 497, 498, 502, 503, 507, 508–509, 514–517, 521, 522–523, 526, 532–533, 534–535
private tours, 505, 527
restaurants, 468, 476–477, 483, 491, 500, 504, 511, 518–519, 523, 528, 537
shopping, 476, 483, 490–491, 499, 504, 510, 518, 523, 527, 536–537
sports and outdoor activities, 500, 527
transportation, 472
Banias Spring, 281
Baptist Church, 278–279
Bæjarins beztu ✕, 604
Barcelona, Spain, 52–61
Barceloneta, 56
Bargello, 131
Bari, Italy, 61–65
Barlingbo, 527
Basilica di San Marco, 230, 231–232
Basilica di San Nicola, 63
Basilica di San Pietro, 84–85
Basilica of the Annunciation, 279
Bastion de l'Étendard, 48
Battisteros, 131, 136
Bayeux, 108–109
Bayeux Tapestry, 108–109
Bead Shop, 363
Beaulieu-Sur-Mer, France, 244
Begijnhof, 462–463
Benaki Museum, 340
Bergen, Norway, 543–548
Bergen Kunstmuseum, 545
Bergenhus Festning, 545
Berlin, Germany, 528–527
Berliner Fernsehturm, 529
Bethlehem, 257–258
Biaxa, 126
Bibliotheca Alexandrina, 251
Birgu, Malta, 223
Bishop Lucey Park, 393
Blarney, Ireland, 395
Blarney Castle, 392, 395

Blarney Stone, *392, 395*
Blue Grotto, *224*
Blue Lagoon, *602*
Blue Mosque, *290–291*
Bølgen & Moi ✕, *548*
Bonifacio, *45, 48*
Bordeaux, France, *65–69*
Brama Wyżynna, *480*
Brama Zielona, *480*
Brama Złota, *480*
Brandenburger Tor, *532, 533*
British Museum, *424–425*
Brīvdabas muzejs, *502*
Brīvības piemineklis, *502*
Broadstairs, U.K., *401*
Brouwersgracht, *376–377*
Bruges, Belgium, *460–466*
Bryggen, *545, 546*
Buckingham Palace, *424, 425*
Burg, *463*
Burrell Collection, *416–417*
Byzantine and Christian
  Museum, *341*
Byzantine Museum (Corfu
  Town), *264*
Byzantine Museum (Paphos),
  326
Byzantine Museum (Rhodes
  Town), *354*

C

Ca N'Alluny, *150*
Cable Car (Gibraltar), *100*
Cabo Girão, Madeira, *582*
Cádiz, Spain, *69–75*
Cádiz Cathedral, *72*
Café Einstein Stammhaus ✕,
  537
CairnGorm Mountain Railway,
  436
Cairngorms National Park, *436*
Cairo, Egypt, *345–351*
Cairo Museum, *348*
Cais da Ribeira, *117*
Cal Pep ✕, *60*
Calanques de Piana, *45*
Calton Hill, *440–441*
Calvi, *45, 49*
Câmara de Lobos, Madeira,
  582
Camogli, Italy, *207*
Campanile, *131, 232*
Campiello, *264*
Camping, *527*
Cannes, France, *76–80*
Canoeing, *527*
Canterbury, U.K., *399–401*
Canterbury Cathedral, *399–400*
Canterbury Roman Museum,
  401
Canterbury Tales, The, *401*
Capo Caccia, *198*
Cappella Sistina, *85*
Cappelle Medicee, *131, 134*
Capri, Italy, *173–182*
Capri Town, *180*
Carlsberg Bryggeri, *473*

Carnival Cruise Lines, *21*
Casa de los Volcanes, *593*
Casa de Vino La Baranda, *608*
Casa Manteca ✕, *75*
Casa Montesdeoca ✕, *590*
Casa Museo Colón, *585*
Casa Museo José Benlliure, *214*
Casa-Museu de Guerra Jun-
  queiro, *117*
Casa-Museu Frederico de Frei-
  tas, *579*
Casa Napoléon, *50*
Casa Rocca Piccola, *220, 222*
Casco Antiguo, *238*
Casemates Square, *100*
Castel del Monte, *64*
Castel Nuovo, *174–175*
Castel Sant'Elmo, *175*
Castell de Bellver, *146*
Castell de Sant Nicolau, *160*
Castello (Trani), *63*
Castello Brown, *205*
Castello Normanno, *165, 166*
Castello Saraceno, *165*
Castello Svevo, *63*
Castelmola, Italy, *166*
Castelsardo, Sardinia, *199*
Castillo de San Antón, *41*
Castillo San Cristóbal, *606*
Castillo San Gabriel, *593*
Catacombe dei Cappuccini, *189*
Catacombs (Rabat), *225*
Catacombs of Kom al-Shoqafa,
  251, 252
Catedral Santa Ana, *585*
Cathach Books (shop), *412*
Cathedral de Majorca, *146*
Cathedral of St. Nicolas, *303*
Cathedral Roofs, *240*
Cathédrale de la Nouvelle
  Major, *153*
Cathédrale Notre-Dame, *109,
  113–114*
Cathédrale Notre-Dame de
  L'Assomption, *45*
Cathédrale St-André, *66*
Cathedrals, *45, 66, 72, 73, 95,
  96, 105, 109, 113–114, 136,
  140, 146, 160, 169, 171, 189,
  214, 225, 237, 238, 301, 303,
  307, 311, 361, 367, 386–387,
  394, 399–400, 417, 427, 456,
  457–458, 481, 498, 502–503,
  507–508, 521, 522, 572,
  581, 585*
Cattedrale (Palermo), *189*
Cattedrale (Trani), *64*
Cattedrale di San Sabino, *63*
Cavafy Museum, *252*
Cawdor Castle, *434–435*
Celebrity Cruises, *21–22*
Center of Hellenic Tradition
  (shop), *343*
Centre de la Vielle Charité,
  153, 154
Centre d'Interpretació Madina
  Yabisa, *105*

Centro Atlántico de Arte Mod-
  erno, *585*
Centro de Arte Contemporáneo,
  139–140
Centro Galego de Arte Contem-
  poránea, *240*
Certosa di San Giacomo, *180*
Čevljarski most, *303*
Chapelle Impériale, *45*
Chappelle St-Pierre, *243*
Charles Fort, *395–396*
Charlotte Square, *441*
Château d'If, *154*
Chawton, U.K., *454, 457*
Christiansborg Slot, *473*
Christianshavn, *473*
Christiansholm Festning, *556*
Church of Paraportiani, *331*
Church of St. Catherine, *257*
Church of St. Gabriel, *280*
Church of St. Lawrenz, *223*
Church of St. Spyridon, *266*
Church of the Holy Sepulcher,
  255, 260
Church of the Nativity, *257*
Church of the Panayia, *357*
Cimiez, France, *186–187*
Çırağan Palace Kempinski
  Istanbul 📷, *294*
Circumetnea railroad, *167*
Citadelle (Calvi), *49*
Citadelle (St-Tropez), *210*
Citadelle St-Elme, *243*
City Hall (Dublin), *406*
City Museum of Ljubljana,
  303–304
Ciutadella, Spain, *160–161*
Ciutat de les Arts i les Ciències,
  216, 217
Cloister (Monreale), *192*
Cobh, Ireland, *390–397*
Cobh Heritage Centre, *392*
Colexiata de Santa Maria do
  Campo, *41*
Collection des Voitures Anci-
  ennes, *171*
Colline de Château, *183*
Colosseo, *84, 85–86*
Commune Libre du Safranier,
  79
Conservatorium Hotel 📷, *381*
Convento de Santa Clara
  (Funchal), *579*
Convento de Santa Clara
  (Menorca), *160*
Copenhagen, Denmark,
  468–477
Corfu, Greece, *263–270*
Corfu Town, *264, 266–267*
Cork, Ireland, *390–397*
Cork City Gaol, *393*
Cospicua, Malta, *223*
Costa Cruises, *22–23*
Costa Smeralda, *197*
Costa Teguise, *593–594*
Cours Masséna, *79*
Cours Saleya, *185*

Court House (Cork), 393
Crawford Art Gallery, 393
Crkva Sv Luke, 310
Crkva Sv Nikole, 311
Crkva Svetog Vlaha, 272
Cruise and Maritime Voyages, 23–24
Cruising, 8–37
 costs, 12
 cruise lines, 18–37
 customs and duties, 17–18
 documents, 14–15
 insurance, 16–17
 itineraries, 9, 12
 money, 15–16
 tips, 13–14
 timing, 12
Crystal Cruises, 23
Cueva de los Verdes, 594
Cuevas de Nerja, 142
Culloden Moor, 434
Cunard Line, 24
Custom House, 406
Customs and duties, 17–18
Cygnaeuksen Galleria, 493
Cyprus Wine Museum, 322

D
Da Baffetto ✕, 89
Da Michele ✕, 182
Dalhem, 527
Dalt Vila, 103, 105
Dam, 377
Daphne's ✕, 344
Dead Sea, Israel, 255, 258–259
Dead Sea Scrolls, 262
D-Day Beaches, 109, 112
Deià, 150
Deichstrasse, 485
Delfshaven, 447
Delft, Netherlands, 448, 449–450
Delos, Greece, 330, 332–333
Den Lille Havfrue (The Little Mermaid), 472, 473–474
Denkmal für die Ermordeten Juden Europas, 532
Dersaadet Hotel 🗒, 294
Designmuseo, 493
Desmond Castle and the International Museum of Wine, 396
Det Gamle Rådhus ✕, 567
Det Hanseatiske Museum, 545–546
Deutsches Historisches Museum, 532
Diamantwijk, 384–385
Diamondland, 384
Dickens House Museum, 401
Dinoris ✕, 357
Dioklecijanova Palača, 365
Disney Cruise Line, 24–25
Diving, 202, 308, 596
Dogsledding, 570
Doma baznīca, 502–503

Dome of the Rock, 255, 260–261
Dominiiklaste Kloostri Muuseum, 521
Dominikanski samostan, 272–273
Dómkirkjan, 600–601
Donners Brunn ✕, 528
Dover, U.K., 397–403
Dover Castle, 399
Dragon Bridge, 304
Dragon Grottoes, 48–49
Dragon tree, 609
Dublin, Ireland, 403–413
Dublin City Gallery, The Hugh Lane, 406–407
Dubrovnik, Croatia, 270–275
Duomo di San Gennaro, 175
Duomos, 136, 163, 175, 191, 192–193, 198
Duquesa de Cardona 🗒, 60
Duties, 17–18
Dvortsovaya Ploshchad, 505, 507
Dwór Artusa, 480

E
East Jerusalem, 259–260
Eastern Mediterranean and Aegean, 248–369
 castles and palaces, 267–268, 273, 285, 290, 291–292, 301, 304, 316, 322, 355, 365
 children, attractions for, 263, 280, 287, 290, 295, 297–298, 301, 303, 323, 324, 327, 341, 356
 churches, mosques, and synagogues, 249, 255, 257, 260–261, 266, 272–273, 274, 278–279, 280, 283–284, 290–291, 303, 304, 307, 310–311, 312, 317, 323, 331, 343, 354, 361, 367
 currency, 249, 255, 264, 271, 276, 282, 286, 294, 300, 305, 309, 314, 319, 328, 335, 345, 352, 357, 358, 364, 365–366
 docking, 249, 255, 257, 264, 271, 276, 283, 286–287, 295, 300, 305, 310, 314, 316, 320, 328, 330, 335, 338, 348, 352, 358, 360, 365
 lodging, 293–294, 345
 museums, 251, 252, 262–263, 264, 267, 268, 273, 274, 278, 287, 290, 298–299, 303–304, 311–312, 313, 322–323, 324, 326, 330–331, 333, 340–342, 348–349, 351, 354, 360–361, 362, 365, 366, 367
 private tours, 255, 258, 286, 309, 314, 319–320, 328
 restaurants, 248, 254, 263, 270, 275, 282, 285, 293, 299, 305, 308–309, 313, 319, 327, 334,

344, 351, 357–358, 363–364, 369
 shopping, 253–254, 269, 275, 292–293, 299, 304, 308, 313, 318, 326–327, 333–334, 343–344, 348, 350–351, 357, 363, 368
 sports and outdoor activities, 308, 334
 transportation, 287, 338
 wine tasting, 307
Edinburgh, Scotland, 437–444
Edinburgh Castle, 440, 441–442
Edvard Grieg Museum, Troldhaugen, 546
Église de l'Immaculée-Conception, 79
Eglise Sainte Marie Majeure, 49
Église St-Jean Baptiste, 46
Egyptian Antiquities Museum, 348–349
Eiffel Tower, 114–115
Eira do Serrado Madeira, 582
Eivissa, 103, 105
Eixample, 56
El Barri Gòtic, 56
El Diablo ✕, 598
Elba, Italy, 200–204
Electra Palace 🗒, 345
Elizabetes Street, 503
English Market, 393
Enrique Becerra ✕, 75
Ephesus, 314–319
Ephesus Archaelogical Site, 317–318
Ephesus Museum, 316
Erkebispegården, 571–572
Ermita de San Telmo, 585
Es Moli de Foc ✕, 162
Escala del Cabirol, 199
Esplanade (Corfu), 266
Esplanāde (Rīga), 502, 503
Estação de São Bento, 117
Estación del Norte, 216
Euromast, 447
Europa Point, 100
European cruise lines, 20
Èze, 245

F
Fantoft Stavkirke, 546
Fårö, 524, 526
Farragut, David Glasgow, monument, 160
Faversham, U.K., 401
Filitosa, 47
Finlandiatalo, 493
Fira, Santorini, 360–361
Firostefani, 361
Fisketorget, 546
Fitzgerald's Park, 394
Fjellheisen, 568
Flåm, 549
Flåmsbana, 549

Flåmsbana Museet, 549
Florence, Italy, 129–137
Fontanna Neptuna, 480–481
Food Market (Ajaccio), 46
Fornells, Spain, 160
Fort George, 434
Fort Qayt Bay, 252
Fort St-Nicolas and Fort St-Jean, 154, 156
Fortaleza de São Tiago, 579
Fortaleza do Pico, 579
Fortnum & Mason (shop), 430
Fotografiska, 514
Fram-Museet, 559, 562
Franciskanska cerkev, 304
Franjevačka Samostan, 273, 284
Fred. Olsen Cruise Lines, 25
Fretheim Hotel ⊞, 549
Funchal, Madeira, 576–583
Fundació Miró, 57
Fundación César Manrique, 594
Fundación Picasso, 140

G

Galata Museo del Mare, 96
Galerija Meštrović, 365–366
Galerija Vidović, 366
Galleria dell'Accademia, 135
Galleria Nazionale, 94
Gallerie dell'Accademia, 232
Gamla Stan, 516
Garachico, 609
Garden of Gethsemane, 259
Gardjola Garden, 223
Gastouri, Greece, 268
Gdańsk, Poland, 477–483
Gedenkstätte Berliner Mauer, 532–533
Geiranger, Norway, 549–550
Gemäldegalerie, 534
Genoa, Italy, 90–97
Genoese castle, 316
George Square, 417
German Colony, 278
Geysir, 603
Ghar Dalam, Malta, 224
Gibralfaro, 140
Gibraltar, 97–102
Gibraltar Museum, 100
Giza, 349–350
Glasgow, Scotland, 413–420
Glasgow Cathedral, 417
Glasgow School of Art, 416, 417–418
Glavna Gradska Vrata, 311
Golan Heights, The, 279, 280–281
Golden Triangle, 600
Golf, 151, 420, 553, 589, 596, 612
Golfe de Porto, 49
Golfo Aranci, Sardinia, 197
Gondolas, 372
González Bypass, 74
Gospa od Skrpjela, 312

Gothem, 527
Gotland, Sweden, 524–527
Gotland Active Store, 527
Gotland Museum, 526
Gradske Zidine, 270, 273, 311
Grafton Street, 407
Gran Canaria, Canary Islands (Las Palmas), 583–590
Gran Teatro Manuel de Falla, 72
Granada, Spain, 138–144
Grand Bazaar, 291
Grand Egyptian Museum, 351
Grand Harbour, 222
Grand Hotel (Oslo) ⊞, 567
Grand Hotel (Stockholm) ⊞, 519
Grand Masters' Palace, 222
Grand Théâtre, 66
Grand Trianon ✕, 254
Graves of the Seven Sleepers, 318
Great Hall, 455–456
Great Siege of Malta and the Knights of St. John, 222
Great Siege Tunnels, 100–101
Great Sphinx, 349–350
Greenock, Scotland, 413–420
Grillmarket ✕, 604–605
Groeningemuseum, 463
Gröna Lund Tivoli, 514
Grote Markt, 385
Grötlingbo, 527
Grotta Azzurra, 181
Grotta di Nettuno, 198–199
Gudvangen, Norway, 550–551
Guinate Tropical Park, 593
Guiness Storehouse, 407–408
Guiseppe Garibaldi's tomb, 196
Gulf of Finland Archipelago, 493
Gullfoss, 603
Guzé ✕, 226–227
Gymnasion, 298

H

Haifa, Israel, 276–282
Hal Saflieni Hypogeum, 224
Hala Sultan Tekke, 323
Hallgrimskirkja, 601
Hamburg, Germany, 484–491
Hamburger Kunsthalle, 488
Hammerfest, Norway, 552–553
Hampshire, U.K., 455
Harrods (department store), 430
Harwich, U.K., 421–431
Hassler ⊞, 90
Haukadalur, 603
Haut-Brion, 67
Haut Ville, 48
Havfruen ✕, 574
Havis Amanda, 493
Heilig Bloed Basiliek, 463–464
Helsingin Taidehalli, 496
Helsinki, Finland, 491–500
Herculaneum, Italy, 173–182

Hermans ✕, 518
Hermes statue, 297
Hermon River (Banias) Nature Reserve, 280–281
High Kirk of St. Giles, 442
Hippodrome, 298
Holiday World, 587
Holland America, 26
Holmenkollbakken og skinmuseet, 562
Holocaust History Museum, 262–263
Honfleur, 108, 112
Honningsvåg, Norway, 544–556
Horseback riding, 558
Hospitaalmuseum, 464
Hostal de los Reyes Católicos, 240
Hotel Continental ⊞, 567
Hôtel de Ville, 46
Hôtel des Invalides, 112
Hotel Neri ⊞, 61
Hötogshallen (market), 518
House of Nero, 298
Houses of Parliament, 425–426
Hunterian Art Gallery, 416, 418
Hurtigruten, 26–27
Hvar, Croatia, 282–285
Hvar Town, 283–284

I

Ia, Santorini, 360, 361–362
Ibiza, Spain, 102–107
Icod de los Vinos, 609
Ida Davidsen ✕, 476
Iglesia de Nuestra Señora de la Concepción, 606
Iglesia de Santiago, 41
Igreja da Misericórdia, 119
Igreja de São Francisco, 119
Igreja e Museu de São Roque, 124, 126
Il Bigo, 95, 96
Il Mare ✕, 204
Ile St-Honorat, 78
Ile Ste-Marguerite, 79
Iles Lérins, France, 76–80
Ilias Lalaounis (shop), 333–334
Imerovigli, Santorini, 361
Inn of France, 354
Inquisitor's Palace, 223
Institut de Thalassothérapie, 51
Institut València d'Art Modern (IVAM), 216
Invergordon, Scotland, 431–437
Inverness, 433–434, 436
Inverness Castle, 434
Inverness Museum and Art Gallery, 434
Irish Museum of Modern Art, 411
Isa Bey Cami, 317
Ishavskatedralen, 568
Israel Museum, 262
Istanbul, Turkey, 286–294

Itineraries, 9, 12
Izola, Slovenia, 301

J
James Joyce Centre, 408
Jane Austen's House, 457
Jardim Botânico (Funchal), 579–580
Jardín Botánico (Tenerife), 608
Jardín Canario Viero y Clavijo, 587
Jardín de Cactus, 593
Jardin Exotique, 245
Jardin Exotique de Monaco, 171
Jardins d'Alfàbia, Spain, 149
Jelsa, Croatia, 284
Jerez de la Frontera, Spain, 69–75
Jerusalem Archaeological Park, 261
Jim Edwards ✕, 396–397
Jüdisches Museum Berlin, 533
Jungfernstieg, 488
Jupiterov Hram, 366–367

K
Kadriorg Palace Foreign Art Museum, 522
Kaiser-Wilhelm-Gedächtnis-Kirche, 533
Kanoni, Greece, 267–268
Kaštelet, 365–366
Kastro ✕, 363–364
Katakolon, Greece, 294–299
Katedra w Oliwie, 481
Katedrala, 307
Katedrala Sv Tripuna, 311
Katedrala Sveti Dujam, 367
Katedrala Sveti Stjepan, 283–284
Katedrala Velika Gospa, 273
Kauppatori, 496
Kayaking, 202, 570
Kazan Cathedral, 507
Kelvingrove Art Gallery and Museum, 416, 418
Kervansaray, 316
Khan al-Khalili (souk), 348, 351
Khorasani ✕, 293
Kidriceva ulica, 301
Kiek-in-de-Kök, 522
Kinderdijk, Netherlands, 448, 450–451
Kinderdijk Windmills, 448, 450–451
Kinsale, Ireland, 395–396
Kition, 324
Knežev Dvor, 273
Kneippbyn, 526
Knifen, 543
Kobilarna Lipica, 301
Kolossi Castle, 322
Kom al-Dikka (Roman Theater), 253

Kongelige Repræsentationlokaler, 473
Kon-Tiki Museum, 562
Koper, Slovenia, 300–305
Koper Old Town, 301
Kopnena Vrata, 307
Korčula, Croatia, 305–309
Korres (shop), 344
Kościół Najświętszej Marii Panny, 481
Kościół świętej Brygidy, 481
Kościół świętej Katarzyny, 482
Kosmos ✕, 500
Kotor, Montenegro, 309–313
Kotor Old Town, 311
Kourion Archaeological Site, 322
Kristiansand, Norway, 556–558
Kristiansand Dyreparken, 556–557
Kristiansand Kanonmuseum, 557
Kristiansten festning, 572
Kuća Marca Pola, 307
Kulturforum, 534
Kulturhuset, 514–515
Kungliga Slottet, 515
Kungsträdgården, 515
Kunsthal, 448
Kuretes Street, 316
Kuşadası, Turkey, 314–319
Kykkos Monastery, 325

L
La Boqueria, 56
La Ciutadella, 56
La Croisette, 77, 78
La Maddalena, Sardinia, 196
La Martorana, 189
La Orotava, 608
La Panier, 153
La Penela ✕, 43
La Rambla, 56, 57
La Sagrada Familia, 57
La Verge del Carme, 158
Lago Martiánez, 609
Lakones, 269
Lanzarote, Canary Islands, 591–598
Larnaca, Cyprus, 323–324
Larnaca District Archaeological Museum, 324
Larnaca Fort, 324
Larnaca Museum, 323
Las Palmas, Gran Canaria, 583–590
Le Fleur de Sel ✕, 115
Le Havre, France, 107–115
Le Louis XV ✕, 172–173
Le Panier, 156
Le Suquet, 77
Le Vailier ✕, 52
Leaning Tower, 136–137
Lefkara, Cyprus, 323, 325
Leith, Scotland, 437–444
Leixões, Portugal, 116–122

Leonidaion, 298
L'Ile Rousse, 50
Lilium ✕, 597
Lilla Karsö, 526
Limanaki ✕, 327
Limassol, Cyprus, 319–327
Limassol Castle, 322
Limassol District Archaeological Museum, 322–323
Limassol Zoo, 323
Lindblad Expeditions, 27
Lindos, Greece, 355, 356–357
Lipica, Slovenia, 301
Lisbon, Portugal, 123–129
Listasafn Reykjavíkur, 601
Liston, 266
Little Mermaid statue, 472, 473–474
Little Venice, 331
Livorno, Italy, 129–137
Livraria Lello e Irmão (shop), 122
Ljubljana, 303–304
Ljubljana Castle, 301
Ljubljanski grad, 304
Llotja, 148
Lo Güeno ✕, 144
Locanda Orseolo ⚏, 235
Loch Ness, 433, 435–436
Loch Ness Centre & Exhibition, 435
Loggia of St. John, 354
Lokanda Peškarija ✕, 275
London, U.K., 421–431
London Eye, 426
Lonja de la Seda, 216
Loro Parque, 609
Los Cristianos and Playa de las Américas, 610
Los Jameos del Agua, 593
Louis Cruises, 27–28
Louvre, 112–113
Lummelundagrottan, 526
Luxury cruise lines, 19–20

M
Madeira Cable Car, 581
Madeira Story Centre, 580
Madonna dell'Orto, 232–233
Magere Brug, 377
Mahón, Spain, 157–162
Mainstream cruise lines, 18–19
Maison Bonaparte, 46
Maison du Vin, 67–68
Málaga, Spain, 138–144
Mallorca, Spain, 145–152
Mando Mavrogenous Square, 331
Manger Square, Bethlehem, 257–258
Manrique, Cèsar, 594, 606
Manzana de la Discòrdia, 57
Marbella, Spain, 138–144
Marché Central, 46
Mariakirken, 546
Marina di Campo, 201

Maritiem Museum Rotterdam, 448
Marjan, 365, 367
Markt (Bruges), 464–465
Marsaxlokk, Malta, 224
Marseille, France, 152–157
Masada, Israel, 259
Maspalomas, Gran Canaria, 587, 588–589
Mathias Dahlgren ✕, 518–519
Mauermuseum-Museum Haus am Checkpoint Charlie, 534
Mavrikos ✕, 358
Mayflower Park and the Pilgrim Fathers' Memorial, 455
Mdina, Malta, 225
Mdina Cathedral, 225
Medieval city walls (Canterbury), 401
Medieval Museum, 324
Melngalvju Nams, 503
Menorca, Spain, 157–162
Mercado de Atarazanas, 140–141
Mercado de Nuestra Señora de Africa, 606
Mercado dos Lavradores, 580
Merrion Square, 408–409
Messina, Italy, 162–168
Meštroviæ Gallery, 365
Metroon, 298
Miguelete Tower, 217
Mirador del Río, 594
Mirador Pico de las Nieves, 587
Mnajdra, 224–225
Mode Museum (MoMu), 385
Moderna Museet, 515
Mon Repos, 267–268
Monaco Cathedral, 169, 171
Monastère de Cimiez, 186
Monastery of the Panayia Tourliani, 332
Monreale, 192–193
Monte, Madeira, 581–582
Monte Capanne, 201
Monte Carlo, Monaco, 168–173
Monte Solaro, 180–181
Montjuïc, 56
Monument du Débarquement, 109
Moorish Castle, 101
Moreška dances, 307, 308
Mosque of Süleyman, 354
Mosta, Malta, 225
Mosteiro dos Jerónimos, 126
Mt. Etna, Italy, 162–168
Mount of Olives and East Jerusalem, 259–260
Mount of Olives Observation Point, 259–260
Mt. Teide, 608, 610
Mövenpick 🍽, 382
MSC Cruises, 28–29
Munchmuseet, 562–563
Municipal Folk Art Museum, 323

Municipal Museum of Natural History, 324
Musée Archéologique, 186
Musée d'Aquitaine, 68
Musée d'Art Contemporain, 68
Musée d'Art Moderne, 185
Musée de la Castre, 77–78
Musée de la Mer, 79
Musée de l'Annonciade, 210–211
Musée Départmental de Préhistoire Corse, 48
Musée des Beaux-Arts (Ajaccio), 46–47
Musée des Beaux-Arts (Bordeaux), 68
Musée des Beaux-Arts Jules-Chéret, 185
Musée d'Histoire de Marseille, 156
Musée d'Orsay, 113
Musée Matisse, 185, 186–187
Musée National Marc-Chagall, 185, 186
Musée Océanographique, 171
Musée Picasso, 78
Musei Capitolini, 87
Musei Vaticani, 86–87
Musej Pravoslavne Crkve, 273
Museo Archeologico, 201
Museo Arqueologico Nazionale, 175, 178
Museo Arqueologico Regionale Salinas, 191
Museo Carmen Thyssen Málaga, 141
Museo de Arte Contemporáneo, 593
Museo de Bellas Artes (Tenerife), 606
Museo de Bellas Artes (Valencia), 216–217
Museo de Cádiz, 72
Museo de la Naturaleza y el Hombre, 606
Museo de las Cortes, 73
Museo de las Peregrinaciones, 237, 240
Museo del Baile Flamenco, 74
Museo dell'Opera del Duomo, 135
Museo di Capodimonte, 178
Museo Diocesano d'Arte Sacra, 199
Museo do Pobo Galego, 240
Museo Nacional de Cerámica, 217
Museo Nazionale, 131
Museo Picasso, 141
Museo Sanna, 198
Museo Taurino, 218
Museu Calouste Gulbenkian, 126
Museu da Quinta das Cruzes, 580
Museu de Arte Contemporânea, 119

Museu de Arte Sacra, 580
Museu d'Es Baluard, 148
Museu d'Història de Catalunya, 57
Museu Fundació Pilar y Joan Miró, 148
Museu Fundación Juan March, 148
Museu Municipal (Funchal), 580
Museu Municipal (Menorca), 160
Museu Nacional d'Art de Catalunya, 58
Museu Nacional de Arte Antiga, 127
Museu Nacional Soares dos Reis, 120
Museu Picasso, 58
Museu Romântico da Quinta da Macierinha, 121
Museum Aan de Stroom (MAS), 384, 386
Museum Boijmans van Beuningen, 448–449
Museum de Dubbelde Palmboom, 449
Museum Het Prinsenhof, 450
Museum het Rembrandthuis, 377–378
Museum Mayer Van den Bergh, 386
Museum of Archaeology, 41
Museum of Cycladic Art, 341
Museum of Decorative Arts, 354
Museum of Post-War Reconstruction, 553
Museum of Prehistoric Thera, 361
Museum van Hedendaagse Kunst (M HKA), 386
Museumsinsel, 533, 534–535
Musiikkitalo, 496
Muzej Grad Perasta, 313
Muzej Hrvatskih Arheološki Spomenika, 367
Muzeum Archeologiczne Gdańska, 482
Muzeum Etnograficzne, 482
Muzeum Morskie, 483
Muzeum Narodowe w Gdańsku, 482
Mykonos, Greece, 328–334
Mykonos Town, 330–331
Mykonos windmills, 331

N

Nacionālā Opera, 503
Naples, Italy, 173–182
Narodni trg, 367
Nasjonalgalleriet, 563
National and University Library, 304
National Archaeological Museum, 341–342
National Gallery, 426–427

National Gallery of Ireland, 409
National Gallery of Scotland, 442
National Museum of Archaeology (Dublin), 409–410
National Museum of Archaeology (Malta), 222
National Museum of Scotland, 442–443
Nationalmuseum, 515
Nature preserves, 49, 101, 280–281, 526
Naval Museum of Thera, 362
Nazareth, 278–280
Nazareth Village, 280
Nea Kameni, Santorini, 362
Nefusot Yehudada Synagogue, 101
Nerja, Spain, 138–144
New Acropolis Museum, 342
New Fortress, 267
Newman House, 410
Nice, France, 182–188
Nidarosdomen, 572
Niguliste Kirik, 522
Nikulásargjá Gorge, 603
Nimrod's Fortress, 281
NK (shop), 518
Nobelmuseet, 515–516
Nordenfjeldske Kunstindustrimuseum, 572
Nordkapp, 554–555
Nordkapphellen, 555
Nordkappmuseet, 554
Normandy, France, 107–115
Norsk Folkenmuseum, 563
North Sea, 372–466
  castles and palaces, 392, 395, 396, 399, 424, 425, 433, 434–435, 440, 441–442, 443
  children, attractions for, 376, 381, 382, 393, 394, 399, 401, 418, 419, 426–428, 434, 435, 441–443, 448
  churches and mosques, 378–379, 384, 386–387, 388–389, 392–393, 394, 399–400, 417, 418, 427, 429, 442, 456, 457–458, 463–464, 465
  currency, 372, 382, 390, 397, 403, 413, 421, 432, 437, 445, 453, 460
  docking, 373, 384, 392, 397–398, 403, 406, 413, 416, 421, 433, 440, 445–447, 453–454, 462
  lodging, 381–382, 403, 431
  museums, 376, 377–378, 379–380, 384, 385–386, 387–388, 392, 393, 396, 401, 406–407, 408, 409–410, 411, 416–418, 419, 424–425, 427–428, 434, 435, 442–443, 448–449, 450, 455–456, 457, 463, 464
  private tours, 373, 382, 390, 413, 432–433, 437, 445, 460
  restaurants, 372, 381, 389–390, 396–397, 402, 412–413, 420, 430–431, 437, 444, 452, 459–460, 466
  shopping, 380–381, 382, 389, 393, 396, 402, 412, 419–420, 429–430, 436, 444, 451–452, 459, 465
  sports and outdoor activities, 420, 465–466
  transportation, 398, 421, 424, 454
Norway, 540–574
  castles and palaces, 559, 564, 571–572
  children, attractions for, 542, 545, 556–557, 559, 562, 563, 564, 562, 563, 564, 566–567, 568, 569, 572–573
  churches and mosques, 546, 551, 557, 568, 572
  currency, 542
  docking, 542, 543, 549, 552, 554, 556, 559, 568, 571
  lodging, 567
  museums, 542, 545–546, 549, 553, 554, 555, 556, 557, 559, 562–564, 568–569, 572–573
  nightlife, 547, 566
  restaurants, 540, 543, 548, 556, 566–567, 570, 573–574
  shopping, 543, 547, 550, 551, 555, 558, 564–565, 570, 573
  sports and outdoor activities, 548, 550, 551, 553, 558, 566, 570, 573
  visitor information, 553
Norwegian Cruise Line, 29
Notre-Dame, 109, 113–114
Notre-Dame-de-la-Garde, 156
Nouveau Musée National de Monaco, 171
Nykytaiteenmuseo (Kiasma), 496
Nymphaion, 298

O

O Plantanos ✕, 344
Obeliski Keisarinnan Kivi, 496
Oceanário de Lisboa, 127
Oceania Cruises, 29–30
O'Connell Street, 410
Oddernes kirke, 557
Öja, 527
Okupācijas muzejs, 503
Olbia, Sardinia, 197
Old City Jerusalem, 260–262
Old Fortress, 267
Old Town (Arrecife), 593
Olde Hansa ✕, 523
Olympia, Greece, 294–299
Omaha Beach, 109
Ons' Lieve Heer op Solder, 378
Onze-Lieve-Vrouwekathedraal, 384, 386–387
Onze-Lieve-Vrouwekerk, 465

Opatska Riznica, 307
Opéra de Monte-Carlo, 172
Operahuset, 563
Operan, 516
Oratorio de la Santa Cueva, 72
Oratorio de San Felipe Neri, 72–73
Orzola, 594
Oslo, Norway, 558–567
Östermalmstorg, 516
Oude Kerk, 378–379
Our Lady of the Rock, 311

P

P & O Cruises, 30
Padrão do Descobrimentos, 127
Pakleni Otoci, Croatia, 284
Paks Margareeta, 522
Palace of Holyroodhouse, 440, 443
Palace of St. Michael & St. George (Museum of Asian Art), 267
Palace of the Grand Masters, 355
Palácio da Bolsa, 120
Palácio da São Lourenço, 581
Palacio de la Condesa de Lebrija, 74
Palacio del Marqués de Dos Aguas, 217
Palacio Episcopal, 141
Palaestra, 298
Palais des Festivals, 78
Palais Princier, 172
Palau de la Música, 217
Palau de la Música Catalana, 58
Palau Salort, 161
Palau Torresana, 161
Palazzina dei Mulini, 201–202
Palazzo Abatellis, 191
Palazzo Bianco, 94
Palazzo Corvaja, 165
Palazzo Ducale, 232
Palazzo Falson, 225
Palazzo Reale (Genoa), 94
Palazzo Reale (Naples), 178
Palazzo Reale (Palermo), 191–192
Palazzo Rosso, 95
Palazzo Stern ⛴, 236
Palazzo Vecchio, 135
Paleokastritsa, Greece, 266, 269
Paleokastritsa Monastery, 269
Palermo, Italy, 188–194
Palma de Mallorca, 146
Palmitos Park, 587
Panayia Angeloktistos, 324
Panayia Ypapantis, 361
Pancake Bakery ✕, 381
Pantheon, 87–88
Paola, Malta, 224
Paphos, Cyprus, 323, 325–326

Paphos District Archaeological Museum, 326
Paphos Fort, 326
Parador Cruz de Tejeda, 587
Paraggi, 205
Paris, France, 107–115
Parque del Castro, 237
Parque Maritimo César Manrique, 606
Parque Nacional del Teide, 610
Parque Nacional Timanfaya, 594, 595
Parque Natural del Torcal de Antequera, 140
Parque Santa Catalina, 585
Parque Santa Catarina, 581
Pasaje Chinitas, 141
Paseo Maritimo, 41–42
Passports and visas, 14–15
Patrick's Bridge, 394
Patrick Street, 392
Paul Gauguin Cruises, 31
Paul Street, 394
Pavilhão do Conhecimento, 127–128
Pazo de Xelmírez, 240–241
Peggy Guggenheim Collection, 233
Pelikan ✕, 519
Pelopeion, 298
Perast, Montenegro, 312–313
Peristil, 367
Perlan, 601
Peter and Paul Fortress, 507–508
Pētera baznīca, 503
Petra Tou Romiou, Cyprus, 325
Pheidias's workshop, 298
Phenomenon (shop), 363
Piazza di Spagna, 88, 89
Piazza Navona, 84, 88
Piazza Pretoria, 192
Piazza San Marco, 231–232
Pierides-Marfin Laiki Bank Museum, 324
Pincio, 88
Þingvallabær, 603
Þingvellir, 602-603
Þingvellir National Park, 602
Piraeus, Greece, 335–345
Pisa, Italy, 129–137
Þjóðminjasafn, 601
Plaça, 274
Plaça de la Conquesta, 159
Plaça de s'Esplanada, 160
Place des Lices, 211
Place Maréchal-Foch, 47
Plage de Pamplonne, 212
Plantin-Moretus Museum/Prentenkabinet, 387
Playa de las Américas, 610
Playa del Inglés, 589
Plaza de España, 606, 608
Plaza de Maria Pita, 42
Plaza de Toros, 218
Plaza del Ayuntamiento, 218
Plaza del Charco, 609

Plaza San Francisco, 73
Plaza Santa Ana, 585
Pod Łososiem ✕, 483
Polaria, 568
Polarmusett, 568–569
Polignano a Mare, 64
Pomorski Muzej, 274
Pomorski Muzej Crne Gore, 311–312
Pompeii, Italy, 173–182
Pompey's Pillar, 253
Pont de Pierre, 68
Ponte de Dom Luis I, 120
Ponte di Rialto, 233
Ponte Vecchio, 135–136
Pontikonisi, 266
Port Said, Egypt, 345–351
Portal de ses Taules, 103
Porte Marine, 79
Porto, Portugal, 116–122
Porto Azzurro, 202
Porto Cervo, Sardinia, 194–200
Porto-Les Calanches, 49
Portoferraio, Italy, 200–204
Portofino, Italy, 204–209
Postojna Cave, 301
Postojnska Jama, 303
Pozo de la Nieve, 587
Praça dos Restauradores, 128
Praça Marquês de Pombal, 128
Praetor's Palace, 301
Premium cruise lines, 19
Princes Square, 420
Princess Cruises, 31–32
Prinsen ✕, 519
Prytaneion, 298
Puerta de San Roque, 159
Puerto Banús, 142–143
Puerto de la Cruz, 608–609
Puerto del Carmen, 594
Puglia, Italy, 63–65
Punta Portofino, 207
Pyramid Plateau, 350
Pyramids, The, 348

Q
Quartier de la Ponche, 211
Queens Cross Church, 418
Queenstown Story at Cobh Heritage Center, 392
Quinta do Palheiro, 581
Qyayt Bay, 251

R
Rabat, Malta, 225
Rachel's Tomb, 258
Rådhuset (Oslo), 563–564
Radisson Blu Plaza Hotel 🖫, 567
Raekoja Plats, 522
Rafting, 551, 558
Ramateulle, France, 212
Rapallo, Italy, 208
Rasmus Meyer Collection, 546
Rathaus, 488, 489
Ratusz Główny, 482

Rautatieasema, 496–497
Ravnedalen, 557
Real Colegio del Patriarca, 218
Real Escuela Andaluza del Arte Ecuestre, 74–75
Regent Seven Seas Cruises, 32
Reial Cartuja, 149
Reichstag, 533, 535–536
Réserve Naturel de Scandola, 49
Restoran Palmižana ✕, 285
Reykjavík, Iceland, 598–605
Rex ✕, 270
Rhodes, Greece, 352–358
Rhodes Town, 354–356
Rīga, Latvia, 500–504
Rīgas motormuzejs, 503
Rijksmuseum, 377, 379
Rio Marina, 202
River cruises, 20
River-Kasematten ✕, 491
Riverside Gallery, 436
Riverside Museum: Scotland's Museum of Transport and Travel, 419
Rocca al Mare, 522–523
Roccia dell'Elefante, 199
Rockoxhuis, 387–388
Roma Kloster Kyrka, 527
Roman Agora, 342–343
Roman Mosaics, 323, 326
Roman Painted House, 399
Rosendals Trädgården, 516
Rosia Bay, 101
Rotterdam, Netherlands, 445–452
Rotunda, 225
Royal Caribbean International, 32–33
Royal Hospital Kilmainham, 411
Royal Scottish Academy, 443
Rúa Pescaderia, 237
Rubenshuis, 388
Rue Obscure, 243–244
Ruins of Bishop Absalon's castle, 473
Runde, 543
Rye, U.K., 400, 402

S
Sa Penya, 103, 105
Sacra Infermeria, 222
Saga Cruises, 33
St. Anne's Church, 394
St. Colman's Cathedral, 392–393
St. Fin Barre's Cathedral, 394
St. Isaac's Cathedral, 508
St. Jacobikirche, 489
St-Jean Baptiste, 49
St-Jean-Cap-Ferrat, 244–245
St. John Basilica, 317
St. John's co-Cathedral, 222, 223
St. John's Fortress, 311
St. Maria Kyrka, 526

St. Mark's Square, 230
St. Michaelis Kirche, 489–490
St. Michael's Cave, 101
St. Mungo Museum of Religious Life and Art, 419
St. Paul's Cathedral, 427
St. Paul's Church, 225
St. Paul's Shipwreck Church, 223
St. Petersburg, Russian Federation, 504–511
St. Stephen's Green, 407, 411
St-Tropez, France, 209–213
Ste-Catherine, 108
Sainte-Chapelle, 114
Salisbury Cathedral, 457–458
Salt Lake, 324
San Cataldo, 192
San Giorgio, 207
San Giovanni degli Eremiti, 192
San Lorenzo, 95, 96
San Mateo, Gran Canaria, 587
San Michele, 181
San Nicolás, 218
San Simplicio, 197
Sanctuary of Apollo, 332
Sant'Agostino, 96
Sant Agusti 📷, 61
Sant Carles, 105
Sant Domingo, 105
Sant Francesc, 148–149
Santa Chiara, 178–179
Santa Croce, 136
Santa Cruz De Tenerife, 605–613
Santa Eulària des Riu, 105
Santa Gertrudis de Fruitera, 105
Santa Margherita Ligure, Italy, 207
Santa Maria, 159
Santa Maria dei Miracoli, 233
Santa Maria del Mar, 57, 58–59
Santa Maria della Salute, 233–234
Santa Maria di Castello, 96–97
Santa Maria Gloriosa dei Frari, 234
Santa Teresa di Gallura, Sardinia, 197
Santiago de Compostela, Spain, 40, 236–241
Santorini, Greece, 358–364
Sartène, 47–48
Sassari, Sardinia, 197–198
Saunas, 500
Scalinata di Spagna 📷, 90
Scandic Grand Central 📷, 519
Scottish National Portrait Gallery, 443
Scuola Grande di San Rocco, 234
Sé, 581
Sé do Porto, 120–121
Sea of Galilee, 281
Sea Satin Market-Caprice ✕, 334

Seabourn Cruise Line, 33–34
SeaCity Museum, 455
SeaDream Yacht Club, 34–35
Selçuk, Turkey, 316–317
Senaatintori, 496, 497
Senglea, Malta, 223
Serra do Monte, 578
Seville, Spain, 69–75
Shepherd's Fields, 258
Shrine of Our Lady of Europe, 101
Siam Park, 610
Silversea Cruises, 35
Sinagoga, 274
Sint-Jacobskerk, 388
Sint-Pauluskerk, 384, 388–389
Skansen, 516–517
Slottet, 564
Solar do Vinho do Porto, 121
Sóller, Spain, 150
Souk, 280
Southampton, U.K., 452–460
Spanish Steps, The, 88
Speicherstadt, 490
Speicherstadtmuseum, 490
Split, Croatia, 364–369
Stadium, 298
Stadshuset, 517
Stalheim Hotel ✕, 550
Star Clippers, 35–36
Stari Grad, Croatia, 284–285
State Hermitage Museum, 507, 508–509
State Museum of Russian Art, 509
Station Building Galleries, 150
Stavrovouni Monastery, 324
Stedelijk Museum of Modern Art, 379–380
Stiftsgården, 572
Stockholm, Sweden, 511–520
Stockholms Stadsbiblioteket, 517
Stocznia Gdańska, 481, 482–482
Stonehenge, 454, 458–459
Stora, 526
Stortorget, 517
Street of the Knights, 355
Strokkur, 603
Süleymaniye Cami, 291
Suomen Kansallismuseo, 497
Suomen Kansallisooppera, 497
Suomenlinna, 497–498
Sverresborg, Trøndelag Folkemuseum, 572–573
Sveti Djordje, 313
Syntagma (Constitution) Square, 343

T
Tábuas de Madeira, 582
Tafira Alta, Gran Canaria, 587
Tahíche, 594
Tallinn, Estonia, 520–523
Taormina, Italy, 162–168

Taormina Mare, 165
Tarxien, Malta, 224
Tarxien Temples, 224
Tate Britain, 427–428
Tate Modern, 428
Taxes, 17, 604
Teatre Principal, 159
Teatro Greco, 165
Teatro Massimo, 192
Teguise, 594
Tejeda, Gran Canaria, 587
Teleférico da Madeira, 581
Temple Expiatori de la Sagrada Familia, 59
Temple Mount, 260–261
Temple of Hera, 298
Temple of Zeus, 297, 298
Temppeliaukio Kirkko, 496, 498
Tenerife, Canary Islands (Santa Cruz De Tenerife), 605–613
Terrace House, 316
Three Cities, The, 223
Thomson Cruises, 36–37
Tiergarten, 536
Tierpark Hagenbeck, 485, 488
Tikotin Museum of Japanese Art, 278
Timing the visit, 12
Tingstäde, 527
Titov trg, 301
Tivoli, 472, 474
Tjörnin Pond, 601
Tomb of Giuseppe Garibaldi, 196
Tombs of the Kings, 326
Toomkirik, 523
Topkapı Sarayı, 290, 291–292
Toranj za sat, 312
Toren op Zuid, 449
Torre de Belém, 128
Torre de Hércules, 42
Torre del Oro, 74
Torre dos Clérigos, 119, 121
Torre Pendente, 136–137
Torre San Giovanni, 199
Torre Tavira, 73
Tour Eiffel, 114–115
Tower of London, 424, 428
Trafalgar Square, 428
Trani, 63–64
Trapholt Museum for Moderne Kunst, 474
Trattoria Altri Tempi ✕, 194
Treasuries, 298
Trevi Fountain, 87
Trg od Oržja, 312
Trg Sveti Stjepan, 283–284
Trinity College Dublin, 411–412
Trīs Brāli, 503
Trollstigveien, 550
Tromsø, Norway, 568–570
Tromsø Museum, 569
Trondheim, Norway, 570–574
Trondheim Kunstmuseum, 573
Troodos Mountains, Cyprus, 325
Trulli, 64

Trullo Sovrano, 65
Turkish Library, 355
Turkish Quarter, 355
Tvrdalj, 284, 285
Tvindefossen, 551
Tvrdjava Sveti Ivana, 312
Twelve Labors of Hercules, 297

U

U.S. Customs, 17
U.S. National Guard Monument, 109
Undredal stavkirke, 551
University College Cork, 394–395
Unter den Linden, 536
Upper Rock Nature Preserve, 101
Urquhart Castle, 433, 435
Uspenskin Katedraali, 498

V

Valencia, Spain, 213–219
Valldemossa, Spain, 149
Valletta, Malta, 219–227
Valsts mākslas muzejs, 504
Value added tax, 17, 604
Vanalinn, 522
Vanha Kauppahalli, 499
Vasamuseet, 516, 517
Venice, Italy, 227–236
Vermeer Centrum, 450
Vest-Agder-museet Kristiansand, 557
Vestibul, 368
Via Dolorosa, 261
Via Sinagoga, 64
Vieux Antibes, 78
Vieux Nice, 183, 1859
Vieux Port (Marseille), 153
Vieux Port (St-Tropez), 211
Vieux Sartène, 48
Vigelandsparken, 562, 564
Vigo, Spain, 236–241
Vikin Sjóminjasafnið í Reykjavik (Viken Maritime Museum), 602
Vikingabyn, 527
Vikingskiphuset, 564
Vila Nova de Gaia, 121
Villa Comunale, 165–166
Villa Ephrussi de Rothschild, 244–245
Villa Kerylos, 244
Villa San Martino, 202
Villefranche-Sur-Mer, France, 241–246

Vini da Gigio ✕, 235
Visby, Sweden, 523–528
Vittoriosa, Malta, 223
Vrata od Pila, 274
Vrata od Ploča, 274

W

Walls of Rhodes, 355–356
War Photo Limited, 274
Warnemünde, Germany, 528–527
Webbes at the Fish Café ✕, 402
West Jerusalem, 262–263
Western Mediterranean, 40–246
castles and palaces, 41, 58, 63, 64, 72, 73, 74, 78, 86, 94, 95, 101, 120, 135, 140, 141, 143, 146, 154, 160, 161, 165, 166, 172, 174–175, 191–192, 201–202, 205, 217, 222, 223, 225, 232, 240–241, 244–245
children, attractions for, 46–47, 48–49, 73, 74–75, 88, 95–96, 115, 121, 127–128, 135, 171, 198, 216, 226, 233
churches and synagogues, 41, 45–46, 49, 57, 58–59, 63, 64, 66, 72–73, 79, 84–85, 95, 96–97, 101, 108, 109, 113–114, 119, 124, 126, 131, 134, 136, 140, 146, 148–149, 153, 156, 158, 159, 163, 175, 178–179, 181, 189, 192–193, 197, 198, 207, 214, 218, 222, 223, 225, 230, 231–234, 243
currency, 40, 43, 52, 61, 66, 69, 76, 81, 91, 98, 103, 107, 116, 123, 130, 138, 145, 152, 157, 162, 168, 173, 182, 188, 194, 201, 204, 209, 213, 219, 227, 236, 242
docking, 41, 43, 45, 53, 62, 66, 70, 76, 81, 91, 94, 98, 103, 107–108, 116–117, 123–124, 130, 138–139, 145, 152–153, 158, 163, 169, 174, 183, 189, 195, 201, 205, 209–210, 214, 220, 227, 230, 237, 243
lodging, 60–61, 89–90, 235–236
museums, 41, 46–47, 48, 57, 58, 59, 68, 72, 74, 77–78, 79, 86–87, 94, 96, 100, 109, 112–113, 117, 119, 120, 121, 124, 126, 127–128, 131, 135, 139–140, 141, 148, 150, 152,

154, 156, 160, 171, 175, 178, 185, 186–187, 198, 199, 201, 210–211, 214, 216–217, 218, 220, 222, 232, 237, 240
private tours, 41, 53, 61, 70, 78, 81, 91, 98, 103, 116, 123, 130, 138, 145, 158, 163, 173, 188, 201, 204, 213, 219, 227, 236
restaurants, 40, 42–43, 51–52, 60, 65, 69, 75, 89, 97, 102, 106–107, 115, 122, 129, 137, 144, 151–152, 157, 162, 168, 172–173, 182, 187–188, 194, 200, 204, 208–209, 212–213, 218–219, 226–227, 235, 246
safety, 52, 173–174
shopping, 42, 46, 50, 59–60, 65, 68–69, 75, 80, 89, 97, 102, 106, 115, 121–122, 128–129, 156–157, 161, 167, 172, 181–182, 187, 193, 199–200, 208, 212, 218, 226, 234–235, 241, 246
sports and outdoor activities, 51, 105, 137, 144, 151, 160, 161, 167, 202, 208
transportation, 53, 56, 78, 124, 230
visitor information, 98
wineries, 67–68, 119, 121
Western Wall, 261
Western Wall Tunnel, 262
Westminster Abbey, 429
White Caves, 551
White Cliffs of Dover, 400
Wied-iz-Zurrieg, 225
Willet-Holthuysen Museum, 380
Winchester, U.K., 454, 455–456
Winchester Cathedral, 456
Windstar Cruises, 37
Windsurfing, 161, 527, 589
Winter Palace, 509–510

Y

Yad Vashem, 262–263
Yaiza, 595

Z

Zecca-Righi funicular, 95
Zeebrugge, Belgium, 460–466
Zlatna Vrata, 368
Zoologischer Garten, 536
Zoos, 323, 485, 488, 536, 556–557, 587
Żuraw Gdański, 483
Zurrieq, Malta, 224–225

PHOTO CREDITS

7, WYSOCKI Pawel/age fotostock. 39, Glen Allison/age fotostock. 247, Peter Adams/age fotostock. 371, Javier Larrea/age fotostock. 467, SuperStock/age fotostock. 539, Sylvain Grandadam/age fotostock. 575, Gonzalo Azumendi/age fotostock.

ABOUT OUR WRITERS

Linda Coffman is a freelance travel writer and the originator of CruiseDiva.com, her Web site, which has been dishing out cruise-travel advice and information since 2000. Before that, she was the cruise guide for About.com. Her columns and articles have appeared in *Cruise Travel, Porthole, Consumers Digest,* and other regional and national magazines; the *Chicago Sun-Times, Denver Post*; and on numerous Web sites, including those for *USA Today,* Fodors.com, and the Travel Channel. She's an avid cruiser, who enjoys sailing on ships of every size to any port worldwide but spends most of her time cruising the Caribbean. Linda thinks cruising is in her Norwegian blood and credits her heritage for a love of all things nautical. When not at sea, she makes her home in Augusta, Georgia, with her husband, Mel. Linda is the primary cruise correspondent for Fodor's and updated all the cruise line and cruise ship sections for this edition.

Although photographer and writer **Victoria Tang** currently calls Paris home, she has lived and traveled internationally since childhood. She's the author of two guidebooks translated into Dutch, Spanish, and Estonian and has written for numerous publications. Victoria covered river and barge cruising for this edition, as well as many of the Europe-based cruise lines, and she updated our coverage of Corsica and Sardinia.

The following writers updated coverage and contributed valuable insights for the European cruise ports of call: Lola Akinmade-Åkerström (Sweden), Alexia Amvrazi and Adrian Vrettos (Greece), Lindsay Bennett (Malta), David Dunne (Finland), Jane Foster (Croatia, Montenegro), Mike Gonzalez (Scotland), Liz Humphreys (Belgium, Cyprus, the Netherlands), Jennifer Ladonne (France), Bruce Leimsidor (Italy, Slovenia), Giulia Pines (Germany), Anne-Sophie Redisch (Norway), Ellin Stein (England), Jessica Steinberg (Israel), Paul Sullivan (Iceland), Joanna Styles (Portugal, Spain), Gelu Sulugiuc (Denmark), Dorota Wąsik (Estonia, Latvia, Lithuania, Poland, and Ukraine).